Praise for Richard Deal's CCNA Study Guide

As a CCIE and instructor, I can personally assure you that the importance of learning the fundamentals cannot be stressed enough. I have instructed certification candidates who were preparing for every level of Cisco certification, from CCNA up to CCIE. Those individuals who took the time to learn the essential technologies have always had a much greater chance of success, both in pursuing certifications and working "real life" in the field. This book is a wonderful tool to help you learn about Cisco networking.

In the years I have known Richard Deal, he has repeatedly impressed me with his technical knowledge and teaching ability. Every time we work together on a project, Richard takes complex subjects and presents them in a way that is understandable. He has a unique ability to enable people to understand complex technical content. Richard has found a way to impress me again by efficiently covering Cisco's large list of exam topics for the new CCNA exams.

This book is much more than the bound paper you are holding in your hands. It contains the Boson NetSim Limited Edition and corresponding labs that are included for critical hands-on experience. The practice exam included on the CD by Richard uses the Boson Exam Engine with the latest in simulation technology. I would recommend taking advantage of the Boson NetSim upgrade and ExSim-Max practice exams prior to your exam date. This will give you maximum exposure to the new topics.

In summary, this book and its enclosed CD-ROM will be a great resource to those preparing for Cisco certification and to those who want to master essential technologies. It will remain accurate reference material about Cisco networking for years to come.

Bryan Baize
CCIE 16139

CCNA® Cisco® Certified Network Associate Study Guide

(Exam 640-802)

Richard Deal

Mc Graw Hill

New York Chicago San Francisco Lisbon London Madrid
Mexico City Milan New Delhi San Juan Seoul Singapore Sydney Toronto

The McGraw·Hill Companies

Cataloging-in-Publication Data is on file with the Library of Congress

McGraw-Hill books are available at special quantity discounts to use as premiums and sales promotions, or for use in corporate training programs. To contact a special sales representative, please visit the Contact Us page at www.mhprofessional.com.

CCNA® Cisco® Certified Network Associate Study Guide (Exam 640-802)

1 2 3 4 5 6 7 8 9 0   DOC DOC   0 1 9 8

ISBN   Book p/n 978-0-07-149730-5 and CD p/n 978-0-07-149731-2
of set 978-0-07-149728-5

MHID   Book p/n 0-07-149730-7 and CD p/n 0-07-149731-5
of set 0-07-149728-5

Sponsoring Editor
Tim Green

Editorial Supervisor
Jody McKenzie

Project Editor
Agatha Kim

Acquisitions Coordinator
Jennifer Housh

Technical Editors
Matthew Walker
Angie Walker

Copy Editor
Lisa Theobald

Proofreader
Paul Tyler

Indexer
Jack Lewis

Production Supervisor
Jim Kussow

Composition
International Typesetting
& Composition

Illustration
International Typesetting
& Composition

Art Director, Cover
Jeff Weeks

Cover Designer
Patti Lee

Information has been obtained by McGraw-Hill from sources believed to be reliable. However, because of the possibility of human or mechanical error by our sources, McGraw-Hill, or others, McGraw-Hill does not guarantee the accuracy, adequacy, or completeness of any information and is not responsible for any errors or omissions or the results obtained from the use of such information.

Boson and the Boson logo, ExSim, and NetSim are trademarks of Boson Holdings, LLC.

About the Author

For more than 10 years, **Richard Deal** has operated his own company, The Deal Group, Inc., in Oviedo, Florida, east of Orlando. Richard has more than 20 years of experience in the computing and networking industry, including networking, training, systems administration, and programming. In addition to earning a B.S. in mathematics from Grove City College, he holds many certifications from Cisco and has taught many beginning and advanced Cisco classes. Richard is the author of *Cisco PIX Firewalls*, an in-depth book on Cisco's PIX firewalls and their implementation, published by McGraw-Hill. Richard is also the author of two books with Cisco Press: *The Complete Cisco VPN Configuration Guide* and *Cisco Router Firewall Security*; the latter book made it to Cisco's CCIE Security recommended reading list.

Richard periodically holds bootcamp classes on the CCNA and CCSP, which provide hands-on configuration of Cisco routers, switches, and security devices. More information on his bootcamp classes can be found at http://home.cfl.rr.com/ dealgroup/.

About the Technical Editors

Matthew Walker is the IA training instructor supervisor and a senior IA analyst at Dynetics, Inc., in Huntsville, Alabama. An IT education professional for more than 15 years, Matt served as the director of the Network Training Center and the curriculum lead and senior instructor for the local Cisco Networking Academy on Ramstein Air Base, Germany. After leaving the US Air Force, Matt served as a network engineer for NASA's Secure Network Systems, designing and maintaining secured data, voice, and video networking for the agency. He has written and contributed to numerous technical training books for Air Education and Training Command, Keesler Air Force Base, Mississippi, and continues to train certification and college-level IT and IA security courses. Matt holds numerous commercial certifications, including Cisco Certified Network Professional (CCNP), Microsoft Certified System Engineer (MCSE), Certified Ethical Hacker (CEH), Certified Network Defense Architect (CNDA), and Certified Pen Test Specialist (CPTS).

Angie Walker is currently the manager of the Information Systems Security (ISS) Office for the Missile Defense Agency (MDA) South, as well as the lead for the MDA Alternate Computer Emergency Response Team (ACERT). Among her many positions throughout the course of her 20-plus years in information technology and information assurance are superintendent of the United States Air Forces in Europe (USAFE) Communications and Information Training Center; Superintendent of the 386 Communications Squadron on Ali Al Saleem Air Base, Kuwait; and Senior Information Security Analyst for Army Aviation Unmanned Aircraft Systems. She holds several industry certifications, including CISSP, Network +, and Security +, and a master's degree in Information Systems Management. With more than nine years of IT and IA educational experience, she has developed and taught courseware worldwide for the US Air Force and several computer science courses as an instructor for the University of Alabama at Huntsville and Kaplan University in Fort Lauderdale, Florida.

CONTENTS

Part I
Introduction to Networking

Part III
Cisco Catalyst Switches

             Self Test Answers   355

12 Initial Switch Configuration **357**

    2960 Overview   358
             2960 Chassis   359
             2960 LEDs and MODE Button   360
             MODE Button   360
    Switch Startup   361
             Switch Bootup Process   362
             System Configuration Dialog   364
    Basic Switch Configuration   367
             IP Address and Default Gateway   367
             Example Configuration   368
             Exercise 12-1: Configuring the Switches   370
    Basic Switch Operation and Verification   372
             MAC Address Table   372
             Static MAC Addresses   373
             Exercise 12-2: CAM Tables   374
    Port Security Feature   375
             Port Security Configuration   375
             Port Security Verification   377
         ✓ Two-Minute Drill   381
    Q&A   Self Test   383
             Self Test Answers   385

13 VLANs and Trunks **387**

    VLAN Overview   388
             Subnets and VLANs   391
             Scalability   392
             VLANs and Traffic Types   393
             VLAN Membership   394
    VLAN Connections   395
             Access-Link Connections   396
             Trunk Connections   396
    VLAN Trunk Protocol   403
             VTP Modes   405
             VTP Messages   406
             VTP Pruning   408

Part IV
Cisco Routers and LANs

15   Routers and Routing **477**

    Routing Introduction 479
        Types of Routes 479
        Autonomous Systems 480
        Administrative Distance 481
    Dynamic Routing Protocols 482
        Routing Metrics 483
        Distance Vector Protocols 484
        Link State Protocols 486
        Hybrid Protocols 489
    Distance Vector Protocol Problems and Solutions 490
        Problem: Convergence 490
        Problem: Routing Loops 496
     ✓ Two-Minute Drill 504
   Q&A Self Test 506
        Self Test Answers 508

16   Initial Router Configuration **511**

    Router Hardware Components 512
        Read-Only Memory (ROM) 512
        Other Components 513
    Router Bootup Process 514
        Bootstrap Program 516
        System Configuration Dialog 519
        Configuration Register 522
    AutoSecure 526
    Router Configuration 531
        Interface Configuration 532
        Subnet Zero Configuration 536
        Static Host Configuration 536
        Exercise 16-1: Using IOS Features 538
    Router-on-a-Stick 540
        Subinterface Configuration 540
        Interface Encapsulation 541
        Router-on-a-Stick Example Configuration 542
     ✓ Two-Minute Drill 546
   Q&A Self Test 548
        Self Test Answers 550

From Boson Software, Inc.

The Cisco CCNA certification requires that you learn and master a number of skills. As you read this book, incorporating Boson NetSim into your learning process will help you successfully complete the CCNA certification track. The Boson NetSim Limited Edition (LE) included with this book will get you started on your way, and additional capability from the full edition is available after purchasing an upgrade.

Boson NetSim will help you with the practical hands-on portion of your education, and it ensures that you not only understand the concepts of routing and switching but that you can actually configure and implement routing and switching on Cisco devices. Once you feel you have mastered both the theory and the practical labs, you can test your knowledge using the exams included with this book and the CD. You may also purchase ExSim-Max practice exams from Boson, available at http://www.boson.com. ExSim-Max is the most realistic practice exam on the market with questions that are well-written, technically accurate, and completely representative of those on the actual exam. With ExSim-Max, you can be sure you are ready to pass the real exam.

Boson NetSim is the most advanced network simulator on the market for learning how to configure a Cisco router and Catalyst switch. Boson NetSim will not only help you become CCNA certified, it will actually help you learn and understand how to configure routers, switches, and networks.

The Boson NetSim LE can be upgraded to the full edition for CCNA at any time at http://www.boson.com/mcgrawhill (with a valid activation code from your qualifying McGraw-Hill book). Upgrading enables all other Boson NetSim labs, commands, telnet, and advanced features. Don't forget to complete your study with ExSim-Max practice exams. Thank you very much, and best wishes in your future studies!

Boson Software, LLC
http://www.boson.com

PREFACE

The primary objective of this book is to help you achieve the Cisco Certified Network Associate (CCNA) certification so that you can enhance your career. I believe that the only way you can increase your knowledge is through theoretical and practical learning. In other words, this book provides the book learning as well as basic hands-on experience that you'll need to pass the exam. However, once you pass the CCNA exam, your journey is just beginning: you'll need to enhance your newly acquired skills with additional reading and a lot of hands-on experience.

You can achieve CCNA certification in two ways:

■ Pass the CCNA (640-802) exam.
■ Pass both the ICNDv1 (640-822) and ICNDv2 (640-816) exams.

The CCNA 640-802 exam includes the same topics covered by the ICNDv1 640-822 and ICNDv2 640-816 exams. Cisco developed the second approach particularly for individuals who are just beginning their journey into networking, especially for people taking the CCNA curriculum at a Cisco Network Academy. The two-test approach is better suited for this environment since it takes a year to two to go through Cisco's CCNA curriculum at the Network Academies. With this approach, you take the ICNDv1 640-822 exam halfway through the curriculum and the ICNDv2 640-816 exam at the end of the curriculum.

Another advantage of taking and passing the ICNDv1 exam is that you have achieved Cisco's newest entry-level certification: CCENT (Cisco Certified Entry Networking Technician). In August 2007, Cisco introduced this certification based on customer and employer demand for a lower level certification demonstrating basic networking and hand-on skills with IOS devices such as routers and switches.

If you already have networking experience, especially if that experience includes configuring Cisco devices, you are better off taking the single CCNA 640-802 exam. The main advantage of this approach is that you have to pay for only one exam. Currently, the exam cost of the ICNDv1 and ICNDv2 exams are $125 US each, while the CCNA 640-802 exam is $150 US (at the time of the printing of this book), but Cisco has changed its pricing scheme in the past and can do so in the future.

This book was primarily written for those individuals wishing to pass the CCNA 640-802 exam. However, this book contains *all* the information that you would need to pass both the ICNDv1 640-822 and ICNDv2 640-816 exams. Therefore, it is up to you to determine which testing approach you take to achieve your CCNA certification.

In This Book

This book covers all the exam objectives posted on Cisco's web site concerning the CCNA 640-802 exam as well as the ICNDv1 640-822 and ICNDv2 640-816 exams. Each chapter covers one or more of the main objectives in this list, especially as it relates to how things work and how to configure them on Cisco's routers and switches. Appendix B has a breakdown of Cisco's objectives and indicates which chapter in this book covers those objectives.

In Every Chapter

I've created a set of chapter components that call your attention to important items, reinforce important points, and provide helpful exam-taking hints. Take a look at what you'll find in every chapter:

- Every chapter begins with the **Certification Objectives**—what you need to know to pass the section on the exam dealing with the chapter topic. The objective headings identify the objectives within the chapter, so you'll always know an objective when you see it!

- **Practice Exercises** are interspersed throughout the chapters. These are step-by-step exercises that allow you to get the hands-on experience you need to pass the exams. They help you master skills that are likely to be an area of focus on the exams. Don't just read through the exercises; they are hands-on practice that you should be comfortable completing. Learning by doing is an effective way to increase your competency with a product. These exercises are directly tied to the McGraw-Hill NetSim Learning Edition simulator, produced by Boson Software and included on the CD. These exercises will always work with the simulator product. Please note that Cisco's real exams contain simulation questions, so it is very important that you practice your skills with either this simulator or with real routers and switches.

- **On the Job** notes describe the issues that come up most often in real-world settings. They provide a valuable perspective on certification- and product-related topics. They point out common mistakes and address questions that have arisen from on-the-job discussions and experience.

- **Exam Watch** notes point out important information you should learn when preparing for your exam.

- Multimedia demonstrations, called **CertCams**, are included on the CD. If you want to see *actual* configurations of Cisco routers and switches in action, you can view these multimedia demonstrations. Throughout each chapter involving configurations are multiple multimedia demonstrations with a pointer to the CD where you can locate and run them. You will need to *read the instructions* included on the CD to run the multimedia demonstrations.

- The **Inside Exam** element appears at the end of each chapter and focuses on important topics mentioned in the chapter, covering procedures you should take to ready yourself for the exam with the information discussed in the chapter. Many tips and tricks are pointed out here to help you pass your exam with confidence.

- The **Two-Minute Drill** at the end of every chapter offers a checklist of the main points of the chapter. It can be used for last-minute review.

- The **Self Test** section at the back of each chapter offers questions similar to those found on the certification exams. The answers to these questions, as well as explanations of the answers, can be found at the end of each chapter. By taking the practice exams after completing each chapter, you'll reinforce what you've learned from that chapter while becoming familiar with the structure of the exam questions.

- The **Exam Readiness Checklist** section at the end of the introduction and in Appendix B is a list of the official exam objectives, presented exactly as the vendor specifies them, cross-listed with the exam objectives as they are presented in the book and chapter references. You should work with this list as you study, noting your familiarity with the objectives by checking off the appropriate box before you review each chapter. The table in the introduction covers exam 640-802. Appendix B covers the objectives for the individual ICNDv1 and ICNDv2 exams.

Some Pointers

Once you've finished reading this book, set aside some time to do a *thorough* review. You might want to return to the book several times and make use of all the methods it offers for reviewing the material:

1. *Re-read all the Two-Minute Drills*, or have someone quiz you. You also can use the drills as a way to do a quick cram before the exam.

2. *Re-read all the Exam Watch notes*. These are important items you should know for the exam. In other words, don't be surprised to see these topics appear on the real exam.

3. *Re-take the Self Test sections at the back of each chapter*. Taking the tests right after you've read the chapter is a good idea, because the questions help reinforce what you've just learned. However, it's an even better idea to return later and go through all the questions in the book in one sitting. Pretend that you're taking the live exam. (When you go through the questions the first time, you should mark your answers on a separate piece of paper. That way, you can run through the questions as many times as you need to until you feel comfortable with the material.)

4. *Use the exam test engine on the CD*. Did you use the test engine on the CD to test your knowledge? The 104 questions in the test engine cover all the topics in the book. You can also purchase additional tests from Boson Software at its web site (www.boson.com).

5. *Do all the practice exercises in each of the chapters*. Some simulation questions appear on the actual CCNA exams. In the simulation questions, you'll be required to perform basic configuration *and* troubleshooting tasks on a Cisco router and/or switch. Therefore, it is important that you have good configuration skills. Use the practice exercises to hone your configuration skills. I have developed two types of simulation questions in this book. All of them have to do with configuring Cisco routers and Catalyst switches; however, some of them also have you troubleshoot networking problems, where two or three configuration errors are introduced into the network and it is your job to track down these configuration errors, using the tools you learned about throughout this book, and fix them.

Basic network
topology for the
practice exercises

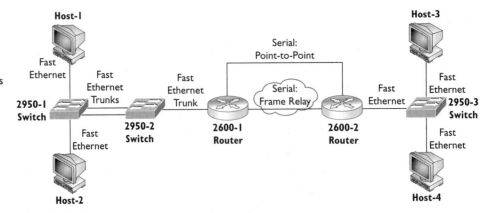

Practice Exams and the Simulator

As I mentioned earlier, it is important that you have hands-on experience not
only for the exam, but also to prepare for working with Cisco equipment in a real
network. A lot of time and effort has been devoted in the creation of the practice
exercises in this book. I have developed Figures 1 and 2 that display the network
topology used with the simulator.

These figures show four PCs, two routers (both 2600s), and three Catalyst 2950
switches. Chapters that have practice exercises will refer you to these figures for the
layout of the network topology and the addressing assigned to the devices in the
topology. Refer to these figures when performing the exercises.

Addressing for
the network
topology used
for the practice
exercises

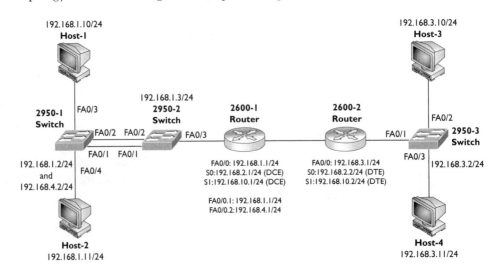

To Natalie, my loving wife, and our two children, Alina and Nika.

ACKNOWLEDGMENTS

I would like to thank the following people:

- This book would not have been possible without the support of my wife, Natalie. A book of this size is very time-consuming, especially when you have to balance a book, a job, and, most importantly, a family. My wife provided endless encouragement to keep me writing when I was pressed to meet deadlines for the book.

- A special thanks to Matt and Angela Walker for providing excellent feedback and encouragement on the technical content of this book. They provided many practical insights for the On the Job notes throughout the book. I would also like to thank Chad Altman and Martin Frank from Boson Software for their assistance in setting up and using the router simulator product and test engine included on the CD.

- The team at McGraw Hill, especially Tim Green, Jennifer Housh, Wilson Drozdowski, and Agatha Kim. I owe a debt of gratitude to this team, especially in pulling all of the pieces together for the CD-ROM material and the final proofing—thanks for your help!

Best wishes to all! And cheers!

Richard A. Deal

How to Take a Cisco Certification Examination

This Introduction covers the importance of your CCNA certification and prepares you for taking the actual examination. It gives you a few pointers on methods of preparing for the exam, including how to study and register, what to expect, and what to do on exam day.

Catch the Wave!

Congratulations on your pursuit of Cisco certification! In this fast-paced world of networking, few certification programs are as valuable as the one offered by Cisco.

The networking industry has virtually exploded in recent years, accelerated by nonstop innovation and the Internet's popularity. Cisco has stayed at the forefront of this tidal wave, maintaining a dominant role in the industry.

The networking industry is highly competitive, and evolving technology only increases in its complexity. The rapid growth of the networking industry has created a vacuum of qualified people: there simply aren't enough skilled networking people to meet the demand. Even the most experienced professionals must keep current with the latest technology in order to provide the skills that the industry demands. Cisco certification programs can help networking professionals succeed as they pursue their careers.

Cisco started its certification program many years ago, offering only the designation Cisco Certified Internetwork Expert (CCIE). Through the CCIE program, Cisco provided a means to meet the growing demand for experts in the field of networking. However, the CCIE tests are brutal, with a failure rate greater than 80 percent, and fewer than 5 percent of candidates pass on their first attempt! As you might imagine, few people attain CCIE status.

In early 1998, Cisco recognized the need for intermediate certifications, and several new programs were created. Four intermediate certifications were added: CCNA (Cisco Certified Network Associate), CCNP (Cisco Certified Network Professional), CCDA

(Cisco Certified Design Associate), and CCDP (Cisco Certified Design Professional). In addition, several specialties were added to the professional and CCIE certification levels since then. Today, Cisco also has Professional and CCIE certifications in Security, Voice, Service Provider, and Network Storage.

---

exam
watch

I would encourage you to take beta tests when they are available. Not only are the beta exams less expensive than the final exams (some are even free), but also, if you pass the beta, you will receive credit for passing the exam. If you don't pass the beta, you will have seen many of the questions in the pool of available questions, and you can use this information when you prepare to take the

exam for the second time. Remember to jot down important information immediately after the exam. You will have to do this after leaving the exam area, since materials written during the exam are retained by the testing center. This information can be helpful when you need to determine which areas of the exam were most challenging for you as you study for the subsequent test.

Why Vendor Certification?

Over the years, vendors have created their own certification programs because of industry demand. This demand arises when the marketplace needs skilled professionals and an easy way to identify them. Vendors benefit because it promotes people skilled in managing their product. Professionals benefit because it boosts their careers. Employers benefit because it helps them identify qualified people.

In the networking industry, technology changes too often and too quickly to rely on traditional means of certification, such as universities and trade associations. Because of the investment and effort required to keep network certification programs current, vendors are the only organizations suited to keep pace with the changes. In general, such vendor certification programs are excellent, with most of them requiring a solid foundation in the essentials as well as their particular product line.

Corporate America has come to appreciate these vendor certification programs and the value they provide. Employers recognize that certifications, like university degrees, do not guarantee a level of knowledge, experience, or performance; rather, they establish a baseline for comparison. By seeking to hire vendor-certified employees, a company can be assured that not only has it found a person skilled in networking, but it has also hired a person skilled in the specific products the company uses.

Technical professionals have also begun to recognize the value of certification and the impact it can have on their careers. By completing a certification program, professionals gain an endorsement of their skills from a major industry source. This endorsement can boost their current position, and it makes finding the next job even easier. Often a certification determines whether a first interview is even granted.

Today a certification may place you ahead of the pack. Tomorrow it will be a necessity to keep from being left in the dust.

---

e x a m

ⓦatch

Signing up for an exam has become easier with a Web-based test registration system. To sign up for the CCNA exams, access Vue's site (http://www .vue.com) and register for the Cisco Career Certification path. You will need to get an Internet account and password, if you do not already have one, for these sites. Just select the option for first-time registration, and the web site will walk you through that process. The registration wizard even provides maps to the testing centers, something that is not available when you call Vue on the telephone. As of 2007, Cisco no longer offers testing through Prometric.

Cisco's Certification Program

Cisco now has a number of certifications for the Routing and Switching career track. While Cisco recommends a series of courses for each of these certifications, they are not required. Ultimately, certification is dependent upon a candidate's passing a series of exams. With the right experience and study materials, you can pass each of these exams without taking the associated class.

Cisco is constantly changing and updating its certification requirements. For more information about Cisco certifications and exams, visit Cisco on the web at http://www.cisco.com/web/learning/index.html.

In addition to the technical objectives that are being tested for each exam, you will find much more useful information on Cisco's web site at http:// www.cisco.com. You will find information on becoming certified, exam-specific information, sample test questions, *demonstration tutorial videos, and the latest news on Cisco certification. This is the most important site you will find on your journey to becoming Cisco certified. The Career and Certification sections of the web site change periodically, so be sure to check for updates regularly!*

Computer-Based Testing

In a perfect world, you would be assessed for your true knowledge of a subject, not simply how you respond to a series of test questions. But life isn't perfect, and it just isn't practical to evaluate everyone's knowledge on a one-to-one basis. (Cisco actually does have a one-to-one evaluation, but it's reserved for the CCIE Laboratory exam.)

For the majority of its certifications, Cisco evaluates candidates using a computer-based testing service operated by Vue. This form of testing service is quite popular in the industry, and it is used for a number of vendor certification programs. Thanks to Vue's large number of facilities, exams can be administered worldwide, and generally in the same town as a prospective candidate.

For the most part, Vue exams work similarly from vendor to vendor. However, there is an important fact to know about Cisco's exams: They use the traditional test format, not the newer adaptive format. This allows Cisco to choose an appropriate number of questions on each objective in order to test your knowledge.

Cisco no longer allows you to mark questions for later review—once *you answer a question, you cannot go back and change your answer.*

To discourage simple memorization, Cisco exams present a different set of questions every time the exam is administered. In the development of the exam, hundreds of questions are compiled and refined using beta testers. From this large collection, a random sampling is drawn for each test. Plus, Cisco has developed simulation questions that require you to place basic configurations on Cisco devices and troubleshoot an existing network topology. These types of questions require a candidate to have hands-on, not just book learning, experience.

Each Cisco exam has a specific number of questions and test duration. Testing time is typically generous (75 to 90 minutes), and the time remaining is always displayed in the corner of the testing screen, along with the number of remaining questions. If time expires during an exam, the test terminates and incomplete answers are counted as incorrect.

At the end of the exam, your test is immediately graded and the results are displayed on the screen. Scores for each subject area are also provided, but the system will not indicate which specific questions were missed. A report is automatically printed at the proctor's desk for your files. The test score is electronically transmitted back to Cisco.

In the end, this computer-based system of evaluation is reasonably fair. You might think that one or two questions were poorly worded; this can certainly happen, but you shouldn't worry too much. Ultimately, it's all factored into the required passing score.

Question Types

Cisco exams pose questions in a variety of formats, most of which are discussed here. As candidates progress toward the more advanced certifications, the difficulty of the exams is intensified, through both the subject matter and the question formats.

exam
watch

To pass these challenging exams, you may want to talk with other test takers to determine what is being tested and what to expect in terms of difficulty. The most helpful way to communicate with other CCNA hopefuls is the Cisco Network Professional Connection. With this bulletin-board system, you can ask questions from other members, including employees of Cisco. These discussions cover everything imaginable concerning Cisco networking equipment and certification. Go to http://forum.cisco.com/eforum/servlet/NetProf?page=main to learn how to access this source of a wealth of information. (Note that at the time of publication, this information was correct. Please contact Cisco directly for the most up-to-date information about Cisco's forums.)

True/False

The classic true/false question format is *not* used in the Cisco exams, for the obvious reason that a simple guess has a 50 percent chance of being correct. Instead, true/false questions are posed in multiple-choice format, requiring the candidate to identify the true or false statement from a group of selections.

Multiple Choice

Multiple-choice is the primary format for questions in Cisco exams. These questions may be posed in a variety of ways.

Select the Correct Answer   This is the classic multiple-choice question, in which the candidate selects a single answer from a minimum of four choices. In addition to the question's wording, the choices are presented in a Windows radio button format, in which only one answer can be selected at a time. The question will instruct you to "Select the best answer" when you need to look for just one answer.

Select the Three Correct Answers   The multiple-answer version is similar to the single-choice version, but multiple answers must be provided. This is an all-or-nothing format; all the correct answers must be selected or the entire question is incorrect. In this format, the question specifies exactly how many answers must be selected. Choices are presented in a checkbox format, allowing more than one answer to be selected. In addition, the testing software prevents too many answers from being selected.

Select All That Apply   The open-ended version is the most difficult multiple-choice format, since the candidate does not know how many answers should be selected. As with the multiple-answer version, all the correct answers must be selected to gain credit for the question. If too many answers or not enough answers are selected, no credit is given. This format presents choices in checkbox format, but the testing software does not advise the candidates whether they've selected the correct number of answers. Cisco's CCIE exams include questions like this. You won't see any questions like this on the CCNA exam.

e x a m

ⓦatch

Make it easy on yourself and find some "braindumps." These are notes about the exam from test takers, which indicate the most difficult concepts tested, what to look out for, and sometimes even what not to bother studying. Several of these can be found at http://www .dejanews.com. Simply do a search for CCNA and browse the recent postings. Another good resource is at http://www .groupstudy.com. Beware, however, of the person that posts a question reported to have been on the test and its answer. First, the question and its answer may be incorrect. Second, this is a violation of Cisco's confidentiality agreement, which you, as a candidate, must agree to prior to taking the exam. Giving out specific information regarding a test violates this agreement and could result in the revocation of your certification status.

Exhibits

Exhibits, usually showing a network diagram or a router configuration, accompany many exam questions. These exhibits are displayed in a separate window, which is opened by clicking the Exhibit button at the bottom of the screen.

Drag-and-Drop

Drag-and-drop questions list terms in one column and descriptions or definitions in another, where you have to click your mouse on a term, drag it, and drop it on the correct definition. With some questions, some terms or definitions might not be used; in others, a term might be used for multiple definitions.

Scenarios

While the normal line of questioning tests a candidate's "book knowledge," scenarios add a level of complexity. Rather than asking only technical questions, they apply the candidate's knowledge to real-world situations. Scenarios generally consist of one or two paragraphs and an exhibit that describes a company's needs or network configuration. This description is followed by a series of questions and problems that challenge the candidate's ability to address the situation. Scenario-based questions are commonly found in exams relating to network design, but they appear to some degree in each of the Cisco exams.

Simulations

The CCNA exam will include a handful of simulation questions. With a simulation question, you will be prompted to put a basic configuration on a Cisco router or switch. This will require you to access the command-line interface (CLI) of the router or switch, access the appropriate mode on the router or switch, supply a basic configuration, and possibly test the configuration. Some simulation questions will already have a preconfiguration on existing Cisco devices, with configuration errors. You will be required to find the configuration errors, fix them, and then test the corrections. While working with the router or switch simulator, you will have the context-sensitive help feature available to you. Before you actually start the exam at a Vue site, you are offered the chance to become more familiar with the look and feel of a simulator question. I highly recommend that you *not* skip this part, especially since the time you spend on this tutorial is *not* counted against you. For a demonstration of what the simulator is like, you can also visit http://www.cisco .com and browse to the certification section to find the demo. This example is very similar to, but not exactly the same as, the simulator that you would see on the real exam. For additional simulation questions that are similar in concept to the actual exam, please be sure to investigate the McGraw-Hill Practice Tests for CCNA included on the CD-ROM.

Testlets

The CCNA and Professional level exams commonly have one testlet question. A testlet question is a multi-part question in which you are given a common scenario and must provide an answer for each question asked. Some testlets are four-part questions and some are six-part. Make sure you answer each of the testlets in the question before proceeding to the next question. Most testlets will require you to answer the questions by examining configurations on Cisco devices. Sometimes the testlets will have you use the CLI and sometimes a GUI interface such as Security Device Manager (SDM).

Studying Techniques

First and foremost, give yourself plenty of time to study. Networking is a complex field, and you can't expect to cram what you need to know into a single study session. It is a field best learned over time, by studying a subject and then applying your knowledge. Build yourself a study schedule and stick to it, but be reasonable about the pressure you put on yourself, especially if you're studying in addition to your regular duties at work.

exam
watch

One easy technique to use in studying for certification exams is the 30-minutes-per-day effort. Simply study for a minimum of 30 minutes every day. It is a small but significant commitment. On a day when you just can't focus, give it at least 30 minutes. On a day when it flows completely for you, study longer. As long as you have more of the flow days, your chances of succeeding are high.

Second, practice and experiment. In networking, you need more than knowledge; you also need understanding. You can't just memorize facts to be effective; you need to understand why events happen, how things work, and (most important) how and why they break.

The best way to gain deep understanding is to take your book knowledge to the lab. Try it out. Make it work. Change it a little. Break it. Fix it. Snoop around "under the hood." If you have access to a network analyzer, such as Ethereal or Wireshark, put it to use. You can gain amazing insight to the inner workings of a network by watching devices communicate with each other.

Unless you have a very understanding boss, don't experiment with router commands on a production router. A seemingly innocuous command can have a nasty side effect. If you don't have a lab, your local Cisco office or Cisco users' group may be able to help. Many training centers also allow students access to their lab equipment during off-hours. Many router and switch simulator products are also available on the market. The simulator included on the CD of this book is a stripped-down version of Boson's NetSim simulator product. It can simulate many router and switch commands for various models of Cisco products. The version included on this CD includes two 2600 series routers as well as three 2950 switches. It comes with a preset topology that includes Fast Ethernet, serial point-to-point connections, and Frame Relay. If you want the full functionality of the simulator product, a voucher is included that gives you a steep discount over buying the product retail. By purchasing the full product, you have access to all of the commands within the product as well as being able to create your own topologies! For hands-on experience, this is a great bargain for the money that you would spend.

Another excellent way to study is through case studies. Case studies are articles or interactive discussions that offer real-world examples of how technology is applied to meet a need. These examples can serve to cement your understanding of a technique or technology by seeing it put to use. Interactive discussions offer added value because you can also pose questions of your own. User groups are an excellent source of examples, since the purpose of these groups is to share information and learn from each other's experiences.

The Cisco Networkers conference is not to be missed. Although renowned for its wild party and crazy antics, this conference offers a wealth of information. Held every year in cities around the world, it includes four to five days of technical seminars and presentations on a variety of subjects. As you might imagine, it's very popular. You have to register early to get the classes you want.

There is also the Cisco web site. This little gem is loaded with collections of technical documents and white papers. As you progress to more advanced subjects, you will find great value in the large number of examples and reference materials available. But be warned: You need to do a lot of digging to find the really good stuff. Often you have to browse every document returned by the search engine to find exactly the one you need. This effort pays off. Most CCIEs I know have compiled six to ten binders of reference material from Cisco's site alone.

Scheduling Your Exam

The Cisco exams are scheduled by calling Vue directly or contacting the company online via its web site. For locations outside the United States, your local number can be found on Vue's web site at http://www.vue.com. Vue representatives can schedule your exam, but they don't have information about the certification programs. Direct questions about certifications to Cisco's education division.

Exams can be scheduled up to a year in advance, although this is really not necessary. Generally, scheduling a week or two ahead is sufficient to reserve the day and time you prefer. When you call to schedule, operators will search for testing centers in your area. For convenience, they can also tell which testing centers you've used before. You can also use Vue's online site, where you can easily search for the test centers closest to your address.

Vue accepts a variety of payment methods, with credit cards being the most convenient. When you pay by credit card, you can take tests the same day you call—provided, of course, that the testing center has room. Vue will e-mail you a receipt and confirmation of your testing date, which typically arrives the same day you schedule the exam. If you need to cancel or reschedule an exam, remember to call at least one day before your exam or you'll lose your test fee.

When you register for the exam, you will be asked for your Cisco testing ID number. This number is used to track your exam results back to Cisco. It's important that you use the same ID number each time you register, so that Cisco can follow your progress. Address information provided when you first register is also used by Cisco to ship certificates and other related material. If this is your first time taking a Cisco exam, Vue will assign you a unique ID number.

You will also be required to provide a valid e-mail address when registering. If you do not have an e-mail address that works, you will not be able to schedule the exam. Once you are registered, you will receive an e-mail notice containing your registration information for your scheduled exam. Examine it closely to make sure that it is correct.

In addition to the Vue testing sites, Cisco also offers facilities for taking exams free of charge or at a greatly reduced rate at each Networkers conference in the United States. As you might imagine, this option is quite popular, so reserve your exam time as soon as you arrive at the conference.

Arriving at the Exam

As with any test, you'll be tempted to cram the night before. Resist that temptation. You should know the material by this point, and if you're too groggy in the morning, you won't remember what you studied anyway. Instead, get a good night's sleep.

Arrive early for your exam; this gives you time to relax and review key facts. Take the opportunity to review your notes. If you get burned out on studying, you can usually start your exam a few minutes early. On the other hand, I don't recommend arriving late. Your test could be canceled, or you might be left without enough time to complete the exam.

When you arrive at the testing center, you'll need to sign in with the exam administrator. You need to provide two forms of identification. Acceptable forms include government-issued IDs (for example, a passport or driver's license) and credit cards. One form of ID must include a photograph.

Aside from a brain full of facts, you don't need to bring anything else to the exam. In fact, your brain is about all you're allowed to take into the exam. All the tests are closed book, meaning that you don't get to bring any reference materials with you. You're also not allowed to take any notes out of the exam room. The test administrator will give you paper and a pencil. Some testing centers may provide a small marker board instead.

Calculators are not allowed, so be prepared to do any necessary math (such as hex-binary-decimal conversions or subnet masks) in your head or on paper. Additional paper is available if you need it.

Leave your pager and cell phone in your car—you are not allowed to take them into the actual testing room. Purses, books, and other materials must be left with the administrator before you enter. While you're in the exam room, it's important that you don't disturb other candidates; talking is not allowed during the exam.

In the exam room, the exam administrator logs you into your exam, and you have to verify that your name and exam number are correct. If this is the first time you've taken a Cisco test, you can select a brief tutorial for the exam software.

Before the test begins, you will be provided with facts about the exam, including the duration, the number of questions, and the score required for passing. Then the clock starts ticking, and the fun begins. Please note that Cisco does not officially publish the number of questions on its exams (typically 55 to 65) or the passing rate (typically between 825 and 850). Cisco changed this philosophy to allow it to dynamically adjust the number of questions and pass rates in order to create a harder or easier exam based on past scores of test-takers. Typically, you'll have about 60 questions with about 75 to 90 minutes to complete the exam. But as I just mentioned, Cisco can change this at any time!

The testing software is Windows-based, but you won't have access to the main desktop or to any of the accessories. The exam is presented in full screen, with a single question per screen. Navigation buttons allow you to move between questions. In the upper-right corner of the screen, counters show the number of questions and time remaining. Make sure you periodically look at the question you are on and the time remaining—you'll want to budget your time appropriately. Also remember that you'll probably need about 5 minutes to complete each of the two or three simulation questions. And once you answer a question and go to the next one, you cannot go back to previous questions! Also, some questions on the exam might be beta questions that are not actually graded; however, Cisco won't state this in the question, so make sure you answer every question.

The Grand Finale

When you're finished, the exam will automatically be graded. After what will seem like the longest 10 seconds of your life, the testing software will respond with your score. This is usually displayed as numbers showing the minimum passing score, your score, and a PASS/FAIL indicator. With some of Cisco tests, the actual score is not displayed on the screen but only on the printed version of your test results.

If you're curious, you can review the statistics of your score at this time. Answers to specific questions are not presented; rather, questions are lumped into categories and results are tallied for each category. This detail is also provided on a report that has been automatically printed at the exam administrator's desk.

As you leave the exam room, you'll need to leave your scratch paper behind or return it to the administrator. (Some testing centers track the number of sheets you've been given, so be sure to return them all.) In exchange, you'll receive a copy of the test report.

You should keep the test results in a safe place. Normally, the results are automatically transmitted to Cisco sometime during the same day you tested, but occasionally you might need the paper report to prove that you passed the exam. Your company's personnel file is probably a good place to keep this report; the file tends to follow you everywhere, and it doesn't hurt to have favorable exam results turn up during a performance review.

Retesting

If you don't pass the exam, don't be discouraged—networking is complex stuff. Try to maintain a good attitude about the experience, and get ready to try again. Consider yourself a little more educated. You know the format of the test a little better, and the report shows which areas you need to strengthen.

If you bounce back quickly, you'll probably remember several of the questions you might have missed. This will help you focus your study efforts in the right area. Serious go-getters will reschedule the exam for five business days after the previous attempt, while the study material is still fresh in their minds—you must wait a minimum of five business days before taking the same exam again. And once you pass the exam, you can resit the exam only once a year.

A new CCNA certification is currently valid for three years. To recertify your CCNA, you can perform any of the following:

- Retake and pass the CCNA exam again.
- Pass any 642-level exam.
- Pass any CCIE written qualification exam.

Performing any of these actions currently recertifies your CCNA. However, Cisco can change the recertification process at any time. You can track your current certification status by going to http://www.cisco.com/go/certifications/login. If you haven't currently set up login credentials, you'll need to do this before logging into the certification site. You'll need to use your Cisco testing ID number to log in.

Ultimately, remember that Cisco certifications are valuable because they're hard to get. After all, if anyone could get one, what value would it have? In the end, it takes a good attitude and a lot of studying, but you can do it!

CCNA 640-802

Exam Readiness Checklist			Beginner	Intermediate	Advanced
Official Objective	**Study Guide Coverage**	**CH #**			
Describe how a network works					
Describe the purpose and functions of various network devices	Networks	1			
Select the components required to meet a network specification	Networks Bridges and Switches Wireless LANs IOS Software Routers and Routing	1 4 5 11 15			
Use the OSI and TCP/IP models and their associated protocols to explain how data flows in a network	OSI Reference Model TCP/IP Internet Layer Sending and Receiving TCP/IP Packets	2 6 10			
Describe common networked applications including web applications	OSI Reference Model TCP/IP Internet Layer	2 6			
Describe the purpose and basic operation of the protocols in the OSI and TCP models	OSI Reference Model TCP/IP Internet Layer TCP/IP Transport Protocols Sending and Receiving TCP/IP Packets	2 6 9 10			
Describe the impact of applications (Voice over IP and Video over IP) on a network	Networks VLANs and Trunks	1 13			
Interpret network diagrams	Layer 2 LAN Technologies Bridges and Switches Sending and Receiving TCP/IP Packets	3 4 10			
Determine the path between two hosts across a network	Bridges and Switches Sending and Receiving TCP/IP Packets Routers and Routing	4 10 15			
Describe the components required for network and Internet communications	Networks	1			
Identify and correct common network problems at layers 1, 2, 3, and 7 using a layered model approach	TCP/IP Internet Layer IOS Device Management	6 17			
Differentiate between LAN/WAN operation and features	WAN Introduction	25			

Exam Readiness Checklist

Official Objective	Study Guide Coverage	CH #	Beginner	Intermediate	Advanced
Configure, verify, and troubleshoot a switch with VLANs and interswitch communications					
Select the appropriate media, cables, ports, and connectors to connect switches to other network devices and hosts	Layer 2 LAN Technologies Bridges and switches	3 4			
Explain the technology and media access control method for Ethernet networks	Layer 2 LAN Technologies	3			
Explain network segmentation and basic traffic management concepts	Bridges and Switches VLANs and Trunks	3 13			
Explain basic switching concepts and the operation of Cisco switches	Bridges and Switches Initial Switch Configuration	3 12			
Perform and verify initial switch configuration tasks including remote access management	Cisco IOS Software Initial Switch Configuration IOS Device Management	11 12 17			
Verify network status and switch operation using basic utilities (including ping, traceroute, telnet, SSH, arp, ipconfig), show and debug commands	TCP/IP Internet Layer Cisco IOS Device Management	6 17			
Identify, prescribe, and resolve common switched network media issues, configuration issues, auto negotiation, and switch hardware failures	Cisco IOS Software Initial Switch Configuration	11 12			
Describe enhanced switching technologies (including VTP, RSTP, VLAN, PVSTP, 802.1q)	VLANs and Trunks Switches and Redundancy	13 14			
Describe how VLANs create logically separate networks and the need for routing between them	VLANs and Trunks	13			
Configure, verify, and troubleshoot VLANs	VLANs and Trunks	13			
Configure, verify, and troubleshoot trunking on Cisco switches	VLANs and Trunks	13			
Configure, verify, and troubleshoot interVLAN routing	VLANs and Trunks Initial Router Configuration	13 16			
Configure, verify, and troubleshoot VTP	VLANs and Trunks	13			

Exam Readiness Checklist

Official Objective	Study Guide Coverage	CH #	Beginner	Intermediate	Advanced
Configure, verify, and troubleshoot RSTP operation	Switches and Redundancy	14			
Interpret the output of various show and debug commands to verify the operational status of a Cisco switched network	Cisco IOS Software Initial Switch Configuration VLANs and Trunks Switches and Redundancy	11 12 13 14			
Implement basic switch security (including port security, trunk access, management VLAN other than VLAN1, etc.)	Initial Switch Configuration VLANs and Trunks	12 13			
Implement an IP addressing scheme and IP services to meet network requirements in a medium-size enterprise branch office network					
Describe the operation and benefits of using private and public IP addressing	TCP/IP Internet Layer Address Translation	6 23			
Explain the operation and benefits of using DHCP and DNS	TCP/IP Internet Layer Sending and Receiving TCP/IP Packets	6 10			
Configure, verify, and troubleshoot DHCP and DNS operation on a router (including CLI/SDM)	SDM	18			
Implement static and dynamic addressing services for hosts in a LAN environment	IP Addressing and Subnetting SDM	7 18			
Calculate and apply an addressing scheme including VLSM IP addressing design to a network	VLSM	8			
Determine the appropriate classless addressing scheme using VLSM and summarization to satisfy addressing requirements in a LAN/WAN environment	VLSM	8			
Describe the technological requirements for running IPv6 in conjunction with IPv4 (including protocols, dual stack, tunneling, etc.)	IPv6	24			
Describe IPv6 addresses	IPv6	24			
Identify and correct common problems associated with IP addressing and host configurations	TCP/IP Internet Layer	6			

Exam Readiness Checklist

Official Objective	Study Guide Coverage	CH #	Beginner	Intermediate	Advanced
Configure, verify, and troubleshoot basic router operation and routing on Cisco devices					
Describe basic routing concepts (including packet forwarding, router lookup process)	VLSM Routers and Routing	8 15			
Describe the operation of Cisco routers (including router bootup process, POST, router components)	Initial Router Configuration	16			
Select the appropriate media, cables, ports, and connectors to connect routers to other network devices and hosts	Layer 2 LAN Technologies	3			
Configure, verify, and troubleshoot RIPv2	Basic Routing	19			
Access and utilize the router to set basic parameters (including CLI/SDM)	Cisco IOS Software Initial Router Configuration SDM	11 16 18			
Connect, configure, and verify operation status of a device interface	Cisco IOS Software	11			
Verify device configuration and network connectivity using ping, traceroute, telnet, SSH, or other utilities	IOS Device Management	17			
Perform and verify routing configuration tasks for a static or default route given specific routing requirements	Basic Routing	19			
Manage IOS configuration files (including save, edit, upgrade, restore)	IOS Device Management	17			
Manage Cisco IOS	IOS Device Management	17			
Compare and contrast methods of routing and routing protocols	Routers and Routing	15			
Configure, verify, and troubleshoot OSPF	OSPF Routing	20			
Configure, verify, and troubleshoot EIGRP	EIGRP Routing	21			
Verify network connectivity (including using ping, traceroute, telnet, or SSH)	IOS Device Management	17			

Exam Readiness Checklist

Official Objective	Study Guide Coverage	CH #	Beginner	Intermediate	Advanced
Troubleshoot routing issues	Routers and Routing Basic Routing OSPF Routing EIGRP Routing	15 19 20 21			
Verify router hardware and software operation using show and debug commands	Cisco IOS Software Initial Router Configuration	11 16			
Implement basic router security	Cisco IOS Software Access Control Lists	11 22			
Explain and select the appropriate administrative tasks required for a WLAN					
Describe standards associated with wireless media (including IEEE WI-FI Alliance, ITU/FCC)	Wireless LANs	5			
Identify and describe the purpose of the components in a small wireless network (including SSID, BSS, ESS)	Wireless LANs	5			
Identify the basic parameters to configure on a wireless network to ensure that devices connect to the correct access point	Wireless LANs	5			
Compare and contrast wireless security features and capabilities of WPA security (including open, WEP, WPA-1/2)	Wireless LANs	5			
Identify common issues with implementing wireless networks (including interface, misconfiguration)	Wireless LANs	5			
Identify security threats to a network and describe general methods to mitigate those threats					
Describe today's increasing network security threats and explain the need to implement a comprehensive security policy to mitigate the threats	Networks	1			
Explain general methods to mitigate common security threats to network devices, hosts, and applications	Networks	1			

Exam Readiness Checklist

Official Objective	Study Guide Coverage	CH #	Beginner	Intermediate	Advanced
Describe the functions of common security appliances and applications	Networks	1			
Describe security recommended practices including initial steps to secure network devices	Networks	1			
Implement, verify, and troubleshoot NAT and ACLs in a medium-size enterprise branch office network					
Describe the purpose and types of ACLs	Access Control Lists	22			
Configure and apply ACLs based on network filtering requirements (including CLI/SDM)	Access Control Lists	22			
Configure and apply an ACL to limit telnet and SSH access to the router using (including SDM/CLI)	Access Control Lists	22			
Verify and monitor ACLs in a network environment	Access Control Lists	22			
Troubleshoot ACL issues	Access Control Lists	22			
Explain the basic operation of NAT	Address Translation	23			
Configure NAT for given network requirements using (including CLI/SDM)	Address Translation	23			
Troubleshoot NAT issues	Address Translation	23			
Implement and verify WAN links					
Describe different methods for connecting to a WAN	WAN Introduction	25			
Configure and verify a basic WAN serial connection	WAN Introduction	25			
Configure and verify Frame Relay on Cisco routers	Frame Relay	25			
Troubleshoot WAN implementation issues	WAN Introduction	25			
Describe VPN technology (including importance, benefits, role, impact, components)	WAN Introduction	25			
Configure and verify a PPP connection between Cisco routers	WAN Introduction	25			

Part I

Introduction to Networking

1

Networks

This chapter offers a brief introduction to networking and some basic networking terms and concepts. This material should be a review of many familiar concepts. You should understand the various networking topologies used in networks, as well as different types of networks, such as local area networks (LANs) and wide area networks (WANs). The last half of the chapter will briefly introduce security and its necessity in today's networks.

CERTIFICATION OBJECTIVE 1.01

Introduction to Networks

A *network* is basically all of the components (hardware and software) involved in connecting computers and applications across small and large distances. Networks are used to provide easy access to information, thus increasing productivity for users. This section covers some of the components involved with networking as well as the basic types of topologies used to connect networking components, including computers. Resources that are commonly shared in a network include data and applications, printers, network storage components (shared disk space), and backup storage components.

Network Characteristics

The following characteristics should be considered in network design and ongoing maintenance:

- **Cost**   Includes the cost of the network components, their installation, and their ongoing maintenance.
- **Security**   Includes the protection of the network components and the data they contain and/or the data transmitted between them.
- **Speed**   Includes how fast data is transmitted between network end points (the data rate).
- **Topology**   Describes the physical cabling layout and the logical way data moves between components.
- **Scalability**   Defines how well the network can adapt to new growth, including new users, applications, and network components.

- **Reliability**   Defines the reliability of the network components and the connectivity between them. Mean time between failures (MTBF) is a measurement commonly used to indicate the likelihood of a component failing.

- **Availability**   Measures the likelihood of the network being available to the users, where downtime occurs when the network is not available because of an outage or scheduled maintenance. Availability is typically measured in a percentage based on the number of minutes that exist in a year. Therefore, uptime would be the number of minutes the network is available divided by the number of minutes in a year.

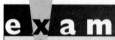

When designing and maintaining a network, remember these *factors: cost, security, speed, topology, scalability, reliability, and availability.*

Designing a network requires a close analysis and balance of cost, security, speed, topology, scalability, reliability, and availability. Every network is different, and the solution that you design will be unique for each situation.

Components

Applications, which enable users to perform various tasks, make up a key component of networking. Many applications are *network-aware*, allowing you to access and use resources that are not located on your local computer. While the number of networking applications ranges in the thousands, some of the more common networking applications include e-mail applications for sending mail electronically, File Transfer Protocol (FTP) applications for transferring files, and web applications for providing a graphical representation of information.

Protocols are used to implement applications. Some protocols are *open standard*, meaning that many vendors can create applications that can interoperate with each other, while others are *proprietary*, meaning that they work only with a particular application. Common protocols used on the Internet are Simple Mail Transfer Protocol (SMTP), Internet Message Access Protocol version 4 (IMAP4), and Post Office Protocol 3 (POP3), which implements e-mail applications such as Sendmail and Microsoft Exchange; File Transfer Protocol (FTP), which implements file transfer programs such as FTP Explorer, Cute FTP, and WSFTP; and Hypertext Transfer Protocol (HTTP), which implements web browsing applications such as

Internet Explorer and Firefox and web server applications such as Microsoft Internet Information Services (IIS) and Apache.

Some applications, such as e-mail, require little bandwidth, while others, such as backup software, video software, and file transfer software, require a lot. Some applications operate in real-time, such as voice over IP (VoIP) and video; some operate interactively, such as instant messaging or database queries; and some operate in a batch mode, requiring little user interaction. Today's networks need to accommodate all these different types of resources and applications, including their specific requirements such as bandwidth for large transfers or minimal delay and latency for VoIP and video. Quality of service (QoS) features are commonly used to meet these requirements.

<table>
<tr><td colspan="2">e x a m
ⓦ a t c h</td></tr>
<tr><td>VoIP and video traffic is sensitive to delay and latency. Therefore, QoS is commonly implemented to ensure</td><td>these applications have enough bandwidth and are prioritized throughout the network to limit the amount of delay they incur.</td></tr>
</table>

To build a network, you need three component categories: computers, networking, and media. Computer components—such as PCs and file servers running Microsoft Windows, Macintosh OS, UNIX (including Linux), or other operating systems—are responsible for providing applications to the users. Networking components—such as hubs, bridges, switches, routers, firewalls, wireless access points, modems, NT1s (Network Terminator Type 1 is an ISDN network termination device), and channel service units/data service units (CSU/DSUs)—are responsible for moving information between computers.

<table>
<tr><td colspan="2">e x a m
ⓦ a t c h</td></tr>
<tr><td>Security appliances are specialized network components that typically provide many security functions, such as Cisco's ASAs and PIXs, Cisco's</td><td>4200 intrusion prevention and detection systems (IPS and IDS), and Cisco's 3000 VPN Concentrators.</td></tr>
</table>

Media types, such as copper or fiber cabling, are needed to connect the computers and networking components so that information can be shared between components. Wireless communication also falls in this category.

TABLE 1-1	Term	Definition
Networking Locations	Small office/home office (SOHO)	Users working from a home or small office (a handful of people)
	Branch office	A small group of users connected in a small area, called a LAN, geographically separated from a corporate office
	Mobile users	Users who can connect to a network from any location, LAN, or WAN
	Corporate or central office	The location where most users in an organization and their resources are located

Watch   *Be sure you can correlate the definition to the appropriate network location in Table 1-1.*

Network Locations

Network components can be found in various locations. Table 1-1 shows some common terms used to describe the location of network components.

Local Area Networks

Local area networks (LANs) are used to connect networking devices that are in a very close geographic area, such as a floor of a building, a building itself, or within a campus environment. In a LAN, you'll find PCs, file servers, hubs, bridges, switches, routers, multilayer switches, voice gateways, firewalls, and other devices. The media types used in LANs include copper and fiber cabling. Ethernet, Fast Ethernet (FE), Gigabit Ethernet (GE), Token Ring, and fiber distributed data interface (FDDI) are frame types used to communicate between components on fiber and copper. Today, most networks use some form of Ethernet (discussed in Chapter 3).

on the **job**   *Ethernet has become the de facto standard for LAN-based networks. Therefore, understanding its topology and workings is very important when it comes to implementation in a company's network.*

Wide Area Networks

Wide area networks (WANs) are used to connect LANs together. Typically, WANs are used when the LANs that must be connected are separated by a large distance.

Whereas a corporation provides its own infrastructure for a LAN, WANs are leased from carrier networks, such as telephone companies and Internet service providers (ISPs). Four basic types of connections, or circuits, are used in WAN services: circuit-switched, cell-switched, packet-switched, and dedicated connections.

> **exam**
> **ωatch**   *LANs provide high-speed bandwidth connections to interconnect components in a geographically close location, such as a building or a campus.*   *WANs provide lower speed bandwidth connections to interconnect multiple locations or sites. WANs involve paying recurring monthly costs to a service provider.*

A wide array of WAN services are available, including analog dialup, asynchronous transfer mode (ATM), dedicated circuits, cable, digital subscriber line (DSL), Frame Relay, Integrated Services Digital Network (ISDN), Switched Multi-megabit Data Services (SMDS), and X.25. Analog dialup and ISDN are examples of circuit-switched services; ATM and SMDS are examples of cell-switched services; and Frame Relay and X.25 are examples of packet-switched services.

Circuit-switched services provide a temporary connection across a phone circuit. In networking, these are typically used for backup of primary circuits and for temporary boosts of bandwidth.

A *dedicated circuit* is a permanent connection between two sites in which the bandwidth is dedicated to that company's use. These circuits are common when a variety of services, such as voice, video, and data, must traverse the connection and you are concerned about delay issues with the traffic and guaranteed bandwidth.

Cell-switched services can provide the same features that dedicated circuits offer. Their advantage over dedicated circuits is that a single device can connect to multiple devices on the same interface. The downside of these services is that they are not available at all locations, they are difficult to set up and troubleshoot, and the equipment is expensive when compared to equipment used for dedicated circuits. *Packet-switched* services are similar to cell-switched services. Whereas cell-switched services switch fixed-length packets called cells, packet-switched services switch variable-length packets. This feature makes them better suited for data services, but they can nonetheless provide some of the QoS features that cell-switched services provide.

Two newer WAN services that are very popular in the United States are DSL and cable. DSL provides speeds up to a few megabits per second (Mbps) and costs much less than a typical WAN circuit from the carrier. It supports both voice and video and doesn't require a dialup connection (it's always enabled). The main disadvantage of DSL is that coverage is limited to about 18,000 feet and the service is not available in all areas. Cable access uses coaxial copper and fiber connections— the same medium used to provide television broadcast services. It supports higher data rates than DSL, but like DSL, it provides a full-time connection. However, it has two major drawbacks: it is a shared service and functions in a logical bus topology much like Ethernet (discussed in Chapter 2), so the more customers in an area that connect via cable, the less bandwidth each customer has; since many people are sharing the medium, it is more susceptible to security risks, such as eavesdropping on other peoples' traffic.

Examples of networking devices used in WAN connections include cable and DSL modems, carrier switches, CSU/DSUs, firewalls, modems, NT1s, and routers.

CERTIFICATION OBJECTIVE 1.02

Network Topologies

When you are cabling up your network components, various types of topologies can be used. A topology defines how the components are connected. Figure 1-1 shows examples of topologies that different media types use.

A *point-to-point* topology has a single connection between two components. In this topology, two components can directly communicate without interference from other components. These types of connections are not common when many components need to be connected together. An example of a point-to-point topology is two routers connected across a dedicated WAN circuit.

In a *star* topology, a central device has many point-to-point connections to other components. Star topologies are used in environments in which many components need to be connected. An example of a media type that uses a star topology is 10BaseT Ethernet. When connecting components together, you connect your computers to a hub or switch (the center of the star). The main problem with a star topology is that if the center of the star fails, no components can communicate with each other. To solve this problem, an extended star topology can be used. An extended star topology is basically multiple interconnected star topologies.

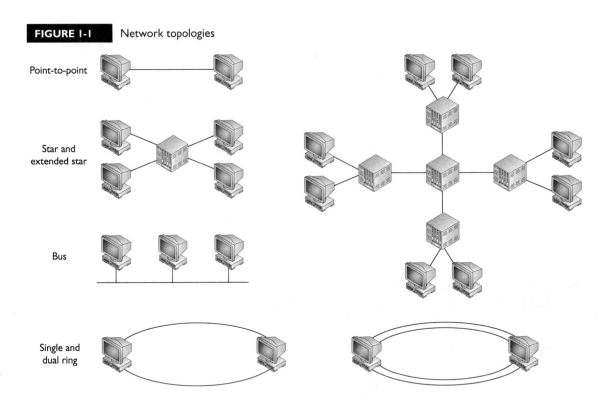

FIGURE 1-1   Network topologies

Point-to-point

Star and
extended star

Bus

Single and
dual ring

In a *bus* topology, all components are connected to and share a single wire. Certain media types, such as 10Base5 and 10Base2 Ethernet, use a bus topology. Typically, special types of connectors or transceivers are used to connect the cables to provide the bus topology. In 10Base5, for example, each device connects to a single strand of coaxial cable via a vampire tap. This device taps into the single strand of coaxial cable and provides the physical connection from a networking device to the single strand of cable.

In a *ring* topology, device one connects to device two, device two connects to device three, and so on to the last device, which connects back to the first device. Ring topologies can be implemented with a single ring or a dual ring. Dual rings are typically used when you need redundancy. For example, if one of the components fails in the ring, the ring can wrap itself, as shown in Figure 1-2, to provide a single, functional ring. Fiber distributed data interface (FDDI) is an example of a media technology that uses dual rings to connect computer components. Single ring topologies lack this type of redundancy feature.

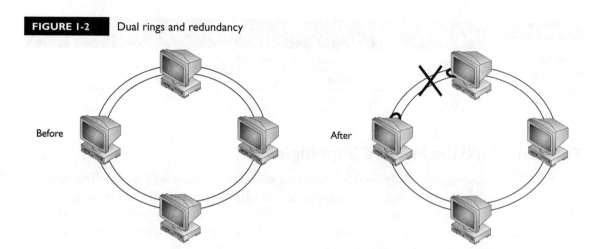

FIGURE 1-2 Dual rings and redundancy

Before

After

Physical and Logical Topologies

A distinction needs to be made between physical and logical topologies. A *physical* topology describes how components are physically cabled together. For instance, 10BaseT has a physical star topology and FDDI has a physical dual ring topology. A *logical* topology describes how components communicate across the physical topology. The physical and logical topologies are independent of each other. For example, any variety of Ethernet uses a logical bus topology when components communicate, regardless of the physical layout of the cabling. This means that in Ethernet, you might be using 10BaseT with a physical star topology to connect components together; however, these components are using a logical bus topology to communicate.

Token Ring is another good example of a communication protocol that has a different physical topology from its logical one. Physically, Token Ring uses a star topology, similar to 10BaseT Ethernet. Logically, however, Token Ring components use a ring topology to communicate between devices. This can create confusion when you are trying to determine how components are connected together and how they communicate. FDDI, on the other hand, is straightforward. FDDI's physical and logical topologies are the same: a ring. Table 1-2 shows common media types and their physical and logical topologies.

exam
watch
Be able to match up the topologies used in Table 1-2 to a given media type.

TABLE 1-2	Media Type	Physical Topology	Logical Topology
Examples of Physical and Logical Topologies	Ethernet	Bus, star, or point-to-point	Bus
	FDDI	Ring	Ring
	Token Ring	Star	Ring

Fully and Partially Meshed Topologies

Meshing generically describes how components are connected together. Two types of meshed topologies are used: partial and full. In a partially meshed environment, every device is *not* connected to every other device. In a fully meshed environment, every component *is* connected to every other component. Figure 1-3 shows examples of these two types of topologies.

Note that like physical and logical topologies, partial and full mesh can be seen from both a physical view and a logical one. For example, in a physical bus topology, all the components are fully meshed, since they are all connected to the same piece of wire—this is both a physical and a logical fully meshed topology and is common in LAN topologies. WANs, on the other hand, because of their cost, commonly use partially meshed topologies to reduce the cost of connecting the components and locations. For example, in the partially meshed network shown at left in Figure 1-3, the top, left, and bottom components can all communicate via the device on the right. This communication introduces a delay in the transmission, but it reduces the cost, since not as many connections are needed.

| FIGURE 1-3 | Partial and full mesh topologies |

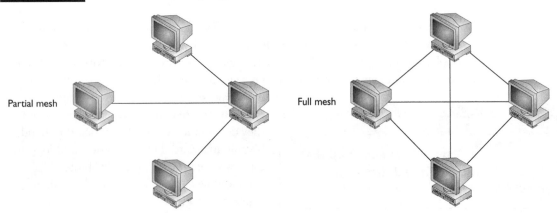

Partial mesh   Full mesh

on the
job

The formula used to determine the number of links needed to fully mesh a WAN is N × (N–1) ÷ 2, where N is the number of locations. For example, if you had 10 locations, you would need 45 links to fully mesh these sites. In addition to cost being an inhibiting factor, the number of interfaces required on WAN devices as well as the management of these connections can quickly become overwhelming as you start interconnecting more and more locations.

CERTIFICATION OBJECTIVE 1.03

Introduction to Network Security

The Computer Security Institute (CSI) has produced many reports on security. One survey revealed that more than 70 percent of the companies surveyed had experienced some kind of security breach. You might think that by setting up a closed network—one not connected to a public network such as the Internet—a company would be safe from most attacks. However, interestingly enough, most (60 to 80 percent) of the breaches or attacks of the surveyed companies occurred *within* the network, not from an external attacker! Because most companies are connected to the Internet and because it is easy to access internal network components within a company, security has played an ever-increasing role in company network designs.

The foundation of security is contained in a company's security policy. A security policy defines what people can and can't do with network components and resources. A security solution is derived from the security policy. A security solution that hinders a company from reaching its business goals, of course, is counterproductive. Therefore, a company must balance security and business plans and goals. This can be difficult when a company's services, such as e-commerce, must be accessed by people over the Internet.

on the
job

Before you even consider designing a security solution for a network, you must have a sound security policy in place. The security policy will determine the security solution you'll design, implement, and maintain. The Securing Cisco Network Devices (SND) course and book briefly talks about security policies. A better reference is RFC 2196 on the Internet Engineering Task Force (IETF) web site (www.ietf.org).

Because most companies' networks are *open*—connected to other public networks such as the Internet—and because most attacks on networks occur from within a company's walls, the need for security is very important. This is apparent when taking a historical look at the sophistication of attacks and hacking tools. In the 1980s, the kinds of threats companies dealt with centered on an attacker manually trying to guess passwords for accounts to break into a network component. Today, most attacks are automated and self-replicating, requiring very little configuration on the attacker's part. Tools such as Metasploit and Core Impact make some hacking, quite literally, as simple as pushing a button—as Metasploit's tagline says, "Point. Click. Root."

Classes of Attacks

To provide an effective security defense, a company must deal with these three things:

- **Adversaries** An adversary is a person or persons interested in attacking your network. Common adversaries include disgruntled employees, unskilled hackers (script kiddies) and skilled hackers, criminals, other countries, terrorists, competing companies, and others.

- **Motivations** Adversaries' motivations range from being challenged (hacker), to gathering or stealing information (competing companies and criminals), to denial of service (terrorists, other countries, and criminals).

- **Classes of attacks** Adversaries can employ five classes of attacks: passive, active, distributed, insider, and close-in.

A *passive* attack monitors unencrypted traffic and looks for clear-text passwords and sensitive information that can be used in other types of attacks. In an *active* attack, the attacker tries to bypass or break into secured systems. This can be done through stealth, viruses, worms, or Trojan horses, or by exploiting a discovered security vulnerability. A *distributed* attack requires that the adversary introduce code, such as a Trojan horse or back-door program, to a "trusted" component or software that will later be distributed to many other companies and users. Installing this component or software then introduces the exploit, unbeknownst to the user and company, into their network. An *insider* attack involves someone from the inside, such as a disgruntled employee, attacking the network. This is the most common type of attack, where the inside attacker attempts to eavesdrop, copy, or cause damage to information. An eavesdropping tool, commonly called a sniffing tool, is Wireshark—it is free to download and can reveal loads of information about what is happening in a company's network. Another common tool is Ettercap; it's also free, but it also allows you to intercept and inject yourself into connections, including Secure Sockets Layer (SSL) connections. A *close-in* attack involves someone attempting to get physically close to network components, data, and systems in order to learn more about a network. This can also lead to the attacker damaging systems, creating a denial of service (DoS).

Common Threats and Mitigation

Four categories of common threats to networks and their components can occur: physical installations, reconnaissance attacks, access attacks, and denial of service (DoS) attacks. The following paragraphs will discuss each of these four threats and mitigation techniques commonly used to thwart and/or defeat these attacks.

Physical Installations

Physical installations involve four types of threats: hardware, electrical, environmental, and maintenance. Hardware threats involve physical damage to network components, such as servers, routers, and switches. To reduce the likelihood of a hardware threat, your critical network components should be placed in a locked room, where only authorized administrators are allowed access. To ensure no entry can be gained to the critical network components, the room should not be accessible by a window, air vents, dropped down ceilings, or raised flooring. To further reduce the likelihood of someone gaining unauthorized access to the secured room, all entry should be monitored, in and out, via electronic access control and video monitoring.

Electrical threats include irregular fluctuations in voltage, such as brownouts and voltage spikes, and complete loss of power. To mitigate these threats, an uninterruptible power supply (UPS) and backup generator system should be installed for critical network components. These should continually be monitored and periodically tested. Also, for critical network components, redundant power supplies should be purchased, if supported by the network components.

on the
!
0 o b

Much confusion exists about the difference between a UPS and a surge protector. A UPS protects equipment against complete loss of power for a short period of time (basically it's a very large battery), whereas a surge protector protects equipment from power spikes and surges. It is common to find products that can perform both functions.

Environmental threats include very low or high temperatures, moisture, electrostatic, and magnetic interference. An adequate temperature and humidity system should be used to ensure that network components are operating in a environment specified by their manufacturers. A monitoring system should be used so that an administrator can take immediate action if anomalies occur in temperature or humidity. No carpeting or similar materials should exist in a room with critical network components, since they can create static electricity that can damage the components when transferred accidentally from a person. Likewise, any device emitting a large amount of magnetic interference should be placed in a separate location to ensure that it doesn't cause damage to network components such as disk drives.

Maintenance threats include not having backup parts or components for critical network components; not labeling components and their cabling correctly, causing problems when performing maintenance in and around network components; and not following electrostatic discharge procedures before handling network components.

To mitigate these threats, an administrator should maintain parts on hand for critical network components. All cables should be clearly labeled and should be neatly run so that tracking cables is an easy matter. Before performing any maintenance on a network component, electrostatic discharge procedures should be followed to minimize the risk that static electricity from your body could damage critical network components. Any login access to a network component should have an idle timeout to ensure that if an administrator temporarily walks away, the network component will sooner rather than later automatically log off the administrator to prevent someone else from gaining unauthorized access to the component. Typically, security controls are either physical or logical. Physical controls are sign in/out logs, locks, guards, and doors. Logical controls would be the idle timeout on logins, passwords, and authentication methods.

Reconnaissance Attacks

A reconnaissance attack occurs when an adversary tries to learn information about your network. He will do this by discovering network components and resources and the vulnerabilities that exist in them. Adversaries will commonly use several tools in their attacks: social engineering (pretending to be a trusted source to gain unauthorized access to information), scanning tools, packet sniffers, and other tools.

To mitigate a social engineering attack, users should have to go through proper training about the kinds of information they can and can't share with other people within and outside of the company. To mitigate scanning and packet sniffing attacks, good access control mechanisms, such as firewalls and IDS/IPS, should be deployed.

Access Attacks

An access attack occurs when someone tries to gain unauthorized access to a component, tries to gain unauthorized access to information on a component, or increases their privileges on a network component. Many kinds of access attacks are used, but the most common kind is a password attack. In a password attack, the adversary tries to guess a valid password for an existing account. She might attempt this kind of attack by using a password cracking program that will use a dictionary to guess common passwords or use a brute-force approach by guessing every combination of numbers, letters, and special characters. A brute-force attack might take a long time to break a password, depending on the length of the password and the computing power used to discover the password. L0ptcrack and Cain & Abel are very good password-cracking programs that support the use of brute force; Cain & Abel is even free to download! More commonly, adversaries will use social engineering to trick a user into revealing passwords or installing a Trojan horse to capture keystrokes from a user's PC, including login credentials. Some adversaries might even use packet sniffers to examine clear-text connections, such as telnet and FTP, for usernames and passwords.

To mitigate these kinds of access attacks, strict access control features should be in place. Access should be restricted to network components and their information through the use of network filters; for example, only accounting people should be able to access accounting servers and data on those servers. This kind of feature can be enforced by access control lists (ACLs) on routers or firewalls, which are covered in more detail in Chapter 22. To mitigate Trojan horse attacks, an IDS/IPS and anti-spyware software should be used. An example of a good (and free) IDS/IPS tool is SNORT, which can run on many UNIX-based and Windows systems. To reduce the likelihood of a brute-force password guessing attack, passwords should contain a combination of letters (upper and lowercase), numbers, and special characters. Passwords should be at least 10 characters long, and users shouldn't be allowed to use the same password on multiple network components. Many companies use token cards, which use one-time passwords (OTPs)—a different, dynamic password is required each time a user logs into a system, making it practically impossible for an adversary to guess the ever-changing dynamic password. Another common solution is to encrypt information between two network components so that login credentials cannot be viewed; for example, it is better to use SSH instead of telnet for remote access because SSH encrypts the session traffic. SSH is discussed in more depth in Chapter 17.

DoS Attacks

DoS attacks involve an adversary reducing the level of operation or service, preventing access to, or completely crashing a network component or service. DoS attacks can involve the flooding of millions of packets or injecting code into an application or overrunning the buffer(s) of an application, causing it to crash. Appropriate firewall access control mechanisms such as packet filtering should be used to control access to a system and mitigate certain kinds of DoS attacks.

Common DoS attacks include flood attacks, such as Internet Control Message Protocol (ICMP) and TCP SYN flooding, as well as buffer overrun attacks (TCP SYNs are discussed in Chapter 9).

Rate limiting and other tools should be used to ensure that a system doesn't become overwhelmed by a flood attack. Intrusion detection and prevention systems should be used to prevent known exploits of vulnerabilities that can cause system crashes, like buffer overrun attacks.

Attack Summary

Table 1-3 sums up the past three sections by listing the attacks, the recommended solutions, the types of devices you would use to implement these solutions, and the chapter or chapters in this book that discuss some of these solutions. Please note that the recommended mitigation solutions discussed in this book are only a few of the tools you can use to deal with the different categories of attacks. Cisco and other vendors have many enhanced products and features that are beyond the scope of this book.

TABLE 1-3	Attack	Recommended Mitigation Solution	Recommended Devices	Chapter
Attacks and Solutions	Reconnaissance	ACLs	IPS, IDS, routers	22
	Access	Authentication, port security, virtual LANs (VLANs), ACLs, virtual private networks (VPNs)	Switches, routers, firewalls, IPS, IDS	11, 12, 13, 22, 25
	DoS	ACLs	IPS, IDS, firewalls, routers	22

INSIDE THE EXAM

Networks, Topologies, and Security

Even though this chapter provides an introduction and overview of networks, topologies, and security, expect to see a few questions on the exam related to this material. Designing and maintaining networks includes factors such as cost, speed, topology type, scalability, reliability, and availability. Certain kinds of traffic, such as VoIP and video, are sensitive to delay and latency and therefore your design should include QoS features to deal with these types of traffic. The kinds of network components you'll see in a network include routers, switches, bridges, hubs, and security appliances such as firewalls and IPS/IDS security appliances.

These devices can be in different geographic locations: mobile user, SOHO, branch office, and/or central or corporate office. Connecting these involves using a WAN service(s).

Ethernet is based on a logical bus topology, but it can use a physical bus, star, or point-to-point topology.

Because most attacks are internal attacks, special planning is needed to deal with physical threats: hardware, electrical, environmental, and maintenance. The three basic kinds of external attacks are reconnaissance, access, and DoS. Easy-to-implement DoS attacks involve flooding a network with thousands or millions of packets, such as a TCP SYN flood attack.

on the job

An IDS/IPS, such as SNORT, is essential in preventing DoS network attacks. While SNORT is a passive, signature-based IDS, you can purchase and implement active IDSs, which will take action to stop the attack instead of simply notifying you that it is happening. NetIQ Security Manager and ARCSight are two IDSs that can be configured to do this.

CERTIFICATION SUMMARY

This chapter focused on three topics: introduction to networks, network topologies, and introduction to network security. A network connects components across a distance, allowing the sharing of resources such as applications and data, printers, and network storage. Characteristics to consider when implementing and maintaining a network design include cost, security, speed, topology, scalability, reliability, and availability. Components common to a network include cabling, computers, switches, routers, firewalls, wireless access points, and others. Networks come in all shapes and sizes: central office, branch office, SOHO, and mobile users.

Network topologies describe how network components are physically cabled and logically how network components communicate with each other. Topology types include point-to-point, star, bus, and ring. Meshing describes how components are interconnected. In a fully meshed topology, every component has direct communication with every other component. In a partially meshed topology, not every component has direct communication with every other component: a component might need to communicate with an intermediate component to get information to the actual destination.

Network security should be a part of every network design and implementation. To implement a secure defense, an administrator needs to consider all adversaries, their motivations, and the classes of attack: passive, active, distributed, close-in, and insider. Common threats to networks include physical installations (hardware, electrical, environmental, and maintenance), reconnaissance attacks, access attacks, and DoS attacks. Appropriate techniques should be deployed to mitigate these threats.

✓ TWO-MINUTE DRILL

Introduction to Networks

❑ A network includes all of the hardware and software components used to connect computers across a distance to provide easy access to information and increase productivity. To build a network, you need computers, networking devices, and media (cable or wireless connections).

❑ A SOHO describes people working from home or a small office. A branch office describes a small group of users connected in a small area. Mobile users connect to a network from any remote location. A central or corporate office is the location of critical services and applications accessed by central office, branch office, SOHO, and mobile users.

Network Topologies

❑ A point-to-point topology uses a single connection between two devices and is typically used in WAN environments. In a star topology, a central device makes many point-to-point connections to other devices. A 10BaseT hub is an example of a central device in a star topology. A bus topology uses a single connection between all devices; Ethernet 10Base5 is an example of this topology. A ring topology connects one device to the next, where the last device is connected to the first. FDDI is an example of a ring topology.

❑ A physical topology defines how the computing devices are physically cabled together. A logical topology describes the method by which devices communicate across a physical topology. The two topologies can vary with the network technology/standard used.

❑ Meshing generically describes how devices are connected. In a partially meshed network, not every device has a connection to every other device. In a fully meshed network, each device is connected to all other devices.

Introduction to Network Security

❑ A security policy is used to implement a security solution and enforce security rules.

❑ An adversary is a person interested in attacking your network; his motivation can range from gathering or stealing information, creating a DoS, or just for the challenge of it. The class of attack can be passive, active, distributed, close-in, or insider.

❑ Hardware threats involve physical damage to network components, so critical components should be placed in a secured room with controlled access. Electrical threats involve fluctuations or loss of power. UPSs, backup generators, and redundant power supplies should be employed. Environmental threats involve wide fluctuations in temperature and humidity, so an appropriate system should be used to control and monitor these. Maintenance threats involve actually working with the equipment, such as unplugging the wrong cable or damaging equipment with static electricity. Proper cable runs and labels should be used, electrostatic discharge procedures should be followed, and careful login and logout procedures should be followed.

❑ Reconnaissance attacks involve learning information about a network. Access attacks involve someone who tries to gain unauthorized access to a component or information on a component or increases her privileges on a network component. A common type of access attack is a password attack. Hard-to-guess passwords or OTP systems should be used to mitigate password attacks. DoS attacks involve reducing the level of operation, preventing access to, or crashing a networking component.

SELF TEST

The following Self Test questions will help you measure your understanding of the material presented in this chapter. Read all the choices carefully, as there may be more than one correct answer. Choose all correct answers for each question.

Introduction to Networks

1. Which of the following network characteristics is concerned about MTBF?
   A. Cost
   B. Security
   C. Reliability
   D. Availability

2. _____ describe(s) users working from home.
   A. SOHO
   B. Branch office
   C. Regional office
   D. Corporate office

Network Topologies

3. A _____ topology uses a single cable to connect all devices together.
   A. Bus
   B. Star
   C. Point-to-point
   D. Ring

4. _____ has both physical and logical ring topologies.
   A. Ethernet
   B. FDDI
   C. Token Ring
   D. Wireless

5. Ethernet _____ has/have both a physical and logical bus topology.
   A. 10BaseT
   B. 10Base2 and 10Base5

    C. 10BaseT and 10Base2

    D. 10BaseT, 10Base2, and 10Base5

6. A _____ topology describes how devices communicate with each other.

    A. Physical

    B. Logical

    C. Layered

    D. Component

Introduction to Network Security

7. What general security term is used to describe a person interested in attacking your network?

    A. Motivator

    B. Adversary

    C. Insider

    D. Distributor

8. What class of attack monitors unencrypted traffic, looking for such things as clear-text passwords?

    A. Passive

    B. Active

    C. Distributed

    D. Close-in

9. Which type of installation threat involves keeping spares on hand to mitigate the threat?

    A. Hardware

    B. Electrical

    C. Management

    D. Maintenance

10. A brute-force password attack would be classified as what kind of attack?

    A. Reconnaissance

    B. Access

    C. Authorization

    D. DoS

SELF TEST ANSWERS

Introduction to Networks

1. ☑ **C.** Mean time between failures (MTBF) is commonly used to measure reliability.
   ☒ **A** defines the total cost of the components, their installation, and ongoing maintenance. **B** defines the protection of network components. **D** measures the uptime of the network.

2. ☑ **A.** The term SOHO describes users working from a home or small office.
   ☒ **B** is a small group of users connected via a LAN at one location. **C** is an office with users who can dynamically connect from either a LAN or a WAN. **D** describes the central site, where most of the users and resources are located.

Network Topologies

3. ☑ **A.** A bus topology uses a single cable to connect all devices together.
   ☒ **B** uses a central device, which has point-to-point connections to other devices. **C** is a single connection between two devices. **D** is where one device is connected to another, which is connected to another, and so on, until the last device is connected to the first device, forming a ring.

4. ☑ **B.** FDDI has both physical and logical ring structures.
   ☒ **A**, depending on the type, uses a physical star or bus topology, but all types use a logical bus topology. **C** uses a physical star topology and a logical ring topology. **D** doesn't have a physical or logical "topology" per se, since it uses airwaves; it definitely doesn't use any type of ring topology, but uses a logical bus topology.

5. ☑ **B.** Ethernet 10Base2 and 10Base5 have both physical and logical bus topologies.
   ☒ **A** has a physical star topology and a logical bus topology. **C** and **D** are incorrect because 10BaseT has a physical star topology and a logical bus topology.

6. ☑ **B.** A logical topology describes how devices communicate with each other.
   ☒ **A** defines how devices are connected to each other. **C** and **D** are nonexistent topology types.

Introduction to Network Security

7. ☑ **B.** An adversary is a general term used to describe an attacker (hacker, criminal, terrorist, company spy, disgruntled employee, and so on).
   ☒ **A** and **D** are not security terms. **C** is a class of attack.

8. ☑ **A.** A passive attack monitors unencrypted traffic looking for clear-text passwords and sensitive information that can be used in other types of attacks.
☒ With **B**, the attacker tries to bypass or break into secured systems. **C** requires the adversary to introduce code, such as a Trojan horse or back-door program, to a "trusted" component or software that will later be distributed to many companies and users. **D** involves someone attempting to get physically close to network components, data, and systems to learn more about a network.

9. ☑ **D.** Maintenance threats include not having backup parts or components for critical network components, not labeling components and their cabling correctly, causing problems when performing maintenance in and around network components, and not following electrostatic discharge procedures before handling network components.
☒ **A** involves physical damage to network components, such as servers, routers, and switches. **B** includes irregular fluctuations in voltage, such as brownouts and voltage spikes, and complete loss of power. **C** is a nonexistent physical threat.

10. ☑ **B.** An access attack occurs when someone tries to gain unauthorized access to a component or information on a component or increases his privileges on a network component; one of the most common types of access attacks is a password attack.
☒ **A** occurs when an adversary is trying to learn information about your network. **C** is a nonexistent security term for attacks. **D** involves an adversary reducing the level of operation or service, preventing access to, or completely crashing a network component or service.

2

OSI Reference Model

B efore you can successfully configure Cisco switches and routers, you must understand some basic networking concepts outlined in this chapter and advanced concepts discussed in later chapters. The Open Systems Interconnection (OSI) Reference Model is the best place to start, since it will help you understand how information is transferred between networking components. Of the seven layers in the OSI Reference Model, you should understand how the bottom three layers function, since most networking components function at these layers. This chapter covers how traffic is generally moved between network components, using the OSI Reference Model to illustrate the encapsulation and de-encapsulation process. Chapter 10 will go into this process in much more depth, focusing on the use of TCP/IP to transmit data between network components.

CERTIFICATION OBJECTIVE 2.01

Introduction to the OSI Reference Model

In 1984, the International Organization for Standardization (ISO) developed the OSI Reference Model to describe how information is transferred from one networking component to another, from the point when a user enters information using a keyboard and mouse to when that information is converted to electrical or light signals transferred along a piece of wire (or radio waves transferred through the air). It is important to understand that the OSI Reference Model describes concepts and terms in a general manner, and that many network protocols, such as Transmission Control Protocol/Internet Protocol (TCP/IP) and Internetwork Packet Exchange (IPX), fail to fit nicely into the scheme explained in ISO's model. Therefore, the OSI Reference Model is most often used as a teaching and troubleshooting tool. By understanding the basics of the OSI Reference Model, you can apply these to real protocols to gain a better understanding of them and to troubleshoot problems more easily. Basically, the OSI Reference Model provides a foundation to use when you are considering what happens between network components when they "talk" to each other.

ISO developed the seven-layer model to help vendors and network administrators gain a better understanding of how data is handled and transported between networking devices, as well as to provide a guideline for the implementation of new networking standards and technologies. To assist in this process, the OSI Reference Model separates the network communication process into seven simple layers. It thus

- Defines the process for connecting two layers together, promoting interoperability between vendors
- Separates a complex function into simpler components
- Allows vendors to compartmentalize their design efforts to fit a modular design, which eases implementations and simplifies troubleshooting
- Provides a teaching tool to help network administrators understand the communication process used between networking components

Remember the advantages the OSI Reference Model provides: *interoperability, simplification, modular design, and training.*

A PC is a good example of a modular device. For instance, a PC typically contains the following components: case, motherboard with processor, monitor, keyboard, mouse, disk drive, CD-ROM drive, floppy drive, RAM, video card, Ethernet card, and so on. If one component breaks, it is easy to figure out which component failed and replace the single component. This simplifies your troubleshooting process. Likewise, when a new CD-ROM drive becomes available, you don't have to throw away the current computer to use the new device—you just need to cable it up and add a software driver to your operating system to interface with it. The OSI Reference Model applies the same thought process to the network: vendors can build and design specific applications and/or hardware in one layer for one purpose without affecting the entire network protocol stack.

CERTIFICATION OBJECTIVE 2.02

Layers of the OSI Reference Model

The OSI Reference Model comprises seven layers, shown in Figure 2-1: application, presentation, session, transport, network, data link, and physical. The functions of the application, presentation, and session layers are typically part of the user's application,

FIGURE 2-1 Layers of the OSI Reference Model

Layer 7	Application
Layer 6	Presentation
Layer 5	Session
Layer 4	Transport
Layer 3	Network
Layer 2	Data link
Layer 1	Physical

such as the Firefox and Internet Explorer web browsers and Microsoft's Outlook e-mail application. The transport, network, data link, and physical layers are responsible for moving data and information back and forth between these higher layers.

on the **Job**

Understanding the functions of each of the OSI Reference Model layers is very important when it comes to troubleshooting connections between network components. Once you understand these functions and the troubleshooting tools available to you at the various layers of the model, troubleshooting problems will be much easier.

Each layer is responsible for a specific process or role. Remember that the seven layers are there to help you understand the transformation process that data will undergo as it is transported to a remote networking component. Not every networking protocol will fit exactly into this model. For example, TCP/IP has four layers. Some layers are combined into a single layer; for instance, TCP/IP's application layer contains the functionality of the OSI Reference Model's application, presentation, and session layers. The following sections go into more detail concerning the seven layers of the OSI Reference Model.

exam

Watch *A good anagram to use to remember the OSI Reference Model layers is "All people seem to need data processing"* *(application, presentation, session, transport, network, data link, and physical).*

Layer 7: The Application Layer

The seventh layer, or topmost layer, of the OSI Reference Model is the *application* layer. It provides the interface that a person uses to interact with the application. This interface can be command-line–based or graphics-based. Cisco Internetwork Operating System (IOS) routers and switches use a command-line interface (CLI), whereas a web browser uses a graphical interface. Cisco routers also have a graphical user interface, called Security Device Manager (SDM), which is introduced in Chapter 18.

Note that in the OSI Reference Model, the application layer refers to applications that are *network-aware*. Of the thousands of existing computer applications, not all can transmit information across a network. This situation is changing rapidly, however. In the 1990s, a distinct line existed between applications that could and couldn't perform network functions. A good example of this was word processing programs, such as Microsoft Word, which were built to perform one process: word processing. Today, however, many applications—Microsoft Word, for instance—have embedded objects that don't necessarily have to be located on the same computer. There are many, many examples of application layer programs. The most common are telnet and Secure Shell (SSH), File Transfer Protocol (FTP), web browsers, and e-mail. You should realize that the applications themselves are not what the OSI Reference Model's application layer is about: the application layer provides a means for the applications to realize that a network is there and to take advantage of it. In other words, the application layer encompasses the protocols and services that the applications will employ to access network resources.

Layer 6: The Presentation Layer

The sixth layer of the OSI Reference Model is the *presentation* layer. The presentation layer is responsible for defining how information is transmitted and presented to the user in the interface that he or she is using. This layer defines how various forms of text, graphics, video, and/or audio information is transmitted and used correctly by the application layer. For example, text is represented in primarily two different forms: ASCII and EBCDIC. ASCII (the American Standard Code for Information Interchange, used by most devices today) uses 7 bits to represent characters. EBCDIC (Extended Binary-Coded Decimal Interchange Code, developed by IBM) is still used in mainframe environments to represent characters. Text can also be shaped by different elements, such as font, underline, italic, and bold.

Many different standards are used for representing graphical information—BMP, GIF, JPEG, TIFF, and others. This variety of standards is also true of audio (WAV and MIDI, for example) and video (WMV, AVI, MOV, and MPEG, for example). Literally hundreds of standards are used to represent information that a user sees in an application. Probably one of the best examples of applications with a very clear presentation layer function is a web browser, since it has many special marking codes, called *tags*, which define how data should be represented to the user. The presentation layer can also provide encryption to secure data from the application layer; however, this is not common with today's methods of security, since this type of encryption is performed in software and requires a lot of CPU cycles to perform.

Layer 5: The Session Layer

The fifth layer of the OSI Reference Model is the *session* layer. The session layer is responsible for initiating the setup and teardown of connections. To perform these functions, the session layer must determine whether data stays local to a computer or must be obtained or sent to a remote networking component. In the latter case, the session layer initiates the connection. The session layer is also responsible for differentiating among multiple network connections, ensuring that data is sent across the correct connection as well as taking data from a connection and forwarding it to the correct local application. The actual mechanics of this process, however, are implemented at the transport layer. To set up connections or tear down connections, the session layer communicates with the transport layer. Remote Procedure Calls (RPCs) are an example of a TCP/IP session protocol; the Network File System (NFS), which uses RPCs, is another example of a protocol at this layer. The session layer is also responsible for error reporting of any issues at the application, presentation, and session layers and for implementing any type of class of service (CoS) to give preference to some types of traffic or connections over others.

The session layer is responsible for setting up, maintaining, *and tearing down network connections. Examples include RPCs and NFS.*

Layer 4: The Transport Layer

The fourth layer of the OSI Reference Model is the *transport* layer. The transport layer is responsible for the actual mechanics of setting up, maintaining, and tearing down a connection, where it can provide both *reliable* and *unreliable* delivery of data. For reliable connections, the transport layer is responsible for error detection and correction: when an error is detected, the transport layer will resend the data, thus providing the correction. For unreliable connections, the transport layer provides only error detection—error correction is left up to one of the higher layers (typically the application layer). In this sense, unreliable connections attempt to provide a best-effort delivery—if the data makes it there, that's great, and if it doesn't, oh well! An example of a reliable transport protocol is TCP/IP's Transmission Control Protocol (TCP). TCP/IP's User Datagram Protocol (UDP) is an example of a protocol that uses unreliable connections.

For people just beginning to learn the mechanics of the OSI Reference Model, it is sometimes difficult to see the delineation between what the session and transport layer actually do. The session layer deals with timeout issues, notifications, hello packets to determine connection issues, and so on; the transport layer entails the actual delivery mechanisms of moving information (at the transport layer) between network components.

The transport layer has five main functions:

- It sets up, maintains, and tears down a session connection between two components.
- It can provide for the reliable or unreliable delivery of data across this connection.
- It segments data into smaller, more manageable sizes.
- It multiplexes connections, allowing multiple applications to send and receive data simultaneously on the same networking device.
- It can implement flow control through ready/not ready signals or windowing to ensure one component doesn't overflow another one with too much data on a connection. Both of these methods typically use buffering and are used to avoid congestion.

The following sections cover these processes in more depth.

Reliable Connections

The transport layer can provide reliable and unreliable transfer of data between networking components. TCP is an example of a transport layer protocol that provides a reliable connection. When implementing a reliable connection, sequence numbers and acknowledgments (ACKs) are commonly used. For example, when information is sent to a destination, the destination will acknowledge to the source what information was received. The destination can examine sequence numbers in the transmitted data segments to determine whether anything was missing (dropped along the way) as well as put the data back in the correct order, if it arrived out of order, before passing it on to the upper-layer application. If a segment is missing, the destination can request that the source resend the missing information. With some protocol stacks, the destination might have the source resend all of the information or parts of the information, including the missing parts.

Some reliable connection protocols might also go through a *handshake* process when initially building a connection. This handshake process determines whether the two networking devices can build the connection and negotiates parameters that should be used to provide a reliable connection. With TCP, this is called the *three-way handshake*. TCP and the three-way handshake are discussed in more depth in Chapter 9.

Unreliable Connections

One of the issues of a connection-oriented service such as TCP is that they typically go through a handshake process before data can be transferred, and then acknowledge that all data sent was received. In some instances, such as file transfers, this makes sense, because you want to ensure that all data for the file is transferred successfully. However, in other cases, when you want to send only one piece of information and get a single reply back, going through a handshake process adds overhead and delay that typically isn't necessary.

In TCP/IP, a domain name service (DNS) query is a good example of when using a connection-oriented service doesn't make sense. With a DNS query, a device is trying to resolve a fully qualified domain name to an IP address. The device sends the single query to a DNS server and waits for the server's response. In this process, only two messages are generated: the client's query and the server's response. Because of the minimal amount of information shared between these two devices, it makes no sense to establish a reliable connection first before sending the query. Instead, the device should just send its information and wait for a response. If a response doesn't come back, the application can send the information again or the user can get involved. With operating systems' implementation of DNS, you can configure two DNS servers in your TCP/IP adapter settings. If you don't get a reply from the first server in an application, the application can try to use the second configured server.

Because no "connection" is built up front, this type of connection is referred to as a *connectionless* service. The TCP/IP protocol stack uses the UDP to provide unreliable or connectionless connections. UDP is discussed in more depth in Chapter 9.

Segmentation

Another function of the transport layer is to set up, maintain, and tear down connections for the session layer—that is, it handles the actual mechanics for the connection. The information transferred between networking devices at the transport layer is called a *segment*. Segmentation is necessary to break up large amounts of data into more manageable sizes that the network can accommodate. A good analogy of this process is "it's easier to pour pebbles down a pipe than giant boulders."

Connection Multiplexing

Because multiple connections may be established from one component to another component or components, some type of multiplexing function is needed to differentiate between data traversing the various connections. This ensures that the transport layer can send data from a particular application to the correct destination and application, and, when receiving data from a destination, get it to the right local application.

To accomplish this feat, the transport layer typically assigns a unique set of numbers for each connection. These numbers are commonly called *port* or *socket* numbers. A source port number and a destination port number are assigned for each connection. The destination port numbers assigned by the source device are sometimes referred to as *well-known* or *reserved* port numbers. The source device uses an appropriate port number in the destination port field to indicate to the destination which application it is trying to access. For example, the TCP/IP protocol stack gives each application a unique port number.

Some well-known port numbers used by TCP/IP applications are FTP (20 and 21), telnet (23), SMTP for e-mail (25), DNS (53), TFTP (69), WWW (80), and POP mail (110). With TCP/IP, port numbers from 0 to 1023 are well-known port numbers. However, some applications have port numbers higher than these numbers. Actually, TCP/IP uses a 16-bit field for the port number, allowing you to reference up to 65,536 different numbers. Port numbers above 1023 are used by the source to assign to the connection as the source port number. Each connection on the source has a unique source port number. This helps the source device differentiate its own connections. This process is discussed in more depth in Chapter 9.

Flow Control

Another function of the transport layer is to provide optional flow control. Flow control is used to ensure that networking components don't send too much information to the destination, overflowing its receiving buffer space and causing it to drop some of the transmitted information. Overflow is not good because the source will have to resend all the information that was dropped. The transport layer can use two basic flow control methods:

- Ready/not ready signals
- Windowing

Ready/Not Ready Signals With *ready/not ready signals*, when the destination receives more traffic than it can handle, it can send a *not ready* signal to the source, indicating that the source should stop transmitting data. When the destination has a chance to catch up and process the source's data, the destination responds back to the source with a *ready* signal. Upon receiving the ready signal, the source can resume sending data.

Two problems are associated with the use of ready/not ready signals to implement flow control. First, the destination may respond to the source with a not ready signal when its buffer fills up. While this message is on its way to the source, the source is *still sending* information to the destination, which the destination will probably have to drop because its buffer space is full. The second problem with the use of these signals is that once the destination is ready to receive more information, it must first send a ready signal to the source, which must receive it before more information can be sent. This causes a delay in the transfer of information. Because of these two inefficiencies with ready/not ready signals, they are not commonly used to implement flow control. Sometimes this process is referred to as *stop/start*, where you stop transmitting for a period and then start retransmitting.

Windowing   *Windowing* is a much more sophisticated method of flow control than using ready/not ready signals. With windowing, a window size is defined that specifies how much data (commonly called *segments* at the transport layer) can be sent before the source has to wait for an acknowledgment (ACK) from the destination. Once the ACK is received, the source can send the next batch of data (up to the maximum defined in the window size).

   Windowing accomplishes two things: First, flow control is enforced, based on the window size. In many protocol implementations, the window size is dynamically negotiated up front and can be renegotiated during the lifetime of the connection. This ensures that the most optimal window size is used to send data without having the destination drop anything. Second, through the windowing process, the destination tells the source what was received. This indicates to the source whether any data was lost along the way to the destination and allows the source to resend any missing information. This provides reliability for a connection as well as better efficiency than ready/not ready signals. Because of these advantages, most connection-oriented transport protocols, such as TCP/IP's TCP, use windowing to implement flow control.

   The window size chosen for a connection impacts its efficiency and throughput in defining how many segments (or bytes) can be sent before the source has to wait for an ACK. Figure 2-2 illustrates the importance of the size used for the window. The top part of the figure shows the connection using a window size of 1. In this instance, the source sends one segment with a sequence number (in this case *1*) and then waits for an acknowledgment from the destination. Depending on the transport protocol, the destination can send the ACK in different ways: it can send back a list of the sequence numbers of the segments it received, or it can send back the sequence number of the next segment it expects. The ACK from the destination has a number 2 in it. This tells the source that it can go ahead and send segment 2. Again, when the destination receives this segment, since the window size is 1, the destination will immediately reply with an acknowledgment, indicating the receipt of this segment. In this example, the destination acknowledges back 3, indicating that segment 3 can be sent, and so on and so forth.

FIGURE 2-2   Window sizes affect efficiency.

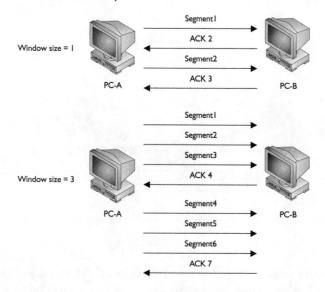

As you can see, with a window size of 1, the flow control process is not very quick or efficient. Let's look at an example with a window size of 3, as illustrated at the bottom of Figure 2-2. With a window size of 3, the source can send three segments at once before waiting for an ACK. Once segments are sent (each with its own unique sequence number: 1, 2, and 3), the source must wait for an acknowledgment. In this instance, the destination sends an ACK back with the number 4 in it, indicating that the fourth segment is expected next. The source can then proceed to send segments 4, 5, and 6, and then wait for the destination's acknowledgment. In this case, having a larger window size is more efficient: only one acknowledgment is required for every three segments that are sent. Therefore, the larger the window size, the more efficient the transfer of information becomes.

However, this is not always the case. For example, let's assume that one segment gets lost on its way to the destination, as is shown in Figure 2-3. In this example, the window size negotiated is 3. PC-A sends its first three segments, which are successfully received by PC-B. PC-B acknowledges the next segment it expects, which is 4. When PC-A receives this acknowledgment, it sends segments 4, 5, and 6. For some reason, segment 4 becomes lost and never reaches the destination, but segments 5 and 6 do arrive. Remember that the destination is keeping track of what was received: 1, 2, 3, 5, and 6. In this example, the destination sends back an ACK of 4, indicating that segment 4 is expected next.

FIGURE 2-3 Lost segments and retransmissions

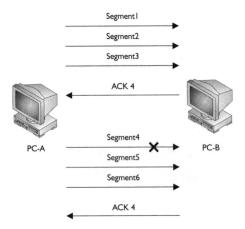

At this point, how PC-A reacts depends on the transport layer protocol that is used. Here are some possible options:

- PC-A understands that only segment 4 was lost and therefore resends segment 4. It then sends segments 7 and 8, filling up the window size.
- PC-A doesn't understand what was or wasn't received, so it sends three segments starting at segment 4, indicated by PC-B.

Of course, if two segments are lost, the first option listed won't work unless the destination can send a list of lost segments. Therefore, most protocol stacks that use windowing will implement the second option. Given this behavior, the size of the window can affect your performance. You would normally think that a window size of 100 would be very efficient; however, if the very first segment is lost, some protocols will have *all* 100 segments resent! As mentioned earlier, most protocol stacks use a window size that is negotiated up front and can be renegotiated at any time. Therefore, if a connection is experiencing a high number of errors, the window size can be dropped to a smaller value to increase efficiency. And once these errors disappear or drop down to a lower rate, the window size can be increased to maximize the connection's throughput.

What makes this situation even more complicated is that the window sizes on the source and destination devices can be *different*. For instance, PC-A might have a window size of 3, while PC-B has a window size of 10. In this example, PC-A is allowed to send 10 segments to PC-B before waiting for an acknowledgment, while PC-B is allowed to send only 3 segments to PC-A.

Flow control through the use of sequence numbers and acknowledgments is covered in more depth in Chapter 9, where TCP is discussed.

Ready/not ready signals and windowing are used to implement flow control. Ready/not ready signals are not efficient, causing drops of unnecessary traffic and delays in the transmission of traffic. Windowing addresses these issues. With windowing, a window size is established, which defines the number of segments that can be transferred before waiting for an acknowledgment from the destination.

Layer 3: The Network Layer

The third layer of the OSI Reference Model is the *network* layer. The network layer provides quite a few functions. First, it provides for a logical topology of your network using logical, or layer 3, addresses. These addresses are used to group networking components together. As you will see in Chapter 7, these addresses have two components: a network and host component. The network component is used to group devices together. Layer 3 addresses allow devices that are on the same or different layer 2 medium or protocol to communicate with each other.

The network layer is responsible for three main functions:

- Defines logical addresses used at layer 3
- Finds paths, based on the network numbers of logical addresses, to reach destination components
- Connects different data link layer types together, such as Ethernet, fiber distributed data interface (FDDI), Serial, and Token Ring

To move information between devices that have different network numbers, a *router* is used. Routers use information in the logical address to make intelligent decisions about how to reach a destination. Routing is discussed in more depth in Part IV of this book. The following sections cover the network layer in more depth.

Layer 3 Addressing

Many protocols function at the network layer, such as AppleTalk, DECnet, TCP/IP, IPX, Vines, XNS, and others. Each of these protocols has its own method of defining logical addressing. Correct assignment of these addresses on devices across your network allows you to build a hierarchical design that can scale to very large sizes. This provides an advantage over layer 2 addressing, which uses a flat design and is not scalable.

All layer 3 addressing schemes have two components: network and host (or node). Each segment (physical or logical) in your network needs a unique network number. Each host on these segments needs a unique host number from within the assigned network number. The combination of the network and host number assigned to a device provides a unique layer 3 address throughout the entire network. For example, if you had 500 devices in your network that were running TCP/IP, each of these devices would need a unique TCP/IP layer 3 address.

This process is different with Media Access Control (MAC) addresses, which are used at layer 2. MAC addresses need to be unique only on a physical (or logical) segment. In other words, within the same broadcast domain, all of the MAC addresses must be unique. However, MAC addresses do *not* need to be unique between two *different* broadcast domains.

A good analogy of unique addresses is the system used by the post office. For example, two homes on the same street cannot have the same house number, such as 1597 Berry Street, since the postal carrier wouldn't know which house using that same address should receive mail. However, if both homes were in different zip codes, but they shared the same street address, the postal carrier would see a difference between the two locations, even though the street names and numbers were the same. MAC addresses are similar: each segment is a separate "neighborhood" with a different "zip code" (different networks); within that "neighborhood," the MAC addresses need to be unique. MAC addresses and broadcasts are discussed in more depth later in the chapter in the "Layer 2: The Data Link Layer" section.

To understand the components of layer 3 addresses, let's look at a few examples. TCP/IP IPv4 addresses are 32 bits in length. To make these addresses more readable, they are broken up into 4 bytes, or *octets*, where any 2 bytes are separated by a period. This is commonly referred to as *dotted decimal notation*. Here's a simple example of an IP address: 10.1.1.1. An additional value, called a *subnet mask*, determines the boundary between the network and host components of an address. When comparing IP addresses to other protocols' addressing schemes, TCP/IP addressing seems the most complicated. IP addressing is thoroughly covered in Chapter 7.

Most other protocols have a much simpler format. For example, IPX addresses are 80 bits in length. The first 32 bits are always the network number, and the last 48 bits are always the host address. IPX addresses are represented in hexadecimal. Here's an example: ABBA.0000.0000.0001. In this example, ABBA is the network number and 0000.0000.0001 is the host number. In IPX's case, the host part defaults to the MAC address on the network interface card (NIC), but this can be overridden by the user or administrator. Every protocol has its own addressing scheme. However, each scheme always begins with a network component followed by a host component.

Routing Tables

Routers are devices that function at the network layer; they use logical network numbers to make routing decisions—how to get information, commonly called a *packet*, to its destination. Routers build a *routing table*, which contains path information. This information includes the network number, which interface the router should use to reach the network number, the metric of the path (what it costs to reach the destination), how the router learned about this network number, and possibly how old the information is. Metrics are used to weight the different paths to a destination. If more than one way can be taken to reach the destination, metrics are used to "rank" each link to determine which path would make the best choice. Using the metrics to make a decision, the router will put the best route to the destination network in its routing table. Many different types of metrics are used, such as bandwidth, delay, and hop count, to name a few. Each routing protocol uses its own metric structure. For instance, TCP/IP's Routing Information Protocol (RIP) uses hop count, while Cisco's EIGRP uses bandwidth, delay, reliability, load, and frame size (maximum transmission unit, or MTU). Routing and routing metrics are discussed in Part IV.

When a router receives an inbound packet, it examines the destination layer 3 address in the packet header. The router then determines the network number in the logical address and then compares this network number to its routing table entries. If the router finds a match, it forwards the packet out of the destination interface. However, if the router does not find a match in its routing table, the router *drops* the packet.

ⓦatch   **Routers make routing decisions based on the network numbers in layer 3 addresses, such as TCP/IP addresses.**   **Locations of networks are stored in a routing table.**

Advantages of Routers

Because routers operate at a higher layer than the data link layer and use logical addressing, they provide many advantages over data link layer devices such as bridges and switches, including the following:

- Logical addressing at layer 3 allows you to build hierarchical networks that scale to very large sizes. This is discussed in Chapters 8, 20, and 21.
- Routers contain broadcasts and multicasts. When a broadcast or multicast is received on an interface, it is *not* forwarded to another interface, by default. Routers are commonly used to solve broadcast problems. (Actually, routers also create separate bandwidth and collision domains, but bridges and switches provide a cheaper solution.) These are discussed later in the "Layer 2: The Data Link Layer" section and in Chapters 3 and 4.
- Routers are better at connecting different layer 2 technologies together, such as Ethernet and Token Ring or FDDI and serial, without any conversion issues.
- Routers can switch packets on the same interface using virtual LANs (VLANs), which are discussed in Chapter 13.
- Routers have advanced features that allow you to implement quality of service using queuing or traffic shaping, filtering traffic using access control lists (ACLs), or protecting traffic using encryption. ACLs are discussed in Chapter 22.

exam

ⓦatch

Remember the bulleted items listing the advantages that routers provide over switches, especially that

routers contain broadcasts: each interface of a router is a separate broadcast and collision domain.

By using logical addresses, routers can create a hierarchical network that supports thousands of network components. Layer 2 components such as bridges and switches, on the other hand, do not support hierarchical addressing: layer 2 MAC addresses support a flat addressing space. In other words, you can't typically change MAC addresses to fit a specific network topology or layout. Also, since routers use logical addresses, it is much easier to implement policy decisions, such as traffic filtering or quality service, since the decisions are made on logical, more easily handled addresses than the physical addresses that bridges and switches use. For example, since logical addresses support a network component, you could filter an entire network number. To accomplish this with a bridge or switch, you would have to filter each individual component's MAC address within the network segment.

Another problem with layer 2 components is that they don't operate very well when connecting different layer 2 technologies or protocols—Ethernet and Token Ring, for instance. At layer 2, this process is called *translational bridging*. Layer 2 devices have issues translating between technologies/protocols for many reasons, but the main reason is that since both topologies are layer 2, the bridge has to translate the layer 2 information between the different protocols. This is process-intensive and can create many problems.

For example, Ethernet supports frame sizes up to 1500 bytes, while Token Ring supports frame sizes up to 16 kilobytes (KB) in size. Therefore, if a large Token Ring frame had to be sent to an Ethernet segment, the bridge or switch would have to fragment the information into two or more Ethernet frames. There might also be a speed difference between the media types: Ethernet supports 10 Mbps (megabits per second), 100 Mbps, 1 Gbps (gigabit per second), and 10 Gbps, while Token Ring supports 4 Mbps, 16 Mbps, and 100 Mbps, and this difference could cause congestion problems on a bridge or switch.

In addition, the translation process between frame types is not always easy. For example, some protocols order their bits from low-to-high, while others order them high-to-low, which can create translation issues. Fortunately, routers provide a clean solution to this translation process. Routers don't actually translate between different frame or layer 2 protocol types; instead, they strip off the layer 2 frame, make a routing decision on the layer 3 packet, and then encapsulate the layer 3 packet in the correct layer 2 frame type for the interface the packet needs to exit. This process is described more thoroughly later in this chapter in the section "Encapsulation and De-Encapsulation" as well as in Chapter 10.

Another advantage routers have over layer 2 components is that they contain broadcast problems. When a router receives a broadcast, it processes that broadcast, but by default, it will not forward the broadcast out any of its other ports. This is different from bridges and switches, which flood broadcast traffic. If broadcasts are affecting the bandwidth and performance of your network, you should break up your network into multiple broadcast domains and use a router to route between the different domains. Each broadcast domain in a network needs a unique layer 3 network number. Broadcasts are discussed later in the chapter in the "Layer 2: The Data Link Layer" section.

on the
job   *Common tools used to troubleshoot layer 3 problems include ping, traceroute, and Address Resolution Protocol (ARP). These tools are discussed in more depth in Chapter 6.*

Layer 2: The Data Link Layer

The second layer in the OSI Reference Model is the *data link* layer. Whereas the network layer provides for logical addresses for components, the data link layer provides for physical, or hardware, addresses. These hardware addresses are commonly called *Media Access Control* (MAC) addresses. The data link layer also defines how a networking component accesses the media to which it is connected and defines the media's frame type and transmission method. The frame includes the fields and components the data link layer uses to communicate with devices on the same wire or layer 2 topology. This communication occurs

e x a m
ⓦ a t c h   *Most wide area network (WAN) protocols primarily function at the data link and physical layers.*

only for components on the same data link layer media type (or same piece of wire), within the same network segment. To traverse layer 2 protocols, Ethernet to Token Ring, for instance, a router is typically used.

The data link layer is also responsible for taking bits (binary 1s and 0s) from the physical layer and reassembling them into the original data link layer frame. The data link layer does error detection and will discard bad frames. It typically does not perform error correction, as some transport layer protocols do; however, some data link layer protocols do support error correction functions.

Examples of data link layer protocols and standards for local area network (LAN) connections include Institute of Electrical and Electronic Engineers (IEEE) 802.2, 802.3, and 802.5; Ethernet II; and ANSI's FDDI. Examples of WAN protocols include Asynchronous Transfer Mode (ATM), Frame Relay, High-Level Data Link Control (HDLC), Point-to-Point Protocol (PPP), Synchronous Data Link Control (SDLC), Serial Line Internet Protocol (SLIP), and X.25. Bridges, switches, and network interface controllers or cards (NICs) are the primary networking components functioning at the data link layer, which is discussed in more depth in Chapter 4.

The data link layer is also responsible for defining the format of layer 2 frames as well as the mechanics of how devices communicate with each other over the physical layer. The data link layer is responsible for the following:

- Defining the MAC or hardware addresses
- Defining the physical or hardware topology for connections
- Defining how the network layer protocol is encapsulated in the data link layer frame
- Providing both connectionless and connection-oriented services

Normally, the data link layer does not provide connection-oriented—that is, reliable—services (those that do error detection and correction). However, in environments that use Systems Network Architecture (SNA) as a data link layer protocol, SNA can provide sequencing and flow control to ensure the delivery of data link layer frames. SNA was developed by IBM to help devices communicate in LANs (predominantly Token Ring) at the data link layer. In most instances, the transport layer provides for reliable connections.

Data Link Layer Addressing

The data link layer uses MAC, or hardware, addresses for communication. For LAN communications, each machine on the same network segment or topology needs a unique MAC address. A MAC address is 48 bits in length and is represented as a hexadecimal number. Represented in hex, it is 12 characters in length. To make it easier to read, the MAC address is represented in a dotted hexadecimal format, like this: FFFF.FFFF.FFFF. It is also common to see MAC addresses formatted in this way: FF:FF:FF:FF:FF:FF. Since the MAC address uses hexadecimal numbers, the values used range from 0 to 9 and A to F, for a total of 16 values for a single digit. For example, a hexadecimal value of A would be *10* in decimal. Hexadecimal numbering is discussed in more depth in Chapter 7. Other types of data link layer addressing are used in addition to MAC addresses. For instance, Frame Relay uses Data Link Connection Identifiers (DLCIs), which are discussed in more depth in Chapter 26.

The first six digits of a MAC address are associated with the vendor, or maker, of the NIC. Each vendor has one or more unique sets of six digits. These first six digits are commonly called the *organizationally unique identifier* (OUI). For example, one of Cisco's OUI values is 0000.0C. The last six digits are used to represent the NIC uniquely within the OUI value. Theoretically, each NIC has a unique MAC address. In reality, however, this is probably not true. What is important for your purposes is that each of your devices has a unique MAC address on its NIC within the same *physical* or *logical* segment. A logical segment is a VLAN and is referred to as a *broadcast domain*, which is discussed in Chapter 13. Some devices allow you to change this hardware address, while others don't.

TABLE 2-1	Address Type	Description
Data Link Address Types	Unicast	Represents a single device on a segment
	Broadcast	Represents every device on a segment
	Multicast	Represents a group of devices on a segment

Each data link layer frame contains two MAC addresses: a source MAC address of the machine creating the frame and a destination MAC address for the device or devices intended to receive the frame. Three general types of addresses are used at the data link layer, as shown in Table 2-1. A source MAC address is an example of a *unicast* address—only one device can create the frame. However, destination MAC addresses can be any of the addresses listed in Table 2-1. The destination MAC address in the data link layer frame helps the other NICs connected to the segment to figure out whether they need to process the frame when they receive it or to ignore it. The following sections cover each of these address types in more depth.

w a t c h *Remember the three types of destination addresses in Table 2-1: unicast, broadcast, and multicast.*

Unicast A frame with a destination *unicast* MAC address is intended for only one network component on a segment. The top part of Figure 2-4 shows an example

FIGURE 2-4	MAC address types

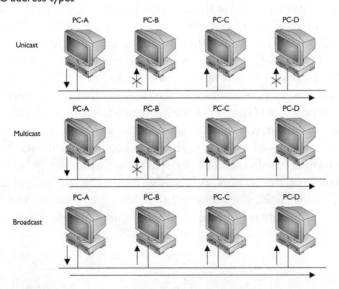

of a unicast. In this example, PC-A creates an Ethernet frame with a destination MAC address that contains PC-C's address. When PC-A places this data link layer frame on the wire, all the devices on the segment receive it. Each of the NICs of PC-B, PC-C, and PC-D examines the destination MAC address in the frame. In this instance, only PC-C's NIC will process the frame, since the destination MAC address in the frame matches the MAC address of its NIC. PC-B and PC-D will ignore the frame.

Multicast   Unlike a unicast address, a *multicast* address represents a group of devices on a segment. The multicast group can contain from no devices to every device on a segment. One of the interesting things about multicasting is that the membership of a group is *dynamic*—devices can join and leave as they please. The detailed process of multicasting is beyond the scope of this book, however.

The middle portion of Figure 2-4 shows an example of a multicast. In this example, PC-A sends a data link layer frame to a multicast group on its segment. Currently, only PC-A, PC-C, and PC-D are members of this group. When each of the PCs receives the frame, its NIC examines the destination MAC address in the data link layer frame. In this example, PC-B ignores the frame, since it is not a member of the group. However, PC-C and PC-D will process the frame.

Broadcast   A *broadcast* is a data link layer frame that is intended for every networking component on the same segment. The bottom portion of Figure 2-4 shows an example of a broadcast. In this example, PC-A puts a broadcast address in the destination field of the data link layer frame. For MAC broadcasts, all of the bit positions in the address are enabled, making the address *FF:FF:FF:FF:FF:FF* in hexadecimal. This frame is then placed on the wire. Notice that in this example, when PC-B, PC-C, and PC-D receive the frame, they *all* process it.

Broadcasts are mainly used in two situations. First, broadcasts are more effective than unicasts if you need to send the same information to every machine. With a unicast, you would have to create a separate frame for each machine on the segment; with a broadcast, you could accomplish the same thing with a single frame. Second, broadcasts are used to discover the unicast address of a device. For instance, when you turn on your PC, initially it doesn't know about any MAC addresses of any other machines on the network. A broadcast can be used to discover the MAC addresses of these machines, since they will all process the broadcast frame. In TCP/IP, the Address Resolution Protocol (ARP) uses this process to discover another device's

MAC address. ARP is discussed in Chapter 6. Other protocols that use broadcasts include Dynamic Host Control Protocol (DHCP) and NetBIOS.

on the **job**

Common tools used to troubleshoot layer 2 problems include ARP (Chapter 6), Cisco's CDP protocol (Chapter 17), switch port address tables (Chapters 4 and 12), and protocol analyzers.

Layer 1: The Physical Layer

The first, or bottommost, layer of the OSI Reference Model is the *physical* layer. The physical layer is responsible for the physical mechanics of a network connection, which include the following:

- The type of interface used on the networking device
- The type of cable used for connecting devices
- The connectors used on each end of the cable
- The pin patterns used for each of the connections on the cable
- The encoding of a message on a signal by converting binary digits to a physical representation based on the media type, such as electrical for copper, light for fiber, or a radio wave for wireless

The type of interface, commonly called a NIC, can be a physical card that you put into a computer, such as a 10BaseT Ethernet card, or a fixed interface on a router, such as a Fast Ethernet port on a Cisco 1841 router.

The physical layer is also responsible for how binary information is converted to a physical layer signal and vice versa. For example, if the cable uses copper as a transport medium, the physical layer defines how binary 1s and 0s are converted into an electrical signal by using different voltage levels. If the cable uses fiber, the physical layer defines how 1s and 0s are represented using an LED or laser with different light frequencies. Binary numbering is discussed in Chapter 7.

Data communications equipment (DCE) terminates a physical WAN connection and provides clocking and synchronization of a connection between two locations and connects to data termination equipment (DTE). The DCE category includes equipment such as CSU/DSUs, NT1s, and modems. A DTE is an end user device, such as a router or a PC, that connects to the WAN via the DCE device. In some cases, the function of the DCE may be built into the DTE's physical interface. For instance, certain Cisco routers can be purchased with built-in

NT1s or CSU/DSUs built into their WAN interfaces. Normally, the terms *DTE* and *DCE* are used to describe WAN components, but they are sometimes used to describe LAN connections. For instance, in a LAN connection, a PC, file server, or router is sometimes referred to as a DTE, and a switch, bridge, or hub is called a DCE.

Examples of physical layer standards include the following cable types (as well as many, many others): Category 3, 5 and 5E; EIA/TIA 232, 449, and 530; multimode and single-mode fiber (MMF and SMF); and Type 1. Interface connectors include the following: attachment unit interface (AUI), bayonet nut coupling (BNC), DB-9, DB-25, DB-60, RJ-11, RJ-45, and others. An Ethernet hub and a repeater are examples of devices that function at the physical layer.

e x a m

w a t c h *The physical layer defines physical properties for connections and communication, including wires (UTP and fiber) and connectors (RJ-45 and DB-9). A hub and a repeater are examples of* *devices that function at the physical layer. A repeater is used to physically extend a single segment, while a hub—known as a multiport repeater—connects many segments together.*

e x a m

w a t c h *Remember the devices listed in Table 2-2 and the layers at which they function.*

Devices

Table 2-2 provides a reminder of the devices that function at various OSI Reference Model layers.

TABLE 2-2	Layer	Name of Layer	Device
Devices and the Layers at Which They Function	3	Network	Routers
	2	Data link	Switches, bridges, NICs
	1	Physical	Hubs and repeaters

CERTIFICATION OBJECTIVE 2.03

Encapsulation and De-encapsulation

Before delving into the mechanics of how information is transferred between computers, you must become familiar with the terminology used to describe the transmitted data. Many of the layers of the OSI Reference Model use their own specific terms to describe data transferred back and forth. As this information is passed from higher to lower layers, each layer adds information to the original data—typically a header and possibly a trailer. This process is called *encapsulation*. The data link layer adds both, where the term *encapsulation* is the most appropriate; however, upper layer protocols add a header, and a few protocols add a trailer, depending on the protocol. Both processes are referred to as *encapsulating* upper layer information and data.

Generically speaking, the term *protocol data unit (PDU)* is used to describe data and its overhead. Table 2-3 describes the terms used at the various layers of the OSI Reference Model. For instance, as data is passed from the session layer to the transport layer, the transport layer *encapsulates* the data PDU in a transport layer segment. For TCP and UDP in the TCP/IP protocol stack, the transport layer adds a header, but no trailer. As the PDU information is passed down, each layer adds its own header and, possibly, trailer to the upper layer PDU.

Once the physical layer is reached, the bits of the data link layer frame are converted into a physical layer signal—a voltage, light source, radio wave, or other source according to the type of physical medium that is employed. When the destination receives the information, it goes through a reverse process of *de-encapsulating* information—basically stripping off the headers and trailers of the PDU information at each layer as the information is passed up from layer to layer of the OSI Reference Model.

TABLE 2-3	PDU Term	OSI Reference Model Layer
	Data	Application, presentation, and session layers
PDU Terms	Segment	Transport layer
	Packet	Network layer (TCP/IP calls this a *datagram*)
	Frame	Data link layer
	Bits	Physical layer

Figure 2-5 shows an example of the process used for encapsulating and de-encapsulating PDUs as data is passed down and back up the OSI Reference Model. In this example, you can see how the application, presentation, and session layers create the data PDU. As this information is passed down from layer to layer, each layer adds its own header (and possibly trailer, as is the case with most layer 2 protocols).

The next few sections will help you better understand the process that devices go through as information is transmitted between computers. The next section covers the details as to how information is encapsulated and sent down the protocol stack and then placed on the wire to the destination. The section following that covers the reverse process: how the information is de-encapsulated at the destination and delivered to the application at the application layer. The last part of the chapter looks at a more complex environment, where bridges, routers, and hubs are involved in the communication process to get information from the source to the destination.

FIGURE 2-5   Encapsulation and de-encapsulation process

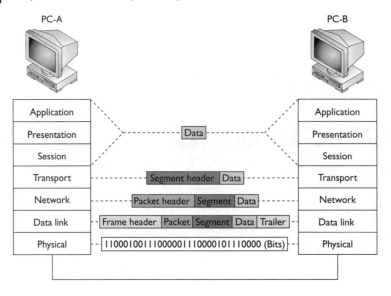

Going Down the Protocol Stack

This section covers the basic mechanics as to how information is processed as it's sent down the protocol stack on a computer. Consult the diagram shown in Figure 2-5 to follow along with this process as PC-A sends data to PC-B. In this example, assume that the data link layer is Ethernet and the physical layer is copper.

The first thing that occurs on PC-A is that the user, sitting in front of the computer, creates some type of information, called *data*, and then sends it to another location (PC-B). This includes the actual user input (application layer), as well as any formatting information (presentation layer). The application (or operating system), at the session layer, then determines whether or not the data's intended destination is local to this computer (possibly a disk drive) or a remote location. In this instance, the user is sending the information to PC-B. We'll assume that the user is executing a telnet connection.

The session layer determines that this location is remote and has the transport layer deliver the information. A telnet connection uses TCP/IP and reliable connections (TCP) at the transport layer, which encapsulates the data from the higher layers into a *segment*. With TCP, as you will see in Chapter 9, only a header is added. The segment contains such information as the source and destination port numbers. As you may recall from the section "Connection Multiplexing," the source port is a number above 1023 that is currently not being used by PC-A. The destination port number is the well-known port number (23) that the destination will understand and forward to the telnet application.

on the **job** *Based on RFC standards, the TCP or UDP source port number really should be above 49,151, but not all operating systems follow this standard verbatim—in many cases, the source port number will be above 1,023.*

The transport layer passes the segment down to the network layer, which encapsulates the segment into a *packet*. The packet adds only a header, which contains layer 3 logical addressing information (source and destination address) as well as other information, such as the upper layer protocol that created this information. In this example, TCP created this information, so this fact is noted in the packet header, and PC-A places its IP address as the source address in the packet and PC-B's IP address as the destination. This helps the destination, at the network layer, to determine whether the packet is for itself and which upper layer process should handle the encapsulated segment. In the TCP/IP protocol stack, the terms *packet* and *datagram* are used interchangeably to describe this PDU. As you will see in Chapter 6, many protocols are within the TCP/IP protocol stack—ARP, TCP, UDP, ICMP, OSPF, EIGRP, and many others.

The network layer then passes the packet down to the data link layer. The data link layer encapsulates the packet into a *frame* by adding both a header and trailer. This example uses Ethernet as the data link layer medium, discussed in more depth in Chapter 3. The important components placed in the Ethernet frame header are the source and destination MAC addresses, as well as a field checksum sequence (FCS) value so that the destination can determine whether the frame is valid or corrupted when it is received. In this example, PC-A places its MAC address in the frame in the source field and PC-B's MAC address in the destination field. FCS's usage is discussed in more depth in Chapter 3.

The data link layer frame is then passed down to the physical layer. At this point, remember that the concept of "PDUs" is a human concept that we have placed on the data to make it more readable to us, as well as to help deliver the information to the destination. However, from a computer's perspective, the data is just a bunch of binary values, 1s and 0s, called *bits*. The physical layer converts these bits into a physical property based on the cable or connection type. In this example, the cable is a copper cable, so the physical layer will convert the bits into voltages: one voltage level for a bit value of 1 and a different voltage level for a 0.

Going Up the Protocol Stack

For sake of simplicity, assume PC-A and PC-B are on the same piece of copper. Once the destination receives the physical layer signals, the physical layer translates the voltage levels back to their binary representation and passes these bit values up to the data link layer.

The data link layer takes the bit values and reassembles them into the original data link frame (Ethernet). The NIC, at the MAC layer, examines the FCS to make sure the frame is valid and examines the destination MAC address to ensure that the Ethernet frame is meant for itself. If the destination MAC address doesn't match its own MAC address, or it is not a multicast or broadcast address, the NIC drops the frame. Otherwise, the NIC processes the frame. In this case, the NIC sees that the encapsulated packet is a TCP/IP packet, so it strips off (de-encapsulates) the Ethernet frame information and passes the packet up to the TCP/IP protocol stack at the network layer. If this were an encapsulated IPX packet, the NIC would pass the encapsulated IPX packet up to the IPX protocol stack at the network layer.

The network layer then examines the logical destination address in the packet header. If the destination logical address doesn't match its own address or is not a multicast or broadcast address, the network layer drops the packet. If the logical address matches, then the destination examines the protocol information in the packet header to determine which protocol should handle the packet. In this example, the logical address matches and the protocol is defined as TCP. Therefore, the network layer strips off the packet information and passes the encapsulated segment up to the TCP protocol at the transport layer.

Upon receiving the segment, the transport layer protocol can perform many functions, depending on whether this is a reliable or unreliable connection. This discussion focuses on the multiplexing function of the transport layer. In this instance, the transport layer examines the destination port number in the segment header. In our example, the user from PC-A was using telnet to transmit information to PC-B, so the destination port number is 23. The transport layer examines this port number and realizes that the encapsulated data needs to be forwarded to the telnet application. If PC-B doesn't support telnet, the transport layer drops the segment. If it does, the transport layer strips off the segment information and passes the encapsulated data to the telnet application. If this is a new connection, a new telnet process is started up by the operating system.

Note that a logical communication takes place between two layers of two devices. For instance, a logical communication occurs at the transport layer between PC-A and PC-B, and this is also true at the network and data link layers.

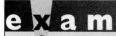

Layers and Communication

As you can see from the encapsulation and de-encapsulation process, *many* processes are occurring on both the source and destination computers to transmit and receive the information. This can become even more complicated if the source and destination are on different segments, separated by other networking devices, such as hubs, switches, and routers. Figure 2-6 shows an example of this process.

In this example, PC-A wants to send data to PC-B. Notice that each device needs to process information at specific layers. For instance, once PC-A places its information on the wire, the switch connected to PC-A needs to process this information. Recall from earlier in this chapter that switches function at layer 2 of

FIGURE 2-6   Multi-segment communications

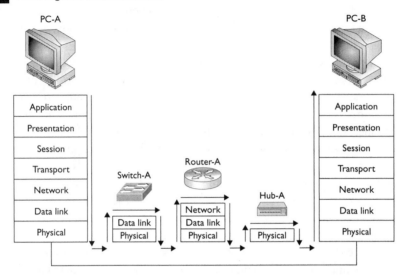

the OSI Reference Model. Whereas routers make path decisions based on destination layer 3 logical addresses, switches make path decisions based on layer 2 destination MAC addresses found in frames. Therefore, the switch's physical layer will have to convert the physical layer signal into bits and pass these bits up to the data link layer, where they are reassembled into a frame. The switch examines the destination MAC address and makes a switching decision, finding the port the frame needs to exit. It then passes the frame down to the physical layer, where the bits of the frame are converted into physical layer signals. Switching is discussed in Chapter 4.

The next device the physical layers encounter is a router. Recall from earlier in the chapter that routers function at layer 3 of the OSI Reference Model. The router first converts the physical layer signals into bits at the physical layer. The bits are passed up to the data link layer and reassembled into a frame. The router then examines the destination MAC address in the frame. If the MAC address doesn't match its own MAC address, the router drops the frame. If the MAC address matches, the router strips off the data link layer frame and passes the packet up to the network layer.

At the network layer, one of the functions of the router is to route packets to destinations. To accomplish this, the router examines the destination logical address in the packet and extracts a network number from this address. The router then compares the network number to entries in its routing table. If the router doesn't find a match, it drops the packet; if it does find a match, it forwards the packet out the destination interface.

To accomplish the packet forwarding, the router passes the packet down to the data link layer, which encapsulates the packet into the correct data link layer frame format. If this were an Ethernet frame, for this example, the source MAC address would be that of the router and the destination would be PC-B. At the data link layer, the frame is then passed down to the physical layer, where the bits are converted into physical layer signals.

---

exam
watch

When sending traffic between two devices on *different* segments, the source device has a layer 2 frame with its own MAC address as the source and the default gateway's (router) MAC address as the destination; however, in the layer 3 packet, the source layer 3 address is the source device and the destination layer 3 address is not the default gateway, but the actual destination the source is trying to reach. Remember that layer 2 addresses are used to communicate with devices on the same physical or logical layer 2 segment/network, and layer 3 addresses are used to communicate with devices across the network (multiple segments). Another way to remember this is that MAC addresses can change from link to link, but layer 3 logical addresses, by default, *cannot*.

Note that routers separate physical or logical segments, while bridges and switches don't. Therefore, if PC-A wants to send traffic to PC-B, PC-A uses the router's MAC (or layer 2) address to get traffic to the exit point of the segment, but it uses PC-B's logical (or layer 3) address to tell the router that this traffic is not for the router but for a machine on a different segment. This process is discussed in more depth in Chapters 3 and 10.

The next device that receives these physical layer signals is the hub. Recall from earlier in the chapter that hubs and repeaters operate at the physical layer. Basically, a hub is a multiport repeater: it repeats any physical layer signal it receives. Therefore, a signal received on one interface of a hub is repeated on all of its other interfaces. These signals are then received by PC-B, which passes this information up the protocol stack as described in the preceding section.

For a more detailed explanation of the process described in this section, please read Chapter 10, which discusses how TCP/IP is used to communicate between devices on *different* Ethernet segments.

INSIDE THE EXAM

Introduction to the OSI Reference Model

Make sure you are familiar with the OSI Reference Model and why it was originally developed.

Layers of the OSI Reference Model

You should know the names and orders of the layers: application, presentation, session, transport, network, data link, and physical. You should also know the kinds of devices that work at various layers (router: network; switch: data link; and hub: physical) and some of the important functions these devices perform. For example, routers switch packets between network segments, they contain broadcasts, they can filter on layer 3 logical addresses, and they determine paths to destination logical networks. You should also be able to name example protocols that function at the various layers. For example, telnet and FTP function at the application layer.

Be especially familiar with the transport, network, and data link layers and their functions. The transport layer, for example, sets up, maintains, and tears down connections. It can provide reliable or unreliable delivery of data. It segments data into smaller, more manageable pieces. It can implement flow control through ready/not ready signals or windowing through the use of sequence and acknowledgment numbers to avoid congestion. It uses buffers to store incoming data and multiplexes multiple connections through

the use of port numbers and layer 3 addresses. TCP and UDP are example protocols that operate at the transport layer.

The network layer defines logical addresses, finds best paths to destination logical addresses through the use of routing tables on routers, and connects different layer 2 link types together. Remember the advantages that routers provide, such as scalability through the use of hierarchical network designs and routing protocols, containment of broadcasts, intelligent path selection, QoS, and traffic filtering.

The data link layer defines how devices connect to a layer 2 media type and how these devices communicate with each other through the use of physical addresses, such as MAC addresses in Ethernet. Know what a MAC address looks like: it's 48 bits long and is represented in hexadecimal.

Encapsulation and De-encapsulation

You should be familiar with the PDU terms used at the various OSI Reference Model layers: segment: transport; packet or datagram: network; frame: data link; and bits: physical. Also be able to describe how devices communicate with others at the various layers: what layer 2 or layer 3 addresses are used between various devices from the source to the destination. Remember that MAC addresses can change from link to link, but layer 3 addresses, such as TCP/IP addresses, typically do not.

CERTIFICATION SUMMARY

The OSI Reference Model defines the process of connecting two layers of networking functions. The application layer provides the user interface. The presentation layer determines how data is represented to the user. The session layer is responsible for setting up and tearing down connections. The transport layer is responsible for the mechanics of connections, including guaranteed services. The network layer provides a logical topology and layer 3 addresses: routers operate here. The data link layer defines MAC addresses and how communication is performed on a specific media type: switches, bridges, and NICs operate here. The physical layer defines physical properties for connections and communication: repeaters and hubs operate here. Wireless solutions are defined at the physical layer.

The transport layer sets up and maintains a session layer connection, and provides for reliable or unreliable delivery of data, flow control, and multiplexing of connections. Reliable connections typically go through a handshake process to establish a connection. Acknowledgments are used to provide reliable delivery. Port or socket numbers are used for connection multiplexing. Ready/not ready signals and windowing are used to implement flow control. Windowing is more efficient than ready/not ready signals.

The network layer defines logical addresses, finds paths to destinations based on the network component of the address, and connects different layer 2 media types together. Routers are used to contain broadcasts. Routers use their routing table, which has a list of destination network numbers, to assist them when finding a destination. If a destination is not found in the routing table, traffic for this destination is dropped.

The data link layer defines hardware addressing. MAC addresses are 48 bits in length in hexadecimal. The first 24 bits (six digits) are the OUI. MAC addresses need to be unique only on a logical segment. In a unicast, one frame is sent to all devices on a segment, but only a single device will process it. In a multicast, one frame is sent to a group of devices. In a broadcast, one frame is sent to all devices.

A PDU describes data and its overhead. A PDU at the application layer is referred to as data; the transport layer PDU is called a segment, the network layer PDU is called a packet or datagram, the data link layer PDU is called a frame, and the physical layer PDU is called bits. As traffic goes down the protocol stack, each layer encapsulates the PDU from the layer above it. At the destination, a de-encapsulation process occurs.

✓ TWO-MINUTE DRILL

Introduction to the OSI Reference Model

❑ The OSI Reference Model provides the following advantages: it promotes interoperability, defines how to connect adjacent layers, compartmentalizes components, allows a modular design, serves as a teaching tool, and simplifies troubleshooting.

Layers of the OSI Reference Model

❑ The application layer (layer 7) provides the user interface. The presentation layer (layer 6) defines how information is presented to the user. The session layer (layer 5) determines whether a network connection is needed and initiates the setup and teardown of connections. The transport layer (layer 4) handles the mechanics of reliable or unreliable services. The network layer (layer 3) creates a logical topology with logical addresses. Routers function at this layer. The data link layer (layer 2) assigns physical (MAC) addresses and defines how devices on a specific media type communicate with each other. Bridges, switches, and NICs operate at this layer. The physical layer (layer 1) handles all physical properties for a connection. Hubs and repeaters function here.

❑ The data link layer defines MAC addresses, the physical or hardware topology, and the framing used; it provides for connection-oriented and connectionless services. MAC addresses are 48 bits in length and are represented in hexadecimal. The first six digits are the OUI (vendor code), and the last six digits represent the NIC within the OUI. A unicast is sent to one destination on a segment, a multicast is sent to a group of devices, and a broadcast (FF:FF:FF:FF:FF:FF) is sent to all devices.

❑ The network layer defines logical addresses, finds paths to destinations using the network number in the logical address, and connects different media types together. Routers function at the network layer. A routing table contains information about destination network numbers and how to reach them. Routers contain broadcasts, allow for scalability through hierarchical designs, make better decisions for reaching a destination than bridges, can switch packets on the same interface using VLANs, and can implement advanced features such as QoS and filtering.

❏ The transport layer sets up and maintains a session connection, segments data into smaller payloads, provides for reliable or unreliable transport of data, implements flow control, and multiplexes connections. Reliable connections use sequence numbers and acknowledgments. TCP is an example. Reliable transport protocols use a handshake process to set up a connection. Unreliable services don't use a connection setup process. UDP is an example. Multiplexing of connections is done with port or socket numbers. Flow control can be implemented with ready/not ready signals or windowing. Windowing is more efficient. The size of the window affects your throughput. Depending on the size, a source can send X segments before having to wait for an acknowledgment.

Encapsulation and De-encapsulation

❏ A protocol data unit (PDU) describes data and its overhead. Each layer has a unique PDU: as data is sent down the protocol stack, it is encapsulated at each layer by adding a header and, possibly, a trailer. The destination de-encapsulates the data as it goes back up the protocol stack.

❏ The transport layer PDU is a segment, the network layer PDU is a packet or datagram, the data link layer PDU is a frame, and the physical layer PDU is bits.

SELF TEST

The following Self Test questions will help you measure your understanding of the material presented in this chapter. Read all the choices carefully, as there may be more than one correct answer. Choose all correct answers for each question.

Introduction to the OSI Reference Model

1. The OSI Reference Model provides for all of the following except which one?
   A. Defines the process for connecting two layers together, promoting interoperability between vendors
   B. Allows vendors to compartmentalize their design efforts to fit a modular design, which eases implementations and simplifies troubleshooting
   C. Separates a complex function into simpler components
   D. Defines eight layers common to all networking protocols
   E. Provides a teaching tool to help network administrators understand the communication process used between networking components

Layers of the OSI Reference Model

2. Put the following in the correct order, from high to low: (a) session, (b) presentation, (c) physical, (d) data link, (e) network, (f) application, (g) transport.
   A. c, d, e, g, a, b, f
   B. f, a, b, g, d, e, c
   C. f, b, g, a, e, d, c
   D. f, b, a, g, e, d, c

3. The _____ layer provides for hardware addressing.
   A. Transport
   B. Network
   C. Data link
   D. Physical

4. MAC addresses are _____ bits in length and are represented in a _____ numbering format.

5. The network layer handles all of the following problems except _____.
   A. Broadcast problems
   B. Conversion between media types
   C. Hierarchy through the use of physical addresses
   D. Splitting collision domains into smaller ones

6. _____ are used to provide a reliable connection.
   A. Ready/not ready signals
   B. Sequence numbers and acknowledgments
   C. Windows
   D. Ready/not ready signals and windowing

7. Connection multiplexing is done through the use of a _____ number.
   A. Socket
   B. Hardware
   C. Network
   D. Session

8. Match the device with the OSI Reference Model at which it primarily functions.
   Devices: (1) Repeater, (2) Router, (3) NIC, and (4) Switch
   Layers: (a) Physical, (b) Data link, (c) Network, and (d) Transport
   Note that not necessarily all layers are used in the answer and that a layer can be used for more than one device.

Encapsulation and De-encapsulation

9. Match the PDU name with the OSI Reference Model at which it is used.
   PDU names: (1) Data, (2) Frame, (3) Packet, (4) Bits, and (5) Segment.
   Layers: (a) Application, (b) Presentation, (c) Session, (d) Transport, (e) Network, (f) Data link, and (g) Physical

10. You have a network with some network components (shown in Figure 2-6). PC-A wants to send data to PC-B. Which of the following statements is true, assuming that the layer 2 medium is Ethernet and TCP/IP is used at layer 3?

 A. When PC-A generates the frame, it puts its MAC address in the source field and the Switch-A's MAC address in the destination field.

 B. When PC-A generates the frame, it puts its MAC address in the source field and the PC-B's MAC address in the destination field.

 C. When PC-A generates the packet, it puts its IP address in the source field and Router-A's IP address in the destination field.

 D. When PC-A generates the packet, it puts Router-A's IP address in the source field and PC-B's IP address in the destination field.

 E. When Router-A generates the frame, it puts its MAC address as the source and PC-B's MAC address as the destination.

SELF TEST ANSWERS

Introduction to the OSI Reference Model

1. ☑ **D.** The OSI Reference Model has seven layers.
   ☒ **A, B, C,** and **E** are functions of the OSI Reference Model and therefore are incorrect answers.

Layers of the OSI Reference Model

2. ☑ **D.** From high to low, the OSI Reference Model has the following layers: application, presentation, session, transport, network, data link, and physical (f, b, a, g, e, d, c).
   ☒ **A** doesn't begin with the application layer. **B**'s second from the top layer is presentation. **C** switches the session and transport layers.

3. ☑ **C.** The data link layer provides for hardware addressing.
   ☒ **A** uses port numbers for multiplexing. **B** defines logical addressing. **D** doesn't have any addressing.

4. ☑ MAC addresses are **48** bits in length and are represented in a **hexadecimal** format.

5. ☑ **C.** The network layer creates a hierarchy through the use of logical, not physical addresses.
   ☒ **A, B,** and **D** are true and thus incorrect.

6. ☑ **B.** Sequence numbers and acknowledgments are used to provide a reliable transport layer connection.
   ☒ **A, C,** and **D** are used for flow control.

7. ☑ **A.** Connection multiplexing is done through the use of a socket or port number.
   ☒ **B** references the data link layer. **C** references the network layer. **D** is a nonexistent type.

8. ☑ **(1)** Repeater: **(a)** Physical; **(2)** Router: **(c)** Network; **(3)** NIC: **(b)** Data link; and **(4)** Switch: **(b)** Data link.

Encapsulation and De-encapsulation

9. ☑ **(1)** Data: **(a)** Application; **(2)** Frame: **(f)** Data link; **(3)** Packet: **(e)** Network; **(4)** Bits: **(g)** Physical; and **(5)** Segment: **(d)** Transport.

10. ☑ **E.** At layer 2, PC-A sends the frame to the router, the router strips off the layer 2 frame and routes the layer 3 packet. When putting it on the second segment, the router puts its MAC address as the source in the frame and PC-B's MAC address as the destination.

    ☒ **A** is incorrect because MAC addresses are used to communicate on the same segment and the switch is on a different segment than PC-A; PC-A should use the router's MAC address as the destination. **B** is incorrect because PC-A should use the router's MAC address as the destination. **C** and **D** are incorrect because layer 3 addresses are used to communicate across networks themselves (that is, multiple segments); therefore, the source IP address should be PC-A and the destination IP address PC-B.

3

Layer 2 LAN Technologies

Y ou'll recall from Chapter 1 that local area networks (LANs) are used to interconnect network components that are geographically close together. Ethernet is one of the most common layer 2 technologies used for connecting the LAN network components, followed by wireless communications. This chapter is devoted to Ethernet, including its operation, the two Ethernet standards, the addressing it uses, and the Ethernet cabling types of copper and fiber. Wireless networking is covered in Chapter 5.

CERTIFICATION OBJECTIVE 3.01

Ethernet Evolution and Standards

A LAN interconnects network components located geographically close, such as the floor of a building, within a building, or on a campus. The LAN infrastructure used is built and owned by a company or other organization. Typically, no external provider, such as a telephone company, is used to connect different parts of the LAN. LANs can scale from very small sizes, such as a small office/home office (SOHO), to a large corporation spanning multiple buildings on a campus, commonly referred to as an enterprise LAN.

Common components you'll find in a LAN include computers (PCs and servers), interconnections (network interface cards and media types such as cabling and wireless), network devices (routers, switches, hubs, firewalls, intrusion detection/ prevention systems, and so on), and protocols (Ethernet and TCP/IP). The main function of all of these components is to allow users to access applications and data, to share resources such as printers and network storage, and to connect to other networks if necessary.

Today, Ethernet is the most common layer 2 LAN protocol implemented in company networks. The precursor to Ethernet was invented by Xerox in 1973. DEC, Intel, and Xerox standardized this precursor in the late 1970s, calling it the *DIX* implementation of Ethernet, based on the names of the three founders. The DIX version specified the transmission of data at 10-megabit-per-second (Mbps) speeds in a shared medium. DIX was then enhanced in 1982 and is now referred to as Ethernet II (version 2), which is commonly used today.

The Institute of Electrical and Electronic Engineers (IEEE), a professional standards organization, defined new standards for Ethernet starting in the mid 1980s. The first two of these standards were 802.3, which deals with the physical layer functions as well as part of the data link layer, and 802.2, which deals with the higher level data link layer functions. IEEE has continually updated the standards to support new functions in Ethernet, such as duplexing and higher data speeds. Both DIX and IEEE standards are discussed in this chapter.

Ethernet Operation

Ethernet is a LAN technology that functions at the data link layer. Ethernet uses the Carrier Sense Multiple Access/Collision Detection (CSMA/CD) mechanism to send information in a *shared* environment. Ethernet was initially developed with the idea that many devices would be connected to the same physical piece of wiring. The acronym CSMA/CD describes the actual process of how Ethernet operates on a shared medium.

Carrier Sense and Multiple Access

In a traditional, or hub-based, Ethernet environment, only one NIC can successfully send a frame at a time. All NICs, however, can simultaneously listen to information on the wire. Before an Ethernet NIC puts a frame on the wire, it will first *sense* the wire to ensure that no other frame is currently on the wire. If the cable uses copper, the NIC can detect this by examining the voltage levels on the wire. If the cable is fiber, the NIC can detect this by examining the light frequencies on the wire. The NIC must go through this sensing process, since the Ethernet medium supports *multiple access*—another NIC might already have a frame on the wire. If the NIC doesn't sense a frame on the wire, it will transmit its own frame; otherwise, if a frame is found on the wire, the NIC will wait for the completion of the transmission of the frame and then transmit its own frame.

Collision Detection

If two or more devices simultaneously sense the wire and see no frame, and each places its frame on the wire, a *collision* will occur. In this situation, the voltage levels on a copper wire or the light frequencies on a piece of fiber get messed up. For example, if two NICs attempt to put the same voltage on an electrical piece of wire, the voltage level will be different from that of only one device. Basically, the two original frames become unintelligible (or indecipherable). The NICs, when they place a frame on the wire, examine the status of the wire to ensure that a collision does not occur: this is the *collision detection* mechanism of CSMA/CD.

If the NICs see a collision for their transmitted frames, they have to resend the frames. In this instance, each NIC that was transmitting a frame when a collision occurred creates a special signal, called a *jam signal*, on the wire. It then waits a small random time period, and senses the wire again. If no frame is currently on the wire, the NIC will then retransmit its original frame. The time period that the NIC waits is measured in microseconds, a delay that can't be detected by a human. Likewise, the time period the NICs wait is random to help ensure a collision won't occur again when these NICs retransmit their frames.

The more devices you place on an Ethernet segment, the more likely you will experience collisions. If you put too many devices on the segment, too many collisions will occur, seriously affecting your throughput. Therefore, you need to monitor the number of collisions on each of your network segments. The more collisions you experience, the less throughput you'll get. Normally, if your collisions are less than one percent of your total traffic, you are okay. This is not to say that collisions are *bad*—they are just part of how Ethernet functions.

Collision Domains

Because Ethernet experiences collisions, networking devices that share the same medium (are connected to the same physical segment) are said to belong to the same *collision* or *bandwidth domain*. This means that, for better or worse, traffic generated by one device in the collision domain can adversely affect other devices in the same domain. Chapter 4 discusses how bridges and switches can be used to solve collision and bandwidth problems on a network segment.

Ethernet Implementations

Two variants of Ethernet exist: IEEE's implementation and Ethernet II. Devices running TCP/IP typically use the Ethernet II implementation. The Ethernet II standard covers both the physical and data link layer functions. The main difference,

TABLE 3-1	IEEE Ethernet Components		
Data Link Layer	**Name**	**IEEE Standard**	**Description**
Top part	Logical Link Control (LLC)	802.2	Defines how to multiplex multiple network layer protocols in the data link layer frame, which doesn't have to be Ethernet. LLC is performed in *software*.
Bottom part	Media Access Control (MAC)	802.3	Defines how information is transmitted in an Ethernet environment and defines the framing, MAC addressing, and mechanics as to how Ethernet works. MAC is performed in *hardware*.

originally, between the two standards was the framing used, and that IEEE split the data link layer into two components to simplify dealing with multiple layer 2 and layer 3 protocols.

The second version of Ethernet was developed by IEEE and is standardized in the IEEE 802.2 and 802.3 standards. IEEE has split the data link layer into two components: Media Access Control (MAC) and Logical Link Control (LLC). These components are described in Table 3-1. The top part of the data link layer is the LLC, and its function is performed in software. The bottom part of the data link layer is the MAC, and its function is performed in hardware.

The LLC performs its multiplexing by using Service Access Point (SAP) identifiers. When a network layer protocol is encapsulated in the 802.2 frame, the protocol number of the network data is placed in the SAP field. When the destination receives the frame, it examines the SAP field to determine which upper-layer network protocol should process the frame. This allows the destination network device to differentiate between TCP/IP, IPX, and other network layer protocols that are being transmitted across the data link layer connection. Optionally, LLC can provide sequencing and flow control to provide a reliable service, as TCP does at the transport layer (this is discussed in Chapter 9). However, most data link layer implementations of Ethernet don't use this function—if a reliable connection is needed, it is provided by either the transport or application layers.

Framing

One of the main differences between IEEE's and Ethernet II's implementation of Ethernet is the framing used. Recall from Chapter 2 that framing defines the format of information as it's carried across a data link layer medium. A frame standardizes the fields in the frame and their lengths so that every device understands how to

FIGURE 3-1

Ethernet frame
types: Ethernet
802.3 and
Ethernet II

Ethernet frame types: Ethernet 802.3 and Ethernet II

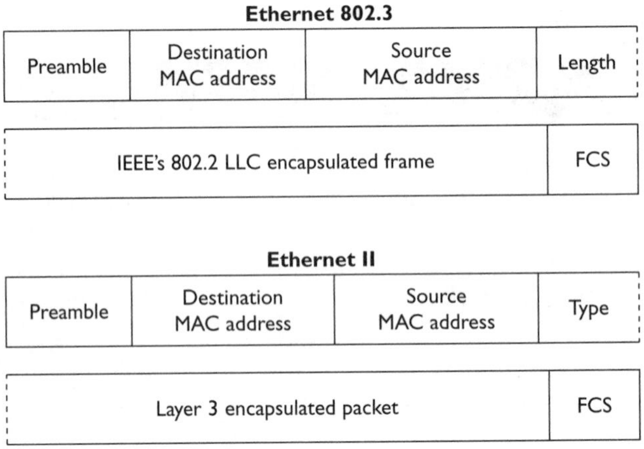

read the contents of the frame. The next sections discuss the framing that IEEE uses
with the 802.3 and 802.2 standards and what Ethernet II uses.

IEEE 802.3

As mentioned in Table 3-1, IEEE 802.3 is responsible for defining the framing used
to transmit information between two NICs. The top part of Figure 3-1 shows the
fields of an 802.3 frame. Table 3-2 explains the fields found in the frame.

TABLE 3-2   Fields in the 802.3 Frame

Field	Length in Bytes	Description
Preamble	7	Identifies the beginning of the 802.3 frame and is a string of 7 bytes of alternating 1s and 0s.
Start of Frame (SOF)	1	Indicates the following byte is the start of the frame. The first 8 bytes are commonly referred to as the preamble, even though this is not quite true.
Destination MAC address	6	The MAC address to which the frame is to be sent.
Source MAC address	6	The MAC address of the source of the frame.
Length	2	Defines the length of the frame from this point to the checksum at the end of the frame.
Data	Variable	The 802.2 LLC encapsulated frame.
FCS (field or frame checksum sequence)	4	A checksum (CRC, or cyclic redundancy check) that is used to ensure that the frame is received by the destination error-free.

The field checksum sequence (FCS) value is used to ensure that when the destination receives the frame, it can verify that the frame was received intact. When generating the FCS value, which is basically a checksum, the NIC takes all of the fields in the 802.3 frame, except the FCS field, and runs them through an algorithm that generates a 4-byte result, which is placed in the FCS field. When the destination receives the frame, it takes the same fields and runs them through the same algorithm. The destination then compares its 4-byte output with what was included in the frame by the source NIC. If the two values don't match, the frame is considered bad and is dropped. If the two values match, the frame is considered good and is processed further.

IEEE 802.2

IEEE 802.2 (LLC) handles the top part of the data link layer. Two types of IEEE 802.2 frames are used: Service Access Point (SAP) and Subnetwork Access Protocol (SNAP). These 802.2 frames are encapsulated (enclosed) in an 802.3 frame when being sent to a destination. Where 802.3 (Ethernet) is used as a transport to get the 802.2 frames to other devices, 802.2 is used to define which network layer protocol created the data that the 802.2 frame will include. In this sense, it serves as a multiplexing function: it differentiates between TCP/IP, IPX, AppleTalk, and other network layer data types. Figure 3-2 shows the two types of 802.2 frames and Table 3-3 lists the fields found in an 802.2 SAP frame.

FIGURE 3-2

IEEE 802.2 frame types: SAP and SNAP

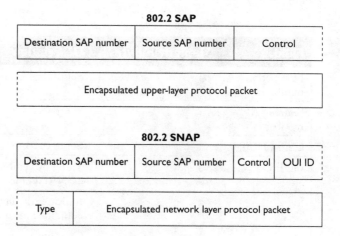

TABLE 3-3	Field	Length in Bytes	Description
802.2 SAP Fields	Destination SAP number	1	Identifies the network layer protocol to which this is to be sent
	Source SAP number	1	Identifies the network layer protocol that originated this data
	Control field	1–2	Determines the fields that follow this field
	Data	Variable	Contains the upper-layer network layer packet

When a destination NIC receives an 802.3 frame, the NIC first checks the FCS to verify that the frame is valid and then checks the destination MAC address in the 802.3 frame to make sure that it should process the frame (or ignore it). The MAC sublayer strips off the 802.3 frame portion and passes the 802.2 frame to the LLC sublayer. The LLC examines the destination SAP value to determine which upper-layer protocol should have the encapsulated data passed to it. Here are some examples of SAP values: TCP/IP uses 0x06 (hexadecimal) and IPX uses 0x0E. If the LLC sees 0x06 in the SAP field, it passes the encapsulated data up to the TCP/IP protocol stack running on the device.

The second frame type supported by 802.2 is SNAP, which is shown in the bottom portion of Figure 3-2. As you can see from this frame, two additional fields are included: *OUI ID* and *Type*. Table 3-4 explains the 802.2 SNAP fields.

One of the issues of the original SAP field in the 802.2 SAP frame is that even though it is 8 bits (1 byte) in length, only the first 6 bits are used for identifying upper-layer protocols, which allows up to 64 protocols. Back in the 1980s, many

TABLE 3-4	Field	Length in Bytes	Description
802.2 SNAP Fields	Destination SAP number	1	Set to 0xAA to signify a SNAP frame
	Source SAP number	1	Set to 0xAA to signify a SNAP frame
	Control field	1–2	Set to 0x03 to signify a SNAP frame
	OUI ID	3	Varies by vendor but is set to 0x0 to signify a SNAP frame
	Type	2	Indicates the upper-layer protocol that is contained in the data field
	Data	Variable	Contains the upper-layer network layer packet

more protocols than 64 were in use, plus there was an expectation that more protocols would be created. SNAP overcomes this limitation without having to change the length of the SAP field.

To indicate a SNAP frame, the SAP fields are set to hexadecimal 0xAA, the control field is set to 0x03, and the OUI field is set to 0x0. The *type* field identifies the upper-layer protocol that is encapsulated in the payload of the 802.2 frame. Since a SAP frame can identify only 64 protocols, the type field was made 2 bytes in length, which theoretically allows the support of up to 65,536 protocols! AppleTalk is an example of a protocol that uses an 802.2 SNAP frame.

Concerning 802.2, other data link layer protocols are available for the LAN besides Ethernet, including Token Ring and fiber distributed data interface (FDDI). IEEE's 802.2 standard supports these sublayer standards at the MAC layer. Token Ring is specified in IEEE's 802.5 standard, and FDDI is specified in an ANSI standard. This book focuses only on Ethernet, however.

w a t c h *802.2 uses a SAP or SNAP field to differentiate between encapsulated layer 3 payloads. With a SNAP frame,* *the SAP fields are set to 0xAA and the type field is used to indicate the layer 3 protocol.*

Ethernet II's Version of Ethernet

Ethernet II was the original Ethernet frame type. Ethernet II and 802.3 are very similar: they both use CSMA/CD to determine their operations. Their main difference is the frames used to transmit information between NICs. The bottom part of Figure 3-1 shows the fields in an Ethernet II frame. Following are the two main differences between an Ethernet II and IEEE:

w a t c h *Be able to compare and contrast the two versions of Ethernet: Ethernet II and 802.2/3.*

- Ethernet II does not have any sublayers, while IEEE 802.2/3 has two—LLC and MAC.

- Ethernet II has a *type* field instead of a length field (used in 802.3). IEEE 802.2 defines the type for IEEE Ethernet.

If you examine the IEEE 802.3 frame and the Ethernet II frame, you can see that they are very similar. NICs differentiate them by examining the value in the type field for an Ethernet II frame and the value in the length field in the IEEE 802.3 frame. If the value is greater than 1,500, then the frame is an Ethernet II frame. If the value is 1,500 or less, the frame is an 802.3 frame.

on the
Ò o b

Both versions of Ethernet can coexist in the same network. However, because of the frame differences between the two types, a NIC running only 802.3 will discard any Ethernet II frames, and vice versa.

CERTIFICATION OBJECTIVE 3.02

Addressing

Recall from Chapter 2 that Ethernet, as well as other LAN technologies such as FDDI and Token Ring, use MAC, or hardware, addresses to uniquely identify devices on a segment (physical or logical). MAC addresses are represented using a hexadecimal addressing scheme. You should be familiar with decimal, binary, and hexadecimal numbering, since you might be expected to convert decimal numbers to binary (and vice versa), decimal to hexadecimal (and vice versa), and binary to hexadecimal (and vice versa).

Bit Values

Before you can begin to understand the conversion process, you need to understand binary mathematics. Computers and networking components process everything in binary. In 1 byte (octet), there are 8 bits. Each bit in a byte, when enabled (turned on), represents a specific decimal value. Table 3-5 shows the conversion of a specific bit position, in a byte, when it is enabled. In this table, the bit positions are labeled from left to right, where the leftmost bit is the *most* significant and the rightmost bit is the *least* significant. A bit can contain one of two values: 0 or 1. If it is enabled (set to 1), then that equates to a particular decimal value, shown in the second row of Table 3-5. If it is disabled (set to 0), then this equates to a decimal value of 0. Higher order bits have a higher-numbered bit position (such as bit position 8), while lower order bits have a lower-numbered bit position (such as bit position 1). To convert the binary byte value to a decimal value, you look at all the bits that are turned on and add up the equivalent decimal values.

TABLE 3-5	Bit Position	8	7	6	5	4	3	2	1
	Decimal Value	128	64	32	16	8	4	2	1

Binary to Decimal
Conversion for
Byte Values

For example, assume that you had a byte with a value of 11000001. Bits 8, 7, and 1 are on, so add up the associated decimal values to get the corresponding decimal equivalent of the byte value: 128 + 64 + 1 = 193. If you had a byte value of 00110011, the decimal value would be 32 + 16 + 2 + 1 = 51. If all the bit positions where set to 0, then the decimal value would be 0. If all the bit positions were set to 1, the equivalent decimal value would be 128 + 64 + 32 + 16 + 8 + 4 + 2 + 1 = 255. Given this, a byte value can range from 0 to 255 in decimal, where 0 is 00000000 in binary and 255 is 11111111.

exam
watch

Remember how to convert a binary 8-bit value to a decimal number and vice versa. As a shortcut, remember that if a binary number ends in 1 *(the least significant bit), the resulting decimal number will be odd; and if it ends in 0, the decimal number will be even.*

Power of 2

Basically, when you look at Table 3-5, the bit positions represent a power of 2. Table 3-6 represents the powers of 2, up to 32 (where $2^0 = 1$).

TABLE 3-6	$2^1 = 2$	$2^9 = 512$	$2^{17} = 131,072$	$2^{25} = 33,554,432$
	$2^2 = 4$	$2^{10} = 1,024$	$2^{18} = 262,144$	$2^{26} = 67,108,864$
Powers of 2	$2^3 = 8$	$2^{11} = 2,048$	$2^{19} = 524,288$	$2^{27} = 134,217,728$
	$2^4 = 16$	$2^{12} = 4,096$	$2^{20} = 1,048,576$	$2^{28} = 268,435,456$
	$2^5 = 32$	$2^{13} = 8,192$	$2^{21} = 2,097,152$	$2^{29} = 536,870,912$
	$2^6 = 64$	$2^{14} = 16,384$	$2^{22} = 4,194,304$	$2^{30} = 1,073,741,824$
	$2^7 = 128$	$2^{15} = 32,768$	$2^{23} = 8,388,608$	$2^{31} = 2,147,483,648$
	$2^8 = 256$	$2^{16} = 65,536$	$2^{24} = 16,777,216$	$2^{32} = 4,294,967,296$

Hexadecimal Conversion

Even though in real life you would probably use a calculator to convert between decimal, binary, and/or hexadecimal, you might be required to perform these kinds of conversions on the exam. Therefore, since part of this chapter deals with numeric conversions, let's briefly cover the process of performing decimal, hexadecimal, and binary conversion, primarily focusing on hexadecimal numbers. You'll be reacquainted with this topic again in Chapter 7 when reading about TCP/IP addressing, where you'll have a lot of practice with decimal and binary conversions.

First, as you already know, binary has two possible values in a bit position and a byte has 8 bit positions, allowing you to represent numbers from 0 to 255 in a byte (8 bits). And in decimal, you have values that range from 0 to 9 (10 values). Hexadecimal has a range of 16 values: 0, 1, 2, 3, 4, 5, 6, 7, 8, 9, A, B, C, D, E, and F. As an example, a decimal *10* is equivalent to *A* in hexadecimal. A decimal *17* is equivalent to *11* in hexadecimal. When dealing with hexadecimal, a hex digit is represented in 4 bits. Table 3-7 lists a handy conversion chart.

	Decimal	Binary	Hexadecimal
TABLE 3-7 Binary to Decimal to Hexadecimal Conversion	0	0000	0
	1	0001	1
	2	0010	2
	3	0011	3
	4	0100	4
	5	0101	5
	6	0110	6
	7	0111	7
	8	1000	8
	9	1001	9
	10	1010	A
	11	1011	B
	12	1100	C
	13	1101	D
	14	1110	E
	15	1111	F

Here's a simple example of converting binary to hexadecimal. If you had an 8-bit value of 10000001, break this up into two 4-bit values, since a hexadecimal value is represented in 4 bits: 1000 and 00001. In hexadecimal, this value would be 8 and 1, or 81. To convert this binary value to decimal, add up the powers of 2 for each bit position: bit 8 is 128 and bit 1 is 1, so the equivalent representation in decimal is 129. If you had an 8-bit value of 11011001, this would be D9 in hexadecimal and 217 in decimal.

MAC Addresses

A MAC address is 48 bits long and is represented as a *hexadecimal* number. Represented in hex, it is 12 characters in length, where each character is 4 bits. To make it easier to read, the MAC address is represented in a dotted hexadecimal format, like this: FFFF. FFFF.FFFF. Some formats use a colon (:) instead; and in some cases, the colon separator is spaced after every two hexadecimal digits, like this: FF:FF:FF:FF:FF:FF.

As mention in Chapter 2, the first six digits of a MAC address are associated with the vendor, or maker, of the NIC. Each vendor has one or more unique sets of six digits. These first six digits are commonly called the *organizationally unique identifier* (OUI). The last six digits are used to represent the NIC uniquely within the OUI value. In theory, each NIC has a unique MAC address. In reality, however, this is probably not true. What is important for your purposes is that each of your NICs has a unique MAC address within the same *physical* or *logical* segment. A logical segment is a virtual LAN (VLAN) and is referred to as a *broadcast domain* (discussed in

Chapter 13). Some devices, such as Cisco routers, might allow you to change the MAC address for a NIC, while others won't.

Every data link layer frame has two MAC addresses: a source MAC address of the host creating the frame and a destination MAC address for the device (or devices, in the cast of a broadcast or multicast) intended to receive the frame. If only one device is to receive the frame, a unicast destination MAC address is used. If all devices need to receive the frame, a destination broadcast address is used. When all the binary bits are enabled for a MAC address, this is referred to as a *local broadcast address*: FFFF. FFFF.FFFF. Unicast, broadcast, and multicast addresses were discussed in Chapter 2.

Local broadcasts, such as FFFF.FFFF.FFFF, are propagated throughout the same broadcast domain: this can be the Ethernet segment or multiple Ethernet segments if they are defined in the same VLAN (see Chapter 13). One important item to point out is that a layer 3 device, such as a router, will not propagate a local broadcast from one layer 3 interface to another. Actually, that's one advantage of using routers: they contain broadcasts.

CERTIFICATION OBJECTIVE 3.03

Ethernet Connections

A NIC, commonly called a LAN adapter, provides the physical connection from a computer or network component to a wired or wireless layer 2 LAN media. A NIC has the following components: interrupt request line (IRQ), an input/output (I/O) address in memory, a driver (software that interfaces with the NIC), and a MAC address. The MAC address is burned into read-only memory (ROM) on the NIC and is commonly called a *burned-in address* (BIA). However, the MAC address is copied into RAM and is then used by the driver software. Some drivers allow the user to change the copied MAC address in RAM (the BIA can't be changed since it is burned into ROM).

Cabling Types

LANs typically use either copper or fiber-optic cabling. Copper cabling can include one strand of copper across which an electrical voltage is transmitted, or many strands of copper. Fiber-optic cabling uses light-emitting diodes (LEDs) and lasers to transmit data. With this transmission, light is used to represent binary 1s and 0s: if light is on the wire, this represents a 1; if there is no light, this represents a 0.

Unshielded Twisted Pair

Between copper and fiber, implementing copper cabling is less expensive. The Ethernet standards define three types of copper cabling:

- **Thicknet**   Uses a thick coaxial cable (no longer used in today's networks)
- **Thinnet**   Uses a thin coaxial cable (no longer used in today's networks)
- **Unshielded Twisted Pair (UTP)**   Uses a four-pair wire, where each pair is periodically twisted

Of the three copper cabling types, only UTP is used today, mainly because it is cheaper than the other two and is easier to install and troubleshoot. Given its advantages, copper cabling, including UTP, has two disadvantages:

- It is susceptible to electromagnetic interference (EMI) and radio frequency interference (RFI).
- Distances of the cable are limited to a short haul.

UTP's internal copper cables are either 22- or 24-gauge in diameter. UTP for Ethernet has 100-ohm impedance, so you can't use just any UTP wiring, like that commonly found for telephones, for example. Each of the eight wires inside the cable is colored: some solid, some striped. Two pairs of the wires carry a true voltage, commonly called "tip" (T1–T4), and the other four carry an inverse voltage, commonly called "ring" (R1–R4). Today, people commonly call these positive and negative wires, respectively. A pair consists of a positive and negative wire, such as T1 and R1, T2 and R2, and so on, where each pair is twisted down the length of the cable.

UTP Categories   To help differentiate between the different kinds of UTP cabling, different categories were created. Table 3-8 shows the categories of UTP cabling.

TABLE 3-8	Category	Description
UTP Categories	Category 1	Used for telephone connections (not suitable for data)
	Category 2	Used for data connections up to 4 Mbps—Token Ring
	Category 3	Used for data connections up to 10 Mbps—Ethernet 10BaseT
	Category 4	Used for data connections up to 16 Mbps—Token Ring
	Category 5	Used for data connections up to 100 Mbps—Ethernet
	Category 5E	Used for data connections up to 1 Gbps (gigabit per second)—Ethernet
	Category 6	Used for data connections up to 1 Gbps (24-gauge)—Ethernet

The two endpoints of a UTP cable have an RJ-45 connector. The RJ-45 connector is a male connector that plugs into a female RJ-45 receptacle. The RJ-45 connector is similar to what you see on a telephone connector (RJ-11), except that the RJ-45 is about 50 percent larger in size.

Cabling Devices   With today's implementation of Ethernet over copper, two components make up the connection: an RJ-45 connector and a Category 5, 5E, or 6 UTP cable. As mentioned earlier, the UTP cable has eight wires in it (four pairs of wires). Two types of implementations are used for the pinouts of the two sides of the wiring: *straight-through* and *crossover*. "Pinout" refers to the color of wire used in the cables and pins in a particular position of the RJ-45 interface. Two standards define the cabling pinouts: 568B is used for both straight-through cables and one end of a crossover cable. 568B wiring colors are listed in Table 3-9.

A straight-through Ethernet UTP cable has pin 1 on one side connected to pin 1 on the other side, pin 2 to pin 2, and so on. A straight-through cable is used for DTE-to-DCE (data termination equipment to data communications equipment) connections. The terms *DTE* and *DCE* are typically used in WAN connections, where the DCE provides clocking. These terms will be discussed in more depth in Chapter 25. However, in LAN terms, a DTE is a router, PC, or file server, and a DCE is a hub or a switch. Here is when you should use a straight-through Ethernet cable, as is shown in Figure 3-3:

- A hub to a router, PC, or file server
- A switch or bridge to a router, PC, or file server

TABLE 3-9	Pin	Color
UTP Pinout Colors	1	White and orange striped
	2	Solid orange
	3	White and green striped
	4	Solid blue
	5	White and blue striped
	6	Solid green
	7	White and brown striped
	8	Solid brown

FIGURE 3-3

Straight-through connections

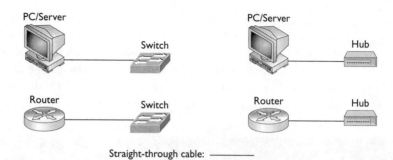

Straight-through cable: —————

A crossover UTP Ethernet cable crosses over two sets of wires: pin 1 on one side is connected to pin 3 on the other and pin 2 is connected to pin 6. Crossover cables should be used when you connect a DTE device to another DTE device or a DCE to another DCE. Use a crossover cable for the following connection types, as shown in Figure 3-4:

- A hub to another hub
- A switch to another switch
- A hub to a switch
- A PC, router, or file server to another PC, router, or file server

FIGURE 3-4

Crossover connections

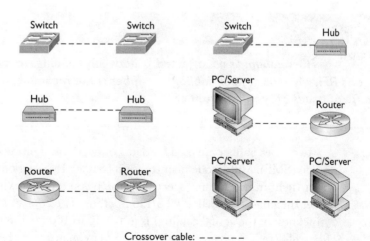

Crossover cable: — — — — —

Sometimes the Ethernet NIC female receptacle will give you a clue as to the type of cable to use. If an X appears on the port and the other port doesn't have an X label, then use a straight-through cable. If neither device has an X or both have an X, then use a crossover cable. In some instances, this setting can be changed in software with a command or in hardware through the use of a dual in-line package (DIP) switch, which allows you to use the cable type that you currently have available.

Fiber

Fiber-optic cabling is typically used to provide very high speeds and to span connections across very large distances. For example, speeds of 100 Gbps and distances greater than 10 kilometers are achievable through the use of fiber—copper cannot come close to these feats. However, fiber-optic cabling does have its disadvantages: it is expensive to implement, difficult to troubleshoot, and difficult to install.

Two types of fiber are used for data connections: multimode (MMF) and single-mode (SMF). Multimode fiber transmits 850 or 1300 nanometer wavelengths of light (light in the infrared spectrum, which you can't see with the naked eye). Fiber thickness for MMF is 62.5/125 microns. The core and cladding diameter (thickness of the actual cabling) is in the 50 to 100 micron range for multimode fiber. 850/1300 nm wavelengths equate to frequencies in the terahertz range. The light is transmitted using a light emitting diode (LED). When transmitting a signal, the light source is bounced off of the inner cladding (shielding) surrounding the fiber. MMF's relatively large core diameter supports the propagation of multiple longitudinal modes (that is, different light paths) at a given wavelength; thus the term *multimode* is used. These multiple modes cause dispersion (signal spreading), which effectively limits the data speeds carried on the fiber to the hundreds-of-Mbps range. A good illustration of this process is when you turn on a flashlight close to a wall; as you move away from the wall, the diameter of the light gets larger and larger, showing dispersion.

Single-mode fiber transmits 1300 or 1550 nm light and uses a laser as the light source. Because lasers provide a higher output than LEDs, SMF can span more than 10 kilometers in distance and have speeds up to 100 Gbps. Due to SMF's very small core diameter, only a single longitudinal mode is propagated at a given wavelength—hence the term *single-mode*. Since only a single mode is propagated, SMF exhibits less dispersion (that is, signal spreading) than MMF, and therefore can support much higher data speeds than MMF (100+ Gbps).

The last few years have seen many advances in the use and deployment of fiber. One major enhancement is wave division multiplexing (WDM) and dense WDM (DWDM). WDM allows more than two wavelengths (signals) on the same piece of fiber, increasing the number of connections. DWDM allows yet more wavelengths, which are more closely spaced together: more than 200 wavelengths can be multiplexed into a light stream on a single piece of fiber. Obviously, one of the advantages of DWDM is that it provides flexibility and transparency of the protocols and traffic carried across the fiber. For example, one wavelength can be used for a point-to-point connection, another for an Ethernet connection, another for an IP connection, and yet another for an Asynchronous Transfer Mode (ATM) connection. Use of DWDM provides scalability and allows carriers to provision new connections *without* having to install new fiber lines, so they can add new connections in a very short period after you order them.

Let's talk about some of the terms used in fiber and how they affect distance and speed. *Cabling* provides the protective outer coating as well as the inner cladding. The inner cladding is denser to allow the light source to bounce off of it. In the middle of the cable is the *fiber* itself, which is used to transmit the signal. The index of refraction (IOR) affects the speed of the light source: it's the ratio of the speed of light in a vacuum to the speed of light in the fiber. In a vacuum, no variables affect the transmission; however, anytime you send something across a medium like fiber or copper, the media itself will exhibit properties that will affect the transmission, causing possible delays. IOR is used to measure these differences: basically, IOR measures the density of the fiber. The denser the fiber is, the slower the light travels through the fiber.

The *loss factor* is used to describe any signal loss in the fiber before the light source gets to the end of the fiber. *Connector loss* is a loss that occurs when a connector joins two pieces of fibers: a slight signal loss is expected. Also, the longer the fiber, the greater the likelihood that the signal strength will decrease by the time it reaches the end of the cable. This is called *attenuation*. Two other terms, *microbending* and *macrobending*, describe signal degradation.

Microbending is when a wrinkle in the fiber, typically where the cable is slightly bent, causes a distortion in the light source. *Macrobending* is when the light source leaks from the fiber, typically from a bend in the fiber cable. To overcome this problem over long distances, *optical amplifiers* can be used. They are similar to an Ethernet repeater or hub. A good amplifier, such as an erbium-doped fiber amplifier (EDFA), coverts a light source directly to another light source, providing for the best reproduction of the original signal. Other amplifiers convert light to an electrical signal and then back to light, which can cause degradation in the signal quality.

Two main standards are used to describe the transmission of signals across a fiber: SONET (Synchronous Optical Network) and SDH (Synchronous Digital Hierarchy). SONET is defined by the Exchange Carriers Standards Association (ECSA) and American National Standards Institute (ANSI) and is typically used in North America. SDH is an international standard used throughout most of the world (with the exception of North America). Both of these standards define the physical layer framing used to transmit light sources, which also includes overhead for the transmission. Three types of overhead are experienced:

- **Section overhead (SOH)** Overhead for the link between two devices, such as repeaters
- **Line overhead (LOH)** Overhead for one or more sections connecting network devices, such as hubs
- **Path overhead (POH)** Overhead for one or more lines connecting two devices that assemble and disassemble frames, such as carrier switches or a router's fiber interface

Typically, either a ring or point-to-point topology is used to connect the devices. With carrier metropolitan area networks (MANs), the most common implementation is through the use of rings. Auto-protection switching (APS) can be used to provide line redundancy: in case of failure on a primary line, a secondary line can automatically be utilized. Table 3-10 contains an overview of the more common connection types for SONET and SDH. Please note that SONET uses STS and that SDH uses STM to describe the signal.

TABLE 3-10	Common Term	SONET Term	SDH Term	Connection Rate
Fiber Connection Types	OC-1	STS-1	n/a	51.84 Mbps
	OC-3	STS-3	STM-1	155.52 Mbps
	OC-12	STS-12	STM-4	622.08 Mbps
	OC-48	STS-48	STM-16	2488.32 Mbps
	OC-192	STS-192	STM-64	9953.28 Mbps

Table 3-11 briefly compares both the copper and fiber cable types.

Ethernet Media Types

Now that you have a better understanding of copper and fiber cabling, let's examine how this is used by the media types that Ethernet supports. The following sections discuss the different implementations of Ethernet based on the cabling and standards used.

Ethernet Physical Layer Properties

Many physical layer standards define the physical properties of an Ethernet implementation. One of the most common is IEEE's 802.3 10Mb. Table 3-12 shows some of the 10Mb standards.

watch
Remember the information in Table 3-12 for the exam.

Ethernet supports a bus topology—physical or logical. In a bus topology, every device is connected to the same piece of wire and all devices see every frame. For example, 10Base5 uses one long, thick piece of coaxial cable. NICs tap into this wire using a device called

TABLE 3-11	Cable	Distance	Data Rates	Comparison
Cable Type Comparisons	UTP	100 meters	10 Mbps–1 Gbps	Easy to install but is susceptible to interference
	Coaxial	500 meters	10–100 Mbps	Easy to install but is difficult to troubleshoot
	Fiber	10 kilometers	10 Mbps–100 Gbps	Difficult and expensive to install, difficult to troubleshoot, but can span very long distances and is not susceptible to interference

TABLE 3-12	10Mb Ethernet Properties				
Ethernet Type	**Distance Limitation**	**Cable Type**	**Interface Type**	**Physical Topology**	**Logical Topology**
10Base5	500 meters	Thick coaxial cable—50 ohm (*thicknet*)	AUI	Bus	Bus
10Base2	185 meters	Thin coaxial cable (*thinnet*)	BNC	Bus	Bus
10BaseT	100 meters	Unshielded twisted pair (UTP) cabling (CAT 3, 4, 5)	RJ-45	Star (Hub)	Bus

a *vampire tap*. With 10Base2, the devices are connected together by many pieces of wire using BNC connectors, commonly called T-taps: one end of the T-tap connects to the NIC and the other two connect to the two Ethernet cables that are part of the bus. Both end points of the cable must be terminated with a terminator cap. With 10BaseT, all devices are connected to a hub, where the hub provides a logical bus topology. All of these 10Mb Ethernet solutions support only half-duplex: they can send *or* receive, but they cannot do both simultaneously. Duplexing is discussed in more depth in Chapter 4.

ⓦatch *Half-duplex connections allow devices either to send or receive in both directions—one direction at a time, though. Additionally, devices using half-duplex experience collisions. Full-duplex* *connections require a point-to-point connection between two devices. With this type of connection, both devices can simultaneously send and receive without any collisions occurring.*

Ethernet 10Base2 and 10Base5 haven't been used in years because of the difficulty in troubleshooting network problems based on the cabling they use. And many 10BaseT networks have been supplanted by higher speed Ethernet solutions, such as Fast Ethernet and Gigabit Ethernet. Ethernet Fast Ethernet and use the same frame types and support the same CSMA/CD operation. However, there are two main differences between the two: Fast Ethernet supports 100 Mbps speeds and the physical layer is implemented differently. Table 3-13 shows the different implementations of Fast Ethernet. Fast Ethernet supports both half- and full-duplex connections. With full-duplex connections, a device can send *and* receive simultaneously but requires a point-to-point connection that doesn't involve a hub.

| TABLE 3-13 | 100Mb Ethernet Properties |

Ethernet Type	Distance Limitation	Cable Type	Cabling	Physical Topology	Logical Topology
100BaseTX	100 meters	UTP CAT 5	RJ-45	Star (hub)	Bus
100BaseFX	400 meters half-duplex, 2000 meters full-duplex	MMF 62.5/125 micron with SC and ST connectors	RJ-45	Star (hub)	Bus
100BaseT4	100 meters	UTP CAT 3, 4, 5	RJ-45	Star (hub)	Bus

on the job

Note that 10Base5 and 10Base2 are rarely used today; even 10BaseT has been supplanted by 100BaseTX and 1000BaseT. For example, my laptop came preinstalled with a 1000BaseT NIC (Gigabit Ethernet).

Gigabit Ethernet is defined in IEEE 802.3z. To achieve 1 Gbps speeds, IEEE adopted ANSI's X3T11 Fiber Channel standard for the physical layer implantation. The physical layer is different from Ethernet and Fast Ethernet in that it uses an 8B/10B encoding scheme to code the physical layer information when transmitting it across the wire. Table 3-14 shows the different implementations of 1 Gbps. One 10 Gbps implementation of Ethernet runs only across fiber. This standard has recently been standardized by IEEE. Gigabit Ethernet connections are commonly use for uplink connections (switch-to-switch) and some server applications.

GBICs

A gigabit interface converter (GBIC) is an I/O device that is plugged into a Gigabit Ethernet interface and provides various interface connector types like those listed in Table 3-14. The advantage of GBICs is that when you purchase a device that supports GBICs, your device comes with a Gigabit Ethernet port and you buy the appropriate GBIC interface connector based on the cabling you'll be using.

TABLE 3-14	Ethernet Type	Distance Limitation	Cable Type
1 Gbps Ethernet Properties	1000BaseCX	25 meters	Shielded twisted pair (STP) copper
	1000BaseLX	3–10 kilometers	SMF
	1000BaseSX	275 meters	MMF
	1000BaseT	100 meters	CAT 5E and CAT 6 UTP (RJ-45)
	1000BaseZX	100 meters	SMF

This means that if you ever need to change your cable requirements, you need to swap only your current GBIC for one that matches your new cabling needs. Most GBICs are *hot-swappable*, but you should always check the device manufacturer's instructions before inserting or removing them.

on the
job

You don't have to use one Ethernet media type and/or speed—it is very common to see a mixture of media types and connection speeds, based on specific needs. For example, it is common to see 100BaseTX using Category 5 or 5E cabling for user connections, 1000BaseTX with Category 5E cabling for server connections, and 1 or 10 Gbps fiber connections for switch-to-switch connections.

INSIDE THE EXAM

Ethernet Evolution and Standards

You should be very familiar with how CSMA/CD operates for Ethernet, which includes Fast Ethernet and Gigabit Ethernet. Remember that there is no prioritization for accessing the Ethernet wire. Less important for the exam are the frame encapsulations for Ethernet II and 802.2/802.3; however, you should be able to compare and contrast the two frame types.

Addressing

You will need to be able to convert binary to decimal (and vice versa), binary to hexadecimal (and vice versa), and decimal to hexadecimal (and vice versa). It would be wise to memorize Tables 3-5 and 3-7. You should know how long a MAC address is, 48 bits; the two components of a MAC address; and what a local broadcast MAC address looks like. Remember that routers don't propagate local broadcasts and that you need unique MAC addresses in the same broadcast domain.

Ethernet Connections

Straight-through unshielded twisted pair (UTP) cables are used for DTE-to-DCE connections, where a DTE is a PC or router and a DCE is a switch or hub. Crossover cables are used for DCE-to-DCE or DTE-to-DTE connections. In a crossover cable, pins 1 and 3, and pins 2 and 6 are crossed. Don't be surprised if you have to match up the cabling type you need to use based on the two devices that you need to connect together.

Fiber-optic cables are best used in environments that have EMI and/or RFI or for connecting components over long distances. Be familiar with the different Ethernet implementations, such as 10BaseT, 100BaseTX, and 1000BaseLX support, including the distances they can span and the kinds of connectors at the ends of their cables. GBICs are used to provide an option of interface connectors for a Gigabit Ethernet interface.

CERTIFICATION SUMMARY

This chapter focused on the Ethernet LAN technology. CSMA/CD is used to implement Ethernet. Ethernet is a shared medium. When a device wants to transmit, it must first listen to the wire to determine whether a transmission is already occurring. If two devices try to send their transmissions simultaneously, a collision occurs. When this happens, a jam signal is created and the two devices back off a random period before trying again.

There are two versions of Ethernet: IEEE 802.2/3 and Ethernet II (or DIX). 802.2 defines the LLC (software) and 802.3 defines the MAC (hardware). 802.2 uses a SAP or SNAP field to designate the layer 3 encapsulated protocol. Ethernet II doesn't have any sublayers and doesn't have a length field; it has a type field instead to designate the encapsulated protocol.

Computers deal with numbers in binary: strings of 0s and 1s. A 1 in a bit position turns on an equivalent decimal value, which is 2 to the power of the bit position. MAC addresses, however, are represented in hexadecimal. Hexadecimal numbers range from 0 through F, where hexadecimal F is 15 in decimal. When all bit positions in a MAC address are enabled—FF:FF:FF:FF:FF:FF—this represents a local broadcast.

Cabling types used in Ethernet networks include copper and fiber. Copper is used to connect components across short distances, and fiber is used to connect them across long distances or when interference, such as EMI, can cause problems with signals traversing a copper wire. The most common copper implementation for Ethernet is UTP Category 5. Two kinds of UTP connections are used: straight-through and crossover. A straight-through cable is used from a switch to either a router or PC. A crossover connection is used between switches, hubs, switches and hubs, a router and PC, two routers, or two PCs.

✓ # TWO-MINUTE DRILL

Ethernet Evolution and Standards

❑ CSMA/CD is used to send information in an Ethernet shared medium.

❑ CSMA/CD senses the wire and then transmits the data; if a collision occurs, it generates a JAM signal and waits a random time interval before transmitting again.

❑ IEEE breaks Ethernet into two components: 802.2 (LLC interfaces with software) and 802.3 (MAC deals with hardware).

❑ Ethernet II doesn't have a sublayer like 802.2 and 802.3, and Ethernet II has a type field instead of a length field.

Addressing

❑ Binary values are read from right to left, where the rightmost bit is the least significant and the leftmost bit the most significant. Each bit position represents a power of 2 in decimal, when turned on (set to 1). Hexadecimal values range from 0 to F.

❑ MAC addresses are 48 bits in length and are represented in hexadecimal. The first six digits are the OUI (vendor code), and the last six digits represent the NIC within the OUI. A local broadcast is represented as FFFF.FFFF.FFFF or FF:FF:FF:FF:FF:FF.

Ethernet Connections

❑ Copper cabling with Ethernet commonly used UTP, a four-pair wire. It's cheap to use and easy to install and troubleshoot. UTP cabling, however, can span only short distances and is susceptible to EMI and RFI. UTP cables use RJ-45 connectors.

❑ Straight-through UTP cables are used between DTE-to-DCE connections. Crossover UTP cables are used between DTE-to-DTE and DCE-to-DCE connections.

❑ Fiber is used to connect devices between buildings or across long distances. Two implementations include MMF and SMF.

❑ Common Ethernet types include standards for Ethernet, such as 10BaseT; Fast Ethernet, such as 100BaseTX; and Gigabit Ethernet, such as 1000BaseLX or 1000BaseSX.

SELF TEST

The following Self Test questions will help you measure your understanding of the material presented in this chapter. Read all the choices carefully, as there may be more than one correct answer. Choose all correct answers for each question.

Ethernet Evolution and Standards

1. Gigabit Ethernet uses which of the following media access methods?
    A. Carrier sense, multiple access, collision detection
    B. Collision sense, multiple access, carrier detection
    C. JAM recovery
    D. Multiple collision and carrier detection

2. Which of the following is *not* a characteristic of Ethernet 802.3?
    A. Contains an LLC
    B. Uses SAPs to multiplex network protocols
    C. Has a type field
    D. Uses FCS to detect invalid frames

3. Which of the following is a valid MAC address?
    A. 00:00:11:GA:7A:34
    B. 00000:CCCCC:ABC12
    C. 00:1F:FF:CE:DA:12
    D. AC:45:32:EE:12:57:34:65

Addressing

4. 11000001 is what in hexadecimal and decimal?
    A. B1, 193
    B. C1, 193
    C. C1, 195
    D. B1, 195

5. 11100111 is what in decimal?
    A. 235
    B. 244
    C. 192
    D. 231

6. Match the following hexadecimal and binary values correctly to their corresponding decimal values:

Decimal	Hexadecimal	Binary
3	A	1110
7	E	1010
10	3	0111
14	7	0011

Ethernet Connections

7. Which of the following is a characteristic of UTP cabling?
    A. Implemented with fiber
    B. Uses two-pair wire
    C. Is susceptible to EMI and RFI
    D. Used between two campus buildings

8. Which cabling would be used for connecting a hub to a switch?
    A. Straight-through UTP
    B. Crossover UTP
    C. Serial
    D. Rollover

9. You need to connect a PC to a hub, the same hub to a switch, the same switch to another switch, and the second switch to a router. What kinds and numbers of UTP cables do you need for this network?
    A. Two straight-through and two crossover
    B. Three straight-through and one crossover
    C. One straight-through and two crossover
    D. Four straight-through

10. Which of the following is a connector on a Category 5 cable with 10BaseT running across it?
    A. AUI
    B. DB-15
    C. RJ-45
    D. SC

SELF TEST ANSWERS

Ethernet Evolution and Standards

I. ☑ **A.** All forms of Ethernet use CSMA/CD: Carrier sense, multiple access, collision detection
☒ **B** and **D** are incorrect because they are the wrong terms. **C** describes how Ethernet recovers from a collision.

2. ☑ **C.** Ethernet II has a type field—802.3 has a length field.
☒ **A, B,** and **D** are true of 802.3 and are therefore incorrect answers.

3. ☑ **C.** MAC addresses are 6 bytes, represented in hexadecimal, which is 12 hexadecimal digits in length.
☒ **A** is incorrect because G is not a hexadecimal character. **B** is incorrect because it has 15 digits. **D** is incorrect because it has 16 digits.

Addressing

4. ☑ **B.** 11000001 is C1 in hexadecimal and 193 in decimal.
☒ **A** and **D** are wrong because B1 is 10110001 in binary. **C** and **D** are wrong because 195 is 11000011 in binary.

5. ☑ **D.** 11100111 is 231 in decimal.
☒ **A** is 11101011 in binary. **B** is 11110100. **C** is 11000000.

6. ☑ Here is the correct matching:

Decimal	Hexadecimal	Binary
3	3	0011
7	7	0111
10	A	1010
14	E	1110

Ethernet Connections

7. ☑ **C.** UTP, which uses copper, is susceptible to EMI and RFI interference.
☒ **A** and **B** are incorrect because UTP uses copper, four-pair wiring. **D** is incorrect because fiber is used in this situation.

8. ☑ **B.** DCE-to-DCE connections, when using UTP, use a crossover cable.

   ☒ **A** is used for a DTE-to-DCE connection. **C** is used with a WAN connection. **D** is used for a Cisco console connection.

9. ☑ **A.** The PC-to-hub and switch-to-router need straight-through cables; the hub-to-switch and switch-to-switch need crossover cables.

   ☒ Since two straight-through and two crossover cables are required, **B**, **C**, and **D** are incorrect.

10. ☑ **C.** 10BaseT with Category 5 uses an RJ-45 connector.

   ☒ **A** is used in 10Base5. **B** is used in AUI as well as some WAN connectors. **D** is used in fiber connectors.

4

Bridges and Switches

CERTIFICATION OBJECTIVES

This chapter provides an introduction to bridges and switches. Bridges and switches are both layer 2 devices, functioning at the data link layer of the OSI Reference Model. Even though they are both layer 2 devices and have many similarities between them, bridges and switches also have many differences. With advancements in hardware and technology, switches perform faster and have many more layer 2 features. However, the basic functions of these two devices are the same.

CERTIFICATION OBJECTIVE 4.01

Problems and Limitations of Ethernet

Even though Ethernet is the main layer 2 technology used in LAN networks for many years, it does have two main disadvantages:

- Distance
- Collisions

The following sections discuss these two problems in depth, and the rest of the chapter will cover some unique solutions commonly found in Ethernet-based networks today.

Distance and Extension of LANs

One of the initial problems with Ethernet was that you were limited to the length of a segment because copper was used as a media type: 10Base5 supported 500 meters and 10Base2 supported 185 meters. When 10BaseT was introduced, using unshielded twisted pair (UTP) cabling, the distance limitation shrunk even further: 100 meters. One issue of using copper as a transmission medium is that as the signal travels down the copper wire, the signal slowly degrades because of noise in the line, the signal losing strength, and issues with devices not specifically following the rules defined by CSMA/CD.

One solution is to use a physical layer repeater to repeat the signal to deal with noise and signal strength. With 10BaseT, a hub, a multiport physical layer repeater, is used to perform this function. A hub takes a signal received on one interface and repeats it across all other available interfaces. The main problem with a hub is that if the signal is bad, the hub repeats the bad signal: bad in, bad out.

CSMA/CD also causes issues. For example, with CSMA/CD, when a device places a frame on a wire, it listens on the wire for a predetermined time period to determine whether a collision occurs. If no collision is detected during this time period, the source assumes that everyone on the segment successfully received the frame. The problem with this implementation is that the longer the cable is, the longer the time period required to accommodate the signal traveling to the two endpoints of the cable. Therefore, the cable can't be of infinite length. Because of this issue, we have different standards of Ethernet that allow for maximum lengths of the cable. If a device has a 10Base5 interface, its NIC knows that it must listen on the wire based on the amount of time it takes for an electrical signal to travel 500 meters, whether or not the cable happens to be this long.

Another solution to deal with the length of an Ethernet segment is to use fiber instead of copper for cabling. Fiber is much more reliable and the signal can travel much father in the same or smaller time period: 100BaseFX can travel 400 meters, for example. The problem with fiber, however, is that it is expensive compared to copper, especially the NICs. Normally, fiber is used only to connect devices between locations, such as two different buildings, or when electromagnetic interference (EMI) or radio frequency interference (RFI) is creating problems in certain areas where copper is deployed.

Collisions, Collision Domains, and Congestion

Another issue with Ethernet is again caused by CSMA/CD: the more devices you put on a segment, the more likely you'll experience collisions, especially among devices that constantly need access to the wire. For example, when two devices are on an Ethernet wire, you would not expect to see that many collisions since it would be unlikely that both devices would need to transmit data simultaneously. However, if 100 devices were on the wire, quite a few might need to send traffic simultaneously. When these devices sense the wire and simultaneously send their traffic, a collision occurs. And the way CSMA/CD works, they need to create a JAM signal and back off a random time interval before sending again. Of course, the more devices present, the more likely that the "random" time interval they choose is the same as another device, thereby creating even more collisions, greatly slowing down a device's access when trying to transmit data. On top of this, high-performance PCs, network-based applications, and high-bandwidth applications such as video can create even more contention for access to a wire.

A collision domain basically includes all the devices that share a media type at layer 1 of the OSI Reference Model—such as all the devices on a single strand of 10Base5 or 10Base2 cabling or all the devices connected to a hub or hubs. In a collision domain, each device on the segment will experience the effects of the collisions. The more devices on the segment, the more likely it is that collisions will create bandwidth problems for these devices. This is not to say that collisions are bad—it's just that collisions are part of how Ethernet functions.

Hubs do not solve collision problems since they replicate physical layer signals. In other words, hubs don't create *extra bandwidth for attached devices. Instead, they extend cable distances and repeat/amplify physical layer signals.*

CERTIFICATION OBJECTIVE 4.02

Solutions to Collision Problems

Bridges were originally used to solve *collision* and *bandwidth* problems. Each port connected to a bridge is a separate collision domain. When a frame is pulled into a port on a bridge, the bridge checks the frame's field checksum sequence (FCS), and if the FCS if valid, the frame is forwarded out of a destination port or ports. Recall from Chapter 3 that the FCS is a checksum to ensure that the destination can check that the Ethernet frame has not been corrupted.

Basically, the bridge is creating the illusion that all physical segments to which it is connected are actually one large *logical* segment. All devices connected to this *logical* segment are in the same broadcast domain—this makes sense because bridges flood broadcasts. Note that if you are having problems with large amounts of broadcasts, bridges will not solve these problems.

Bridges

Bridges are data link layer devices that switch frames between different layer 2 segments or cables. They perform their switching in software, and their switching decisions are based on the destination MAC address in the header of the data link layer frame.

Bridges perform three main functions:

- They learn where devices are located by placing the MAC address of a NIC and the identifier of the bridge port to which it is connected in a port address table.
- They forward traffic intelligently, drawing on information they have in their port address table.
- They remove layer 2 loops by running the Spanning Tree Protocol (STP).

Actually, these three functions are implemented in bridges that perform transparent bridging. Other types of bridging include translational bridging, source route bridging, source route transparent bridging, and source route translational bridging. However, this book focuses on transparent bridging.

The three main functions of a bridge are to learn the MAC addresses and port locations of devices, intelligently forward traffic to a specific destination or flood broadcasts and multicasts, and remove layer 2 loops.

Learning Function

One of the three functions of a bridge is to learn which devices are connected to which ports of the bridge. The bridge then uses this information to switch frames intelligently. When a bridge receives a frame, it reads the source MAC address in the frame and compares it to a local MAC address table, called a *port address table*. If the address is not already in this table, the bridge adds the address and the port identifier or number on which the frame was received. If the address is already in the table, the bridge resets the timer for the table entry. Entries in the table remain there as long as the bridge sees traffic from them; otherwise, the bridge ages out the old entries to allow room for newer ones.

Forwarding Function

The second function of a bridge is to forward traffic intelligently. To do this, the bridge uses the port address table to help it find where destinations are located. When a frame is received on a port, the bridge first performs its learning function and then performs its forwarding function. The bridge examines the destination MAC address in the frame header and looks for a corresponding entry in the port address table. If the bridge finds a matching entry, the bridge forwards the frame out of the specified port. If the port is the same port on which the frame was received (the source and destination are connected to the same port), the bridge drops the frame. If the bridge doesn't find an entry, or if the destination MAC address is a broadcast or multicast address, the bridge *floods* the frame out all of the remaining ports.

ⓦatch *Remember that these three types of traffic are always flooded: unknown unicast addresses, broadcasts, and multicasts.*

Removing Loops

The third function of a bridge is to remove layer 2 loops. To see the problem that layer 2 loops can cause, consider Figure 4-1. One advantage of using two bridges to connect two segments together, as shown in Figure 4-1, is that it creates redundancy.

FIGURE 4-1

Layer 2 loops and redundancy

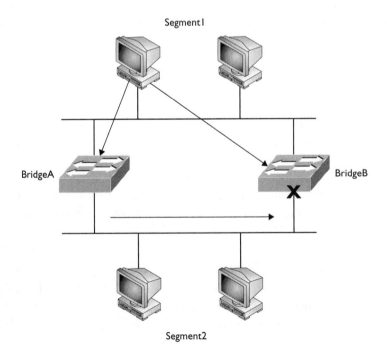

But these loops also create problems. For instance, a bridge always floods traffic that has a destination address that is an unknown unicast, a broadcast, or a multicast address. And this traffic will continually circle around the loop—possibly forever. For example, in Figure 4-1, assume that a PC generates a broadcast on Segment1. When BridgeA and BridgeB receive the broadcast, they flood it out all of their remaining ports. This means that the same broadcast will appear twice on Segment2. Each bridge sees the other's broadcast on Segment2 and forwards this back to Segment1. This process will go on ad infinitum. This process not only wastes bandwidth on your LAN segments but also affects the CPU cycles of all devices on these segments, since all NICs will accept the broadcast and pass it up the protocol stack for further processing.

STP is used to remove loops in your layer 2 network. When STP runs, one of the ports of the bridges in a loop is disabled in software. In Figure 4-1, this is the port on BridgeB that is connected to Segment2. Any user traffic is ignored if it is received on this port and is not forwarded out of this port. Going back to our broadcast example, if a PC on Segment1 generated a broadcast, both bridges, again, would receive it. BridgeA would flood the broadcast to Segment2, but BridgeB would not, since the port is in a *blocked* state. STP is discussed in much more depth in Chapter 14.

Switches

Switches, like bridges, operate at the data link layer. The three main functions of a bridge are also true of a switch: they learn, forward, and remove loops. However, switches have many more features than bridges; for instance, they make their switching decisions in hardware by using application-specific integrated circuits (ASICs). ASICs are specialized processors built to perform very few specific tasks. Because they do only a few things, ASICs are much more cost-effective than a generic processor, such as the one in your PC. Cisco, like most networking vendors, extensively uses ASICs throughout its switching products.

CERTIFICATION OBJECTIVE 4.03

Bridges versus Switches

The main function of bridges and switches is to solve bandwidth, or collision, problems. Remember that in Ethernet, multiple devices can share the same segment, so there is a chance that more than one device might try to transmit at the same time, creating a collision and a retransmission. The more devices you have in a shared medium, the more likely collisions will occur.

In the old days of networking you used hubs to connect devices together or used 10Base5 or 10Base2 cabling (where many devices would share one wire). If you experienced constant or excessive amounts of collisions, you could use bridges (and later on, switches) to break up the user devices to multiple physical segments, where each segment would have fewer users and thus fewer collisions. You could also use a router to perform this function; however, the disadvantage of a router is that it costs a lot more than a bridge or switch. This section provides a brief overview of bridges and switches.

e x a m

w a t c h   *Hubs cannot solve bandwidth or collision problems. Bridges and switches, on the other hand, can. Bridges and switches take one large collision domain and split it into a bunch of smaller ones. In this sense, they create extra* *collision domains, since each interface of the layer 2 device is a separate collision domain. This process is called microsegmentation. Routers, at the network layer, can also solve collision problems, but they cost more than bridges or switches.*

Even though bridges and switches both operate at layer 2, there are many differences between them. Switches have many advantages over bridges, including the following:

- Full-duplex support to allow a device to send and receive simultaneously
- Support for different Ethernet speeds on different switch ports, such as 10BaseT, 100BaseTX, and Gigabit Ethernet
- Dedicated connections between a router, PC, or server to a port on the switch
- Multiple, simultaneous session transmissions between different switch ports

Table 4-1 compares other differences between bridges and switches.

e x a m

w a t c h   *Remember the advantages of switches outlined in the bullet points.*

Perhaps the biggest difference between the bridges and switches is performance. Bridges switch frames in software, providing a frame rate between 10,000 and 50,000 frames per second (fps). Switches, on the other hand, perform their switching in hardware, using

TABLE 4-1	Functions	Bridges	Switches
Bridge and Switch Comparison	Form of switching	Software	Hardware (in ASICs)
	Method of switching	Store and forward	Store and forward, cut-through, fragment-free
	Ports	2–16	Possibly hundreds
	Duplexing	Half	Half and full
	Collision/bandwidth domains	1 per port	1 per port
	Broadcast domains	1	1 per VLAN
	STP instances	1	1 per VLAN

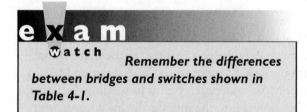

ASICs. ASICs are specialized processors, and in the switching world, they are built to do one thing: switch frames very, very fast. As an example, the Catalyst 2960 switch has a frame rate of 2.7 *million* fps, which is more than 50 times faster than the fastest bridge! Note that the 2960 is a low-end switch; Cisco's Catalyst 6500 has a rate of 400 million fps!

Methods of Switching

Another difference between bridges and switches is in how they switch frames. The switching method affects how a layer 2 device receives, processes, and forwards a frame. Bridges support only one switching method, store-and-forward, while switches might support one, two, or three different switching methods. The three switching methods that might be supported by layer 2 devices include the following:

- Store-and-forward
- Cut-through
- Fragment-free

The following sections cover these three switching methods.

Store-and-Forward

Store-and-forward switching is the most basic form of switching. With store-and-forward switching, the layer 2 device must pull in the entire frame into the buffer of the inbound port and check the FCS (checksum) of the frame before the layer 2 device will perform any additional processing of the frame. When checking the FCS, commonly called a *cyclic redundancy check* (CRC), the layer 2 device will calculate a CRC value, just as the source device did, and compare this value to what was included in the frame. If they are the same, the frame is considered good and the layer 2 device can start processing the frame, including forwarding the frame out the correct destination port of the layer 2 device. If the FCS value in the frame and the frame value it computes are different, the layer 2 device will drop the frame.

Bridges support only the store-and-forward switching method. All switches support store-and-forward. However, some switches, such as Cisco's older Catalyst 1900 series, may support additional switching methods; but this is dependent on the actual switch model and vendor.

Cut-Through

Some switches, such as the older Catalyst 1900, support *cut-through* switching. With cut-through switching, the switch reads only the very first part of the frame before making a switching decision. Once the switch device reads the destination MAC address (8-byte preamble and 6-byte MAC address), it begins forwarding the frame (even though the frame may still be coming into the interface). One advantage of cut-through switching over store-and-forward is that it is faster. Its biggest problem, though, is that the switch may be switching bad frames since the header could be legible, but the rest of the frame corrupted from a late collision.

Most vendors solve this problem by supporting a dynamic switching method. When performing cut-through switching, the switch will still examine the CRC of the frame as it is being switched, looking for bad frames. Even though the frame may be bad, it is still switched. However, the switch keeps a count of these bad frames. If over a certain period of time, the switch reaches a threshold of switching bad frames, the switch will dynamically switch its method from cut-through to store-and-forward. This function, though, is entirely dependent on whether or not the vendor included it in its switching product.

Fragment-Free

Fragment-free switching is a modified form of cut-through switching. Whereas cut-through switching reads up to the destination MAC address field in the frame before making a switching decision, fragment-free switching makes sure that the frame is at least 64 bytes long before switching it (64 bytes is the minimum legal size of an Ethernet frame). The goal of fragment-free switching is to reduce the number of Ethernet *runt frames* (frames smaller than 64 bytes) that are being switched. Sometimes fragment-free switching is also called *modified cut-through* or *runtless* switching.

Even with fragment-free switching, a switch could still be switching corrupt frames (frames with a bad FCS), since the switch is checking only the first 64 bytes, and the FCS is at the end of the frame. To overcome this problem, many vendors implement dynamic switching methods, as discussed in the preceding section. At least with fragment-free switching, most collisions typically create runts, and this switching method would prevent the forwarding of these frames, unlike cut-through switching.

Store-and-forward switching pulls in the whole frame, checks the FCS, and then switches the frame. This increases latency for switching but reduces the number of bad frames in the network. Bridges support only this mode, as does the Catalyst 2960 switch. Cut-through switching switches a frame as soon as it sees the destination MAC address in the frame (first 14 bytes). Fragment-free switching will switch a frame after the switch sees at least 64 bytes, which prevents the switching of runt frames.

on the
Job
Even though the Catalyst 2960 switch doesn't support cut-through and fragment-free switching like the 1900, it still switches frames faster (the 1900 has a frame rate of 500,000 fps). This is because the 2960 has much faster ASICs than the 1900 switch. Therefore, you shouldn't judge a switch by its switching method, but by a combination of factors, such as price, performance, and features.

Duplexing

Duplexing affects how a device can send and receive frames in Ethernet. Two modes are used in duplexing: half and full. With half-duplex, the device can either send or receive—it cannot do both simultaneously. Half-duplex connections are used in a shared medium, such as 10Base2, 10Base5, and Ethernet hub connections. In this environment, one device sends while all other devices in the collision domain listen for and receive the frame. In a shared environment like this, you can typically get 40 to 60 percent utilization out of your Ethernet segment. Note, however, that every situation is different and these numbers are under normal, or average, conditions.

on the **Job** *If your utilization in a half-duplex environment starts eclipsing the 40–60 percent utilization range, or your collisions exceed 2 percent of total traffic, you should consider either using full-duplex, increasing the speed of the link (by using Fast or Gigabit Ethernet), or breaking up the collision domain with switches.*

Full-duplex, unlike half-duplex, allows a device to send *and* receive frames simultaneously. However, this will work only if two devices are using the connection, such as a PC connected to a switch or a switch connected to a router. This is called a *point-to-point connection*. You cannot use a hub in a full-duplex connection. To set up a full-duplex connection, both devices need to support full-duplexing. Table 4-2 compares half- and full-duplex connections.

exam **Watch** *Remember the information in Table 4-2. Also remember that full-duplex gives you more bandwidth than half-duplex since both devices can simultaneously transmit and receive without any collisions.*

As Table 4-2 points out, one main advantage full-duplex connections have over half-duplex connections is that full-duplex connections do not experience collisions. Basically, the transmit circuit on one side is wired to the receive circuit on the other side, and vice versa. In this situation, the Ethernet NIC disables the collision detection mechanism, since it isn't needed. Full-duplex connections are supported

TABLE 4-2		Half-Duplex	Full-Duplex
Half-Duplex and Full-Duplex Comparison	Send and/or receive	Send or receive	Send and receive
	Connection type	Hub, 10Base2, 10Base5	Point-to-point
	Collisions	Yes	No
	CSMA/CD	Enabled	Disabled
	Requirements	Hub or wire tap	Dedicated switch port

with the following media types: 10BaseT, 100BaseTX, 100BaseFX, and Gigabit Ethernet. Connections using 10Base5, 10BaseFL, and 10Base2 support only half-duplexing. Note that some older 10BaseT NICs may not support full-duplex. An example of this is the 10BaseT interfaces on Cisco 2500 series routers, which support only half-duplex.

When dealing with bridges and switches, bridges support only half-duplex connections, while most switches support both. For instance, the 2960 switches support both connection types. Most switches and NICs will autosense the duplexing and configure it appropriately.

If one side is configured as full-duplex and the other half-duplex, expect to experience problems with collisions, since the full-duplex side has CSMA/CD disabled. Cisco recommends that you let ports autosense the duplexing to alleviate this kind of problem.

CERTIFICATION OBJECTIVE 4.04

Switching Functions

With all of these differences between bridges and switches, they are still, at heart, both layer 2 devices and perform the same three basic network functions:

- **Learning** They learn what device is connected to which port.
- **Forwarding** They intelligently switch frames to the port or ports where the destination is located.
- **Removing layer 2 loops** They remove loops with the Spanning Tree Protocol (STP), so that frames don't continually circle around the network.

These functions are functions of *transparent* bridges. Other types of bridging include source route bridging, source route transparent bridging, and source route translational bridging, which appear in mixed-media networks, such as Ethernet, Token Ring, and fiber distributed data interface (FDDI). However, since the CCNA exam focuses on transparent bridging, and Token Ring and FDDI are basically dead LAN technologies, this book focuses only on transparent bridging.

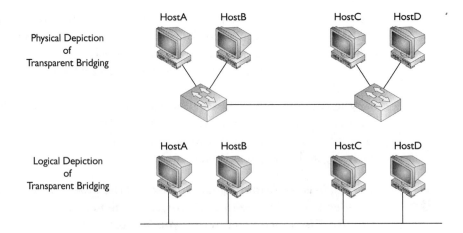

Physical
and logical
descriptions of
a transparently
bridged network

The term *transparent* appropriately describes a transparently bridged network: the devices connected to the network are unaware that the bridge, or switch, is a part of the network and is forwarding frames to destinations. Basically, transparent-bridge networks physically look like a bunch of star topologies connected together. However, transparent bridges give the appearance to connected devices that every device in the broadcast domain is on the same logical segment, as shown in Figure 4-2.

The following sections cover the three main functions of transparent bridges and switches in more depth. As you read through these sections, you'll see the term *switch* used to describe the layer 2 device; however, the terms *bridge* and *switch* are interchangeable when it comes to the three main functions.

Learning Function

One of the three main functions of a transparent switch is to learn which device is connected to each of the active ports of the switch. As a frame comes into the port of a switch, the switch examines the source MAC address of the frame and compares it to its switch table, commonly referred to as a *content addressable memory* (CAM) table or *port* or *MAC address* table. In the old days of bridging, CAM was a special form of high-speed memory that facilitated the switching function in a bridge when it had to forward a frame out of the correct destination port. Today, switches use RAM to store the MAC addresses, but the term CAM is still commonly used.

When the switch receives a frame on a port, and as it examines the source MAC address in the frame and doesn't see a corresponding entry in the CAM table, the switch will add the address to the table, including the source port identifier or number. If the address is already in the CAM table, the switch compares the incoming port with the port already in the table. If they are different, the switch updates the CAM table with the new port information. This is important because you might have moved the device from one port to another port, and you want the switch to learn where the new location is and have the switch forward frames to the device correctly (not to the old port).

Any time the switch updates an entry in the CAM table, the switch also resets the timer for the specific entry. Switches use timers to age out old information in the CAM table, allowing room to learn new MAC addresses. Each switch has different default timers for the aging process. Aging is important because, once a CAM table is full, the switch will not be able to learn any new addresses. For MAC addresses it can't learn, traffic sent to these addresses will have to be flooded, affecting the bandwidth on all the switch's or bridge's interfaces. A switch will also reset the timer for an entry in the CAM table if it sees traffic from a source MAC address that is currently in the CAM table. In this manner, devices that are constantly sending information will always remain in the CAM table and devices that are not sending traffic will eventually be aged out of the table (removed from the table).

The CAM table can be built statically or dynamically. By default, when you turn on a switch, the CAM table is empty unless you have configured static entries in it. As traffic flows through the switch, the switch will begin building its CAM table. This dynamic building process is a very nice feature. In the old days of bridging, only two kinds of bridges were used: learning and nonlearning. Learning bridges function as I have just described—they dynamically learn addressing locations by examining the source MAC addresses in the Ethernet frames. Nonlearning bridges, by contrast, do not have a dynamic learning function. Instead, you must statically configure each device's MAC address and the port to which it is connected. Of course, if you had 1000 devices in your non-learning bridged network, you would be very busy building and maintaining these tables, which would be an arduous task. Today, switches support both functions. Normally, you would use static configurations for security purposes. Static configurations are covered in Chapter 12.

exam
ⓦatch

Switches place learned source MAC addresses and their corresponding ports in a CAM or port address table. This feature is used to forward frames intelligently. Switches will never learn a broadcast or multicast address since these should never be seen in the source MAC address field in the frame header.

Forwarding Function

The second major function of a switch is to forward traffic intelligently. Whenever a frame comes into a port on the switch, the switch not only examines the source MAC address so that it can perform its learning function, it also examines the destination MAC address to perform its forwarding function. It examines the destination MAC address and compares this address to the addresses in its CAM table to determine which interface it should use when forwarding the frame to the destination.

If the destination address is found in the CAM table, the forwarding process is easy: the switch forwards the frame out the port for the corresponding CAM entry. If the switch examines the destination address and finds that the destination is associated with the same port as the source of the frame, the switch will drop the frame. In this situation, you might have a hub connected to this port of the switch, and both the source and destination are connected to this hub. Given this, the switch shouldn't forward any frames between these two machines to other switch segments, since this would be wasting bandwidth in your network. As you can see, the switch is *intelligently* forwarding traffic, thereby creating a *separate* bandwidth domain per port.

Frame Types

Three different MAC address destination types are available: *unicast*, *broadcast*, and *multicast*. Depending on the type of destination address, in certain situations, the switch will have to flood the frame out of all of its ports (with the exception of the port on which the frame was received). Here are the three frame types that are always flooded:

- **Broadcast address**   Destination MAC address of FFFF.FFFF.FFFF
- **Multicast address**   Destination MAC addresses between 0100.5E00.0000 and 0100.5E7F.FFFF
- **Unknown unicast destination MAC addresses**   The destination MAC address is not found in the CAM table

Unicast Frames   With a unicast, the source device sends a separate copy of each frame to each destination. So, as an example, if a device needs to send the same information to 50 different destinations, the device would have to create 50 frames, with 50 different destination MAC addresses. When a switch receives a frame with a unicast address as the destination, the switch looks for the address in its CAM table to make a switching decision. If the switch doesn't have the address in its CAM table, the switch will flood the frame out all of its other ports. If the address is found in the table, the switch will forward the frame out one port: the one with the destination address behind it.

It's important to remember that you are dealing with a *transparent* switch when dealing with the forwarding process. Therefore, if the switch doesn't know where the destination is, and obviously the source is assuming that the device is on the same "logical" segment, the switch will have to flood the frame to ensure that the destination, if it is somewhere in the broadcast domain, will receive the source's frame. This process, hopefully, won't happen every time. If the destination receives the frame, the destination will probably send a response frame back to the source. Through the switch's learning process, it now knows where the destination is located, and any further frames sent from the source to the destination and back can be intelligently forwarded instead of flooded.

One issue with this process, however, occurs if your CAM table is filled to capacity and your switch can't add new entries to the table; in this case, the switch will *always* flood traffic to new destinations that it couldn't fit into the CAM table. Therefore, it is very important that when you purchase a switch, you select one that will be able to handle the number of devices that you'll have in your switched network. You'll be creating problems if you have 2000 devices in your switched network but your CAM table on each switch can hold only 1000 entries. In this situation, the switches will be flooding traffic for half of the destinations, creating serious bandwidth and performance problems in your network.

Broadcast and Multicast Frames   A *broadcast* is a frame that is sent to all devices in a broadcast domain. As an example, if a source device needed to send the same information to 50 destinations, the source would create only one frame, and every destination would process this frame with the destination MAC address of FFFF.FFFF.FFFF. Remember to think of the switched network as a logical bus, where it appears that everyone is on the same piece of wire. Therefore, when a switch receives a broadcast, it needs to ensure that all machines will receive it, and thus the switch will flood this frame to make sure all devices receive the broadcast.

A *multicast* is a frame addressed to a group of devices, where the group consists of devices interested in receiving the multicast data. This group can contain no devices, all devices, or some devices in the broadcast domain. In a standard switch configuration, when the switch receives a multicast frame, it floods it out all its ports. Only the devices configured to use the multicast address actually process the frame; all other devices drop it. The problem of using unicast frames to disseminate certain types of information is that it can negatively impact the performance of your network. For instance, imagine that you have a network where you want 10 devices to receive a specific multicast stream, such as a real-time video presentation. One solution would be to have the video server use unicasts and send 10 copies of the same information to each destination. Of course, if the multimedia stream is running at 5 Mbps, then this would require the server to generate 50 Mbps worth of traffic.

Another solution would be to use a broadcast. In this situation, the multicast server generates only one stream of information. The problem with this is twofold, however. First, the switched infrastructure would flood this traffic to every destination, including the 10 devices that are interested in seeing it, wasting a lot of bandwidth. Second, because broadcast frames are addressed FF:FF:FF:FF:FF:FF, each device must waste processing cycles to process them. The third solution is to use multicast frames. With multicasting, switches also flood the frames; however, they *can* learn which devices want to receive multicast traffic and therefore forward the multicast frames only to those devices that want to see the multicast traffic. This topic is beyond the scope of this book, but it is covered in Cisco's Switching exam for the CCNP certification.

o n t h e
ⓙ o b   *If you have a large multicast solution deployment, you will definitely want to make sure that your switches support advanced multicast features that allow them to forward multicast traffic intelligently instead of having to flood it. You want to have the switch forward multicast frames to end stations that are running a multicast application that need to see the multicast stream—you don't want your switch to flood multicasts to all end stations, especially if the multicast traffic is video.*

Switch Example

To help you understand what happens when a switch forwards rather than floods, the example in Figure 4-3 shows a hub and a switch, with various PCs connected to these two devices.

Let's assume that the switch was just turned on, which means that its CAM table is empty. PC-A generates a frame destined for PC-C. When the switch receives the frame, it looks in its CAM table and does not see the source MAC

FIGURE 4-3   Transparent switch forwarding example

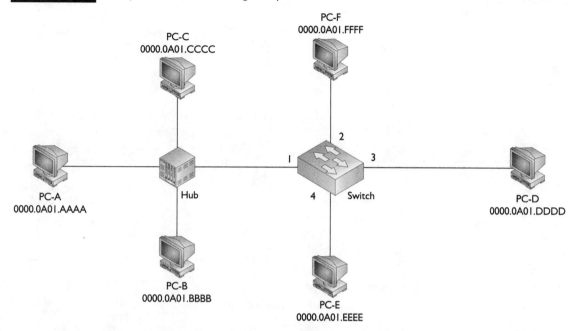

address (0000.0A01.AAAA), so it adds it along with port 1. It also examines the destination MAC address (0000.0A01.CCCC) and does not see this address in its CAM table, so the switch floods the frame out all of its remaining ports: 2, 3, and 4.

In this example, the switch did not need to do this because PC-C is connected to the same hub as PC-A; however, the switch doesn't know this yet. This is an example of flooding an unknown destination unicast address. Figure 4-4 shows an example of the switch adding the entry to its CAM table and flooding the frame. You can see from this figure that the switch now has one entry in its CAM table (PC-A's) as well as the flooding process that it performed. Since the destination, PC-C, is connected to the same hub as PC-A, it obviously receives the frame.

PC-C now responds back to PC-A with a unicast frame: the source MAC address is 0000.0A01.CCCC and the destination MAC address is 0000.0A01.AAAA. The switch performs its learning process, and since PC-C's MAC address is not in its CAM table, it adds it, as is shown in Figure 4-5. Now the switch has two entries in its CAM table: PC-A's and PC-C's. To perform the forwarding process, the switch examines the destination MAC address, 0000.0A01.AAAA. It finds a match in its CAM table and finds that the destination MAC address is associated with the same port as the source MAC address of PC-C's. Therefore, the switch drops the frame: it does not forward it out of any of its ports, as can be seen from Figure 4-5.

FIGURE 4-4   Adding PC-A's MAC address to the CAM table

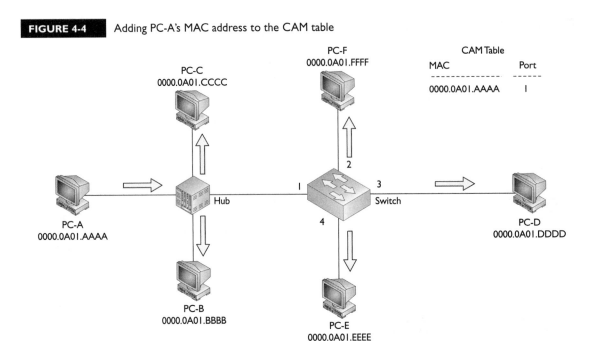

PC-B now sends a unicast frame to PC-F: These PCs are connected to different ports of the switch. When the switch receives the frame from PC-B, it again performs its learning process. Since PC-B is not in its CAM table, the switch adds 0000.0A01.BBBB along with port 1 to its table. Now the switch performs its forwarding function: Since the destination MAC address 0000.0A01.FFFF is not in the CAM table, the switch floods the frame out all ports except the source, port 1. This process can be seen in Figure 4-6.

The switch now has three MAC addresses in its CAM table. PC-F receives the frame and responds with an answer to PC-B. The switch again performs its learning function: since 0000.0A01.FFFF is not in its CAM table, it adds it. Now the switch performs its forwarding function. It sees 0000.0A01.BBBB in its CAM table with the port number of 1 and therefore forwards the frame out of port 1 *only*. This process can be seen in Figure 4-7.

In this last example, PC-E generates a broadcast (FFFF.FFFF.FFFF). When the switch receives the broadcast frame, it performs its learning function by adding 0000.0A01.EEEE to its CAM table. The switch then floods the frame, since it is a broadcast. This process can be seen in Figure 4-8.

From this simple example, you can see that the role of the switch is not a complicated one. First, the switch examines the source MAC address in the frame and updates the

FIGURE 4-5   Adding PC-C's MAC address to the CAM table

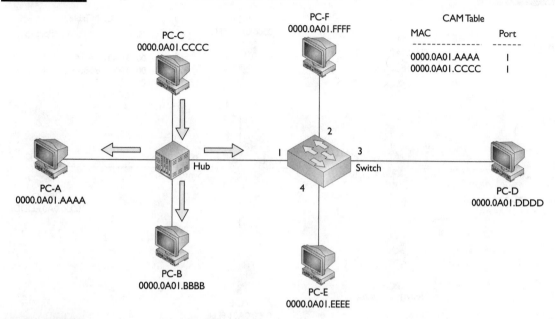

FIGURE 4-6   Adding PC-B's MAC address to the CAM table

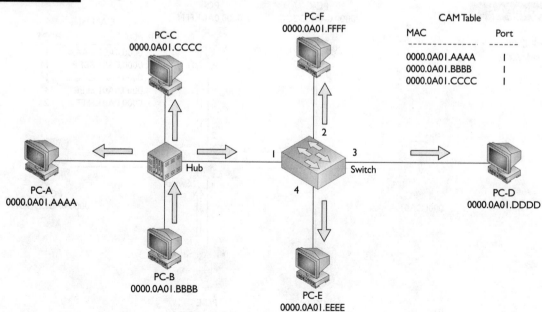

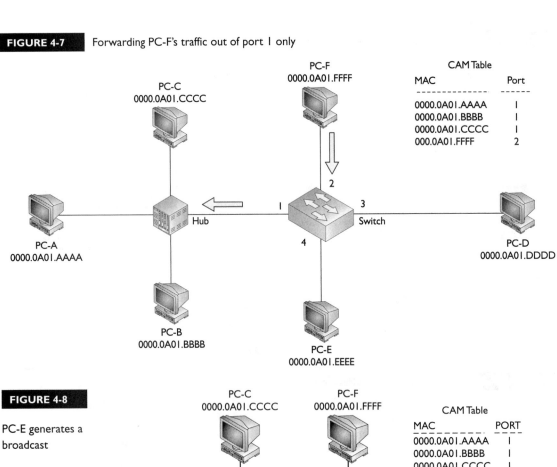

FIGURE 4-7 Forwarding PC-F's traffic out of port 1 only

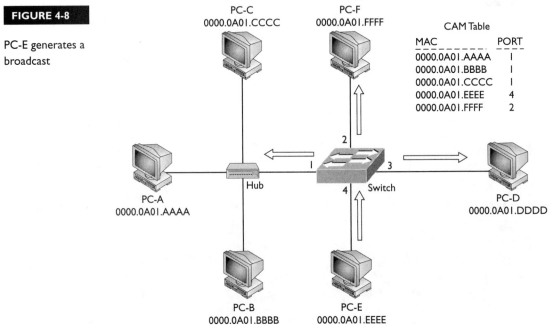

FIGURE 4-8

PC-E generates a broadcast

CAM table if necessary. Second, the switch examines the destination MAC address in the frame and makes a forwarding decision. As you will see in the next section, the switch's function becomes more complicated when more than one switch resides in the network, and layer 2 loops are between the switches.

exam

watch

You will need to be able to determine how many collision/bandwidth domains, as well as broadcast domains, exist in a network diagram. For example, in Figure 4-8, four collision/bandwidth domains (one for each port on the switch) exist, but only one broadcast domain. Each interface off a layer 3 device, such as a router, on the other hand, would be a separate broadcast domain.

Loops

At the backbone of your network, or at least where your critical resources are located, you'll probably incorporate some type of redundancy in your design. This might include redundancy with your switches at layer 2, creating layer 2 loops in your network as shown in Figure 4-9. The problem with loops in your network is that when the switch floods certain types of traffic, such as broadcasts or multicasts, you don't want this traffic going around and around the loop forever, creating serious utilization problems.

Plus, for unknown destinations, as the frame is going around the loop, the switches update their CAM tables with the source address, which eventually shows up as connected to another connected switch, creating confusion about where the source device really is located. For example, if a device is connected to Switch 3,

FIGURE 4-9

Looped layer 2 topology

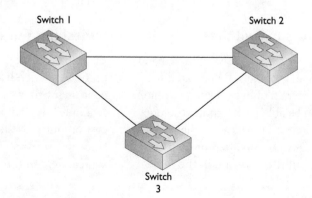

Switch 1

Switch 2

Switch 3

when the device generates a frame, Switch 3 adds the source MAC address to its CAM table and notes that it is connected to the incoming port. If Switch 3 doesn't know where the destination is located, it will flood the frame to Switches 1 and 2 on its two uplink ports. If both Switches 1 and 2 don't know where the destination is, they also flood the frame across the link between them, and will then flood it back to Switch 3. This presents a problem: When Switch 3 receives these flooded frames and performs its learning function, it now looks as if the device is connected to not the original port, but one of the two uplink ports to Switch 1 or 2.

INSIDE THE EXAM

Problems and Limitations of Ethernet

Remember that all devices connected to a hub are in the *same* collision domain. Hubs solve distance and signal degradation problems.

Solutions to Collision Problems

Know the three kinds of traffic flooded by a switch: unknown unicasts, broadcasts, and multicasts.

Bridges versus Switches

Bridges and switches are used to solve bandwidth/collision problems. Be prepared to examine a diagram of hubs, switches, routers, and PCs and be able to determine the number of collision and broadcast domains: each port off of a switch is a different collision domain, but all the ports are in the same broadcast domain unless VLANs are used; each port off of a router is a separate collision *and* broadcast domain. Be able to compare bridges and switches, using Table 4-1. Also be familiar with the three switching methods, store-and-forward, cut-through, and fragment free, as well as the differences between half- and full-duplex, as compared in Table 4-2.

Switching Functions

Be prepared for exam questions that test you on how a switch learns and forwards MAC addresses. Study the example in the "Switch Example" section. Remember that a broadcast or multicast address is never learned since it is seen in the destination, not the source, field in the MAC address header.

STP is used to prevent these problems from occurring. STP removes loops in your network but still allows for redundancy. Actually, the loop removal process is done in software—you don't have to disconnect wires between your switches physically to remove the loops. Chapter 14 focuses on redundancy in more depth, including the STP protocol.

CERTIFICATION SUMMARY

This chapter focused on the advantages that bridges and switches provide in a network. Ethernet has problems dealing with collisions. Originally, bridges were used to solve this problem; today, switches have supplanted bridges because of their many advantages, including support for a large number of ports, full duplexing, different Ethernet speeds, dedicated connections, simultaneous session transmissions, and very fast switching of frames.

Switches switch frames in hardware using ASICs and support both full- and half-duplex connections. Full-duplex allows you to send and receive simultaneously but requires a point-to-point connection. Three switching modes are used: store-and-forward (reads whole frame), cut-through (reads up to the destination MAC address), and fragment-free (reads the first 64 bytes).

Bridges and switches have three main functions: learn, forward, and remove loops. They learn by placing source MAC addresses and associated bridge ports in a port address or CAM table. They will flood traffic if the destination address is a multicast, broadcast, or unknown destination. STP is used to remove loops.

✓ TWO-MINUTE DRILL

Problems and Limitations of Ethernet

❑ Ethernet is limited in distance based on its CSMA/CD implementation.

❑ Hubs and repeaters can be used to extend the distance of an Ethernet segment, but since they only repeat physical layer signals, they don't solve collision problems.

Solutions to Collision Problems

❑ Bridges and switches help solve bandwidth and collision issues.

❑ Each port off of a bridge or switch is a separate bandwidth/collision domain.

Bridges versus Switches

❑ With store-and-forward switching, the layer 2 device must pull the entire frame into port and check the FCS before any additional processing of the frame is done. With cut-through switching, the switch reads up to and including the destination MAC address in the frame before switching the frame. Fragment-free switching makes sure that the frame is at least 64 bytes before switching it.

❑ In half-duplex connections, a device can either send or receive at one time. In full-duplex connections, a device can simultaneously send and receive. Full-duplex connections don't experience collisions and therefore have the collision detection mechanism disabled in the NIC.

❑ Bridges switch frames in software, use store-and-forward switching, use half-duplex connections, and support a small number of ports. Switches switch frames in hardware (ASICs), use multiple switching methods, support both half- and full-duplex connections, and can support hundreds of ports.

Switching Functions

❑ The three main functions of layer 2 devices are learning, forwarding, and removing loops.

❑ During the learning process, layer 2 devices add the source MAC address of the frame and the incoming port number to the port address, or CAM, table.

❑ Three types of frames are flooded: broadcast (all devices), multicast (a group of devices), and unknown (one device) destination.

SELF TEST

The following Self Test questions will help you measure your understanding of the material presented in this chapter. Read all the choices carefully, as there may be more than one correct answer. Choose all correct answers for each question.

Problems and Limitations of Ethernet

1. Which devices cannot solve collision problems?
    A. Hubs
    B. Switches
    C. Switches and hubs
    D. Routers and hubs

Solutions to Collision Problems

2. Which is not one of the three main functions of a layer 2 device?
    A. Learning
    B. Forwarding
    C. Listening
    D. Loop removal

3. Which type of traffic is not flooded by a switch?
    A. Multicast
    B. Known unicast
    C. Broadcast
    D. Unknown unicast

Bridges versus Switches

4. Examine the top part of Figure 4-2. How many collision and broadcast domains are there?
    A. 1, 5
    B. 5, 1
    C. 4, 1
    D. 0, 5

5. Which of the following is true concerning bridges?
    A. They switch frames in hardware.
    B. They support half- and full-duplexing.

C. They support one collision domain for the entire bridge.

D. They do only store-and-forward switching.

6. With _____ switching, the switch reads the destination MAC address of the frame and immediately starts forwarding the frame.

   A. Store-and-forward

   B. Cut-through

   C. Fragment-free

   D. Runtless

7. Which of the following is true concerning full-duplexing on a NIC?

   A. It can either send or receive frames, but not both simultaneously.

   B. It can be used with hubs.

   C. It can be used with 10Base5 cabling.

   D. It uses point-to-point connections.

Switching Functions

8. Which of the following is true concerning the switch learning process?

   A. Known destination MAC addressing information is updated in the port address table.

   B. Unknown destination MAC addresses are intelligently forwarded by the switch.

   C. A broadcast MAC address can be learned by the switch.

   D. Unknown destination MAC addresses are dropped by the switch.

9. When would you see multiple copies of the same unicast frame being transmitted in a switched network?

   A. A port is misconfigured in half-duplex on one side and full-duplex on the other.

   B. This is impossible.

   C. The switching mode is configured as runtless.

   D. An inadvertent layer 2 loop exists.

10. Examine Figure 4-6. Which of the following statements would be false?

    A. If PC-B sends a frame to PC-C, the frame would be dropped by the switch.

    B. If PC-B is moved to port 3 of the switch, the switch will automatically update its CAM table when PC-A sends a frame to PC-B.

    C. If PC-C sends out a broadcast, the switch will still learn the MAC address of the source.

    D. PC-D can set its interface to full-duplex if the switch port supports full-duplexing.

SELF TEST ANSWERS

Problems and Limitations of Ethernet

1. ☑ **A.** Hubs cannot solve collision problems since they replicate signals—they are used to extend cable distances and to repeat/amplify physical layer signals.
   ☒ **B, C,** and **D** are incorrect because switches and routers can be used to solve collision problems.

Solutions to Collision Problems

2. ☑ **C.** Listening is an STP port state, not one of the three main functions of a layer 2 device.
   ☒ **A, B,** and **D** are the three main functions of a layer 2 device.

3. ☑ **B.** Known unicast traffic is not flooded if the destination MAC address is in the CAM table.
   ☒ **A, C,** and **D** are incorrect because multicast, broadcast, and unknown unicast traffic is always flooded, to maintain the transparency of the layer 2 device.

Bridges versus Switches

4. ☑ **B.** There are 5 collision domains and 1 broadcast domain: each port off of a switch (the segment associated with it) is a separate collision domain and all ports in a layer 2 network are in the same broadcast domain.
   ☒ **A, C,** and **D** have either the wrong number of collision domains or the wrong number of broadcast domains.

5. ☑ **D.** Bridges support only the store-and-forward switching method.
   ☒ **A** and **B** are done by switches, not bridges. **C** is incorrect because each port on a bridge or switch is a separate collision domain.

6. ☑ **B.** With cut-through switching, the switch reads the destination MAC address of the frame and immediately starts forwarding the frame.
   ☒ With **A**, store-and-forward, the entire frame is read and the CRC is checked before further processing. **C** and **D**, fragment-free and runtless, are the same thing—once the first 64 bytes of the frame are read, the switch begins to forward it.

7. ☑ **D.** Full-duplex connections require point-to-point connections and cannot involve hubs.
   ☒ **A, B,** and **C** are true of half-duplex connections.

Switching Functions

8. ☑ **A.** If a MAC address is already in the CAM table and is seen again, the switch will update the CAM table appropriately, including a different port number if the MAC address is seen off of a different port.
    ☒ **B** and **D** are incorrect because unknown destination MAC addresses are flooded. **C** is incorrect because you should never see a broadcast address as a source MAC address under normal operating conditions.

9. ☑ **D.** If you are seeing multiple copies of the same unicast frame in a switched network, it is probably because STP is disabled or a misconfiguration of the switches is causing a layer 2 loop.
    ☒ **A** would cause an increase in collisions on the segment. **B** is incorrect because this problem can exist. **C** actually prevents frames less than 64 bytes from being switched, typically solving late collision problems on the connected segment.

10. ☑ **B.** The switch will only update the CAM table for PC-B when it sees a frame coming *from* PC-B.
    ☒ Since PC-C is in the CAM table, the switch would not flood the frame, making **A** an incorrect answer. **C** is incorrect because the source address is PC-C, which it will still learn since it is a unicast address. **D** is incorrect because if two devices support full-duplexing on a point-to-point link, it can be used.

5
Wireless

This chapter provides an introduction to wireless communications. Wireless transmission has been used for a long time to transmit data by using infrared radiation, microwaves, or radio waves through a medium such as air. With this type of connection, no wires are used. Wireless LANs (WLANs) are becoming more and more common in companies' networks, especially in small offices/home offices (SOHOs): instead of designing and implementing an Ethernet-based network, requiring the laying of cabling, it can be more cost effective to use wireless communications, or a combination of wired and wireless. This can be true in older buildings where the physical infrastructure makes it difficult, if not impossible, to run Ethernet cables to each room or area. And on top of this, many companies are deploying mobile services, such as PDAs, smart phones, and laptops that require constant access to e-mail and web-based services. This chapter discusses the differences between LANs and WLANs, the common standards that are used, security concerns when using wireless, and common types of devices you'll find in a WLAN.

CERTIFICATION OBJECTIVE 5.01

Wireless LAN Technologies

Before we begin a discussion of the actual standards used in a WLAN, you need to understand some of the technologies used in wireless communications. This section introduces you to three groups of wireless technologies: narrowband, broadband, and circuit/packet data solutions. Narrowband is the most common solution deployed in WLANs, so this chapter focuses on the technology and standards used in WLANs today.

Narrowband, Broadband, and Packet Data Solutions

When you are choosing a wireless solution for your WAN or LAN, you should always consider the following criteria: speed, distance, and number of devices to connect.

Narrowband solutions typically require a license and operate at a low data rate. Only one frequency is used for transmission of the wireless traffic: 900 MHz, 2.4 GHz, or 5 GHz. Other technologies—household wireless phones, for instance—also use these technologies. Through the use of *spread spectrum*, higher data rates can be achieved by spreading the signal across multiple frequencies. However, transmission of these signals is typically limited to a small area, such as a small campus network.

The *broadband* solutions fall under the heading of a *Personal Communications Service* (PCS). They provide lower data rates than narrowband solutions and cost about the same, but they provide broader coverage. With the right provider, you can obtain national coverage. Sprint PCS is an example of a carrier that provides this type of solution.

Circuit and packet data solutions are based on cellular technologies. They provide lower data rates than the other two and typically have higher fees for each megabit transmitted; however, you can easily obtain nationwide coverage from almost any cellular phone company. 3G is one of the more popular implementations used by cellular phone companies today; many cell phone companies even charge a flat rate for unlimited usage.

CSMA/CA

Recall from Chapter 3 that Ethernet uses Carrier Sense Multiple Access/Collision Detection (CSMA/CD) to control access to a wire. WLANs use a similar mechanism called *Carrier Sense, Multiple Access/Collision Avoidance* (CSMA/CA). Unlike Ethernet, it is impossible to detect collisions in a wireless medium. In a WLAN, a device cannot simultaneously send or receive and thus cannot detect a collision: it can only do one or the other.

To avoid collisions, a device will use Ready-to-Send (RTS) and Clear-to-Send (CTS) signals. When a device is ready to transmit, it first senses the airwaves for a current signal. If there is none, it generates an RTS signal, indicating that data is about to send. It then sends its data and finishes by sending a CTS signal, indicating that another wireless device can now transmit.

WLAN devices also have another similarity to Ethernet LANs: they use an access point to connect devices together logically. The access point serves a function similar to that of a hub in Ethernet. One problem with a WLAN implementation, like Ethernet, is that it is a shared medium: the more devices in the topology, the less throughput each device individually gets because they have to *share* the finite amount of bandwidth and because of the increased collisions that can occur when devices simultaneously sense the airwaves and send an RTS signal. Another problem with WLANs is security. Unlike Ethernet, anyone with a compatible device can sniff the airwaves and eavesdrop on communications; at least with Ethernet, this would require someone to have access to the Ethernet cable the traffic was traversing. The most common method of dealing with this problem is to *encrypt* the wireless traffic.

Radio Frequency Transmission Factors

Radio frequencies (RF) are generated by antennas that propagate the waves into the air. As they are being propagated, various factors can reflect or deflect the signal, affecting its quality and strength.

on the **()** o b

Antennas fall under two different categories: directional and omni-directional. Directional antennas are commonly used in point-to-point configurations (connecting two distant buildings), and sometimes point-to-multipoint (connecting two WLANs). An example of a directional antenna is a Yagi antenna: this antenna allows you to adjust the direction and focus of the signal to intensify your range/reach. Omni-directional antennas are used in point-to-multipoint configurations, where they distribute the wireless signal to other computers or devices in your WLAN. An access point would use an omni-directional antenna. These antennas can also be used for point-to-point connections, but they lack the distance that directional antennas supply.

Three main factors influence signal distortion:

- **Absorption** Objects that absorb the RF waves, such as walls, ceilings, and floors
- **Scattering** Objects that disperse the RF waves, such as rough plaster on a wall, carpet on the floor, or drop-down ceiling tiles
- **Reflection** Objects that reflect the RF waves, such as metal and glass

e x a m

ⓦ a t c h *Common objects that will cause RF distortion problems include walls, ceilings, floors, glass windows, metal* *objects such as desks and file cabinets, and many others.*

CERTIFICATION OBJECTIVE 5.02

WLAN Standards

Typically, government agencies control the use of RF bands. For example, in the United States, the Federal Communications Commission (FCC) regulates wireless transmissions, which includes new transmission methods, frequencies, and modulations; in Europe, the European Telecommunications Standards Institute (ETSI) is the regulator. However, one international agency, the International Telecommunication Union-Radio Communication Sector (ITU-R) is responsible for managing the radio frequency (RF) spectrum and satellite orbits for wireless communications: its main purpose is to provide for cooperation and coexistence of standards and implementations across country boundaries.

Two standards bodies are primarily responsible for implementing WLANs: the Institute of Electrical and Electronic Engineers (IEEE) and the Wi-Fi Alliance. IEEE defines the mechanical process of how WLANs are implemented in the 802.11 standards so that vendors can create compatible products. The Wi-Fi Alliance basically certifies companies by ensuring that their products follow the 802.11 standards, thus allowing customers to buy WLAN products from different vendors without having to be concerned about any compatibility issues. Cisco is a founding member of the Wi-Fi Alliance. You can find a list of certified vendor products at www.wi-fi.com.

RF Bands

Wireless communications can use various RF bands. Some of these are licensed (you have to pay a governmental agency to use them) and some are unlicensed. For example, radio broadcasts, such as AM and FM, are licensed through your country's government. Other bands, such as the 802.11 bands, are unlicensed, so you don't have to buy a license from the government to use these frequencies. However, unlicensed bands are still regulated by governments, which might define restrictions in their usage. WLANs use three unlicensed bands:

- **900 MHz** Used by older cordless phones
- **2.4 GHz** Used by newer cordless phones, WLANs, Bluetooth, microwaves, and other devices
- **5 GHz** Used by the newest models of cordless phones and WLAN devices

A *hertz* (Hz) is a unit of frequency that measures the change in a state or cycle in a wave (sound or radio) or alternating current (electricity) during 1 second. A *megahertz* (MHz) is 1 million cycles per second and a *gigahertz* (GHz) is 1 billion cycles per second. The word *hertz* is from Heinrich Hertz, a German physicist who first discovered that you could send and receive waves through the air.

The 900 MHz and 2.4 GHz frequencies are commonly referred to as the *Industrial, Scientific, and Medical* (ISM) bands and the 5 GHz frequency the *Unlicensed National Information Infrastructure* (UNII) band.

e x a m

ⓦatch

The advantage of using unlicensed bands for WLANs is that you, as a company, don't have to pay a license fee to the government to use these frequencies. However, their main drawback is that many types of devices use them, such as cordless phones, microwave ovens, and Bluetooth devices, which can create interference for WLAN devices using the same RF band.

802.11 Standards

Wireless is becoming very popular in today's LANs, since little cabling is required. Four basic standards are currently in use: 802.11a, 802.11b, 802.11g, and 802.11n, as shown in Table 5-1.

e x a m

ⓦatch

Be familiar with the contents of Table 5-1, especially the data rates: 802.11b—11 Mbps; 802.11a—54 Mbps; and 802.11g—54 Mbps. Remember that 802.11b and 802.11g support DSSS and 802.11a and 802.11g support OFDM.

on the ⓙob

The speeds listed in Table 5-1 are optimal speeds based on the specifications— the actual speeds that you might achieve in a real network vary according to the number of devices you have, the distance that they are from an access point, and any physical obstructions or interference that might exist.

TABLE 5-1	WLAN Standards			
	802.11a	**802.11b**	**802.11g**	**802.11n**
Data Rate	54 Mbps	11 Mbps	54 Mbps	248 Mbps (with 2×2 antennas)
Throughput	23 Mbps	4.3 Mbps	19 Mbps	74 Mbps
Frequency	5 GHz	2.4 GHz	2.4 GHz	2.4 and/or 5 GHz
Compatibility	None	With 802.11g and the original 802.11	With 802.11b	802.11a, b, and g
Range (meters)	35–120	38–140	38–140	70–250
Number of Channels	3	Up to 23	3	14
Transmission	OFDM	DSSS	DSSS/OFDM	MIMO

Direct Sequence Spread Spectrum (DSSS) uses one channel to send data across all frequencies within that channel. Complementary Code Keying (CCK) is a method for encoding transmissions for higher data rates, such as 5.5 and 11 Mbps, but it still allows backward compatibility with the original 802.11 standard, which supports only 1 and 2 Mbps speeds. 802.11b and 802.11g support this transmission method. OFDM (Orthogonal Frequency Division Multiplexing) increases data rates by using a spread spectrum: modulation. 802.11a and 802.11g support this transmission method. 802.11n uses MIMO (Multiple Input Multiple Output) transmission, which uses DSSS and/or OFDM by spreading its signal across 14 overlapping channels at 5 MHz intervals. Use of 802.11n requires multiple antennas.

Of the four IEEE 802.11 standards, 802.11b has been deployed the most, with 802.11g being the most common one sold today. 802.11n is very new and not commonly found in company networks, but is slowing making its way into SOHO networks; its main drawback is that 802.11n hasn't been ratified as a standard yet—it's still in a draft state. One advantage that 802.11b and 802.11g devices have over 802.11a is that 802.11b and 802.11g can interoperate, which makes migrating from an all-802.11b network to an 802.11g network an easy and painless process. Note that 802.11g devices are compatible with 802.11b devices (but not vice versa) and 802.11a devices are *not* compatible with the 802.11b and 802.11g standards. 802.11n is backward compatible with all three standards; however, when running it in compatibility mode, you will not reach its maximum data rate or throughput. 802.11n is currently in a draft state and should be ratified as a standard in 2008 or 2009; therefore, you might experience compatibility issues between different vendors if using 802.11n equipment.

Typically, your throughput on any given wireless network is half of the overall bandwidth. For example, an 802.11b network usually runs with only 5.5 Mbps throughput. The overhead bandwidth involved really makes a difference.

CERTIFICATION OBJECTIVE 5.03

WLAN Security

One of the biggest problems of wireless networks is security. *War driving* is a term used in the old days of hacking when a person would continually dial phone numbers until he eventually dialed a number of a computer system and then would try to hack into it using various methods. Today, the term is commonly used to describe hackers that roam around with a laptop and 802.11b/g NIC trying to find WLANs to break into. Most WLAN solutions support some form of security features; however, it is really surprising about the number of SOHO companies and home users that don't implement these features, basically allowing someone who is driving by to get free Internet access or worse, opening up their network to other forms of attacks. The following sections discuss some common threats WLANs face and security solutions you can implement to mitigate these threats.

WLAN Client Access to the Network

Before learning about security solutions available for your WLAN networks, you should understand how an end user client with a WLAN NIC accesses a LAN or other wireless services via an access point (AP). To allow clients to find the AP easily, the AP periodically broadcasts beacons, announcing its Service Set Identifier (SSID), data rates, and other WLAN information. SSID is a naming scheme for WLANs to allow an administrator to group WLAN devices together. To discover APs, clients will scan all channels and listen for the beacons from the AP(s). By default, the client will associate itself with the AP that has the strongest signal. When the client associates itself with the AP, it sends the SSID, its MAC address, and any other security information that the AP might require based on the authentication method configured on the two devices. Once connected, the client periodically monitors the signal strength of the AP to which it is connected;

if the signal strength becomes too low, the client will repeat the scanning process to discover an AP with a stronger signal. This process is commonly called *roaming*.

802.11 defines only two authentication methods for APs to authentication clients:

■ **Open Authentication** Exchanging four hello packets that contain no verification (basically no security at all)

■ **Shared Key Authentication** A static encryption key is used with the Wireless Equivalency Privacy (WEP, or sometimes referred to as the Wireless Encryption Protocol), which is very weak by today's standards

The following sections discuss in depth the security solutions available in a WLAN environment.

Security Solutions

A good WLAN security solution should provide for the following:

■ **Encryption** Protect data transmitted between the edge WLAN device and the access point, providing privacy and confidentiality

■ **Authentication** Control who is allowed to access LANs behind the WLAN access points

■ **Intrusion prevention system (IPS)** Protect the network by detecting and preventing network and unauthorized access attacks

A brief overview of some of these solutions is found in Table 5-2. The following sections discuss methods available for securing your wireless network.

TABLE 5-2 Common WLAN Security Solutions

	WEP	**802.1x EAP**	**WPA**	**802.11i/WPA2**
Introduced	1997	2001	2003	2004
Encryption	Static keys, breakable	Dynamic keys	Dynamic, per packet	Dynamic, per packet, most secure
User Authentication	None (optional MAC address filtering)	Usernames/ passwords, certificates, pre-shared keys (PSK)	Usernames/ passwords, certificates, PSK	Usernames/ passwords, certificates, PSK

SSID and MAC Address Filtering

When implementing SSIDs, the AP and client must use the same SSID value to authenticate. By default, the access point broadcasts the SSID value, advertising its presence, basically allowing anyone access to the AP. Originally, to prevent rogue devices from accessing the AP, the administrator would turn off the SSID broadcast function on the AP, commonly called *SSID cloaking*. To allow a client to learn the SSID value of the AP, the client would send a null string value in the SSID field of the 802.11 frame and the AP would respond; of course, this defeats the security measure since through this query process, a rogue device could repeat the same process and learn the SSID value. Therefore, the APs were commonly configured to filter traffic based on MAC addresses. The administrator would configure a list of MAC addresses in a security table on the AP, listing those devices allowed access; however, the problem with this solution is that MAC addresses can be seen in clear-text in the airwaves. A rogue device can easily sniff the airwaves, see the valid MAC addresses, and change its MAC address to match one of the valid ones. This is called MAC *address spoofing*.

If broadcast beaconing is disabled on the AP, the client will manually have to configure the SSID to match that of the AP.

WEP

WEP (Wired Equivalent Privacy) was one of the first security solutions for WLANs that employed encryption. WEP uses a static 64-bit key, where the key is 40 bits long, and a 24-bit initialization vector (IV) is used. Because repetitious data will eventually allow a person to discover the key, a random IV value is added to the data and included in the encryption; however, the IV is sent in clear-text. Because WEP uses RC4 as an encryption algorithm and the IV is sent in clear-text, WEP can be broken. To alleviate this problem, the key was extended to 104 bits with the IV value. However, either variation can easily be broken in minutes on laptops and computers produced today.

Because WEP can easily be broken, it is not recommended to be used in company networks. However, in SOHO networks it is still commonly used because of its simplicity to implement; to add an extra level of security, it is commonly combined with MAC address filtering. Even so, a determined attacker/hacker can easily bypass both methods.

Because of the security issues prevalent in WEP, Cisco enhanced it with a proprietary solution called Temporal Key Integrity Protocol (TKIP). TKIP does per-packet keying and Cisco Message Integrity Check (CMIC), which basically does per-packet keying and hashing. With TKIP, every packet has a unique encryption key, and each packet is digitally signed to validate the source of the sender before decrypting it, to make sure the packet is valid and that it's coming from a trusted source and not being spoofed.

802.1x EAP

The Extensible Authentication Protocol (EAP) is a layer 2 process that allows a wireless client to authenticate to the network. There are two varieties of EAP: one for wireless and one for LAN connections, commonly called EAP over LAN (EAPoL). One of the concerns in wireless is allowing a WLAN client to communicate to devices behind an AP. Three standards define this process: EAP, 802.1x, and Remote Authentication Dial In User Service (RADIUS). EAP defines a standard way of encapsulating authentication information, such as a username and password or a digital certificate that the AP can use to authenticate the user. EAP is basically an extension of the Point-to-Point Protocol (PPP) and one of the first forms of EAP was EAP-MD5, which used Challenge Handshake Authentication Protocol (CHAP) for authentication (CHAP is discussed in more depth in Chapter 25). Here are some of the extensions of EAP:

- **EAP-MD5** Supports CHAP with static passwords for authentication
- **EAP-TLS** Supports x.509v3 digital certificates for authentication
- **LEAP (Lightweight EAP)** Supports static passwords and allows for per-session WEP keys
- **PEAP (Protected EAP)** Supports static and one-time passwords (OTP), where SSL secures the connection so that MS-CHAP can be used for authentication and the username and password are encrypted to protect them from an eavesdropping attack (a digital certificate is required only on the server)
- **EAP-FAST** Supports faster authentication, where a shared secret key is used to encrypt authentication information (similar to PEAP)
- **EAP-GTC** Supports authentication via a generic token card server

Some of these EAP methods support authentication as well as keying information to encrypt the wireless transmissions between the client and AP.

FIGURE 5-1

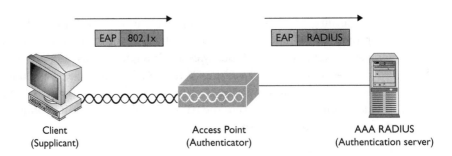

EAP operation
and devices

Client (Supplicant)   Access Point (Authenticator)   AAA RADIUS (Authentication server)

802.1x and RADIUS define how to packetize the EAP information to move it across the network. The use of the three standards is shown in Figure 5-1. 802.1x describes how the client, commonly called the *supplicant*, transports the EAP information to the network access device, commonly called an *authenticator*. The network access device can be an AP, switch, router, VPN gateway, or other similar device. The authenticator passes this information using the RADIUS protocol to an *authentication server*, which will validate the supplicant's access to the network. Note that the authenticator doesn't typically have the user's credentials defined locally—it usually looks these up from the authentication server.

WPA

Wi-Fi Protected Access (WPA) was designed by the Wi-Fi Alliance as a temporary security solution to provide for the use of 802.1x and enhancements in the use of WEP until the 802.11i standard would be ratified. Authentication is handled by 802.1x and TKIP is used with WEP; however, the TKIP used by WPA is not compatible with Cisco's older and proprietary form of TKIP.

WPA can operate in two modes: personal and enterprise mode. Personal mode was designed for home or SOHO usage. A pre-shared key is used for authentication, requiring you to configure the same key on the clients and the AP. With this mode, no authentication server is necessary as it is in the official 802.1x standard. Enterprise mode is meant for large companies, where an authentication server will centralize the authentication credentials of the clients.

WPA2

WPA2 is the IEEE 802.11i implementation from the Wi-Fi Alliance. Instead of using WEP, which uses the weak RC4 encryption algorithm, the much more secure Advanced Encryption Standard (AES)–counter mode CBC-MAC Protocol (CCMP)

TABLE 5-3	Mode	WPA	WPA2
WPA and WPA2 Comparison	Enterprise	802.1x with EAP authentication and WEP/TKIP for encryption	802.1x with EAP authentication and AES encryption
	Personal	PSK authentication and WEP/TKIP for encryption	PSK authentication and AES-CCMP encryption

algorithm is used. AES is used for encryption with a 128-bit key. AES-CCMP incorporates two cryptographic techniques—counter mode and CBC-MAC—and adapts them to wireless frames to provide a robust security protocol between the client and AP. Even though AES itself is a strong encryption algorithm, the use of counter mode makes it much more difficult for an eavesdropper to spot patterns in the encrypted data, and the CBC-MAC message integrity method ensures that wireless frames haven't been tampered with and are coming from a trusted source.

Table 5-3 compares the implementations of WPA and WPA2. As you can see, the main difference between the two is the use of AES for encryption in WPA2 over WEP/RC4 encryption for WPA.

ⓦatch   *WPA uses WEP/TKIP (dynamic, per-packet keying) for encryption while WPA2 uses AES-CCMP.*   *Both support pre-shared keys (PSK) in personal mode but rely on 802.1x for authentication in enterprise mode.*

CERTIFICATION OBJECTIVE 5.04

WLAN Implementation

Now that you have a better understanding how a client connects to an AP, let's talk about more of the mechanics involved in designing a WLAN implementation. The following sections discuss the access modes and coverages commonly used, as well as how data rates are handled with wireless connections.

Access Modes

Two 802.11 access modes can be used in a WLAN:

- Ad hoc mode
- Infrastructure mode

Ad hoc mode is based on the Independent Basic Service Set (IBSS). In IBSS, clients can set up connections directly to other clients without an intermediate AP. This allows you to set up peer-to-peer network connections and is sometimes used in a SOHO. The main problem with ad hoc mode is that it is difficult to secure since each device you need to connect to will require authentication. This problem, in turn, creates scalability issues.

Infrastructure mode was designed to deal with security and scalability issues. In infrastructure mode, wireless clients can communicate with each other, albeit via an AP. Two infrastructure mode implementations are in use:

- Basic Service Set (BSS)
- Extended Service Set (ESS)

In BSS mode, clients connect to an AP, which allows them to communicate with other clients or LAN-based resources. The WLAN is identified by a single SSID; however, each AP requires a unique ID, called a Basic Service Set Identifier (BSSID), which is the MAC address of the AP's wireless card. This mode is commonly used for wireless clients that don't roam, such as PCs.

on the job *If your computer is running Wireless Zero Configuration (on by default in most current Windows installs), any computer with a wireless NIC in ad hoc mode can connect directly to you, without your approval. By default, your wireless NIC will start in infrastructure mode, looking for the strongest signal, and so on. A good article on this topic, "How WiFi Ad-Hoc Networks Are Like Zombies," can be found at https://edge.arubanetworks.com/article/how-wifi-ad-hoc-networks-are-zombies-or-free-public-wifi-phenomenon-0.*

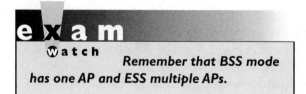

In ESS mode, two or more BSSs are interconnected to allow for larger roaming distances. To make this as transparent as possible to the clients, such as PDAs, laptops, or mobile phones, a single SSID is used among all of the APs. Each AP, however, will have a unique BSSID.

Coverage Areas

A WLAN coverage area includes the physical area in which the RF signal can be sent and received. As mentioned previously, various factors can affect the strength and distance of an RF signal, such as walls and ceilings, windows, metal objects, microwave ovens, certain types of wireless phones, and so on. Two types of WLAN coverages are based on the two infrastructure mode implementations:

■ Basic Service Area (BSA)
■ Extended Service Area (ESA)

The terms BSS and BSA, and ESS and ESA, can be confusing. BSS and ESS refer to the building topology whereas BSA and ESA refer to the actual signal coverage, as shown in Figure 5-2.

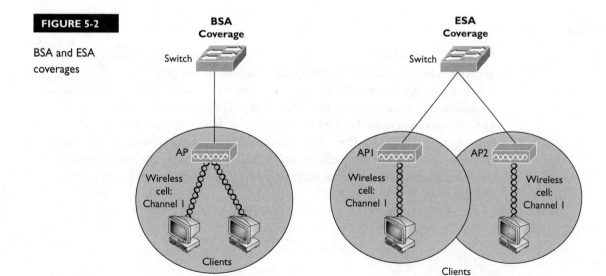

FIGURE 5-2

BSA and ESA coverages

BSA

With BSA, a single area called a *cell* is used to provide coverage for the WLAN clients and AP, as shown on the left side of Figure 5-2. The AP advertises the cell through an SSID value, where the SSID logically separates the different WLAN BSAs. Since BSA uses BSS, infrastructure mode is used: clients that need to communicate with other clients must do this via an AP. To improve coverage, a client can be configured without an SSID, allowing the client to learn all of the APs and their associated SSIDs and choose the one that has the strongest signal and/or data rate. This approach will work, however, only if the APs are configured to advertise their SSID.

ESA

With ESA, multiple cells are used to provide for additional coverage over larger distances or to overcome areas that have or signal interference or degradation, as shown in the right side of Figure 5-2. When designing a WLAN with ESA coverage, it is recommended to overlap cells by 10 to 15 percent so that data devices can roam between cells without losing a signal. If you are using voice over wireless, it is recommended that you have 15 to 50 percent overlap between cells.

When using ESA, remember that each cell should use a different radio channel.

Data Rates

As WLAN clients are transmitting data or moving around within or between cells, the clients can automatically change data rates to fit the current signal quality. For example, when using 802.11b, a device can start with 11 Mbps, but if a problem is encountered, it can slow its rate to 5.5 Mbps, and then down to 2 Mbps or 1 Mbps. This allows clients to send data without losing their connection to the AP. Rate-shifting is supported on a transmission-by-transmission basis, which means different clients or the same client can be using different speeds each time they need to transmit data, allowing each client to adapt to ongoing changes of the signal quality.

CERTIFICATION OBJECTIVE 5.05

WLAN Devices

Most companies, when deploying wireless, use enterprise mode with ESA, where multiple APs provide coverage for the WLAN clients. The following sections discuss the basic configuration tasks for the APs and the clients, as well as common troubleshooting tips when clients have problems connecting to or communicating with APs.

Access Points

Cisco's APs can be configured using a command-line interface (CLI), but it is actually much easier to use a graphical user interface (GUI). Cisco routers that support wireless include a component of Security Device Manager (SDM) that provides a GUI component for the wireless configuration component of the router. SDM is discussed in Chapter 18.

APs are layer 3 devices, and as such, they need a layer 3 address. Since TCP/IP is the de facto standard layer 3 protocol in the world today, your APs will need IP addressing information. This includes an IP address, a subnet mask, and a default gateway address. The default gateway is a layer 3 LAN device providing access to a company's LAN-based resources. This is commonly a router, a layer 3 switch, or a firewall. This information can be assigned statically or dynamically using Dynamic Host Control Protocol (DHCP), which is discussed in more depth in Chapters 6 and 7.

For the wireless communications, you'll need to determine the protocol you'll use for the APs: 802.11b, 802.11a, 802.11b/g, 802.11a/b/g, or possibly 802.11n. Finding APs that do 802.11a as well as other protocols requires that you have two radios in the AP. Cisco's Aironet products support this feature as an option. You also might have to adjust the radio channels on the APs, the power adjustment, and the type of antennae if you are having signal problems.

on the **job**

If you use 802.11b and 802.11g in a mixed mode, your throughput will be decreased. When running in this type of compatibility mode, the AP must implement a Ready-to-Send/Clear-to-Send protocol for each. Therefore, it is recommended that all your wireless devices use the same 802.11 protocol.

To secure your WLAN implementation, you'll need to determine the following:

- The SSID that will represent your WLAN
- The security implementation:
    - WPA in either enterprise (preferably) or personal mode
    - WPA2 in either enterprise (preferably) or personal mode

Clients

Clients will need a wireless card, a driver for the card, and software to configure the card. Some operating systems include a utility for the software configuration, such as Microsoft Windows XP: Wireless Zero Configuration (WZC). WZC allows clients to discover the SSIDs within range automatically and to connect automatically to the AP that has the strongest signal. Clients, like APs, also need IP addressing information. For a SOHO network, it is common to set up the single AP as a DHCP server and have the AP assign addressing information to the clients; however, this does not scale well, nor work well, when using ESA with multiple APs. In this scenario, it is more common to have the AP forward DHCP requests from the clients to a real DHCP somewhere on the LAN network.

Troubleshooting

Most wireless problems for new clients occur because either the AP or, more commonly, the user misconfigured the wireless setup. The most common misconfiguration problem is where the client chooses a security implementation that is different from the AP: for example, the user chooses WPA but the AP is configured for WPA2. If you've verified the settings on both sides and still have problems connecting to the WLAN, you might also want to check the firmware on your wireless NICs to make sure they are running the latest code.

on the
Ĵob

One common oversight of administrators when they are experiencing a problem with a new client they are adding to the network is to verify that the client's NIC is running the latest firmware revision on the NIC. I once had a problem with an Intel wireless NIC that would constantly disconnect and reconnect to my home AP every 5 minutes; a firmware upgrade quickly fixed this problem.

TABLE 5-4	WLAN Problem	Troubleshooting Tip
WLAN Troubleshooting	Weak signal causing intermittent loss of connectivity	Check the placement of the AP and make sure it is in a central location; check the antenna on the AP and point it in the correct direction; make sure the AP is of similar height as the clients (within 20 vertical feet)
	Signal degradation	Check to see if an object is causing interference, such as a metal file cabinet, window, microwave oven, or cordless phone

Other problems you might experience include those shown in Table 5-4. Based on the problems, an appropriate troubleshooting tip is provided. One quick test to ensure that clients and the AP can communicate is to place the client physically close to the AP and see how successful your connection is and then slowly move the client away from the AP, in different directions, to see what might be interfering with the signal. In some instances, you'll need an expensive wireless sniffer to troubleshoot certain connectivity problems. For a smaller company, in this situation, it would make sense to hire an experienced professional for assistance.

If you are experiencing slow performance and connection drops, you should check the direction of the *AP's antenna. If you are having consistent problems, you might want to replace your antenna with a better type.*

INSIDE THE EXAM

Wireless LAN Technologies and WLAN Standards

The CCNA exam focuses on the technology used with WLANs: you will not be expected to understand the configuration and maintenance of Cisco's APs and other wireless products. You should be familiar with the kinds of objects that can distort RF signals, such as microwave ovens, metal file cabinets, cordless phones, windows, and so on. You should be familiar with the 802.11 standards and be able to compare and contrast them as shown in Table 5-1. Be especially familiar with their data rates and transmission methods.

WLAN Security

You should be able to compare and contrast the various security solutions available in WLANs. Tables 5-2 and 5-3 are a good place to start. Remember that if you disable the SSID broadcast function on the AP, clients won't automatically learn the SSID: you'll have to configure it manually.

WLAN Implementation

Understand the differences between ad hoc (IBSS) and infrastructure modes. Be able to compare BSS/BSA and ESS/ESA: one versus multiple APs. When using ESS/ESA, each cell should use a different radio channel.

WLAN Devices

You should be familiar with the kinds of problems you'll face in a WLAN and common troubleshooting tips to help solve these problems. For weak signal problems, the most common solution is to adjust the direction of the radio antenna or to upgrade the antenna to a more powerful one.

CERTIFICATION SUMMARY

This chapter focused on the technology of WLANs, which are becoming more and more common in SOHO and company networks today. WLAN implementations fall under three general categories: narrowband, broadband, and packet data solutions. CSMA/CA is used in wireless to send an RF signal: a device will use Ready-to-Send (RTS) and Clear-to-Send (CTS) signals. This is similar to Ethernet's CSMA/CD. Many factors can affect signal distortion, including absorption (walls), scattering (rough plaster walls), and reflection (metal file cabinets).

Two main standards bodies affect wireless: IEEE with its 802.11 standard and the Wi-Fi Alliance. RF bands commonly used for wireless include 900 MHz, 2.4 GHz, and 5.0 GHz. 802.11 standards defined for WLANs include 802.11b (2.4 GHz at 11 Mbps), 802.11a (5 GHz at 54 Mbps), and 802.11g (2.4 GHz at 54 Mbps). 802.11b uses DSSS as a transmission method, 802.11a uses OFDM, and 802.11g supports both.

A good wireless security solution should include these components: authentication, encryption, and IPS. An SSID is used to identify a group of devices in a WLAN. APs can disable the broadcast of this, but then you must manually configure this value on the clients. WEP is not recommended for use today since its encryption process can be easily broken. 802.1x provides for secure authentication. WPA enhances WEP by performing dynamic per-packet keying for encryption. WPA2 offers the most security, relying on AES-CCMP for encryption. Personal mode uses PSKs for authentication while enterprise mode uses user credentials such as a username and password.

Two access modes for WLANs are used: ad hoc (IBSS) and infrastructure. Ad hoc is a point-to-point connection between two clients while infrastructure mode uses an AP to interconnect devices. The two infrastructure mode implementations are BSS/BSA and ESS/ESA. ESS/ESA uses multiple APs, where each cell—each individual AP—should use a different RF channel.

TWO-MINUTE DRILL

Wireless LAN Technologies

❑ Three types of wireless technologies are used: narrowband, broadband, and packet data.

❑ CSMA/CA uses RTS and CTS RF signals to transmit data.

❑ Factors that influence signal distortion include absorption, scattering, and reflection: floors, walls, ceilings, and metal desk and file cabinets.

Wireless Standards

❑ The main standards bodies responsible for WLANs are IEEE and Wi-Fi Alliance.

❑ The unlicensed bands used by WLANs include 900 MHz, 2.4 GHz, and 5 GHz.

❑ Popular WLAN standards include 802.11a, 802.11b, and 802.11g.

❑ 802.11a uses OFDM as a transmission method, uses a 5 GHz frequency, and has 54 Mbps throughput.

❑ 802.11b uses DSSS as a transmission method, uses a 2.4 GHz frequency, and has 11 Mbps throughput.

❑ 802.11g uses DSSS/OFDM as a transmission method, uses a 2.4 GHz frequency, has 54 Mbps throughput, and is backward compatible with 802.11b.

WLAN Security

❑ An SSID represents a group of devices in a WLAN; APs automatically broadcast this, but if disabled, the WLAN clients must manually configure the SSID value. The original security for wireless commonly used MAC address filtering to supplement SSIDs.

❑ WEP specifies the use of RC4 encryption and is easily breakable with today's desktop computers and laptops.

❑ 802.11x, EAP, and RADIUS are protocols that define how to perform user authentication before allowing a client to transmit data through an AP.

❏ WPA uses RC4 for encryption but makes it more difficult to break since each packet is encrypted with a different key: TKIP.

❏ WPA2 replaces RC4 with AES-CCMP for an encryption algorithm and is the recommended security solution, as well as 802.1x, for an enterprise WLAN solution.

WLAN Implementation

❏ Ad hoc mode (IBSS) allows clients to set up connections directly to other clients.

❏ Infrastructure mode uses an AP to interconnect clients. With BSS/BSA, a single AP is used. With ESS/ESA, multiple APs are used. Each cell in an ESS/ESA topology should be configured with a different RF channel.

WLAN Devices

❏ The most common problem with connecting to a WLAN is client misconfiguration.

❏ To provide for a better signal, change the direction of the AP's antenna or upgrade it to a better one.

SELF TEST

The following Self Test questions will help you measure your understanding of the material presented in this chapter. Read all the choices carefully, as there may be more than one correct answer. Choose all correct answers for each question.

Wireless LAN Technologies

1. Which of the following is true concerning WLAN wireless transmissions?
   A. A device can send and receive simultaneously.
   B. CSMA/CD is used to detect and transmit a signal.
   C. A wireless device will use RTS and CTS signals to avoid collisions.
   D. Reflection issues are caused by rough plaster on a wall, carpet, and drop-down ceiling tiles.

WLAN Standards

2. You are experiencing intermittent connection and signal quality problems with your WLAN implementation. Which of the following would typically not be causing this problem?
   A. Computer USB headset
   B. Cordless phone
   C. Microwave oven
   D. Rogue AP

3. Which of the following is not true concerning 802.11b?
   A. Maximum transmission rate of 11 Mbps
   B. Backward compatible with the original 802.11 standard
   C. Uses OFDM as a transmission method
   D. Is an IEEE standard

4. Which of the following IEEE standards support(s) the OFDM transmission method and can transmit data at 54 Mbps using a 5 GHz frequency?
   A. 802.11b
   B. 802.11a
   C. 802.11g
   D. 802.11a and g

WLAN Security

5. Which of the following Wi-Fi standards supports PSK authentication and RC4 encryption with TKIP?
   A. WEP
   B. 802.1x
   C. WPA
   D. WPA2

6. If you disable broadcast beaconing on an AP, which of the following is true?
   A. You need to configure MAC address filtering to allow clients to talk to the AP.
   B. You need to disable MAC address filtering to allow clients to talk to the AP.
   C. You must define the IBSS on each client, matching it to the configured value on the AP.
   D. You must define the SSID on each client, matching it to the configured value on the AP.

7. Which WLAN security solution uses 802.1x authentication with AES-CCMP for encryption?
   A. Personal WPA
   B. Personal WPA2
   C. Enterprise WPA
   D. Enterprise WPA2

WLAN Implementation

8. Which 802.11 access mode is based on IBSS?
   A. Ad hoc
   B. Infrastructure
   C. BSA
   D. ESA

9. Three APs make up your WLAN network with roaming devices. Which of the following is true concerning the setup of the three APs?
   A. They should use different SSID values.
   B. ESA coverage should be used.
   C. They should all use the same RF channel.
   D. They should use different RF frequencies.

WLAN Devices

10. You are experiencing consistent connection drops and poor performance on your WLAN SOHO network in a small three-room plaza store. Which of the following would you do to solve this problem? (choose two)

    A. Buy an AP for each room and set them up using ESA coverage.

    B. Place the AP in a central location between the three rooms.

    C. Check the direction of the antennas on the AP and possibly upgrade the antennas to get better signal coverage.

    D. Replace the AP with a better product.

SELF TEST ANSWERS

Wireless LAN Technologies

1. ☑ **C.** A wireless device will use Ready-to-Send (RTS) and Clear-to-Send (CTS) signals to avoid collisions, using a similar process to CSMA/CD in Ethernet.
    ☒ **A** is wrong because a wireless device cannot do both simultaneously. **B** is wrong because CSMA/CA (collision avoidance) is used. **D** is wrong because these things refer to scattering.

WLAN Standards

2. ☑ **A.** A wireless headset, like Bluetooth, could cause these kinds of problems, not a corded one using USB.
    ☒ **B, C,** and **D** are types of devices that can cause problems with wireless transmissions.

3. ☑ **C.** 802.11b uses DSSS as a transmission method.
    ☒ **A, B,** and **D** are true of 802.11b and thus are incorrect answers.

4. ☑ **B.** 802.11a supports the OFDM transmission method and can transmit data at 54 Mbps using a 5 GHz frequency.
    ☒ **A** is wrong because it supports DSSS at 11 Mbps at 2.4 GHz. **C** and **D** are wrong because 802.11g uses a 2.4 GHz frequency.

WLAN Security

5. ☑ **C.** WPA supports PSK authentication and RC4 encryption with TKIP.
    ☒ **A** is incorrect because WEP doesn't support authentication and doesn't define TKIP (Cisco has a proprietary solution that does, however). **B** is incorrect because 802.1x is an IEEE standard and only defines authentication. **D** is incorrect because it supports AES-CCMP for encryption.

6. ☑ **D.** If you disable broadcast beaconing on the AP, you must define the SSID on each client, matching it to the configured value on the AP.
    ☒ **A** and **B** have nothing to do with broadcast beaconing, but MAC address filtering can be used to enhance the security of a WLAN implementation. **C** refers to ad hoc mode and has nothing to do with SSID values.

7. ☑ **D.** Enterprise mode for WPA2 uses 802.1x authentication with AES-CCMP for encryption.
    ☒ **A** and **B** are incorrect because personal mode uses PSKs. **C** is incorrect because it uses WEP/RC4 for encryption.

WLAN Implementation

8. ☑ **A.** Ad hoc mode is based on the Independent Basic Service Set (IBSS).

   ☒ **B** uses an AP for non-point-to-point connections. **C** and **D** are based on using an AP.

9. ☑ **B.** When you have more than one AP, ESA coverage should be used.

   ☒ **A** is incorrect because they are all in the same network and should have the same SSID value. **C** is incorrect because each cell (each AP and its clients) should have different RF channels. **D** is incorrect because they would be using the same RF frequency, such as 2.4 GHz for 802.11b or g.

WLAN Devices

10. ☑ **B** and **C.** Check the placement of the AP and the direction of its antennas. Possibly upgrade the antennas to provide for better signal coverage.

    ☒ **A** is incorrect given the small coverage area: one AP should be more than sufficient. **D** is incorrect assuming that you have a correct design: if anything, you might have to upgrade the antennas, not replace the AP with a different product.

Part II

TCP/IP Protocol Suite

6

TCP/IP and the Internet Layer

The Transmission Control Protocol/Internet Protocol (TCP/IP) is a standard that includes many protocols. It defines how machines on an internetwork can communicate with each other. It was initially funded by and developed for the Defense Advanced Research Projects Agency (DARPA), which is a conglomeration of US military and government organizations. Developed initially for the government, it was later made available to the public, mainly seen on Unix systems. First specified in RFC 791, it has become the de facto standard for networking protocols. The Internet uses TCP/IP to carry data between networks, and most corporations today use TCP/IP for their networks. This chapter provides an overview of TCP/IP version 4 (IPv4), focusing on layer 3, the Internet layer. Chapters 7, 8, and 9 expand upon TCP/IP, covering IP addressing, the transport layer, and how TCP/IP communications occur. Chapter 24 covers the newest version of TCP/IP, IP version 6 (IPv6).

CERTIFICATION OBJECTIVE 6.01

TCP/IP Protocol Stack

To help clarify how data moves between devices running TCP/IP, a model was developed that resembles the OSI Reference Model discussed in Chapter 2. Figure 6-1 compares the two models. As you can see, the two models are different. Where the OSI model has seven layers, the TCP/IP protocol stack only has four layers. Its application layer covers the application, presentation, and session layers of the OSI Reference Model, its network layer uses the term *Internet* to describe layer 3, and the network access layer includes both the data link and physical layers. The TCP/IP protocol stack actually doesn't define the components of the network access layer in the TCP/IP standards, but it uses the term to refer to layer 2 and layer 1 functions.

watch **The TCP/IP protocol stack has four layers: application, transport, internet, and network access.**

Internet Layer

The rest of this chapter focuses on the Internet layer, layer 3 of the TCP/IP protocol stack. The corresponding layer in the OSI Reference Model is the network layer. IP protocols at the Internet layer include Address Resolution Protocol (ARP), Reverse Address Resolution Protocol (RARP), Internet Control Management Protocol

FIGURE 6-1

OSI Reference Model and TCP/IP protocol stack

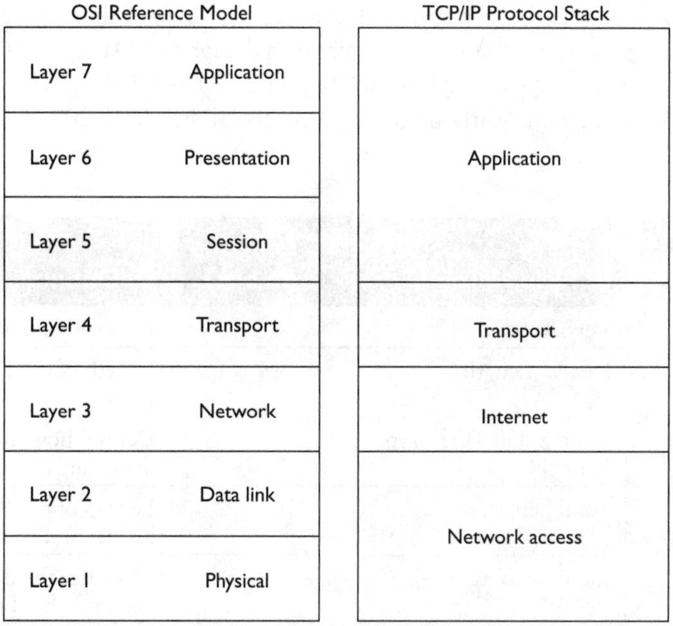

OSI Reference Model		TCP/IP Protocol Stack
Layer 7	Application	Application
Layer 6	Presentation	
Layer 5	Session	
Layer 4	Transport	Transport
Layer 3	Network	Internet
Layer 2	Data link	Network access
Layer 1	Physical	

(ICMP), Open Shortest Path First (OSPF), and many others. The next few sections explain the components of an IP packet and some of the protocols that function at the Internet layer.

on the job

The Internet Protocol (IP) is just one of the protocols that reside at the Internet layer. It is common in the industry to hear people refer to TCP/IP as just IP; however, this is a misnomer, since IP is just one of many protocols within the TCP/IP protocol suite.

The IP protocol is mainly responsible for these functions:

- Connectionless data delivery: best effort delivery with no data recovery capabilities
- Hierarchical logical addressing to provide for highly scalable internetworks

exam

watch   *IP provides a connectionless, unreliable delivery to other devices at layer 3. It treats packets individually. If reliability and flow control are required, TCP, at the transport layer, can provide this function. TCP is discussed in Chapter 9.*

Where the transport layer uses segments to transfer information between machines, the Internet layer uses datagrams. Datagram is just another word for *packet*, if you recall from Chapter 2. Table 6-1 shows the components of the IP datagram. Without any options, the IP header is 20 bytes in length.

TABLE 6-1			
IP Datagram Components	**IP Field Name**	**Length (in bits)**	**Definition**
	Version	4	IP version number, such as IPv4
	Header Length	4	Length of the IP header in 32-bit word values
	Priority and TOS (Type of Service)	8	Defines how the IP network should treat the datagram
	Total Length	16	Length of the IP datagram, including the header and encapsulated data
	Identification	16	Identifies the datagram component if the datagram has been fragmented
	Flags	3	Is set if the datagram is a fragment; also used for other purposes
	Fragment Offset	13	Defines information about the datagram if it is a fragment
	TTL (Time-To-Live)	8	Sets the number of allowed layer 3 hops the datagram is allowed to traverse
	Protocol	8	Identifies the protocol (such as TCP, UDP, ICMP, OSPF, etc.) that was used to encapsulate payload information. A complete list of IP protocols and their numbers can be found at www.iana.org/assignments/protocol-numbers.
	Header Checksum	16	Checksum on just the IP header fields
	Source IP Address	32	IP address of the source device
	Destination IP address	32	IP address of the destination device
	Options	0–32	Allows IP to support various options, such as security
	Data		Protocol information (such as an encapsulated TCP or UDP segment or ICMP packet information)

The main function of the IP datagram is to carry protocol information for either Internet layer protocols (other TCP/IP layer 3 protocols) or encapsulated transport layer protocols (TCP and User Datagram Protocol, or UDP). To designate what protocol the IP datagram is carrying in the data field, the IP datagram carries the protocol's number in the Protocol field.

ⓦatch *IP uses a TTL field to limit the number of hops a datagram can travel. This is discussed in more depth in Chapters 15 and 19. Here are some* *common IP protocols and their protocol numbers: ICMP (1), IPv6 (41), TCP (6), UDP (17), Enhanced Interior Gateway Routing Protocol (EIGRP) (88), and OSPF (89).*

Introduction to TCP/IP Addressing

Probably one of the most confusing aspects of the TCP/IP stack is the addresses used at the Internet layer, referred to as *IP addresses*. This chapter introduces you to IPv4 addressing; however, the details of IP addressing are discussed in later chapters. Note that two different versions of TCP/IP exist: IPv4 and IPv6. IPv4 addressing is covered in Chapter 7 and IPv6 in Chapter 24.

IPv4 addresses are 32 bits in length. However, to make the addresses readable, they are broken into 4 bytes (called *octets*), with a period (decimal) between each byte. Remember that there are 8 bits in a byte (this was discussed in Chapter 3). So that the address is understandable to the human eye, the four sets of binary numbers are then converted to decimal. Let's look at a simple example: 111111111111111 11111111111111111, which is 32, 1s. This is broken up into four octets, like this: 11111111.11111111.11111111.11111111. Then each of these octets is converted into decimal, resulting in an IP address of 255.255.255.255. The format of this address is commonly called *dotted decimal*.

Types of Addresses

Many different types of IP addresses exist. Table 6-2 offers a brief description of these types.

TABLE 6-2	IP Address Type	Definition
Types of IP Addresses	Reserved	Addresses that cannot be assigned to a network component, such as a network address, a broadcast, or Class D and E addresses
	Network ID	The network number assigned to a segment or VLAN
	Host ID	The host component of an IP address
	Directed Broadcast	The broadcast address of a network ID—these can be routed by routers
	Local Broadcast	The "all hosts" address for everyone on the same segment: 255.255.255.255 (routers will not route this type of address)
	Loopback	The internal address of a device used for testing functions (127.0.0.1)
	Autoconfigured	An address automatically assigned to a network component (DHCP is an example of this type of addressing)
	Public	An address used to access devices across the Internet or other public networks
	Private	An address to access devices in a local network, which cannot be used to access public networks

Classes of Addresses

Recall from Chapter 2 that logical, or layer 3, addresses have two components: a network number and a host number. When dealing with IP addresses, the address is broken into two components:

- **Network component**   Defines on what segment, in the network, a device is located
- **Host component**   Defines the specific device on a particular network segment

The network number uniquely identifies a segment in the network and a host number uniquely identifies a device on a segment. The combination of these two numbers must be unique throughout the entire network. TCP/IP uses the same two components for addressing, but it adds a twist by breaking up network numbers into five classes: A, B, C, D, and E. Each of these classes has a predefined network and host boundary:

- **Class A address**   The first byte is a network number (8 bits) and the last 3 bytes are for host numbers (24 bits).
- **Class B address**   The first 2 bytes are a network number (16 bits) and the last 2 bytes are for host numbers (16 bits).

- **Class C address** The first 3 bytes are a network number (24 bits) and the last 1 byte is for host numbers (8 bits).
- **Class D and E addresses** Used for multicasting and Class E addresses are reserved.

Given the distinctions discussed so far, it would seem that addressing for IPv4 is easy. However, what distinguishes the different classes of addresses are the settings to which the first bit to 5 bits are set:

- Class A addresses always begin with a *0* in the highest order bit.
- Class B addresses always begin with *10* in the highest order bits.
- Class C addresses always begin with *110* in the highest order bits.
- Class D addresses always begin with *1110* in the highest order bits.
- Class E addresses always begin with *11110* in the highest order bits.

When talking about the highest order bit or bits, this includes *all* 32 bits. Therefore, this would be the very first bit on the *left* of the address (the most significant bit). If the first octet contains *1000001*, this represents *129* in decimal, which would be a Class B address.

Given these distinctions with the assigned high order bit values, it is easy to predict, for a given address, to what class of network numbers it belongs:

- Class A addresses range from 1 to 126: 0 is reserved and represents all IP addresses; 127 is a reserved address and is used for testing, such as a loopback on an interface.
- Class B addresses range from 128 to 191: binary 10000000-10111111.
- Class C addresses range from 192 to 223: binary 11000000-11011111.
- Class D addresses range from 224 to 239: binary 11100000-11101111.
- Class E addresses range from 240 to 254: 255 is a reserved address and is used for local broadcasting purposes.

Given these restrictions with beginning bit values, it is fairly easy to predict what address belongs to what class. Simply look at the first number in the dotted-decimal notation and see which range it falls into.

Class A addresses range from 1 to 126, Class B from 128 to 191, Class C from 192 to 223, Class D from 224 to 239, and Class E from 240 to 254. 127 is reserved for the loopback interface (internal testing). Also remember the ranges *in binary. Remember the binary values that IP addresses begin with, and you should be able to determine, by looking at the first binary byte, whether the address is a Class A, B, C, D, or E address.*

When you are dealing with IP addresses, two numbers are always reserved for each network number: the first address in the network represents the network's address, and the last address in the network represents the broadcast address for this network, commonly called a *directed broadcast*. When you look at IP itself, two IP addresses are reserved: 0.0.0.0 (the very first address), which represents all IP addresses, and 255.255.255.255 (the very last address), which is the local broadcast address (all devices should process this datagram). Don't get too worried at this point if this is confusing, because Chapter 7 will delve into IPv4 addressing in a lot of depth.

Public and Private Addresses

As to assigning addresses to devices, two general types of addresses can be used: public and private. Public addresses are Class A, B, and C addresses that can be used to access devices in other public networks, such as the Internet. The Internet Assigned Numbers Authority (IANA) is ultimately responsible for handing out and managing public addresses. Normally you get public addresses directly from your ISP, which, in turn, requests them from one of five upstream address registries:

- American Registry for Internet Numbers (ARIN)
- Reseaux IP Europeans Network Coordination Center (RIPE NCC)
- Asia Pacific Registry for Internet Numbers (APNIC)
- Latin American and Caribbean Internet Address Registry (LACNIC)
- African Network Information Centre (AfriNIC)

Within this range of addresses for Class A, B, and C addresses are some reserved addresses, commonly called *private addresses*. All the other addresses in these classes are called *public addresses*. Anyone can use private addresses; however, this creates a problem if you want to access the Internet. Remember that each device in the network (in this case, this includes the Internet) must have a unique IP address. If two networks are using the same private addresses, you would run into reachability issues. To access the Internet, your source IP addresses must have a unique Internet public address. This can be accomplished through address translation. Here is a list of private addresses that are assigned in RFC 1918:

- Class A: 10.0.0.0–10.255.255.255 (1 Class A network)
- Class B: 172.16.0.0–172.31.255.255 (16 Class B networks)
- Class C: 192.168.0.0–192.168.255.255 (256 Class C networks)

Private and public addresses, as well as address translation, are discussed in Chapter 23.

ⓦatch   **Remember the list of** **172.16.0.0–172.31.0.0, and 192.168.0.0–**
private networks, which must be translated **192.168.255.0.**
when accessing public networks: 10.0.0.0,

DNS

One of the problems with using IP addresses to access destinations is that as a person, it can be difficult to remember dozens of addresses of devices. People tend to be better at remembering names than lists of dotted-decimal numbers. However, since network components are uniquely identified by IP addresses, something is needed to translate names to addresses, which is what the *Domain Name System (DNS)* does. DNS is used to resolve names to IP addresses. DNS is a TCP/IP application that other applications such as File Transfer Protocol (FTP) applications, telnet, web browsers, and e-mail use to resolve the names a user enters to real IP addresses.

To use DNS, a network component needs to define a DNS server that will handle the resolution process. Most components, such as Windows PCs, allow two DNS servers to be configured for redundancy. You can manually define the DNS servers to use or acquire them dynamically via Dynamic Host Configuration Protocol (DHCP, discussed a bit later).

CERTIFICATION OBJECTIVE 6.02

TCP/IP Internet Protocols

Many, many protocols function at the Internet layer. If you go out to IANA's web site, you'll see more than 100 protocols defined for the Internet layer. The most commonly used of these protocols is IP, which is used to transport data for these other protocols. This part of the chapter will discuss some of the more common ones: Dynamic Host Configuration Protocol (DHCP), Address Resolution Protocol (ARP), and Internet Control Message Protocol (ICMP).

DHCP

DHCP allows devices to acquire their addressing information dynamically. Originally defined in RFC 2131 and updated in 2939, DHCP is actually based on the Bootstrap Protocol (BOOTP). It is built on a client/server model and defines two components:

- **Server** Delivering host configuration information
- **Client** Requesting and acquiring host configuration information

DHCP provides the following advantages:

- It reduces the amount of configuration on devices.
- It reduces the likelihood of configuration errors on devices acquiring address information.
- It gives you more administrative control by centralizing IP addressing information and management.

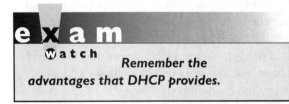

e x a m

ⓦ **a t c h**   *Remember the advantages that DHCP provides.*

Most networks today employ DHCP because it is easy to implement and manage. Imagine you work for a company that is bought by another company and you must re-address your network, which contains 2000 devices. If you previously configured the IP addresses on these machines manually, then you now must manually change each device's configuration. However, if you were using DHCP, you have to change the

TABLE 6-3	Allocation Type	Explanation
	Automatic	Server assigns a permanent IP address to the client
DHCP Address Allocation Types	Dynamic	Server assigns an IP address to a client for a period of time, referred to as a *lease*
	Manual	IP address is manually configured on the client, and DHCP is used to convey additional addressing information and verification

configuration on only the DHCP servers, and when the clients either reboot or must renew their addressing information, they'll acquire the addressing information from the new addressing scheme.

As mentioned, DHCP contains two types of devices: servers and clients. Cisco IOS routers support both functions. Servers are responsible for assigning addressing information to clients, and clients request addressing information from servers. A DHCP server can use three mechanisms, which are described in Table 6-3, when allocating address information. Most DHCP implementations use the dynamic allocation type.

When acquiring addressing information, a DHCP client goes through four steps:

1. A client generates a DHCPDISCOVER local broadcast to discover who the DHCP servers are on the LAN segment.

2. All DHCP servers on the segment can respond to the client with a DHCPOFFER unicast message, which offers IP addressing information to the client. If a client receives messages from multiple servers, it chooses one (typically the first one). DHCPOFFER server messages include the following information: IP address of the client, subnet mask of the segment, IP address of the default gateway, DNS domain name, DNS server address or addresses, WINS server address or addresses, and TFTP server address or addresses. Note that this is not an all-encompassing list.

3. Upon choosing one of the offers, the client responds to the corresponding server with a DHCPREQUEST message, telling the server that it wants to use the addressing information the server sent. If only one server is available and the server's information conflicts with the client's configuration, the client will respond with a DHCPDECLINE message.

4. The DHCP server responds with a DHCPACK, which is an acknowledgment to the client indicating that it received the DHCPREQUEST message and that the client accepted the addressing information. The server can also respond with a DHCPNACK, which tells the client the offer is no longer valid and the client should request addressing information again. This can happen if the client is tardy in responding with a DHCPREQUEST message after the server generated the DHCPOFFER message.

e x a m

watch
Remember the four steps that DHCP goes through when a client requests addressing information as well as the information that can be included in a DHCPOFFER message: an IP address and a subnet mask; a default gateway; DNS server, TFTP server, and WINS server addresses; and a domain name.

When a client shuts down gracefully, it can generate a DHCPRELEASE message, telling the server it no longer needs its assigned IP address. Most DHCP configurations involve a lease time, which specifies a time period that the client is allowed to use the address. Upon reaching this time limit, the client must renew its lease with the current server or get new IP addressing information.

on the job
If a server does not respond to the client, the client's TCP/IP protocol stack will automatically pick an IP address from the range of this Class B network: 169.254.0.1–169.254.255.254, based on the RFC. This process is referred to as Automatic Private IP Addressing (APIP). However, I know of only Microsoft Windows operating systems that perform APIP; other operating systems, such as Linux, won't enable the NIC if they can't obtain IP addressing for the NIC.

ARP

The Address Resolution Protocol (ARP) is an Internet layer protocol that helps TCP/IP network components find other devices in the same broadcast domain. ARP uses a local broadcast (255.255.255.255) at layer 3 and FF:FF:FF:FF:FF:FF at layer 2 to discover neighboring devices. Basically stated, you have the IP address you want to reach, but you need a physical (MAC) address to send the frame to the destination at layer 2. ARP resolves an IP address of a destination to the MAC address of the destination on the same data link layer medium, such as Ethernet. Remember that for two devices to talk to each other in Ethernet (as with most layer 2 technologies), the data link layer uses a physical address (MAC) to differentiate the machines on the segment. When Ethernet devices talk to each other at the data link layer, they need to know each other's MAC addresses.

Single-Segment ARP Example

The top part of Figure 6-2 shows an example of the use of ARP. In this example PC-A wants to send information directly to PC-B. PC-A knows PC-B's IP address (or has DNS resolve it to an IP address); however, it doesn't know PC-B's Ethernet MAC address. To resolve the IP to a MAC address, PC-A generates an ARP request. In the ARP datagram, the source IP address is 10.1.1.1 and the destination is 255.255.255.255 (the local broadcast represents every device on the

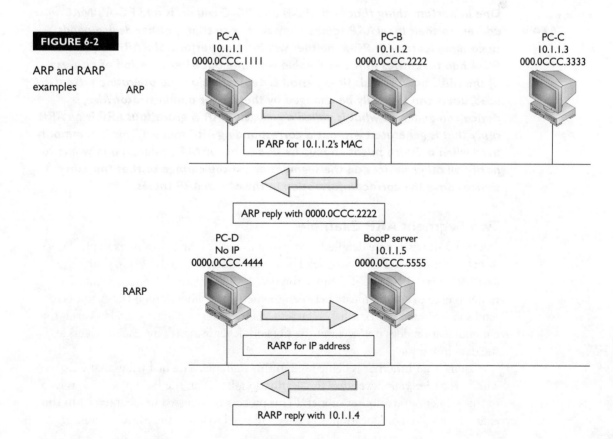

FIGURE 6-2

ARP and RARP examples

Ethernet segment). PC-A includes PC-B's IP address in the data field of the ARP datagram. This is encapsulated into an Ethernet frame, with a source MAC address of 0000.0CCC.1111 (PC-A's MAC address) and a destination MAC address of FF:FF:FF:FF:FF:FF (the local broadcast address) and is then placed on the Ethernet segment. Both PC-B and PC-C see this frame. Both devices' NICs notice the data link layer broadcast address and assume that this frame is for them since the destination MAC address is a broadcast, so they strip off the Ethernet frame and pass the IP datagram with the ARP request up to the Internet layer. Again, there is a broadcast address in the destination IP address field, so both devices' TCP/IP protocol stacks will examine the data payload. PC-B notices that this is an ARP and that this is its own IP address in the query, and therefore responds directly back to PC-A with PC-B's MAC address. PC-C, however, sees that this is not an ARP for its MAC address and ignores the datagram.

on the
job

One important thing that both PC-B and PC-C will do is add PC-A's MAC address to their local ARP tables. They do this so that if either device needs to communicate with PC-A, neither will have to perform the ARP request as PC-A had to. Entries in the ARP table will time out after a period of non-use of the MAC address. This time period is dependent on the operating system used, but it can typically be changed by the user or administrator. Also, a device can generate what is called a gratuitous *ARP. A gratuitous ARP is an ARP reply that is generated without a corresponding ARP request. This is commonly used when a device might change its IP address or MAC address and wants to notify all other devices on the segment about the change so that the other devices have the correct information in their local ARP tables.*

Two-Segment ARP Example

Figure 6-3 shows a more detailed example of the use of ARP. In this example, PC-A wants to connect to PC-B using IP. The source address is 1.1.1.1 (PC-A) and the destination is 2.2.2.2 (PC-B). Since the two devices are on different networks, a router is used to communicate between the networks. Therefore, if PC-A wants to send something to PC-B, it has to be sent via the intermediate router. However, this communication does not occur at the network layer using IP; instead, it occurs at the data link layer.

Assume that Ethernet is being used in this example. The first thing that PC-A will do is to determine whether the destination, based on the layer 3 address, is local to this subnet or on another subnet. (This process is discussed in Chapter 7.) In this example, it's a remote location, so PC-A will need to know the MAC address of

FIGURE 6-3   ARP example with a router

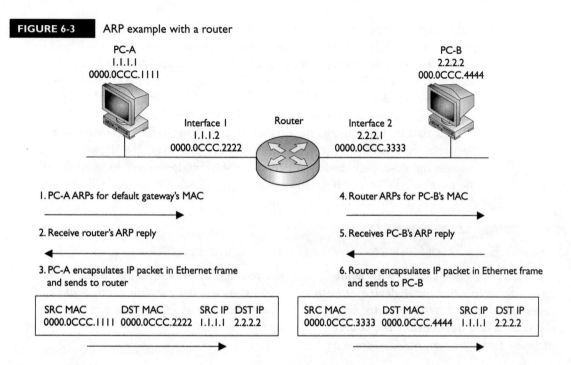

1. PC-A ARPs for default gateway's MAC

2. Receive router's ARP reply

3. PC-A encapsulates IP packet in Ethernet frame and sends to router

4. Router ARPs for PC-B's MAC

5. Receives PC-B's ARP reply

6. Router encapsulates IP packet in Ethernet frame and sends to PC-B

SRC MAC	DST MAC	SRC IP	DST IP
0000.0CCC.1111	0000.0CCC.2222	1.1.1.1	2.2.2.2

SRC MAC	DST MAC	SRC IP	DST IP
0000.0CCC.3333	0000.0CCC.4444	1.1.1.1	2.2.2.2

the default gateway router. If the address isn't already in its local ARP table, PC-A will ARP for the default gateway's MAC address. (Note that one thing you must configure on PC-A, other than its own IP address and subnet mask, is the default gateway address, or you must acquire this information via DHCP.) This is shown in step 1 of Figure 6-3. In step 2, the router responds with the MAC address of its Ethernet interface connected to PC-A. In step 3, PC-A creates an IP packet with the source and destination IP addresses (the source is 1.1.1.1 and the destination is 2.2.2.2, PC-B) and encapsulates this in an Ethernet frame, with the source MAC address of PC-A and the destination MAC address of the *router*. PC-A then sends the Ethernet frame to the router.

When the router receives the Ethernet frame, the router compares the frame to the MAC address on its Ethernet interface, which it matches. The router strips off the Ethernet frame and makes a routing decision based on the destination address of 2.2.2.2. In this case, the network is directly connected to the router's second interface, which also happens to be Ethernet. In step 4, if the router doesn't have PC-B's MAC address in its local ARP table, the router ARPs for the MAC address of PC-B (2.2.2.2) and receives the response in step 5. The router then encapsulates the original IP packet in a new Ethernet frame in step 6, placing its second interface's MAC address, which is sourcing the frame, in the source MAC address field and PC-B's MAC address in the destination field. When PC-B receives this, it knows the frame is for itself (matching destination MAC address) and that PC-A originated the IP packet that's encapsulated based on the source IP address in the IP header at layer 3.

Note that in this example, the original IP addressing in the packet was not altered by the router, but two Ethernet frames are used to get the IP packet to the destination. Also, each device will keep the MAC addresses in a local ARP table, so the next time PC-A needs to send something to PC-B, the devices will not have to ARP other intermediate devices again.

---

exam
ⓦatch

Be familiar with what device talks to what other device at both layer 2 and layer 3. With a router between the source and destination, the source at layer 2 uses its own MAC address as the source but the default gateway MAC address as the destination. Note that the IP addresses used at layer 3 are not changed by the router.

The assumption with ARP is that the device being ARPed is on the same segment. For example, in Figure 6-4, PC-A assumes 1.1.1.2 (the router's IP address) is in the same broadcast domain based on the IP address of the router, which is true. If PC-A generated a broadcast ARP for the router's MAC address, the router would see the request. However, you might encounter a situation in which you've moved a device from one part of the network to another, but you must keep the device's original IP address when moving it.

---

exam
ⓦatch

Proxy ARP allows the router to respond with its own MAC address in an ARP reply for a device on a different network segment. Proxy ARP is used when you need to move a device from one segment to another but cannot change its current IP addressing information.

If you examine Figure 6-4, you can see that PC-C was moved from the left-hand segment to the right-hand segment, but its IP address was kept the same.

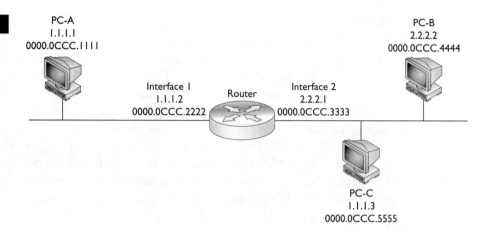

FIGURE 6-4

Proxy ARP
example

However, PC-A still assumes that PC-C is on the local segment. To solve this reachability problem, two things need to occur:

■ The router will need a static host route that directs traffic sent to the host address that was moved to the devices' new network segment.

■ The proxy ARP must be enabled on the router's interface that's connected to the original network segment.

Proxy ARP is a feature that allows a router to reply with its own MAC address to an ARP query when the destination device isn't on the same segment. For example, in Figure 6-4, since PC-C won't see the local broadcast ARP query from PC-A, and the router has a static host route for 1.1.1.3 that points to the right-hand segment, when the router receives the ARP request for 1.1.1.3, the router will respond with its own MAC address (0000.0CCC.2222). This creates the illusion for PC-A that PC-C is still on the same segment. PC-A will then forward its traffic to the router (thinking that it is actually sending it directly to PC-C), and the router will then route the traffic to the correct network segment.

on the job

The example shown in Figure 6-4 is not a recommended practice in a network: if you move a device from one segment to another, you should change its IP addressing information to match the network number of the new segment. The only two times that you might need Proxy ARP are if an application has hard-coded the IP address and therefore you can't change it when moving the server to a different network number; and in certain cases with assigning of IP addressing information to remote access IPSec clients.

RARP

RARP is sort of the reverse of an ARP. In an ARP, the device knows the layer 3 address, but not the data link layer address. With a RARP, the device doesn't have an IP address and wants to acquire one. The only address that this device has is a MAC address. Common protocols that use RARP are BOOTP and DHCP.

The bottom part of Figure 6-2 shows a RARP example. In this example, PC-D doesn't have an IP address and wants to acquire one. It generates a data link layer broadcast (FF:FF:FF:FF:FF:FF) with an encapsulated RARP request. This example assumes that the RARP is associated with BOOTP. If there is a BOOTP server on the segment, and if it has an IP address for this machine, it will respond. In this example, the BOOTP server, 10.1.1.5, has an address (10.1.1.4) and assigns this to PC-D, sending this address as a response to PC-D.

ICMP

ICMP is used to send error and control information between TCP/IP devices at the Internet layer. ICMP, originally defined in RFC 792, includes many different messages that devices can generate or respond to. Here is a brief list of these messages: Address Reply, Address Request, Destination Unreachable, Echo, Echo Reply, Information Reply, Information Request, Parameter Problem, Redirect, Subnet Mask Request, Time Exceeded, Timestamp, and Timestamp Reply.

One of the most common applications that uses ICMP is *ping*. Ping uses a few ICMP messages, including echo, echo request, destination unreachable, and others. Ping is used to test whether or not a destination is available. A source generates an ICMP echo packet. If the destination is available, it will respond with an echo reply packet. If an intermediate router doesn't know how to reach the destination, it will respond with a destination unreachable message. However, if the router knows how to reach the destination, but the destination host doesn't respond to the echo packets, you'll see a request timed out message. *Traceroute*, sometimes called trace, is an application that will list the IP addresses of the routers along the way to the destination, displaying the path the packet took to reach the destination. Some traceroute applications use ICMP messages, while others use UDP to transport their messages. These tools are discussed in more depth in the next section, as well as in Chapter 17.

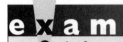

CERTIFICATION OBJECTIVE 6.03

TCP/IP Tools for Windows PCs

You can use various tools on a device to check its IP configuration, as well as to test connectivity to and between devices. This part of the book will focus on tools you can use on a Windows-based PC: **ipconfig**, **ping**, **tracert**, and **arp**.

ipconfig Command

The **ipconfig** command is a CLI tool that displays your PC's IP configuration. To execute the command, you must open up a command window: Go to Start | Run, and enter **cmd.exe** in the Open text box. Then click the OK button. To see all of the optional parameters available to you, execute **ipconfig /all** from the CLI. The available options are shown in Table 6-4.

TABLE 6-4   `ipconfig` Command Options

Option	Description
/all	Displays the complete TCP/IP configuration for all adapters in the PC; omitting this parameter displays only the IP address, subnet mask, and default gateway setting for each adapter.
/renew [*adapter*]	Renews a DHCP acquired address for all adapters or the specified adapter.
/release [*adapter*]	Has the PC send a DHCPRELEASE message to the DHCP server indicating that the PC is no longer using the address; it also causes the PC to disable the use of DHCP to acquire addressing information.
/flushdns	Flushes the PC's DNS cache of resolves names and addresses.
/displaydns	Displays the PC's local DNS cache of resolved names and addresses.
/registerdns	Initiates dynamic DNS, having the PC publish its name and IP address to a DNS server. This is commonly used when PCs are acquiring their IP addresses dynamically via DNS, where their addresses can differ over time, but the PC's name remains the same.
/showclassid [*adapter*]	Displays the DHCP class ID.
/setclassid [*adapter* [*classID*]]	Sets the DHCP class ID value to be used, which can be sent to a DHCP server to help it in assigning the right addressing information to the PC.

Here is an example using the **/all** parameter:

```
C:\> ipconfig /all
Windows IP Configuration
        Host Name . . . . . . . . . . . . : D620
        Primary Dns Suffix  . . . . . . . :
        Node Type . . . . . . . . . . . . : Hybrid
        IP Routing Enabled. . . . . . . . : No
        WINS Proxy Enabled. . . . . . . . : No

Ethernet adapter Wireless:
        Connection-specific DNS Suffix  . :
        Description . . . . . . . . . . . : Intel(R) PRO/Wireless 3945ABG
                Network Connection
        Physical Address. . . . . . . . . : 00-18-DE-8A-52-A6
        Dhcp Enabled. . . . . . . . . . . : No
        IP Address. . . . . . . . . . . . : 192.168.1.66
        Subnet Mask . . . . . . . . . . . : 255.255.255.0
        Default Gateway . . . . . . . . . : 192.168.1.1
        DNS Servers . . . . . . . . . . . : 4.2.2.1
                                            4.2.2.2
```

Notice that in this example, the IP addressing information has been manually configured on the PC for the wireless adapter—DHCP is not being used to acquire addressing information. If DHCP were used, you would also see when the address was obtained and when the lease would expire for the IP addressing information.

on the **job**

***ipconfig* is used for Windows NT machines and later; Windows 98 and earlier machines use the *winipcfg* command.**

In addition to using the **ipconfig** CLI command, you can also view information about the configuration of an adapter from the Network Connection tab in Windows. In Windows XP, to pull up this window, choose Start | Connect To | Show All Connections. Double-click the name of an adapter in the Network Connections window and then click the Properties button. Click Internet Protocol (TCP/IP) and then click the Properties button. If the radio buttons Obtain An IP Address Automatically and Obtain DNS Server Address Automatically are selected, DHCP will be used to acquire the IP addressing information for the adapter.

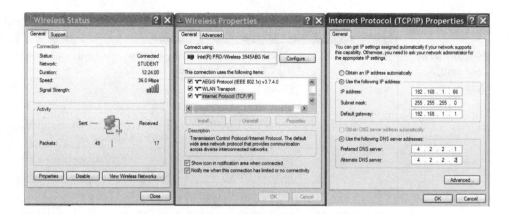

on the job *CompTIA recommends that you systematically test connectivity by pinging from local to remote networks or destinations.*

The ping Command

The Windows `ping` command is used to test layer 3 connectivity between two devices. The source sends an ICMP echo message and if the destination is reachable, it replies with an ICMP echo reply message. If the destination is not reachable and an intermediate router is between the source and destination, the router closest to the problem will send back an appropriate ICMP message. If the router is connected to the same segment as the destination device and the destination device is not reachable, the router will respond with an ICMP destination host unreachable message; otherwise, if the router doesn't have a route to the destination network, it will reply with an ICMP destination network unreachable message.

exam watch *Ping uses ICMP echo messages to initiate the test. If the destination is reachable, the destination responds with an echo reply message for each echo sent by the source. Both the Windows PC* ping *and* tracert *commands test layer 3 connectivity.*

TABLE 6-5	Option	Description
Windows ping Command Options	-t	Sends a continuous string of echo request messages to the destination: use CTRL-C to abort the process.
	-a	Performs a reverse name lookup, resolving the entered IP address to a fully qualified domain name.
	-n count	Sends the specified number of echo request messages; if you omit this parameter, the default is 4 echo requests.
	-l size	Specifies the size, in bytes, of the echo request message; if you omit this parameter, the default is 32 bytes.
	-f	Sets the don't fragment flag in the IP header.
	-w seconds	Specifies the number of seconds to wait for an echo reply message before giving up on the reply; if you omit this parameter, the default is 2 seconds.

The Windows **ping** command is executed from the CLI command prompt. Table 6-5 lists the more common options you can specify with the command.

exam
watch

When troubleshooting PC problems, first determine whether the user can ping the loopback address: ping 127.0.0.1. If this fails, then something is wrong with the TCP/IP stack installation on the PC. Next, have the user try to ping the locally configured IP address.

If this fails, something is wrong with the IP address configuration on the PC. Next, have the user ping the default gateway. If this fails, then something is wrong with the configured default gateway address, the default gateway itself, or the subnet mask value configured on the user's PC.

Here is an example of using the **ping** command:

```
C:\ > ping 4.2.2.2
Pinging 4.2.2.2 with 32 bytes of data:
Request timed out.
Reply from 4.2.2.2: bytes=32 time=20ms TTL=53
Reply from 4.2.2.2: bytes=32 time=22ms TTL=53
Reply from 4.2.2.2: bytes=32 time=20ms TTL=53
```

```
Ping statistics for 4.2.2.2:
    Packets: Sent = 4, Received = 3, Lost = 1 (25% loss),
Approximate round trip times in milli-seconds:
    Minimum = 20ms, Maximum = 25ms, Average = 21ms
```

Notice that the first echo request message timed out, but the following three were successful—this is probably because this PC, as well as intermediate routers, had to perform ARPs to find the next hop layer 3 device's MAC address, causing the time to exceed 2 seconds. In the successful echo replies, you can see the time it took for the round-trip between the source and destination; for example, the last echo request and reply took 20 milliseconds to complete.

e x a m

ⓦatch
If the first echo request times out, but the rest of the echo requests are successful, the first request probably timed out because the source and possibly intermediate devices were performing ARPs. If you see intermixed echo replies and destination unreachable messages, *you know that either a lot of traffic lies between you and the destination, causing a large delay in the returning echo replies, or a physical layer problem exists somewhere between the source and destination causing corruption of sent data.*

The tracert Command

One limitation of **ping** is that this command will not tell you, between you and the destination device, where layer 3 connectivity is broken. The Windows **tracert** command (short for traceroute), on the other hand, will list each router along the way, including the final destination. Therefore, if a layer 3 connection problem exists, with traceroute, you'll know at least where the problem begins. Table 6-6 lists the more common options you can specify with the **tracert** command.

TABLE 6-6	Option	Explanation
Windows **tracert** Command Options	**-d**	Specifies that a reverse DNS lookup should not be performed for each hop to, and including, the destination
	-h *maximum_hops*	Specifies the maximum number of hops that the trace can traverse to the destination
	-w *timeout*	Specifies the number of seconds to wait for an echo reply message before giving up on the reply; if you omit this parameter, the default is 2 seconds

Here is an example of the use of the **tracert** command:

```
C:\ > tracert -d 4.2.2.2
Tracing route to 4.2.2.2 over a maximum of 30 hops
  1     1 ms     1 ms     1 ms   192.168.1.1
  2     8 ms     7 ms     9 ms   10.122.208.1
  3    10 ms    20 ms    12 ms   24.95.231.65
  .
  .
  .
  8    27 ms    26 ms    20 ms   4.68.103.68
  9    21 ms    20 ms    24 ms   4.2.2.2
Trace complete.
```

In this example, it took nine hops to reach the destination (4.2.2.2). Three probes were sent to each next-hop layer 3 device, which the round-trip time, in milliseconds, displayed for each probe. If you see an asterisk (*) for the probe reply, either the traceroute probe message reply came back after the timeout period or it didn't come back at all.

on the !ob *I highly recommend that you use the -d parameter when executing the* ***tracert*** *command; this disables the reverse DNS lookup to find the name of each layer 3 device along the way to the destination. If you don't use this option, your trace will take much longer to finish.*

The arp Command

The Windows **arp** command allows you to display the ARP table, delete entries in it, or add static entries to it. The more common parameters to the command are shown in Table 6-7.

TABLE 6-7	Option	Description
Windows **arp** Command Options	**-a** or **-g**	Displays the entries in the ARP table.
	-d [*inet_addr*]	Deletes all the entries in the ARP table unless a specific IP address is entered.
	-s *inet_addr eth_addr*	Adds a static ARP entry, where you need to specify the IP and MAC addresses, in that order, of the destination device. This is normally not configured unless for security purposes.

Here is an example of the use of the Windows **arp** command:

```
C:\> arp -a
Interface: 192.168.1.66 --- 0x3
   Internet Address       Physical Address     Type
   192.168.1.1            00-14-a4-24-10-30    dynamic
   192.168.1.12           00-0f-66-84-8b-94    dynamic
```

In this example, two entries are in the ARP table, where both entries were learned dynamically. The Internet Address column lists the IP addresses of destination devices, and the Physical Address column lists the corresponding MAC addresses of these devices.

INSIDE THE EXAM

TCP/IP Protocol Stack

For the exam, you should be able to compare the OSI Reference Model and the layers in the TCP/IP protocol stack. Know that IP is a connectionless protocol that does not provide data correction. You should be familiar with some IP protocol numbers used by various layer 3 TCP/IP protocols, such as UDP, TCP, and ICMP, among others.

IP addresses are logical layer 3 addresses. You need to know the five classes of addresses and, if given a specific address, what kind of address it is. You might be given an IP address in binary and be asked to choose what class it belongs to; therefore, be familiar with the bit values that the classes of address begin with. Don't get tricked when picking addresses: any answer that has an octet with a number 256 or higher is invalid. Also be familiar with the RFC 1918 private addresses reserved for use within a company.

TCP/IP Internet Protocols

You need to remember what DHCP is used for and the kinds of addressing information assigned by the DHCP server to the client. Also be familiar with the four DHCP messages used in the address request process. You might be given scenarios on the exam about devices trying to communicate with other devices at layer 2 and layer 3. Therefore, you should be very familiar with how ARP functions and what MAC addresses are used when devices are communicating with each other. Remember that when devices on different segments need to communicate with each other, at layer 2 they need to communicate with an intermediate layer 3 device, such as a router, and would therefore use the router's MAC address to get the layer 3 packet to a different segment.

(continued)

ICMP is commonly used to test connectivity at layer 3. If you receive a destination unreachable message, an intermediate layer 3 device is indicating that either no path exists to the destination or the destination itself is not reachable. Traceroute is used to determine where a layer 3 problem exists between two devices.

TCP/IP Tools for Windows PCs

You need to be familiar with the Windows commands to troubleshoot connectivity, especially **ping**. Remember that pinging 127.0.0.1 tests whether or not the TCP/IP protocol stack has or hasn't been installed successfully on a local device. Also remember the different scenarios as to when you might see "request timeout": ARPs, physical layer problems, and/or delay issues.

CERTIFICATION SUMMARY

TCP/IP has four layers: application, transport, internet, and network access. IP functions at the Internet layer and transports protocols such as ICMP, ARP, RARP, OSPF, EIGRP, and others. ICMP is used to test connections. IP provides a best effort, connectionless delivery of datagrams with no data recovery capabilities. Through hierarchical addressing, IP can scale networks to very large sizes.

IP addresses are 32 bits in length and are broken up into 4 bytes, with a period between the bytes. This format is referred to as dotted decimal. There are five classes of IP addresses: A (1–126), B (128–191), C (192–223), D (224–239), and E (240–254). Class A, B, and C addresses have two components, network and host, where the combination of these components must be unique in the network. Class A addresses have 1 network byte and 3 host bytes. Class B addresses have 2 network and 2 host bytes. Class C addresses have 3 network bytes and 1 host byte. Private IP addresses include networks 10.0.0.0, 172.16.0.0–172.31.0.0, and 192.168.0.0–192.168.255.0. Address 127.0.0.0 is reserved for loopback functions on devices to perform local testing. To make dealing with IP addresses easier, names can be used to access remote devices instead of addresses; in this instance, DNS will resolve the name to its corresponding IP address.

DHCP is used to assign addressing information dynamically to devices. This can include an IP address, a subnet mask, a default gateway address, two DNS server addresses, two WINS server addresses, a TFTP server address, and the length of the lease. ARP resolves an IP address to a MAC address. RARP, used by BOOTP and DHCP, resolves a MAC address to an IP address (used to acquire IP addressing information on a device). ICMP is used to send control and error information between devices. The most common application that uses ICMP is ping, which is used to test connectivity between devices. Common Windows commands to troubleshoot layer 3 connectivity include **`ipconfig`**, **`ping`**, **`tracert`**, and **`arp`**.

✓ TWO-MINUTE DRILL

TCP/IP Protocol Stack

❑ The TCP/IP protocol stack has the following four layers: network access, internet, transport, and application.

❑ The Internet layer corresponds to the network layer of the OSI Reference Model, where the IP protocol resides.

❑ IP provides connectionless, best effort delivery of datagrams.

❑ Common TCP/IP protocols include IP, ICMP, TCP, UDP, EIGRP, and OSPF.

❑ The TTL field in the IP header is used to restrict the maximum number of hops a datagram can travel.

❑ IP addresses are 32 bits in length and are broken into 4 bytes (8 bits) with a period between the bytes. This format is called dotted decimal.

❑ IP addresses are broken into five classes: A (1–126), B (128–191), C (192–223), D (224–239), and E (240–254). IP addresses are broken into two components: network and host. With Class A addresses, the first byte is a network number, Class B, the first 2 bytes are network numbers, and Class C, the first 3 bytes are network numbers.

❑ A Class A, B, and C address has two components: network and host. The combination of these must be unique throughout the network.

❑ Private addresses include 10.0.0.0-10.255.255.255, 172.16.0.0–172.31.255.255, and 192.168.0.0–192.168.255.255

❑ Network 127.0.0.0 is reserved for loopback testing on a device. If you can ping 127.0.0.1 on your device, the TCP/IP protocol stack is installed and operational.

TCP/IP Internet Protocols

❑ Many protocols function at the Internet layer, such as ARP, RARP, and ICMP. ARP resolves IP to MAC addresses, RARP is used by BOOTP and DHCP to help a device acquire an IP address, and ICMP is used to send error and control information. The ping application uses ICMP.

❑ DHCP allows clients to acquire their addressing dynamically, reducing the amount of configuration on a device and the likelihood of user error.

❑ When requesting an address, DHCP goes through four steps. DHCP addressing information sent to a client can include an IP address and subnet mask, a default gateway address, one or two DNS server addresses, a WINS server address, and a TFTP server address.

❑ ARP resolves layer 3 IP addresses to layer 2 MAC addresses: The source sends out a layer 2 local broadcast with the encapsulated ARP packet to discover the layer 3 address of a destination on the same segment or broadcast domain.

❑ If a router sits between the source and destination, the IP addresses are the actual source and destination, but two Ethernet frames are used. The first frame has a source MAC address of the source and a destination MAC address of the router; the second frame has a source MAC address of the router and a destination MAC address of the actual destination.

❑ ICMP is used to test layer 3 connectivity between network components.

TCP/IP Tools for Windows PCs

❑ `ipconfig` allows you to view a Windows PC TCP/IP configuration.

❑ `ping` and `tracert` allow you to test layer 3 connectivity on a Windows PC.

❑ `arp` allows you to view, modify, and delete ARP table entries on a Windows PC.

SELF TEST

The following Self Test questions will help you measure your understanding of the material presented in this chapter. Read all the choices carefully, as there may be more than one correct answer. Choose all correct answers for each question.

TCP/IP Protocol Stack

1. How many layers does the TCP/IP protocol stack have?
   A. 3
   B. 4
   C. 5
   D. 7

2. Which of the following is not true concerning the IP protocol and the TCP/IP protocol stack?
   A. The Internet layer corresponds to layer 3 of the OSI Reference Model.
   B. The IP protocol provides for connectionless delivery of datagrams.
   C. The IP protocol provides for best effort delivery, with data recovery capabilities.
   D. The source and destination address in an IP header totals 64 bits.

3. A Class A address has _____ host bits.
   A. 8
   B. 16
   C. 20
   D. 24

4. 191.75.39.24 is a Class _____ address.
   A. A
   B. B
   C. C
   D. None of the above

5. 172.16.240.256 is a Class _____ address.
   A. A
   B. B
   C. C
   D. None of the above

6. Which of the following is a private IP address?

   A. 10.189.289.66

   B. 172.32.18.19

   C. 192.169.1.1

   D. None of the above

TCP/IP Internet Protocols

7. You are testing connectivity with the `ping` command and getting a "request timeout" or "destination unreachable" message in reply. At what layer of the OSI Reference Model does this indicate a problem?

   A. Transport or lower

   B. Data link or lower

   C. Network or lower

   D. Application or lower

8. Examine Figure 6-3. PC-A wants to send a packet to PC-B. When PC-A ARPs for the correct MAC address, what will the response be in the ARP reply?

   A. 0000.0CCC.1111

   B. 0000.0CCC.2222

   C. 0000.0CCC.3333

   D. 0000.0CCC.4444

TCP/IP Tools for Windows PCs

9. You execute `ping 127.0.0.1` on your Windows PC and you get echo replies to the ping. What does this behavior indicate?

   A. You have connectivity to other layer 3 devices.

   B. You have connectivity to other hosts on the same segment or broadcast domain.

   C. You have correctly installed TCP/IP on your PC.

   D. You have correctly configured your DNS and default gateway settings on your PC.

10. You execute the Windows `ping` command. The first echo request times out, but the last three are successful. What would typically cause this problem?

   A. DHCP is occurring.

   B. ARP is occurring.

   C. The routers are running a routing protocol to find a destination.

   D. There is an application layer problem.

SELF TEST ANSWERS

TCP/IP Protocol Stack

1. ☑ **B.** The TCP/IP protocol stack has four layers: network access, internet, transport, and application.
   ☒ **A, C,** and **D** are incorrect.

2. ☑ **C.** The IP protocol does not provide for data recovery capabilities—if this is needed, TCP is used.
   ☒ **A, B,** and **D** are true and are therefore incorrect answers.

3. ☑ **D.** Class A addresses have 24 host bits and 8 networking bits.
   ☒ **A** is true for Class C networks. **B** is true for Class B networks. **C** can only be true for subnetted Class A and B networks.

4. ☑ **B.** 191.75.39.24 is a Class B network. Class B networks range from 128 to 191.
   ☒ **A** addresses range from 1 to 126. **C** addresses range from 192 to 223. Since there is an answer, **D** is incorrect.

5. ☑ **D.** It's impossible to represent 256 in a byte value (see the fourth octet)—the values range from 0 to 255 in a byte value.
   ☒ **A, B,** and **C** are incorrect.

6. ☑ **D.** None of the answers are correct.
   ☒ **A** is incorrect because 289 cannot be represented in a byte (the maximum number is 256). **B** is incorrect because the reserved range of Class B addresses are 172.16.0.0 to 172.31.255.255. **C** is incorrect because the reserved range of Class C addresses are 192.168.0.0 to 192.168.255.255.

TCP/IP Internet Protocols

7. ☑ **C.** Ping uses the ICMP protocol, which operates at layer 3, the network or Internet layer, and is used to discover problems at this layer or lower.
   ☒ **A, B,** and **D** are incorrect because ICMP functions at the network layer.

8. ☑ **B.** The next-hop layer 3 device will respond with the MAC address of the NIC connected to the source device.
   ☒ **A** is incorrect because this is the source itself. **C** and **D** are incorrect because these are on a different segment/broadcast domain than the source, PC-A.

TCP/IP Tools for Windows PCs

9. ☑ **C.** 127.0.0.1 is a loopback address and represents the local device itself—if you can ping this address, then you have correctly installed the TCP/IP protocol stack on the device.

☒ **A** and **B** are incorrect because 127.0.0.1 represents the local host, not other devices. **D** is incorrect because you would ping the DNS server or default gateway addresses to test connectivity with these devices.

10. ☑ **B.** If the first echo request times out, and the rest are successful, this typically indicates that the first echo request timed out because of the ARP process taking place for devices to talk to each other on each segment/broadcast domain.

☒ **A** is incorrect because DHCP is used to acquire addressing information, not to test connectivity. **C** is incorrect because if a router doesn't have a path to a destination, it drops the packet and sends a "destination unreachable" message, which you would expect for all the echo requests sent by ping. **D** is incorrect because ping operates at the Internet layer, not the application layer.

7

IP Addressing and Subnetting

Probably one of the most confusing aspects of the TCP/IP protocol stack is the addressing structure used at the Internet layer, referred to as *IP addressing*. Chapter 6 briefly discussed IP addresses and their classes. This chapter focuses on IP addressing, its components, and how to plan for addressing. Note that two different versions of TCP/IP addressing are in use: IPv4 and IPv6. This chapter focuses on 32-bit IPv4 addressing; Chapter 24 focuses on 128-bit IPv6 addressing. Before beginning this chapter, you should go back to Chapter 3 and review the binary and decimal conversion process, since these concepts are used heavily in this chapter.

CERTIFICATION OBJECTIVE 7.01

IP Addressing Review

Recall from Chapter 6 that IPv4 addresses are 32 bits long, broken up into 4 bytes, and separated by decimals, commonly called the *dotted decimal format*. Two components make up the address: a *network* and *host number*. The combination of these two numbers must be unique in the entire network. You can compare an IP address to the United States postal system: The IP address works like a ZIP code. When you address a letter and put it in the mailbox, the clerk at your post office doesn't care *who* you're sending it to or their street address. He *does* pay attention to the ZIP code, however. He'll have several containers behind him and will drop the letter into the appropriately numbered one. If the ZIP starts with a *3*, for example, he'll put it in the container headed to the southeastern United States. At the regional post office, they'll drop the letter into the state container (*32* for Florida), and so on and so on, until it reaches to the post office closest to the recipient (*32765*, in Oviedo, Florida).

If IP addressing were this easy, a lot of network administrators would be unemployed. However, to complicate matters, IP addresses are broken down into address classes: A, B, C, D, and E. Each A, B, and C class address has a predefined network boundary, shown in Table 7-1. Class D addresses are used for multicasting and Class E for research purposes.

exam

🐵 **a t c h**
Remember the five classes of IP addresses, and the fact that Class A addresses have, by default, 8 network bits,
Class B addresses have 16 bits, and Class C addresses have 24 bits.

TABLE 7-1	Address Class	Network Bytes	Host Bytes	Beginning Bit Values	Addresses (First Octet)
Network and Host Boundaries	A	1 (8 bits)	3 (24 bits)	0	1–126; 0 and 127 are reserved
	B	2 (16 bits)	2 (16 bits)	10	128–191
	C	3 (24 bits)	1 (8 bits)	110	192–223
	D	N/A	N/A	1110	224–239
	E	N/A	N/A	11110	240–254; 255 is reserved

Distinguishing Between Classes of Addresses

Given the aforementioned class distinctions, it would seem that addressing for IP is easy. However, what distinguishes the different classes of addresses are the values to which the first to fifth bits are set, as shown in Table 7-1. When you're talking about the highest order bit or bits, this includes *all* 32 bits of the IP address. Therefore, the address's class can be determined by looking at the very first bit to the *left* of the address (the most significant bit). If the first octet contains 10000001, this represents 129 in decimal, which would be a Class B address. Given the aforementioned distinctions with the assigned high-order bit values, it is easy to tell which class of network numbers a particular address belongs to.

In Class A addresses, *0* (in the first octet) is reserved; it represents "all" IP addresses and is commonly used as a default route. The address *127* is also reserved for a loopback, which is used for local testing function. In Class E, *255* is reserved and is used as a local broadcast—all IP devices in a broadcast domain, such as a segment or virtual LAN (VLAN). Also, remember that there are three classes of private addresses: Class A, 10.0.0.0; Class B, 172.16.0.0–172.31.0.0; and Class C, 192.168.0.0–192.168.255.0. Recall from Chapter 6 that private addresses can be used internally in a network, but they must be translated to a public address space before being transmitted to a public network such as the Internet (discussed in Chapter 23).

exam

ⓦatch

Remember the binary values that IP addresses begin with and be able to determine, by looking at the first binary byte, whether the address is a Class A, B, C, D, or E address.

IP Address Components

Two components make up a Class A, B, and C IP address: *network* and *host*. The host portion is actually broken into three subcomponents: the *network address*, the *host address*, and the *directed broadcast address*.

The first address in a network number is called the *network address*, or *wire number*. This address is used to uniquely identify one segment or broadcast domain/VLAN from all the other segments in the network. The last address in the network number is called the *directed broadcast address* and is used to represent all hosts on this network segment. A directed broadcast is similar to a local broadcast. The main difference is that routers will not propagate local broadcasts between segments, but they will, by default, propagate directed broadcasts. Any address between the network address and the directed broadcast address is called a *host address* for the segment. You assign these middle addresses to host devices on the segment, such as PCs, servers, routers, and switches.

---

e x a m

ⓦatch
Each network has two reserved addresses: a network number (the first address) and a directed broadcast (the last address). Any addresses between *these two values can be assigned to networking devices on the segment and are called host addresses.*

Network and Directed Broadcast Addresses

When dealing with a network address, all the host bits in the host portion of the address are set to 0s (zeros). If all the host bits in a network number are set to 1s (ones), making it the very last address, then this is the *directed broadcast* address. Any combination of bit values between these two numbers in the *host* portion of the address is considered a *host* address.

Here's an example: 192.1.1.0 is a Class C address and is also a network number. Recall from the table that the Class C addresses range from 192 to 223 in the first octet or byte and the network number is 3 bytes long. Therefore, *192.1.1* is the network number. The last byte is the host address. This byte is 0 (all bits are zero), which is the very *first* address in the network. Therefore, the network address is *192.1.1.0*. If you would set the last 8 bits to all 1s (all the host bits), which is equivalent to 255 in decimal, this would be the directed broadcast (192.1.1.255) for the network.

Host Addresses

Any number between the network address and the directed broadcast address is a host address. In the preceding example, any number between 0 and 255 is a host address for the network 192.1.1.0: 192.1.1.1–192.1.1.254. An important item to point out about this process is that for any given network number, you *lose* two addresses. The first address in a network is reserved for the network number itself and the last address is reserved for the directed broadcast address for the network. A formula can be used to define the number of available host addresses, assuming that you know the number of bits that can be used for host numbers: $2^H - 2$. At the beginning of this formula, 2 is raised to the power of H, where H is the number of host bits.

So, for example, a Class C network has a 24-bit network number component and an 8-bit host component. Therefore, for a Class C network, the lowest address in this fourth octet is 0 and the last address in this octet is *255* (all 8 bits are set to *1*). All numbers between 1 and 254 are host addresses for the Class C network. Using the addressing formula, you can easily show that a Class C network has 254 host addresses: $2^H - 2 = 2^8 - 2 = 256 - 2 = 254$ available host addresses. For a Class B network, the number of host addresses is 65,534: $2^H - 2 = 2^{16} - 2 = 64,536 - 2 = 65,534$. And for a Class A network, the number of host addresses is 16,777,214: $2^H - 2 = 2^{24} - 2 = 16,777,216 - 2 = 16,777,214$. See Chapter 3 for a review of powers of 2.

CERTIFICATION OBJECTIVE 5.02

Subnetting

One of the problems with the original IP addressing scheme was that for Class A and B networks, address efficiency was an issue. In other words, how many hosts can you physically put on a network segment or broadcast domain? Even with the advent of VLANs, this number did not increase dramatically. With IP, you can get 200 to 500 devices in a single broadcast domain before experiencing broadcast problems. This is one to two Class C networks. If you would assign a Class B network for this broadcast domain, you'd be wasting more than 65,000 addresses.

To overcome this deficiency issue, subnetting was introduced. Subnetting allows you to take some of the *higher-order host* bits in a network number and use them to create more networks. In the process of creating more networks, each of these additional networks has a lesser number of hosts. These smaller networks are commonly called *subnets*. One disadvantage of subnetting is that you are losing more addresses, because each of these subnets has a network and directed broadcast address. However, the advantage of subnetting is that you now can more efficiently use your addresses for a class network.

Let's look at an example. A Class C network has 8 host bits, giving you a total of 256 addresses. Of these 256 addresses, you can use only 254 for host devices, such as PCs, routers, and servers. Let's assume that you use the highest order bit to create more networks, leaving 7 bits for host addresses. With this example, you are creating two subnets: $2^1 = 2$. In this formula, the *1* is the number of subnet bits. In each of these subnets you have 126 host addresses: $2^7 - 2 = 126$. Originally, you lost two addresses in a Class C network. Now that you have two subnets, you are losing a total of four addresses. However, the advantage of subnetting is that you now have two networks instead of one!

Or suppose you have two segments in your network with 100 hosts each on them. You could assign a separate Class C network to each of these segments, but this would be a very inefficient use of your addresses. By using subnetting, you can more efficiently use your addresses. In this example, one Class C network, subnetted with one subnet bit, creates two subnets with 126 host addresses each. So in this example, you are wasting a smaller number of addresses.

Subnet Masks

TCP/IP is unique among most layer 3 addressing schemes. When dealing with TCP/IP addresses, each address actually has three components: a network component, a host component, and a *subnet mask*. The function of the subnet mask is to differentiate among the network address, the host addresses, and the directed broadcast address. Subnetting was originally defined in RFC 950.

Like an IP address, a subnet mask is 32 bits long. In binary, a *1* in a bit position in the subnet mask represents a network component and a *0* in a bit position represents a host component. One restriction of subnet masks is that all the network bits (1s) must be contiguous and all the host bits (0s) are contiguous. This is true not only in a single octet, but across all the bits in all four octets. A subnet mask of 11110000.00001111.11111111.11111111 (240.31.255.255) would be invalid since all the 1s are not contiguous. A subnet mask of 11111111.11111111.11111111.11111000 (255.255.255.248), however, is valid.

You can actually use four methods to represent a subnet mask. Here is a list with a demonstration using a Class C network:

- **Dotted-decimal**   192.168.1.0 255.255.255.0
- **Number of networking bits**   192.168.1.0/24
- **Hexadecimal**   192.168.1.0 0xFFFFFF00
- **Binary**   192.168.1.0 11111111111111111111111100000000

The most common of these formats is the dotted-decimal and the number of networking bits used (the first two listed above). Hexadecimal and binary are rarely used.

Subnet mask values, binary 1s and 0s, must be contiguous in order to be considered as a valid subnet mask. When representing subnet masks, be very familiar with both the dotted-decimal and number of networking bits nomenclature.

Any subnet mask using a number not listed in Table 7-2 is invalid.

Subnet Mask Values

Given the fact that subnet mask values must have all 1s contiguous and all 0s contiguous, Table 7-2 shows some valid decimal numbers for subnet masks in an octet.

TABLE 7-2	00000000 = 0	11100000 = 224	11111100 = 252
Valid Subnet Mask	10000000 = 128	11110000 = 240	11111110 = 254
Values in an Octet	11000000 = 192	11111000 = 248	11111111 = 255

For a Class A network, the default subnet mask is 255.0.0.0: the first octet (byte) is the network number and the last three octets are the host numbers. For a Class B network, the default subnet mask is 255.255.0.0: the first two octets are the network number and the last two octets are the host numbers. For a Class C network, the default subnet mask is 255.255.255.0: the first three octets are the network numbers and the last octet is the host number.

One important item to point out is that the subnet mask, in and of itself, means nothing without the context of the IP address associated with it. For example, most people would assume that when you see a subnet mask of 255.255.255.0, you are dealing with a Class C network. However, remember that you can perform subnetting on any class address: A, B, and C. So a subnet mask of 255.255.255.0 can also be used for Class A and B networks. Therefore, the IP address and subnet mask have a symbiotic relationship. The following sections will show you the valid subnet mask values for Class A, B, and C networks.

---

e x a m

ⓦatch
When subnetting, depending on the device, the very first and last subnet in a network, referred to as subnet 0, might or might not be valid. For the exam, remember this, since the *exam may or may not tell you one way or the other. However, when looking for an answer, you'll never see both as a valid answer; either the answer will include the first and last subnet or it won't.*

Subnet Masks for Class A Networks

Table 7-3 shows valid subnet masks for Class A networks. In this table, the number of networking bits is the total number of bits used in networking, including both the network and subnet bits. This is also true in Tables 7-4 and 7-5.

---

e x a m

ⓦatch
The best subnet mask for a point-to-point link, for which *you need only two host addresses, is 255.255.255.252.*

TABLE 7-3	Subnet Mask	Networking Bits	Number of Subnets	Number of Hosts per Subnet
Valid Subnet Masks for Class A Networks	255.255.255.252	/30	4,194,304	2
	255.255.255.248	/29	2,097,152	6
	255.255.255.240	/28	1,048,576	14
	255.255.255.224	/27	524,288	30
	255.255.255.192	/26	262,144	62
	255.255.255.128	/25	131,072	126
	255.255.255.0	/24	65,536	254
	255.255.254.0	/23	32,768	510
	255.255.252.0	/22	16,384	1022
	255.255.248.0	/21	8192	2046
	255.255.240.0	/20	4096	4094
	255.255.224.0	/19	2048	8190
	255.255.192.0	/18	1024	16,382
	255.255.128.0	/17	512	32,766
	255.255.0.0	/16	256	65,534
	255.254.0.0	/15	128	131,070
	255.252.0.0	/14	64	262,142
	255.248.0.0	/13	32	524,286
	255.240.0.0	/12	16	1,048,574
	255.224.0.0	/11	8	2,097,150
	255.192.0.0	/10	4	4,194,302
	255.128.0.0	/9	2	8,388,606
	255.0.0.0	/8	1	16,777,216

e x a m
ⓦ a t c h   *You should be very familiar with subnet masks for a given address and the number of networks that a subnet mask creates, as well as the number of host addresses for each network.*

Subnet Masks for Class B Networks

Table 7-4 shows valid subnet masks for Class B networks.

Subnet Masks for Class C Networks

Table 7-5 shows valid subnet masks for Class C networks.

TABLE 7-4	Subnet Mask	Networking Bits	Number of Subnets	Number of Hosts per Subnet
Valid Subnet Masks for Class B Networks	255.255.255.252	/30	32,768	2
	255.255.255.248	/29	8192	6
	255.255.255.240	/28	4096	14
	255.255.255.224	/27	2048	30
	255.255.255.192	/26	1024	62
	255.255.255.128	/25	512	126
	255.255.255.0	/24	256	254
	255.255.254.0	/23	128	510
	255.255.252.0	/22	64	1022
	255.255.248.0	/21	32	2046
	255.255.240.0	/20	16	4094
	255.255.224.0	/19	8	8190
	255.255.192.0	/18	4	16,382
	255.255.128.0	/17	2	32,764
	255.255.0.0	/16	1	65,534

As you can see from Tables 7-3, 7-4, and 7-5, you can't choose just any subnet mask and apply it to any class of addresses: Some masks are valid for some classes, but not valid for others. For instance, 255.255.0.0 is a valid mask for Class A and B networks, but it is an *invalid* mask for Class C networks.

TABLE 7-5	Subnet Mask	Networking Bits	Number of Subnets	Number of Hosts per Subnet
Valid Subnet Masks for Class C Networks	255.255.255.252	/30	64	2
	255.255.255.248	/29	32	6
	255.255.255.240	/28	16	14
	255.255.255.224	/27	8	30
	255.255.255.192	/26	4	62
	255.255.255.128	/25	2	126
	255.255.255.0	/24	1	254

on the **ob** *Starting in IOS 12.0, Cisco routers and switches automatically support the use of subnet 0 (the first and last subnets). Prior to this, the use of subnet 0 was, by default, disabled, but you could enable it to use on a router or switch.*

CERTIFICATION OBJECTIVE 5.03

IP Address Planning

When it comes to addressing, dealing with protocols such as AppleTalk, IPX, and XNS is easy: each has a distinct network and host component. With these protocols, there is no such thing as a subnet mask that can change the boundary between network and host numbers. When I started out with TCP/IP, one of the most difficult tasks I faced in my networking career was tackling and understanding how to handle subnetting and IP addressing. To make matters worse, IP addressing has its roots in binary mathematics, since this is how computing devices deal with numbers. And considering that I have a degree in mathematics, and that I had trouble with IP addressing, imagine how strange IP addressing must be to the layperson!

Through my years of experience dealing with TCP/IP and teaching Cisco-related courses, however, I've developed a simplified six-step approach to help students plan for their IP addressing needs in their networks:

1. Determine network and host requirements.
2. Satisfy host and network requirements.
3. Determine the subnet mask.
4. Determine the network addresses.
5. Determine the directed broadcast addresses for your networks.
6. Determine the host addresses for your networks.

The following sections will cover the six steps in depth.

exam

watch

Be very familiar with these six steps and how to plan out IP addressing. Many questions on the exam will have you perform this process—perhaps multiple times for a single question!

Step 1: Determine Network and Host Requirements

In this step, you need to do two things:

- Determine the number of hosts that do, or will, exist on the largest segment in your network.
- Determine the maximum number of segments that you have in your network—this will tell you how many networks, or subnets, you'll need.

If you are dealing with an existing network, you have a lot of analysis ahead of you. And, of course, if you're taking the exam, Cisco will fortunately supply this information to you. You'll need to perform the above two tasks, counting hosts on each segment and the number of segments that you have. Remember that when you are counting hosts, each device with a connection to the segment needs to be counted—this includes PCs, servers, routers, switches, printers, and other devices. Remember that a segment could be used in a logical sense, like all the ports off a switch, or a VLAN, as discussed in Chapter 13. You might even want to leave some room for growth by taking your final numbers and adding to them.

ⓦatch *All devices on a segment—router, switches, PCs, servers, and so on—need a host address from a network or subnet number.*

To assist with the remaining five steps, I'll create an imaginary network. This network has 14 segments and the largest segment has 14 devices on it. You've been assigned a single Class C network number (192.168.1.0) to complete the task. Now you're ready to proceed to step 2.

Step 2: Satisfy Host and Network Requirements

In the second step, you'll use three formulas:

- 2^S >= number of networks you need (S represents subnet bits)
- $2^H - 2$ >= number of hosts on your largest segment (H represents host bits)
- $S + H$ <= total number of host bits you have for a class of address

In the first step, you need to figure out how many bits you need to steal from the host bits to create your subnets. In the second step, you need to figure out how many host bits you need to accommodate your host requirements. And last, you need to make sure that when you add up the bits that you stole for subnets and the bits that you need for your hosts, you don't exceed the original number of host bits that you started out with, based on the Class A, B, or C network.

As an example, if you had a Class C network and were subnetting it and needed 5 bits for subnets and 4 bits for hosts, this would total 9 bits. Unfortunately, Class C networks have only 8 host bits to begin with, so this wouldn't work. In this situation, you would need either a Class B network or two Class C networks. As another example, if you had the same Class C network and were subnetting it, and you needed 3 bits for subnets and 4 bits for host addresses, this would total 7 bits. In this situation, the Class C network has 8 bits, and you need only 7. This gives you some flexibility—you could use the extra bit either to create more subnets or have subnets with more hosts.

Let's go back to the original example of 192.168.1.0, where you need 14 subnets with a maximum of 14 hosts on each:

1. 2^S >= 14 subnets; in this example, $S = 4$, which would result in 16 subnets.

2. $2^H - 2$ >= 14 hosts; in this example, $H = 4$, which would result in 14 hosts.

3. $S + H <= 8$ (Class C network); in this example $4 + 4$ is less than or equal to 8.

Let's break this down step-by-step.

In the first step, you need to find a power of 2 that will provide a number that is either greater than or equal to the number of subnets that you need. In our example, the power of 2 needs to be 4: 2^4 >= 16. This meets your subnet requirements, since you need only 14 subnets (there are only 14 segments). If subnet 0 were not available, then you would need 5 subnet bits instead of 4, since you would lose the first and last subnets; however, I'm assuming that subnet 0 is available in this example.

In the second step, you need to figure out your host bits by using the formula $2^H - 2$ >= 14 required hosts, where H is the necessary number of host bits. In this example, $2^4 - 2 = 14$, so you need 4 host bits to get your required 14 hosts. Remember that you need to subtract 2 since the first address in the network is the network address and the last is the directed broadcast address.

And third, since you are dealing with a Class C network, you have only 8 original host bits. You need to make sure that the total of your subnetting and host bits does not exceed this original value. In your case, $4 + 4 = 8$, so you're okay. If the number of bits totaled more than 8, you would need two Class C networks or a Class B network. If the number of bits were less than 8, you could allocate the extra bit or bits to create more subnets and/or hosts. Remember that if you are ever in a situation where you have extra bits to deal with, you need to examine your network closely and figure out, based on future growth, whether you should create more subnets or allow for more hosts on a subnet.

Step 3: Determine the Subnet Mask

Now that the hardest part is over, the remaining four tasks are easy. At this point, you know the number of subnet bits you need. However, when dealing with networking and subnet masks, a subnet mask's network portion contains both network *and* subnet bits. Remember the default number of networking bits for a class address: A is 8, B is 16, and C is 24.

Given this, you can just add the class address bits to the subnet bits, and this gives you the total number of *networking* bits. In this example, 24 + 4 = 28. To make the remaining three steps easier, you can convert the number of bits of the subnet mask to a dotted-decimal mask. Tables 7-3, 7-4, and 7-5 show the lists of subnet masks if you need help. However, this process is not too difficult. First, remember that a subnet mask, just like an IP address, is represented in a dotted-decimal format, with 8 bits in each octet. That means, for a Class C mask, the first 24 bits are set to 1. In other words, the mask at least begins with 255.255.255. Your job is to figure out the mask in the last octet. Remember that the four highest bits are for subnetting, so just add up these decimal values: 128 + 64 + 32 + 16 = 240.

You can also use a shortcut (which I always use). Recall from the example that the number of host bits that are used are the four lower order bits. Add up these values: 1 + 2 + 4 + 8 = 15. The largest number represented by a byte is 255. Since you're not using these bits, just subtract this value from 255, which will give you the mask value in this byte of 255 − 15 = 240. I find it easier to add up the small values and subtract them from 255 than to add up the larger bit-decimal values. Eventually, you won't have to do this mathematical trick as you become accustomed to performing IP addressing and dealing with subnetting. Going back to our example, our subnet mask for network 192.168.1.0 is *255.255.255.240*, or 192.168.1.0/28.

Step 4: Determine the Network Addresses

In step 4, you need to figure out the networks that you created with your new subnet mask. Since IP addressing is done in binary, network addresses will always increment in a multiple of something. You can use this to your advantage when figuring out what your network numbers are for your Class C network. Remember that the network number has all the host bits set to 0s.

Actually, you already know what this multiplier is: you figured this out in the second part of step 2, using the $2^H - 2 = 14$ formula. The *14* is the number of valid host values for a subnet; however, this is *not* the total number of addresses for the subnet. The subnet also has a network and broadcast address, which is the reason the formula subtracts 2 (since you can't use these addresses for host devices). Therefore, in this example, each network has a total of *16* addresses and increments by *16* from subnet-to-subnet.

You can use another method of verifying your multiplying value. In a byte, you can have numbers ranging from 0 to 255, resulting in a total of 256 numbers. For this verification, take the subnet mask decimal value in the interesting octet and subtract it from 256. The interesting octet is the octet that contains the network and host boundary. In our case, this is the fourth octet. Therefore, using this trick, $256 - 240 = 16$. When you compare this number to the number in the last paragraph, you can be assured that you have done your math correctly.

Now that you have figured out the multiplier, write down the very first network, and then start adding *16* to the interesting octet. Table 7-6 lists the subnet numbers for 192.168.1.0. In this table, notice something interesting concerning the last subnet: 192.168.1.240. The network number in the last octet matches the interesting octet in your subnet mask (240). This will *always* be true when you perform subnetting.

Another important item needs to be mentioned about subnetting. In the original RFC for subnetting, you were not allowed to use the first and last subnet. For instance, in our example, you would not be able to use 192.168.1.0/28 and 192.168.1.240/28. However, today, assuming that your TCP/IP protocol stack supports subnet 0 (this refers to these two subnets—first and last), you can use 192.168.1.0/28 and 192.168.1.240/28, and this has been true since the mid-1990s. You need to make sure, though, that each device on the segment that will have one of these subnets supports this function. In today's age, this shouldn't be an issue for computers and networking devices.

TABLE 7-6	192.168.1.0	192.168.1.64	192.168.1.128	192.168.1.192
	192.168.1.16	192.168.1.80	192.168.1.144	192.168.1.208
Network Numbers for	192.168.1.32	192.168.1.96	192.168.1.160	192.168.1.224
192.168.1.0	192.168.1.48	192.168.1.112	192.168.1.176	192.168.1.240

Step 5: Determine the Directed Broadcast Addresses

After figuring out all of your subnets, you next need to determine the directed broadcast address for each subnet. This is very simple. The directed broadcast of a subnet is *one number less* than the next network number. Also, the broadcast address has all of its hosts bits (in the subnet) set to binary 1s. Table 7-7 shows our network numbers and directed broadcast addresses. For the last table entry, the directed broadcast address will be the highest possible value in a byte: 255.

As a shortcut, remember that the directed broadcast address is one number less than the network address of the next subnet number.

TABLE 7-7	Network Address	Mathematics	Directed Broadcast Address
Network and Directed Broadcast Addresses for 192.168.1.0/28	192.168.1.0	16 – 1	192.168.1.15
	192.168.1.16	32 – 1	192.168.1.31
	192.168.1.32	48 – 1	192.168.1.47
	192.168.1.48	64 – 1	192.168.1.63
	192.168.1.64	80 – 1	192.168.1.79
	192.168.1.80	96 – 1	192.168.1.95
	192.168.1.96	112 – 1	192.168.1.111
	192.168.1.112	128 – 1	192.168.1.127
	192.168.1.128	144 – 1	192.168.1.143
	192.168.1.144	160 – 1	192.168.1.159
	192.168.1.160	176 – 1	192.168.1.175
	192.168.1.176	192 – 1	192.168.1.191
	192.168.1.192	208 – 1	192.168.1.207
	192.168.1.208	224 – 1	192.168.1.223
	192.168.1.224	240 – 1	192.168.1.239
	192.168.1.240		192.168.1.255

Step 6: Determine the Host Addresses

Step 6 is the easiest step. Recall that any address between the network and directed broadcast address is a host address for a given network. You can then complete the rest of your addressing for 192.168.1.0, as shown in Table 7-8. If you look at the first subnet in this table, 192.168.1.0, you'll see that it has a total of 14 host addresses, which you can see using our formula $2^H - 2$: $2^4 - 2 = 14$ hosts.

on the **Job**

For the CCNA exam, you will definitely need to understand how to figure IP addressing, and quickly. Of course, on the job, you can cheat and use an IP subnet calculator. One of my favorites is from a company called Boson Software, which offers a free download of its subnet calculator (www.boson .com). Boson's subnet calculator will even do route summarization, which is discussed in the next chapter.

TABLE 7-8	Network Number	Host Address	Directed Broadcast Address
Addressing for 192.168.1.0/28	192.168.1.0	192.168.1.1–192.168.1.14	192.168.1.15
	192.168.1.16	192.168.1.17–192.168.1.30	192.168.1.31
	192.168.1.32	192.168.1.33–192.168.1.46	192.168.1.47
	192.168.1.48	192.168.1.49–192.168.1.62	192.168.1.63
	192.168.1.64	192.168.1.65–192.168.1.78	192.168.1.79
	192.168.1.80	192.168.1.81–192.168.1.94	192.168.1.95
	192.168.1.96	192.168.1.97–192.168.1.110	192.168.1.111
	192.168.1.112	192.168.1.113–192.168.1.126	192.168.1.127
	192.168.1.128	192.168.1.129–192.168.1.142	192.168.1.143
	192.168.1.144	192.168.1.145–192.168.1.158	192.168.1.159
	192.168.1.160	192.168.1.161–192.168.1.174	192.168.1.175
	192.168.1.176	192.168.1.177–192.168.1.190	192.168.1.191
	192.168.1.192	192.168.1.193–192.168.1.206	192.168.1.207
	192.168.1.208	192.168.1.209–192.168.1.222	192.168.1.123
	192.168.1.224	192.168.1.225–192.168.1.238	192.168.1.239
	192.168.1.240	192.168.1.241–192.168.1.254	192.168.1.255

EXERCISE 7-1

Planning IP Addressing Exercise

This exercise will help reinforce the concepts you've learned in this chapter, including the six steps that you should use to come up with an appropriate subnet mask value and network, directed broadcast, and host addresses.

1. You are given a Class C network (192.168.1.0) and you have four segments in your network, where the largest segment has 50 hosts. What subnet mask should you use and what is the layout of your addresses?

    Performing the six steps, the subnet mask is 255.255.255.192 (/26), giving you four network numbers: 192.168.1.0, 192.168.1.64, 192.168.1.128, and 192.168.1.192. Each of these four networks has a total of 64 addresses, of which 62 can be used for host devices.

2. You are given a Class B network (172.16.0.0) and you have 490 segments in your network, where the largest segment needs 112 host addresses. What subnet mask should you use and what is the layout of your addresses?

    Performing the six steps, the subnet mask is 255.255.255.128 (/25), giving you 512 network numbers: 172.16.0.0, 172.16.0.128, 172.16.1.0, 172.16.1.128, 172.16.2.0, 172.16.2.128, and so on and so forth. Each of these 512 subnets has 128 addresses, of which 126 can be used to assign addressing information to host devices.

3. You are given a Class A network (10.0.0.0) and you have 9000 segments in your network, where the largest segment needs 560 host addresses. What subnet mask should you use and what is the layout of your addresses?

    Performing the six steps, the subnet mask is 255.255.252.0 (/22), giving you 16,384 network numbers: 10.0.0.0, 10.0.4.0, 10.0.8.0, 10.0.12.0, 10.0.16.0, 10.0.20.0, 10.0.24.0, and so on and so forth. Each of these 16,384 subnets has 1024 addresses, of which 1022 can be used to assign addressing information to host devices.

Now you should be more comfortable with planning IP addressing. In the next section, you will see how to determine whether an IP address is a network, directed broadcast, or host address.

e x a m

Make sure that you
practice, practice, and do more practice
on exercises like those presented here
when preparing for your exam. This is very
important. Use a subnet calculator to
check your results. Many are available on
the Internet for free; Boson's calculator

is one example. On the exam, you might
have to perform many subnet calculations
to answer a single question, so time is your
enemy in these situations: practice until
you can perform the subnetting process
quickly! Many people fail the CCNA exam
because they run out of time!

CERTIFICATION OBJECTIVE 7.04

Determining IP Address Components

For purposes of the CCNA exam, you might not be given an assignment like the
one described in the preceding section. However, you will have to know how to
figure out how many host addresses are in a particular subnet, how many subnets
you can create with a particular mask, and, given a specific IP address, whether it
is a network, host, or directed broadcast address. The last section described how to
plan IP addressing. This section teaches you to use a few tools to figure out these
questions—more specifically, given a certain address, what type of address it is:
network, host, or directed broadcast.

Recall from the last section that three types of addresses are used for each
network: network, directed broadcast, and host addresses. The trick to figuring this
out goes back to step 4. You need to figure out the number by which networks are
incrementing. For exam purposes, you may be given an IP address and a subnet
mask. Convert the decimal subnet mask to the number of bits in the mask. In the
previous example, for instance, 255.255.255.240 is a 28-bit mask. Take this number
and subtract it from 32. In our example, this gives you 4 bits. Since the first 28 bits
are network numbers, the last 4 bits are host addresses.

Remember that every subnet has the same number of addresses. So all you need
to do is raise this value to the power of 2 to figure out how many addresses are in a
network, and therefore you know by how much each network number is incrementing.

In our example, 2^4 gives you a total of 16 addresses in the subnet, including the network, host, and directed broadcast addresses. Based on this information, it is easy to figure out what type of address the exam is asking about.

As you will learn, subnetting is not a difficult task, but it does take *a lot of practice*. I've developed six steps to help you out, which are covered in the following sections.

Six-Step Approach for Determining IP Address Components

When you are given a particular address and subnet mask, and asked whether the address is a network, host, or directed broadcast address, you should use the following six steps:

1. You need an IP address and a subnet mask (this is the easy part).

2. Examine the subnet mask and find the interesting octet. The interesting octet in the mask is the one in which the network and host boundary are found. This includes the following mask values in an octet: 0, 128, 192, 224, 240, 248, 252, and 254. It does *not* include 255—an octet with a mask value of 255 (all 8 bits are 1s) indicates that this octet is part of the network number. Only when an octet contains one or more binary 0s does it have a host component.

3. Subtract the interesting octet in the subnet mask from 256. This will give you the increment by which network numbers are increasing in the interesting octet.

4. On a piece of paper, start writing down the network numbers, starting with the first subnet (0), and working your way up to a network number that is higher than the address in question.

5. After you have written down the network numbers, beside each of these, write down their corresponding broadcast addresses. Remember that the broadcast address is one number less than the *next* network number. You don't have to do this with every network number—just the networks near the network number in question.

6. Between the network and broadcast addresses, write down the host addresses. Host addresses are any number between the network and directed broadcast addresses.

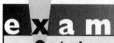

Based on these six steps, you should be able to figure out whether your address is a host, network, or broadcast address. Note that these six steps are somewhat similar to the six steps used in the "IP Address Planning" section. However, the steps in this section are for CCNA test purposes and the steps in the previous section are for design purposes.

Example #1 for Determining IP Address Components

To help you out with the six steps, take a look at an example as an illustration. In step 1, you have an IP address and subnet mask. Assume that this is 192.168.1.37 255.255.255.224 (or 192.168.1.37/27). This is a Class C network. Remember this shortcut: if it's an odd address, it's either a directed broadcast or host address. Therefore, you know this address is not a network address.

In step 2, you need to find the interesting octet in the subnet mask. This is the octet where the boundary exists between network and host bits. In this example, this is the fourth octet: *224*. In step 3, you need to find the increment by which network numbers are increasing. To perform this step, subtract the interesting octet from 256: 256 − 224 = 32. Therefore, there are 32 addresses in each network, and each network is incrementing by 32 in the interesting octet (fourth octet).

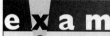

In step 4, write down the network numbers starting with the first subnet and work your way up. Here is the list of network numbers for our example: 192.168.1.0, 192.168.1.32, 192.168.1.64, 192.168.1.96, 192.168.1.128, 192.168.1.160, 192.168.1.192, and 192.168.1.224. In this example, there are eight subnets. Mathematically, this makes sense. There are 32 addresses per subnet, with a total of 256 addresses (0–255) in a Class C network. 256 ÷ 32 = 8! Remember that the interesting octet in the subnet mask will be the subnet number in the last subnet of the IP class address.

In step 5, list the directed broadcast address beside each network number. And in step 6, list the host addresses for each network. Remember that the broadcast address for a network is one number less than the next network number and that the host addresses are any IP addresses between the network and directed broadcast addresses. Table 7-9 shows the completion of steps 5 and 6.

Considering Table 7-9, the host address of 192.168.1.37 is a *host* address, since it falls in the rage of host addresses for subnet 192.168.1.32/27.

exam ⓦatch

When you are taking the CCNA exam, don't build the entire table. Instead, list the network numbers until you have a network number greater than the address in the question. Once this is done, for the last three network numbers, list the directed broadcast and host addresses, and then you'll know the answer to the exam question. In the above example, these networks would be 192.168.1.0, 192.168.32.0 and 192.168.64.0.

TABLE 7-9

Network, Broadcast, Directed, and Host Addresses of 192.168.1.0/27

Network Address	Host Address	Directed Broadcast Address
192.168.1.0	192.168.1.1–192.168.1.30	192.168.1.31
192.168.1.32	192.168.1.33–192.168.1.62	192.168.1.63
192.168.1.64	192.168.1.65–192.168.1.94	192.168.1.95
192.168.1.96	192.168.1.97–192.168.1.126	192.168.1.127
192.168.1.128	192.168.1.129–192.168.1.158	192.168.1.159
192.168.1.160	192.168.1.161–192.168.1.190	192.168.1.191
192.168.1.192	192.168.1.193–192.168.1.222	192.168.1.223
192.168.1.224	192.168.1.225–192.168.1.254	192.168.1.255

Example #2 for Determining IP Address Components

Let's look at another example to help clarify the six steps. For step 1, you are given the following address and subnet mask: 192.168.1.132 255.255.255.192 (/26), which is a Class C address. Remember the shortcut from earlier: if the last octet is even, it's either a network or host address. Therefore, you know it's not a directed broadcast address.

In the second step, you need to find the interesting octet in the subnet mask. This is the last octet. For a Class C network, this will *always* be the last octet. The value in this mask is *192*, indicating that the first two high-order bits in the octet are part of the network component and the last six low-order bits are the host component. In step 3, you need to determine by what number the network addresses are increasing. To do this step, subtract the value in the subnet mask's interesting octet from 256: 256–192 = 64. Therefore, network addresses are incrementing by 64 numbers and each network contains 64 addresses: a network address, a directed broadcast address, and 62 host addresses. Remember that since the interesting octet is in the fourth octet, the network addresses are increasing by 64 in the *interesting* (fourth) octet.

In step 4, write down the network numbers. In our example, this gives you four networks: 192.168.1.*0*, 192.168.1.*64*, 192.168.1.*128*, and 192.168.1.*192*. In the interesting octet, 2 bits are used for networking and 6 bits for host addresses. With 2 bits of networking, this gives you four networks ($2^2 = 4$), and with 6 bits of host addresses and 64 addresses in a network, it's $2^6 = 64$.

The address in question, 192.168.1.132, is between two networks: 192.168.1.128 and 192.168.1.192. This means that you should have to perform steps 5 and 6 only on these two networks, and possibly the network before it. However, go ahead and complete steps 5 and 6 for all of the networks since this is good practice. Remember that the directed broadcast address for a network is one number less than the next network number and that the addresses between the network and directed broadcast addresses are host addresses. Table 7-10 shows the addressing for the Class C address. Our address, 192.168.1.132, is a *host* address based on this table, where its network number is 192.168.1.128 and its directed broadcast is 192.168.1.191.

TABLE 7-10	Network Address	Host Address	Directed Broadcast Address
Network, Broadcast, Directed, and Host Addresses of 192.168.1.0/26	192.168.1.0	192.168.1.1–192.168.1.62	192.168.1.63
	192.168.1.64	192.168.1.65–192.168.1.126	192.168.1.127
	192.168.1.128	192.168.1.129–192.168.1.190	192.168.1.191
	192.168.1.192	192.168.1.193–192.168.1.253	192.168.1.254

Example #3 for Determining IP Address Components

The first two examples were fairly simple, since the addresses were from a Class C network. In this example, let's complicate matters by using a Class B network. In step 1, the address assigned is 172.16.5.0 255.255.254.0, which can also be represented as 172.16.5.0/23. This is an excellent example of an address that most test-takers would incorrectly identify on a test. Right now, try and guess what type of address this is (network, directed broadcast, or host) and then work through it step-by-step to come up with an answer. However, if you remember the shortcut from earlier, since the host portion of the address is an even number, you at least know that the address is not a directed broadcast, narrowing your choice down to two possibilities.

In step 2, you need to find the interesting octet—where the network and host boundary resides. In this case, it happens to be the *third* octet (254) of the subnet mask. It is important to point out that *all* of the *fourth* octet represents host addresses. In step 3, you need to find the increment by which network numbers are increasing: 256 – 254 = 2. *Network numbers are incrementing by 2 in the third octet.* This last sentence is very important. Remember that the entire fourth octet is the host component since the subnet mask value in this position is set to 0 (all 8 bits are 0).

In step 4, you need to write down your network numbers, starting with the first subnet, and work your way up until you go past the IP address in question: 172.16.0.0, 172.16.2.0, 172.16.4.0, 172.16.6.0, 172.16.8.0, and so on and so forth. Remember that with a Class B address, there are 16 bits in the host component. With this subnet mask, you're using 7 bits for subnets and 9 bits for hosts. Therefore, with 7 bits for subnets, you have a total of 128 subnets, where each subnet has 512 total addresses. Each network really has 510 *host* addresses, where the first and last addresses are used for the network and directed broadcast addresses, respectively. Looking at the address, 172.16.5.0, you can tell that it at least is *not* a network address.

Go ahead and do steps 5 and 6, listing the directed broadcast addresses and host addresses for these subnets, as shown in Table 7-11. Looking at this table, you can see that 172.16.5.0 is a *host* address! Even 172.16.0.255 is a host address! This example illustrates that you should *never* make assumptions about what type an address is without considering the subnet mask. Always remember that the subnet mask puts a context on the IP address and determines its type: network, directed broadcast, or host address.

For the CCNA exam, I would expect a trick question like this. In real life, I would typically not use addresses like 172.16.5.0 or 172.16.0.255 because this would *confuse* many network administrators. I've actually had to argue with people over the validity of these kinds of addresses as host addresses in network planning sessions!

TABLE 7-11	Network Address	Host Address	Directed Broadcast Address
Network, Broadcast, Directed, and Host Addresses of 172.16.0.0/23	172.16.0.0	172.16.0.1–172.16.1.254	172.16.1.255
	172.16.2.0	172.16.2.1–172.16.3.254	172.16.3.255
	172.16.4.0	172.16.4.1–172.16.5.254	172.16.5.255
	172.16.6.0	172.16.6.1–172.16.7.254	172.16.7.255
	172.16.8.0	172.16.8.1–172.16.9.254	172.16.9.255

I've learned, though, that it's pretty hard to teach an old dog new tricks, so instead of wasting my time arguing or explaining the address validity, I just don't use them. For test purposes, though, they *are* valid host addresses!

EXERCISE 7-2

ON THE CD

Determining Network, Directed Broadcast, and Host Components

These last few sections deal with how to determine the type of address: network, directed broadcast, or host address. The following exercises will help you practice your IP addressing skills.

1. You are given the following address: 192.168.1.63/255.255.255.248. What type of address is this—network, directed broadcast, or host?

   The interesting octet is the *fourth*: 248. Subtract this from 256: 256 – 248 = 8. Network numbers are incrementing by 8: 192.168.1.0, 192.168.1.8, 192.168.1.16, 192.168.1.24, 192.168.1.32, 192.168.1.40, 192.168.1.48, 192.168.1.56, 192.168.1.64, and so on and so forth. After writing down the directed broadcast addresses, you'll see that the network 192.168.1.56 has a directed broadcast address of 192.168.1.63 and host address of 57–62. Therefore, this is a broadcast address.

2. You are given the following address: 172.16.4.255/255.255.252.0. What type of address is this—network, directed broadcast, or host?

The interesting octet is the *third*: 252. Subtract this from 256: 256 − 252 = 4. Network numbers are incrementing by 4 in the third octet: 172.16.0.0, 172.16.4.0, 172.16.8.0, 172.16.*12*.0, and so on and so forth. After writing down the directed broadcast addresses, you'll see that the network 172.16.4.0 has a directed broadcast address of 172.16.7.255 and host addresses of 172.16.4.1–172.16.7.254. Therefore, this is a host address.

INSIDE THE EXAM

IP Addressing Review

I cannot stress enough how important it is for you to know IP addressing inside and out for the CCNA exam—whether you're taking the two-exam or one-exam approach. Out of all of the topics in this book, those covered in this chapter are probably the most important. Therefore, be familiar with the classes of addresses, including the default bit lengths and beginning bit values for each address class. Also understand the three kinds of addresses in a network: network address, host addresses, and directed broadcast address. Each network loses two addresses for host purposes: the first and last.

Probably the main reason that most test takers fail any of the three CCNA exams is that they run out of time: they know the material, but when it comes to IP addressing and subnetting, they're taking too much time to answer the questions. Therefore, you need to read this chapter a few times and practice, and practice exercises like those found in the

"IP Address Planning" and "Determining IP Address Components" sections until you can do these things in your sleep.

Subnetting

You need to be highly proficient in subnetting. Be able to pick out invalid masks and be able to determine the number of networks and hosts available based on a particular subnet mask value (whether it's displayed in a dotted-decimal format or by the number of networking bits). 255.255.255.252 is a good mask for point-to-point links, since it offers two hosts for the subnet. Typically, when given a subnet question, the exam will tell you whether or not subnet 0 is valid—however, in those questions where it isn't stated, you'll need to look close at the answers to determine how to answer the question, which to me is unfair.

(continued)

IP Address Planning

Don't be surprised to see a simulation question on the exam, for which you need to configure one or more routers as well as design an appropriate IP addressing scheme. The question will tell you how many devices need to be on each segment, and you can easily count the number of segments in the network diagram. The question will also tell you the network number—you need to come up with a subnet mask that will work for the question as well as do the subnetting, logically assign the subnets to each of the segments, and give the router interfaces a host address from each of the subnets. Therefore, make sure you practice and practice the six steps described in this section until you have subnetting down pat.

Determining IP Address Components

You might see some questions on the exam for which you have to choose the network addresses, host addresses, or directed broadcast addresses from a list of addresses. This means you'll have to figure out the address components multiple times to choose the correct answer or answers. Remember the trick to eliminate some of the answers right away: network addresses are always even numbered, directed broadcast addresses are always odd numbered, and host addresses can be either.

CERTIFICATION SUMMARY

IP addresses are 32-bits in length and are broken up into 4 bytes, with a period between the bytes. This format is referred to as dotted-decimal. There are five classes of IP addresses: A (1–126), B (128–191), C (192–223), D (224–239), and E (240–254). Class A addresses have 1 network byte and 3 host bytes. Class B addresses have 2 network and 2 host bytes. Class C addresses have 3 network bytes and 1 host byte. Private IP addresses include networks 10.0.0.0/8, 172.16.0.0/16–172.31.0.0/16, and 192.168.0.0/24–192.168.255.0/24.

IP addresses have three components: network, host, and broadcast. The first number in a network is the network or wire number. The very last address is the broadcast address of the network. Any addresses between the network and broadcast addresses are host addresses. What differentiates network, host, and broadcast addresses is the context the subnet mask places on the address. The subnet mask is used to mark the boundary between the network and host bits.

TWO-MINUTE DRILL

IP Addressing Review

❑ IP addresses are 32 bits in length and are broken into 4 bytes (8 bits) with a period between the bytes. This format is called dotted-decimal.

❑ IP addresses are broken into five classes: A (1–126), B (128–191), C (192–223), D (224–239), and E (240–254). IP addresses are broken into two components: network and host. With Class A addresses, the first byte is a network number, Class B, the first 2 bytes, and Class C, the first 3 bytes.

❑ The first few bits in the first octet identity the class of address. Class A addresses begin with 0, Class B with 10, Class C with 110, Class D with 1110, and Class E with 11110.

❑ Each network has three components to its address: network, directed broadcast, and host. The first number in the network is the network address, the last is the directed broadcast address, and any addresses between these two are host addresses.

Subnetting

❑ Subnetting allows you to break up and use an addressing space more efficiently. Basically, subnetting steals the higher-order bit or bits from the host component and uses these bits to create more subnets with a smaller number of host addresses in each of these subnets.

❑ Subnet masks are 32 bits long and are typically represented in dotted-decimal (such as 255.255.255.0) or the number of networking bits (such as /24). The networking bits in a mask must be contiguous and the host bits in the subnet mask must be contiguous. 255.0.255.0 is an invalid mask.

IP Address Planning

❑ Six steps are required for designing a network with IP addresses: 1) Figure out your network and host requirements; 2) satisfy host and network requirements; 3) figure out the subnet mask; 4) figure out the network addresses; 5) figure out the directed broadcast addresses; 6) figure out the host addresses.

❏ When satisfying your host and networking requirements, you need to determine how many bits you need to meet your network segment requirements and how many bits you need to satisfy the maximum number of hosts on the largest segment in your network. When you add these two values together, they shouldn't exceed the original number of host bits in the host component of the address.

Determining IP Address Components

❏ Use six steps to figure out the type of address: 1) List the IP address and mask; 2) find the interesting octet in the subnet mask; 3) subtract the interesting octet from 256, which gives you the increment that network addresses are increasing by in the interesting octet; 4) write down the network addresses; 5) beside each network address, write down its directed broadcast address; 6) host addresses are addresses between the network and directed broadcast addresses.

❏ When figuring out directed broadcast addresses, they will be one number less than the next network address.

❏ Network addresses are even numbers, directed broadcast addresses are odd numbers, and host addresses can be either.

❏ Subnet masks determine the context of IP addresses—whether an address is a network, broadcast, or host address.

222 Chapter 7: IP Addressing and Subnetting

SELF TEST

The following Self Test questions will help you measure your understanding of the material presented in this chapter. Read all the choices carefully, as there may be more than one correct answer. Choose all correct answers for each question.

IP Addressing Review

1. A Class B address has _____ host bits.
   A. 8
   B. 16
   C. 20
   D. 24

2. 192.168.256.135 is a Class _____ address.
   A. A
   B. B
   C. C
   D. None of the above

Subnetting

3. Which of the following is a valid subnet mask value?
   A. 255.0.255.255
   B. 0.0.0.255
   C. 255.255.254.0
   D. 255.255.255.256

4. The function of a _____ is to differentiate between the network address, the host addresses, and the directed broadcast address.

IP Address Planning

5. You are given a Class C network with 25 bits for networking. How many subnets do you have?
   A. 1
   B. 2
   C. 3
   D. 4

6. You are given a Class C network with a subnet mask of 255.255.255.248. How many host addresses are there on each subnet?

   A. 4
   B. 6
   C. 8
   D. 14

7. You are given a Class B network with a subnet mask of 255.255.255.192. How many host addresses are there on each subnet?

   A. 30
   B. 62
   C. 126
   D. 254

Determining IP Address Components

8. You are given the following addressing information: 192.168.37.192/25. What type of address is this?

   A. Network
   B. Directed broadcast
   C. Host

9. You are given the following addressing information: 172.17.16.255/23. What type of address is this?

   A. Network
   B. Directed broadcast
   C. Host

10. You are given the following addressing information: 10.0.8.0/22. What type of address is this?

   A. Network
   B. Directed broadcast
   C. Host

SELF TEST ANSWERS

IP Addressing Review

1. ☑ **B.** Class B addresses have 16 host bits and 16 networking bits.
    ☒ **A** is true for Class C networks. **C** is true only for subnetted Class A and B networks. **D** is for Class C networks and subnetted Class A and B networks.

2. ☑ **D.** It's impossible to represent 256 in a byte (see the third octet)—the values range from 0 to 255.
    ☒ **A, B,** and **C** are incorrect.

Subnetting

3. ☑ **C.** 255.255.254.0 is a valid subnet mask—the 1s and 0s must be contiguous.
    ☒ **A** has noncontiguous 1s. **B** is an inverted mask, with the network and host bits reversed. **D** has an invalid mask value in the fourth octet: 256.

4. ☑ The function of a *subnet mask* is to differentiate between the network address, the host addresses, and the directed broadcast address.

IP Address Planning

5. ☑ **B.** Class C networks have 24 bits—this example steals 1 bit. 2 raised to the power of 1 equals 2 subnets.
    ☒ **A, C,** and **D** are incorrect.

6. ☑ **B.** There are 3 host bits, with 2 raised to the power of 3 resulting in 8 addresses in a network, but you lose 2 for the network and directed broadcast address, resulting in 6 host addresses. You could also subtract 248 from 256, resulting in a total of 8 addresses per network, of which the first and last are reserved.
    ☒ **A, C,** and **D** are incorrect.

7. ☑ **B.** There are 6 host bits, with 2 raised to the power of 6, resulting in 64 addresses in a network, but you lose 2 for the network and directed broadcast address, resulting in 62 host addresses. You could also subtract 192 from 256, resulting in a total of 64 addresses in a network—but you can't use the first and the last, so the answer is 62.
    ☒ **A, C,** and **D** are incorrect.

Determining IP Address Components

8. ☑ **C.** There is 1 subnet bit for this Class C network, resulting in two networks—192.168.37.0 and 192.168.37.128—making 192.168.37.192 a host address. Host addresses for this subnet range from 192.168.37.129 to 192.168.37.254.

☒ **A** is true for 192.168.37.0 and 192.168.37.128. **B** is true for 192.168.37.127 and 192.168.37.255.

9. ☑ **C.** Network addresses are incrementing by 2 in the *third* octet. 172.17.16.255 is a host address. Host addresses range from 172.17.16.1 to 172.17.17.254.

☒ **A** is true for 172.17.16.0. **B** is true for 172.17.17.255.

10. ☑ **A.** Network addresses are incrementing by 4 in the third octet. 10.0.8.0 is a network address. Other network addresses include 10.0.0.0, 10.0.4.0, 10.0.8.0, 10.0.12.0, and so on and so forth.

☒ **B** is true for 10.0.3.255, 10.0.7.255, 10.0.11.255, 10.0.15.255, and so on and so forth. **C** is true for 10.0.8.1 to 10.0.11.255, as well as other host addresses in other subnets.

8

VLSM

In Chapter 7, you were introduced to IP addressing and subnetting, including such topics as classes of addresses, address components (network, host, and directed broadcast), and IP address planning. This chapter expands on the topic of IP addressing and introduces two new subjects: *Variable Length Subnet Masks* (VLSM) and route summarization. Because both of these topics expand upon the information you learned in Chapter 7, if you are still trying to grasp the mechanics of IP addressing, please re-read Chapter 7 and practice some more before proceeding to this chapter. You'll need a solid understanding of subnetting to perform VLSM tasks and/or route summarization.

CERTIFICATION OBJECTIVE 8.01

VLSM

VLSM, originally defined in RFC 1812, allows you to apply *different* subnet masks to the *same* class address space. For instance, a good mask for point-to-point links is 255.255.255.252, which provides for two host addresses in each subnet. A good mask for a LAN connection might be 255.255.255.192, which provides for 62 host addresses for each network segment. Using a 255.255.255.252 mask for a LAN connection will not give you enough host addresses, and using a 255.255.255.192 mask on a point-to-point connection wastes addresses. One solution would be to divide the mask values in the middle to limit the waste of addresses, but this doesn't scale well. VLSM solves this problem by letting you use different subnet mask values on the *same* class address space. The following sections cover the advantages that VLSM provides as well as how to use VLSM in your own network.

<table>
<tr><td>w a t c h</td><td>*Remember that the best subnet mask for point-to-point links is 255.255.255.252 (130).*</td></tr>
</table>

Features of VLSM

VLSM lets you have more than one mask for a given class of address, be it a Class A, B, or C network number. Classful protocols, such as Routing Information Protocol (RIP) v1, do not support VLSM. Deploying VLSM requires a routing protocol that is *classless*—Border Gateway Protocol (BGP), Enhanced Interior Gateway Routing Protocol (EIGRP), Intermediate System-Intermediate System (IS-IS),

Open Shortest Path First (OSPF), or RIPv2, for instance. VLSM provides two major advantages:

- Efficient use of addressing in large-scale networks
- Ability to perform route summarization, or route aggregation, to reduce the size of the routing tables in your routers

As these advantage points suggest, VLSM allows you to make more efficient use of IP addressing. Figure 8-1 shows a simple before-and-after example of using VLSM. In this example, a router at the corporate site (RouterA) has point-to-point WAN

FIGURE 8-1   Using VLSM

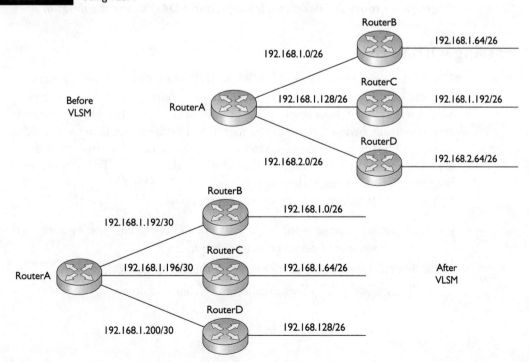

Before VLSM

- 192.168.1.0/26 — RouterB — 192.168.1.64/26
- 192.168.1.128/26 — RouterC — 192.168.1.192/26
- 192.168.2.0/26 — RouterD — 192.168.2.64/26

RouterA

After VLSM

RouterA
- 192.168.1.192/30 — RouterB — 192.168.1.0/26
- 192.168.1.196/30 — RouterC — 192.168.1.64/26
- 192.168.1.200/30 — RouterD — 192.168.128/26

connections to the remote office routers (RouterB, RouterC, and RouterD). The LAN segments at these remote sites have about 50 devices (thus the /26 mask). In the *before* design, a single subnet mask is chosen—255.255.255.192—which allows 62 hosts per subnet. Because of the number of segments, two Class C networks are needed. On the WAN segments, this wastes a lot of addressing space since you need only two host addresses on a point-to-point link.

The bottom part of Figure 8-1 shows a more efficient use of addressing by using VLSM. In this example, the three remote sites have a 255.255.255.192 mask, but the last subnet, 192.168.1.192/26, is assigned a *different* subnet mask. And these little subnetted subnets are then assigned to the point-to-point links of the WAN connections. Given the VLSM solution, only one Class C network is needed to assign addressing to this network. The second advantage of VLSM, route summarization, is discussed later in this chapter.

on the ** Job** *The way subnet zero should be used when performing VLSM is divided into two camps of people. Half prefer using subnet zero as the "subnetted subnet." This was a popular choice a while back when certain operating systems didn't necessarily support subnet zero, but network equipment, such as routers, could. The other half say that today it doesn't matter, since all modern TCP/IP stacks (even those for desktops, laptops, and PDAs) support subnet 0.*

Addressing with VLSM

To use VLSM, you must be very familiar with IP addressing and normal subnetting, as discussed in the last chapter. If you have not yet fully grasped these concepts, VLSM will be out of your reach. If you are still uncomfortable with IP addressing and subnetting, review Chapter 7. As mentioned in the example in the preceding section, VLSM basically means taking a subnet (not a network number) and applying a different subnet mask to this, and only this, subnet. This section covers how to create an efficient addressing scheme using VLSM.

You should follow these steps when performing VLSM:

1. Find the largest segment in the network address space—the segment with the largest number of devices connected to it.

2. Find the appropriate subnet mask for the largest network segment.

3. Write down your subnet numbers to fit your subnet mask.

4. For your smaller segments, take one of these newly created subnets and apply a different, more appropriate, subnet mask to it.

5. Write down your newly subnetted subnets.

6. For even smaller segments, go back to step 4 and repeat this process.

Actually, you can take a subnetted subnet and subnet it again! With this process, you can come up with a very efficient addressing scheme to accommodate addressing needs in your network.

Here's an example: Assume that you have a Class C network (192.168.1.0/24) and three LAN segments—one with 120 hosts, one with 60 hosts, and one with 30 hosts. Assume that subnet 0 is valid. In steps 1 and 2, you find the largest segment and an appropriate subnet mask for it. This would be the segment with 120 hosts. To accommodate the 120 hosts, you would need a subnet mask of 192.168.1.0/25. If you recall from Chapter 7, a /25 subnet mask is 255.255.255.128 in decimal, and with a Class C network, this provides for two subnets with 126 host addresses each. In step 3, write down the newly created subnets: 192.168.1.0/25 and 192.168.1.128/25. You'll assign the first subnet to the large LAN segment. You now have two segments left: 60 and 30 hosts. Again, start with the larger segment first. Next, perform step 4. Which subnet mask is appropriate for 60 devices? If you guessed /26 (255.255.255.192), then you guessed correctly—this gives you 62 host addresses. Apply this subnet mask to the original *remaining* subnet. In step 5, you write down your newly created subnetted subnets by subnetting 192.168.1.128/25: 192.168.1.128/26 and 192.168.1.192/26. Then assign 192.168.1.128/26 to the segment with 60 devices.

This leaves you with one extra subnet. You could easily assign it to this segment, but this segment needs only 30 hosts and the mask has 62 hosts, which is not the most efficient mask. If you want, you can go back to step 4 and repeat the process for this subnet. The subnet mask /27 (255.255.255.224) is a subnet mask that results in 30 host addresses, resulting in two more smaller subnets from the original 192.168.1.192/26 subnet: 192.168.1.192/27 and 192.168.1.224/27. In this example, you have one extra subnet remaining that you could use for future growth! As you can see, with VLSM, you can be very efficient in your IP addressing design.

on the
! o b

You should leave room in each subnet for future growth. For instance, in the preceding example, using a mask of /27 on the 192.168.1.192 subnet creates two more subnets, each with 30 host addresses. If you use this address scheme and the 30-host segment grows, you'll have to go back and re-address a portion of your network, which is not fun.

VLSM Example 1

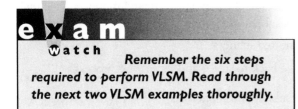

Now that you understand the basics of performing VLSM, let's look at a more difficult example. Consider the network shown in Figure 8-2. In this example, you are given a Class C network: 192.168.2.0/24. You are tasked with using VLSM to accommodate the following requirements: each remote site (total of seven sites) has no more than 30 hosts and this isn't expected to grow in the future. The links between the central and remote routers are point-to-point connections.

You first need to be concerned with handling the largest segments, which are the remote sites with 30 hosts. To handle 30 hosts, you need a 225.255.255.224 (/27) subnet mask. This mask results in the following subnets: 192.168.2.0/27, 192.168.2.32/27, 192.168.2.64/27, 192.168.2.96/27, 192.168.2.128/27, 192.168.2.160/27, 192.168.2.192/27, and 192.168.2.224/27. Assume that subnet 0 is valid for this example.

FIGURE 8-2

VLSM example 1

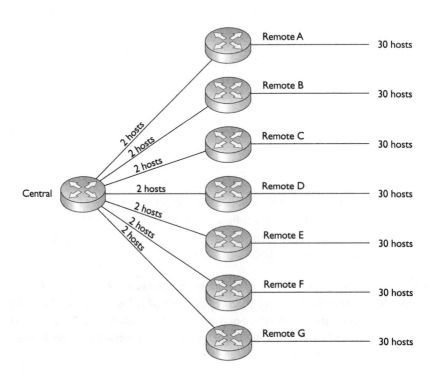

With a /27 mask, you have actually created eight subnets; however, you need only seven for the remote offices. This leaves you one remaining subnet, but you still need to address the seven point-to-point links between the central and remote routers.

Assign the first seven subnets for the remote LAN segments and use the last subnet (192.168.2.224/27) for VLSM and the point-to-point links. To accommodate the point-to-point links, use a 255.255.255.252 (/30) subnet mask, which results in the following subnetted subnets: 192.168.2.224/30, 192.168.2.228/30, 192.168.2.232/30, 192.168.2.236/30, 192.168.2.240/30, 192.168.2.244/30, 192.168.2.248/30, and 192.168.2.252/30.

With a /30 mask on the 192.168.2.224 subnet, you have created eight little subnets with two hosts each. You need only seven subnets for the point-to-point links, which leaves one small subnet remaining. Figure 8-3 shows the actual networking layout based on this example. Notice that this example used two subnet mask values, 255.255.255.224 and 255.255.255.252, with the same Class C network, 192.168.2.0/24.

FIGURE 8-3

VLSM example 1 address design

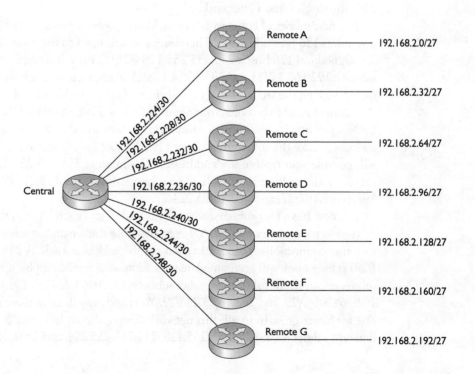

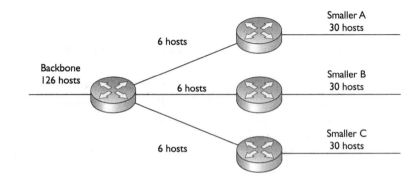

FIGURE 8-4

VLSM example 2

VLSM Example 2

Here's another example, shown in Figure 8-4. You have been given a Class C network: 192.168.3.0/24, with the addressing requirements shown in the figure. You need to come up with a VLSM solution to accommodate all of the network segments with the single Class C network.

The first subnet of concern is the backbone router segment, since it is the largest: it requires 126 host addresses. Therefore, you will need to use a subnet mask that accommodates 126 hosts: 255.255.255.128 (/25). This subnet mask results in two subnets: 192.168.3.0/25 and 192.168.3.128/25. Assign the first subnet to the backbone router, leaving the second subnet for further subnetting with VLSM.

You next need to be concerned about the second largest subnet: the smaller router LAN segments. Each of these locations needs networks that will accommodate 30 host addresses. Take the remaining subnet (192.168.3.128/25) and apply a mask to it that will provide your remote site's addresses. The mask of 255.255.255.224 (/27) will do this for you, resulting in the following subnets: 192.168.3.128/27, 192.168.3.160/27, 192.168.3.192/27, and 192.168.3.224/27.

You now have four subnets, with 30 host addresses each. Assign the first three subnets to your smaller router LAN segments. Use the remaining subnet for your router-to-router connections. These links need six host addresses each. A 255.255.255.248 (/29) subnet mask will accommodate your addressing needs. Applying this to the fourth subnet results in the following smaller subnets: 192.168.3.224/29, 192.168.3.232/29, 192.168.3.240/29, and 192.168.3.248/29. You need only three of these subnets, leaving one for future growth. In all, this network design, shown in Figure 8-5, used three different subnet masks: 255.255.255.128, 255.255.255.224, and 255.255.255.248.

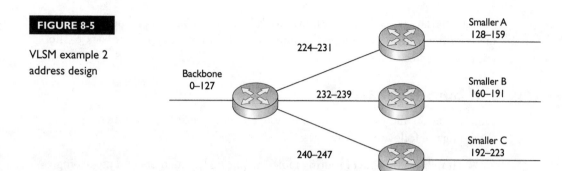

FIGURE 8-5

VLSM example 2 address design

CERTIFICATION OBJECTIVE 8.02

Route Summarization

Route summarization is the ability to take a bunch of contiguous network numbers in your routing table and advertise these contiguous routes as a single summarized or aggregated route. VLSM allows you to summarize subnetted routes back to the class boundary. For instance, if you have 192.168.1.0/24 and have subnetted it to 192.168.1.0/26, giving you four networks, you could summarize these subnets in your routing table and advertise them as the Class C network number 192.168.1.0/24, as shown in Figure 8-6. In this example, the routing entries are reduced from four down to one in your routing updates. Notice in the preceding example that the same class network, 192.168.1.0, has two masks associated with it: 255.255.255.192 and 255.255.255.0.

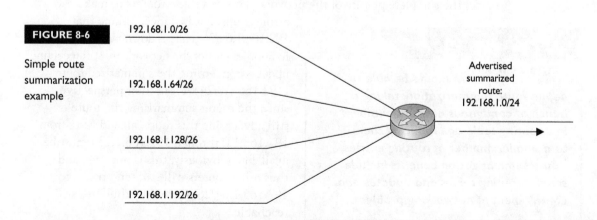

FIGURE 8-6

Simple route summarization example

Summarization is a form of VLSM. With VLSM, you are extending the subnet mask farther to the right, but with summarization, you're collapsing it back to the left of the address.

Advantages of Summarization

Summarization allows you to create a more efficient routing environment by providing the following advantages:

- It reduces the size of routing tables, requiring less memory and processing.
- It reduces the size of routing updates, requiring less bandwidth.
- It contains network problems such as routing flapping.

As you can see from the design shown in Figure 8-6, the size of the routing table update was reduced from four routes to one route, which requires less processing for any routers receiving this information. Thus, less bandwidth is required to advertise the update, and less memory and processing are required on the receiving routers to process the update.

Another advantage of route summarization is that it helps contain certain kinds of network problems. For example, assume that 192.168.1.64/26 was going up and down, up and down (a flapping route). This condition obviously affects the connected router and any router that knows about this specific subnet: every time the route goes up or down, other routers have to incorporate the change in their routing tables. However, routers that know only the summarized route are not affected by the subnet that is flapping. For these routers to be affected, all four subnets would have to fail, causing the router performing the summarization to stop advertising the summarized route.

This, obviously, is an advantage, but it does have a downside. Route summarization *hides* the complete picture of the network. This can cause routers to make bad assumptions. For instance, assume that 192.168.1.64/26 really is down but that routers in another part of the network are still receiving updates concerning the summarized route (192.168.1.0/24). From their perspective, since the router summarizing the route is still advertising this route, all addresses from 192.168.1.0 through 192.168.1.255 must be available. Obviously, this is not true, and thus other routers will still send traffic to 192.168.1.64/26, since they think it's still reachable.

eʂⓧⓐⓜ

ⓦ a t c h **You should be able to define route summarization: taking a bunch of contiguous network numbers in a routing table and reducing them to a smaller number of routing entries. Route summarization benefits include smaller routing tables and updates and containment of networking problems.**

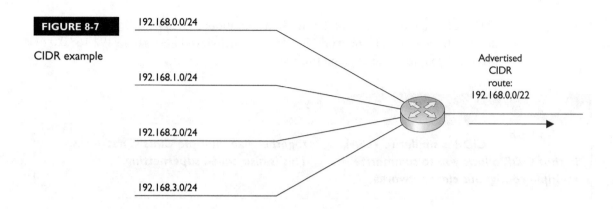

FIGURE 8-7

CIDR example

Classless Interdomain Routing

Classless Interdomain Routing

Classless Interdomain Routing (CIDR), specified in RFC 2050, is an extension to VLSM and route summarization. With VLSM, you can summarize subnets back to the Class A, B, or C network boundary. For example, if you have a Class C network 192.168.1.0/24 and subnet it with a 26-bit mask, you have created four subnets. Using VLSM and summarization, you can summarize these four subnets back to 192.168.1.0/24. CIDR takes this one step further and allows you to summarize a block of contiguous Class A, B, and/or C network numbers. This practice is commonly referred to as *supernetting*. Today's classless protocols support supernetting. However, it is most commonly configured by ISPs on the Internet who use BGP as a routing protocol.

Figure 8-7 shows an example of CIDR. In this example, a router is connected to four Class C networks: 192.168.0.0/24, 192.168.1.0/24, 192.168.2.0/24, and 192.168.3.0/24. The router is summarizing these routes into a single entry: 192.168.0.0/22. Table 8-1 illustrates the bits that are in common in this example. In the first 2 bytes, all bits in the four networks match (192.168). In the third octet, the first 6 bits match, totaling

TABLE 8-1

Common Bits in Summarization

Third Octet Bits								
192.168.0.0	0	0	0	0	0	0	0	0
192.168.1.0	0	0	0	0	0	0	0	1
192.168.2.0	0	0	0	0	0	0	1	0
192.168.3.0	0	0	0	0	0	0	1	1
Bits in Common								

22 bits. Notice the subnet mask for this summarization: 255.255.252.0. This mask, along with the beginning network, 192.168.0.0, includes addresses from 192.168.0.0 to 192.168.3.255, which are behind this router.

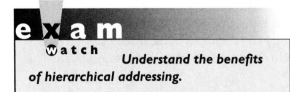

CIDR is similar to VLSM, in that CIDR allows you to summarize multiple contiguous class networks together, like multiple Class C networks. This is also called supernetting.

Hierarchical Addressing

To perform route summarization, you will need to set up your addressing in a hierarchical fashion. Hierarchical addressing provides the following benefits:

- It enables more efficient routing.
- It uses route summarization to decrease the size of routing tables.
- It decreases the amount of memory needed to store the smaller routing tables.
- It decreases the impact on the router when needing to rebuild the routing table.
- It provides a design to simplify your troubleshooting process.

Understand the benefits of hierarchical addressing.

Figure 8-8 shows a simple example of hierarchical addressing. In this example, the network is using 10.0.0.0/8. This is summarized before being sent to another network. This addressing space is broken up into three campuses: 10.1.0.0/16, 10.2.0.0/16, and 10.3.0.0.16. Each of these sets of addresses is summarized when sharing routes between the campuses. Within each campus, the addressing is further broken up for the two buildings: 10.x.1.0/24, 10.x.2.0/24, and so on.

To implement a hierarchical addressing design and to take advantage of route summarization, you'll need a routing protocol that supports VLSM: BGP, EIGRP,

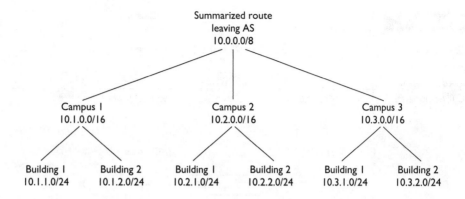

FIGURE 8-8

Simple
hierarchical
addressing
example

IS-IS, OSPF, or RIPv2. When implementing route summarization, you'll need to consider the following:

- The routing protocol must carry the subnet mask with the corresponding network entries it will be advertising.
- Routing decisions must be made on the entire destination IP address.
- To summarize routing entries, they must have the same highest order matching bits (see Table 8-1 as an example).

Routing and Subnet Masks

Remember the three bulleted points dealing with implementation of route summarization.

As mentioned in the preceding section, the routing protocol must carry the subnet mask with the corresponding network entries if you want to take advantage of route summarization. Otherwise, if you had more than one subnet mask applied to a class network number, the router wouldn't know which mask to use when routing a packet to a destination.

A good example of this problem is apparent in classful protocols, such as RIPv1, and how you lay out your IP addresses in your network. With classful protocols, routing updates are sent out with only network entries: no subnet masks are included in the routing updates. The assumption is that the routers on other segments are connected to the same class network and thus know about the subnet mask since it is configured on their interfaces.

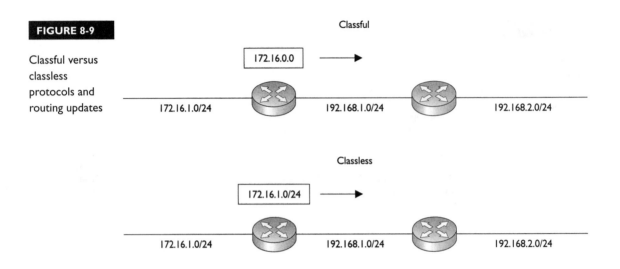

FIGURE 8-9

Classful versus
classless
protocols and
routing updates

If a network number crosses boundaries from one class network to another,
the classful protocol will automatically summarize it to the class address network
number (Class A, B, or C), as is shown in the top part of Figure 8-9. As you can see,
the classful protocol advertises just the network number (172.16.0.0) without any
subnet mask. Plus, since the network number crosses a class boundary (172.16.0.0 to
192.168.1.0), the subnet (172.16.1.0) is not advertised, but instead the class network
number (172.16.0.0) is. The bottom part of Figure 8-9 shows how classless protocols
react when crossing a class boundary (either by default or with configuration). Notice
two things: the subnet mask is included in the routing update, and the routing update
is *not* automatically summarized across the class boundary.

on the
ئ o b

RIPv2 and EIGRP act as classful protocols, by default, and will therefore
automatically summarize across network class boundaries; this can be
manually disabled. You can also configure specific summarized routes.
OSPF, on the other hand, acts as a classless protocol by default and will not
automatically summarize any type of routing information; with OSPF, you
must manually configure summarization.

Given the routing behavior of classful routing protocols, certain addressing designs
will create problems. Consider the network shown in the top part of Figure 8-10.
With a classful protocol like RIPv1, the routers, when advertising networks across a
class boundary, summarize the networks back to their class boundary. In this example,
both RouterA and RouterB advertise 172.16.0.0—they don't advertise their specific

subnets for 172.16.0.0. This creates a problem with RouterC, which receives two routes for 172.16.0.0. If RouterC wanted to reach 172.16.1.0/24, it really wouldn't know to which router (RouterA or RouterB) to send its packets.

Actually, it's a bit more complicated than this. For a basic RIP implementation, the last update received by RouterC would be placed in the route table and the packet would be delivered out the interface to that router. However, half the time it would go to RouterA, and the other half to RouterB, depending on when the route updates were received by RouterC. Were EIGRP used as a routing protocol, though, the metric might make one route better than another, and every packet would go to the one associated with the best metric.

This network design is referred to as a *discontiguous* subnet design—not all of the subnets are connected together. In this network, 172.16.1.0/24 and 172.16.2.0/24 are not connected via another 172.16.0.0 subnet number. This creates routing problems for other routers not connected to the 172.16.0.0 network, and therefore, discontiguous subnet designs are not recommended with classful protocols.

Discontiguous subnets *are*, however, supported by *classless* protocols. As is shown in the bottom part of Figure 8-10, classless protocols include the subnet mask in the routing updates. In this example, RouterC knows exactly where 172.16.1.0/24

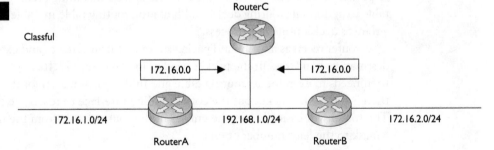

FIGURE 8-10

Discontiguous subnets

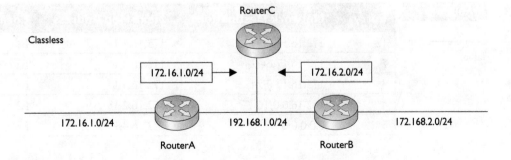

and 172.16.2.0/24 are located, since the mask is included in the routing updates. However, discontiguous subnets are not recommended even with classless protocols, since they limit your ability to summarize routing information in the most efficient fashion. Routing protocols and how routing tables are built are covered in Chapters 15, 19, 20, and 21. For now, keep in mind the main point here: classful routing protocols always advertise the classful network number across network boundaries.

e x a m

ⓦatch

Discontiguous subnets are not supported by classful protocols but are supported by classless protocols.

Classful protocols do not include the subnet mask when advertising network and subnet numbers.

The Routing Table

When implementing route summarization, you'll also need to consider that routing decisions made by a router must be made on the entire destination IP address in the IP packet header. The router always uses the longest matching prefix in the routing table to perform its routing decision. I'll use the routing table in Table 8-2 to illustrate a router's decision-making process.

A router receives an inbound packet on one of its interfaces and examines the destination IP address in the packet header: in this case, 172.16.17.65. The router then needs to examine its routing table and find the *best* match for this packet, and then it routes the packet out the corresponding interface to reach the destination. The router will basically sort the entries in the routing table from the most bits in a mask to the least number of bits.

TABLE 8-2	Entry	Network Destination	Next-Hop Address	Local Interface
Example Routing Table	1	172.16.17.66/32	172.16.1.1	E1
	2	172.16.17.64/24	172.16.2.1	E2
	3	172.16.17.0/24	172.16.3.1	E3
	4	172.16.0.0/16	172.16.2.1	E2
	5	0.0.0.0/0	172.16.4.1	E4

In the preceding routing table, entry 1 isn't a valid match since the mask for the entry indicates a *host* address (32-bit subnet mask). When comparing all 32 bits of 172.16.17.66 with all 32 bits of 172.16.17.65, no match is found. Typically, host address routes are placed in the routing table whenever you have moved a host from its native network segment to another, but, for logistical purposes, you cannot change the address on the host to correspond to its new segment. In other words, you need this host to retain its old IP address.

When comparing entry 2 in the routing table, the router is comparing the first 27 bits of 172.16.17.64 with the first 27 bits of 172.16.17.65, which *do* match. When comparing entry 3, the router compares the first 24 bits of 172.16.17.0 with the first 24 bits of 172.16.17.64, which *also* match. When comparing entry 4, the router compares the first 16 bits of 172.16.0.0 with the first 16 bits of 172.16.17.65, which also match.

When comparing entry 5, the router finds that the entry is a default route and matches any packet. Given this example, the first entry doesn't match, but the last four do match. The router needs to pick *one* entry and use it to route the packet to the destination. When picking an entry, the router uses the one that best matches—the one with the longest number of matching bits. Therefore, the router will use entry 2 in the routing table to route this packet to the corresponding destination.

Performing Summarization

As mentioned earlier, to summarize routing entries, they must have the same highest-order matching bits. In other words, you can perform summarization when the network numbers in question fall within a range of a power-of-2 number—such as 2, 4, 8, 16, and so on—or within a range of a multiple of a power of 2. For example, assume a network number is 4, which is a power of 2. Valid multiples of this value would be 4, 8, 12, 16, and so on. So with network 4, you could include networks 4, 5, 6, and 7 with the correct summarization mask. The network boundary is based on the subnet mask.

For example, if you have a subnet mask of 255.255.255.240, you cannot start the summarization on a network number that is not a multiple of 16 (the number of addresses in a network accommodated by a mask of /28). For instance, 192.168.1.16/28 is a valid summarization for this mask, while 192.168.1.8/28 is not (it doesn't start on a multiple of 16). If the increment is not a power of 2 or a multiple of a power of 2, you can sometimes summarize the addresses into a set of smaller routes. The list of power-of-2 numbers in this case is 0, 2, 4, 8, 16, 32, 64, and 128. Also, when performing summarization, you want to make sure that *all* of the routes that are aggregated are associated with the router (or behind the router) that is advertising the summarized route.

Summarization and Powers of 2

When summarizing, however, remember that you can summarize routes only on a bit boundary (power of 2) or a multiple of a power-of-2 boundary. The trick to summarization is to look at your subnet mask options: 0, 128, 192, 224, 240, 248, 252, 254, and 255. Each of these masks covers a range of numbers, as is shown in Table 8-3. For instance, suppose you have a set of Class C subnets: 192.168.1.0/30 and 192.168.1.4/30. These networks contain a total of eight addresses and start on a power-of-2 boundary: 0. Therefore, you could summarize these as 192.168.1.0/29, which encompasses addresses from 192.168.1.0 through 192.168.1.7.

Let's take a look at another example. Say you have a set of Class C subnets: 192.168.1.64/26 and 192.168.1.128/26. Each of these networks has 64 addresses, for a total of 128 addresses. A mask value that accommodates 128 addresses in a Class C network is 255.255.255.128 (25 bits). However, this subnet mask poses

TABLE 8-3	Mask Value	Range of Numbers	Number of Bits
Summarizing Network Numbers	0	256 numbers	0
	128	128 numbers	1
	192	64 numbers	2
	224	32 numbers	3
	240	16 numbers	4
	248	8 numbers	5
	252	4 numbers	6
	254	2 numbers	7
	255	1 number	8

a problem, since the bit value must be a power of 2 *and* start on a power-of-2 network boundary. With a 25-bit mask, there are only two network numbers: 192.168.1.0/25 and 192.168.1.128/25. The address 192.168.1.64/26 falls under the first network number, and the 192.168.1.128/26 falls under the second one—so even though the two networks are contiguous, they can't be summarized with a 25-bit mask (255.255.255.128). You could use a 24-bit mask (255.255.255.0); however, this includes a total of 256 addresses, not just the 128 addresses in question.

on the
Job

You should summarize only *for addresses that are connected to or behind your router. Otherwise, you could be propagating bad routing information—routes in another part of your network that your router is not connected to. In the just-mentioned example, if 192.168.1.0/26 and 192.168.1.192/26 were also behind your router, you could then summarize all four of these as 192.168.1.0/24.*

All of this can be very confusing for someone just introduced to subnetting and summarization. Summarization is nothing more than listing all the routes and choosing the highest order bits that match to advertise, making sure to exclude those outside your coverage. Summarization usually gets difficult only when you have a poor addressing design in the first place—like the examples you might see on the CCNA exam. In a nutshell, remember that you can create a summary route when the total number of addresses is a power of 2. If it is not a power of 2, you'll have to divide the addresses into smaller groups and summarize them separately. For the purposes of the CCNA exam, simply do the following:

1. Write all possible subnet IDs from the existing diagram, including those outside the router's coverage.

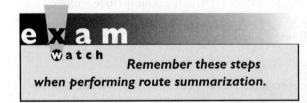

e x a m
ⓦatch
Remember these steps when performing route summarization.

2. Pick the highest order bits that match for only the routes you're summarizing. You will easily see in your bit chart which ones overlap (like that in Table 8-1).

3. Create as many summary routes as you can.

4. Advertise the single (leftover) routes separately.

Summarization Difficulties

The first two summarization examples were pretty simple. Let's look at a more complicated example to illustrate how difficult summarization can be if you don't lay out your addressing correctly in your network. In the network shown

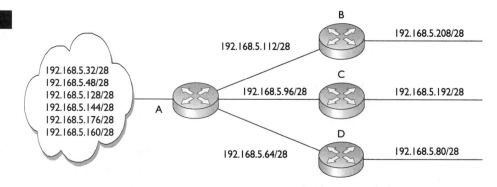

in Figure 8-11, Router A needs to summarize routes to which it and Routers B, C, and D are connected, realizing that other networks reside to the left of Router A. The goal is to have Router A advertise the least number of routes to routers to the networking cloud on the left. Remember that Router A should create summarizations only for the routes that it is connected to or that are behind it (Routers B, C, and D). Also remember that these summarizations should either be a power of 2 or start on a power-of-2 networking boundary.

In this example, the first thing you want to do is put the routes that Router A knows about (those to its right) in numerical order: 192.168.5.64/28, 192.168.5.80/28, 192.168.5.96/28, 192.168.5.112/28, 192.168.5.192/28, and 192.168.5.208/28. Note that other subnets of 192.168.5.0 reside to the left of Router A that should not be included in the summarization. In this example, subnets 64, 80, 96, and 112 are contiguous, and if you use a 26-bit summarization mask, this would accommodate addresses from 64 through 127. These addresses are contiguous, and the summarization mask starts on a power-of-2 network boundary (address 64). To summarize subnets 192 and 208, you would need a 27-bit mask (255.255.255.224), which would include a block of 32 addresses: from 192 through 223.

Router A can advertise the following summarized routes to the left network cloud:

- **192.168.5.64/26**   This covers addresses 64–127, which are to the right of Router A.
- **192.168.5.192/27**   This covers addresses 192–223, which are also to the right of Router A.

As you can see, the number of network entries Router A originally advertised was six network numbers. Through summarization, this was reduced to two summarized routes.

Understand the **exercise to prepare for similar scenarios on**
summarization examples in this section and **the real exam.**
practice summarization in the following

EXERCISE 8-1

ON THE CD

Performing Route Summarization

The preceding sections dealt with route summarization and its advantages and disadvantages. This exercise will reinforce this material by having you look at an example network and come up with summarized routes for a router to reduce the number of routes it advertises to neighboring routers. You'll use the network shown in Figure 8-12. In this example, you need to summarize the routes to the right of Router A, making sure that these summarizations don't overlap any of the addresses in the network to the left of Router A. Please note that there is no guarantee that you can end up with one summary route or that any specific route can be summarized.

1. Write down your networks (to the right of Router A) in numerical order:

   Here are the networks that you want to summarize: 192.168.5.8/29, 192.168.5.16/29, 192.168.5.24/29, 192.168.5.32/29, 192.168.5.40/29, and 192.168.5.56/29.

FIGURE 8-12

Summarization exercise

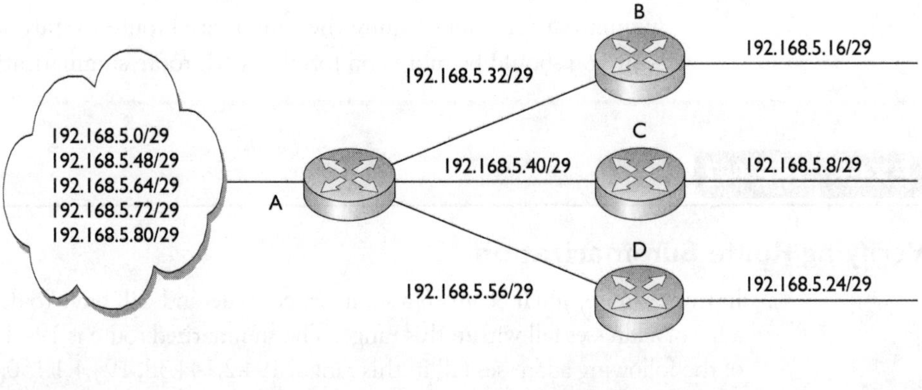

B
192.168.5.16/29

192.168.5.32/29

192.168.5.0/29
192.168.5.48/29
192.168.5.64/29   C
192.168.5.72/29   192.168.5.40/29   192.168.5.8/29
192.168.5.80/29
A

D

192.168.5.56/29   192.168.5.24/29

2. Break up the networks into contiguous blocks of addresses, starting on a power-of-2 network boundary.

    Given that the subnet mask is 255.255.255.248 (29 bits), here are the blocks of addresses:

    ■ 192.168.5.8/29

    ■ 192.168.5.16/29, 192.168.5.24/29

    ■ 192.168.5.32/29, 192.168.5.40/29

    ■ 192.168.5.56/29

    Notice that even though subnets 8 and 16 are contiguous, a summarized mask would have to include subnet 0, which is to the left of Router A. Remember that the summarization must begin on a power-of-2 boundary (or multiple of this) and must correspond to valid network numbers for this mask value.

3. Assign an appropriate *summarized* mask to each of the following contiguous blocks. For the given subnets, here is a list of those that can and can't be summarized, as well as the summarized masks:

    ■ **192.168.5.8/29**   Can't be summarized

    ■ **192.168.5.16/29, 192.168.5.24/29**   Can be summarized:
      192.168.5.16/28

    ■ **192.168.5.32/29, 192.168.5.40/29**   Can be summarized:
      192.168.5.32/28

    ■ **192.168.5.56/29**   Can't be summarized

    The subnet 192.168.5.8/29 can't be summarized, since when you shift one bit to the left in the subnet mask, this would include network 192.168.5.0/29, which is to the left of Router A. Remember that on a 28-bit mask, the networks increase in multiples of 16, starting at 0: 0, 16, 32, 48, 64, and so on. This is also true with 192.168.5.56. Shifting one bit to the left in the summarization would require the summarized route to start at 192.168.5.48. Now you should be more comfortable with route summarization.

EXERCISE 8-2

ON THE CD

Verifying Route Summarization

In this exercise, you'll be given a summarized route and will have to determine whether a list of addresses fall within this range. The summarized route is 194.1.128.0/18. Which of the following addresses fall in this range? 194.2.144.38, 194.1.1.150, 194.1.129.36,

194.1.191.88, or 194.1.64.31. You could approach this solution using one of two methods: Use the subnetting method discussed in Chapter 7 or the method shown in Table 8-1. The first method is shown in step 1 and the second in step 2. For the exam, use the method that is easier for you; however, using step 1 is the quicker of the two choices.

1. List the addresses in numerical order. Based on the subnet mask value, figure out the beginning address in the summarized route and the ending one. Choose the answers that fall between these.

   Here are the addresses in numerical order: 194.1.1.150, 194.1.64.31, 194.1.129.36, 194.1.191.88 and 194.2.144.38. The bit mask is /22; this is 255.255.192.0 in decimal. The summarization is occurring in the *third* octet, where the numbers are incrementing by 64 (256–192). This means the addresses range from 194.1.128.0 to 194.1.191.255. Therefore, the answers are 194.1.129.36 and 194.1.191.88.

2. Your second option is to create a table similar to Table 8-1. Break out the third octet of the summarized route and do the same for the addresses in question. Compare them to determine whether they are included in the summarized route.

   You don't need to write down 194.2.144.38, since its second octet is different from the second octet in the summarized route. Table 8-4 has the binary breakout of the third octet of the summarized route and the remaining addresses shown. Notice that the first two addresses below the summarized route have the first two highest-order binary bits (based on the summarized subnet mask) being different, so they are not included in the summarized route; however, the last two addresses have the two highest order bits matching, so they are included in the summarized route.

TABLE 8-4	Third Octet Bits							
194.1.128.0/18	1	0	0	0	0	0	0	0
194.1.1.150	0	0	0	0	0	0	0	1
194.1.64.31	0	1	0	0	0	0	0	0
194.1.129.36	1	0	0	0	0	0	0	1
194.1.191.255	1	0	1	1	1	1	1	1

Exercise 8-2
Summarization
Comparison

INSIDE THE EXAM

VLSM

You will need to be very comfortable not just with subnetting IP networks, but also with using VLSM to create efficient subnets. Remember the advantages of VLSM: efficient addressing, route summarization, and containment of layer 3 network problems. You need to know how to do VLSM, so remember the 6 steps: 1) find the largest segment; 2) choose a mask for this segment; 3) write down the network numbers; 4) take one of the subnets and apply a different mask to it; 5) write down the newly subnetted subnets; and 6) restart with step 4, if necessary. You will probably have to do something similar to this on the exam.

Route Summarization

Classless protocols, such as EIGRP, OSPF, RIPv2, IS-IS, and BGP, support VLSM and CIDR with route summarization.

Classless protocols advertise network numbers and subnet masks in their routing updates. Remember the advantages of route summarization. Understand the issues of discontiguous subnets and routing.

Routers make routing decisions based on all 32 bits of a destination IP address, looking for the most number of matching bits for a network number and mask in the routing table. Don't be surprised if you see a question on the exam that asks about what route in a routing table will be used to reach a destination.

Practice summarizing routes. Make sure you work through Exercises 8-1 and 8-2 and other exercises like them, since you might see questions similar to these on the exam. Remember that you are limited in time and can't afford to spend more than a minute or two on this process to answer such questions. Practice, practice, and more practice!

CERTIFICATION SUMMARY

VLSM allows you to apply more than one subnet mask to the same class address. VLSM's advantages include more efficient use of addressing and route summarization. Only classless protocols such as RIPv2, EIGRP, OSPF, IS-IS, and BGP support VLSM. To perform VLSM, find the segment with the largest number of devices. Find an appropriate mask for the segment and write down all of your network numbers using this subnet mask. Take one of these newly subnetted network numbers and apply a different subnet mask to it to create more, yet smaller, subnets.

Route summarization is the ability to take a group of contiguous network or subnet entries in your routing table and advertise these entries as a single summarized routing update. Through proper configuration of summarization, your routing table sizes will decrease, the number of advertised network numbers will decrease, and you'll be able to contain certain networking problems, especially flapping routes. CIDR is a special type of route summarization. VLSM allows you to summarize back only to the class boundary of the network: the Class A, B, or C network number. CIDR allows you to summarize a group of contiguous class network numbers.

Summarization can be achieved only by using a hierarchical addressing design in your network. Used with a proper address design, hierarchical addressing allows for more efficient routing: it decreases routing table sizes, the amount of memory for routing, the number of processing cycles required, and simplifies routing troubleshooting. When implementing route summarization, note that the routing protocol must carry the subnet mask along with the routing entry: only classless protocols allow this process. And since the mask is carried with the network number, discontiguous subnets are supported with classless protocols, but not classful ones. When the router makes routing decisions, it will use the entire destination IP address to make them.

When creating summarized entries, note that the network numbers being summarized must have the same highest order matching bits. Remember that you can summarize routes only on a bit boundary, which is a power of 2, or a multiple of a power of 2. When summarizing, you need to know the ranges of addresses a mask value in an octet covers; for example, a subnet mask value of 192 covers 64 numbers.

✓ # TWO-MINUTE DRILL

VLSM

❑ VLSM allows you to have different subnet masks applied to the same class address.

❑ Classless protocols, such as BGP, IS-IS, OSPF, and RIPv2, support VLSM.

❑ VLSM uses addressing more efficiently and allows you to configure route summarization.

❑ When setting up a network with VLSM, first find the largest segment. Then find an appropriate subnet mask for this network. Write down the subnet numbers according to this mask. For smaller segments, take one of the subnets and subnet it further, writing down your newly subnetted subnets.

Route Summarization

❑ Route summarization is the ability to take a bunch of contiguous network numbers in your routing table and advertise these contiguous routes as a single summarized route. The summarization must begin on a power-of-2 boundary (or a multiple of a power of 2).

❑ Summarization reduces the routing table size, reduces the bandwidth required for routing updates, and contains network problems. Proper summarization requires a hierarchical addressing design in your network.

❑ CIDR, commonly called supernetting, allows you to summarize routes to the left of the class boundary, such as a group of Class C networks.

❑ Routing protocols must carry the subnet mask with the network entry to perform route summarization. Routing decisions must be made on the entire destination IP address. Summarization requires that the routing entries have the same highest order matching bits.

❑ Classful protocols have problems with discontiguous subnet masks; classless protocols do not.

SELF TEST

The following Self Test questions will help you measure your understanding of the material presented in this chapter. Read all the choices carefully, as there may be more than one correct answer. Choose all correct answers for each question.

VLSM

1. Which protocol supports VLSM?
   A. RIPv2
   B. IGRP
   C. RIP and IGRP
   D. None of these

2. You are given a Class C network, 192.168.1.0/24. You need one network with 120 hosts and two networks with 60 hosts. How many subnet masks do you need?

   A. 1
   B. 2
   C. 3
   D. 4

3. You are given a Class C network, 192.168.1.0/24. You need one network with 120 hosts and three networks with 60 hosts. What subnet mask values would you use?
   A. 255.255.255.128 and 255.255.255.192
   B. 255.255.255.128
   C. 255.255.255.192
   D. None of these

4. You are given a Class C network, 192.168.1.0/24. You need three networks with 60 hosts and two networks with 30 hosts. What are the subnet mask values you could use? (Choose two answers.)
   A. 255.255.255.128 and 255.255.255.192
   B. 255.255.255.224 and 255.255.255.240
   C. 255.255.255.192 and 255.255.255.224
   D. None of these

5. You are given this address space: 172.16.5.0/25. You need one network with 64 hosts and two with 30 hosts. What are the most specific subnet mask values to use?

   A. /25 and /26

   B. /26 and /27

   C. /27 and /28

   D. None of these

6. You are given a Class C network and you have four LAN segments with the following numbers of devices: 120, 60, 30, and 30. What subnet mask values would you use to accommodate these segments?

   A. /24, /25, and /26

   B. /25, /26, and /27

   C. /26, /27, and /28

   D. None of these

Route Summarization

7. VLSM allows you to summarize _____ back to the Class A, B, or C network boundary.

   A. Subnets

   B. Networks

8. Which of the following is not an advantage of route summarization?

   A. It requires less memory and processing.

   B. It supports smaller routing update sizes.

   C. It helps contain network problems such as flapping routes.

   D. It supports discontiguous subnets.

9. _____ allows you to create this summarization: 10.0.0.0/7.

   A. Subnetting

   B. CDR

   C. Supernetting

   D. VLSM

10. Which of the following are classless protocols?

    A. IGRP

    B. EIGRP

    C. IGRP and EIGRP

    D. Neither IGRP or EIGRP

11. A routing protocol that supports route summarization must perform all except which of the following?

    A. Carry the subnet mask with the network entry.

    B. Make routing decisions based on the entire destination IP address.

    C. Summarize entries so that the same lowest order bits match.

    D. None of these is correct.

12. You have the following two routes: 192.168.1.64/27 and 192.168.1.96/27. Enter the most specific summarized route for these two subnets: _____.

13. You have the following four routes: 192.168.1.32/30, 192.168.1.36/30, 192.168.1.40/30, and 192.168.1.44/30. Enter the most specific summarized route for these four subnets: _____.

SELF TEST ANSWERS

VLSM

1. ☑ **A.** RIPv2 supports VLSM (RIPv1 does not).
   ☒ **B** is classful and doesn't support VLSM. **C** includes a classful protocol. **A** is a correct answer, so **D** is incorrect.

2. ☑ **B.** You need two subnet masks: 255.255.255.128 (/25) and 255.255.255.192 (/26). This creates three networks, for instance, 192.168.1.0/25, 192.168.128/26, and 192.168.1.192/26.
   ☒ Therefore answers **A**, **C**, and **D** are incorrect.

3. ☑ **D.** None of these answers is correct because this is impossible with a single Class C network. This is impossible because 120 hosts require a 255.255.255.128 mask, which is half a Class C network; 60 hosts require a 255.255.255.192 mask, but you need three of these, which is three-quarters of a Class C network.
   ☒ **A** is incorrect because it accommodates only the 120-host and two 60-host segments. **B** is incorrect because it accommodates only two subnets. **C** is incorrect because it accommodates the three 60-host segments, but not the 120-host segment.

4. ☑ **A and C.** Answer **A** creates one 126-host segment and two 62-host segments. Answer **C** creates three 62-host segments and two 30-host segments.
   ☒ **B** is incorrect because the second mask supports only 14 hosts. **D** is incorrect because A and C are correct answers.

5. ☑ **D.** None of these answers is correct. Sixty-four hosts require a 25-bit mask, and you are only given this to begin with—62 hosts would work with a 26-bit mask.
   ☒ **A**, **B**, and **C** don't support enough addresses.

6. ☑ **B.** A bit mask of 25 creates two networks: 0 and 128. If you take one of these subnets and apply a 26-bit mask, you have two more networks, such as 128 and 192. Taking one of these two subnets, applying a 27-bit mask creates two more subnets, such as 192 and 224.
   ☒ **A** and **C** don't support enough addresses to accommodate all four LAN segments. **D** is incorrect because B is the correct answer.

Route Summarization

7. ☑ **A.** VLSM allows you to summarize subnets back to the Class A, B, or C network boundary.
   ☒ **B** is a non-subnetted address space and therefore is a Class A, B, or C network number and can't be summarized with VLSM, but it can be summarized with CIDR.

8. ☑ **D.** Discontiguous subnets are supported by classless protocols, but they are not an advantage of summarization. Actually, summarization is more difficult if you have discontiguous subnets.
    ☒ **A**, **B**, and **C** are advantages of route summarization.

9. ☑ **C.** Supernetting, or CIDR, supports summarization of contiguous blocks of Class A, B, or C networks.
    ☒ **A** is the opposite of summarization. **B** should be CIDR, not CDR. **D** is incorrect because VLSM allows you to summarize subnets, not networks.

10. ☑ **B.** EIGRP, as well as IS-IS, BGP, OSPF, and RIPv2, is a classless protocol.
    ☒ **A** is incorrect because IGRP is not a classless protocol. **C** is incorrect because the answer includes a classful protocol (IGRP). **D** is incorrect because B is the correct answer.

11. ☑ **C.** Summarized entries must have the same *highest*-order matching bits, not lowest.
    ☒ **A** and **B** are things a routing protocol supporting route summarization must perform. **D** is incorrect because answer C is correct.

12. ☑ **192.168.1.64/26**: this includes addresses from 192.168.1.64 through 192.168.1.127.

13. ☑ **192.168.1.32/28**: this includes addresses from 192.168.1.32 through 192.168.1.47.

9

TCP/IP and the Transport Layer

C hapters 6 and 7 focused on TCP/IP's Internet layer—comparable to layer 3 of the OSI Reference Model. This chapter moves up one layer and talks about how the transport layer functions at layer 4. It discusses two additional TCP/IP protocols: the Transmission Control Protocol (TCP) and the User Datagram Protocol (UDP). These two protocols are responsible for moving user data between network components.

CERTIFICATION OBJECTIVE 9.01

Transport Layer Functions

The TCP/IP transport layer is responsible for providing a *logical* connection between two hosts and can provide these functions:

- Flow control (through the use of windowing)
- Reliable connections (through the use of sequence numbers and acknowledgments)
- Session multiplexing (through the use of port numbers and IP addresses)
- Segmentation (through the use of segment protocol data units, or PDUs)

TCP/IP's transport layer can provide for flow control, reliable connections, session multiplexing, and segmentation.

Flow Control

Flow control, introduced in Chapter 2, is used to ensure that the destination doesn't become overwhelmed by the source sending too much information at once. Two kinds of flow control exist: ready/not-ready signals and windowing. Recall from Chapter 2 that ready/not-ready signals are not very efficient when a lot of delay is present in the data transmission. For example, if the destination's receive buffer fills up and the destination sends a not-ready signal to the source, the source could still be sending data that the destination would have to drop. And when the destination is ready to start receiving again, the destination sends a ready signal to the source to start sending stuff, introducing a delay before the source can actually begin sending again. This delay can be significant, causing the throughput of the session to drop dramatically.

Windowing is a much more efficient process, since the size of the window determines how many segments can be sent before waiting for an acknowledgment to send the next batch of segments. A good windowing flow control implementation will use a sliding scale, allowing for the size of the window to change based on events occurring at both the source and destination and any congestion or extra bandwidth available between these devices.

Reliability

Reliability is not necessary in all communications. For example, in a voice or video conversation, missing a packet every now and then will probably not be noticeable to the receiver. However, if a file was being transferred, missing even one packet would corrupt the entire file.

When reliability is necessary, it should cover these four items:

- Recognizing lost packets and having them re-sent
- Recognizing packets that arrive out of order and reordering them
- Detecting duplicate packets and dropping the extra ones
- Avoiding congestion

Most protocols with built-in reliability use sequence and acknowledgment numbers to deal with the first three bullet points. However, how they deal with resending any missed data depends on the protocol's implementation, as was discussed in Chapter 2. In a best case scenario, the source will resend only those PDUs that were not received by the destination: the destination sends a list of sequence numbers not received and the source resends only those. Most reliable protocols, however, use a simpler but less efficient approach: the destination will send the sequence number of the very first PDU not received and the source will resend that PDU and all subsequent PDUs. A large window size can be efficient if the source is constantly sending a large batch of PDUs, but if the lost PDU is toward the beginning in the sequencing, lots of unnecessary retransmissions result.

Multiplexing

Multiplexing is the ability of a single host to have multiple concurrent sessions open to one or many other hosts. A *session* occurs when the source opens a connection by sending one or more PDUs and typically, but not always, receives a reply from the destination. A session can be reliable or unreliable and may or may not involve flow control. To handle multiplexing, a transport layer protocol must be able to distinguish between each session to each destination host. Some protocols assign a number to the session, called a *session number*, to identify the session uniquely. TCP/IP uses a more complicated process that accomplishes basically the same thing.

Segmentation

Segmentation is the process of breaking up data into smaller, identifiable PDUs at the transport layer. In TCP/IP, the transport layer packages application layer data into *segments* to send to a destination device. The remote destination is responsible for taking the data from these segments and directing it to the correct application. One component of the segment must contain information that will help the destination in the forwarding process, such as specifying the application that is supposed to process the encapsulated data.

CERTIFICATION OBJECTIVE 9.02

Transport Layer Protocols

TCP/IP uses two transport layer protocols: TCP and UDP. The following two sections discuss these protocols in depth and describe their characteristics and the segmentation they use, including the layout of their segment headers.

Transmission Control Protocol

TCP uses a reliable delivery system to deliver layer 4 segments to the destination. This would be analogous to using a certified, priority, or next-day service with the US Postal Service. For example, with a certified letter, the receiver must sign for it, indicating the destination actually received the letter: proof of the delivery is provided. TCP operates under a similar premise: it can detect whether or not the destination received a sent segment. With the postal example, if the certified letter got lost, it would be up to you to resend it; with TCP, you don't have to worry about what was or wasn't received—TCP will take care of all the tracking and any necessary resending of lost data for you.

TCP's main responsibility is to provide a reliable full-duplex, connection-oriented, logical service between two devices. TCP goes through a three-way handshake to establish a session before data can be sent (discussed later in the "TCP's Three-Way Handshake" section). Both the source and destination can simultaneously send data across the session. It uses windowing to implement flow control so that a source device doesn't overwhelm a destination with too many segments. It supports data recovery, where any missed or corrupted information can be re-sent by the source. Any packets that arrive out of order, because the segments traveled different paths to reach the destination, can easily be reordered, since segments use sequence numbers to keep track of the ordering.

TCP transmits information between devices in a data unit called a segment, as mentioned earlier. Recall from Chapter 6 that the IP datagram contains a protocol field, indicating the protocol that is encapsulated in the payload. In the case of TCP, the protocol field contains 6 as a value, indicating that a TCP segment is encapsulated.

Table 9-1 shows the components of a segment. The segment is composed of a header, followed by the application data. Without any options, the TCP header is 20 bytes in length.

TABLE 9-1		TCP Segment Components
TCP Field Name	**Length (in bits)**	**Definition**
Source Port	16	Identifies which application is sending the information
Destination Port	16	Identifies which application is to receive the information
Sequence Number	32	Maintains reliability and sequencing
Acknowledgment Number	32	Used to acknowledge received information
Header Length	4	Number of 32-bit words that make up the header
Reserved Field	3	Currently not used (set to all zeroes)
Code Bits	9	Defines control functions, such as synchronization
Window Size	16	Indicates the number of segments allowed to be sent before waiting for an acknowledgment from the destination
Checksum	16	Cyclic redundancy check (CRC) of the header and encapsulated application data
Urgent Field	16	Points to any urgent data in the segment
Options	0–32	The only option currently defined is the maximum TCP segment size to use for the session
Data	Variable	Application data (not part of the TCP header)

User Datagram Protocol

UDP uses a best-effort delivery system, similar to how first class and lower postal services of the US Postal Service work. With a first class letter, you place the destination address and return address on the envelope, put it in your mailbox, and hope that it arrives at the destination. With this type of service, nothing guarantees that the letter will actually arrive at the destination, but in most instances, it does. If, however, the letter doesn't arrive at the destination, it's up to you, the letter writer, to resend the letter: the post office isn't going to perform this task for you. UDP operates under the same premise: it does not guarantee the delivery of the transport layer segments.

While TCP provides a reliable connection, UDP provides an unreliable connection. UDP doesn't go through a three-way handshake to set up a connection—it simply begins sending the data. Likewise, UDP doesn't check to see whether sent segments were received by a destination; in other words, it doesn't use an acknowledgment process. Typically, if an acknowledgment process is necessary, the transport layer (UDP) won't provide it; instead, the application itself, at the application layer, will provide this verification.

Given these deficiencies, UDP does have an advantage over TCP: it has less overhead. For example, if you need to send only one segment and receive one segment in reply, and that's the end of the transmission, it makes no sense to go through a three-way handshake to establish a connection and then send and receive the two segments; this is not efficient. DNS queries are a good example in which the use of UDP makes sense. Voice and video are two other applications that commonly use UDP; assuming that the network path to the destination is fairly reliable and not many packets are dropped, the listener in a phone conversation or the viewer in a video application probably won't notice that every now and then a packet is lost. Of course, if you are sending a large amount of data to a destination, and you need to verify that all of it was received, TCP would be a better transport mechanism.

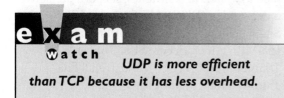

e x a m

⒲ a t c h *UDP is more efficient than TCP because it has less overhead.*

When transmitting a UDP segment, an IP header will show *17* as the protocol number in the protocol field. Table 9-2 shows the components of a UDP segment. Notice the many differences between UDP and TCP segments. First, since UDP is connectionless, sequence and acknowledgment numbers are not necessary. Second, since there is no flow control, a window size field is not needed. As you can see, UDP is a lot simpler and more efficient than TCP. Its only reliability component, like TCP, is a checksum field, which allows UDP, at the destination, to detect a bad UDP segment and then drop it. Any control functions or other reliability functions that need to be implemented for the session are not accomplished at the transport layer; instead, these are handled at the application layer.

TABLE 9-2			
UDP Field Name	**Length (in bits)**	**Definition**	
Source Port	16	Identifies the sending application	
Destination Port	16	Identifies the receiving application	
Length	16	Denotes the size of the UDP segment	
Checksum	16	Provides a CRC on the complete UDP segment	
Data	Variable	Application data (not part of the UDP header)	

UDP Segment Components

CERTIFICATION OBJECTIVE 9.03

TCP and UDP Applications

One main difference between the OSI Reference Model and TCP/IP's model is that TCP/IP lumps together the application, presentation, and session layers into one layer, called the *application layer*, as discussed in Chapter 6. Hundreds and hundreds of TCP/IP applications are available. The most common ones are used to share information, such as file transfers, e-mail communications, and web browsing.

<table>
<tr><td></td><td>

Some applications encrypt their data, such as SSH and HTTPS (HTTP with SSL).
</td></tr>
</table>

Table 9-3 briefly describes some of the applications and their usage. Here are some common TCP/IP applications, Cisco devices, such as routers and switches, support: domain name service (DNS), HTTP and HTTPS, Simple Network Management Protocol (SNMP), telnet, Secure Shell (SSH), File Transfer Protocol (FTP), and Trivial File Transfer Protocol (TFTP).

TABLE 9-3	Application Usage	Applications/Protocols
Common TCP/IP Applications and Protocols	File transfers	FTP, TFTP, Network File System (NFS), Remote Procedure Call (RCP)
	Content	HTTP, HTTPS, gopher (HTTPS encrypts traffic)
	E-mail	SMTP, Post Office Protocol 3 (POP)3, Internet Message Access Protocol version 4 (IMAP4)
	Remote login	Telnet, rlogin, RSH, SSH (of these, only SSH encrypts traffic, the rest send traffic in clear text)
	Network management	SNMP
	Name management	DNS
	Voice	Skinny Station Protocol, Session Initiation Protocol (SIP), H.323
	Video	Real Time Streaming Protocol (RTSP), H.323

Ports

TCP/IP's transport layer uses port numbers and IP addresses to multiplex sessions between multiple hosts. If you look back at Tables 9-1 and 9-2, you'll see that both the TCP and UDP headers have two port fields: a source port and a destination port. These, as well as the source and destination IP addresses in the IP header, are used to identify each session uniquely between two or more hosts. As you can see from the port number field, the port numbers are 16 bits in length, allowing for port numbers from 0 to 65,535 (a total of 65,536 ports).

Port numbers fall under three types:

- **Well-known** These port numbers range from 0 to 1023 and are assigned by the Internet Assigned Number Authority (IANA) to applications commonly used on the Internet, such as HTTP, DNS, and SMTP.

- **Registered** These port numbers range from 1024 to 49,151 and are assigned by IANA for proprietary applications, such as Microsoft SQL Server, Shockwave, Oracle, and many others.

- **Dynamically assigned** These port numbers range from 49,152 to 65,535 and are dynamically assigned by the operating system to use for a session.

When you want to connect to an application on a destination host, the source port field in the TCP or UDP header will have a dynamically assigned port; the destination port field will have either a well-known or registered port number, depending on the application to which you are connecting. The destination host can use this information to determine what application needs to process the session data.

You can find a list of the port numbers and names at www.iana.org/assignments/port-numbers. Note that some of the applications support TCP, some UDP, and some both, such as DNS. DNS uses UDP for DNS queries and resolutions, but it uses TCP to copy name resolution tables between DNS servers.

e x a m

Ⓦ a t c h *Remember a few examples of applications (and their ports) that use TCP: HTTP (80), FTP (21), POP3 (110), SMTP (25), SSH (22), and telnet (23). Remember a few examples of UDP applications, along with their assigned port numbers: DNS queries (53), RIP (520), SNMP (161), and TFTP (69).*

Application Mapping

TCP and UDP provide a multiplexing function for simultaneously supporting multiple sessions to one or more hosts: This allows multiple applications to send and receive data to many devices simultaneously. With these protocols, port numbers (at the transport layer) and IP addresses (at the Internet layer) are used to differentiate the sessions.

As shown in Tables 9-1 and 9-2, however, two port numbers are included in the segment: source and destination. When you initiate a connection to a remote application, your operating system should pick a currently unused dynamic port number from 49,152 to 65,535 and assign this number as the source port number in the TCP or UDP header. Based on the application that is running, the application will fill in the destination port number with the well-known or registered port number of the application. When the destination receives this segment, it looks at the destination port number and knows by which application this segment should be processed. This is also true for traffic returning from the destination.

Let's look at an example, shown in Figure 9-1, that uses TCP for multiplexing sessions. In this example, PC-A has two telnet connections between itself and the server. You can tell these are telnet connections by examining the destination port number (23). When the destination receives the connection setup request, it knows that it should start up the telnet process. Also notice that the source port number is *different* for each of these connections (50,000 and 50,001). This allows both the PC and the server to differentiate between the two separate telnet sessions. This is a simple example of multiplexing connections.

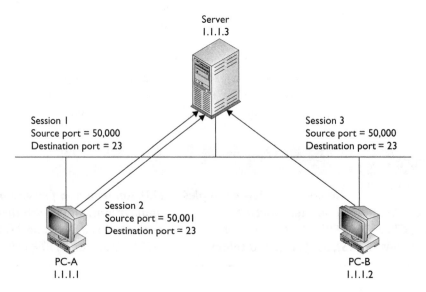

FIGURE 9-1

Multiplexing connections

Of course, if more than one device is involved, things become more complicated. In the example shown in Figure 9-1, PC-B also has a session to the server. This connection has a source port number of 50,000 and a destination port number of 23—another telnet connection. This brings up an interesting dilemma. How does the server differentiate between PC-A's connection that has port numbers 50,000/23 and PC-B's, which has the same? Actually, the server uses not only the port numbers at the transport layer to multiplex sessions, but also the *layer 3* IP addresses of the devices associated with these sessions. In this example, notice that PC-A and PC-B have *different* layer 3 addresses: 1.1.1.1 and 1.1.1.2, respectively.

Figure 9-2 shows a simple example of using port numbers between two computers. PC-A opens up two telnet sessions to PC-B. Notice that the source port numbers on PC-A are different, which allows PC-A to differentiate between the two telnet sessions. The destination ports are 23 when sent to PC-B, which tells PC-B which application should process the segments. Notice that when PC-B returns data to PC-A, the port numbers are reversed, since PC-A needs to know what application this is from (telnet) and which session is handling the application.

e✗am

ⓦatch

No matter where a session begins, or how many sessions a device encounters, a host can easily differentiate between various sessions by examining the *source and destination port numbers as well as the source and destination layer 3 IP addresses.*

FIGURE 9-2

Using port numbers

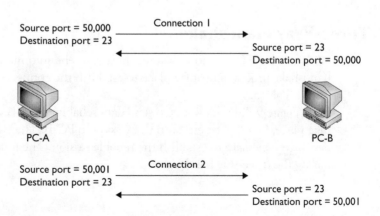

CERTIFICATION OBJECTIVE 9.04

Session Establishment

TCP and UDP use completely different processes when establishing a session with a remote peer. As you probably already have guessed, UDP uses a fairly simple process. With UDP, one of two situations will occur that indicate that the session is established:

- The source sends a UDP segment to the destination and receives a response
- The source sends a UDP segment to the destination

As to which of the two are used, that depends on the application. And as to when a UDP session is over, that is also application-specific:

- The application can send a message, indicating that the session is now over, which could be part of the data payload
- An idle timeout is used, so if no segments are encountered over a predefined period, the application assumes the session is over

TCP, on the other hand, is much more complicated. It uses what is called a *defined state machine*. A defined state machine defines the actual mechanics of the beginning of the state (building the TCP session), maintaining the state (maintaining the TCP session), and ending the state (tearing down the TCP session). The following sections cover TCP's mechanics in much more depth.

TCP's Three-Way Handshake

With reliable TCP sessions, before a host can send information to another host, a handshake process must take place to establish the connection. Figure 9-3 shows the steps involved.

In Figure 9-3, PC-A wants to send data reliably to PC-B via TCP. Before this can take place, PC-A must establish the session to PC-B. The two hosts go through a *three-way handshake* to establish the reliable session. The following three steps occur during the three-way handshake:

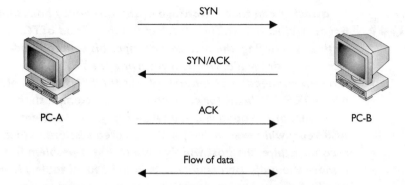

FIGURE 9-3

Setting up
a reliable
connection: three-
way handshake

1. The source sends a synchronization (SYN) segment (where the SYN control flag is set in the TCP header) to the destination, indicating that the source wants to establish a reliable session.

2. The destination responds with both an acknowledgment and synchronization in the same segment. The acknowledgment indicates the successful receipt of the source's SYN segment, and the destination's SYN flag indicates that a session can be set up (it's willing to accept the setup of the session). Together, these two flag settings in the TCP segment header are commonly referred to as SYN/ACK; they are sent together in the same segment header.

3. Upon receiving the SYN/ACK, the source responds with an ACK segment (where the ACK flag is set in the TCP header). This indicates to the destination that its SYN was received by the source and that the session is now fully established.

Once the three-way handshake has occurred, data can be transferred across the session. Because the connection was established first, this type of service is referred to as *connection-oriented*. Remember that this type of connection always goes through a three-way handshake before one device can start sending and receiving information from another.

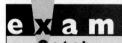

*TCP uses a three-step,
three-way handshake to set up a*

*reliable connection: SYN, SYN/ACK,
and ACK.*

on the
job

An attacker can take advantage of the three-way handshake process to wreak havoc against a host. The attacker spoofs a flood of TCP SYN segments to a victim. In spoofing, the attacker changes his source IP address to something else—valid or invalid. The host receiving the TCP SYNs assumes that each one is a new connection attempt: it places the SYNs in a local table and responds with a TCP SYN/ACK for each connection attempt; then it waits for the third part of the handshake, an ACK reply. The problem with this is that an ACK reply will never arrive for the spoofed sessions. Typically, after 30 to 60 seconds expire, the host will figure out that a problem has occurred and will remove the half-open connection from its local table. However, the local table can fit only so many connections before it begins to deny new ones—both spoofed and valid ones. This is a problem with TCP. A good firewall or intrusion prevention/detection system solution should be able to deal with this problem effectively.

TCP's Sequencing and Acknowledgments

One of the ways TCP provides a reliable session between devices is by using sequence numbers and acknowledgments. Every TCP segment sent has a sequence number in it. This not only helps the destination reorder any incoming segments that arrived out of order, but it also provides a method of verifying whether all the sent segments were received. The destination responds to the source with an acknowledgment indicating receipt of the sent segments.

Before TCP can provide a reliable session, it has to go through a synchronization phase—the three-way handshake. Let's expand upon that process by introducing sequence and acknowledgment numbers to the process:

1. The source sends a synchronization frame with the SYN bit marked in the Code field. This segment contains an initial sequence number. This is referred to as a *SYN segment*.

2. Upon receipt of the SYN segment, the destination responds with its own segment, with its own initial sequence number and the appropriate value in the Acknowledgment field indicating the receipt of the source's original SYN segment. This notifies the source that the original SYN segment was received. This is referred to as a *SYN/ACK segment* and the appropriate bits in the Code field are marked.

3. Upon receipt of the SYN/ACK segment, the source will acknowledge receipt of this segment by responding to the destination with an ACK segment, which has the Acknowledgment field set to an appropriate value based on the destination's sequence number and the appropriate bit set in the Code field.

Here is a simple example of a three-way handshake with sequence and acknowledgment numbers:

1. Source sends a SYN: sequence number = 1
2. Destination responds with a SYN/ACK: sequence number = 10, acknowledgment = 2
3. Source responds with an ACK segment: sequence number = 2, acknowledgment = 11

In this example, the destination's acknowledgment (step 2) number is one greater than the source's sequence number, indicating to the source that the next segment expected is 2. In the third step, the source sends the second segment, and, within the same segment in the Acknowledgment field, indicates the receipt of the destination's segment with an acknowledgment of 11—one greater than the sequence number in the destination's SYN/ACK segment.

exam
⑩atch

When acknowledging a received segment, the destination returns a segment with a number in the *acknowledgment field that is one number higher than the received sequence number.*

TCP's Flow Control and Windowing

TCP allows the regulation of the flow of segments, ensuring that one host doesn't flood another host with too many segments, overflowing its receiving buffer. TCP uses a sliding windowing mechanism to assist with flow control. For example, if the window size is 1, a host can send only one segment and must then wait for a corresponding acknowledgment before sending the next segment. If the window size is 20, a host can send 20 segments and must wait for the single acknowledgment of the sent 20 segments before sending 20 additional segments. Windowing is discussed in Chapter 2.

TCP employs a positive acknowledgment with retransmission (PAR) mechanism to recover from lost segments. The same segment will be repeatedly re-sent, with a delay between each segment, until an acknowledgment is received from the destination. The acknowledgment contains the sequence number of the segment received and verifies receipt of all segments sent prior to the retransmission process. This eliminates the need for multiple acknowledgments and resending acknowledgments.

The larger the window size for a session, the less number of acknowledgments sent, thus making the session more efficient. Too small a window size can affect throughput, since a host has to send a small number of segments, wait for an acknowledgment, send another bunch of small segments, and wait again. The trick is to figure out an optimal window size that allows for the best efficiency based on the current conditions in the network and on the two hosts' current capabilities.

A nice feature of this TCP windowing process is that the window size can be dynamically changed through the lifetime of the session. This is important because many more sessions may arrive at a host with varying bandwidth needs. Therefore, as a host becomes saturated with segments from many different sessions, it can, assuming that these sessions are using TCP, lower the window size to slow the flow of segments it is receiving. Likewise, a congestion problem might crop up in the network between the source and destination, where segments are being lost; the window size can be lowered to accommodate this problem and, when the network congestion disappears, can be raised to take advantage of the extra bandwidth that now exists in the network path between the two.

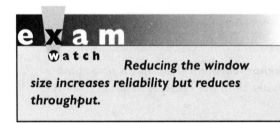

Reducing the window size increases reliability but reduces throughput.

What makes this situation even more complicated is that the window sizes on the source and destination hosts can be *different* for a session. For instance, PC-A might have a window size of 3 for the session, while PC-B has a window size of 10. In this example, PC-A is allowed to send ten segments to PC-B before waiting for an acknowledgment, while PC-B is allowed to send only three segments to PC-A.

INSIDE THE EXAM

TCP/IP's Transport Layer

At this point, after detailing some of the basics in Chapter 2 concerning the transport layer, a lot of this material should be familiar to you. Don't expect many questions on the exam related to information in this chapter. The exam questions should be fairly simple and straightforward.

Be familiar with the common applications that use TCP and UDP as well as their port numbers. Understand how TCP sessions get built with the three-way handshake and how TCP implements windowing. Know the differences between the TCP and UDP headers.

CERTIFICATION SUMMARY

TCP/IP has five layers: application, transport, Internet, data link, and physical. This chapter focuses on protocols used at the transport layer: TCP and UDP. TCP provides a reliable connection through the use of sequence numbers and acknowledgments. TCP uses a three-way handshake when establishing a connection: SYN, SYN/ACK, and ACK. TCP uses PAR to recover lost segments, resending segments with a delay between transmissions, until an acknowledgment is received. Applications that use TCP include FTP (21), HTTP (80), SMTP (25), SSH (22), and telnet (23). UDP provides unreliable connections and is more efficient than TCP. Examples of applications that use UDP include DNS (53), RIP (520), SNMP (161), and TFTP (69).

✓ TWO-MINUTE DRILL

Transport Layer Functions

❑ The transport layer provides for flow control through windowing and acknowledgments, reliable connections through sequence numbers and acknowledgments, session multiplexing through port numbers and IP addresses, and segmentation through segment PDUs.

❑ Transport reliability should deal with out-of-order packets, duplicate packets, and congestion avoidance.

Transport Layer Protocols

❑ TCP provides connection-oriented, reliable connections by using sequence numbers and acknowledgments, windowing, and error detection and correction.

❑ The TCP header is 20 bytes long and contains two port fields, sequence and acknowledgment number fields, code bit fields, a window size field, a checksum field, and others.

❑ UDP provides a best effort delivery and is more efficient than TCP because of its lower overhead.

❑ The UDP header has source and destination port fields, a length field, and a checksum field.

TCP and UDP Applications

❑ Most TCP and UDP applications/protocols send traffic in clear text, but applications such as HTTPS and SSH encrypt their traffic.

❑ Well-known (0 to 1023) and registered (1024 to 49,151) port numbers are assigned to applications; dynamic port numbers (49,152 to 65,535) are assigned by the operating system to the source connection of a session.

❑ Common TCP applications/protocols and their ports are 21 (FTP), 22 (SSH), 23 (telnet), 25 (SMTP), and 80 (HTTP). Common UDP applications/ protocols and their ports are 53 (DNS), 69 (TFTP), and 161 (SNMP).

❑ Multiplexing sessions are achieved through source and destination port numbers and IP addresses.

Session Establishment

❑ TCP goes through a three-way handshake: SYN, SYN/ACK, and ACK.

❑ When acknowledging the receipt of all sequence segments, the destination responds with an acknowledgment number one higher than the last valid sequence number.

❑ If a segment is lost, TCP resends that segment and all proceeding segments up to the last one in the window size by using PAR.

SELF TEST

The following Self Test questions will help you measure your understanding of the material presented in this chapter. Read all the choices carefully, as there may be more than one correct answer. Choose all correct answers for each question.

Transport Layer Functions

1. Flow control is commonly implemented through which of the following mechanisms?
   A. Windowing
   B. Sequence numbers and acknowledgments
   C. Port numbers and IP addresses
   D. Segment PDUs

2. A PDU at the transport layer is called a _____.
   A. frame
   B. datagram
   C. packet
   D. segment

Transport Layer Protocols

3. TCP has all of the following characteristics except which?
   A. Connection-oriented
   B. Windowing
   C. Best-effort delivery
   D. Reordering packets

4. Which of the following is *not* a common field found in both TCP and UDP headers?
   A. Source Port
   B. Code Bits
   C. Length
   D. Checksum

5. Which of the following is the correct order for a three-way handshake?
   A. SYN, ACK, SYN/ACK
   B. SYN, ACK/SYN, ACK
   C. SYN/ACK, SYN/ACK, ACK
   D. SYN, SYN/ACK, ACK

TCP and UDP Applications

6. Which TCP/IP applications send traffic in clear text? (choose two)

    A. telnet

    B. SSH

    C. HTTPS

    D. FTP

7. Which of the following has an incorrect application-to-well-known-port mapping?

    A. SNMP: 161

    B. TFTP: 21

    C. telnet: 23

    D. SMTP: 25

8. What port number and application does a DNS query use?

    A. 53, TCP

    B. 69, UDP

    C. 520, UDP

    D. 53, UDP

Session Establishment

9. An application is using TCP with a window size of 10. The source sends 10 segments, but segments 5, 6, and 7 are lost. What number does the destination acknowledge with?

    A. 4

    B. 5

    C. 6

    D. 7

    E. 8

10. When a PC opens up two telnet connections to a server, what does the server use to determine that these sessions are different from each other?

    A. Destination IP address

    B. Destination port number

    C. Source port number

    D. Source IP address

SELF TEST ANSWERS

Transport Layer Functions

1. ☑ **A.** Flow control is commonly implemented through the use of windowing.
    ☒ **B** refers to reliable connections, **C** refers to session multiplexing, and **D** refers to segmentation.

2. ☑ **D.** A PDU at the transport layer is called a segment.
    ☒ **A** refers to the data link layer and **B** and **C** refer to the network/Internet layer.

Transport Layer Protocols

3. ☑ **C.** Best-effort delivery is used by UDP.
    ☒ **A, B,** and **D** are implemented in TCP.

4. ☑ **B.** The Code Bits field is found only in TCP and defines control functions, such as synchronization and acknowledgment functions.
    ☒ **A, C,** and **D** are found in both TCP and UDP headers.

5. ☑ **D.** The correct order of the three-way handshake is SYN, SYN/ACK, and ACK.
    ☒ **A, B,** and **C** are invalid orders for the code flags in the three-way handshake.

TCP and UDP Applications

6. ☑ **A** and **D.** Telnet and FTP send their application data in clear text.
    ☒ **B** and **C** encrypt their traffic.

7. ☑ **B.** TFTP is assigned port 69 and FTP 21.
    ☒ **A, C,** and **D** have the correct application-to-port mappings.

8. ☑ **D.** DNS queries use UDP with port 53.
    ☒ **A** is used by DNS zone transfers between servers. **B** is used by TFTP. **C** is used by the RIP routing protocol.

Session Establishment

9. ☑ **B.** The destination always acknowledges the next segment expected, which is 5 (the first one lost).
    ☒ Therefore **A, C, D,** and **E** are incorrect.

10. ☑ **C.** Since it's the same source, the dynamically assigned port numbers will be different numbers.
    ☒ **A** is incorrect because it's the same IP address—the server. **B** would be the same port number—23. **D** would be the same—the PC's IP address.

10

Sending and Receiving TCP/IP Packets

T his chapter offers a review of previous chapters, pulling together everything you've learned so far about network components at layers 1, 2, and 3 of the OSI Reference Model and how they interoperate and intercommunicate. The first part of the chapter is a quick review on the network components at the various OSI Reference Model layers, including the addressing used at layers 2 and 3. The last part of the chapter illustrates the process of how a PC acquires its IP addressing information and how it communicates, using TCP/IP, to a host on a remote segment.

CERTIFICATION OBJECTIVE 10.01

Network Components and Addressing Review

Following is a quick review of the first three layers of the OSI Reference Model (physical, data link, and network) and the network components used at each. It reviews layers 2 and 3 addressing and some TCP/IP protocols used for communications.

Layer 1 Components

Recall from Chapter 2 that the physical layer defines the physical properties of transmitting data between network components: electrical, mechanical, functional, and so on. This can include the kind of wiring (or wireless communications), interfaces, and other hardware components. One type of layer 1 device is an Ethernet hub. A hub replicates any signal it receives—good or bad. An Ethernet hub can be used to connect many devices to the bus topology, as well as to extend the distance between devices.

Layer 2 Components

The data link layer defines how devices communicate across a physical layer medium. Ethernet is one of the more common layer 2 standards. Common devices that operate primarily at layer 2 include network interface cards (NICs) and switches. A NIC, commonly called an *interface*, provides a connection to a wired or wireless network, such as Ethernet.

Unlike hubs, switches do not extend a single collision domain. Instead, they create multiple collision domains—a separate collision domain off each port. All devices connected to a hub are in the same collision domain. Switches, therefore, create more, yet smaller, collision domains, and thus provides more bandwidth in a network. To switch (forward) frames intelligently, switches learn which MAC addresses are attached to which interfaces and store these in content addressable memory (CAM) or a port address table. Frames always flooded (sent out all ports with the exception of the received port) by the switch include unknown unicast destinations, multicasts, and local broadcasts. Because of this interconnectivity, all devices in the switched layer 2 network must have unique MAC addresses.

MAC addresses can be duplicated if the devices with the identical MAC addresses are in different broadcast domains.

Switches can also have a MAC address or addresses, and they are required for Spanning Tree Protocol (STP) to elect a root switch and to communicate directly with the switch for remote management functions. Because redundancy can be important, loops can exist in layer 2 switched networks. MAC addresses associated with the switch typically come from the switch's backplane or from a supervisor module installed in the switch: the switch ports themselves typically don't have individual MAC addresses.

Layer 3 Components

Routers are the primary layer 3 network components. Routers connect different broadcast domains together, whether they are different Ethernet segments or different VLANs. Logical addresses are used to implement a hierarchical, scalable network. TCP/IP is an example of a protocol with logical addressing. Recall from Chapter 7 that an IP address has two components: network and host. A subnet mask is used to differentiate between these two components.

One of a router's main responsibilities is to find the best path to a destination and switch packets appropriately. Routers have a list of destination layer 3 networks and subnets in a routing table. As you will see in Chapter 15, the routing table can have entries that you manually enter (static routes) or entries that it learns with a dynamic routing protocol, where networks and their locations are automatically shared between routers.

Default Gateway

If devices on a segment want to reach devices in a different broadcast domain—that is, a different network—they must know to which default gateway to forward their traffic. A default gateway is basically a router that knows how to get the local broadcast domain's traffic to remote destinations. Local devices will need to learn the default gateway dynamically or have it statically defined on them.

on the **job**

One way of telling whether or not a default gateway is defined on a host is to ping the default gateway's address from the host. If you are successful, try pinging a different address (on a different subnet) on the same default gateway router. If this is not successful, and you are certain that the other interface on the default gateway is operational, you probably don't have a default gateway address defined on your PC. If you see a "destination unreachable" message, this is an Internet Control Message Protocol (ICMP) reply from an intermediate layer 3 device indicating that a network problem has prohibited the ping from reaching the destination; if you see a "request timeout" message, your device is not receiving any type of ICMP reply to your original ping.

TCP/IP Protocols

Many protocols are used in TCP/IP to transport information between hosts. The three commonly used protocols are Dynamic Host Control Protocol (DHCP), domain name service (DNS), and Address Resolution Protocol (ARP), which were discussed in Chapter 6. Transmission Control Protocol (TCP) and User Datagram Protocol (UDP), discussed in Chapter 9, are used to transmit data, such as file transfers and e-mails, between hosts.

Here's a quick overview of the protocols:

- **DHCP**   Dynamically acquires IP addressing information on a host, including an IP address, subnet mask, default gateway address, and a DNS server address.
- **DNS**   Resolves names to layer 3 IP addresses.
- **ARP**   Resolves layer 3 IP addresses to layer 2 MAC addresses so that devices can communicate in the same broadcast domain.
- **TCP**   Reliably transmits data between two devices. It uses a three-way handshake to build a session and windowing to implement flow control, and it can detect and resend lost or bad segments.
- **UDP**   Delivers data with a best effort. No handshaking is used to establish a session—a device starts a session by sending data.

CERTIFICATION OBJECTIVE 10.02

End-to-End Delivery Example

This part of the chapter illustrates how devices communicate with each other using TCP/IP. The network shown in Figure 10-1 is used to illustrate the example. Notice that there are three Ethernet network segments (broadcast domains) containing the following devices:

- **10.0.1.0/24**   PC-A, Switch-A, and Router-A
- **10.0.2.0/24**   Router-A, Hub-A, and Router-B
- **10.0.3.0/24**   Router-B, Switch-B, and PC-B

FIGURE 10-1

Example TCP/IP communications

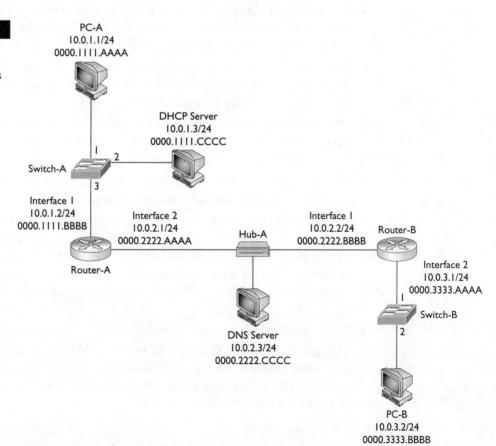

The remainder of this chapter covers how PC-A acquires its IP addressing information using DHCP, how DNS works to resolve names, how PC-A and PC-B use TCP to perform telnet, how the three-way handshake occurs, how the switches switch frames, and how the routers route the packets. In this example, assume that the routers have static routes defined to reach the IP destinations and that the two switches have just booted up and haven't learned any MAC addresses.

PC-A Acquires Addressing Information

Recall from Chapter 6 that one way of acquiring IP addressing information on a device is to use DHCP. Let's assume PC-A hasn't acquired its IP addressing information yet and will be using DHCP. As soon as PC-A's NIC becomes operational and the TCP/IP stack has been loaded, PC-A will go through the eight-step DHCP process:

1. PC-A creates an Ethernet frame with an encapsulated DHCP Discover packet. The source MAC address in the frame is PC-A's 0000.1111.AAAA, and the destination is a broadcast of FFFF.FFFF.FFFF.

2. When Switch-A receives the frame, it performs its learning process, adding 0000.1111.AAAA and port 1 to the CAM table. Since it is a broadcast, the switch floods the frame out ports 2 and 3.

3. Off port 3, when the router receives the frame, it processes it at layer 2, since the destination MAC address is a broadcast; but then it drops the frame at layer 3, since it isn't a DHCP server.

4. Off port 2, when the DHCP server receives the frame, it processes it at layer 2, since it is a local broadcast, and forwards it up to layer 3.

5. Assuming the DHCP server has a free address in its pool, the DHCP server responds with a DHCP OFFER message with IP addressing information: IP address of 10.0.1.1/24, DNS server address of 10.0.2.3, and a default gateway of 10.0.1.2. This is encapsulated in an Ethernet frame with a source MAC address of the server's 0000.1111.CCCC and a destination MAC address of PC-A, 0000.1111.AAAA.

6. When Switch-A receives the OFFER message, it does its learning function, adding 0000.1111.CCCC and port 2 to the CAM table. It then does its forwarding function, comparing the destination MAC address of 0000.1111 .AAAA to the CAM table and sees that this is associated with port 1; so the switch forwards the frame out that port.

7. PC-A receives the frame. The NIC compares its MAC address to the destination MAC address and sees a match, so it passes the IP packet up to layer 3, where the PC accepts the OFFER by sending a DHCP REQUEST message directly to the DHCP server: Switch-A switches the frame directly between these MAC addresses. PC-A also incorporates the IP addressing information into its NIC configuration.

8. The DHCP server responds with a DHCP ACK message directly to PC-A, which the switch again directly switches to port 1.

Now that PC-A has IP addressing information, it can begin communicating, via TCP/IP, to other IP-enabled devices.

PC-A Opens Up a Session to PC-B

The remainder of this example, covered in the next few sections, illustrates PC-A opening up a telnet session to PC-B, including how DNS is used, how the TCP connection is built, and how it is torn down.

PC-A Resolving PC-B's Name

Assume that PC-A doesn't know the IP address of PC-B, but it does know its name. So from the Windows command prompt, the user on PC-A types in the following:

```
C:\> telnet PC-B
```

Since a name is used, DNS must be used to resolve it to an IP address. PC-A creates a DNS query for the name *PC-B* and sends this to the DNS server. Notice that since the DNS server is in a different subnet, the frame must be forwarded to the router first; therefore, the destination MAC address needed is Router-A's MAC address. Since this is not originally known, PC-A will have to ARP for the MAC address associated with 10.0.1.2, the default gateway. The source MAC address in the ARP is PC-A's, and the destination MAC address is a broadcast, which Switch-A will flood. Router-A will respond to the ARP with the correct IP addressing information. (The router will also add PC-A's IP and MAC addresses to its local ARP table.) In the Ethernet frame, the source MAC address will be the router's destination MAC address, PC-B. The switch will perform its learning function, adding 0000.1111.BBBB (the router's MAC address) to the CAM table. At this point, the switch knows all the MAC address within the broadcast domain and can intelligently forward unicast frames without having to resort to flooding them.

						Src.	Dest.
PDU	**Dest. MAC**	**Src. MAC**	**Src. IP**	**Dest. IP**	**Protocol**	**Port**	**Port**
1	0000.1111.BBBB	0000.1111.AAAA	10.0.1.1	10.0.2.3	UDP	50000	53
2	0000.2222.CCCC	0000.2222.AAAA	10.0.1.1	10.0.2.3	UDP	50000	53
3	0000.2222.AAAA	0000.2222.CCCC	10.0.2.3	10.0.1.1	UDP	53	50000
4	0000.1111.BBBB	0000.1111.AAAA	10.0.2.3	10.0.1.1	UDP	53	50000

TABLE 10-1   DNS PDUs

When PC-A receives the ARP reply, it can build the DNS query and forward it to the switch. The partial Ethernet frame, IP packet, and UDP segment headers (in the displayed order) are shown in PDU 1 of Table 10-1. The layers 3 and 4 information is stored in a local connection table so the PC knows what do with the DNS reply when it arrives.

on the   *You can see the local connection on a PC by using the* `netstat` *command.*
ⓘob

exam
ⓦatch   *When sending an IP packet across the network, with the exception of the TOS and TTL fields, nothing else changes on a hop-by-hop basis as the packet travels across the layer 3 network. The same cannot be said about the layer 2*   *framing, which changes on each segment. Therefore, for a PC to send a packet to a PC on another segment, the source PC must use a layer 2 frame with the default gateway as the destination.*

Switch-A forwards the frame out port 3 directly to the router. Router-A, upon receiving the frame, examines the destination MAC address and sees that it matches the local interface's MAC address. Router-A strips off the Ethernet frame and passes it up the TCP/IP stack. Since the destination IP address doesn't match its own interface 1 address, the router examines its local routing table and notices that it is directly connected to subnet 10.0.2.0/24 on interface 2. Therefore Router-A knows that to get the frame to 10.0.2.3, the router will have to know the corresponding

MAC address of the DNS server. If the router doesn't have it in its local ARP table, the router will have to ARP for it. Notice that a hub connects Router-A, Router-B, and the DNS server. Hubs are physical layer devices, so when the hub receives the frame from Router-A, it repeats the signal out to all remaining interfaces. Therefore, both Router-B and the DNS server will receive the ARP. Unlike a switch, no learning process takes place here since the hub isn't looking at the layer 2 information—only the physical layer signal. The DNS server will add Router-A to its local ARP table and send an ARP reply to Router-A containing the DNS server's MAC address.

Router-A can now forward the DNS query to the DNS server, using the information in PDU 2 in Table 10-1. Notice that the only thing that has changed from PDU 1 to PDU 2 is the Ethernet frame header information—the original IP packet and encapsulated UDP segment are still the same.

When the DNS server receives the Ethernet frame, the NIC sees a match in the destination MAC address, strips off the Ethernet header, and forwards the IP packet up the protocol stack. The Internet layer compares the destination IP address with the server's address, sees a match, sees that the protocol is UDP, and passes this up to the transport layer. The transport layer sees a destination port number of 53 and knows that the DNS application on the server should process the DNS query. The server looks up the name and then sends back an appropriate DNS reply, with an IP address of 10.0.3.2 for the PC-B lookup. PDU 3 in Table 10-1 shows the Ethernet, IP, and UDP header for the reply. Assume that the default gateway address for the DNS server is Router-A. Notice two things about this: first, the destination MAC address is Router-A, the exit point for the Ethernet segment; second, notice that the source and destination UDP port numbers are reversed from the original DNS query. The source port number is the number the source uses, which is 53 in this case since the connection was directed to this port. The destination port number is 50,000, which PC-A is listening on for the returning UDP DNS reply.

When Router-A receives the frame, it does its MAC comparison, strips off the Ethernet frame, does its route lookup, determines that the destination is directly off interface 1, examines the ARP table and sees the MAC address, and then re-encapsulates the DNS reply in a new Ethernet frame with a source MAC address of 0000.1111.BBBB and a destination MAC address of 0000.1111.AAAA. This is shown in PDU 4 of Table 10-1. The switch intelligently forwards the frame out of port 1. PC-A receives the frame, passes it up to layer 3, passes it up to layer 4, and sees the destination port of 50,000. PC-A compares this to its local connection table and knows that this is the DNS reply it's waiting for, so it now knows the IP address of PC-B.

PC-A Sending a TCP SYN to PC-B

Now that PC-A knows the IP address of PC-B, the telnet application can proceed with the actual telnet. Telnet uses TCP at the transport layer, so the three-way handshake must take place first. The first step is for PC-A to send a TCP segment with the SYN code (commonly called a flag) set. It uses a dynamic port above 49,151 and a destination, the well-known port of 23 for telnet. PDU 1 in Table 10-2 shows the Ethernet frame, IP packet, and TCP header information. Notice that the next-hop layer 2 address is Router-A, the default gateway. When the router receives this and processes the information, at layer 3 the router notices that the destination IP address is not its own; so the router does a lookup in its routing table and sees that the next-hop at layer 3 is Router-B.

| TABLE 10-2 | | TCP SYN to PC-B |

PDU	Dest. MAC	Src. MAC	Src. IP	Dest. IP	Proto.	Src. Port	Dest. Port	TCP Code
1	0000.1111.BBBB	0000.1111.AAAA	10.0.1.1	10.0.3.2	TCP	50001	23	SYN
2	0000.2222.BBBB	0000.2222.AAAA	10.0.1.1	10.0.3.2	TCP	50001	23	SYN
3	0000.3333.BBBB	0000.3333.AAAA	10.0.1.1	10.0.3.2	TCP	50001	23	SYN

exam
watch

Don't be surprised if you see a question on the exam that asks you to figure out, based on the link an Ethernet frame is traversing, the contents of the fields in the Ethernet header, IP header, and TCP/UDP header, as shown in Tables 10-1, 10-2, and 10-3.

If Router-A doesn't know the IP-to-MAC address mapping of Router-B, it will ARP for it. Router-A then re-encapsulates the IP packet in a new Ethernet frame, shown in PDU 2 in Table 10-2: the IP and TCP headers remain the same, but a new frame header was generated to get it information across the 10.0.2.0/24 subnet.

When Router-B receives the frame, it notices that the IP address doesn't match its own, so Router-B looks in its routing table to see where the packet should be forwarded. In this case, Router-B is directly connected to the destination subnet, 10.0.3.0/24. If Router-B doesn't know the IP-to-MAC address mapping for PC-B, Router-B will ARP for it. During the ARP request process, Switch-B will learn about Router-B's MAC address and add it and port 1 to its CAM table (if it hasn't already done this). Likewise, Switch-B will learn PC-B's MAC address during the ARP reply process, if it doesn't know it already. Router-B then encapsulates the IP packet in a new frame to get the data to PC-B. The Ethernet frame header, IP packet header, and TCP segment header are shown in PDU 3 of Table 10-2.

One important item to point out about the sending of the preceding SYN segment is that the only thing that changed from PC-A to PC-B was the Ethernet framing information—three Ethernet frames were used, but the original IP packet stayed the same.

PC-B Sending a TCP SYN/ACK to PC-A

At this point, PC-B is processing the frame, sending the IP packet up to layer 3, and then sending the TCP segment up to layer 4. At the transport layer, PC-B notices that this is a new connection based on the TCP SYN code and that the application that should handle it is telnet. Assuming that a telnet server is running on the host, PC-B will add the connection to its local connection table and reply back with a TCP SYN/ACK segment. You can see this in PDU 1 in Table 10-3. The source port is 23 (the server) and the destination port is 50001, PC-A. The process basically works in reverse when sending the SYN/ACK back to PC-A: the source and destination addresses and ports are reversed. Also, no ARPs need to be performed since this was already done in the PC-A-to-PC-B direction. Also, both switches have the destination MAC addresses in their CAM tables, so no flooding will occur.

Completing the Session

The last part of the handshake is the ACK, which, with the exception of the ACK flag being set instead of the SYN flag, is the process described earlier in the "PC-A Sending a TCP SYN to PC-B" section. Again, no ARPs are necessary, nor does the switch need to do any re-learning, since this already occurred when PC-A sent the SYN to PC-B.

Once the telnet is completed and the user types `exit` to end the telnet session, the session will be gracefully torn down. PC-A sends a special TCP segment with the FIN flag set (FIN is short for finish). Upon receiving this teardown message, PC-B will respond with a TCP segment where the FIN and ACK (FIN/ACK) flags are set, indicating that the telnet session is now over. A flag or code of RST is used to indicate that a session is being abnormally terminated.

TABLE 10-3　TCP SYN/ACK Reply to PC-A

PDU	Dest. MAC	Src. MAC	Src. IP	Dest. IP	Proto.	Src. Port	Dest. Port	TCP Code
1	0000.3333.AAAA	00003333.BBBB	10.0.3.2	10.0.1.1	TCP	23	50001	SYN/ACK
2	0000.2222.AAAA	0000.2222.BBBB	10.0.3.2	10.0.1.1	TCP	23	50001	SYN/ACK
3	0000.1111.AAAA	0000.1111.BBBB	10.0.3.2	10.0.1.1	TCP	23	50001	SYN/ACK

INSIDE THE EXAM

End-to-End Delivery Example

You should focus primarily on the "End-to-End Delivery Example" in this chapter. If you don't understand what was discussed here, you can refer to Chapters 2, 3, 4, 6, 7, and 9, where this information is discussed in more depth. This chapter is included in the book for two reasons: First, you can probably expect to see a few questions on the exam related to PDUs and how they are created as traffic is transmitted across the network. Therefore, you should carefully review this section and the information in Tables 10-1, 10-2, and 10-3. Know what MAC addresses are placed in the Ethernet header, as well as port numbers used for TCP: source and destination. Also know how PDUs are

built in both the source-to-destination and destination-to-source directions.

Second, this chapter pulls all the information from previous chapters and puts it into perspective in a real-life situation, which will help you troubleshoot issues. You might expect to see some questions on the exam related to troubleshooting issues, such as "what would you see if an intermediate router doesn't know how to reach a destination?"; or "how would you know your NIC had a problem?"; or "how would you know that the TCP/IP stack on your host was operational?" Know how ICMP works and the kinds of messages you can see. You can review all of this in Chapter 6.

CERTIFICATION SUMMARY

This chapter focused on how PDUs are transmitted across an Ethernet-based network using TCP/IP. It provided a quick review of the devices that function at the physical, data link, and network layers—hubs, NICs and switches, and routers, respectively—as well as MAC addressing and TCP/IP addressing. The remainder of the chapter detailed how a device acquires its IP addressing information via DHCP, how names are resolved to IP addresses using DNS, and how a telnet is established and torn down with TCP. All this information was covered in Chapters 2, 3, 4, 6, 7, and 9; however, pulling all of this information together in a detailed example helps you understand the complete process as to how the network components interact with each other and how the PDUs are created for each of the segments across which data is transmitted.

✓ TWO-MINUTE DRILL

Network Components and Addressing Review

❏ Hubs repeat signals at the physical layer; switches and NICs deal with Ethernet frames and MAC addresses at the data link layer; and routers deal with packets and IP addressing at the network/Internet layer.

End-to-End Delivery Example

❏ When sending an IP packet across multiple Ethernet segments/broadcast domains, the only thing that changes in the IP packet is the TTL and, possibly, the TOS fields in the IP header—the IP addressing and the encapsulated payload are not altered.

❏ When sending an IP packet across multiple subnets, the MAC addresses in the Ethernet frame change on a subnet-by-subnet basis.

❏ Pinging 127.0.0.1 tests whether or not the local TCP/IP stack is operational.

❏ Pinging your own IP address tests for a physical layer problem of your NIC and the device to which it is directly connected.

❏ A "destination unreachable message" with a corresponding source IP address indicates that the specific router is telling you it doesn't know how to reach the destination, or, if the router is connected to the same host, the host is not responding to an ARP query and is therefore probably not functioning.

❏ Be familiar with the ports used in the TCP and UDP headers. The device originating the session uses a dynamic source port greater than 49,151 and a well-known or reserved destination port (such as 80, if HTTP). When the destination service responds, the source and destination port values are flipped (reversed) in the TCP or UDP header, indicating that the receiving host is sending a reply to the originating host.

SELF TEST

The following Self Test questions will help you measure your understanding of the material presented in this chapter. Read all the choices carefully, as there may be more than one correct answer. Choose all correct answers for each question.

Network Components and Addressing Review

1. Hubs make switching decisions based on which of the following?

    A. Frames

    B. Datagrams

    C. Segments

    D. None of the above

2. Which of the following is a true statement?

    A. MAC addresses must be unique for devices connected to the same switch port.

    B. MAC devices must be unique throughout the world.

    C. MAC devices must be unique within a network.

    D. MAC addresses must be unique in a broadcast domain.

3. Which IP protocol maps a layer 2 to a layer 3 address?

    A. ARP

    B. DHCP

    C. ICMP

    D. None of the above

End-to-End Delivery Example

4. Examine Figure 10-1. PC-B pings the DNS server. What source MAC address does DNS server's NIC see?

    A. 0000.2222.BBBB

    B. 0000.2222.AAAA

    C. 0000.2222.CCCC

    D. 0000.3333.BBBB

5. Examine Figure 10-1. PC-B opens up a web session to a web service running on PC-A. In the SYN/ACK, what would be the source port number in the TCP segment header?

A. 69

B. 80

C. Greater than 49,151

D. Greater than 1023

6. Examine Figure 10-1. What would PC-A ping to see whether its TCP/IP protocol stack is operational?

A. 172.0.0.1

B. 10.0.1.1

C. 10.0.1.2

D. None of the above

7. Examine Figure 10-1. If PC-A could ping 10.0.1.2, but got a destination unreachable message when pinging 10.0.2.1, what could cause this issue?

A. The connection between Router-A and Router-B is down.

B. The connection between Router-A and the hub is down.

C. The connection between Router-A and the switch is down.

D. The connection between Switch-A and PC-A is down.

8. Examine Figure 10-1. PC-A pings 10.0.1.1 and is successful. PC-A pings 10.0.1.2 and is successful. PC-A pings 10.0.2.1 and is not successful. PC-A pings 10.0.3.1 and is successful. What could be the issue with this scenario?

A. The hub is down.

B. Switch-A is down.

C. The DNS server is down.

D. Router-A is down.

9. In Figure 10-1, Router-B needs to forward PDU information from PC-B to PC-A. What MAC address would it place in the source MAC address field in the Ethernet header?

A. 0000.2222.AAAA

B. 0000.2222.BBBB

C. 0000.3333.AAAA

D. 0000.3333.BBBB

SELF TEST ANSWERS

Network Components and Addressing Review

1. ☑ **D.** Hubs are physical layer repeaters and don't care what bits and bytes are being transmitted.

   ☒ **A** refers to the data link layer; **B** refers to the network layer; and **C** refers to the transport layer.

2. ☑ **D.** MAC addresses must be unique in a broadcast domain (Ethernet segment).

   ☒ **A, B,** and **C** are not true since duplicate MAC addresses can exist across different broadcast domains.

3. ☑ **D.** None of these answers is correct. Reverse Address Resolution Protocol (RARP) maps a layer 2 to a layer 3 address.

   ☒ **A** maps a layer 3 to a layer 3 address. **B** assigns addressing information to a host. **C** is used to share control and error information between network components.

End-to-End Delivery Example

4. ☑ **A.** On the 10.0.2.0/24 subnet, Router-B needs to forward the Ethernet frame to the DNS server, so Router-B's MAC address would be in the source field of the Ethernet header.

   ☒ **B** would be true if Router-A were sending the frame. **C** is the destination MAC address. **D** is the source MAC address of PC-B when it sends the frame to Router-B.

5. ☑ **B.** Since the web server is responding, the ports are reversed and the well-known/reserved port number (80) is the source.

   ☒ **A** is incorrect because port 69 is for TFTP. **C** would be the destination port number when returning to the originator of the session. **D** includes both reserved and dynamic port numbers.

6. ☑ **D.** None of these answers is correct. PC-A would ping 127.0.0.1, the local loopback address.

   ☒ **A** is a B class network, not 127.0.0.1. **B** would be the dynamically or statically assigned address and would test whether the interface was operational if pinged. **C** is the default gateway and tests connectivity across the broadcast domain.

7. ☑ **B.** The interface or the connection between Router-A and the hub is down.

   ☒ **A** is not true because if the connection between Router-A and the hub was up, PC-A would receive an echo reply even if the connection between the hub and Router-B was down. **C** and **D** are not true because PC-A can ping interface 1 of Router-A.

8. ☑ **C.** Either the DNS server is down or the link between the DNS server and the hub is not operational.

☒ **A, B,** and **D** must be up if PC-A can ping 10.0.2.1 and 10.0.3.1.

9. ☑ **B.** Since Router-B needs to forward information to the next-hop Router-A, the source MAC address used would be Router-B's interface 1's MAC address, which is 0000.2222.BBBB.

☒ **A** is the destination MAC address in this frame. **C** is what PC-B fills in for the destination MAC address to get it to the default gateway. **D** is the source MAC address that PC-B uses.

Part III

Cisco Catalyst Switches

11

Cisco IOS Software

T his chapter begins with a discussion of the applied side of networking. It focuses on the command-line interface (CLI) of Cisco's routers and switches, including using a console connection to perform basic configuration on these devices.

This book emphasizes the fundamental and important concepts of accessing, configuring, and managing Cisco routers and switches. These discussions assume that you have never configured a Cisco router or switch; you'll therefore begin with the basics, learning the operating system (OS) used by these devices, the advantages provided by Cisco's OS, and the use of commands to configure a Cisco device. The remaining chapters in Part 3 focus specifically on Cisco switch features, while Part 4 focuses on routers.

CERTIFICATION OBJECTIVE 11.01

Introduction to Cisco Device Configuration

One of the main reasons that Cisco is number one in the enterprise networking marketplace is its *Internetwork Operating System (IOS)*. The IOS provides a function similar to that provided by Microsoft Windows XP or Linux: it controls and manages the hardware on which it is running. Basically, the IOS provides the interface between you and the hardware, enabling you to execute commands to configure and manage your Cisco device. Originally, the IOS was developed for Cisco routers, but over the last few years, Cisco has been porting the IOS to its other platforms, including the Catalyst switches.

Cisco has spent many years tweaking and tuning the IOS, and it has added new features as new technologies are introduced to the marketplace. Following are some advantages of the IOS:

- **Features** The IOS includes a wide array of features for protocols and functions that provide connectivity, scalability, reliability, and security solutions for networks of any size.

- **Connectivity** The IOS supports a variety of data link layer technologies for LAN and WAN environments, including copper and fiber wiring as well as wireless support.

- ■ **Scalability** The IOS supports both fixed and modular chassis platforms, enabling you to purchase the appropriate hardware to meet your needs, yet still allowing you to leverage the same IOS CLI to reduce management costs.
- ■ **Reliability** To ensure that your critical resources are always reachable, Cisco has developed many products and IOS features to provide chassis and network redundancy.
- ■ **Security** With the IOS, you can strictly control access to your network and networking devices in accordance with your internal security policies.

Because of the success of its IOS software, Cisco has grown from a garage-based router company to one of the largest companies in the world in a little more than a decade. Most enterprise networks, as well as ISPs, use Cisco products in one form or another. Actually, a large portion of the Internet backbone is composed of Cisco products. With the IOS coupled to a first-class service and support team, few companies compare to Cisco when it comes to customer satisfaction.

Router and Switch Connections

Cisco's routers and switches support two types of external connections: *ports* (referred to as *lines*) and *interfaces*. Physical ports are used for management purposes and provide an out-of-band method for managing your Cisco product. Every Cisco router and switch has a console (con) port; some have an auxiliary (aux) port. *Out-of-band* means that your management tasks do not affect traffic that is flowing through your Cisco product. Interfaces are used to connect networking devices together, such as a switch and router or a switch and a PC. Interfaces are connected to the backplane of the switch or router. You can also use interfaces for management purposes, but doing so might affect the performance of your IOS device. These types of connections are called *in-band* connections. The following sections will cover the console port as well as interfaces on your Cisco devices.

Console Connection

The console port is used to establish an out-of-band connection in order to access the CLI to manage your Cisco device locally. Once you have placed a basic configuration on your Cisco device (assigning it IP addressing information, for instance), you can then come in via one of its interfaces to manage your product in-band. Some methods of in-band management include telnet, a web browser, Simple Network Management Protocol (SNMP), and CiscoWorks and Cisco Managed Services Solutions.

Assuming that your Cisco device has an RJ-45 console port, you will need to use two components to manage your Cisco device from your PC:

- An RJ-45 rollover cable
- An RJ-45–to–DB-9 or RJ-45–to–DB-25 terminal adapter: determined by the number of pins that your COM port has on your PC

If your router has a DB-25 console port, you'll also need a DB-25–to–RJ-45 modem adapter, which is plugged into the console port of the router.

The rollover cable used for the console connection looks similar to every other UTP/STP connecting cable; however, this cable is proprietary to Cisco and will not work for other types of connections, such as Ethernet connections. The rollover cable has eight wires inside its plastic shielding and two RJ-45 connectors at each end. Each side of the rollover cable reverses the pins compared to the other side: pin 1 on one side is mapped to pin 8 on the other side, pin 2 is mapped to pin 7, pin 3 is mapped to pin 6, pin 4 is mapped to pin 5, pin 5 is mapped to pin 4, pin 6 is mapped to pin 3, pin 7 is mapped to pin 2, and pin 8 is mapped to pin 1.

e x a m
ⓦatch

Most console connections to Cisco devices require an RJ-45 rollover cable and an RJ-45–to–DB9 terminal adapter. Today, Cisco's console cables actually have the RJ-45–to–DB9 adapter built into the cable. The rollover cable pin-outs are reversed on the two sides.

Once you have connected one end of the rollover cable (the RJ-45 end) to the console port of your Cisco device and the other end into the terminal adapter and into the COM port of your PC (or terminal), you are ready to set up your PC to access the Cisco device. You will need a terminal emulation package to do this. Many products are available, including HyperTerminal, which comes standard with Microsoft Windows operating systems. However, two of my personal favorites are PuTTY and Tera Term: they're both free! Within your terminal emulation software, you will need to set the parameters shown in Table 11-1 to the specified values.

TABLE 11-1	COM Component	Setting
COM Port Settings	Speed	9600 bps
	Data bits	8
	Stop bits	1
	Parity	None
	Flow control	None

Once you have configured these settings, you should be able to press the ENTER key a few times to gain access to the CLI. At this point, you are accessing the Cisco product using an out-of-band approach.

Hardware Interfaces

This section covers the nomenclature that Cisco uses for switch and router interfaces. This is important information to know when it comes to configuring the components of a specific interface, such as its duplexing, or connecting a cable to it. As you will see under the following two headings, some minor differences exist between these two types of products.

Switch Interface Nomenclature   The Catalyst 2950 and 2960 switches support only fixed interfaces, while some of Cisco's higher end switches, such as the 6500s, support modular slots with interface cards. Like their modular router counterparts, the nomenclature of an interface is *type slot_#/port_#*. The type of interface is the media type, such as *ethernet*, *fastethernet*, or *gigabit*. Following this is the slot number. For all fixed interfaces on a Cisco switch, the slot number is always *0*.

The port number is the number of the port in the specified slot. Unlike Cisco router ports, switch port numbers start at *1* and work their way up. For instance, on a 2960, the very first port is *fastethernet 0/1*, the second port is *fastethernet 0/2*, and so on. Some 2960 switches support Gigabit Ethernet interfaces, so the nomenclature for the interface would look like this: *gigabitethernet 0/1*.

Router Interface Nomenclature Depending on the Cisco router product you purchased, the interfaces are either fixed, modular, or a combination of the two. When referring to fixed interfaces on a Cisco product, the interface numbers *always* begin with 0 (not 1, like the switches) and work their way up within a particular interface type. Unlike switches, routers support many different data link layer media types, depending on their model. These types can include the following: atm, asynch, bri, ethernet, fastethernet, gigabitethernet, and serial, as well as many others.

For routers that have only fixed interfaces, the interface nomenclature is *type port_#*. For example, if a router has two fixed Ethernet interfaces and two fixed serial interfaces, they would be called *ethernet 0* and *ethernet 1* and *serial 0* and *serial 1*. As you can see in this example, the port numbers begin at 0 within *each* interface type. Through use of an interface type and a number, each of the interfaces can be uniquely identified.

However, if a router has modular slots, and you can insert interface cards into these slots, the interface nomenclature is similar to the Catalyst switches: *type slot_#/ port_#*. Each slot has a unique slot number beginning with 0, and within each slot, the ports begin at 0 and work their way up. For example, if you had a modular router with two slots, the first slot would be 0 and the second 1. If the first slot had four serial interfaces, the interface numbers would be *0–3*, and if the second slot had two Ethernet interfaces, the interface numbers would be 0 and 1.

Here's an example of a four-port serial module in the third slot of a 3640 router: *serial 2/0*, *serial 2/1*, *serial 2/2*, and *serial 2/3*. Some examples of routers with modular interfaces follow: 1800, 2600, 2800, 3700, 3800, 7200, 7300, and 7600. The exception to this is the 1700 routers; even though they are modular, you don't configure any slot number when specifying a particular interface.

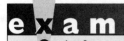

Device Startup

You can access and configure a Cisco device in many ways, including the following:

- Console port
- Auxiliary port (only certain Cisco products)
- Telnet
- Secure Shell (SSH)
- Web browser
- SNMP management station

A console interface provides serial connection access to a Cisco device—with console access, you can enter commands in a text-based mode. To manage your Cisco device from a remote station, however, you first need to create a basic configuration, including IP addressing on the device. Therefore, to perform your initial configurations, you need access to the console port of your Cisco device.

Before you can begin configuring your Cisco device, you must first connect it to your network and set up a terminal connection to its console interface, as described earlier in the "Console Connection" section. Here are the three steps your Cisco device goes through when booting up:

1. Perform hardware tests.
2. Locate and load the IOS.
3. Locate and execute the device's configuration file.

Once you power on your Cisco device, hardware tests are performed to ensure that it is operating correctly. These tests, power-on self tests (POSTs), are discussed in Chapters 12 (switches) and 16 (routers). After these tests have completed, the Cisco device finds and locates the IOS and then proceeds to load it. Once the IOS is loaded, the IOS then searches for the device's configuration and executes it. With steps 2 and 3, the Cisco device typically goes through fallback measures if it cannot find an IOS or locate a configuration file.

As you will see in this chapter, and as you work with Cisco devices in a production environment, each Cisco product is unique and may have its own methods for finding and loading its IOS and configuration files. As an example, a Catalyst 2960 switch, direct from Cisco, comes with a default configuration already on it. This configuration is enough to allow the switch to perform basic switching functions right out of the box. A Cisco router, by contrast, requires some basic configuration to route traffic between interfaces.

ⓦatch *When an IOS device boots up, it runs POST, finds and loads the IOS, and then finds and loads the device's configuration file.*

CERTIFICATION OBJECTIVE 11.02

Command-Line Interface (CLI)

How you access the IOS CLI on a Cisco device for the first time depends on the kind of device you are configuring. In almost every case, you will use the console interface initially to interact with the device; however, gaining access to the CLI from the console port can be different from one device to another. On a Cisco router, for instance, you are taken directly to the IOS CLI when you log in from the console port. If the IOS cannot find a configuration file for the router or switch, the IOS takes you through *Setup* mode (commonly called the System Configuration Dialog), which is a basic configuration script that prompts you for information on how you want to configure your IOS device (discussed in Chapter 16).

Once you have configured your Cisco device via the console port, you can then use other methods of accessing and changing its configuration, such as telnet or SSH—Cisco calls this *virtual type terminal (VTY)* access—Trivial File Transfer

Protocol (TFTP), Simple Network Management Protocol (SNMP), or a web browser (Security Device Manager, or SDM, for routers). Cisco has a variety of management products that can be used to configure and manage your Cisco device, such as CMS; however, this book focuses primarily on the IOS CLI. SDM for routers is discussed in Chapter 18.

IOS Differences

In this and subsequent chapters, you will see that even though both Cisco routers and switches run the IOS, the commands used by these products are frequently different! In other words, how you configure a feature on a Cisco router might be different from how you configure the same feature on a Catalyst switch. However, how you access the IOS and maneuver around the IOS access levels, as well as how you use many of the management commands, are performed the same way on *all* IOS products. This can become confusing to a Cisco novice, as one command for a particular feature is the same on all Cisco products, but configuring another feature might differ between a Cisco router and a Catalyst switch.

In addition to command differences between different products, such as routers and switches, command differences may exist within a product line, such as Cisco routers, for instance. For example, Cisco sells different flavors of its IOS software for routers, depending on the features that you need. Or because of hardware differences, some commands work on some routers but not on others.

Interacting with the IOS

The CLI is a character- or text-based interface. To interact with the CLI, you simply need to type in commands, just as you would do when typing an essay in a text editor or a message in an e-mail program. You can even use functions such as cut and paste with the IOS CLI: you can copy the complete configuration from a router using a terminal emulator's copy function, paste this into a text editor, make changes to the configuration, select and copy the new configuration, and paste all of these commands back into the CLI.

The CLI supports a command parser. Whenever you press the ENTER key, the IOS parses the command and parameters that you entered and checks for correct syntax and options. When you paste multiple commands into the CLI, the IOS still performs this process for each command that is included in the paste function. If you make a mistake with one command, the CLI parser will display an error message, but it will continue with the next command in the pasted list.

on the
!
Ü o b

Before making any configuration changes on your IOS device, you must first back it up! You'll learn how to do this across the network in Chapter 17, but you could easily do this by executing the show running-config *command, copying this, and pasting it into a backup text file on your PC: make sure you don't modify this configuration. The backup text file can then be used if any changes you make don't behave the way you expect and you don't remember how to revert your running configuration back to the way it was before your changes. To do a restore, erase the configuration on your IOS device (*erase startup-config*), reboot your IOS device (*reload*), enter configuration mode once it boots up (*enable and* configure terminal*), and then paste in your backed-up configuration. By default, the interfaces on routers will be disabled and will have to be enabled (*no shutdown*). The IOS commands mentioned here are discussed later in this chapter and in Chapter 17.*

CLI Access Modes

Each Cisco device supports several access modes. For CLI interaction, four modes are supported:

- **User EXEC**   Provides basic access to the IOS with limited command availability (basically simple monitoring and troubleshooting commands)
- **Privilege EXEC**   Provides high-level management access to the IOS, including all commands available at User EXEC mode
- **Configuration**   Allows configuration changes to be made to the device
- **ROMMON**   Loads a bootstrap program that allows for low-level diagnostic testing of the IOS device, performing the password recovery procedure, and performing an emergency upgrade

Of the four modes, the first three apply to the IOS. While in ROMMON mode, the IOS has not loaded and therefore packets are not moved between interfaces of the device. Both EXEC modes can be password-protected, allowing you to limit the people who can access your device to perform management, configuration, and troubleshooting tasks. The next two sections introduce the two EXEC modes.

User EXEC Mode

Your initial access to the CLI is via the User EXEC mode, which has only a limited number of IOS commands you can execute. Depending on the Cisco device's configuration, you might be prompted for a password to access this mode.

This mode is typically used for basic troubleshooting of networking problems. You can tell that you are in User EXEC mode by examining the prompt on the left side of the screen:

```
IOS>
```

If you see a > character at the end of the information, you know that you are in User EXEC mode. The information preceding the > is the name of the Cisco device. For instance, the default name of all Cisco routers is *Router*, whereas the 2960 switch's User EXEC prompt looks like this: Switch>. These device names can be changed with the **hostname** command, which is discussed later in this chapter. In the preceding example, I renamed the device *IOS*.

Privilege EXEC Mode

Once you have gained access to User EXEC mode, you can use the **enable** command to access Privilege EXEC mode:

```
IOS> enable
IOS#
```

Once you enter the **enable** command, if a Privilege EXEC password has been configured on the Cisco device, you will be prompted for it. Upon successfully authenticating, you will be in Privilege EXEC mode. You can tell that you are in this mode by examining the CLI prompt. In the preceding code example, notice that the > changed to a #.

When you are in Privilege EXEC mode, you have access to all of the User EXEC commands as well as many more advanced management and troubleshooting commands. These commands include extended ping and trace abilities, managing configuration files and IOS images, and detailed troubleshooting using **debug** commands. About the only thing that you can't do from this mode is change the configuration of the Cisco device—this can be done only from Configuration mode.

If you wish to return to User EXEC mode from Privilege EXEC mode, use the **disable** command:

```
IOS# disable
IOS>
```

Again, by examining the prompt, you can tell that you are now in User EXEC mode.

Know the three different modes in the IOS—User EXEC, Privilege EXEC, and Configuration modes—and what you can do in each mode. Use the enable *command to go from User EXEC* *mode to Privilege EXEC mode. Use the* disable *command to go from Privilege EXEC to User EXEC modes, and use the* exit *command to log out of the IOS device from either of these two modes.*

Logging Out of Your Device

You can log out of your Cisco device from either User or Privilege EXEC mode by using the **logout** or **exit** command:

```
IOS# logout
   -or-
IOS# exit
```

CertCam

11.01. The CD includes a multimedia demonstration of logging in and out of a Cisco router.

CERTIFICATION OBJECTIVE 11.03

IOS Basics

Now that you know how to log in to and out of a Cisco IOS device, the next few sections describe some of the features built into the CLI that will make your configuration and management tasks easier. These features include how to abbreviate commands, how to bring up detailed help on commands and their specific parameters, the output of commands, recalling commands, and editing commands.

Command Abbreviation and Completion

The CLI of the IOS allows you to abbreviate commands and parameters to their most unique characters. This feature is useful for those who are physically challenged at typing. As an example, you could type **en** instead of **enable** when you want to go from User EXEC to Privilege EXEC mode, like this:

```
IOS> en
IOS#
```

The Cisco device, internally, completes the command for you. However, the characters that you enter must make the command unique. As an example, you couldn't type just the letter *e*, since other commands being with the letter *e*, such as **exit**.

Context-Sensitive Help

One of the more powerful features of the IOS is context-sensitive help. Context-sensitive help is supported at all modes within the IOS, including User EXEC, Privilege EXEC, and Configuration modes. You can use this feature in a variety of ways. If you are not sure what command you need to execute, at the prompt, type either **help** or **?**. The Cisco device then displays a list of commands that can be executed at the level in which you are currently located, along with a brief description of each command. Here is an example from a router's CLI at User EXEC mode:

```
Router> ?
Exec commands:
  access-enable     Create a temporary Access-List entry
  cd                Change current device
  clear             Reset functions
  .
  .
  .
-- More --
```

w a t c h   *Use the* `help` *command or the* ? *to pull up context-sensitive help. Also, you can abbreviate commands to their most unique characters.*

If you see -- More -- at the bottom of the screen, this indicates that more help information is available than can fit on the current screen. On a Cisco device, if you press the SPACEBAR, the IOS pages down to the next screen of help information; if you press the ENTER key, help scrolls down one line at a time. Any other keystroke breaks out of the help text.

For more detailed help, you can follow a command or parameter with a space and a **?**. This causes the CLI to list the available options or parameters that are included for the command. For instance, you could type **erase** followed by a space and a **?** to see all of the parameters available for the **erase** command:

```
Router# erase ?
  /all              Erase all files(in NVRAM)
  flash:            Filesystem to be erased
  nvram:            Filesystem to be erased
  pram:             Filesystem to be erased
  slot0:            Filesystem to be erased
  slot1:            Filesystem to be erased
  startup-config  Erase contents of configuration memory
Router# erase
```

In this example, you can see at least the first parameter necessary after the **erase** command. Please note that additional parameters may appear after the first one, depending on the next parameter that you enter.

If you're not sure how to spell a command, you can enter the first few characters and immediately follow these characters with a **?**. Typing **e?**, for instance, lists all the commands that begin with *e* at the current mode:

```
Router# e?
enable  erase  exit
Router# e
```

This example shows that three commands begin with the letter *e* in Privilege EXEC mode.

11.02. The CD includes a multimedia demonstration of using context-sensitive help on a Cisco router.

Error Messages

Errors inevitably creep up when you enter commands. Whenever you mistype a command, the IOS tells you that it has encountered a problem with the previously executed command. For instance, this message indicates a CLI input error:

```
% Invalid input detected at '^'.
```

You should examine the line between the command that you typed in and the error message. Somewhere in this line, you'll see a ^ character. This is used by the IOS to indicate that an error exists in the command line at that spot.

Here is another CLI error message:

```
% Incomplete command.
```

This error indicates that you have not entered all the necessary parameters for the command. The syntax of the command is correct, but more parameters are necessary. In this case, you can use the context-sensitive help feature to help you figure out what parameter or parameters you forgot.

You see an error message similar to the following if you do not type in enough characters to make a command or parameter unique:

```
% Ambiguous command: "show i"
```

In this example, apparently, more than one parameter for the **show** command begins with the letter *i*. Again, you can use context-sensitive help to figure out what parameter to use:

```
Router# show i?
idb  interfaces  ip  ipv6
Router# show i
```

If you enter a command that the IOS does not understand, you'll see this error message:

```
% Unknown command or computer name, or unable to find computer address
```

If you see this, use the context-sensitive help to figure out the correct command to enter.

Entering Commands

Four key features included in the IOS relate to entering commands:

- Symbolic translation
- Command prompting
- Syntax checking
- Command recall

Whenever you enter a command in the CLI, the command-line parser dissects the command, making sure that it is a valid command with valid parameters. In the case of Cisco routers only, if the CLI parser cannot find the actual command, the IOS assumes that you are trying to telnet to a machine by that name and attempts a DNS resolution of the name to an IP address. This process, called *symbolic translation*, can be annoying at times. But it does make telnetting to a remote machine easier, since you only have to type the name or IP address of the machine instead of using the **telnet** command, as discussed in Chapter 17.

on the
Job

Use the `no ip domain-lookup` *Configuration mode command to disable DNS lookups on your IOS device. This is typically one of the first commands I configure on a router; by doing this, any time you type an invalid command, the IOS won't do a DNS lookup, but will return an invalid command message. The downside of this command is that the IOS device will no longer do DNS lookups of any kind, but this is typically not an issue in most situations.*

You have already been presented with the *command prompting* feature—this is most commonly seen when using the context-sensitive help, such as the following:

```
Router# show ?
  aaa                       Show AAA values
  aal2                      Show commands for AAL2
  access-expression         List access expression
  access-lists              List access lists
  accounting                Accounting data for active sessions
  .
  .
  .
Router# show
```

In this example, after you use the context-sensitive help with the **show** command, the command **show** is left on the command line after the displayed output. The IOS is assuming that you are entering one of the parameters of this command and thus re-enters the command on the CLI. This can be annoying if you forget that the router is performing this function and re-enter the command again, like this:

```
Router# show show
```

The CLI always parses your commands and checks their validity by using the *syntax checking* feature. Any nonexistent commands or improperly entered commands cause the IOS to generate an error message with an appropriate error description.

on the
Job

Whenever you enter a command correctly, will you rarely see any output from the IOS, unless the command you typed in somehow changes the state of the router or one of its components, such as an interface coming up or going down. Therefore, you should be concerned primarily after you enter a command and the IOS displays a message—you should assume that a problem may exist.

Of course, when you are configuring an IOS device, you will sometimes make typing mistakes or enter invalid commands. If you typed in a 20-parameter command and made a mistake in the very last character, it would be sadistic on Cisco's part to make you type the complete command again. The *command recall* feature is extremely useful as it allows you to recall and edit previously executed commands. The next two sections discuss how to recall and edit previous (or current) commands.

Command-Line History

On any IOS device, you can use the **show history** command to see your previously entered commands:

```
IOS# show history
  enable
  show interface
  show version
  show history
IOS#
```

By default, an IOS device stores the last 10 commands that you executed. You can recall these commands by pressing either CTRL-P or the UP ARROW key. If you accidentally go past the command that you want to edit or re-execute, press CTRL-N or the DOWN ARROW key.

You can increase the size of the history buffer from 10 commands up to 256 by using the **terminal history size** command:

```
IOS# terminal history size #_of_commands
```

11.03. The CD includes a multimedia demonstration of using the history function on a Cisco router.

Editing the Command Line

Table 11-2 shows the control or command sequences that you can use to edit information on the command line.

TABLE 11-2	Editing Control Sequences for IOS Devices

Control Sequence	Description
CTRL-A	Moves the cursor to the beginning of the line
CTRL-E	Moves the cursor to the end of the line
ESC-B	Moves the cursor back one word at a time
ESC-F	Moves the cursor forward one word at a time
CTRL-B or LEFT ARROW	Moves the cursor back one character at a time
CTRL-F or RIGHT ARROW	Moves the cursor forward one character at a time
CTRL-P or UP ARROW	Recalls the last command
CTRL-N or DOWN ARROW	Recalls the most previously executed command
CTRL-D	Deletes the character the cursor is under
BACKSPACE	Deletes the character preceding the cursor
CTRL-R	Redisplays the current line
CTRL-U	Erases the line completely
CTRL-W	Erases the word the cursor is under
CTRL-Z	Takes you from Configuration mode back to Privilege EXEC mode
TAB	Once you enter a few characters and press the TAB key, the IOS device completes the word, assuming that you typed in enough characters to make the command or parameter unique.
$	When this appears at the beginning of a command line, it indicates that there are more characters to the right of the $.

e**x**am

ⓦatch   *Remember the basic editing*   *last 10 executed commands. You can use*
control sequences for editing commands   *the TAB key to auto-complete commands.*
in the CLI. By default, the IOS stores the

11.04. The CD includes a multimedia demonstration of using the command-line editing features on a Cisco router.

IOS Feature Example

This example uses the **clock** command to illustrate the helpfulness of some of the IOS's command-line features. This command is used on a router to set the current date and time. As an example, let's assume that English isn't your native language and that you are not sure how to spell "*clock,*" but you do know that it begins with the letters "*c* and *l*." Here's the example:

```
IOS# cl?
clear     clock
IOS# cl
```

Notice two things about the output in this example. First, two commands begin with **cl**: **clear** and **clock**. Second, notice the CLI after the help output—the IOS kept the **cl** on the command line. Some administrators like this feature and some hate it. I'm in the latter camp, since I commonly forget that the IOS device is doing this and I start typing from the beginning, like this:

```
IOS# clclock
Translating "clclock"
% Unknown command or computer name, or unable to find computer address
IOS#
```

If you haven't already guessed, this is an invalid command. Now that you know how to spell "*clock,*" if you don't know what parameter(s) to type after the **clock** command, you can use context-sensitive help:

```
IOS# clock ?
  set  Set the time and date
IOS# clock
```

The first column is the name of the parameter, and the second column is description. In this case, the IOS wants the word *set*:

```
IOS# clock set ?
  hh:mm:ss  Current Time
IOS# clock set
```

The next parameter wants the current time. This is based on UTC (unless you've changed the device's time zone) and is in a 24-hour format. For example, 3 P.M. would be 15:00:00. Again, use context-sensitive help to figure out if more parameters are required:

```
IOS# clock set 15:00:00 ?
  <1-31>  Day of the month
  MONTH   Month of the year
IOS# clock set 15:00:00
```

Whenever you see a range of numbers inside angle brackets, you must choose a value in this range. If you see a parameter in all caps, such as MONTH, you must supply a *name*. In this clocking example, the IOS wants the number of the day or name of the month, such as "May"—with this command, the router isn't picky about in which order either of these parameters is entered, but in many cases the order does matter. Again, using context-sensitive help, indicate the number of the year following the name of the month:

```
IOS# clock set 15:00:00 23 May ?
  <1993-2035>  Year
IOS# clock set 15:00:00 23 May
```

Again, use context-sensitive help to see what's next:

```
IOS# clock set 15:00:00 23 May 2004 ?
  <cr>
IOS# clock set 15:00:00 23 May 2004
IOS#
```

The <cr> means that you can press the ENTER key and the IOS device will accept the command. On an IOS router, use the **show clock** command to see your current time and date:

```
IOS# show clock
15:00:02.187 UTC Fri May 23 2003
IOS#
```

11.05. The CD includes a multimedia demonstration of using a combination of the command-line editing features on a Cisco router.

EXERCISE 11-1

Using IOS Features

So far in this chapter, you've learned how to use the IOS features on your Cisco devices. You can perform the following exercises on a Cisco router to enforce your skills. You can use the router simulator included on the CD-ROM, or you can use a real Cisco router. You can find a picture of the network diagram for the simulator in the Introduction to this book.

  1. Access the simulator and click the Lab Navigator button.

  2. Double-click Exercise 11-1, click the Load Lab button, and then click OK.

3. Click the eRouters button and choose 2600-1.

4. If you are currently logged into the router and see "Router#" as the prompt, type **exit** to log out.

5. Access User EXEC mode on your router by pressing the ENTER key. You should see the EXECprompt: Router>.

6. Pull up the list of commands available at this mode. Type in the ?. Press the SPACE key to page through the help information.

7. Go to Privilege EXEC mode. Use the **enable** command and your prompt should look like this: Router#.

8. On one command line, type **show interfaces**. Press the SPACE key to page through the help information.

9. On the next command line, type **show running-config**. Press the SPACE key to page through the help information.

10. Use the CLI editing features of your router by changing the **show running-config** command to **show startup-config** and execute this.

    Use the command recall (UP ARROW) to recall the **show running-config** command. Edit this command and replace **running** with **startup**. Press the LEFT ARROW to move over to the - and press BACKSPACE to delete the word **running**. Then type **startup**. Press CTRL-E to go to the end of the line and press the ENTER key to execute the command. Press the SPACE key to page through the help information.

11. Log out of the router using the **exit** command.

Now you should be more comfortable with the CLI of the IOS. The next section shows you how to create a basic configuration on your IOS device.

CERTIFICATION OBJECTIVE 11.04

Basic IOS Configuration

Here you'll learn the basics of accessing the IOS software and creating a simple configuration on your IOS device. Many of the configuration commands are the same on Cisco routers and switches, simplifying a basic setup of these devices;

however, as you'll see in subsequent chapters, certain features are specific to each product type, and thus each product has unique configuration commands.

Accessing Configuration Mode

All system/operating changes in the IOS must occur within Configuration mode. To access this mode, you must first be at Privilege EXEC mode and use this command:

```
IOS# configure terminal
IOS(config)#
```

a t c h   *Remember that you use the `configure terminal` command to enter global Configuration mode. Your prompt will change and contain (config)#.*

Notice that the prompt changed from # to (config)#, indicating the change in modes. You can abbreviate **configure terminal** to **conf t**. Configuration mode allows you to execute commands that change your router's or switch's configuration; however, you cannot actually view the changes from within this mode, as this is done from Privilege EXEC mode. To exit Configuration mode and return to Privilege EXEC mode, either type **end** or press CTRL-Z.

Device Identification

One of your first tasks is to change the name of your IOS device. This has only local significance and is used for management purposes. For instance, the Cisco Discovery Protocol (CDP) uses this device name. (CDP is discussed in Chapter 17.) On both routers and switches, the **hostname** command is used to change the name of the device. Here is a simple example of changing the name on a router:

```
Router(config)# hostname Perimeter
Perimeter(config)#
```

First, notice that the name of the device is placed after the command. As soon as you press ENTER, the new CLI prompt is immediately changed—it contains the device's new name.

To undo changes or negate a command on an IOS device, you can precede the command with the **no** parameter. As an example, to change the hostname back to the factory default, use this command:

```
Perimeter(config)# no hostname Perimeter
Router(config)#
```

In certain cases, you don't have to include the parameters of the command when negating it. In the preceding example, you could easily have typed in **no hostname** to accomplish the change, but in other cases, you must type in **no** and follow it with the entire configuration command.

Subconfiguration Modes

Certain configuration commands on IOS devices take you into a specific Subconfiguration mode, commonly referred to as a subcommand mode. Table 11-3 shows a few Subconfiguration modes that you might see on IOS devices.

NOTE: Not all Subconfiguration modes are supported on all IOS devices. When you are working in a Subconfiguration mode, the commands you enter affect only a specific component of the router or switch.

To leave a Subconfiguration mode and return to Global Configuration mode, use the **exit** command. Using the **end** command or pressing CTRL-Z will always take you back to Privilege EXEC mode no matter what Configuration mode you are currently working in. Here is an example of going from a subcommand mode to Global Configuration mode:

```
IOS(config)# line con 0
IOS(config-line)# exit
IOS(config)#
```

In many cases, when you are working in a Subconfiguration mode and type in a Global Configuration mode command, the IOS executes it and the mode changes to Global Configuration mode, like this:

```
IOS(config)# line con 0
IOS(config-line)# hostname 2960
2960(config)#
```

TABLE 11-3	IOS Prompt	Subconfiguration Mode
Subconfiguration Modes on IOS Devices	`(config-if)#`	Interface Subconfiguration mode
	`(config-subif)#`	Subinterface Subconfiguration mode
	`(config-line)#`	Line Subconfiguration mode
	`(config-controller)#`	Controller Subconfiguration mode
	`(config-router)#`	IP Routing Protocol Subconfiguration mode

Notice that when the **hostname** command was executed in Line Subconfiguration mode, the switch changed its name as well as the mode. Sometimes, you'll get an invalid command response from the router; in this case you'll have to exit out of Subconfiguration mode before executing the Global command.

11.06. The CD includes a multimedia demonstration of using Configuration and Subconfiguration modes on an IOS device.

Line Configuration

Lines on IOS devices provide access to an EXEC shell; sometimes this is called *character mode access*, since it deals with a CLI. Table 11-4 shows the supported line types. The **line** command is used to reference a line in Configuration mode. You must specify the type of line you want to configure as well as the line number, where line numbers begin at 0 and work their way up. Note that the console and auxiliary lines have only one line number: 0. When configuring VTYs and TTYs, you can specify a range of numbers. Executing the **line** command takes you into Subconfiguration mode, where the commands you enter affect that particular line or possibly multiple lines with VTYs and TTYs.

Changing the Inactivity Timeout

By default, the IOS device automatically logs you off after 10 minutes of inactivity. You can change this using the **exec-timeout** Line Subconfiguration mode command:

```
IOS(config)# line line_type line_#
IOS(config-line)# exec-timeout minutes seconds
```

TABLE 11-4	IOS Line Types	

Line Type	Description	Command Nomenclature
Console	Physical port that provides the initial CLI access; used for troubleshooting when remote access to the IOS device isn't functioning; only one is supported on a device.	`line con 0`
Auxiliary	Backup physical port typically used for dialup into the IOS device; not all devices have an auxiliary port and only one is supported per device.	`line aux 0`
Virtual Type Terminal (VTY)	Logical port that allows for remote access connections such as telnet and SSH to gain access to the CLI; many VTYs are supported on an IOS device, and the number is dependent on the device, model, and software version.	`line vty 0 4`
Teletype Terminal (TTY)	Physical port used for connecting to a modem for a terminal service or for access to the console ports of other devices. These ports are found only on routers and the number supported depends on the router model.	`line tty 0 31`

Remember that this changes the configuration only for the line (or lines) you've specified—other lines will still use the default idle time. If you don't want a particular line to time out ever, you can set the minutes and seconds values to 0, like this:

```
IOS(config)# line console 0
IOS(config-line)# exec-timeout 0 0
```

on the **Job**

Disabling the timeout for a line is not recommended in a production environment, since it creates security issues. However, for training purposes, such as studying for the CCNA exam, this is okay.

If you want to disable the use of a line completely, use this configuration:

```
IOS(config)# line line_type line_#
IOS(config-line)# no exec
```

To verify your line configuration, use the **show line** command:

```
IOS# show line con 0
 Tty Typ  Tx/Rx A Modem Roty AccO AccI Uses Noise Overruns
*  0 CTY         -  -     -    -    -    0    0    0/0
```

```
Line 0, Location: "", Type: ""
Length: 24 lines, Width: 80 columns
Status: Ready, Active
Capabilities: none
Modem state: Ready
Special Chars: Escape Hold Stop Start Disconnect Activation
               ^^x    none   -    -     none
Timeouts: Idle EXEC  Idle Session  Modem Answer  Session  Dispatch
          never       never                       none     not set
Session limit is not set.
Time since activation: 0:04:49
Editing is enabled.
History is enabled, history size is 10.
Full user help is disabled
Allowed transports are pad telnet mop.  Preferred is telnet.
No output characters are padded
No special data dispatching characters
```

In this example, notice that the timeout value is set to never.

on the **Job**

Notice that the show command is not entered from Configuration mode.
To enter User and Privilege EXEC mode commands in Configuration mode,
preface the commands with the word do, like so: do show line con 0.

11.07. The CD includes a multimedia demonstration of changing the idle
timeout on a Cisco device.

CLI Output

One nice feature of an IOS device is that when certain types of events occur, such as an interface going down or up, an administrator making a configuration change, or output of **debug** commands, the IOS device, by default, prints an informational message on the console line. It won't, however, display the same messages if you happen to have logged into the IOS device via telnet or SSH or accessed the device via the auxiliary or TTY lines.

If the latter is the case, you can have the IOS display these messages on your screen by executing the Privilege EXEC **terminal monitor** command, as shown here:

```
IOS# terminal monitor
```

You must execute this command after you have logged into the IOS from the VTY, TTY, or auxiliary lines. Once you log out, however, this command does not apply to anyone else logging into the IOS device on the same line; each individual line session must re-execute this command.

One annoying problem with the information messages displayed on your CLI screen is that if you are typing in an IOS command, when the device displays the message, it starts printing it right where the cursor is, making it difficult to figure out where you left off typing. If you remember, just keep typing your command, or press CTRL-C to abort the command. A better approach, though, is to set up the IOS so that after the message prints in your window, the IOS redisplays what you have already entered on a new CLI prompt. The **logging synchronous** command accomplishes this:

```
IOS(config)# line line_type line_#
IOS(config-line)# logging synchronous
```

Notice that this command is executed under the Line Subconfiguration mode. If you want to implement this feature, you'll need to set it up under all the lines from which you'll be accessing your IOS device, including your VTYs and console port. You can also press CTRL-R to refresh the screen.

11.08. The CD includes a multimedia demonstration of using `logging` `synchronous` **on a Cisco router.**

Interface Configuration

To configure an interface, you must first enter Interface Subconfiguration mode:

```
IOS(config)# interface type [slot_#/]port_#
IOS(config-if)#
```

You must specify two components to the **interface** command: the *type* and the *location*. When you enter the complete **interface** command, notice that the prompt changes, signifying that you are in Interface Subconfiguration mode for the specified interface, `(config-if)#` in this example.

on the job *You can't determine what interface you are working in by examining the prompt. If you aren't sure, use the history recall feature to recall the* `interface` *command and re-execute it.*

When specifying the interface, you can use any of the following nomenclatures:

```
IOS(config)# interface ethernet 0/1
IOS(config)# interface ethernet0/1
IOS(config)# int e 0/1
IOS(config)# int e0/1
```

You can separate the type and location with a space, or concatenate the two together. Likewise, you can abbreviate the commands and parameters.

Enable and Disable

On the Catalyst switches, the interfaces are *enabled* by default; on Cisco routers, the interfaces are *disabled* by default. You can disable interfaces with the **shutdown** Interface Subconfiguration mode command:

```
IOS(config)# interface type slot_#/port_#
IOS(config-if)# shutdown
```

To re-enable the interface, use the **no shutdown** command.

Remember how to enable and disable an interface on an IOS	*device:* `no shutdown` *and* `shutdown`, *respectively.*

Whenever the interface changes status, the router prints a message on the screen telling you so. Here is an example in which an interface on a router is being activated:

```
IOS(config)# interface fastethernet0/1
IOS(config-if)# no shutdown
1w0d: %LINK-3-UPDOWN: Interface FastEthernet0/1, changed state to up
1w0d: %LINEPROTO-5-UPDOWN: Line protocol on Interface
      FastEthernet0/1, changed state to up
IOS(config-if)#
```

In this example, the first information line indicates that the physical layer is activated. The second information line indicates that the data link layer is enabled.

When copying and pasting a configuration file into the router, and the router interface is disabled with the `shutdown` *command, the pasted configuration file must contain the* `no shutdown` *command in order to active the interface. This is a common problem when copying and pasting a configuration file from an old router to a new router, where the interfaces on the new router are disabled by default.*

Description

You can add a description to any interface by using the **description** command:

```
IOS(config)# interface type [slot_#/]port_#
IOS(config-if)# description interface_description
```

The **description** command supplies a one-line description of the device to which the interface is connected, or whatever description you want to assign. This description appears in the output of the **show interfaces** command discussed later in the chapter.

Speed and Duplexing for Ethernet Interfaces

To set the speed and duplexing speeds of Ethernet-based interfaces, use the following configuration:

```
IOS(config)# interface ethernet_type [slot_#/]port_#
IOS(config-if)# speed 10|100|1000|auto
IOS(config-if)# duplex full|half|auto
```

on the Job

For 10/100 or 10/100/1000 Ethernet ports, it is no longer recommended that you hard code the speed and duplexing with the speed *and* duplex *commands; instead, let the interface autosense these settings from the directly connected device.*

CertCam

11.09. The CD includes a multimedia demonstration of configuring interfaces on IOS devices.

Serial Interfaces on Routers

When connecting a serial cable to the serial interface of a router, clocking is typically provided by an external device, such as a modem or a channel service unit/data service unit (CSU/DSU). The router is the data termination equipment (DTE) and the external device is the data communications equipment (DCE), where the DCE provides the clocking. This type of WAN connection is discussed in Chapter 25.

In some cases, however, you might connect two routers back-to-back using the routers' serial interfaces. For instance, if you are building your own lab to practice CCNA commands, you'll more than likely connect the routers back-to-back to reduce equipment costs. In this situation, each router, by default, is a DTE. Since clocking is required for the interface to be enabled, one of the two routers will have to perform the function of an external DCE. This is accomplished by using the **clock rate** Interface Subconfiguration mode command on the serial interface:

```
Router(config)# interface serial [slot_#/]port_#
Router(config-if)# clock rate rate_in_bits_per_second
```

When entering the clock rate, you can't choose any arbitrary value. Use context-sensitive help to find out which clock rates your serial interface supports. Here are some possible values: 1200, 2400, 4800, 9600, 19200, 38400, 56000, 72000, 125000, 148000, 500000, 800000, 1000000, 1300000, 2000000, and 4000000.

Note that that you can't choose an arbitrary router in the back-to-back connection to be the DCE—this is based on how the two routers are cabled. One end of the cable is physically the DTE, and the other is the DCE. Some cables are marked and some are not, depending on where they were purchased. If you are not sure which router has the DTE end of the cable and which has the DCE end, you can determine this with the **show controller** command:

```
Router> show controller serial [slot_#/]port_#
```

This is one of the few commands in which you *cannot* concatenate the type and the port number—you must separate them by a space. Here is an example of the use of this command:

```
Router> show controller serial 0
HD unit 0, idb = 0x121C04, driver structure at 0x127078
buffer size 1524 HD unit 0, DTE V.35 serial cable attached
   .
   .
   .
```

Notice that the second line of this example holds two important pieces of information: the connection type (DTE) and the type of cable (V.35).

Here is an example of an interface connected to the end of a DCE cable:

```
Router> show controller serial 0
HD unit 0, idb = 0x1BA16C, driver structure at 0x1C04E0
buffer size 1524  HD unit 0, V.35 DCE cable, clockrate 64000
   .
   .
   .
```

In this example, the clocking has already been configured: 64,000 bps (bits per second).

11.10. The CD includes a multimedia demonstration of setting the clocking on a serial interface on a Cisco router.

CERTIFICATION OBJECTIVE 11.05

Basic IOS Security Configuration

The Computer Security Institute (CSI) is an organization that provides education and training on network security fundamentals. Periodically it performs market research studies on security issues with companies. In one study, more than 70 percent of all the companies polled reported experiencing some kind of security breach. Knowing this information, as a network administrator, one of your roles will be to ensure that access to your networking devices is strictly controlled. The following sections will introduce you to securing your IOS device.

NOTE: The information introduced in this chapter is only the beginning of security features you'll set up on your IOS devices; many more of these features are discussed throughout the book, such as port security on the switches in Chapter 12, Security Device Manager (SDM) in Chapter 18, and access control lists (ACLs) in Chapter 22, to name a few.

Physical and Environmental Threats

Many network administrators forget that the first line of defense in securing their network devices includes protecting against physical and environmental threats, including the following:

- **Hardware** Restricting physical access to the router via physical measures, such as locked doors, key cards, video cameras, and so on
- **Electrical** Ensuring that equipment is protected from power surges/spikes, brownouts, and loss of power

- ■ **Environmental**   Protecting equipment from temperatures that are too cold or too hot or from too much humidity
- ■ **Maintenance**   Ensuring that you follow electrostatic discharge procedures when handling sensitive electronic parts, have spares on hand for critical parts, and properly label equipment and cables

An in-depth discussion of these issues is beyond the scope of this book; however, it is covered in a little bit more depth in Cisco's Securing Network Devices (SND) course.

Passwords

The most common way of restricting physical access to IOS devices is to use some type of user authentication. For example, you can configure passwords to restrict access to the lines on IOS devices (User EXEC mode) as well as access to Privilege EXEC mode. Configuring passwords on Catalyst IOS switches, such as the 2950s and 2960s, is the same as configuring passwords on IOS routers. The following sections discuss the configuration of passwords on IOS devices.

User EXEC Password Protection

Controlling access to User EXEC mode on an IOS device is accomplished on a line-by-line basis: console, auxiliary, TTYs, and VTYs. Remember that not all devices support auxiliary ports, only routers support TTYs, and the number of VTYs an IOS device supports is product-dependent, ranging from five VTYs (0–4) to almost a thousand.

To secure the console port, you must first go into the console's Line Subconfiguration mode with the **line console 0** command to configure the line password:

```
IOS(config)# line console 0
IOS(config-line)#  password console_password
```

The **0** in the first command specifies the console port. Lines and interfaces are numbered from 0 upward. Even though the IOS devices have only a single console port, it is designated as 0. Next, notice that the prompt on the second line changed. Once you are in Line Subconfiguration mode, you can use the **password** command to assign the console password. Passwords on IOS devices are *case-sensitive*. Remember that the **password** command, when executed under **line console 0**, sets the User EXEC password for someone trying to access the IOS device from the console port only.

The auxiliary port is typically used as a backup console port or a remote access port with a modem attached to it. The following code shows the syntax for setting up password authentication on the auxiliary port:

```
Router(config)# line aux 0
Router(config-line)# password console_password
Router(config-line)# exit
```

To set up a telnet password for your VTYs, use this configuration:

```
IOS(config)# line vty 0 15
IOS(config-line)# password telnet_password
IOS(config-line)# login
```

The **vty** parameter in this command refers to *virtual terminal*, a fancy name for telnet or SSH access. The 2950 and 2960 switches support up to 16 simultaneous VTY sessions, where each connection is internally tracked by a number: 0–15. Depending on the router model and IOS software version, this number might range from 5 (0–4) on up to almost 1000. You could assign a different password to each VTY, but then you wouldn't know which password to use when telnetting into the IOS device. However, the IOS allows you to specify all 16 VTYs with the **line** command, simplifying your configuration, as in the preceding configuration: **line vty 0 15**. You need to specify the beginning and ending VTY numbers on the same line. Once you are in Line Subconfiguration mode, use the **password** command to set your password. You also need to enter the **login** command to allow remote access to the IOS—this tells the IOS to use the password configured with the **password** command on the specified line.

---

e x a m

ⓦ a t c h   *By default, only the first five VTYs (0–4) are enabled. On devices that support more VTYs, they must manually be enabled. When you remotely log into your IOS device using telnet, and you see the message "Password required but none set,"* *then you have not configured a password on the line with the* password *command and won't be able to log in until you configure it. Remember that you should secure your VTYs with a password and login process.*

Other ways of validating access are available, such as a local username database or through an external authentication server. (The configuration of an authentication server is beyond the scope of this book. For an in-depth discussion, see my book

Cisco Router Firewall Security from Cisco Press.) A local username database is a database on the router that allows you to specify both a username and a password to restrict access to the lines on the IOS device. Using usernames and passwords is recommended over using only passwords on lines: the advantage of this approach is that each user can have his or her own password instead of sharing a password, providing for more accountability. The following commands illustrate the setup of a local username database and its use on VTYs:

```
IOS(config)# username name secret|password password
IOS(config)# line vty 0 15
IOS(config-line)# login local
```

The **username** command specifies the name and password for the user. The main difference between the **secret** and **password** parameters is that the **secret** parameter tells the IOS to encrypt the password with an MD5 hash, and the **password** parameter doesn't (the password is stored in clear text). This is true of the Line Subconfiguration mode **password** command: it also is stored in clear text.

NOTE: The `login local` command can be used on any of the lines on the router to perform user authentication: console, auxiliary, VTYs, and TTYs.

Privilege EXEC Password Protection

Along with protecting access to the lines on an IOS device, you can also control access to Privilege EXEC mode by assigning a password to it. Two configuration options are shown here:

```
Switch(config)# enable password Privilege_EXEC_password
```

or

```
Switch(config)# enable secret Privilege_EXEC_password
```

Both of these commands configure the Privilege EXEC password. The main difference between the two, as with the **username** command, is that the **secret** parameter encrypts the Privilege EXEC password and the **password** parameter doesn't. If you configure both of these commands, the password configured with the **enable secret** command always takes precedence over the **enable password** command.

Password Encryption

Passwords that are not encrypted can be encrypted by using the **service password-encryption** Global Configuration mode command. However, the **enable secret** command's encryption is much stronger than using the **service password-encryption** command to do the encryption.

on the
job

I recommend against *using the* `enable password` *command or the* *username command with the* `password` *parameter, along with* `service` `password-encryption`, *since several easily accessible utilities on the Internet can be used to break this encryption: just do a search on "Cisco password cracker" using a search engine and you'll find a lot of them. And even with a password-cracking program such as Cain and Abel or L0phtcrack, given enough time, the MD5 hashed encryption using the* `secret` *keyword can also be broken. If someone steals your configuration file, you're vulnerable to an access attack. The best defense is protecting any access to your configuration file.*

CertCam

11.11. The CD includes a multimedia demonstration of configuring passwords on an IOS device.

Login Banners

You can set up a login banner on your IOS device that will display a message to every user attempting to access User EXEC mode. The **banner motd** command is used to create the login banner:

```
IOS(config)# banner motd delimiting_char your_banner delimiting_char
IOS(config)#
```

The **motd** (message of the day) is a carryover from the UNIX world. After the **banner motd** command, you must enter the delimiting character, which is used to signify the beginning and ending of the banner—it cannot appear in the actual banner. Once you enter the delimiting character, when the IOS CLI parser sees this character later in your text, the IOS terminates the banner and returns you to the CLI prompt. One nice feature of the banner is that pressing the ENTER key doesn't terminate the banner, so you can have banners that span multiple lines. Whenever you have completed your banner, type the delimiting character to end the command. Here is an example of setting up a login banner:

```
IOS(config)# banner motd $
This is a private system and only authorized individuals
          are allowed!
All others will be prosecuted to the fullest extent of the law!
$
IOS(config)#
```

In this example, the banner spans multiple lines and the delimiting character is the dollar sign ($). A banner doesn't have to span multiple lines, but it can be placed on a single line, as in this example:

```
IOS(config)# banner motd 'Keep Out!'
IOS(config)#
```

In this example, the single quote (') is the delimiting character. Once you have created a login banner, test it by logging out of the IOS device and logging back in. You should see your banner appear *before* the User EXEC password prompt.

ⓦatch *Remember that the banner motd command displays a banner before you are authenticated on a line; the* banner exec *command displays a banner after you log in, but before you get a User EXEC prompt.*

Besides the MOTD banner, you can create other types of banners. The MOTD banner is displayed before the login process occurs. An EXEC banner allows you to display a message after authentication occurs and before the User EXEC prompt is displayed. To create an EXEC banner, replace the **motd** parameter in the **banner motd** command with **exec**.

on the ❗**ⓙob** *You should not use such words as* welcome *or any type of welcoming salutation in your banner; using such words can be misconstrued and allow real attackers to defend their actions by the welcoming salutation in your login banner.*

11.12. The CD includes a multimedia demonstration of setting up a login banner on a Cisco router.

CERTIFICATION OBJECTIVE 11.06

IOS Operation and Verification

Once you have configured your IOS device, many commands are available to use to examine and troubleshoot your configuration. This section covers some of the basic **show** commands available. Subsequent chapters will discuss additional commands you can use to help troubleshoot more complex problems.

Show and Debug Command Overview

You can use two basic commands to troubleshoot problems on an IOS device:

- **show** Takes a snapshot of a particular process and displays information about it; the information displayed is static and will not refresh itself unless you re-execute the command (you can use your command-line history feature to do this).
- **debug** Displays how a particular process is currently operating, showing information as it basically happens, in real-time.

The **show** commands require little processing on the IOS device to perform and allow you to get a quick idea as to how something is configured (the configuration in RAM, a routing protocol, or STP) or the current state of a process (such as an interface, a routing table, or a port address table). Unfortunately, **show** commands sometimes don't provide enough information, in certain instances, to diagnose a problem and fix it correctly.

The **debug** commands, on the other hand, display how a process is currently running or behaving, such as the contents of a routing update received by a neighboring router, and are therefore typically more useful in troubleshooting difficult problems. The main disadvantage of **debug** commands is that they are process-intensive on the IOS device and should be used with care.

Running and Startup Configuration

A configuration file contains the commands used by an IOS device. By default, two configurations are possible on an IOS device:

■ **running-config**   This file contains the actual configuration running in RAM of the IOS device (the one it is currently using).

■ **startup-config**   This file contains the backed-up configuration in NVRAM or flash of an IOS device.

Configuration files can reside in many locations, including RAM, nonvolatile RAM (NVRAM), or a TFTP server, among other places. Whenever you make changes to an IOS's configuration by typing in commands from Configuration mode, these changes are made in RAM. These changes can then be saved to NVRAM, which is a static form of memory in which, when the Cisco device is turned off, the contents are not erased and are available upon a power-up. IOS devices do *not* automatically back up the configuration file from RAM to NVRAM; this must be done *manually*. Configuration changes can also be saved to an external server using Trivial File Transfer Protocol (TFTP), File Transfer Protocol (FTP), and Secure Copy Protocol (SCP)—this, however, requires that you configure IP addressing and possibly a default gateway address on your IOS device. (These topics are discussed in Chapters 12, 16, and 17.)

The following sections discuss how you view your IOS device's configuration files as well as how to back up and restore your configuration files locally on your IOS device.

Viewing Configurations

To examine the active or running configuration on an IOS device, use the **show running-config** command. You must be in Privilege EXEC mode to execute this command. Here is an example of this command from a Cisco router:

```
Router# show running-config
Building configuration...
Current configuration:
!
version 12.0
no service udp-small-servers
no service tcp-small-servers
!
hostname Router
 .
 .
 .
```

Notice the references to Building configuration... and Current configuration in this example. Both of these refer to the configuration in RAM.

Backing Up Your Configuration File Locally

Configuration files are stored in NVRAM for both switches and routers. When an IOS device boots up, the IOS operating system loads the configuration from NVRAM and places it in RAM. However, as mentioned in the "Running and Startup Configuration" introduction to this section, the running configuration in RAM is not automatically saved to NVRAM: if you turn off your IOS device without saving its configuration, your newly implemented changes will disappear. To save the active configuration to NVRAM, you must execute the **copy running-config startup-config** Privilege EXEC mode command. Upon executing this command, the IOS device takes the active configuration in RAM and saves it to NVRAM. In this process, the old configuration file in NVRAM is overwritten. Here is an example of this command:

```
IOS# copy running-config startup-config
Destination filename [startup-config]?
Building configuration...
[OK]
IOS#
```

When executing this command, you are asked for a filename for the configuration file—the default is "*startup-config*." This is the filename the IOS looks for when booting up. You can change the name for backup revisioning purposes (different versions of the backed-up configuration), but make sure that your most current configuration is saved as startup-config. On the IOS device, you can view the saved configuration in NVRAM with the **show startup-config** Privilege EXEC mode command.

on the **job**

A shortcut to save the IOS's configuration to NVRAM is the write memory *command: you can abbreviate this to just* wr. *However, this command is not supported on the exam. On real IOS devices, I use* wr *all the time to quickly save a configuration.*

To see the configuration file stored in NVRAM, use this command:

```
Router# show startup-config
Using 4224 out of 65536 bytes
!
version 11.3
```

```
no service udp-small-servers
no service tcp-small-servers
!
hostname Router
 .
 .
 .
```

One difference between this output and that from the **show running-config** command is the first line of output. Using 4224 out of 65536 bytes refers to the amount of NVRAM currently used by the saved configuration file.

11.13. The CD includes a multimedia demonstration of configuring and manipulating configuration files on an IOS device.

You should know that IOS devices do not automatically save configuration changes. You must manually enter the copy running-config startup-config command from Privileged EXEC mode. This command backs up your configuration to NVRAM.

Also, any time you want to examine or manipulate a configuration, you must be in Privilege EXEC mode. The show running-config command displays the IOS device's currently running configuration in RAM.

Restoring Your Configuration File Locally

To restore your configuration from NRAM to RAM, use the **copy startup-config running config** command from Privilege EXEC mode, like this:

```
IOS# copy startup-config running-config
Destination filename [running-config]?
947 bytes copied in 0.320 secs (2959 bytes/sec)
IOS#
```

One important thing to note is that when you take a configuration file from any location and copy it to RAM, the IOS uses a merge process to load in the configuration file from the source, overwriting matching commands in RAM and adding new commands that don't exist in RAM, but not deleting commands that don't exist in NVRAM but do exist in RAM. Chapter 17 will go into this process in more depth.

Device Version Information

If you want to see general information about your IOS device—its model number, the types of interfaces, the different kinds and amounts of memory, its software version, where the IOS located and loaded itself and its configuration file, as well as the configuration settings—you can use the **show version** command.

e x a m
ⓦatch   *Be familiar with the output*   *the uptime, the amount of RAM, NVRAM,*
of the show version *command, including*   *flash, the type and number of interfaces,*
what is displayed, such as the IOS version,   *and the configuration register value.*

Here is an example of this command on a Cisco router:

```
Router> show version
Cisco Internetwork Operating System Software
IOS (tm) 3600 Software (C3640-JS-M), Version 12.0(3c), RELEASE SOFTWARE (fc1)
Copyright (c) 1986-1999 by cisco Systems, Inc.
Compiled Tue 13-Apr-99 07:39 by phanguye
Image text-base: 0x60008918, data-base: 0x60BDC000

ROM: System Bootstrap, Version 11.1(20)AA2, EARLY DEPLOYMENT
RELEASE SOFTWARE (fc1)

Router uptime is 2 days, 11 hours, 40 minutes
System restarted by power-on
System image file is "flash:c3640-js-mz.120-3c.bin"

cisco 3640 (R4700) processor (revision 0x00) with 49152K/16384K
bytes of memory.
.
.
.
1 FastEthernet/IEEE 802.3 interface(s)
8 Low-speed serial(sync/async) network interface(s)
1 Channelized T1/PRI port(s)
DRAM configuration is 64 bits wide with parity disabled.
125K bytes of non-volatile configuration memory.
32768K bytes of processor board System flash (Read/Write)

Configuration register is 0x2102
```

The last line of this output is the configuration register value. This value determines how the router will boot up, including how it will find its IOS and its configuration file. The bootup process of the router is discussed in more depth in Chapter 16.

11.14. The CD includes a multimedia demonstration of using the* show *version *command on a Cisco router.

Interface Information

One common networking problem occurs when you enable an interface: it might not always come up. In Ethernet, this could be caused by using the wrong cable type (crossover versus straight-through), a mismatch in the speed or duplex settings, or a bad cable. This section will discuss how to diagnose these problems with the **show interfaces** command.

Viewing Interface Information

One of the most common commands that you will use on an IOS device is the **show interfaces** command. This command allows you to see the status and configuration of your interfaces, as well as some statistical information. Here is the syntax of this command:

```
IOS> show interfaces [type [slot_#/]port_#]
```

If you don't specify a specific interface, the IOS device displays all of its interfaces—those enabled as well as those disabled. Here is an example of the output of this command on a router:

```
Router# show interfaces e0
Ethernet 0 is up, line protocol is up
  Hardware is MCI Ethernet, address is 0000.0c00.1234
                                (bia 0000.0c00.1234)
  Internet address is 172.16.16.2, subnet mask is 255.255.255.252
  MTU 1500 bytes, BW 10000 Kbit, DLY 100000 usec, rely 255/255,
                  load 1/255
  Encapsulation ARPA, loopback not set, keepalive set (10 sec)
  ARP type: ARPA, ARP Timeout 4:00:00
  Last input 0:00:00, output 0:00:00, output hang never
  Last clearing of "show interface" counters 0:00:00
  Output queue 0/40, 0 drops; input queue 0/75, 0 drops
  Five minute input rate 0 bits/sec, 0 packets/sec
  Five minute output rate 4000 bits/sec, 8 packets/sec
```

```
2240375 packets input, 887359872 bytes, 0 no buffer
Received 722137 broadcasts, 0 runts, 0 giants
0 input errors, 0 CRC, 0 frame, 0 overrun, 0 ignored, 0 abort
10137586 packets output, 897215078 bytes, 0 underruns
4 output errors, 1037 collisions, 3 interface resets,
                    0 restarts
```

Troubleshooting Interface Problems

One of the first things that you want to examine in this display is the status of the interface: Ethernet0 is up, line protocol is up. The first up refers to the status of the physical layer, and the second up refers to the status of the data link layer. Here are the possible values for the physical layer status:

- Up   The device is sensing a physical layer signal on the interface.
- Down   The device is not sensing a physical layer signal on the interface, a condition that can arise if the attached device is turned off, there is no cable attached, or you are using the wrong type of cable.
- Administratively down   You used the **shutdown** command to disable the interface.

Here are the possible values for the data link layer status:

- Up   The data link layer is operational.
- Down   The data link layer is not operational, a condition that can be caused by missed keepalives on a serial link, no clocking, an incorrect encapsulation type, or a disabled physical layer.

If the interface status is "up and up," the interface is operational; if it is "up and down," it signals a problem with the data link layer (layer 2); if it is "down and down," there is a physical layer problem (layer 1). If it is "administratively down and down," the interface was disabled with the shutdown command.

The "Hardware is" refers to the physical (layer 1) properties of the interface and the "Encapsulation" refers to the data link (layer 2) properties of the interface. If the hardware type for an interface says "LANCE", then the interface is a Fast Ethernet interface.

The second line of output from the **show interfaces** command has the hardware interface type (in this example, it's an Ethernet controller). This is followed by the MAC address on the interface. The third line has the IP address and subnet mask configured on the interface (you won't see this on a layer 2 switch's interface). The fourth line has the MTU Ethernet frame size as well as the routing protocol metrics. (These metrics are discussed in depth in Chapters 15, 19, 20, and 21, which discuss routing protocols.) Notice the BW parameter in this line. Referred to as the *bandwidth* of the link, this is used by some routing protocols, such as Open Shortest Path First (OSPF) and Enhanced Interior Gateway Routing Protocol (EIGRP), when making routing decisions. For Ethernet, this is 10,000 Kbps. The line after this refers to the layer 2 encapsulation (frame) type used; with Ethernet, this can be ARPA (used with TCP/IP), Subnetwork Access Protocol (SNAP), or SAP.

Table 11-5 explains some of the elements that you may see with the **show interfaces** command. Note that depending on the kind of IOS device and type of interface, the output displayed in the **show interfaces** command may differ slightly.

TABLE 11-5   Explanation of the Elements in the **show interfaces** Command

Element	Description
Address	The MAC address of the interface; BIA (burnt-in address) is the MAC address burnt into the Ethernet controller—this can be overridden with the Interface **mac-address** command.
Last input/output	The last time a packet was received on or sent out of the interface—can be used to determine whether the interface is operating or not.
Last clearing	Indicates the last time the **clear counters** command was executed on the interface.
Output queue	Indicates the number of packets waiting to be sent out the interface—the number after the slash (/) is the maximum size of the queue and then the number of packets dropped because the queue was full.
Input queue	Indicates the number of packets received on the interface and waiting to be processed—the number after the slash (/) is the maximum size of the queue and then the number of packets dropped because the queue was full.
No buffers (input)	Number of received packets dropped because the input buffer was filled up.
Runts (input)	Number of packets received that were less than the minimum for the encapsulation type (64 bytes for Ethernet).

| TABLE 11-5 | Explanation of the Elements in the `show interfaces` Command (*Continued*) |

Element	Description
Giants (input)	Number of packets received that were greater than the maximum allowed size (1518 bytes for Ethernet).
Input errors	The total number of input errors received on the interface.
CRC (input)	Indicates packets received that had checksum errors.
Frame (input)	Indicates the number of packets received that had both CRC errors and cases where the length of the frame was not on a byte boundary.
Overruns (input)	Number of times the inbound packet rate exceeded the capabilities of the interface to process the traffic.
Ignored (input)	Number of inbound packets that were dropped because of the lack of input buffer space.
Aborts (input)	Number of received packets that were aborted.
Collisions (output)	Number of times the interface tried transmitting a packet, but a collision occurred—this should be less than 0.1% of total traffic leaving the interface.
Interface resets (output)	Number of times the interface changed state by going down and then coming back up.
Restarts (output)	Number of times the controller was reset because of errors—use the **show controllers** command to troubleshoot this problem.

11.15. The CD includes a multimedia demonstration of displaying interface statistics on an IOS device.

Remember that if devices connected to a subnet can ping each other, but devices cannot ping the router connected to the same subnet, use the `show interfaces` *command to verify that the interface is operational and that the router has the right IP address configured on it.*

EXERCISE 11-2

Using the CLI to Set Up a Basic Router Configuration

In this exercise, you will use the CLI to create a basic configuration. You'll perform these steps on the routers and switches using Boson's NetSim simulator. (You can find a picture of the network diagram for the simulator in the Introduction section of this book.) After starting up the simulator, do the following:

1. Click the LabNavigator button. At the top of the simulator in the menu bar, click the eRouters icon and choose 2600-1.

2. Starting with the 2600-1 router, go to Privilege EXEC mode and then enter Configuration mode: At the top of the simulator's toolbar, click the eRouters icon and select 2600-1. On the 2600-1 router, access User EXEC mode and use **enable** to go to Privilege EXEC mode, and then use **configure terminal** to access Configuration mode.

3. Assign a hostname of *2600-1*: Use the **hostname 2600-1** command and examine the prompt.

4. Set a User EXEC password of *cisco* for telnet access: Enter the **line vty 0 4** command and follow it with the **login** and **password cisco** commands. Exit this subcommand mode: **exit**.

5. Assign an encrypted Privilege EXEC password of *cisco*: Enter **enable secret cisco**.

6. Check whether or not the serial 0 interface is DTE or DCE. If it is DCE, assign a clock rate of 64,000: Check the controller from Privilege EXEC mode using **show controller serial 0**.

7. If it's the DCE, configure the clock rate by performing the following. Enter the interface with **configure terminal** and **interface serial 0**. Configure the clock rate: **clock rate 64000**.

8. Enable the fastethernet0/0 interface: **interface fastethernet0/0**, **no shutdown**, and **exit**.

9. Enable the serial0 interface: **interface serial0**, **no shutdown**, and **exit**. Exit to Privilege EXEC mode: **end**.

10. Use a command to display all of the interfaces, their IP addresses, and their statuses on one screen and then show the details of `fastethernet0/0` and `serial0` separately: Use the **show interfaces** command followed by **show interface fa0/0** and **show interface s0**. fa0/0 should be "up and up"; but since the 2600-2's s0 interface hasn't been configured yet, this should be "up and down."

11. Save your configuration to NVRAM and view the active configuration: Save it with **copy running-config startup-config** and view it with **show running-config**.

12. Configure the 2600-2 router. At the top of the simulator in the menu bar, click the eRouters icon and choose 2600-2.

13. First set the hostname (*2600-2*): At the top of the simulator's toolbar, click the eRouters icon and select 2600-2. On the 2600-2 router, access User EXEC mode and use **enable** to go to Privilege EXEC mode and then **configure terminal** to access Configuration mode. Use the **hostname 2600-2** command and examine the prompt. Enter the **line vty 0 4** command and follow it with the **login** and **password cisco** commands. Exit the subcommand mode: **exit**.

14. Then set the telnet (*cisco*) and enable secret passwords (*cisco*): Enter **enable secret cisco**.

15. For the interfaces, enable `fastethernet0/0` and `serial0`. Set the clock rate to 64,000 bps if necessary on the serial interface: Enter the interface with **interface fastethernet 0/0**. Use the **no shutdown** command to enable the interface. Exit Configuration mode (**end**) and check the `serial0` controller: **show controller serial 0**. If it's a DCE, configure the following. Enter the interface with **configure terminal** and **interface serial 0**. Configure the clock rate: **clock rate 64000**. Use the **no shutdown** command to enable the s0 interface. Exit to Privilege EXEC mode: **end**.

16. Then view the router's interface status: **show interfaces**. Make sure fa0/0 and s0 are "up and up."

17. Save the router's configuration by running **copy running-config startup-config**.

18. Configure the 2950-1 switch: At the top of the simulator in the menu bar, click the eSwitches icon and choose 2950-1.

19. Set the hostname (*2950-1*) as well as the telnet (*cisco*) and enable secret passwords (*cisco*): At the top of the simulator's toolbar, click the eSwitches icon and select 2950-1. On the 2950-1 switch, access User EXEC mode and use **enable** to go to Privilege EXEC mode; then use **configure terminal** to access Configuration mode. Use the **hostname 2950-1** command and examine the prompt. Enter the **line vty 0 4** command and follow it with the **login** and **password cisco** commands. Enter **enable secret cisco**. Exit Configuration mode: **end**.

20. Verify the interface's operation: View the switch's interface status by using the **show interfaces** command for **fa0/1** (connected to 2950-2), **fa0/2** (connected to 2950-2), **fa0/3** (connected to Host-1), and **fa0/4** (connected to Host-2).

21. Save the switch's configuration: **copy running-config startup-config**.

22. Repeat this process (steps 18 to 21) for the 2950-2 switch (with a hostname of *2950-2*) and the 2950-3 switch (with a hostname of *2950-3*).

You should now be comfortable with creating a basic configuration on a router and switch from the CLI.

INSIDE THE EXAM

Introduction to Cisco Device Configuration

This chapter covers some important aspects required for the exam, and configuring commands as listed here will probably be included as part of a simulation question. You'll probably need to configure more things in the simulation question, such as an IP address and default gateway on a switch, and an IP address and static or dynamic routing on a router or routers, but these are covered in later chapters. You need to practice, practice, practice the commands you've learned about in this chapter.

You might see some questions that ask you to match up a cable type to the type of connection required: remember where a rollover, a straight-through, and a crossover cable are used.

Command-Line Interface (CLI)

In the simulation questions you experience on the exam, you will need to be able to move easily between User EXEC, Privilege EXEC, and Configuration modes, and then back to

Privilege EXEC mode. You'll also need to know how to log out of the IOS device.

IOS Basics

In the exam simulation questions, the CLI works almost the same as you would experience with a real Cisco router or switch. Therefore, take advantage of the CLI features such as context-sensitive help (**?**) to figure out the commands and parameters as well as the TAB key to autocomplete commands. These very powerful tools will definitely assist you in the simulation questions, given that you might not remember all the commands for the exam!

Basic IOS Configuration

In addition to making the basic IOS configurations in this section, you will be required to configure other commands on a handful of switches and routers in a possible simulation question—so practice configuring and securing your lines and interfaces.

Basic IOS Security Configuration

One of the first things you would do in real life is secure your IOS device with passwords; you should expect to see some questions about how your VTYs are secured, including the differences between the **login** and **login local** parameters. Remember that passwords are *case-sensitive* when configured. Part of a simulation question you might see will require this kind of configuration, as well as other configuration tasks. Remember the differences between the two kinds of banners.

IOS Operation and Verification

Remember the differences between the running-config and startup-config files, and know how to use the **copy** command to back up the configuration in RAM to NVRAM. You should be very familiar with the output of the **show interfaces** command and be able to decipher the status of the physical and data link layers of an interface. Don't be surprised to see two or three questions related to interface problems or statuses on the exam.

CERTIFICATION SUMMARY

This chapter introduced you to the IOS's CLI and how to make basic configurations on Cisco's switches and routers. The Cisco console port requires an RJ-45 rollover cable and, possibly, an RJ-45–to–DB-9 terminal adapter. The rollover cable pins are reversed on the two sides. Your terminal emulator on your PC will need to be configured for 9600 bps, 8 data bits, 1 stop bit, no parity, and no flow control for a console connection.

The nomenclature of a switch interface is this: `type slot_#/port_#`. The type of interface is the media type, such as `ethernet`, `fastethernet`, or `gigabit`. Following this is the slot number. For all fixed interfaces on the 2960 switches, the slot number is always 0. All switch port numbers start at 1 and work their way up. The nomenclature of a router interface is either `type slot_#/port_#` or `type port_#`. The type of interface is the media type, such as `ethernet`, `fastethernet`, `gigabitethernet`, and `serial`, as well as many others. Following this is the slot number for modular routers. The slot numbers start at 0 and work their way up. All port router numbers within a slot and type start at 0 and work their way up, which is different from the Catalyst switches.

The IOS provides a CLI with many features, including context-sensitive help accessed by using **help** or **?**, command history, and advanced editing features, which are available at all modes, including the User and Privilege EXEC and Configuration modes. Within Configuration mode are Subconfiguration modes. To access Privilege EXEC mode, use the **enable** command, and to access Configuration mode, use **configure terminal**.

You can protect access to your Cisco device by assigning User EXEC and Privilege EXEC passwords. Use the Line Subconfiguration mode **password** command and the **enable secret** or **enable password** command for the two respective levels. The **service password encryption** command encrypts clear-text passwords on the IOS device. The **banner motd** command displays a login banner before any username or password prompt.

To view the active configuration, use the **show running-config** command. On IOS devices, you must manually save your configuration to NVRAM with the **copy running-config startup-config** command.

Switch interfaces are enabled by default, but router interfaces need to be enabled with the **no shutdown** command. For DCE serial interfaces, routers need a clock rate applied with the **clock rate** command. Use the **show interfaces** command to view the status and configuration of your interfaces.

✓ TWO-MINUTE DRILL

Introduction to Cisco Device Configuration

❑ Out-of-band management occurs through the console or auxiliary ports; in-band occurs through an interface.

❑ Console port connections require an RJ-45 rollover cable and, possibly, an RJ-45–to–DB-9 terminal adapter. In your terminal emulation package, set the following: speed to 9600 bps, data bits to 8, stop bits to 1, parity to none, and flow control to none.

❑ Interfaces have a name, possibly a slot number, and a port number. The slot number of the 2960 is 0; port numbers start at 1. Router slot numbers begin with 0; port numbers start at 0 and restart with each type within each slot.

Command-Line Interface (CLI)

❑ Four CLI access modes exist: User EXEC (`IOS>`), Privilege EXEC (`IOS#`), Configuration (`IOS(config)#`), and ROMMON mode (`>`).

❑ The **enable** command moves you from User EXEC to Privilege EXEC mode. The **exit** command logs you out of the IOS device.

IOS Basics

❑ Use the **?** to display context-sensitive help in any mode of a router; it lists available commands and their valid parameters.

❑ If you execute a command and see the resulting output of the command, examine the output to ensure that no error is present in the command you entered.

❑ You can use the arrow keys on your keyboard to recall and edit commands.

❑ Use the TAB key to autocomplete a command.

Basic IOS Configuration

❑ Use the Privilege EXEC **configure terminal** command to enter Configuration mode.

❑ The **hostname** command assigns a locally significant name to the router. The **no** parameter negates/undoes a configuration change.

❑ The **no shutdown** command enables an interface; interfaces on switches are enabled by default, but router interfaces are disabled. The **clock rate** command specifies the speed of a DCE serial interface on a router and is required when connecting two serial interfaces, back-to-back, without using external clocking devices such as CSU/DSUs. Use the **show controller** command to verify whether or not the serial interface is a DTE or DCE.

Basic IOS Security Configuration

❑ Lines (access to User EXEC mode) can be secured with the **password** command. Access to Privilege EXEC mode can be secured with either the **enable password** or **enable secret** command; the former is unencrypted and the latter is strongly encrypted.

❑ Clear-text passwords can be encrypted with the **service password-encryption** command.

❑ You can display a login banner before a username/password prompt with the **banner motd** command; after the authentication takes place and before the user sees an EXEC prompt, you can display a banner with the **banner exec** command.

IOS Operation and Verification

❑ You must be at Privilege EXEC mode to manipulate configuration files. The **show running-config** command displays the running configuration in RAM. The **show startup-config** command displays the backed-up configuration in NVRAM.

❑ IOS devices do not automatically save their configurations from RAM to NVRAM; use the **copy running-config startup-config** command to do this.

❑ Use the **show version** command to see the IOS version of the device as well as its hardware characteristics.

❑ The **show interfaces** command is used to see the operational status of the physical and data link layers of an IOS device's interface.

SELF TEST

The following Self Test questions will help you measure your understanding of the material presented in this chapter. Read all the choices carefully, as there may be more than one correct answer. Choose all correct answers for each question.

Introduction to Cisco Device Configuration

1. A _____ cable is used to connect to the console port of your IOS device.

Command-Line Interface (CLI)

2. Match the device modes with commands or processes associated with that mode. Device modes: User EXEC, Privilege EXEC, Configuration, and ROMMON. Commands or processes: **show running-config**, **enable**, password recovery, **line vty 0 4**.

IOS Basics

3. Which of the following allows you to use context-sensitive help? (choose two)
   A. **help**
   B. **show**
   C. **?**
   D. **verify**

4. Which control sequence takes you to the beginning of the CLI?
   A. CTRL-E
   B. CTRL-A
   C. ESC-B
   D. CTRL-B

Basic IOS Configuration

5. Enter the IOS command that will change the device name to "*Perimeter*": _____.

6. Match the following commands to their description. Commands: **shutdown**, **show controller**, **login local**, and **clock rate**. Descriptions: Shows if an interface is DTE/DCE; specifies the use of an IOS database for authentication; specifies the speed of a serial interface; disables an interface.

7. You execute the **line console 0** command from *Configuration* mode. What will the router's prompt be?

   A. Router(config)#

   B. Router(config-line)#

   C. Router(config-interface)#

   D. Router#(config-if)

Basic IOS Security Configuration

8. Enter the IOS command that will encrypt unencrypted passwords: _____.

9. Which IOS command would display a message of "This is Router5" after a user logs in?

   A. **banner motd**

   B. **login exec**

   C. **banner exec**

   D. **login motd**

IOS Operation and Verification

10. You examine your interfaces, and the **Ethernet 0** interface status says **Ethernet 0 is up, line protocol is down**. What does this indicate?

    A. A physical layer problem

    B. A data link layer problem

    C. A network layer problem

    D. There is no problem.

11. What IOS command saves the active configuration to NVRAM?

    A. **copy nvram startup-config**

    B. **copy startup-config running-config**

    C. **copy running-config nvram**

    D. **copy running-config startup-config**

SELF TEST ANSWERS

1. ☑ A *rollover* cable is used to provide your initial access to an IOS device via the console port/line.

2. ☑ User EXEC: **enable**; Privilege EXEC: **show running-config**; Configuration: **line vty 0 4**; and ROMMON: password recovery.

3. ☑ A and C. The **?** and **help** commands allow you to use the context-sensitive help feature.
   ☒ B is incorrect because the **show** command displays how a feature is configured or operating. D is incorrect because **verify** is an invalid command.

4. ☑ B. Pressing CTRL-A takes you to the beginning of the CLI.
   ☒ A is incorrect; pressing CTRL-E takes you to the end of the CLI. C, ESC-B, moves the cursor back one word at a time. D, CTRL-B, moves the cursor back one character at a time.

5. ☑ The **hostname Perimeter** command will change the device name to *Perimeter*.

6. ☑ The **show controller** command shows whether an interface is DTE/DCE; **shutdown** disables an interface; **login local** specifies the use of an IOS database for authentication; **clock rate** specifies the speed of a serial interface.

7. ☑ B. When you execute the **line console 0** command, your prompt changes to `Router(config-line)#`.
   ☒ A is incorrect because this is Global Configuration mode. D represents Interface Subconfiguration mode, and C is a nonexistent prompt.

8. ☑ The **service password-encryption** command will encrypt unencrypted passwords.

9. ☑ C. The **banner exec** command displays a banner after the user authenticates, but before the EXEC prompt is displayed.
   ☒ A, **banner motd**, displays a banner before the username and password prompt. B and D are invalid commands.

10. ☑ B. The `line protocol is down` refers to a problem in the data link layer.
    ☒ A is incorrect because the physical layer is up. C is incorrect because the status refers only to the physical and data link layers. Since there is a correct answer, D is incorrect.

11. ☑ D. Use the **copy running-config startup-config** command to back up your configuration from RAM to NVRAM.
    ☒ B is incorrect because **copy startup-config running-config** restores your configuration to RAM. A and C are incorrect because these commands use nonexistent parameters.

12

Initial Switch
Configuration

T he 2940, 2955, and 2960 series of switches are Cisco's current desktop and workgroup switching solution; they replace the 1900 and 2950 switches. The new switches support Fast Ethernet and Gigabit Ethernet interfaces. This book, and the CCNA exam, focus on the end-of-sale 2950 and the newer 2960 switches, but the topics and configuration commands discussed in this chapter apply to all of Cisco's Catalyst switches running the Internetwork Operating System (IOS).

CERTIFICATION OBJECTIVE 12.01

2960 Overview

The 2960 series of switches comes with the LAN-based software image, which provides advanced quality of service, rate limiting, access control list (ACL), and many other features. Table 12-1 compares the 2960 switches and their port types and capacities. The dual-purpose Gigabit Ethernet (GE) port supports a 10/100/1000 port and an SFP (fiber) port, where *one* of the two ports (not both) can be used. If a 2960 supports dual-ports, this is displayed in the Dual-Purpose column of Table 12-1. The 2960 series supports an optional external redundant power supply (RPS) that can be attached to the rear of the chassis.

TABLE 12-1

2960 Models

Switch	10/100 BaseTX	10/100/1000 BaseTX	Dual-Purpose GE
WS-C2960-8TC-L	8	0	1
WS-C2950-24TT-L	24	2	0
WS-C2960-48TT-L	48	2	0
WS-C2950-24TC-L	24	0	2
WS-C2960-48TC-L	48	0	2
WS-C2960G-8TC-L	0	7	1
WS-C2960G-24TC-L	0	20	4
WS-2960G-48TC-L	0	44	4

Before you begin connecting any cables to your Cisco switches, you should become familiar with their chassis and interfaces. First, you should understand how to turn on your Cisco device, what interfaces it has, and the meanings of the various LEDs (light-emitting diodes) on the chassis. The next few sections cover this in more depth for the 2960.

2960 Chassis

Figure 12-1 shows illustrations of the front (at top) and rear (at bottom) views of a 2960-24TT switch. For the front view, the ports on the left are the 10/100 BaseTX ports and the two on the right are the two 10/100/1000 BaseTX ports. For the 10/100 ports, the ports are numbered in the first column, 1 at the top and 2 at the bottom; in the second column, 3 at the top and 4 at the bottom; and so on. The front of the chassis contains the MODE button as well as the LEDs.

The rear of the chassis has the management connections. You'll notice that no toggle switch is included to turn the switch on or off. To turn the switch on, plug one end of the power cable into the back of the switch and the other into a power outlet. To turn the switch off, unplug the power cable from either end. The 2960 supports an RJ-45 console interface, which uses a *rollover* cable for connectivity to a terminal or terminal emulation device for console access.

FIGURE 12-1

A 2950-24TT switch

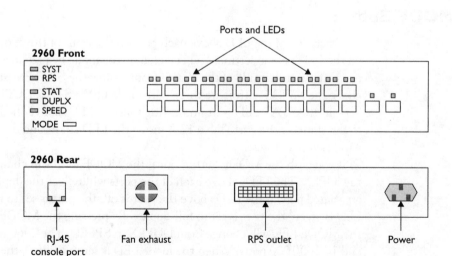

	LED	Color	Description
TABLE 12-2 2960 SYSTEM and RPS LEDs	SYSTEM	Green	The system is up and operational.
		Amber	The system experienced a malfunction.
		Off	The system is powered down.
	RPS	Green	The RPS is attached and operational.
		Amber	The RPS is installed but is not operational. Check the RPS to ensure that it hasn't failed.
		Flashing amber	Both the internal power supply and the external RPS are installed, but the RPS is providing power.
		Off	The RPS is not installed.

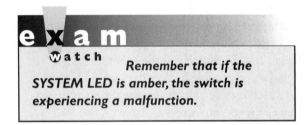

2960 LEDs and MODE Button

The front of the 2960 chassis has many LEDs that you can use to monitor the switch's activity and performance. At the top-left of the 2960's front chassis are the SYSTEM and RPS LEDs. The colors of these LEDs and their meanings are shown in Table 12-2.

MODE Button

The meaning of the LED above each port on the front of the 2960's chassis depends on the LED's mode setting. You can change the mode by pressing the MODE button on the bottom-left side of the chassis front, below the SYSTEM and RPS LEDs. Just above the MODE button are three port-mode LEDs: STAT, DUPLX, and SPEED. By default, the STAT LED is lit, indicating that the LEDs above the Ethernet ports refer to the status of the port. Table 12-3 shows the LED colors and descriptions for the various port statuses.

If you push the MODE button once, the MODE LED will change from STAT to DUPLX. The LEDs above each of the ports will reflect the duplex setting of the associated port. If the LED above the port is off, the port is set to half-duplex; if the LED is green, the port is set to full-duplex. By pressing the MODE button again, the MODE LED will change from DUPLX to SPEED. The 2960 supports 10/100 and 10/100/1000 ports. When the mode LED is set to SPEED, the LEDs above the port refer to the speed at which the port is operating. If the LED is off, the port is operating at 10 Mbps; if solid green, 100 Mbps; and if blinking green, 1 Gbps.

TABLE 12-3	LED Color	LED Meaning
Status Mode and Port LEDs	Green	A powered-up physical layer connection to the device is attached to the port.
	Flashing green	Traffic is entering and/or leaving the port.
	Flashing green and amber	An operational problem is occurring with the port—perhaps excessive errors or a connection problem.
	Amber	The port has been disabled manually (shut down), disabled because it is in a blocking STP state, or disabled because of a security issue.
	Off	No powered-up physical layer connection exists on the port.

If you press the MODE button again, the MODE LED will change back to STAT. As you can see, the use of the MODE button allows you to cycle through the different mode settings. If the MODE LED is either DUPLX or SPEED, it will automatically change back to STAT after 1 minute.

ⓦatch   *If you don't have connectivity through the switch and the switch port LEDs are all off, make sure the switch is powered on. Reseat the cable*   *connectors in their ports. Also check the cables to make sure they are the correct type: straight versus cross-through.*

CERTIFICATION OBJECTIVE 12.02

Switch Startup

Now that you have a basic understanding of the chassis of the 2960, you are ready to learn about the bootup process of the switch: this includes the running of hardware tests, loading the IOS, and finding and applying a configuration file. The following sections discuss these processes.

Switch Bootup Process

For your initial access to the switch, make sure you plug the rollover cable into the switch's console port and the other end into the COM port of your computer. Start up a terminal emulation program such as HyperTerminal, Tera Term, or PuTTY to view the command-line interface (CLI) output of the switch. When power is applied to the 2960, the switch will begin its bootup process. Flash is first validated, and then the IOS is found, uncompressed, and loaded.

POST is then run to verify that the different components of the switch are operational. When POST begins, the SYSTEM LED is off. Once POST completes all testing, and all tests have passed, the SYSTEM LED should turn green. If the LED is amber, you know that at least one test has failed during POST, which is usually catastrophic for the switch: in other words, the switch won't boot up. Running POST takes about a minute.

Assuming that the POST tests pass, at least the critical ones, the IOS continues executing. Once the IOS completely loads, a configuration is found and applied to the switch, and you'll be presented with the User EXEC prompt, assuming you are connected to the console port of the switch. An example of the 2960's bootup process is shown here:

```
Base ethernet MAC Address: 00:1c:f6:89:97:00
Xmodem file system is available.
The password-recovery mechanism is enabled.
Initializing Flash...
flashfs[0]: 602 files, 19 directories
flashfs[0]: 0 orphaned files, 0 orphaned directories
  .
  .
  .
flashfs[0]: flashfs fsck took 10 seconds.
...done Initializing Flash.
Boot Sector Filesystem (bs) installed, fsid: 3
done.
Loading "flash:c2960-lanbasek9-mz.122-40.SE/c2960-lanbasek9-
mz.12240.SE.bin"...@@@@@@@@@@@@@@@@@@@@@@@@@@@@@@@@@@@@@@@@@@@@@@@
@@@@@@@@@@@@@@@@@@@@@@@@@@@@@@@@@@@@@@@@@@@@@@@@@@@@@@@@@@@@@@@@@
  .
  .
  .
File "flash:c2960-lanbasek9-mz.122-40.SE/c2960-lanbasek9-mz.
     122-40.SE.bin" uncompressed and installed, entry point:
     0x3000
```

```
executing...

                    Restricted Rights Legend
Use, duplication, or disclosure by the Government is
subject to restrictions as set forth in subparagraph
(c) of the Commercial Computer Software - Restricted
Rights clause at FAR sec. 52.227-19 and subparagraph
(c) (1) (ii) of the Rights in Technical Data and Computer
Software clause at DFARS sec. 252.227-7013.

             Cisco Systems, Inc.
             170 West Tasman Drive
             San Jose, California 95134-1706

Cisco IOS Software, C2960 Software (C2960-LANBASEK9-M),
      Version 12.2(40)SE, RELEASE SOFTWARE (fc3)
Copyright (c) 1986-2007 by Cisco Systems, Inc.
Compiled Fri 24-Aug-07 01:55 by myl
Image text-base: 0x00003000, data-base: 0x00FC0000

Initializing flashfs...
flashfs[1]: 602 files, 19 directories
flashfs[1]: 0 orphaned files, 0 orphaned directories
flashfs[1]: Total bytes: 32514048
.
.
.
flashfs[1]: Initialization complete....done Initializing
flashfs.
POST: CPU MIC register Tests : Begin
POST: CPU MIC register Tests : End, Status Passed
POST: PortASIC Memory Tests : Begin
POST: PortASIC Memory Tests : End, Status Passed
POST: CPU MIC interface Loopback Tests : Begin
POST: CPU MIC interface Loopback Tests : End, Status Passed
POST: PortASIC RingLoopback Tests : Begin
POST: PortASIC RingLoopback Tests : End, Status Passed
POST: PortASIC CAM Subsystem Tests : Begin
POST: PortASIC CAM Subsystem Tests : End, Status Passed
POST: PortASIC Port Loopback Tests : Begin
POST: PortASIC Port Loopback Tests : End, Status Passed

Waiting for Port download...Complete
```

```
This product contains cryptographic features and is subject
to United States and local country laws governing import,
export, transfer and use. Delivery of Cisco cryptographic
.
.
.
cisco WS-C2950-24TT-L (PowerPC405) processor (revision D0)
with 61440K/4088K bytes of memory.
Processor board ID FOC1131W4NR
Last reset from power-on
1 Virtual Ethernet interface
24 FastEthernet interfaces
2 Gigabit Ethernet interfaces
The password-recovery mechanism is enabled.

64K bytes of flash-simulated non-volatile configuration memory.
Base ethernet MAC Address        : 00:1C:F6:89:97:00
Motherboard assembly number      : 73-10390-04
Power supply part number         : 341-0097-02
Motherboard serial number        : FOC11305QDR
Power supply serial number       : AZS113104M2
Model revision number            : D0
Motherboard revision number      : A0
Model number                     : WS-C2950-24TT-L
System serial number             : FOC1131W4NR
Top Assembly Part Number         : 800-27221-03
Top Assembly Revision Number     : A0
Version ID                       : V03
CLEI Code Number                 : COM3L00BRB
Hardware Board Revision Number   : 0x01

Switch   Ports  Model         SW Version   SW Image
------   -----  -----         ----------   ----------
*   1    26     WS-C2950-24TT-L  12.2(40)SE  C2960-LANBASEK9-M
Press RETURN to get started!
```

on the job *I prefer using PuTTY as my management program. It supports COM terminal emulation, telnet, and SSH functions—and it's free!*

System Configuration Dialog

If no configuration is found, the IOS will run the setup script, commonly called the *System Configuration Dialog*. This script asks you questions to help it create a basic configuration on the switch. When posing questions, the setup script uses brackets ([and]) to indicate default values. Leaving these answers blank (that is, not supplying an answer) results in the script accepting the value indicated in brackets for the configuration component. In the script, you can configure the switch's hostname, set up a Privilege EXEC password, assign a password for the virtual type terminals (VTYs), and set up an IP address for a VLAN interface to manage the switch remotely.

e x a m
ᴡatch   *If a switch boots up without   (System Configuration Dialog) will be*
a configuration in NVRAM, the setup script   presented to the administrator.

Here's an example of this script:

```
Would you like to enter the initial configuration dialog? [yes/no]: yes
At any point you may enter a question mark '?' for help.
Use ctrl-c to abort configuration dialog at any prompt.
Default settings are in square brackets '[]'.

Basic management setup configures only enough connectivity
for management of the system, extended setup will ask you
to configure each interface on the system

Would you like to enter basic management setup? [yes/no]: yes
Configuring global parameters:
  Enter host name [Switch]:
  The enable secret is a password used to protect access to
  privileged EXEC and configuration modes. This password, after
  entered, becomes encrypted in the configuration.
  Enter enable secret: cisco
  The enable password is used when you do not specify an
  enable secret password, with some older software versions, and
  some boot images.
  Enter enable password: boson
  The virtual terminal password is used to protect
  access to the router over a network interface.
  Enter virtual terminal password: sanjose
  Configure SNMP Network Management? [no]:

Current interface summary
```

```
Interface              IP-Address      OK? Method Status         Protocol
Vlan1                  unassigned      YES unset  up             down
FastEthernet0/1        unassigned      YES unset  down           down
FastEthernet0/2        unassigned      YES unset  down           down
.
.
.
FastEthernet0/24       unassigned      YES unset  down           down
GigabitEthernet0/1     unassigned      YES unset  down           down
GigabitEthernet0/2     unassigned      YES unset  down           down

Enter interface name used to connect to the
management network from the above interface summary: vlan1

Configuring interface Vlan1:
  Configure IP on this interface? [no]: yes
    IP address for this interface: 192.168.1.253
    Subnet mask for this interface [255.255.255.0] :
    Class C network is 192.168.1.0, 24 subnet bits; mask is /24
Would you like to enable as a cluster command switch? [yes/no]: no

The following configuration command script was created:

hostname Switch
enable secret 5 $1$.N.L$t4q9Jw5DTffPTPE.KkKNX/
enable password boson
line vty 0 15
 password sanjose
no snmp-server

interface Vlan1
 no shutdown
 ip address 192.168.1.253 255.255.255.0
!
interface FastEthernet0/1
.
.
.
interface GigabitEthernet0/1
!
interface GigabitEthernet0/2
end
[0] Go to the IOS command prompt without saving this config.
[1] Return back to the setup without saving this config.
[2] Save this configuration to nvram and exit.
Enter your selection [2]: 2
```

12.01. The CD contains a multimedia demonstration of the bootup process of a 2950 switch.

At the end of the script, type 2 to accept and activate your changes, as well as save the configuration to NVRAM. Entering 0 aborts the script and 1 starts the script over, remembering what you just entered, as the defaults, for the questions you were just asked.

on the
Job

One problem with this script is that once you answer a question—correctly or incorrectly—there is no way of going back to the question. To abort the script, press CTRL-C and start over. To run the script from the CLI without rebooting the switch, go to Privilege EXEC mode and execute the setup *command.*

CERTIFICATION OBJECTIVE 12.03

Basic Switch Configuration

Common IOS configuration tasks for switches and routers, such as assigning a hostname, setting up passwords for User and Privilege EXEC access, and configuring hardware characteristics for interfaces (speed and duplexing), were discussed in Chapter 11. This section addresses how to assign an IP address and default gateway address to your switch so that you can access it remotely. You'll also see a quick and basic initial switch configuration based on the commands in Chapter 11 and this chapter.

on the
Job

Remember that you don't have to enable interfaces manually on your Catalyst switches: they are enabled by default.

IP Address and Default Gateway

If you want to manage your layer 2 switch remotely, you need to assign it IP addressing information. For example, if you want to telnet or SSH to your switch, remotely manage it from a web browser or SNMP management station, or back up and restore configuration files or upgrade the switch, you'll need to set up IP addressing information on the switch: an IP address associated with an interface and a default gateway address. Here's the configuration you'll use:

```
Switch(config)# interface vlan VLAN_#
Switch(config-vlan)# ip address IP_address subnet_mask
Switch(config-vlan)# exit
Switch(config)# ip default-gateway router's_IP_address
```

With layer 2 switches such as the 2960, you must go into the VLAN interface with which you want the IP address to be associated—this will be the management VLAN in which your administrative PC is located. The System Configuration Dialog assumes this will be VLAN 1, but you can use any VLAN you want; however, you must first create the VLAN (see Chapter 13.) Once you're working in the VLAN interface, use the **ip address** command to assign the address and subnet mask. Next, assign the default gateway: **ip default-gateway**. This command is necessary if the switch needs to communicate with other devices, via IP, that are located in other subnets.

For the switch to access devices in other VLANs, you need to assign it an IP address and a default gateway: use the `ip address` **and** `ip` **default-gateway commands. Hosts should not use a layer 2 switch's address as a default gateway.**

Example Configuration

Now let's pull together the basic configuration tasks from Chapter 11 as well as the above configuration in a simple example, using the network shown in Figure 12-2:

```
Switch(config)# hostname Switch-A
Switch-A(config)# line console 0
Switch-A(config-line)# exec-timeout 5 0
Switch-A(config-line)# password consolepass123
Switch-A(config)# exit
Switch-A(config)# line vty 0 15
Switch-A(config-line)# password telnetpass123
Switch-A(config-line)# exec-timeout 5 0
```

FIGURE 12-2

Simple switch
configuration
example

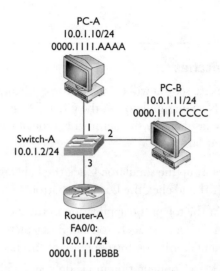

PC-A
10.0.1.10/24
0000.1111.AAAA

PC-B
10.0.1.11/24
0000.1111.CCCC

Switch-A
10.0.1.2/24

Router-A
FA0/0:
10.0.1.1/24
0000.1111.BBBB

```
Switch-A(config-line)# login
Switch-A(config-line)# exit
Switch-A(config)# enable secret secretpass123
Switch-A(config)# service password-encryption
Switch-A(config)# banner motd $
This is a private system and only authorized individuals
          are allowed!
All others will be prosecuted to the fullest extent of the law!
$
Switch-A(config)# interface vlan 1
Switch-A(config-vlan)# ip address 10.0.1.2 255.255.255.0
Switch-A(config-vlan)# exit
Switch-A(config)# ip default-gateway 10.0.1.1
Switch-A(config)# end
Switch-A# copy running-config startup-config
```

In this example, the switch was given a hostname (Switch-A), passwords for the
console, VTYs, Privilege EXEC mode, a login banner, an IP address for VLAN 1,
and a default gateway; plus, I saved the switch's configuration to NVRAM.

CertCam

*12.02. The CD includes a multimedia demonstration of placing a basic
configuration on a 2950 switch.*

EXERCISE 12-1

Configuring the Switches

In this exercise, you will create a basic configuration on the 2950 switches using Boson's NetSim simulator on the CD-ROM switch. If you have closed the simulator since the last lab, the simulator will automatically load Chapter 11's completed configuration.

1. Start up the simulator. Click the LabNavigator button. Double-click Exercise 12-1 and click the Load Lab button.

2. At the top of the application in the menu bar, click the eSwitches icon and choose 2950-1. You can find a picture of the network diagram for the simulator in the Introduction to this book.

3. Go to Configuration mode on your 2950-1 switch. Assign an IP address of 192.168.1.2/24 to the 2960 in VLAN 1, with a default gateway of 192.168.1.1.

4. Access User EXEC mode. Type **enable** to go to Privilege EXEC mode and then type **configure terminal** to access Configuration mode. Your prompt should look like this: Switch(config)#.

5. Enter the VLAN interface with **interface vlan1**.

6. Enter the addressing information: **ip address 192.168.1.2 255.255.255.0**. Enable the interface: **no shutdown**.

7. Exit the interface with the **exit** command and configure the default gateway: **ip default-gateway 192.168.1.1**.

8. Save your configuration to NVRAM and view the configuration in NVRAM. Test connectivity by pinging the Host-1 and Host-2 PCs. Return to Privilege EXEC mode with the **end** command.

9. Save the configuration with **copy running-config startup-config** and view it with **show startup-config**.

10. Test connectivity to Host-1: **ping 192.168.1.10**. The ping should be successful.

11. Test connectivity to Host-2: **ping 192.168.1.11**. The ping should be successful.

Now configure the 2950-2 switch. The commands are the same, except use the appropriate configuration information: the IP address is 192.168.1.3/24. Test connectivity to the Host-1 PC and 2950-1 switch.

1. Click the eSwitches icon in the toolbar and choose 2950-2.

2. On the 2950-2 switch, access User EXEC mode, and then enter the following: **enable, configure terminal, interface vlan1, ip address 192.168.1.3 255.255.255.0, no shutdown, exit, ip default-gateway 192.168.1.1, end, copy running-config startup-config**, and **show startup-config**. Make sure you configured the right IP address.

3. Test connectivity by pinging Host-1 and the 2950-1 switch: **ping 192.168.1.10** and **ping 192.168.1.2**. The pings should be successful.

Now configure the 2950-3 switch. The commands are the same, except use the appropriate configuration information: the IP address is 192.168.3.2/24. Test connectivity to the 2600-1 and Host-4.

1. Click the eSwitches icon in the toolbar and select 2950-3.

2. On the 2950-3 switch, access User EXEC mode, and then enter the following: **enable, configure terminal, interface vlan1, ip address 192.168.3.2 255.255.255.0, no shutdown, exit, ip default-gateway 192.168.3.1, end, copy running-config startup-config**, and **show startup-config**. Make sure you configured the right IP address.

3. Test connectivity by pinging the Host-3 and Host-4 PCs: **ping 192.168.3.10** and **ping 192.168.3.11**. The pings should be successful.

Now you should be comfortable with the basic configuration of the Catalyst IOS switches.

CERTIFICATION OBJECTIVE 12.04

Basic Switch Operation and Verification

This section focuses on the basic operations of a switch, such as learning MAC addresses and basic verification commands.

MAC Address Table

You'll recall that one of the three main functions of a switch is to learn which devices—that is, MAC addresses—are associated with which interfaces or ports. This information is stored in a port address, or content addressable memory (CAM), table. The learning process was discussed in Chapter 4. You can view the CAM table by using the **show mac-address-table** command. Here is an example of the use of this command, based on the network shown in Figure 12-2:

```
Switch> show mac address-table
          Mac Address Table
-------------------------------------------
Vlan    Mac Address       Type        Ports
----    -----------       ----        -----
All     0000.0000.0001    STATIC      CPU
All     0000.0000.0002    STATIC      CPU
 .
 .
 .
  1     0000.1111.AAAA    DYNAMIC     FA0/1
  1     0000.1111.CCCC    DYNAMIC     FA0/2
  1     0000.1111.BBBB    DYNAMIC     FA0/3
Total Mac Addresses for this criterion: 12
```

In this example, all the STATIC entries represent the switch itself. The last three entries represent the MAC addresses learned from the first three interfaces of the switch. By default, the 2960 can fit 8192 MAC addresses in its CAM table. To clear dynamically learned entries from the CAM table, use the **clear mac-address-table** command from Privilege EXEC mode.

on the
()ob

You shouldn't see a broadcast or multicast addresses in the port address table since these are not seen as source addresses in frames and thus aren't learned by the switch.

exam
ⓦatch

Be familiar with the output of the `show mac-address-table` *command. If a destination MAC address is* *not in the table (unknown), the switch will flood it.*

Static MAC Addresses

In addition to having the switches learn MAC addresses dynamically, you can manually create static entries. You might want to do this for security reasons. If a user moves her connection from one switch port to another, her traffic won't be forwarded correctly if you had statically configured her address to the old port. For traffic to flow correctly again, you would have to change the old entry to reflect the user's new interface. You may want to do this to ensure that the user doesn't unplug her connection from one port and connect it to another port, where the user might have access to more networking resources.

Unlike dynamic entries in a CAM table, static entries do not age out. This is true even if you reboot the switch (assuming your configuration has been saved). Also, if you have a static entry for a device and you move that device to a different port, even though the switch will see the change, the static entry will always override the learning function of the switch.

On a 2960 switch, use the following command to create a static entry in the CAM table:

```
Switch(config)# mac-address-table static MAC_address
                vlan VLAN_#
                interface type module/port_#
```

In addition to specifying the MAC address of the device and the interface where the device is located, you must also specify the VLAN in which the device is located (see Chapter 13). Use the **show mac-address-table** command to view your new entries. To remove a static entry from the CAM table, preface the preceding command with the **no** parameter.

on the
ⓙob

Statically configuring MAC addresses on the switch is not very common today. If configured, static entries are typically used for network devices, such as servers and routers. If you are concerned about controlling what user device is located from which interface on a switch, either use the port security feature or 802.1x authentication.

EXERCISE 12-2

CAM Tables

The following sections deal with the CAM table and port security. This exercise will help you become more familiar with the CAM table on a 2950 switch. You'll perform this lab using Boson's NetSim simulator. You can find a picture of the network diagram for the simulator in the Introduction of this book.

1. Start up the simulator and click the Lab Navigator button.

2. Double-click Exercise 12-2 and click the Load Lab button. This will load the lab configuration based on Exercise 12-1.

3. On the 2950-1 switch, access Privilege EXEC mode and examine the CAM table. If any entries appear, clear them.

4. At the top of the simulator in the menu bar, click the eSwitches icon and choose 2950-1.

5. Enter Privilege EXEC mode by typing **enable**. View the CAM table by typing **show mac-address-table**.

6. Clear the CAM table by typing **clear mac-address-table dynamic**.

7. On the 2950-1, ping Host-1: type **ping 192.168.1.10**. Examine the CAM table: **show mac-address-table**. What is the MAC address of Host-1? The MAC address will be different for each computer on which NetSim is installed. With what interface is it associated (should be fastethernet0/3)?

8. On the 2950-1, ping Host-2: type **ping 192.168.1.11**. Examine the CAM table: **show mac-address-table**. What is the MAC address of Host-2? With what interface is it associated (should be fastethernet0/4)?

9. Verify the MAC address on Host-1.

10. At the top of the simulator in the menu bar, click the eStations icon and choose Host-1. Enter **ipconfig /all** and compare the MAC address of the PC to that learned by the 2950-1 switch on fastethernet0/3.

11. Verify the MAC address on Host-2.

12. At the top of the simulator in the menu bar, click the eStations icon and choose Host-2. Enter `ipconfig /all` and compare the MAC address of the PC to that learned by the 2950-1 switch on `fastethernet0/4`.

You should be more comfortable with the CAM table on Cisco switches.

CERTIFICATION OBJECTIVE 12.05

Port Security Feature

Port security is a switch feature that allows you to lock down switch ports based on the MAC address or addresses associated with the interface, preventing unauthorized access to a LAN. For example, if MAC address 0001.001c.dddd is supposed to be off of fa0/1, but it is seen off of fa0/2, this would be considered a security violation. Or, if more addresses are seen off the interface than you allow, this would also be considered a violation. As an administrator, you control what should happen when a violation occurs, be it generating a notification about the issue, dropping traffic for the MAC address that caused the violation, or completely disabling the port where the violation occurred.

The port security feature will not work on trunk ports (Chapter 13), switch port analyzer ports (SPANs), and EtherChannel ports (Chapter 14). However, it is compatible with 802.1x (Chapter 5) and Voice VLANs (Chapter 13).

exam

Watch   *Port security and/or 802.1x can be used lock down ports on a switch, preventing unauthorized access to your LAN network.*

Port Security Configuration

Starting in IOS 12.1(6)EA2, Cisco standardized how port security is configured on its switches. The entire configuration is performed on an interface-by-interface basis by using the **switchport** commands:

```
switch(config)# interface fastethernet|gigabit 0/port_#
switch(config-if)# switchport mode access
switch(config-if)# switchport access vlan VLAN_#
```

```
switch(config-if)# switchport port-security
switch(config-if)# switchport port-security maximum value
switch(config-if)# switchport port-security violation
                   protect|restrict|shutdown
switch(config-if)# switchport port-security mac-address MAC_address
switch(config-if)# switchport port-security mac-address sticky
```

exam

watch   *Be familiar with configuring   limiting the MAC addresses, violation mode,
port security with the* switchport   *and sticky learning).*
port-security *commands (enabling it,*

First, you must enter the appropriate interface where you want to set up restricted security. The first command, **switchport mode access**, defines the interface as a host (access) port instead of a trunk port (trunking is explained in Chapter 13). The second command places the access port in a specific VLAN (also discussed

exam

watch   *Set the maximum to
1 address for an interface to prevent
spoofing of MAC addresses: only one
MAC address is learned.*

in Chapter 13). The third command on the interface, **switchport port-security**, enables port security (it is disabled, by default). The fourth command, **switchport port-security maximum**, specifies the maximum number of devices that can be associated with the interface. This defaults to 1 and can range from 1 to 132.

The fifth command on the interface specifies what should occur if a security violation occurs—the MAC address is seen connected to a different port. Three options are possible:

■ **protect**   When the number of secure addresses reaches the maximum number allowed, any additionally learned addresses will be dropped. This applies only if you have enabled the sticky option, discussed in the next paragraph.

■ **restrict**   Causes the switch to generate a security violation alert.

■ **shutdown**   Causes the switch to generate an alert and to disable the interface. The only way to re-enable the interface is to use the **no shutdown** command. This is the default violation mode if you don't specify the mode.

When an interface is disabled because of a violation with port security, you can reset the interface with this Configuration mode command: `errdisable recovery cause psecure-violation`.

The last two commands in the preceding code listing affect how the switch learns the secure MAC addresses on the interface. The first one has you specify the exact MAC address that is allowed to be associated with this interface—this is statically defining the MAC addresses allowed off of the port. The second command uses the sticky feature, which allows the switch to dynamically learn the MAC address(es) associated with the interface and convert these dynamic entries to static entries. The interface will learn MAC addresses only up to the maximum configured value for that interface. After you save your configuration (`copy running-config startup-config`), and when you reboot your switch, the sticky-learned addresses appear as statically secure addresses. Basically, sticky learning lets you avoid having to configure the MAC addresses associated with the interface.

If you don't statically define the MAC addresses or use sticky learning to learn them with port security, dynamic learning is used. Dynamic learning is similar to sticky learning in that the switch will learn the MAC addresses dynamically off of the interface up to the maximum defined; however, unlike sticky learning, these addresses are not saved: every time the switch boots up or the interface is reset, the MAC addresses are relearned for the interface.

Port Security Verification

To verify your configuration, use the **show port-security interface** command:

```
switch# show port-security interface fa0/2
Port Security : Enabled
Port status : SecureUp
Violation mode : Restrict
Maximum MAC Addresses : 1
Total MAC Addresses : 1
```

```
Configured MAC Addresses : 1
Aging time : 0 mins
Aging type : Absolute
SecureStatic address aging : Disabled
Security Violation count : 0
```

In this example, you can see that port security is enabled, the violation mode is restrict, the maximum number of MAC addresses that can be connected to the port is 1, and one MAC address has to be statically configured for the port. At the bottom of the output, you can see that no security violations have occurred on the port.

To see an overview configuration of port security on your switch, use the **show port-security** command:

```
switch# show port-security
Port   MaxSecureAddr CurrentAddr SecurityViolation Security Action
          (Count)      (Count)        (Count)
-----------------------------------------------------------------
Fa0/1      10           10              0            Shutdown
Fa0/2       1            1              0            Restrict
.
.
.
-----------------------------------------------------------------
Total Addresses in System :21
Max Addresses limit in System :6176
```

In this example, 10 MAC addresses can be learned off of FA0/1, 10 have been learned, and the violation mode is shut down; but currently no violations have occurred on the port.

To see the MAC addresses statically defined or dynamically learned with port security, use the **show port-security address** command:

```
IOS# show port-security address
Secure Mac Address Table
-----------------------------------------------------------------
Vlan   Mac Address    Type              Ports Remaining Age
                                               (mins)
----   -------------- ----------------- ----- -------------
1      0001.0001.0011 SecureDynamic     Fa0/1  15 (I)
1      0001.0001.0022 SecureDynamic     Fa0/1  15 (I)
1      0001.0001.1144 SecureConfigured  Fa0/1  -
.
.
.
-----------------------------------------------------------------
Total Addresses in System :21
Max Addresses limit in System :6176
```

In this example, three MAC addresses are off of FA0/1, where the first two were learned dynamically and the last one was statically configured.

12.03. The CD contains a multimedia demonstration of configuring and verifying port security on a switch.

INSIDE THE EXAM

2960 Overview

Be familiar with the LEDs on the 2900 series switches, including the SYSTEM and PORT LEDs and their colors.

Switch Startup

Understand when the setup script automatically runs.

Basic Switch Configuration

Be able to put a basic configuration on a switch: hostname, passwords, assigning an IP address to a VLAN interface, and assigning a default gateway address. Know when you must configure a default gateway address on a switch.

Basic Switch Operation and Verification

Understand how to view the MAC addresses in the MAC address table

(`show mac-address-table`) and how to compare incoming frames to the table to determine how the switch will forward the frame.

Port Security Feature

Of the five sections in this chapter, this section is probably the most emphasized on the exam. Understand why port security is used as well as the commands to configure it. Know why the maximum addresses for an interface is set to 1. Remember the three violation modes, as well as what they do. Be able to compare and contrast dynamic, sticky, and static learning and when each is used. And be able to configure this feature on a switch, since you might see it on a simulation question!

CERTIFICATION SUMMARY

This chapter focused on basic configuration tasks specific to Cisco Catalyst switches. The 2960 switches were introduced, including the meaning of their LEDs and the use of the MODE button. When a switch boots up, it runs POST, loads the IOS, and then loads its configuration. If the IOS can't find a configuration file, it runs the System Configuration Dialog.

To manage the switch remotely, minimally it will need an IP address associated with a VLAN (**interface vlan** and **ip address**) and a default gateway address (**ip default-gateway**). To view the MAC addresses the switch learns, use the **show mac-address-table** command.

Port security can be used to prevent unauthorized access to a LAN. Addresses can be learned dynamically (not saved), using sticky learning (saved), or statically configured. A violation occurs when more MAC addresses are off of an interface than are specified or when a MAC address is seen off of a different interface than expected. Violation modes are restrict, protect, and shutdown. Port security can be configured only on access (non-trunk) ports with the **switchport port-security** commands.

✓ TWO-MINUTE DRILL

2960 Overview

- ❏ The 2960 switches support Fast Ethernet and/or Gigabit Ethernet interfaces.
- ❏ The SYSTEM LED will be amber if the switch experiences a malfunction.
- ❏ The MODE button is used to change the meanings of the port LEDs.
- ❏ If a port LED is flashing amber/green, there is an operational problem with the port; if it is amber, the port has been disabled: shutdown, STP blocking, or port security violation.

Switch Startup

- ❏ When a switch boots up, POST is run, the IOS is found and loaded, and the configuration is found and loaded.
- ❏ If a configuration file cannot be found when booting up, the System Configuration Dialog questions can be answered to place a basic configuration on the switch.

Basic Switch Configuration

- ❏ An IP address can be assigned to a VLAN interface on a switch for accessing it remotely via telnet or SSH, or to back up its configuration or upgrade its IOS using the `ip address` command.
- ❏ The `ip default-gateway` command assigns a router address the switch should use to access other subnets.

Basic Switch Operation and Verification

- ❏ The `show mac-address-table` command displays the port address table of the switch.

Port Security Feature

- ❏ Port security is used to prevent unauthorized access to a LAN on access interfaces (non-trunk connections).
- ❏ The `switchport port-security` commands are used to configure it.

❑ The defaults for port security are learning one MAC address on the interface with a violation mode of shutdown.

❑ Sticky learning allows a switch to dynamically learn which MAC addresses are associated with an interface, as well as saving these in the running configuration of the switch.

SELF TEST

The following Self Test questions will help you measure your understanding of the material presented in this chapter. Read all the choices carefully, as there may be more than one correct answer. Choose all correct answers for each question.

2960 Overview

1. The SYSTEM LED will be _____ if the switch has experienced a malfunction.
   A. green
   B. off
   C. amber
   D. red

2. Two PCs are connected to a switch configured in the same subnet, but they can't ping each other. 100BaseTX is used for connectivity. What would *not* indicate a problem?
   A. The PORT LED is off on one of the two PCs' switch port connections.
   B. The PORT LED is amber on one of the two PCs' switch port connections.
   C. The SYSTEM LED is off.
   D. The MIC connectors on the Ethernet cables are not seated correctly in the switch ports.

Switch Startup

3. Which of the following is *not* asked for during the System Configuration Dialog script?
   A. Enabling interfaces
   B. Default gateway address
   C. VLAN interface to use for management functions
   D. Enable secret password

Basic Switch Configuration

4. In which configuration mode is the default gateway address configured for a switch?
   A. Interface
   B. Line
   C. Global
   D. Port

5. Your switch is in the management subnet (192.168.1.0/25). The switch should have the second to the last valid host address in the subnet in the management VLAN, which is VLAN 5. The router in the subnet uses the last valid host address in the subnet, which is the switch's default gateway. Configure the switch to allow it to reach other subnets.

Basic Switch Operation and Verification

6. Enter the switch command that allows you to see the contents of the port address table: _____.

7. Examine the following MAC address table on a switch. What will happen if a switch sees a frame with a destination MAC address of 0000.1111.DDDD?

```
Switch> show mac address-table
Vlan    Mac Address      Type       Ports
----    -----------      ----       -----
   1    0000.1111.AAAA   DYNAMIC    FA0/1
   1    0000.1111.CCCC   DYNAMIC    FA0/2
   1    0000.1111.BBBB   DYNAMIC    FA0/3
```

   A. Flood it
   B. Drop it
   C. Forward it out FA0/1
   D. Forward it out of FA0/1 and FA0/2

Port Security Feature

8. Which switch feature is used to prevent unauthorized access to a LAN?
   A. Port security
   B. Port security and 802.1Q
   C. VTY passwords
   D. Enable password

9. Which of the following is *not* a default configuration for port security?
   A. 1 MAC address per interface
   B. Violation mode shutdown
   C. Sticky learning
   D. Disabled by default

10. What learning mode should you use to associate a server with a switch port when port security is enabled?
   A. Dynamic
   B. Automatic
   C. Sticky
   D. Static

SELF TEST ANSWERS

2960 Overview

1. ☑ **C.** The SYSTEM LED will be amber if the switch has experienced a malfunction.
    ☒ **A** is incorrect because green indicates that the switch is operational. **B** is incorrect because the LED is off when the switch is turned off. **D** is not a valid color for the system LED.

2. ☑ **D.** 100BaseTX uses RJ-45 connectors, not MIC connectors. MIC connectors are used for fiber connections.
    ☒ **A**, **B**, and **C** would indicate a problem and are thus incorrect answers.

Switch Startup

3. ☑ **A.** Enabling the interfaces is *not* asked for during the System Configuration Dialog script: interfaces are enabled by default on Cisco switches.
    ☒ **B**, **C**, and **D** are asked for and are thus incorrect answers.

Basic Switch Configuration

4. ☑ **C.** The `ip default-gateway` command is a Global configuration mode command.
    ☒ **A** is incorrect because the Interface mode is used to assign an IP address to a VLAN interface. **B** is incorrect because Line mode is used to restrict User EXEC access to the switch. **D** is a nonexistent configuration mode.

5. ☑ Here is how to configure the switch to allow it to reach other subnets:

```
interface vlan 5
      ip address 192.168.1.125 255.255.255.128
      exit
ip default-gateway 192.168.1.126
```

Notice that the subnet mask is not /24, but /25!

Basic Switch Operation and Verification

6. ☑ `show mac-address-table` allows you to see the contents of the port address table.

7. ☑ **A.** Unknown unicast destination MAC addresses are flooded.
    ☒ **B** is true of routers, not switches. **C** and **D** are incorrect because the frame is flooded since the destination is unknown.

Port Security Feature

8. ☑ **A.** Port security is used to prevent unauthorized access to a LAN.

☒ **B** is incorrect because 802.1Q is a VLAN trunking protocol. **C** and **D** are used to restrict access to the switch, not to the LAN for which the switch provides connectivity.

9. ☑ **C.** Dynamic, not sticky, learning is the default.

☒ **A**, **B**, and **D** are defaults and thus incorrect.

10. ☑ **D.** You should statically define MAC addresses of servers and routers when using port security.

☒ **A** and **C** are used for user ports. **B** is a nonexistent learning mode.

13
VLANs and Trunks

CERTIFICATION OBJECTIVES

A s was mentioned in Chapters 2 and 4, layer 2 devices, including bridges and switches, always propagate certain kinds of traffic in the broadcast domain: broadcasts, multicasts, and unknown destination traffic. This process impacts every machine in the broadcast domain (layer 2 network). It impacts the bandwidth of these devices' connections as well as their local processing. If you were using bridges, the only solution available to solve this problem would be to break up the broadcast domain into multiple broadcast domains and interconnect these domains with a router. With this approach, each new broadcast domain would be a new logical segment and would need a unique network number to differentiate it from the other layer 3 logical segments.

Unfortunately, this is a costly solution, since each broadcast domain, each logical segment, needs its own port on a router. The more broadcast domains that you have from bridges, the bigger the router required: an interface for each broadcast domain. As you will see in this chapter, switches also have the same problem with traffic that must be flooded. You will see, however, that switches have a unique solution to reduce the number of router ports required and thus the cost of the layer 3 device that you need to obtain: virtual LANs and trunking.

CERTIFICATION OBJECTIVE 13.01

VLAN Overview

A *virtual LAN* (VLAN) is a logical grouping of network devices in the same broadcast domain that can span multiple physical segments. The top part of Figure 13-1 shows an example of a simple VLAN, where every device is in both the same collision and broadcast domains. In this example, a hub is providing the connectivity, which represents, to the devices connected to it, that the segment is a logical segment.

The bottom part of Figure 13-1 shows an example of a switch with four PCs connected to it. One major difference between the switch and the hub is that all devices connected to the hub are in the same collision domain, whereas in the switch example, each port of the switch is a separate collision domain. By default, all ports on a switch are in the same broadcast domain. In this example, however, the configuration of the switch places PC-E and PC-F in one broadcast domain (VLAN) and PC-G and PC-H in another broadcast domain.

Switches are used to create VLANs, or separate broadcast domains. VLANs are not restricted to any physical boundary in the switched network, assuming that all

FIGURE 13-1   VLAN examples

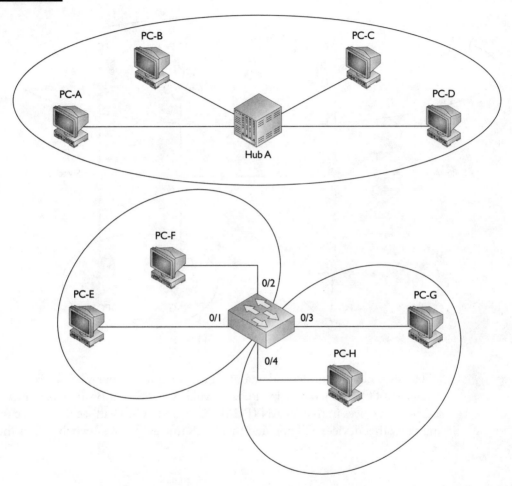

the devices are interconnected via switches and that there are no intervening layer 3 devices. For example, a VLAN could be spread across multiple switches, or it could be contained in the same switch, as is shown in Figure 13-2. This example shows three VLANs. Notice that VLANs are not tied to any physical location: PC-A, PC-B, PC-E, and PC-F are in the same VLAN but are connected to different ports of different switches. However, a VLAN could be contained to one switch, as PC-C and PC-D are connected to SwitchA.

FIGURE 13-2   Physical switched topology using VLANs

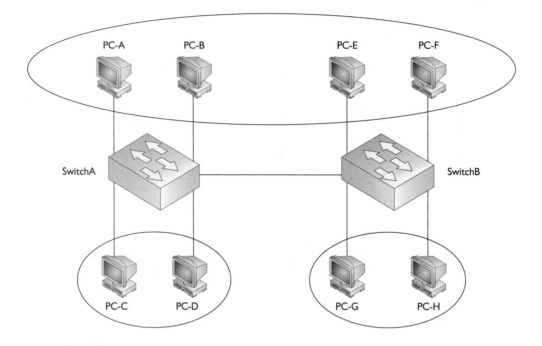

The switches in your network maintain the integrity of your VLANs. For example, if PC-A generates a broadcast, SwitchA and SwitchB will make sure that only other devices in that VLAN (PC-B, PC-E, and PC-F) will see the broadcast, and that other devices will not, and that holds true even across switches, as is the case in Figure 13-2.

exam
ⓦatch

A VLAN is a group of devices in the same broadcast domain or subnet. VLANs are good at logically separating traffic between different groups of users. VLANs contain/isolate broadcast traffic, where you need a router to move traffic between VLANs.

Subnets and VLANs

Logically speaking, VLANs are also subnets. A subnet, or a network, is a contained broadcast domain. A broadcast that occurs in one subnet will not be forwarded, by default, to another subnet. Routers, or layer 3 devices, provide this boundary function. Each of these subnets requires a unique network number. And to move from one network number to another, you need a router. In the case of broadcast domains and switches, each of these separate broadcast domains is a separate VLAN; therefore, you still need a routing function to move traffic between different VLANs.

From the user's perspective, the physical topology shown in Figure 13-2 would actually look like Figure 13-3. And from the user's perspective, the devices know that to reach another VLAN (subnet), they must forward their traffic to the default gateway address in their VLAN—the IP address on their router's interface.

FIGURE 13-3   Logical topology using VLANs

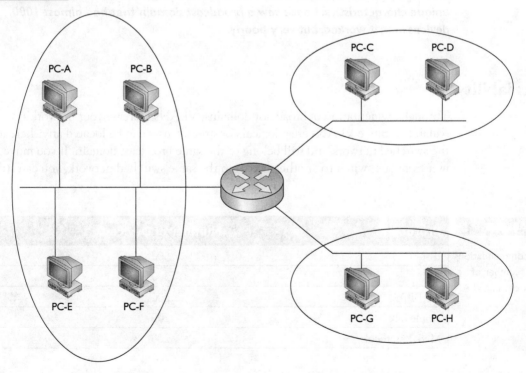

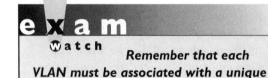

One advantage that switches have over bridges, though, is that in a switched VLAN network, assuming your routing function supports VLANs, the switch can handle multiple VLANs on a single port and a router can route between these VLANs on the same single port. This special kind of connection is called a *trunk* and is discussed in more depth later in the "VLAN Connections" section. With a bridge, each VLAN must be placed on a separate port of a router, increasing the cost of your routing solution.

Cisco has recommendations as to the number of devices in a VLAN, which are shown in Table 13-1. Remember that these numbers are only recommendations from Cisco; however, they are backed by many years of designing and implementing networks.

on the ⓘob *Remember that the information listed in Table 13-1 represents recommendations only: every network and its components are unique. Each network has its own unique characteristics. I once saw a broadcast domain that had almost 1000 devices in it; it worked, but very poorly.*

Scalability

Through segmentation of broadcast domains, VLANs increase your network's scalability. Since VLANs are a logical construct, a user can be located anywhere in the switched network and still belong to the same broadcast domain. If you move a user from one switch to another switch in the same switched network, you can still

TABLE 13-1	Protocol	Number of Devices
Recommendations for Number of Devices in a VLAN	IP	500
	IPX	300
	NetBIOS	200
	AppleTalk	200
	Mixed protocols	200

keep the user in his or her original VLAN. This includes a move from one floor of a building to another floor, or from one part of the campus to another. The limitation is that the user, when moved, must still be connected to the same layer 2 network.

VLANs provide for location independence in a switched network. This flexibility makes adds, changes, and moves of networking devices a simple process. It also allows you to group people together, perhaps according to their job function, which makes implementing your security policies easier. Logically separating people using VLANs provides additional security, since traffic must traverse a layer 3 device to go from one VLAN to another, where you can use an access control list (Chapter 22) to filter traffic.

VLANs and Traffic Types

Many network administrators use VLANs not only to separate different types of user traffic (commonly separated by job function), but also to separate it based on the type of traffic, placing network management, multicast, and voice over IP (VoIP) traffic into their own distinctive VLANs.

Network management traffic includes Simple Network Management Protocol (SNMP); Remote Monitoring (RMON); Spanning Tree Protocol (STP); Bridge Protocol Data Units (BPDUs), discussed in Chapter 14; Cisco Discovery Protocol (CDP) messages, discussed in Chapter 17; syslog messages; Network Time Protocol (NTP) updates; configuration backups of network devices, discussed in Chapter 17; and network device operating system upgrades, discussed in Chapter 17.

Multicast traffic is commonly used by video applications to transmit video streams intelligently from a server to one or more clients interested in seeing it, where UDP is used as a transport for the video stream. An example of a video solution that uses multicasts is Cisco's IP/TV server. Video traffic is delay sensitive—too much delay can be noticeable by the end user, where the actual video picture looks jumpy and jagged. By separating this traffic from other types through VLANs, and by setting up the necessary quality of service (QoS) for this VLAN traffic, you can help minimize or prevent delay issues.

VoIP traffic includes two kinds of traffic: signaling information sent from the VoIP phones to the VoIP gateway products, such as Cisco's Call Manager, and the actual voice conversations, which use UDP as a transport between VoIP phones and/or digital phones connected to VoIP PBXs. One issue with VoIP traffic is that it is delay-sensitive, so mixing this kind of traffic with other data types can cause performance issues that are very noticeable on voice connections; separating this traffic in its own VLAN and using QoS to ensure that this kind of traffic is given higher priority than other types is an important design consideration. Some Cisco Catalyst switches support a special type of VLAN, called a *voice VLAN*. With the voice VLAN feature, switches will automatically place a Cisco VoIP phone automatically into the voice VLAN once the VoIP phone is plugged into the switch. The advantage of this approach is that you, as an administrator, no longer have to worry, when a VoIP phone is added to the network, that you need to configure the switch to place the phone into the correct VLAN.

---

e x a m

ⓦatch

Different data types, such as voice, video (multicast), network management, and data application traffic, should be separated into different VLANs via connected switches to prevent problems *in one data type affecting others. QoS can be used to prioritize traffic types like VoIP and video to ensure that they receive the necessary bandwidth and are prioritized over other types of data traffic.*

VLAN Membership

A device's membership in a VLAN can be determined by one of three methods: static, dynamic, or voice. These methods affect how a switch will associate a port in its chassis with a particular VLAN. When you are dealing with static VLANs, you must manually assign a port on a switch to a VLAN using an *Interface Subconfiguration* mode command. VLANs configured in this way are typically called *port-based* VLANs.

With dynamic VLANs, the switch automatically assigns the port to a VLAN using information from the user device, such as its MAC address, IP address, or even directory information (a user or group name, for instance). The switch then consults a policy server, called a *VLAN membership policy server (VMPS)*, which contains a mapping of device information to VLANs. One of the switches in your network must be configured as this server. Low-end Cisco switches cannot serve as a VMPS server switch, but other switches, such as the Catalyst 6500, can. In this situation, the low-end switches act as clients and use the 6500 to store the dynamic VLAN membership information.

Another option is to use 802.1x authentication, briefly discussed in Chapter 5, which is used to authenticate a device's access to a switch or wireless access point. The authentication credentials are stored on an authentication server. One policy you can assign the user account (associated with the authenticating device) on the authentication server is the VLAN to which the device belongs—the server can pass this to the layer 2 device, which, in turn, can associate the VLAN to the port with which the authenticated device is associated.

Dynamic VLANs have one main advantage over static VLANs: they support plug-and-play movability. For instance, if you move a PC from a port on one switch to a port on another switch and you are using dynamic VLANs, the new switch port will automatically be configured for the VLAN to which the user belongs. About the only time that you have to configure information with dynamic VLANs is if you hire an employee and the employee leaves the company or changes job functions.

If you are using static VLANs, not only will you have to configure the switch port manually with this updated information, but if you move the user from one switch to another, you will also have to perform this manual configuration to reflect the user's new port. One advantage, though, that static VLANs have over dynamic VLANs is that since they have been around much longer than dynamic VLANs, the configuration process is easy and straightforward. Dynamic VLANs require a lot of initial preparation involving matching users to VLANs. (This book focuses exclusively on static VLANs, as dynamic VLANs are beyond the book's scope.)

Voice VLANs are unique. They are associated to ports that have VoIP phones attached. Some VoIP phones might have a multiport switch attached to them, to allow other devices to connect to the switch via the phone. In this instance, the phone might tag frames to indicate which device is sending the traffic—phone or computer—that the switch can then use to deal with the traffic correctly.

CERTIFICATION OBJECTIVE 13.02

VLAN Connections

When dealing with VLANs, switches support two types of switch ports: access-links and trunks. When setting up your switches, you will need to know what type of connection an interface should use and configure it appropriately. As you will see, the configuration process for each type of interface is different. This section discusses the two types of connections.

Access-Link Connections

An *access-link* connection is a connection to a device that has a standardized Ethernet NIC that understands only standardized Ethernet frames—in other words, a normal NIC card that understands IEEE 802.3 and Ethernet II frames. Access-link connections can be associated only with a single VLAN (voice VLAN ports are an exception to this). This means that any device or devices connected to this port will be in the same broadcast domain.

For example, if ten users are connected to a hub, and you plug the hub into an access-link interface on a switch, then all of these users will belong to the same VLAN that is associated with the switch port. If you wanted five users on the hub to belong to one VLAN and the other five to a different VLAN, you would need to purchase an additional hub and plug each hub into a different switch port. Then, on the switch, you would need to configure each of these ports with the correct VLAN identifier.

Trunk Connections

Unlike access-link connections, *trunk* connections are capable of carrying traffic for multiple VLANs. To support trunking, the original Ethernet frame must be modified to carry VLAN information, commonly called a *VLAN identifier* or number. This ensures that the broadcast integrity is maintained. For instance, if a device from VLAN 1 has generated a broadcast and the connected switch has received it, when this switch forwards it to other switches, these switches need to know the VLAN origin so that they can forward this frame out only VLAN 1 ports and not other VLAN ports.

Cisco supports two Ethernet trunking methods:

■ Cisco's proprietary InterSwitch Link (ISL) protocol for Ethernet
■ IEEE's 802.1Q, commonly referred to as *dot1q* for Ethernet

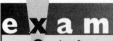

Cisco's high-end switches, such as the Catalyst 6500s, support both types; however, Cisco's low-end switches support only 802.1Q: ISL is being phased out by Cisco. This book focuses on the use of the latter trunk method, dot1q.

Trunk Tagging

Trunking methods create the illusion that instead of a single physical connection between the two trunking devices, a separate logical connection exists for each VLAN between them. When trunking, the switch adds the source port's VLAN identifier to the frame so that the device (typically a switch) at the other end of the trunk understands what VLAN originated this frame and the destination switch can make intelligent forwarding decisions on not just the destination MAC address, but also the source VLAN identifier.

Since information is added to the original Ethernet frame, normal NICs will not understand this information and will typically drop the frame. Therefore, you need to ensure that when you set up a trunk connection on a switch's interface, the device at the other end also supports the same trunking protocol and has it configured. If the device at the other end doesn't understand these modified frames or is not set up for trunking, it will, in most situations, drop them.

The modification of these frames, commonly called *tagging*, is done in hardware by application-specific integrated circuits (ASICs). ASICs are specialized processors. Since the tagging is done in hardware at faster than wire speeds, no latency is involved in the actual tagging process. And to ensure compatibility with access-link devices, switches will strip off the tagging information and forward the original Ethernet frame to the device or devices connected to access-link connections. From the user's perspective, the source generates a normal Ethernet frame and the destination receives this frame, which is an Ethernet 802.3 or II frame coming in and the same going out. In reality, this frame is tagged as it enters the switched infrastructure and sheds the tag as it exits the infrastructure: the process of tagging and untagging the frame is hidden from the users connected to access-link ports.

Trunk-Capable Devices

Trunk links are common between certain types of devices, including switch-to-switch, switch-to-router, and switch-to-file server connections. Using a trunk link on a router is a great way of reducing your layer 3 infrastructure costs. For instance, in the old days of bridging, in order to route between different broadcast domains, you needed a *separate* physical router interface for each broadcast domain. So if you had two broadcast domains, you needed two router ports; if you had 20 broadcast domains, you needed 20 router ports. As you can see, the more broadcast domains you had with bridges, the more expensive the router would become.

Today, with the advent of VLANs and trunk connections, you can use a single port on a router to route between your multiple broadcast domains. If you had 2 or 20 broadcast domains, you could use just one port on the router to accomplish the routing between these different subnets. Of course, you would need a router and an interface that supported trunking. Not every Cisco router supports trunking; you would need at least a 1751 or higher router with the correct type of Ethernet interface. If your router didn't support trunking, you would need a separate router interface for each VLAN you had created to route between the VLANs. Therefore, if you have a lot of VLANs, it makes sense to economize and buy a router and the correct type of interface that supports trunking.

You can also buy specialized NICs for PCs or file servers that support trunking. For instance, suppose you want multiple VLANs to access a file server. You could use a normal NIC and set this up with an access-link connection to a switch. Since this is an access-link connection, the server could belong only to one VLAN. The users in the same VLAN, when accessing the server, would have all their traffic switched via layer 2 devices to reach it. Users in other VLANs, however, would require that their traffic be routed to this server via a router, since the file server is in a different broadcast domain.

If throughput is a big concern, you might want to buy a trunk NIC for the file server. Configuring this NIC is different from configuring a normal NIC on a file server. For each VLAN in which you want the file server to participate, you would create a virtual NIC, assign your VLAN identifier and layer 3 addressing to the virtual NIC for the specific VLAN, and then associate it with the physical NIC. Once you have created all of these logical NICs on your file server, you need to set up a trunk connection on the switch to the server. And once you have done this, members of VLANs in the switched network will be able to access the file server directly without going through a router. Since these cards can be expensive, many administrators will purchase these devices only for critical services.

on the
Öob
A good example of a device that might need a trunk-capable NIC is a DHCP server, since it might need to assign IP addresses to users across multiple VLANs. If you don't have a trunk-capable NIC, but users are spread across multiple VLANs, you could use the IP helper feature on a Cisco router connected to the users' VLANs and have the router forward the DHCP broadcasts to the DHCP server located in a different VLAN.

If the same VLANs are
on two connected switches, use a trunk
connection between the switches to
allow the associated VLANs on each
side to communicate with each other.
Trunk connections are commonly used on
routers so that a router, via subinterfaces,

can route between the VLANs. The
configuration of trunking on a router's
interface is discussed in Chapter 16. The
trunking encapsulation, though, must
match between the two trunking devices
(such as using 802.1Q on both sides, or ISL
on both sides).

Trunking Example

Figure 13-4 shows an example of a trunk connection between SwitchA and SwitchB
in a network that has three VLANs. In this example, PC-A, PC-F, and PC-H belong
to one VLAN; PC-B and PC-G belong to a second VLAN; and PC-C, PC-D, and
PC-E belong to a third VLAN. The trunk between the two switches is also tagging
VLAN information so that the remote switch understands the source VLAN of the
originator.

FIGURE 13-4   Trunking example

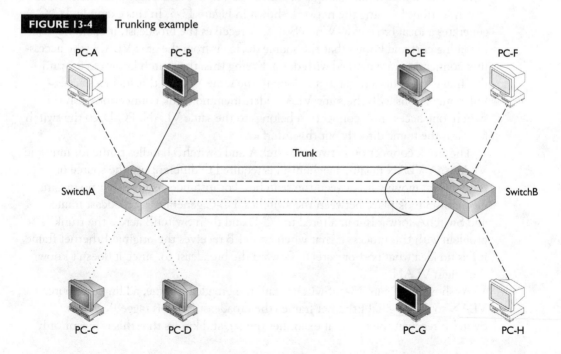

FIGURE 13-5

Broadcast traffic
example

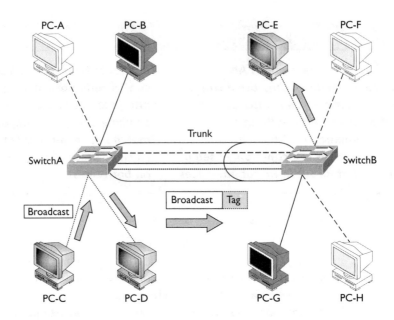

Let's take a look at an example of the use of VLANs and the two different types of connections by using the network shown in Figure 13-5. In this example, PC-C generates a local broadcast. When SwitchA receives the broadcast, it examines the incoming port and knows that the source device is from the gray VLAN (the access-link connections are marked with dots). Seeing this, the switch knows to forward this frame only out of ports that belong to the same VLAN: this includes access-link connections with the same VLAN identifier and trunk connections. On this switch, one access-link connection belongs to the same VLAN, PC-D, so the switch forwards the frame directly out this interface.

The trunk connection between SwitchA and SwitchB handles traffic for multiple VLANs. A VLAN tagging mechanism is required to differentiate the source of traffic when moving it between the switches. For instance, assume that no tagging mechanism took place between the switches. PC-C generates a broadcast frame, and SwitchA forwards it unaltered to PC-D and then SwitchB across the trunk. The problem with this process is that when SwitchB receives the original Ethernet frame, it has no idea what port or ports to forward the broadcast to, since it doesn't know the origin VLAN.

As shown in Figure 13-5, SwitchA tags the broadcast frame, adding the source VLAN to the original Ethernet frame (the broadcast frame is tagged). When SwitchB receives the frame, it examines the tag and knows that this is meant only for the VLAN to which PC-E belongs. Of course, since PC-E is connected via an access-link connection, SwitchB first strips off the tagging and then forwards the original Ethernet frame to PC-E. This is necessary because PC-E has a standard NIC and doesn't understand VLAN tagging. Through this process, both switches maintained the integrity of the broadcast domain.

802.1Q

ISL, which is Cisco proprietary, is being phased out in Cisco's products and being replaced with IEEE's 802.1Q trunking standard, which was introduced in 1998. One of the advantages provided by the IEEE standard is that it allows trunks between different vendors' devices, whereas ISL is supported only on certain Cisco devices. Therefore, you should be able to implement a multivendor trunking solution without having to worry about whether or not a specific type of trunk connection is or is not supported. The 2960 switches, as well as Cisco's higher-end switches such as the 6500 series, support 802.1Q. Actually, the 2960 switches support *only* 802.1Q trunking—they don't support ISL. 802.1Q trunking is supported on switch ports that are capable of either Fast or Gigabit Ethernet speeds.

802.1Q trunks support two types of frames: tagged and untagged. An untagged frame does not carry any VLAN identification information in it—basically, this is a standard, unaltered Ethernet frame. The VLAN membership for the frame is determined by the switch's port configuration: if the port is configured in VLAN 1, the untagged frame belongs to VLAN 1. This VLAN is commonly called a *native* VLAN. A tagged frame contains VLAN information, and only other 802.1Q-aware devices on the trunk will be able to process this frame.

One of the unique aspects of 802.1Q trunking is that you can have *both* tagged and untagged frames on a trunk connection, such as that shown in Figure 13-6. In this example, the white VLAN (PC-A, PC-B, PC-E, and PC-F) uses tagged frames on the trunk between SwitchA and SwitchB. Any other device that is connected on this trunk line would have to have 802.1Q trunking enabled to see the tag inside the frame to determine the source VLAN of the frame. In this network, a third device is connected to the trunk connection: PC-G. This example assumes that a hub connects the two switches and the PC together.

PC-G has a normal Ethernet NIC and obviously wouldn't understand the tagging and would drop these frames. However, this presents a problem: PC-G belongs to the dark VLAN, where PC-C and PC-D are also members. Therefore, in order for frames to be forwarded among these three members, the trunk must also support untagged frames so that PC-G can process them. To set this up, you would configure

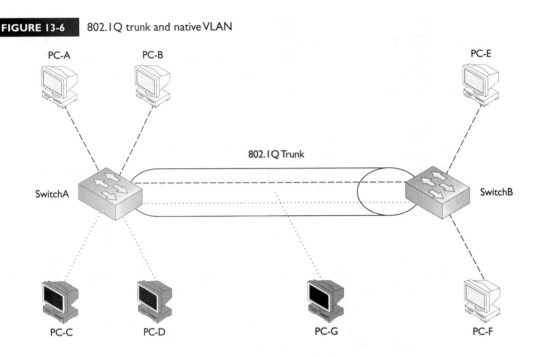

FIGURE 13-6 802.1Q trunk and native VLAN

the switch-to-switch connection as an 802.1Q trunk but set the native VLAN as the dark one, so that frames from this VLAN would go untagged across it and allow PC-G to process them.

One restriction placed on an 802.1Q trunk configuration is that it must be the *same* on both sides. In other words, if the dark VLAN is the native VLAN on one switch, the switch at the other end must have the native VLAN set to the dark VLAN. Likewise, if the white VLAN is having its frames tagged on one switch, the other switch must also be tagging the white VLAN frames with 802.1Q information.

With the 802.1Q tagging method, the original Ethernet frame is modified. A 4-byte field, called a *tag* field, is *inserted* into the header of the original Ethernet frame, and the original frame's FCS (checksum) is recomputed on the basis of this change. The first 2 bytes of the tag are the protocol identifier. For instance, an Ethernet type frame has a protocol identifier value of 0x8100, indicating that this is an Ethernet tagged frame. The next 3 bits are used to prioritize the frame, which is defined in the IEEE 802.1p standard. The fourth bit indicates if this is an encapsulated Token Ring frame (Cisco no longer sells Token Ring products), and the last 12 bits are used for the VLAN identifier (number).

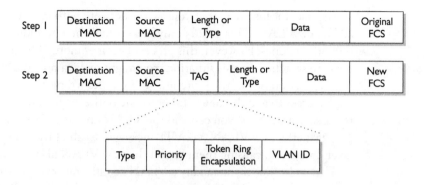

FIGURE 13-7

802.1Q framing process

Figure 13-7 shows the process that occurs when tagging an Ethernet frame by inserting the 802.1Q field into the Ethernet frame header. As you can see in this figure, step 1 is the normal, untagged Ethernet frame. Step 2 inserts the tag and recomputes a new FCS value. Below step 2 is a blow-up of the actual Tag field. As you can see in this figure, the tag is inserted directly after the source and destination MAC addresses in the Ethernet header.

802.1Q is a standardized trunking method that inserts a 4-byte field into the original Ethernet frame and recalculates the FCS. The 2950s and 2960s support only 802.1Q trunking. The native VLAN contains untagged frames, even on trunk connections.

One advantage of using this tagging mechanism is that since you are adding only 4 bytes, your frame size will not exceed 1518 bytes, and thus you could actually forward 802.1Q frames through the access-link connections of switches, since these switches would forward the frame as a normal Ethernet frame.

CERTIFICATION OBJECTIVE 13.03

VLAN Trunk Protocol

The VLAN Trunk Protocol (VTP) is a proprietary Cisco protocol used to share VLAN configuration information between Cisco switches on trunk connections. VTP allows switches to share and synchronize their VLAN information, which ensures that your network has a consistent VLAN configuration.

Assume, for instance, that you have a network with two switches and you need to add a new VLAN. This could easily be accomplished by adding the VLAN manually on both switches. However, this process becomes more difficult and tedious if you have 30 switches. In this situation, you might make a mistake in configuring the new VLAN on one of the switches, giving it the wrong VLAN identifier, or you might forget to add the new VLAN to one of the 30 switches. VTP can take care of this issue. With VTP, you can add the VLAN on one switch and have this switch propagate the new VLAN, via VTP messages, to all of the other switches in your layer 2 network, causing them to add the new VLAN also.

This is also true if you modify a VLAN's configuration or delete a VLAN—VTP can verify that your VLAN configuration is consistent across all of your switches. VTP can even perform consistency checks with your VLANs, to make sure that all the VLANs are configured identically. For instance, some of these components of a VLAN include the VLAN number, name, and type. If you have a VLAN number of 1 and a name of "admin" on one switch, but a name of "administrator" on a second switch for this VLAN, VTP can check for and fix these kinds of configuration mismatches.

VTP messages will propagate *only* across *trunk* connections, so you will need to set up trunking between your switches in order to share VLAN information via VTP. VTP messages are propagated as layer 2 multicast frames. Therefore, if a router separates two of your switches, the router will *not* forward the VTP messages from one of its interfaces to another.

In order for VTP to function correctly, you must associate your switch with a VTP domain. A *domain* is a group of switches that have the same VLAN information applied to them. Basically, a VTP domain is similar to an autonomous system, which some routing protocols use (autonomous systems and routing protocols are introduced in Chapter 15). A switch can belong only to a single domain. Domains are given names, and when switches generate VTP messages, they include the domain name in their messages. An incoming switch will not incorporate the VLAN changes in the received VTP message if the domain name in the message doesn't match the domain name configured on itself. In other words, a switch in one domain will ignore VTP messages from switches in other domains. The following sections cover the components and messages that VTP uses, as well as some of the advantages that it provides, such as pruning.

VTP Modes

When you are setting up VTP, you can choose from three different modes for your switch's configuration:

- *Client*
- *Server*
- *Transparent*

Table 13-2 shows the differences between these VTP modes.

A switch configured in either VTP server or transparent mode can add, modify, and delete VLANs. The main difference between these modes is that the configuration changes made to a transparent switch affect only *that* switch and no other switch in the network. A VTP server switch, however, will make the change and then propagate a VTP message concerning the change on all of its trunk ports. If a server switch receives a VTP message, it will incorporate the update and forward the message out its remaining trunk ports. A transparent switch, on the other hand, ignores VTP messages—it will accept them on trunk ports and forward them out its remaining trunk ports, but it will not incorporate the changes in the VTP message in its local VLAN configuration. In this sense, transparent switches are like little islands, where changes on a transparent switch affect no one else but the transparent switch itself, and changes on other switches do not affect transparent switches.

A VTP client switch cannot make changes to its VLAN configuration itself—it requires a server switch to tell it about the VLAN changes. When a client switch receives a VTP message from a server switch, it incorporates the changes and then floods the VTP message out its remaining trunk ports.

TABLE 13-2		Server	Client	Transparent
Description of VTP Modes	Can add, modify, and delete VLANs	Yes	No	Yes
	Can generate VTP messages	Yes	No	No
	Can propagate VTP messages	Yes	Yes	Yes
	Can accept changes in a VTP message	Yes	Yes	No
	Default VTP mode	Yes	No	No
	Saves VLANs to NVRAM	Yes	No	Yes

Normally, you would set up one switch in server mode and all other switches in client mode. Then you would control who could make changes on the server switch. However, you should keep in mind that if you make a VLAN configuration mistake on the server switch, this mistake is *automatically propagated* to all the client switches in your network. Imagine that you accidentally deleted a VLAN on your server switch, and this VLAN had 500 devices in it. When this occurs, all the switches remove the VLAN from their configuration.

Given this problem, some administrators don't like to use VTP server and client modes; they prefer to configure all of their switches in transparent mode. The problem with transparent mode is that it isn't very scalable; if you need to add a VLAN to your network and your network has 20 switches, you would have to add the VLAN manually to each individual switch, which is a time-consuming process. Of course, the advantage of this approach is that if you make a mistake on a transparent switch, the problem is *not* propagated to other switches: it's localized.

You could also set up all of your switches in server mode, which is the default setting for VTP. As you can see, a wide range of VTP configuration options is available. You could even mix and match these options. Set up a couple of server switches, and have the remaining switches as clients, or set your switches initially as servers and clients, add all your VLANs on the server switch, allow the clients to acquire this information, and then change all the switches to transparent mode. This process allows you to populate your switches' configurations easily with a consistent VLAN configuration during the setup process. Note that if you don't specify the VTP mode for your switch, it will default to *server*.

VTP Messages

If you use a client/server configuration for VTP, these switches can generate three types of VTP messages:

- Advertisement request
- Subset advertisement
- Summary advertisement

An *advertisement request* message is a VTP message a client generates to acquire VLAN information, to which a server will respond. When the server responds to a client's request, it generates a *subset advertisement*. A subset advertisement contains detailed VLAN configuration information, including the VLAN numbers, names, types, and other information. The client will then configure itself appropriately.

A *summary advertisement* is also generated by a switch in VTP server mode. Summary advertisements are generated every 5 minutes (300 seconds) by default, or when a configuration change takes place on the server switch. Unlike a subset advertisement, a summary advertisement contains only summarized VLAN information.

When a server switch generates a VTP advertisement, it can include the following information:

- The number and name of the VLAN
- The MTU size used by the VLAN
- The frame format used by the VLAN
- The Security Association ID (SAID) value for the VLAN (needed if it is an 802.10 VLAN, which is implemented in networks using FDDI)
- The configuration revision number
- The name of the VTP domain

This list includes a couple of important items that should be discussed further. Switches in either server or client mode will process VTP messages if they are in the same VTP domain; however, some restrictions are placed on whether the switch should incorporate the changes or not. For instance, one function of the VTP summary advertisements is to ensure that all of the switches have the most current changes. If you didn't make a change on a server switch in the 5-minute update interval, when the countdown timer expires, the server switch still sends out a summary advertisement with the same exact summary information. It makes no sense to have other switches, which have the most up-to-date information, incorporate the same information in their configuration.

To make this process more efficient, the *configuration revision number* is used to keep track of what server switch has the most recent changes. Initially this number is set to zero (0). If you make a change on a server switch, it increments its revision number and advertises this to the other switches across its trunk links. When a client or server switch receives this information, it compares the revision number in the message to the last message it received. If the newly arrived message has a higher number, this server switch must have made changes. If the necessary VLAN information isn't in the VTP summary advertisement, all client and server switches will generate an advertisement request and the server will respond with the details in a subset advertisement.

If a server switch receives a VTP message from another server, and the advertising server has a lower revision number, the receiving server switch will respond to the advertising server with a VTP message with its current configuration revision number. This will tell the advertising server switch that it doesn't have the most up-to-date VLAN information and should request it from the server that does. In this sense, the revision number used in a VTP message is somewhat similar to the sequence number used in TCP. Also, remember that transparent switches are not processing these VTP advertisements—they simply passively forward these messages to other switches on their trunk ports.

on the

ⓙob

IOS switches save the VLAN database and revision value in the vlan.dat file, not the startup-config file: server, transparent, and client mode switches. The `erase startup-config` *command will not delete this file. Therefore, it is possible that if you boot up a switch that has a higher revision number than an existing server switch in a domain, the switch's VLAN configuration could overwrite the existing VLAN information in the domain. You should delete the vlan.dat file on the switch* before *adding it to an existing network. This is done from* Privilege EXEC *mode with this command:* `delete vlan.dat`. *You must press* ENTER *twice after executing the command to confirm your option.*

VTP Pruning

VTP pruning is a Cisco feature that allows your switches dynamically to delete or add VLANs to a trunk, creating a more efficient switching network. By default, all VLANs are associated with a trunk connection. This means that if a device in *any* VLAN generates a broadcast, multicast, or an unknown unicast, the switch will flood this frame out all ports associated with the source VLAN port, including trunks. In many situations, this flooding is necessary, especially if the VLAN spans multiple switches. However, it doesn't make sense to flood a frame to a neighboring switch if that switch doesn't have any active ports in the source VLAN.

Trunking Without Pruning

Let's take a look at a simple example by examining Figure 13-8. In this example, VTP pruning is not enabled. PC-A, PC-B, PC-E, and PC-F are in the same VLAN. If PC-A generates a broadcast, SwitchA will forward this to the access link to which PC-B is connected as well as the trunk (since a trunk is a member of all VLANs, by default). This makes sense, since PC-E and PC-F, connected to SwitchB, are in the same VLAN.

Figure 13-8 shows a second VLAN with two members: PC-C and PC-D. If PC-C generates a local broadcast, SwitchA will obviously send to this to PC-D's port. What doesn't make sense is that SwitchA will flood this broadcast out its trunk port to SwitchB, considering that no devices on SwitchB are in this VLAN. This is an example of wasting bandwidth and resources. A single broadcast isn't a big problem; however, imagine this were a video multicast stream at 5 Mbps coming from PC-A.

FIGURE 13-8 Without VTP pruning

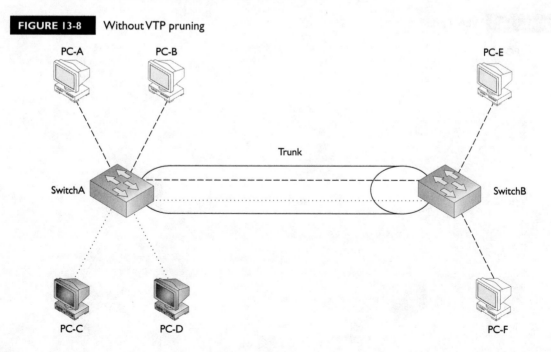

This network might experience throughput problems on the trunk, since a switch treats a multicast just like a broadcast—it floods it out all ports associated with the source port's VLAN.

You could use one of two methods to fix this problem: static and dynamic VLAN pruning. With a static configuration, you would manually prune the inactive VLAN off the trunk on both switches, as shown in Figure 13-9. Notice that in this figure, the dark VLAN (indicated by dotted lines) has been pruned from the trunk. The problem with manual pruning is that if you add a dark VLAN member to SwitchB, you will have to log into both switches and manually add the pruned VLAN back to the trunk. This can become very confusing in a multi-switched network with multiple VLANs, where every VLAN is not necessarily active on every switch. It would be easy to accidentally prune a VLAN from a trunk that shouldn't have been pruned, thus creating connectivity problems.

Trunking with Pruning

The VTP pruning feature allows the switches to share additional VLAN information and allows them to prune inactive VLANs dynamically from trunk connections. In this instance, the switches share which VLANs are active. For example, SwitchA

FIGURE 13-9 VLAN pruning

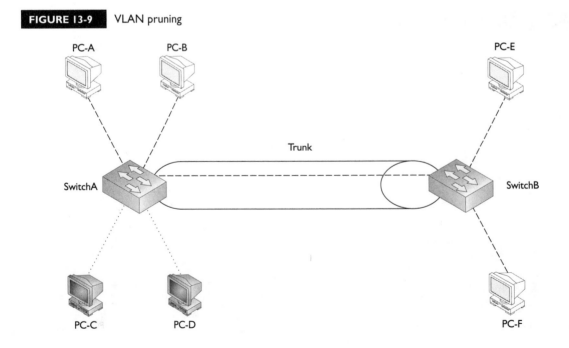

FIGURE 13-10   VTP pruning activating a VLAN on a trunk

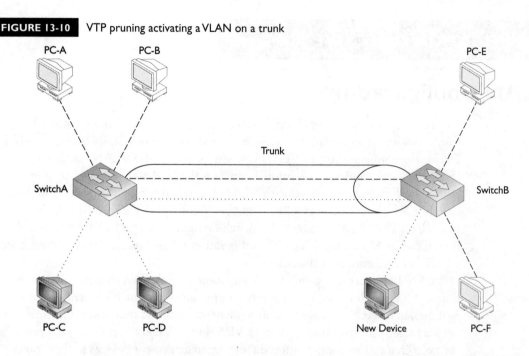

tells SwitchB that it has two active VLANs (the white one and the dark one). SwitchB, on the other hand, has only one active VLAN, and it shares this fact with SwitchA. Given the shared information, both SwitchA and SwitchB realize that the dark VLAN is inactive across their trunk connection and therefore the dark VLAN should be dynamically removed from the trunk's configuration.

The nice thing about this feature is that if you happen to activate the dark VLAN on SwitchB by connecting a device to a port on the switch and assigning that port to the dark VLAN, SwitchB will notify SwitchA about the newly active VLAN and both switches will dynamically add the VLAN back to the trunk's configuration. This will allow PC-C, PC-D, and the new device to send frames to each other, as is shown in Figure 13-10.

Only a VTP switch in *server* mode can enable VTP pruning, and the remaining switches in the domain must be either in VTP server or client mode. If you have transparent mode switches, you'll have to prune VLANs off their trunk links manually.

exam
ⓦatch   *By default, all VLANs can traverse a trunk. VTP pruning is used on trunk connections to dynamically remove VLANs not active between the two switches. It must be enabled on a VTP server switch and the other switches must be either servers or clients.*

CERTIFICATION OBJECTIVE 13.04

VLAN Configuration

Unlike Cisco routers, every Cisco switch comes with a default configuration. For instance, some preconfigured VLANs are already on the switch, including VLAN 1. During the configuration, all VLAN commands refer to the VLAN number, even though you can configure an optional name for the VLAN. Every port on your switch, by default, is associated with VLAN 1. And all communications from the switch itself—VTP messages, Cisco Discovery Protocol (CDP) multicasts (discussed in Chapter 17), and other traffic the switch originates—occur in VLAN 1. Recall from Chapter 12 that the 2960's IP configuration is based on the VLAN interface for which you configure your IP address.

VLAN 1 is sometimes called the *management VLAN*, even though you can use a different VLAN. It is a common practice to put all of your management devices— switches, manageable hubs, and management stations—in their own VLAN. If you decide to put your switch in a different VLAN than VLAN 1, it is recommended that you change this configuration on all your management devices so that you can more easily secure them, since other VLANs would have to go through a layer 3 device to access them; and on this layer 3 device, you can set up access control lists to filter unwanted traffic (discussed in Chapter 22).

It's important that all your switches are in the same VLAN, since many of the switches' management protocols, such as CDP, VTP, and the Dynamic Trunk Protocol (DTP), which is discussed later in this chapter, occur within the switch's management VLAN. If one switch had its management VLAN set to 1 and another connected switch had it set to 2, the two switches would lose a lot of inter-functionality.

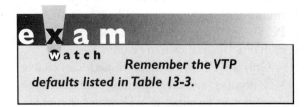

Remember the VTP defaults listed in Table 13-3.

Configuring VTP

One of the very first VLAN configuration tasks you'll perform on your switch is to set up VTP. Table 13-3 shows the default VTP configuration of the 2960 switches. The following sections cover the configuration of VTP on the two switches.

TABLE 13-3	VTP Component	2960
	Domain name	None
VTP Default Configuration Values	Mode	Server
	Password	None
	Pruning	Disabled
	Version	1

Your VTP configuration is done from *Global Configuration* mode on the 2960:

```
switch(config)# vtp domain VTP_domain_name
switch(config)# vtp mode server|client|transparent
switch(config)# vtp password VTP_password
switch(config)# vtp pruning
```

The **vtp domain** command defines the domain name for your switch. Remember that in order for switches to share VTP information, they must be in the same domain. Messages received from other domains are ignored. If you don't configure a domain name, the switch will learn this from a server advertisement.

The rest of the commands in the configuration are optional. The second **vtp** command defines the VTP mode of the switch. If you don't configure this command, the default mode is **server**. You can configure a VTP MD5 password for your switches, which must match the password configured on every switch in the domain. Switches will use this password to verify VTP messages from other switches; if the created hashed values placed in VTP messages (generated by taking the VTP message and password and running it through MD5 to create the hash signature) can't be verified, the switches ignore the VTP messages. On the 2960 switches, pruning is disabled by default, but you can disable or enable it with the **vtp pruning** command. It is important to note that if pruning is enabled on a server switch, the server switch will propagate this to all other server and client switches in the same domain.

Once you are done configuring VTP, use this command to check your configuration:

```
switch# show vtp status
VTP Version : 1
Configuration Revision : 17
Maximum VLANs supported locally : 255
Number of existing VLANs : 7
VTP Operating Mode : Server
VTP Domain Name : dealgroup
```

```
VTP Pruning Mode : Enabled
VTP V2 Mode : Disabled
VTP Traps Generation : Disabled
MD5 digest : 0x95 0xAB 0x29 0x44 0x32 0xA1 0x2C 0x31
Configuration last modified by 0.0.0.0 at 3-1-03 15:18:37
Local updater ID is 192.168.1.4 on interface Vl1
    (lowest numbered VLAN interface found)
```

In this example, 17 configuration changes have occurred (examine the
`Configuration Revision` field). The switch is operating in server mode in
the *dealgroup* domain.

The `vtp password` command is used to authenticate VTP messages between switches. The `show vtp status` command will display the VTP	mode in which the switch is operating, the configuration revision number, and the VTP domain to which the switch belongs.

The following command displays VTP statistics concerning VTP messages sent
and received:

```
switch # show vtp counters
VTP statistics:
  Summary advertisements received : 12
  Subset advertisements received : 0
  Request advertisements received : 0
  Summary advertisements transmitted : 7
  Subset advertisements transmitted : 0
  Request advertisements transmitted : 0
  Number of config revision errors : 0
  Number of config digest errors : 0
  Number of V1 summary errors : 0
  .
  .
  .
```

In this example, you can see that the switch has sent and received VTP summary
advertisements.

*13.01. The CD contains a multimedia demonstration of configuring and
verifying VTP on a switch.*

Configuring Trunks

This section covers the setup of trunk connections on your switches using the 802.1Q trunking protocol. Before getting into the configuration, however, you should first be familiar with a protocol that is used to form a trunk between two devices: the Dynamic Trunk Protocol (DTP). One limitation of trunks is that they don't work with the port security and 802.1x authentication features; these features are used on access-links.

Dynamic Trunk Protocol (DTP)

Cisco's proprietary trunking protocol is used on trunk connections to form trunks dynamically. DTP is used to form and verify a trunk connection dynamically between two Cisco switches. DTP supports five trunking modes, shown in Table 13-4.

If the trunk mode is set to *on* or *trunk* for an interface, this causes the interface to generate DTP messages on the interface and to tag frames on the interface, based on the trunk type (802.1Q on the 2960s). When set to *on*, the trunk interface always assumes the connection is a trunk, even if the remote end does not support trunking. Some of Cisco's switches use the term *trunk* instead of *on*, like the 2960s.

If the trunk mode is set to *desirable*, the interface will generate DTP messages on the interface, but it will make the assumption that the other side is not trunk-capable and will wait for a DTP reply message from the remote side. In this state, the interface starts as an access-link connection. If the remote side sends a DTP message, and this message indicates that trunking is compatible between the two switches, a trunk will be formed and the switch will start tagging frames on the interface. If the other side does not support trunking, the interface will remain as an access-link connection.

If the trunk mode is set to *auto*, the interface passively listens for DTP messages from the remote side and leaves the interface as an access-link connection. If the interface receives a DTP message, and the message matches trunking capabilities of the interface, then the interface will change from an access-link connection to a

TABLE 13-4	DTP Mode	Generate DTP Messages	Default Frame Tagging
DTP Modes and Operation	On or trunk	Yes	Yes
	Desirable	Yes	No
	Auto	No	No
	Off	No	No
	No-negotiate	No	Yes

trunk connection and start tagging frames. This is the default DTP mode for a Cisco switch interface that is trunk-capable.

If an interface is set to *no-negotiate*, the interface is set as a trunk connection and will automatically tag frames with VLAN information; however, the interface will not generate DTP messages: DTP is disabled. This mode is typically used when connecting trunk connections to non-Cisco devices that don't understand Cisco's proprietary trunking protocol and thus won't understand the contents of these messages.

If an interface is set to *off*, the interface is configured as an access-link. No DTP messages are generated in this mode, nor are frames tagged.

Table 13-5 shows when switch connections will form a trunk. In this table, one side needs to be configured as either *on* or *desirable* and the other side as *on*, *desirable*, or *auto*, or both switches need to be configured as *no-negotiate*. Note that if you use the no-negotiate mode, trunking is formed but DTP is not used, whereas if you use on, desirable, or auto, DTP is used. One advantage that DTP has over no-negotiate is that DTP checks for the trunk's characteristics: if they don't match on the two sides (for instance, as to the type of trunk), then the trunk will not come up and the interfaces will remain as an access-link connection. With no-negotiate, if the trunking characteristics don't match on the two sides, the trunk connection will probably fail.

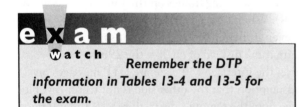

Switch Trunk Configuration

Setting up a trunk on a 2960 is the same as most of Cisco's IOS switches:

```
switch(config)# interface type slot_#/port_#
switch(config-if)# switchport mode trunk|dynamic desirable|
                        dynamic auto|nonegotiate
switch(config-if)# switchport trunk native vlan VLAN_#
```

TABLE 13-5	Your Switch	Remote Switch
Forming Trunks	On	On, desirable, auto
	Desirable	On, desirable, auto
	Auto	On, desirable
	No-negotiate	No-negotiate

All ports on a 2960 switch support trunking. Remember that the 2960 supports only 802.1Q trunking, so you must set up a trunk connection only to other 802.1Q trunking devices. If you want a trunk to be in an *on* state, use the **trunk** parameter. For a *desirable* DTP state, use **dynamic desirable**, and for an *auto* state, use **dynamic auto**. The default mode is auto. If you don't want to use DTP but still want to perform trunking, use the **nonegotiate** parameter. For 802.1Q trunks, the native VLAN is VLAN 1. You can change this with the **switchport trunk native vlan** command, but then you'll need to match up the native VLAN on all switches in the layer 2 network.

Use the switchport *mode command to enable trunking on a switch.*

After you have configured your trunk connection, you can use this command to verify it:

```
switch# show interfaces type 0/port_# switchport|trunk
```

Here's an example using the **switchport** parameter:

```
switch# show interface fastEthernet0/1 switchport
Name: Fa0/1
Switchport: Enabled
Administrative mode: trunk
Operational Mode: trunk
Administrative Trunking Encapsulation: dot1q
Operational Trunking Encapsulation: dot1q
Negotiation of Trunking: Disabled
Access Mode VLAN: 0 ((Inactive))
Trunking Native Mode VLAN: 1 (default)
Trunking VLANs Enabled: ALL
Trunking VLANs Active: 1,2
Pruning VLANs Enabled: 2-1001
Priority for untagged frames: 0
Override vlan tag priority: FALSE
Voice VLAN: none
```

In this example, FA0/1's trunking mode is set to trunk (on), with the native VLAN set to 1. Here's an example using the trunk parameter:

```
switch# show interfaces trunk
Port    Mode        Encapsulation   Status      Native vlan
Fa0/1   on          802.1q          trunking    1
Port    Vlans allowed on trunk
```

```
Fa0/1    1-4094
Port     Vlans allowed and active in management domain
Fa0/1    1-2
Port     Vlans in spanning tree forwarding state and not pruned
Fa0/1    1-2
```

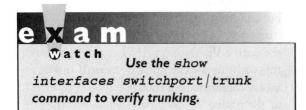

w a t c h *Use the show interfaces switchport/trunk command to verify trunking.*

In this example, one interface is trunking—fa0/1: the trunking mode is on, the trunking protocol is 802.1Q, and the native VLAN is 1.

13.02. The CD contains a multimedia demonstration of configuring trunking on a switch.

EXERCISE 13-1

Configuring Trunks on Your Switches

The last few sections dealt with setting up trunks on Cisco switches. You'll perform this lab using Boson's NetSim simulator. This exercise has you set up a trunk link between the two 2950 switches (2950-1 and 2950-2). You can find a picture of the network diagram for the NetSim simulator in the Introduction of this book. After starting up the simulator, click the Lab Navigator button. Next, double-click Exercise 13-1 and click the Load Lab button. This will load the lab configuration based on the exercises in Chapters 11 and 12.

1. On the 2950-1 switch, set the trunk mode to trunk for the connection between the two 2950 switches and examine the status. Does the trunk come up?

   At the top of the simulator in the menu bar, click the eSwitches icon and choose 2950-1. Access Configuration mode: **enable** and **configure terminal**. Go into the interface: **interface fa0/1**. Set the trunk mode to trunk: **switchport mode trunk**. Exit Configuration mode: **end**. Use the **show interfaces trunk** command to verify the status.

You might have to wait a few seconds, but the trunk should come up. If one side is set to *on*, or *desirable*, and the other is set to *on*, *desirable*, or *auto* (default), then the trunk should come up.

2. Save the configuration on the switch: `copy running-config startup-config`.

3. On the 2950-2 switch, set the trunk mode to trunk for the connection between the two 2950 switches and verify the trunking status of the interface.

    At the top of the simulator in the menu bar, click the eSwitches icon and choose 2950-2. Access Configuration mode: `enable` and `configure terminal`. Go into the interface: `interface fa0/1`. Set the trunk mode to trunk: `switchport mode trunk`. Exit Configuration mode: `end`. Use the `show interfaces trunk` command to verify the status.

4. Save the configuration on the switch: `copy running-config startup-config`.

Now you should be more comfortable with setting up trunks on your switches. In the next section, you will be presented with setting up VLANs and associating interfaces to your VLANs.

Creating VLANs

This section covers how you can create VLANs on your switches and then statically assign access-link connections (interfaces) to your newly created VLANs. Here are some guidelines to remember when creating VLANs:

- The number of VLANs you can create is dependent on the switch model and IOS software.
- Some VLANs are preconfigured on every switch, including VLAN 1 and 1002–1005 (1002–1005 are used in Token Ring and FDDI networks only).
- To add or delete VLANs, your switch must use either VTP server or transparent mode.
- VLAN names can be changed; VLAN numbers can't: you must delete a VLAN and re-add it in order to renumber it.
- All interfaces, by default, belong to VLAN 1.

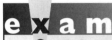

- CDP, DTP, and VTP advertisements are sent in the native VLAN, which is VLAN 1, by default.
- Before deleting VLANs, reassign any ports from the current VLAN to another; if you don't, any ports from the deleted VLAN will be inoperable.

Table 13-6 lists the VLAN capabilities of the 2960 switches.

You can use two methods—an old one and a new one—to create VLANs on your 2960 switch. The old method requires you to go into the VLAN database in Privilege EXEC mode and create the VLAN, like this:

```
switch# vlan database
switch(vlan)# vlan VLAN_# [name VLAN_name]
```

Starting in IOS 12.1(9)EA1 and later, you can use this configuration:

```
switch(config)# vlan VLAN_#
switch(config-vlan)# name VLAN_name
```

When you execute the **vlan** command, you are taken into VLAN Subconfiguration mode, where you can enter your configuration parameters for the VLAN, such as its name. Use the **no** parameter in front of the **vlan** command to delete it.

on the
job
*Cisco recommends you use the newer method to create VLANs on your switches: the Global configuration **vlan** command. The former method of using the Privilege EXEC **vlan database** command is not available on newer IOS versions. Remember that your switch must be a VTP server or transparent switch to create or delete VLANs on it. Also, before you delete a VLAN, move all ports in the VLAN to a different one; otherwise, ports associated with a deleted VLAN will not be able to communicate with other ports until you either re-add the VLAN number back or move the ports to an existing VLAN. When this happens, the port LED(s) will be solid amber.*

TABLE 13-6	Switch Model	Software Revision	Number of VLANs
VLAN Capabilities of the 2960 Cisco Switches	2960	LAN Lite	64
	2960	LAN Base	255

Once you have created your VLANs, you need to assign your VLANs to your switch's interfaces using the following configuration:

```
switch(config)# interface type 0/port_#
switch(config-if)# switchport mode access
switch(config-if)# switchport access vlan VLAN_#
```

The first thing you must do is specify that the connection is an access-link connection with the **switchport mode access** command. The **switchport access vlan** command assigns a VLAN to the access-link connection.

Once you have created and assigned your VLANs, you can use various **show** commands to review and verify your configuration. The **show vlan** command displays the list of VLANs and which ports are assigned to them:

```
switch# show vlan
VLAN Name            Status    Ports
---- --------------- --------- ------------------------------
1    default         active    Fa0/1, Fa0/2, Fa0/3, Fa0/4
                               Fa0/5, Fa0/6, Fa0/7, Fa0/8
                               Fa0/9, Fa0/10, Fa0/11, Fa0/12
                               Fa0/13, Fa0/14, Fa0/15, Fa0/16
                               Fa0/17, Fa0/18, Fa0/19, Fa0/20
                               Fa0/21, Fa0/22, Fa0/23, Fa0/24
                               Gi0/1, Gi0/2
1002 fddi-default    act/unsup
 .
 .
 .
```

In this example, all the ports are assigned to VLAN 1. You can add the **brief** parameter to this command and it will not display the details for each VLAN at the bottom of the display. You can also use the **show interface switchport** command to see a specific interface's VLAN membership information. This command was shown earlier in the chapter in the "Switch Trunk Configuration" section.

13.03. The CD contains a multimedia demonstration of configuring VLANs on a switch.

Basic Troubleshooting of VLANs and Trunks

Now that you know how to set up a VLAN-based network, you will eventually run into a problem that is related to your VLAN configuration. Basically, you should check the following, in order, to determine the cause of the problem:

1. Check the status of your interface to determine whether it is a physical layer problem.
2. Check your switches' and routers' configuration to make sure nothing was added or changed.
3. Verify that your trunks are operational.
4. Verify that your VLANs are configured correctly and that the spanning tree protocol (STP), discussed in Chapter 14, is functioning correctly.

The following sections cover some of the basic things that you should check whenever you experience switching problems.

Performance Problems

If you are experiencing slow performance or intermittent connection problems, you should first check the statistics on the interfaces of your switch with the **show interfaces** command. Are you seeing a high number of errors, such as collisions?

A few things can cause these problems. The most common is a mismatch in either the duplexing or the speed on a connection. Examine the settings on both sides of the connection. Also make sure that you are using the correct cabling type: straight for a DTE-to-DCE connection and crossover for a DTE-to-DTE or DCE-to-DCE connection (as covered in Chapter 4). And make sure that the cable does not exceed the maximum legal limit. Also, make sure that the connected IC is not experiencing a hardware problem or failure.

Local Connection Problems

If you are attempting to access the console port of a switch or router, and all you see is garbage in your terminal session, this could indicate an incorrect terminal setting. Usually the culprit is an incorrect baud rate. Some devices allow you to perform an operating system upgrade via the console port, and an administrator might change it to the highest possible value but forget to change it back to 9600 bps. If you suspect this, keep on changing your baud rate until you find the right speed.

If you are having problems accessing devices in the switched network, you can look at a few options. First, is the device you are trying to reach in the same VLAN? If so, make sure that you are using the correct IP addressing scheme in the VLAN and that the two devices trying to share information have their ports in the same VLAN. If the two devices are Cisco devices, you can use CDP to elicit some of this information, for instance the IP address, by using the **show cdp** commands (discussed in Chapter 17). Is the switch learning about the devices in your network? You might want to examine your CAM tables and make sure that a port security violation is not causing your connectivity problem (see Chapter 12).

For VLAN information, use the **show** commands on your switches to check your VLAN configuration. Also check the VLAN configuration on each switch and make sure the VLANs are configured with the same parameters by using the **show vlan** command. If the port LED is solid amber, your problem could be that the port's VLAN was deleted and the port wasn't reassigned. Other problems can also cause the port LED to turn amber, such as STP placing the port in a blocking state (Chapter 14) or port security has disabled the port because of a security violation (Chapter 12). Actually, if you see that a lot of port LEDs are amber, a deleted VLAN is probably the problem. Use the **show interface switchport** command to determine whether a deleted VLAN is the problem: if you see that the VLAN assigned to the port is inactive, like this, then you've identified the culprit:

```
switch# show interface fastEthernet0/1 switchport
Name: Fa0/1
Switchport: Enabled
Administrative mode: static access
Operational Mode: static access
Administrative Trunking Encapsulation: dot1q
Operational Trunking Encapsulation: native
Negotiation of Trunking: Off
Access Mode VLAN: 5 (Inactive)
Trunking Native Mode VLAN: 1 (default)
.
.
.
```

Notice that in the above example VLAN 5 is inactive, indicating that the interface is assigned to the VLAN, but the VLAN was deleted, making the interface inoperable.

If you are using trunks between the switches, make sure that the trunks are configured correctly: **show interface trunk**. Make sure that the native VLAN number matches on both ends of the trunk: if they are mismatched, a trunk will not form.

Also check VTP (if you are using it) by executing the **show vtp** commands. Make sure you have trunk connections between your switches, since VTP messages only traverse trunks. When using a server/client implementation, make sure that the domain name and, if using the password option, the password match among the VTP switches. Also, all switches must be running the same VTP version (by default this is version 1).

Inter-VLAN Connection Problems

If you are having problems reaching devices in other VLANs, make sure that, first, you can ping the default gateway (router) that is your exit point from the VLAN. A common misconfiguration on a user's PC is a misconfigured default gateway. If you can't ping the default gateway, then go back to the preceding section and check local VLAN connectivity issues. If you can ping the gateway, check the router's configuration and its interface (Chapter 16). Also make sure that the router has a route to the destination VLAN (**show ip route**). This is covered in Chapters 19, 20, and 21. If you do have a route to the destination, make sure the destination VLAN is configured correctly and that the default gateway in that VLAN can reach the destination device.

<table>
<tr><td>e x a m
ⓦatch   Remember the commands you should use to troubleshoot VLAN problems and trunk connection issues.</td></tr>
</table>

EXERCISE 13-2

Configuring VLANs on Your Switches

The last few sections dealt with the creation of VLANs and the assignment of interfaces to them. This lab builds upon this information and allows you to perform some of these configurations. You can find a picture of the network diagram for the simulator in the Introduction of this book. After starting up Boson's NetSim simulator, click the LabNavigator button. Next, double-click Exercise 13-2 and click the Load Lab button. This will load the lab configuration based on Exercise 13-1.

1. From the 2950-1, verify that you can ping Host-1 connected to `fa0/3`. Also ping Host-2 connected to 2950-1's `fa0/4` interface.

   At the top of the simulator in the menu bar, click the eSwitches icon and choose 2950-1. Access the CLI of the 2950-1. Execute **ping 192.168.1.10** and **ping 192.168.1.11**. Both should be successful.

2. On the 2950-1, create VLAN 2. Then assign `fa0/3` to VLAN 2 as an access-link port. Examine your VLANs.

   Access Configuration mode: **enable** and **configure terminal**. Use the **vlan 2** command to create your VLAN. Go into the interface: **interface fastethernet0/3**. Assign the VLAN: **switchport mode access** and **switchport access vlan 2**. Exit out of Configuration mode: **exit** and **exit**.

3. View your VLANs on the 2950-1: **show vlan**. Make sure that all interfaces are in VLAN 1 except for `fa0/3`, which should be in VLAN 2.

4. From Host-1, ping Host-2 (192.168.1.11) connected to the 2950-1 switch. Is the ping successful?

   At the top of the simulator in the menu bar, click the eStations icon and choose Host-1. Execute **ping 192.168.1.11**. The ping should fail, since Host-2 is in VLAN 1, while Host-1 is in VLAN 2.

5. On the 2950-1 switch, move Host-2 to VLAN 2 and verify your configuration.

   At the top of the simulator in the menu bar, click the eSwitches icon and choose 2950-1. On the 2950-1, go into the Host-2 interface: **configure terminal** and **interface fa0/4**. Assign the VLAN: **switchport mode access, switchport access vlan 2**, and **exit**. Exit out of Configuration mode: **exit** and **exit**.

6. View your VLANs: **show vlan**. Make sure that `fa0/3` and `fa0/4` are in VLAN 2.

7. From Host-1, ping Host-2 (192.168.1.11), which is connected to the 2950-1 switch. Is the ping successful? Can Host-1 ping the 2950-1 or 2950-2 switches?

   At the top of the simulator in the menu bar, click the eStations icon and choose Host-1. Execute **ping 192.168.1.11**. The ping should be successful, since all connections from Host-1 to Host-2 are in VLAN 2. Execute **ping 192.168.1.2** and **ping 192.168.1.3**. Both should fail, since both switches IP addresses are in VLAN 1 and the hosts are in VLAN 2.

Now you should be more comfortable with configuring VLANs on your switches.

INSIDE THE EXAM

VLAN Overview

Interestingly, the information in this chapter is emphasized a bit more than that of other chapters on the CCNA exam. The exam focuses primarily on VLAN concepts and troubleshooting connectivity problems, but you might see a few questions on VLAN configurations. Understand what VLANs are, the benefits they provide, that they represent subnets, and when they are used. Know that a router is needed to route between VLANs. Understand why VLANs are used to separate different kinds of traffic: data, voice, and video.

VLAN Connections

Understand the difference between an access link and a trunk, and what each type can be connected to: switches, routers, and servers. Be familiar with 802.1Q, how it tags frames, and what the native VLAN is.

VLAN Trunk Protocol

Be *very* familiar with VTP, since it is probably the most emphasized topic in this chapter.

Understand its function: consistent VLAN configuration. Be able to compare and contrast the VTP modes a switch can operate in—server, client, and transparent—and what a switch will do with a VTP message based on the mode in which it is operating. Understand what the VTP password, domain, and configuration revision number are used for. Be familiar with how VTP pruning works.

VLAN Configuration

You should be familiar with the syntax of **vtp** commands, setting up a trunk port, and setting up an access-link and assigning a VLAN to it. Understand how DTP works and the modes that can be used to form a trunk. Be *very* familiar with the output of the **show vtp status, show interface switchport, show interface trunk**, and **show vlan** commands to identify how a switch is configured with VLAN information and to troubleshoot configuration problems.

CERTIFICATION SUMMARY

A VLAN is a group of devices in the same broadcast domain (subnet). To move among VLANs, you need a router. Static VLAN assignment to devices is also called port-based VLANs. An access-link is a connection to a device that processes normal frames. Trunk connections modify frames to carry VLAN information. Ethernet trunking methods include ISL and 802.1Q. The 802.1Q method inserts a 4-byte field and recomputes the FCS for Ethernet frames; the 2960 switches support only 802.1Q.

VTP is a Cisco-proprietary protocol that transmits VLAN information across trunk ports. Switches must be in the same domain to share messages. There are three modes for VTP: client, server, and transparent. Server and transparent switches can add, change, and delete VLANs, but server switches advertise these changes. Clients can accept updates only from server switches. There are three VTP messages: advertisement request, subset advertisement, and summary advertisement. Servers generate summary advertisements every 5 minutes on trunk connections. The configuration revision number is used to determine which server switch has the most current VLAN information. VTP pruning is used to prune off VLANs that are not active between two switches, but it requires switches to be in server and/or client mode.

On the 2960, use the **vtp domain** command and **vtp server|client| transparent** commands to configure VTP. The default mode is server. To configure a VTP password, use the **vtp password** command.

DTP is a Cisco-proprietary trunking protocol. There are five modes: on (or trunk), off, desirable, auto, and no-negotiate. On and desirable actively generate DTP messages. auto is the default. Use no-negotiate for non-Cisco switch connections. On the 2960, use the **switchport mode** command to set trunking and the **show interfaces switchport|trunk** command to verify it.

By default, all interfaces are in VLAN 1. On the 2960, use the **vlan** command at Global Configuration mode command to create VLANs. Use the **switchport mode access** and **switchport access vlan** commands to associate an interface with a VLAN. The **show vlan** command displays your VLAN configuration.

✓ TWO-MINUTE DRILL

VLAN Overview

❑ A VLAN is a group of devices, in the same broadcast domain, that have the same network or subnet number. VLANs are not restricted to physical locations: users can be located anywhere in the switched network.

❑ Static, or port-based, VLAN membership is manually assigned by the administrator. Dynamic VLAN membership is determined by information from the user device, such as its MAC address or 802.1x authentication credentials.

VLAN Connections

❑ An access-link is a connection to another device that supports standard Ethernet frames and supports only a single VLAN. A trunk is a connection that tags frames and allows multiple VLANs. Trunking is supported only on ports that are trunk-capable: not all Ethernet ports support trunking.

❑ IEEE 802.1Q is a standardized trunking method. The 2960 supports only this method. The 802.1Q method inserts a VLAN tag in the middle of the frame and recomputes the frame's checksum. It supports a native VLAN—this is a VLAN that is not tagged on the trunk link. On Cisco switches, this defaults to VLAN 1.

VLAN Trunk Protocol

❑ VTP is used to share VLAN information to ensure that switches have a consistent VLAN configuration.

❑ VTP has three modes: server (allowed to make and accept changes, and propagates changes), transparent (allowed to make changes, ignores VTP messages), and client (accepts changes from servers and doesn't store this in NVRAM). The default mode is server.

❑ VTP messages are propagated only across trunks. For a switch to accept a VTP message, the domain name and optional password must match. There are three VTP messages: advertisement request (client or server request), subset advertisement (server response to an advertisement), and summary advertisement (server sends out every 5 minutes). The configuration revision number is used in the VTP message to determine whether it should be processed or not.

❑ VTP pruning allows for the dynamic addition and removal of VLANs on a trunk based on whether or not there are any active VLANs on a switch. Requires switches to be in server and/or client mode.

VLAN Configuration

❑ To configure VTP, use the **vtp domain** command to assign the domain, the **vtp mode** command to assign the mode, and **vtp password** to authenticate VTP messages. Use the **show vtp status** command to verify your VTP configuration.

❑ DTP is a Cisco-proprietary protocol that determines whether two interfaces on connected devices can become a trunk. There are five modes: on, desirable, auto-negotiate, off, and no-negotiate. If one side's mode is on, desirable, or auto, and the other is on or desirable, a trunk will form. No-negotiate mode enables trunking but disables DTP.

❑ To enable trunking on a 2960's interface, use **switchport mode trunk**. To verify trunking, use the **show interfaces switchport|trunk** command.

❑ All ports on a switch are automatically placed in VLAN 1. To add a VLAN on a 2960, use the **vlan** command. To assign an interface to a VLAN, use **switchport mode access** and **switchport access vlan**. To view your VLANs and the ports assigned to them, use **show vlan**.

SELF TEST

The following Self Test questions will help you measure your understanding of the material presented in this chapter. Read all the choices carefully, as there may be more than one correct answer. Choose all correct answers for each question.

VLAN Overview

1. Which of the following is false concerning VLANs?
   A. A VLAN is a broadcast domain.
   B. A VLAN is a logical group of users.
   C. A VLAN is location-dependent.
   D. A VLAN is a subnet.

2. Two groups of users are connected to a switch: sales and marketing. You are concerned about marketing and sales people seeing each others' traffic. What solutions would you use to prevent this? (choose two)
   A. VLANs
   B. Hubs
   C. MAC address filtering
   D. Router with ACLs

VLAN Connections

3. A connection that supports multiple VLANs is called a _____.

4. Which of the following is true concerning 802.1Q?
   A. It supports hub connections.
   B. It is not supported on the 2960 switches.
   C. The native VLAN is tagged.
   D. The original Ethernet frame is not modified.

VLAN Trunk Protocol

5. The _____ is a proprietary Cisco protocol used to share VLAN configuration information between Cisco switches on trunk connections.

6. Which VTP mode(s) will propagate VTP messages?

    A. Client and server

    B. Server

    C. Client, server, and transparent

    D. Transparent

7. You have a server switch with VLANs accounting, HR, and executives on one switch with a configuration revision value of 55 and another server switch with VLANs engineering, sales, and marketing with a configuration revision value of 57. Currently the two switches are not connected together. You connect them together. What can happen? (choose two)

    A. If the domain names don't match, nothing occurs.

    B. If the domain names don't match, the VLANs on the higher revision switch are used and the other ones are deleted.

    C. If the domain names match, the engineering, sales, and marketing VLANs are deleted.

    D. If the domain names match, the accounting, HR, and executives VLANs are deleted.

VLAN Configuration

8. Enter the switch command to set the VTP mode to transparent mode: _____.

9. Which switch command enables trunking on a 2960 switch?

    A. `switchport mode trunk`

    B. `trunking on`

    C. `trunking enable`

    D. `switchport trunk on`

10. Which 2960 command assigns a VLAN to an interface?

    A. `vlan-membership static`

    B. `vlan`

    C. `switchport access vlan`

    D. `switchport mode access`

SELF TEST ANSWERS

1. ☑ **C.** VLANs are location-*independent*, assuming the devices are connected via layer 2.
   ☒ **A, B,** and **D** are true, and thus incorrect answers.

2. ☑ **A and D.** When using switches, to logically segregate traffic, use VLANs. To control access between them, use a router with ACLs.
   ☒ **B** is incorrect because hubs place people in the same broadcast domain. **C** is incorrect because filtering at layer 3 is more manageable than layer 2.

3. ☑ A connection that supports multiple VLANS is called a *trunk*.

4. ☑ **A.** 802.1Q, because it supports a native VLAN, can use point-to-point and multipoint (hub) connections.
   ☒ **B** is false, since the 2960 does support it. **C** is incorrect because the native VLAN is not tagged. **D** is incorrect because the original Ethernet frame is modified—a VLAN field is inserted and a new FCS is computed.

5. ☑ The *VLAN Trunk Protocol (VTP)* is a proprietary Cisco protocol used to share VLAN configuration information between Cisco switches on trunk connections.

6. ☑ **C.** Switches in all VTP modes will propagate VTP messages; however, only client and server switches will process these messages.
   ☒ **A** is incorrect because it doesn't include transparent. **B** is incorrect because it doesn't include client and transparent. **D** is incorrect because it doesn't include server and client.

7. ☑ **A and D.** If the domain names don't match, they ignore each other's VTP messages. If the domain names match, the switch with the highest revision number is used; the switch with the lowest revision number will have its VLANs deleted.
   ☒ **B** is incorrect because domain names must match for VTP messages to be processed. **C** is incorrect because the lower numbered revision switch will have its VLANs deleted.

8. ☑ `vtp transparent`

9. ☑ **A.** The `switchport mode trunk` command enables trunking on a 2960 switch.
   ☒ **B** enables trunking on a 1900 switch. **C** and **D** are nonexistent commands.

10. ☑ **C.** The `switchport access vlan` command assigns a VLAN to an interface on a 2960 switch.
    ☒ **A** is incorrect because `vlan-membership static` assigns a VLAN to an interface on a 1900. **B** in incorrect because `vlan` creates a VLAN. **D** is incorrect because `switchport mode access` sets the interface as an access-link, versus a trunk, connection.

14

Switches and Redundancy

T his chapter is the last chapter on layer 2 functions. Most larger networks implement redundancy in case of failures, whether it be multiple WAN connections, multiple paths in your layer 3 network, and/or multiple paths in your layer 2 network. This chapter focuses on layer 2 redundancy and the issues involved with layer 2 loops, including two features that are commonly used to solve these problems: the Spanning Tree Protocol (STP) and EtherChannels.

CERTIFICATION OBJECTIVE 14.01

Layer 2 Redundancy

Cisco has developed a three-layer hierarchical model to help you design campus networks. Cisco uses this model to simplify designing, implementing, and managing large-scale networks. With traditional network designs, it was common practice to place the networking services at the center of the network and the users at the periphery. However, many things in networking have changed over the past decade, including advancements in applications, developments in graphical user interfaces (GUIs), the proliferation of multimedia applications, the explosion of the Internet, and fast-paced changes in your users' traffic patterns. Cisco's model was designed to accommodate these rapid changes.

Hierarchical Campus Design

Cisco's enterprise campus hierarchical model, shown in Figure 14-1, contains three layers: core, distribution, and access. A well-designed campus network typically follows this topology. The core layer, as its name suggests, is the backbone of the network. It provides a high-speed connection between the different distribution layer devices. Because of the need for high-speed connections, the core consists of high-speed *switches* and will not, typically, perform any type of packet or frame manipulations, such as filtering. Layer 2 or layer 3 switches (more commonly the latter) are used at the core with Gigabit connectivity, sometimes using EtherChannels (discussed at the end of the chapter). The traffic that traverses the core is typically intending to access enterprise corporate resources: connections to the Internet, WAN connections, and applications on servers in the campus server farm.

FIGURE 14-1

FIGURE 14-1

Cisco's
hierarchical
model

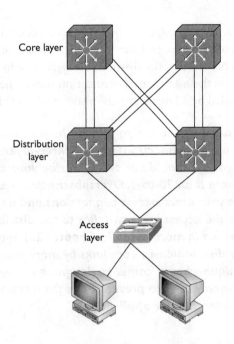

Core layer

Distribution
layer

Access
layer

on the
Job

A layer 3 switch is basically a router that performs its switching using application-specific integrated circuits (ASICs) instead of a central CPU (ASICs are discussed in Chapter 4). Some of Cisco's switches support this feature, from the Catalyst 3500s and higher with the right IOS image.

Layer 3 switches are most commonly used at the distribution layer to connect the access layers to the core. Fast Ethernet, but more commonly Gigabit Ethernet, connections are used for this connectivity. For smaller networks, sometimes layer 2 switches are used. The responsibilities of the distribution layer include the following:

- Containing broadcasts between the model layers via layer 3 separation, such as VLANs
- Securing traffic between subnets using access control lists (ACLs are discussed in Chapter 22)
- Providing a hierarchy through layer 3 logical addressing and route summarization
- Translating between different media types

Layer 3 separation is provided between the access layers and the core; however, between the distribution layer switches and the access layer switches, layer 2 is used, creating a layer 2 loop.

The bottom layer of the three-layer hierarchical model is the access layer. Actually, the access layer is at the periphery of your campus network, separated from the core layer by the distribution layer. The main function of the access layer is to provide the user's initial connection to your network. Typically, this connection is provided by a layer 2 switch or sometimes a wireless access point.

on the Job *Cisco has online design tools to help you choose the appropriate devices and uplink connections in your three-layer hierarchical network. In a basic design, you should not oversubscribe your access-to-distribution layer links by more than 20-to-1. Oversubscription occurs when too much traffic comes from your users' access connections and not enough bandwidth is available from the access layer switches to the distribution layer (oversubscription is discussed in more depth in Chapter 26). You should also not oversubscribe your distribution-to-core links by more than 4-to-1. However, every situation is unique when it comes to designing the appropriate solution. Rate limiting is commonly used to prevent users from oversubscribing and creating problems for other users or applications.*

Layer 2 Issues

As you can see in Figure 14-1, a redundant design was implemented: two links exist from the access layer switch up to the distribution layer, with multiple layer 2 connections (in most cases an EtherChannel) between the distribution layer switches. This redundancy commonly introduces layer 2 loops into a network design, which can create these layer 2 problems:

- Multiple frame copies
- Broadcast storms
- Mislearning MAC addresses

The following three sections will discuss these problems, using the simple example in Figure 14-2 to illustrate the issues these problems create.

Multiple Frame Copies and Broadcast Storms

Recall from Chapter 4 that a switch will flood three kinds of frames: broadcast, multicast, and unknown destination unicast frames. In the case of broadcast and multicast traffic, this can create serious performance issues with a layer 2 network that has loops. For example, imagine that PC-A in Figure 14-2 performs an ARP

Simple layer 2
loop example

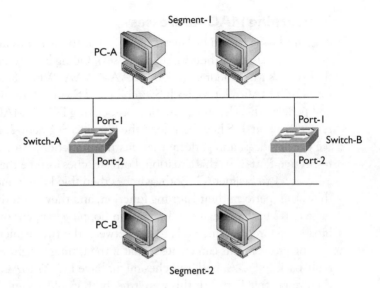

for PC-B's MAC address. Recall from Chapter 6 that Address Resolution Protocol (ARP) uses a broadcast mechanism to learn the MAC address that corresponds to a device's IP address. In Figure 14-2, both switches would receive this frame and flood it to Segment-2, since the frame is a broadcast.

The first problem this creates is that although PC-A generates one frame, Segment-2, along with PC-B, sees two frames. PC-B sees these as two distinct ARPs and will reply twice. On top of this, depending on the application receiving the traffic, PC-B might see multiple copies of the same frame as an error and reset its connection to the source of the transmissions, creating connectivity issues.

The bigger issue here, however, is that both switches, on their Segment-2 ports, would again see the flooded ARP request and flood it back to Segment-1. Basically these broadcasts would continue to be flooded between the two segments, affecting all devices. Devices are affected since their NICs would be processing all of these broadcasts; as more devices generate ARPs and other types of broadcast frames, the bandwidth is eventually gobbled up by these broadcasts. In this scenario, the network will crash and the devices will run out of CPU cycles to process the broadcasts!

Recall from Chapter 4 that multicasts are only processed by NICs in which the user has an application running that needs to see the specific multicast traffic: It notifies the NIC about the multicast address or addresses to listen for and process. So a flood of multicasts won't affect the CPU cycles of devices not running an application that uses multicasting. However, multicasts still affect everyone's bandwidth, since switches flood this kind of traffic; and if the multicasts are part of a high-speed video stream, this quickly gobbles up the bandwidth.

Mislearning MAC Addresses

The third issue caused by layer 2 loops is that the switches mislearn the location of devices (based on their MAC addresses). Going back to Figure 14-2, assume that PC-A's MAC address is 0000.01AA.AAAA. When PC-A generates an ARP for PC-B's MAC address, both Switch-A and Switch-B receive the ARP request and perform their learning function, associating PC-A's MAC address with their respective Port-1. They then flood the frame to Segment-2. Again, both switches see the broadcast and perform their learning function, associating PC-A with their respective Port-2. In this situation, both switches assume that PC-A moved from Segment-1 to Segment-2. Both switches then flood the frame to Segment-1, where they again perform their learning function, and they again think PC-A moved from Segment-2 back to Segment-1. This flip-flopping happens over and over as the two broadcasts circle around and around between the two segments.

One problem this can create is that if the timing is right and PC-B sends an ARP reply back to PC-A, both switches might have PC-A's MAC address associated with their respective Port-2. If this were true, both would assume PC-A was on Segment-2 and would drop and not forward the frame. Thus, PC-A wouldn't get the reply to its ARP request and then couldn't communicate with PC-B. Of course, PC-A could perform the ARP request again, but this would just make the problem worse, since now instead of two broadcasts circling around the loop, it would double to four!

CERTIFICATION OBJECTIVE 14.02

Spanning Tree Protocol

The main function of the Spanning Tree Protocol (STP) is to remove layer 2 loops from your topology, logically speaking. DEC, now a part of HP, originally developed STP. IEEE enhanced the initial implementation of STP, giving us the 802.1d standard. The two different implementations of STP, DEC and 802.1d, are not compatible with each other—you need to make sure that all of your devices support either one or the other. All of Cisco's switches use IEEE's 802.1d protocol, which is enabled, by default, on their switches. If you have a mixed-vendor environment where some devices are running 802.1d and others are running DEC's STP, you might run into layer 2 looping problems.

Bridge Protocol Data Units

For STP to function, the switches need to share information about themselves and their connections. What they share are *Bridge Protocol Data Units (BPDUs)*, which are sent out as *multicast* frames to which only other layer 2 switches or bridges are listening. Switches will use BPDUs to learn the topology of the network: what switch is connected to other switches, and whether any layer 2 loops are based on this topology.

If any loops are found, the switches will logically disable a port or ports in the topology to ensure that there are no loops. Note that they don't actually shut down the ports, but they place the port or ports in a special disabled state for user traffic, as discussed later in the "Port States" section. Based on this port disabling process—in other words, from one device to any other device in the layer 2 network—only one path can be taken. If any changes occur in the layer 2 network—such as when a link goes down, a new link is added, a new switch is added, or a switch fails—the switches will share this information, causing the STP algorithm to be re-executed, and a new loop-free topology is then created.

By default, BPDUs are sent out every 2 seconds. This helps speed up convergence. *Convergence* is a term used in networking to describe the amount of time it takes to deal with changes and get the network back up and running. The shorter the time period to find and fix problems, the quicker your network is back online. Setting the BPDU advertisement time to 2 seconds allows changes to be quickly shared with all the other switches in the network, reducing the amount of time any disruption would create.

BPDUs contain a lot of information to help the switches determine the topology and any loops that result from that topology. For instance, each bridge has a unique identifier, called a *bridge* or *switch ID*. This is typically the priority of the switch and the MAC address of the switch itself. When switches advertise a BPDU, they place their switch ID in the BPDU so that a receiving switch can tell from which switch it is receiving topology information. The following sections cover the steps that occur while STP is being executed in a layer 2 network.

Root Switch

The term *Spanning Tree Protocol* describes the process that is used to find and remove loops from a layer 2 network. The STP algorithm is similar to how link state routing protocols, such as Open Shortest Path First (OSPF), ensure that no layer 3 loops are created; of course, STP deals only with layer 2 loops (link state routing protocols are discussed in Chapters 15 and 20).

A spanning tree is first created. Basically, a spanning tree is an inverted tree. At the top of the tree is the root, or what is referred to in STP as the *root bridge* or *switch*. From the root switch, branches (physical Ethernet connections) extend and connect to other switches, and branches from these switches connect to other switches, and so on.

Take a look at the physical topology of a network, shown in Figure 14-3, to demonstrate a spanning tree. When STP is run, a logical tree structure is built, like that shown in Figure 14-4. As you can see from Figure 14-4, Switch-A is the root switch and is at the top of the tree. Underneath it are two branches connecting to Switch-B and Switch-C. These two switches are connected to Switch-E, creating a loop. Switch-B is also connected to Switch-D. At this point, STP is still running, and a loop still exists. As STP runs, the switches will determine, out of the four switches—Switch-A, Switch-B, Switch-C, and Switch-E—which port on these switches will be logically disabled in order to remove the loop. This ensures that from one device to any other device in the network, only one path will be used to connect the devices.

Actually, the very first step in STP is to elect the root switch. BPDUs are used for the election process. As mentioned earlier, when a device advertises a BPDU, the switch puts its switch ID in the BPDU. The switch ID is used to elect the root switch.

FIGURE 14-3

Physical layer 2 looped topology

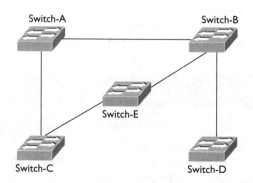

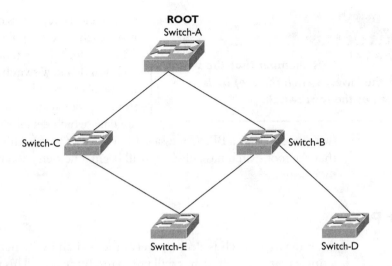

FIGURE 14-4

Logical layer 2
STP topology

The switch with the *lowest* switch ID is chosen as root. The switch ID is made up of two components:

- The switch's priority, which defaults to 32,768 on Cisco switches (2 bytes in length)
- The switch's MAC address (6 bytes in length)

With Cisco's switches, the default priority is 32,768, which is defined by IEEE 802.1d. Assuming that all your switches are Cisco switches and you don't change the default priority, the switch with the *lowest* MAC address will be chosen as the root switch. You can override the election process by changing the priority value assigned to a switch. If you want one switch to be the root, assign it a priority value that is lower than 32,768. Through the sharing of the BPDUs, the switches will figure out which switch has the lowest switch ID, and that switch is chosen as the root switch. Note that this election process is taking place almost simultaneously on each switch, where each switch will come up with the same result. In other words, the switch that has the lowest switch ID is not advertising to other switches that it has the lowest ID value and thus everyone else should be a non-root switch.

For Catalyst switches that implement VLANs (discussed in Chapter 13), the switches will have a different switch ID *per* VLAN, and a *separate* instance of STP *per* VLAN. Each VLAN has its own root switch (which can be the same switch for all VLANs, or different switches for each VLAN). And within each VLAN, STP will run and remove loops in that particular VLAN. Cisco calls this concept *per-VLAN STP (PVST)*. This topic is discussed later in the "Per-VLAN STP Plus" section.

The election process of the root switch takes place each time a topology change occurs in the network, such as the root switch failing or the addition of a new switch. All the other switches in the layer 2 topology expect to see BPDUs from the root switch within the *maximum age time,* which defaults to 20 seconds. If the switches don't see a BPDU message from the root within this period, they assume that the root switch has failed and will begin a new election process to choose a new root switch.

Root Port

After the root switch is elected, every other switch in the network needs to choose a single port, on itself, that it will use to reach the root. This port is called the *root port.* For some switches, such as Switch-D in Figure 14-4, this is very easy—it has only one port it can use to access the switched topology. However, other switches, such as Switch-B, Switch-C, and Switch-E in Figure 14-4, might have two or more ports that they can use to reach the root switch. If multiple port choices are available, an intelligent method needs to be used to choose the best port. With STP, a few factors are taken into consideration when choosing a root port. It is important to note that the root switch itself will never have a root port—it's the root, so it doesn't need a port to reach itself!

Port Costs and Priorities

First, each port is assigned a cost, called a *port cost.* The lower the cost, the more preferable the port. The cost is an inverse reflection of the bandwidth of the port. Two sets of costs exist for 802.1d's implementation of STP—one for the old method of calculation and one for the new, as is shown in Table 14-1. Cisco's discontinued Catalyst 1900 switch uses the old 802.1d port cost values, while Cisco's other Catalyst switches, including those currently sold today (such as the 2960 and 6500), use the newer cost values. Switches always prefer lower cost ports over higher cost ones. Each port also has a priority assigned to it, called a *port priority* value, which defaults to 32. Again, switches will prefer a lower priority value over a higher one.

TABLE 14-1	Connection Type	New Cost Value	Old Cost Value
Port Costs for STP	10 Gbps	2	1
	1 Gbps	4	1
	100 Mbps	19	10
	10 Mbps	100	100

One of the main reasons for replacing the old cost method with a newer one is the inherent weakness in the algorithm used to calculate the port cost: 1000 divided by the port speed. The assumption was that no port would have a speed greater than 1 Gbps (1000 Mbps). As you can see from today's Ethernet standards, 10 Gbps is making its way into corporate networks. With the old port cost method, 1 Gbps and 10 Gbps links were treated as having the same speed.

Path Costs

Path costs are calculated from the root switch. A path cost is basically the accumulated port costs from the root switch to other switches in the topology. When the root advertises BPDUs out its interfaces, the default path cost value in the BPDU frame is 0. When a connected switch receives this BPDU, it increments the path cost by the cost of its local incoming port. If the port was a Fast Ethernet port, then the path cost would be figured like this: 0 (the root's path cost) + 19 (the switch's port cost) = 19. This switch, when it advertises BPDUs to switches behind it, will include the updated path cost. As the BPDUs propagate further and further from the root switch, the accumulated path cost values become higher and higher.

Remember that path costs are incremented as a BPDU comes into a port, not when a BPDU is advertised out of a port.

Root Port Selection

If a switch has two or more choices of paths to reach the root, it needs to choose one path and thus have one root port. A switch will go through the following STP steps when choosing a root port:

1. Choose the path with the *lowest* accumulated path cost to the root when it has a choice between two or more paths to reach the root.

2. If multiple paths to the root are available with the same accumulated path cost, the switch will choose the neighboring switch (that the switch would go through to reach the root) with the *lowest* switch ID value.

3. If multiple paths all go through the same neighboring switch, it will choose the local port with the lowest priority value.

4. If the priority values are the same between the ports, it will choose the physically lowest numbered port on the switch. For example, on a 2960, that would be FastEthernet 0/1 or Gigabit 0/1.

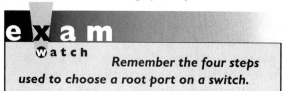

Remember the four steps used to choose a root port on a switch.

After going through this selection process, the switch will have one, and only one, port that will become its root port.

Designated Port

You now know that each switch has a single root port that it uses to reach the root switch. In addition to each switch having a root port, each segment also has a single port that is uses to reach the root, and this port is called a *designated port*. For example, imagine that a segment has two switches connected to it. Either one or the other switch will forward traffic from this segment to the rest of the network.

The third step in running STP is to elect a designated port on a single switch for each segment in the network. The switch (and its port) that is chosen should have the best path to the root switch. Here are the steps taken by switches in determining which port on which switch will be chosen as the designated port for a particular LAN segment.

1. The connected switch on the segment with the lowest accumulated path cost to the root switch will be used.

2. If there is a tie in accumulated path costs between two switches, the switch with the lowest switch ID will be chosen.

3. If it happens that it is the same switch, but with two separate connections to the LAN segment, the switch port with the lowest priority is chosen.

4. If there is still a tie (the priorities of the ports on this switch are the same), the physically lowest numbered port on the switch is chosen.

After going through these steps for each segment, each segment will have a single designated port on a connected switch that it will use to reach the root switch. Sometimes the switch that contains the designated port is called a *designated switch*.

This term is misleading, though, since it is a port on the switch that is responsible for forwarding traffic. A switch may be connected to two segments, but it may be the designated switch for only one of those segments; another switch may provide the designated port for the second segment.

Interestingly enough, *every* active port on the *root switch* is a designated port. This makes sense because the cost of the attached network segments to reach the root is 0, the lowest accumulated cost value. In other words, each of these LAN segments is directly attached to the root switch, so in reality, it costs nothing for the segment to reach the root switch itself.

Port States

A port can be in one of five states when it is participating in STP:

- Blocking
- Listening
- Learning
- Forwarding
- Disabled

Of the five states, only the first four are used when the algorithm is running. The following sections cover these port states for STP.

Blocking

Ports will go into a *blocking* state under one of three conditions:

- During election of a root switch (for instance, when you turn on all the switches in a network)
- When a switch receives a BPDU on a port that indicates a better path to the root switch than the port which the switch is currently using to reach the root
- If a port is not a root port or a designated port

A port in a blocking state will remain there for 20 seconds by default (the maximum age timer). During this state, the port is listening to and processing only BPDUs on its interfaces. Any other frames that the switch receives on a blocked port are dropped. In a blocking state, the switch is attempting to figure out which port is going to be the root port, which ports on the switch need to be designated ports, and which ports will remain in a blocking state to break up any loops.

Listening

After the 20-second timer expires, a root port or a designated port will move to a *listening* state. Any other port will remain in a blocking state. During the listening state, the port is still listening for BPDUs and double-checking the layer 2 topology. Again, the only traffic that is being processed on a port in this state consists of BPDUs; all other traffic is dropped. A port will stay in this state for the length of the *forward delay timer*. The default for this value is 15 seconds.

Learning

From a listening state, a root and designated ports move into a *learning* state. During the learning state, the port is still listening for and processing BPDUs on the port; however, unlike while in the listening state, the port begins to process user frames. When processing user frames, the switch is examining the source addresses in the frames and updating its MAC or port address table, but the switch is still not forwarding these frames out destination ports. Ports stay in this state for the length of the forward delay time (which defaults to 15 seconds).

Forwarding

Finally, after the forward delay timer expires, ports that were in a learning state are placed in a *forwarding* state. In a forwarding state, the port will process BPDUs, update its MAC address table with frames that it receives, *and* forward user traffic through the port.

Disabled

The *disabled* state is a special port state. A port in a disabled state is not participating in STP. This could be because the port has been manually shut down by an administrator, manually removed from STP, disabled because of security issues, or rendered nonfunctional because of a lack of a physical layer signal (such as the patch cable being unplugged).

Four major port states are used in STP: blocking (20 seconds), listening (15 seconds), learning (15 seconds), and forwarding. It can take 30 to 50 seconds for STP convergence to take place. STP must recalculate if a new root is discovered or a topology change occurs in the network (a new switch added or a change in the state of a port on a switch). In blocking and listening states, only BPDUs are processed. In a learning state, the MAC address table is being built. In a forwarding state, user frames are moved between ports. STP leaves ports in a blocking state to remove loops.

Layer 2 Convergence

As you should have noticed in the last section, STP goes through a staged process, which *slows* down convergence. For switches, convergence occurs once STP has completed: a root switch is elected, root and designated ports have been chosen, the root and designated ports have been placed in a forwarding state, and all other ports have been placed in a blocking state.

If a port has to go through all four states, convergence takes 50 seconds: 20 seconds in blocking, 15 seconds in listening, and 15 seconds in learning. If a port doesn't have to go through the blocking state but starts at a listening state, convergence takes only 30 seconds. This typically occurs when the root port is still valid, but another topology change has occurred. Remember that during this time period (until the port reaches a forwarding state), no user traffic is forwarded through the port. So, if a user was performing a telnet session, and STP was being recalculated, the telnet session, from the user's perspective, would appear stalled or the connection would appear lost. Obviously, a user will notice this type of disruption.

STP convergence has occurred when all root and designated ports are in a forwarding state and all other ports are in a blocking state.

PortFast Overview

The faster that convergence takes place, the less disruption it will cause for your users. You can reduce the two timers to speed up your convergence time, but this can create more problems if you aren't aware of what you are doing when you change them. For user ports, you can use the *PortFast* feature to speed up convergence. PortFast should be used only on ports that will not create layer 2 loops, such as ports connected to PCs, servers, and routers (sometimes referred to as a user, or edge, ports).

A port with PortFast enabled is always placed in a forwarding state—this is true even when STP is running and the root and designated ports are going through their different states. So, when STP is running, PortFast ports on the same switch can still forward traffic among themselves, limiting your STP disruption somewhat. However, if these devices wanted to talk to devices connected to other switches, they would have to wait until STP completed and the root and designated ports had moved into a forwarding state.

Ports connected to non-switch or non-bridge devices should be configured with PortFast, such as PCs, servers, and routers. However, make sure that you don't enable PortFast on a port connected to another layer 2 switch, since you might inadvertently be creating a layer 2 loop, which will create broadcast storms and mislearning of MAC addressing information.

PortFast Configuration

PortFast works with all versions of STP supported by Cisco switches. Configuring the PortFast feature is simple, and you can enable it globally or on an interface-by-interface basis. To enable it globally, use this command:

```
Switch(config)# spanning-tree portfast default
```

This command enables PortFast on all non-trunking ports on the switch.
To enable PortFast on an interface, use this configuration:

```
Switch(config)# interface type [slot_#/]port_#
Switch(config-if)# spanning-tree portfast [trunk]
```

The optional **trunk** parameter enables PortFast on trunk connections to non-switch devices, such as a router or server with a trunk card.

14.01. The CD contains a multimedia demonstration of configuring PortFast.

Per-VLAN STP Plus

STP doesn't guarantee an optimized loop-free network. For instance, take a look at the network shown in Figure 14-5. In this example, the network has two VLANs, and the root switch is Switch-8. The Xs are ports placed in a blocked state to remove any loops. If you look at this configuration for VLAN 2, it definitely isn't optimized. For instance, VLAN 2 devices on Switch-1, if they want to access VLAN 2 devices on Switch-4, have to go to Switches-2, -3, -6, -9, -8, and then -4. Likewise, VLAN 1 devices on either Switch-5 or Switch-7 that want to access VLAN 1 devices on Switch-4 must forward their traffic first to Switch-8 and then to Switch-4.

When one instance of STP is running, this is referred to as a *Common Spanning Tree (CST)*. Cisco also supports a process called *Per-VLAN Spanning Tree Plus (PVST+)*. With PVST+, *each* VLAN has its own instance of STP, with its own root switch, its own set of priorities, and its own set of BPDUs. In this scenario, the BPDUs have an additional field that is a component of the switch or bridge ID: switch priority, extended system ID, and switch's MAC address. The extended system ID is a new field and carries the VLAN ID (VID) for the instance of STP.

With the addition of this field, it is possible to have different priorities on switches in different VLANs; thus you have the capability of having multiple root switches—one per VLAN. Each VLAN in PVST+, by default, will develop its own loop-free topology. Of course, PVST+, just like CST, doesn't create an optimized

FIGURE 14-5

STP and VLANs

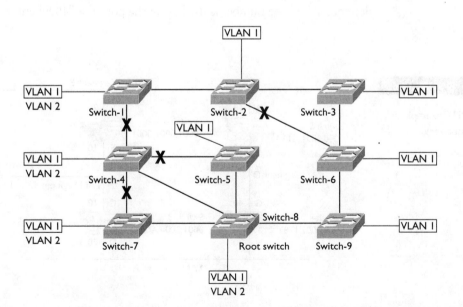

loop-free network; however, you can make STP changes in *each* VLAN to optimize traffic patterns for each separate VLAN. It is highly recommended that you tune STP for each VLAN to optimize it. Another advantage that PVST+ has is that if STP changes are occurring in one VLAN, they do not affect other instances of STP for other VLANs, making for a more stable topology. Given this, it is highly recommended that you implement VTP pruning to prune off VLANs from trunks of switches that are not using those VLANs. Pruning was discussed in the Chapter 13.

The downside of PVST+ is that since each VLAN has its own instance of STP, more overhead is involved: more BPDUs and STP tables are required on each switch. Plus, it makes no sense to use PVST+ unless you tune it for your network, which means more work and monitoring on your part.

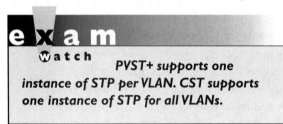

PVST+ supports one instance of STP per VLAN. CST supports one instance of STP for all VLANs.

Simple STP Example

To help you get more familiar with the workings of 802.1d STP, take a look at an example of STP in action. Use the network shown in Figure 14-6 as a starting point and assume that these switches do not support Rapid STP (RSTP), discussed later in the chapter, but only 802.1d STP. I'll also assume that there is only one VLAN. The ports on each switch are labeled with a letter and a number. The letter is the port designator, and the number is the cost of the port as a BPDU enters the port.

FIGURE 14-6

STP example network

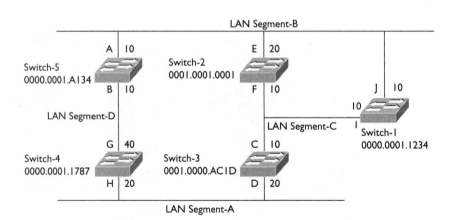

Electing the Root Switch

The first thing that occurs once all these switches are booted up is the election of the root switch. The switches share BPDUs with one another to elect the root. In this example, all of the switches are using the default priority (32,768). Remember that the switch with the lowest switch ID is elected as root. Since all of the switches have the same priority, the switch with the lowest MAC address, which is Switch-1, is chosen as the root switch. Based on the election process, the new network topology looks like that shown in Figure 14-7.

Choosing Root Ports for Each Switch

After the root switch is elected, each non-root switch must choose one of its ports that it will use to reach the root, called the *root port*. Let's take this one switch at a time so that you can see the decision process in detail. With Switch-1, which is the root switch, there are no root ports—if you recall, all ports on the root switch are designated ports.

Switch-2 has two ports to use to reach the root: E and F. When Switch-1 generates its BPDUs on ports I and J, the original path cost is set to 0. As these BPDUs are received by other switches, the receiving switch increments the path cost by the cost of the port on which the BPDU was received. As the BPDU comes into port E, Switch-2 increments the path cost to 20 and for port F, 10. The first check that Switch-2 makes is to compare the path costs. Port F has the best path cost and therefore is chosen as the root port, which is shown as *RP* in Figure 14-8. Switch-3 also has two paths to reach the root: via ports C and D. Port C's accumulated path cost is 10, while D's cost is 70.

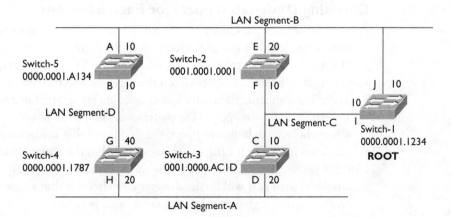

FIGURE 14-7

Root switch election

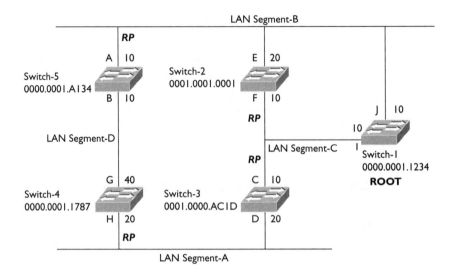

FIGURE 14-8

Root ports

Therefore, port C is chosen as the root port. Switch-4 also has two ports to use to access the root: H and G. Port H has an accumulated path cost of 30, while G has a cost of 50, causing Switch-4 to choose port H as the root port. Switch-5's two ports, A and B, have accumulated path costs of 10 and 40, respectively, causing Switch-5 to choose Port A as the root port. Note that all the switches in the network are simultaneously running STP and figuring out for themselves who the root switch is and which port on themselves should be the root port. This is also true for choosing a designated port on a segment, discussed in the next section.

Choosing Designated Ports for Each Segment

After the root ports are chosen, each switch will figure out, on a segment-by-segment basis, whether its connected port to the segment should be a designated port or not. Remember that the designated port on a segment is responsible for moving traffic back and forth between the segment and the rest of the layer 2 network. The segments themselves, of course, are completely unaware of this process of choosing a designated port—the switches are figuring this out.

When choosing a designated port, the first thing that is examined is the accumulated path cost for the switch (connected to the segment) to reach the root. For two switches connected to the same segment, the switch with the lowest accumulated path cost will be the designated switch for that segment and its port connected to that segment becomes a designated port.

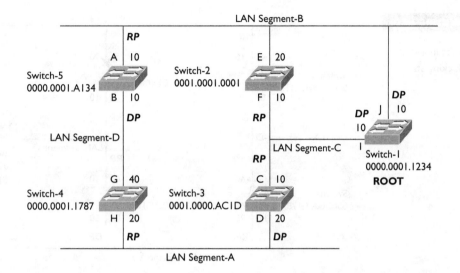

FIGURE 14-9

Root and
designated ports

Going back to our network example, let's start with the easiest segments: B and C. For Switch-1, the accumulated path cost for LAN Segment-B is 0, Switch-2 is 20, and Switch-5 is 10. Since the root switch (Switch-1) has the lowest accumulated path cost, its local port (J) becomes the designated port for LAN Segment-B. This process is also true for LAN Segment-C—the root switch has the lowest accumulated path cost (0), making port I on Switch-1 the designated port for LAN Segment-C.

LAN Segment-A has two choices: Switch-3's D port and Switch-4's H port. Switch-3 has the lower accumulated path cost: 10 versus Switch-4's 50. Therefore, Switch-3's D port becomes the designated port for LAN Segment-A.

LAN Segment-D also has two choices for a designated port: Switch-5's B port and Switch-4's G port. Switch-5 has an accumulated path cost of 10, and Switch-4 has a cost of 30. Therefore Switch-5's B port becomes the designated port for LAN Segment-D.

Figure 14-9 shows the updated STP topology for our network, where DP represents the designated ports for the LAN segments.

Changing Port States

After the designated ports are chosen, the switches will move their root and designated ports through the various states: blocking, listening, learning, and forwarding, whereas any other ports will remain in a blocked state. Figure 14-10 shows the ports in a blocking state, designated by an X. Remember that on Switch-2,

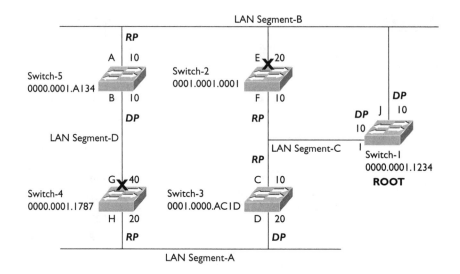

FIGURE 14-10

Ports in a
blocking state

only Port F (the root port) is in a forwarding state: Port E will remain in a blocking state. In this example, two ports are left in a blocking state: Switch-2's E port and Switch-4's G port.

on the
Job

STP guarantees only a layer 2 loop-free topology—it does not guarantee an optimal topology! For example, in the network shown in Figure 14-10, networking devices on LAN Segment-A would have to go through Switches 3, 1, and 5 in order to reach LAN Segment-D, since Switch-4's G port is in a blocked state.

CERTIFICATION OBJECTIVE 14.03

Rapid Spanning Tree Protocol

The 802.1d standard was designed back when waiting for 30 to 50 seconds for layer 2 convergence wasn't a problem. However, in today's networks, this can cause serious performance problems for networks that use real-time applications, such as voice over IP (VoIP) or video. To overcome these issues, Cisco developed proprietary bridging features called PortFast (discussed earlier), UplinkFast, and BackboneFast. The problem with these features, however, is that they are proprietary to Cisco.

The Rapid Spanning Tree Protocol (RSTP) is an IEEE standard, defined in 802.1w, which is interoperable with 802.1d and an extension to it. With RSTP, there are only three port states:

- Discarding
- Learning
- Forwarding

A port in a discarding state is basically the grouping of 802.1d's blocking, listening, and disabled states. The following sections cover some of the enhancements included in RSTP.

Additional Port Roles

With RSTP, there is still a root switch and there are still root and designated ports, performing the same roles as those in 802.1d. However, RSTP adds two additional port types: *alternate* ports and *backup* ports. These two ports are similar to the ports in a blocking state in 802.1d. An alternate port is a port that has an alternative path or paths to the root but is currently in a discarding state. A backup port is a port on a segment that could be used to reach the root switch, but an active port is already designated for the segment. The best way to look at this is that an alternate port is a secondary, unused root port, and a backup port is a secondary, unused designated port.

Given these new port roles, RSTP calculates the final spanning tree topology the same way as 802.1d. Some of the nomenclature was changed and extended, and this is used to enhance convergence times, as you will see later in the "RSTP Convergence Features" section.

RSTP BPDUs

The 802.1w standard introduced a change with BPDUs. Some additional flags were added to the BPDUs, so that switches could share information about the role of the port the BPDU is exiting or leaving. This can help a neighboring switch converge faster when changes occur in the network.

In 802.1d, if a switch didn't see a root BPDU within the maximum age time (20 seconds), STP would run, a new root switch would be elected, and a new loop-free topology would be created. This is a time-consuming process. With 802.1w, if a BPDU is not received in three expected hello periods (6 seconds), STP information can be aged out instantly and the switch considers that its neighbor is lost and actions should be taken. This is different from 802.1d, where the switch had to miss the BPDUs from the root—here, if the switch misses three consecutive hellos from a neighbor, actions are immediately taken.

RSTP Convergence Features

The 802.1w standard includes new convergence features that are very similar to Cisco's proprietary UplinkFast and BackboneFast features. The first feature, which is similar to Cisco's BackboneFast feature, allows a switch to accept *inferior BPDUs*.

Look at Figure 14-11 to understand the inferior BPDU feature. In this example, the root bridge is Switch-A. Both of the ports on Switch-B and Switch-C directly connected to the root are root ports. For the segment between Switch-B and Switch-C, Switch-B provides the designated port and Switch-C provides a backup port (a secondary way of reaching the root for the segment). Switch-B also knows that its designated port is an alternative port (a secondary way for the switch to reach the root), via Switch-C from Switch-C's BPDUs.

Following the example in Figure 14-11, the link between the root and Switch-B fails. Switch-B can detect this by either missing three hellos from the root port or detecting a physical layer failure. If you were running 802.1d, Switch-B would see an inferior root BPDU (worse cost value) coming via Switch-C, and therefore all ports would have to go through blocking, listening, and learning states, which would take 50 seconds, by default, to converge. With the inferior BPDU feature, assuming that Switch-B knows that Switch-C has an alternate port for their directly connected segment, then Switch-B can notify Switch-C to take its alternate port and change it to a designated port, and Switch-B will change its designated port to a root port. This process takes only a few seconds, if even that.

The second convergence feature introduced in 802.1w is *rapid transition*. Rapid transition includes two new components: edge ports and link types. An edge port is

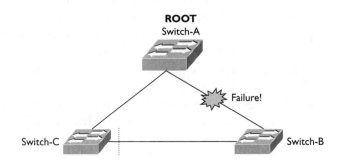

FIGURE 14-11

Accepting
inferior BPDUs

a port connected to a non–layer 2 device, such as a PC, server, or router. RSTP with rapid transition of edge ports to a forwarding state is the same as Cisco's proprietary PortFast. Changes in the state of these ports do not affect RSTP to cause a recalculation, and changes in other port types will keep these ports in a forwarding state.

Rapid transition can take place in RSTP only for edge ports and links that are point-to-point. The link type is automatically determined in terms of the duplexing of the connection. Switches make the assumption that if the port is configured for full-duplex between the two switches, the port can rapidly transition to a different state without having to wait for any timers to expire. If they are half-duplex, this feature won't work by default, but you can manually enable it for point-to-point half-duplex switch links.

Let's take a look at an example of rapid transition of point-to-point links by using the topology in Figure 14-12. The topology in Figure 14-12 is the same as that shown in Figure 14-11. In this example, however, the link between Switch-A (the root) and Switch-C fails. When this happens, Switch-C can no longer reach Switch-A on its root port. However, looking at the BPDUs it has been receiving from Switch-A and Switch-B, Switch-C knows that the root is reachable via Switch-B and that Switch-B provides the designated port (which is in a forwarding state) for the segment between Switch-B and Switch-C. Switch-C, knowing this, changes the state of the backup port to a root port and places it immediately into a forwarding state, notifying Switch-B of the change. This update typically takes less than a second, assuming that the failure of the segment between the root and Switch-C is a physical link failure, instead of three missed consecutive hello BPDUs.

RSTP Configuration

Cisco switches support three types of STP, as displayed in Table 14-2. The default configuration on Cisco switches is a separate instance of STP per VLAN, one root switch for all the VLANs, and no load sharing.

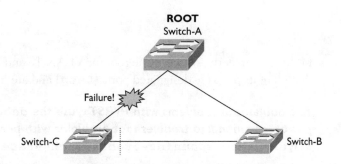

FIGURE 14-12

Rapid transition example

ROOT
Switch-A

Failure!

Switch-C

Switch-B

TABLE 14-2	STP	Description
STP Types	PVST+	802.1d per VLAN with Cisco-proprietary extensions (PortFast, UplinkFast, BackboneFast)
	PVRST+	802.1w (RSTP) per VLAN
	Multiservice Transport Platform (MSTP)	802.1s, referred to as multiple STP, combines Cisco's PVST+ with IEEE standards

This book focuses only on PVRST+, and briefly at that. To enable PVRST+, use the following command:

```
Switch(config)# spanning-tree mode rapid-pvst
```

Once enabled, you can view the STP on a per-VLAN basis with this command:

```
Switch# show spanning-tree vlan VLAN_# [detail]
```

Here's an example of this command:

```
Switch# show spanning-tree vlan 10
VLAN0010
Spanning tree enabled protocol rstp
Root ID Priority 32768
This bridge is root
Hello Time 2 sec Mag Age 20 sec Forward Delay 15 sec
Bridge ID Priority 32768 (priority 32768 sys-id-ext 10)
Address 0000.01c1.1111
Hello Time 2 sec Mag Age 20 sec Forward Delay 15 sec
Aging Time 300
Interface   Role   Sts   Cost   Pior.Nbr   Type
---------   ----   ---   ----   --------   ----
Fa0/1       Desg   FWD   19     128.1      P2p
Fa0/2       Desg   FWD   19     128.2      P2p
Fa0/3       Desg   FWD   19     128.3      P2p
  .
  .
  .
```

In this example, the switch is the root for VLAN 10 and RSTP is being used. Notice that all of its ports are designated ports (Desg) and are in a forwarding state (FWD).

on the
ⓘob

To troubleshoot problems with PVRST+, use the `debug spanning-tree pvst+` command; to troubleshoot problems with ports changing state within STP, use `debug spanning-tree switch state`.

PVST+ and RSTP Optimization

To understand the advantages offered by PVST+ and RSTP, examine Figure 14-13. This example shows two VLANs, numbered 1 and 2. The default behavior with Cisco's switches is that a single root switch is used for all VLANs, based on the switch with the lowest switch ID. In this instance, this is Switch-A. Notice that based on RSTP's calculation, Switch-C disabled its port to Switch-B for both its VLANs. The downside of this design is that of the two connections to the distribution layer, only one is being utilized on the access switch.

A better design is shown in Figure 14-14. However, to obtain this kind of topology, you must tune your network, making sure that Switch-A is the root for VLAN 1 and Switch-B is the root for VLAN 2. With this kind of design, you can actually utilize both of your uplink connections on your access layer switch up to the distribution layer switches. In Figure 14-14, VLAN 1 will use the left-hand uplink connection and VLAN 2 the right-hand uplink connection.

on the

Job

Based on the design in Figure 14-14, make sure the default gateway for VLAN 1 is Switch-A (assuming it's a layer 3 switch) and for VLAN 2 Switch-B (assuming it's a layer 3 switch). If you don't configure it this way, but have the default gateway associated with Switch-A, VLAN 2's traffic will have to go from the access layer switch, to Switch-B, and then across the EtherChannel to Switch-A before leaving the subnet. You can learn more about this in Cisco's CCNP Switching course.

FIGURE 14-13

PVST+ and RSTP non-optimized

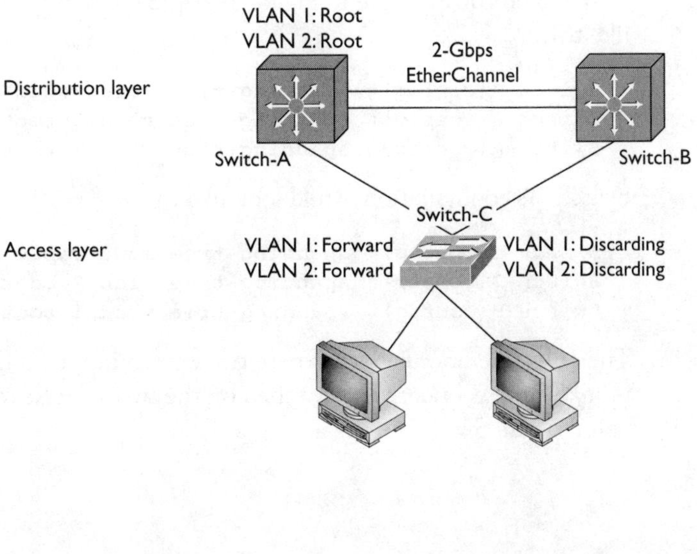

FIGURE 14-14

PVST+ and
RSTP optimized

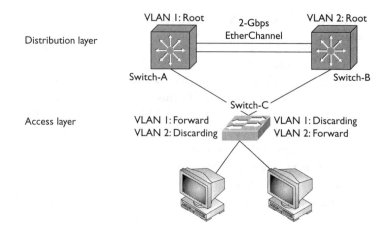

Remember that the topology in Figure 14-14 is created by you: you must manually change each switch's priority to create the desired topology. The commands to accomplish this include the following:

```
Switch(config)# spanning-tree vlan VLAN_# root primary
Switch(config)# spanning-tree vlan VLAN_# root secondary
Switch(config)# spanning-tree vlan VLAN_# priority priority_#
```

Remember that the default priority for a switch is 32,768. The first command changes the switch's priority to 4096 for the specified VLAN. The second command changes it to 8192 for the specified VLAN. The third allows you to customize the priority for the specified VLAN.

Based on the example in Figure 14-14, Switch-A's configuration would look like this:

```
Switch-A(config)# spanning-tree mode rapid-pvst
Switch-A(config)# spanning-tree vlan 1 root primary
Switch-A(config)# spanning-tree vlan 2 root secondary
```

Switch-B's configuration would look like this:

```
Switch-B(config)# spanning-tree mode rapid-pvst
Switch-B(config)# spanning-tree vlan 2 root primary
Switch-B(config)# spanning-tree vlan 1 root secondary
```

The only difference between these two configurations is that the priorities for the primary and secondary are switched on the two VLANs to allow for the use of both uplinks from Switch-C, the access layer switch.

Any STP configuration changes you make on your switches are effected immediately, which means that layer 2 will have to re-converge, causing a brief disruption in your layer 2 network.

14.02. The CD contains a multimedia demonstration of configuring an optimized PVRST+ topology.

EXERCISE 14-1

ON THE CD

Examining STP Information on Your Switches

The last few sections dealt with the operation of STP. This lab builds upon this information and allows you to view STP in operation on switches. You can find a picture of the network diagram for the simulator in the Introduction of this book. After starting up Boson's NetSim simulator, click the LabNavigator button. Next, double-click Exercise 14-1 and click the Load Lab button. This will load the lab configuration based on Chapter 12.

1. From the 2950-1, verify that you can ping the Host-1 PC and the 2950-2 switch. At the top of the simulator in the menu bar, click the eSwitches icon and choose 2950-1. Access the CLI of the 2950-1. Execute **ping 192.168.1.10** and **ping 192.168.1.3**. Both should be successful.

2. From Privilege EXEC mode, view the STP operation for VLAN 1: **show spanning-tree vlan 1**.

3. Compare the root ID and bridge ID at the top of the display: if they are the same, then this is the root switch, which means interfaces fa0/1 and fa0/2 (connected to 2950-2) should be in a forwarding state. If the IDs are different, then this is not the root switch and fa0/2 should be in a blocking state (BLK).

4. At the top of the simulator in the menu bar, click the eSwitches icon and choose 2950-2. Access the CLI of the 2950-2. From the 2950-2, view the STP operation for VLAN 1.

5. From Privilege EXEC mode, view the STP operation for VLAN 1: **show spanning-tree vlan 1**. Examine the IDs and the fa0/1 and fa0/2 interfaces, as described in step 3.

Now you should be more comfortable with STP on your Catalyst IOS switches.

CERTIFICATION OBJECTIVE 14.04

EtherChannels

It is common to need higher bandwidth speeds for certain kinds of connections in your network, such as connections from the access layer to the distribution layer, between distribution layer switches, between distribution and core layer switches, and between certain servers or routers and their connected switches. For example, in Figures 14-1 and 14-14 you can see dual layer 2 connections between the two distribution layer switches as well as between the distribution and core layer switches. The problem with this type of design, however, is that it creates layer 2 loops; and with STP running, STP will ensure that only one path is active between two devices, limiting you to the bandwidth of one of possibly multiple connections.

EtherChannel Overview

An EtherChannel is a layer 2 solution that allows you to aggregate multiple layer 2 Ethernet-based connections between directly connected devices. Basically, an EtherChannel bundles together multiple Ethernet ports between devices, providing what appears to be single logical interface. From STP's perspective, it sees the EtherChannel as a single logical connection between the connected devices, which means that you can actually use all of the individual connections, simultaneously, in the channel you've created.

EtherChannels provide these advantages:

- **Redundancy** If one connection in the channel fails, you can use other connections in the channel.
- **More bandwidth** Each connection can be used simultaneously to send frames.
- **Simplified management** Configuration is done on the logical interface, not on each individual connection in the channel.

EtherChannel Restrictions

Interfaces in an EtherChannel must be configured identically: speed, duplexing, and VLAN settings (in the same VLAN if they are access ports, or the same trunk properties) must be the same. When setting up EtherChannels, you can use up to eight interfaces bundled together:

- Up to eight Fast Ethernet connections, providing up to 800 Mbps
- Up to eight Gigabit Ethernet connections, providing up to 8 Gbps
- Up to eight 10-Gigabit Ethernet connections, providing up to 80 Gbps

You can have a total of six EtherChannels on a switch.

EtherChannel Operations

Channels can be formed dynamically between devices by using one of two protocols: Port Aggregation Protocol (PAgP) or Link Aggregation Control Protocol (LACP), compared in Table 14-3. Remember that ports participating in a channel must be configured identically.

Once a channel is formed, load balancing can be used by the connected devices to utilize all the ports in the channel. Load balancing is performed by reducing part of the binary addressing in the frame or packet to a numeric value and then associating the numeric value to one of the ports in the channel. Load balancing can use MAC or IP addresses, source or destination addresses, or both source and destination address pairs. With this fashion, you are guaranteed that all links in the channel will be utilized; however, you are not guaranteed that all the ports will be utilized the same.

For example, if you are load balancing based on source addresses, you are guaranteed that different source MAC addresses will use different ports in the channel. All traffic from a single-source MAC address, however, will always use the same port in the channel. Given this situation, if you have one device generating a lot of traffic, that link will possibly be utilized more than other links in the channel. In this situation, you might want to load balance based on destination or both source and destination addresses.

TABLE 14-3	Protocols	Description
EtherChannel Protocols	PAgP	Proprietary to Cisco. It allows connected devices to group similarly configured ports dynamically into a single channel.
	LACP	Defined in the IEEE 802.3ad standard. Like PAgP, it learns from a connected device which ports between the two are identically configured and dynamically forms a channel between them.

on the
job *To configure load balancing properly for a channel, you must understand the traffic patterns in your network. Once you understand your traffic patterns, you can get the most utilization out of your channel by choosing the correct load balancing type.*

EtherChannel Configuration

As mentioned, you should make sure that all interfaces in the channel are configured identically (configuring interface properties were discussed in Chapter 11); otherwise, a channel might not form. Here is the configuration to set up an EtherChannel:

```
Switch(config)# interface type [slot_#/]port_#
Switch(config-if)# channel-group group_# mode mode
Switch(config-if)# port-channel load-balance {dst-ip|dst-mac|
                                  src-dst-ip|src-dst-mac|src-ip|src-mac}
```

The *group_#* specifies the channel group to which the interface belongs, which can be from 1 to 6 (remember that you can have up to six EtherChannels on your switch). The mode can be one of those listed in Table 14-4. When using PAgP, one side needs to be configured as *desirable* and the other side as *desirable* or *auto*; or you can configure both sides to be *on*. When using LACP, one side needs to be *active* and the other side can be *active* or *passive*.

The **port-channel load-balance** command configures the type of load balancing you want to use on the channel. If you omit this command, it defaults to load balancing based on source MAC addresses (**src-mac**).

TABLE 14-4	EtherChannel Modes

Mode	Protocol	Description
auto	PAgP	Passively listens for PAgP queries from a Cisco device configured with either *desirable* or *on*. By default the interface is not part of a channel.
desirable	PAgP	Generates PAgP queries to form a channel, but by default is not part of a channel.
on	PAgP	Generates PAgP queries and assumes the port is part of a channel.
active	LACP	Enables a channel if the other side responds to its LACP messages.
passive	LACP	Passively listens for LACP messages to form a channel from an active port.

CERTIFICATION OBJECTIVE 14.05

STP Troubleshooting

Troubleshooting problems created by loops can be a difficult task. This section covers some simple steps you can take to identify and fix layer 2 loop problems.

Loop Identification

One indication of a broadcast storm is very high CPU and port utilization on your switches. The best way to identify a layer 2 loop is to capture and analyze traffic with a protocol analyzer to determine whether the same packet appears multiple times. This is typically done by connecting your protocol analyzer to a switch and using the Switch Port Analyzer (SPAN) feature on your switch, which copies frames from an interface or VLAN to the SPAN port. A good protocol analyzer should be able to see that a loop exists and notify you of this problem.

Once a loop is identified, to restore connectivity quickly, you should start disabling ports that are part of the loop; then diagnose the problem to determine whether a configuration issue on your part or the addition of a new layer 2 device is causing the problem. If you are having problems identifying what is causing the loop, turn on debug for STP (**debug spanning-tree events**).

Configuration Remedies

To simplify your troubleshooting process, disable as many features as necessary. For example, if you have EtherChannels enabled, disabling the channel will help determine whether the channel itself is not functioning correctly and possibly creating the layer 2 loop.

If you are not certain which switch is the root switch, log into the switch that logically should be the root and force it to become the root by changing its priority to 1 with the **spanning-tree vlan *VLAN_#* priority** command.

on the
job

A good step on your part should be to include the MAC addresses of each switch in your network topology diagram. Then, when troubleshooting loop problems, you'll find it much easier to determine whether a rogue switch was introduced into the topology that might be creating the loop.

Make sure that all your switches are running either 802.1d or 802.1w (RSTP), preferably the latter. Use the `show spanning-tree` command to verify this as well as whether or not the switch is playing the role of root for a VLAN.

INSIDE THE EXAM

Layer 2 Redundancy

Cisco's exam focuses more on the concepts of this chapter, rather than on the configuration. Be familiar with Cisco's three-layer hierarchy, since you might see it in illustrations on the exam. Understand the three issues with layer 2 loops (multiple frame copies, broadcast storms, and mislearning MAC addresses) and the problems these issues create.

Spanning Tree Protocol

Understand how STP works: how the root switch is elected, how root and designated ports are chosen, and the different states a port can be in. Don't be surprised if you are presented with a diagram and must choose answers dealing with these functions on the exam: Review the "Simple STP Example" section until you are comfortable with the STP terms and how the STP functions are derived. Remember that the switch ID is created from the switch's priority *and* MAC address. Be familiar with how long a port stays in a particular state for 802.1d STP.

Understand when PortFast is best used and the advantages that PVST+ provides when implementing VLANs.

Rapid Spanning Tree Protocol

Be familiar with the port states with RSTP: discarding, learning, and forwarding. Understand the difference between an alternate and a backup port. The configuration and tuning of RSTP is not emphasized on the exam.

EtherChannels

The configuration of EtherChannels is not emphasized on the exam; however, you need to understand what they are and when they are used.

STP Troubleshooting

Remember what symptoms you look for to identify a layer 2 loop. Be familiar with the configuration remedies in dealing with layer 2 loops.

CERTIFICATION SUMMARY

Bridges have three main functions: learn, forward, and remove loops. They learn by placing source MAC addresses and associated bridge ports in a port address or CAM table. They will flood traffic if the destination address is a multicast, broadcast, or unknown unicast destination. STP is used to remove layer 2 loops.

BPDUs are used by STP to learn about other neighboring switches. These are generated every 2 seconds as multicasts. When running STP, a root switch is elected—the one with the lowest switch or bridge ID. The switch ID is composed of a priority and the switch's MAC address. Each switch chooses a root port to reach the root switch—the one with the lowest accumulated path cost. Each segment has one port on one switch that becomes a designated port, which is used to forward traffic to and from the segment. This is typically the port on the switch with the lowest accumulated path cost. There are five port states: blocking (20 seconds), listening (15 seconds), learning (15 seconds), forwarding, and disabled. PortFast puts a port immediately into forwarding mode and should be used only on non-switch ports. PVST+ has an instance of STP running per VLAN—this is proprietary to Cisco but standardized by IEEE with MSTP.

RSTP reduces convergence to a few seconds by having switches determine valid alternate root ports and backup designated ports that they can use when topology changes take place. PVST+ with RSTP is enabled with the **spanning-tree mode rapid-pvst** command.

EtherChannels bundle layer 2 connections between devices, creating a single logical port from STP's perspective. Load balancing can then be performed on the ports in the channel. PAgP or LACP are used to form the channel. No more than eight interfaces can be part of a channel.

If your CPU and/or port utilization is high, you might have a layer 2 loop. Typically you should use a protocol analyzer and look for multiple copies of the same frame in your frame captures.

✓ # TWO-MINUTE DRILL

Layer 2 Redundancy

❏ There are three layers to a campus design: access, distribution, and core.

❏ Redundancy in layer 2 networks can create loops that can cause multiple frame copies, broadcast storms, and/or mislearning MAC addresses.

Spanning Tree Protocol

❏ STP is defined in 802.1d. It removes loops from your network.

❏ The switch with the lowest switch ID (priority + MAC address) is elected as the root.

❏ Each switch chooses the best path to the root, and this port is called a root port. Each segment needs a switch port to access the rest of the network—this port is called a designated port.

❏ BPDUs are used to elect root switches and to share topology information. BPDUs are multicasts that are advertised every 2 seconds.

❏ There are five STP port states: blocking (only processing BPDUs—20 seconds), listening (only processing BPDUs—15 seconds), learning (processing BPDUs and building the CAM table—15 seconds), forwarding (processing BPDUs, building the CAM table, and forwarding user traffic), and disabled (the port is not enabled). Root and designated ports will eventually move into a forwarding state, which can take between 30 and 50 seconds.

❏ PortFast keeps a port in a forwarding state when STP is recalculating; it should *not* be used on switch-to-switch connections and thus could lead to inadvertent loops.

❏ PVST+ is proprietary to Cisco and allows for a separate STP instance per VLAN.

Rapid Spanning Tree Protocol

❏ RSTP has three port states: discarding, learning, and forwarding.

❏ RTSP supports two additional port types: alternate (secondary to a root port) and backup (secondary to a designated port).

EtherChannels

❑ From STP's perspective, an EtherChannel, which is a grouping of layer 2 physical connections between devices, is seen as a single logical connection.

❑ Ports must be configured identically in an EtherChannel. PAgP or LACP can be used to form a channel.

STP Troubleshooting

❑ Look for high CPU and/or port utilization as a symptom of a broadcast storm.

❑ Use a protocol analyzer and look for multiple frame copies to determine whether you have a loop.

SELF TEST

The following Self Test questions will help you measure your understanding of the material presented in this chapter. Read all the choices carefully, as there may be more than one correct answer. Choose all correct answers for each question.

Layer 2 Redundancy

1. Which of the following would not be a symptom of a layer 2 loop?
   A. Broadcast flooding
   B. Multiple frame copies
   C. Learning MAC addresses on incorrect ports
   D. None of these

Spanning Tree Protocol

2. The root switch is the one elected with the _____.
   A. lowest MAC address
   B. highest MAC address
   C. lowest switch ID
   D. highest switch ID

3. The switch port that is chosen to forward traffic for a segment is called a _____.
   A. root port
   B. alternate port
   C. backup port
   D. designated port

4. Which is true concerning a port in a listening state? (choose two)
   A. It remains there for 15 seconds.
   B. It forwards BPDUs and builds the CAM table.
   C. It remains there for 20 seconds.
   D. It forwards BPDUs.

Rapid Spanning Tree Protocol

5. How many port states are there in RSTP?
   A. 3
   B. 4

    C. 5

    D. 6

6. What port role will be assigned to a port that has the second best path to the root switch?

    A. Root

    B. Designated

    C. Alternate

    D. Backup

7. Which command enables RSTP with PVRST+ on a switch?

    A. `spanning-tree mode rapid-pvst`

    B. `spanning-tree state rapid-pvst`

    C. `stp state rapid-pvst`

    D. `spanning-tree mode rtsp`

EtherChannels

8. Which of the following is true concerning EtherChannels?

    A. You can have up to six ports in a channel.

    B. You can have up to eight channels on a switch.

    C. Ports must be configured identically to form a channel.

    D. RSTP dynamically groups ports into a channel.

STP Troubleshooting

9. What symptom should you look for to determine whether you have a layer 2 loop?

    A. High number of broadcast and/or multicast frames

    B. High port utilization

    C. User switch interfaces dropping and reconnecting

    D. Port address tables not being updated

10. What tool would you use to determine whether you had a broadcast storm caused by a layer 2 loop?

    A. `show interface` command

    B. Protocol analyzer

    C. `debug broadcast` command

    D. `traceroute` command

SELF TEST ANSWERS

Layer 2 Redundancy

1. ☑ **A.** Switches flood broadcasts by default; seeing the *same* broadcast again and again could indicate a broadcast storm and a layer 2 loop.
   ☒ **B** and **C** are symptoms of a layer 2 loop. Since there is an incorrect answer, **D** is incorrect.

Spanning Tree Protocol

2. ☑ **C.** The switch with the lowest switch ID is elected as the root switch.
   ☒ **A** and **B** are incorrect because the decision is based on the switch ID, which includes the switch's priority and MAC address. **D** is incorrect because it is the lowest, not the highest switch ID.

3. ☑ **D.** The switch port that is chosen to forward traffic for a segment is called a designated port.
   ☒ **A** is incorrect because the root port is the port that the switch uses to reach the root. **B**, the alternate port, is used in RSTP and is a secondary root port, and **C**, the backup port, is used in RSTP and is a secondary designated port.

4. ☑ **A** and **D.** In a listening state, the port processes and forwards BPDUs. A port stays in the listening state for 15 seconds.
   ☒ **B** occurs in the learning state. **C** is the time period for the blocking state.

Rapid Spanning Tree Protocol

5. ☑ **A.** There are 3 port states in RSTP: discarding, learning, and forwarding.
   ☒ Since there are only 3 states, **B**, **C**, and **D** are incorrect.

6. ☑ **C.** An alternate port has the second best path to the root switch.
   ☒ **A** is the best path to the root. **B** is the best path for a segment to the root. **D** is the second best path for a segment to the root.

7. ☑ **A.** The **spanning-tree mode rapid-pvst** command enables RSTP with PVST+ on a Catalyst switch.
   ☒ **state** is an invalid parameter, making **B** incorrect. **C** is an invalid command. **D** has an invalid **mode** parameter.

EtherChannels

8. ☑ **C.** Ports must be configured identically to form a channel.

☒ **A** is incorrect because you can have up to eight ports in a channel. **B** is incorrect because the limit is six channels per switch. **D** rapidly converges STP: PAgP and LACP dynamically form channels.

STP Troubleshooting

9. ☑ **B.** If you have a layer 2 loop, the switch's CPU and/or port utilization will be very high.

☒ **A** is true only if you are seeing duplicate broadcast/multicast frames, not just a high number of these. **C** would be indicative of a physical layer problem such as a cable issue. Port address tables would be constantly updated with correct and incorrect information, making **D** incorrect.

10. ☑ **B.** When using a protocol analyzer to troubleshoot layer 2 loop problems, look for the same frame being repeated constantly.

☒ **A** will show an inordinate amount of statistical traffic on the interface, but it doesn't clarify it as broadcast or part of a loop. **C** is an invalid command. **D** is used to troubleshoot layer 3, not layer 2, problems.

Part IV

Cisco Routers and LANs

15

Routers and Routing

T he preceding part of the book focused on switches and protocols that function at layer 2. This part of the book moves up one layer in the OSI Reference Model to discuss layer 3, the network layer. Layer 3 devices are generically called *routers*. Routers basically have two functions:

- To find a layer 3 path to a destination network
- To move packets from one interface to another to get a packet to its destination

To accomplish the first function, a router will need to do the following:

- Learn about the routers to which it is connected to determine the networks that are reachable.
- Find locations of destination network numbers.
- Choose a *best* path to each destination.
- Maintain the most up-to-date routing information about how to reach destination networks.

To accomplish the second function, a router will need to examine the destination IP address in an incoming IP packet, determine the network number of the destination, look in its routing table, and switch the packet to an outgoing interface.

As you will see in this chapter, the routing table contains a list of destination network numbers, the status of these networks, which interface the router should use to reach the destination, and which neighboring router the router should use if the destination is more than one hop away. This chapter introduces routing and the types of dynamic routing protocols: distance vector, link state, and hybrid protocols.

CERTIFICATION OBJECTIVE 15.01

Routing Introduction

Before a discussion of routers and routing protocols begins, you need a fundamental understanding of the types of routes that can exist on a router and how a router uses routes that it learns. The following sections discuss two learning methods (static and dynamic), how routers are grouped together (autonomous systems), and how routing protocols are weighed by the router when choosing a path between multiple routing protocols.

Types of Routes

A router can learn a route using one of two methods: *static* and *dynamic*. The following two sections discuss the two types.

Static Routes

A router can learn a static route in two ways: First, a router will look at its active interfaces, examine the addresses configured on the interfaces and determine the corresponding network numbers, and populate the routing table with this information. This is commonly called a *connected* or *directly connected* route. The second way that a router can learn a static route is for you to configure it manually. One special type of static route is called a *default route*, commonly called the *gateway of last resort*. If the specified destination is not listed in the routing table, the default route can be used to route the packet. A default route has an IP address of 0.0.0.0 and a subnet mask of 0.0.0.0, often represented as 0.0.0.0/0. Default routes are commonly used in small networks on a perimeter router pointing to the directly connected ISP router. The configuration of static and default routes is discussed in Chapter 19.

Dynamic Routes

A router learns dynamic routes by running a routing protocol. Routing protocols will learn about routes from other neighboring routers running the same routing protocol. Dynamic routing protocols share network numbers known by the router and reachability information concerning these networks. Through this sharing

TABLE 15-1	Routed Protocols	Routing Protocols
Routed and Routing Protocols	IP	RIP, IGRP, OSPF, EIGRP, BGP, IS-IS
	IPX	RIP, NLSP, EIGRP
	AppleTalk	RMTP, AURP, EIGRP

process, a router will eventually learn about all of the reachable network and subnet numbers in the network.

You should know that the terms *routing* protocol and *routed* protocol have two different meanings. A *routing* protocol learns about routes for a *routed* protocol. A routed protocol is a layer 3 protocol, such as Transmission Control Protocol/Internet Protocol (TCP/IP) or Internetwork Packet Exchange (IPX). A routed protocol carries user traffic such as e-mail, file transfers, and web downloads. Table 15-1 shows some common routed protocols and the routing protocols that they use. This book

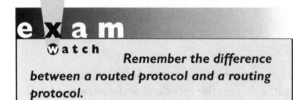

focuses only on routing for IP traffic and covers the basics of the following dynamic IP routing protocols: Routing Information Protocol (RIP) v1 and v2 in Chapter 19, Open Shortest Path First (OSPF) in Chapter 20, and Enhanced Interior Gateway Routing Protocol (EIGRP) in Chapter 21.

w a t c h *Remember the difference between a routed protocol and a routing protocol.*

Autonomous Systems

Some routing protocols understand the concept of an autonomous system, and some do not. An *autonomous system (AS)* is a group of networks under a single administrative control, which could be your company, a division within your company, or a group of companies. An *Interior Gateway Protocol (IGP)* refers to a routing protocol that handles routing within a single autonomous system. IGPs include RIP, EIGRP, OSPF, and Intermediate System-Intermediate System (IS-IS). An *Exterior Gateway Protocol (EGP)* handles routing between different autonomous systems. Today, only one EGP is active: the Border Gateway Protocol (BGP). BGP is used to route traffic across the Internet backbone between different autonomous systems.

Not every routing protocol understands the concept of an AS. An AS can provide distinct boundaries for a routing protocol, and thus provides some advantages. For instance, you can control how far a network number is propagated by routers. Plus, you can control what routes you will advertise to other autonomous systems and what routes you'll accept from these systems.

To distinguish one autonomous system from another, an AS can be assigned a unique number from 1 to 65,535. The Internet Assigned Numbers Authority (IANA) is responsible for assigning these numbers. Just like the public and private IP addresses defined in RFC 1918, there are public and private AS numbers. If you will be connected to the Internet backbone, are running BGP, and want to accept BGP routes from the Internet, you will need a public AS number. However, if you only need to break up your internal network into different systems, you can use private AS numbers. Routing protocols that understand the concept of an AS are EIGRP, OSPF, IS-IS, and BGP. RIP doesn't understand autonomous systems, while OSPF does; but OSPF doesn't require you to configure the AS number, whereas other protocols, such as EIGRP, do. Cisco's CCNP certification spends a lot of time discussing autonomous systems and routing between them. The CCNA exam focuses only on the basics of IGPs and routing within an AS.

watch *An autonomous system (AS) is a group of networks under a single administrative control. Each AS is assigned a unique number that differentiates it from other autonomous systems.*

Administrative Distance

As mentioned in the chapter introduction, each router needs to choose a *best* path to a destination. This process can become somewhat complicated if the router is receiving routing update information for a single network from multiple sources, such as connected, static, and IGP routing protocols, and must choose *one* of these sources as the best and place this choice in the router's routing table. As you will see in the next few sections, a router looks at two items when choosing a *best* path: administrative distance and routing metrics. The first item a router looks at is the administrative distance for a route source. Administrative distance is a Cisco-proprietary mechanism used to rank the IP routing protocols. As an example, if a router was running two IGPs, RIP and EIGRP, and was learning network 10.0.0.0/8 from both of these routing protocols, which one should the router pick and place in its routing table? Which one should the router *believe* more? Actually, the term *administrative distance* is somewhat misleading, since the term has nothing to do with measuring distance. The term *believability* better describes the process.

TABLE 15-2	Administrative Distance	Route Type
	0	Connected interface route
	0 or 1	Static route
	90	Internal EIGRP route (within the same AS)
	110	OSPF route
	120	RIPv1 and v2 route
	170	External EIGRP (from another AS)
	255	Unknown route (is considered an invalid route and will not be used)

Administrative Distance Values

Administrative distance ranks the IP routing protocols, assigning a value, or weight, to each protocol. Distances can range from 0 to 255. A smaller distance is more believable by a router, with the best distance being 0 and the worst, 255. Table 15-2 displays some of the default administrative distances Cisco has assigned to its IP routing protocols. Going back to the previous example of a router learning network 10.0.0.0/8 from RIP and EIGRP, since RIP has a value of 120 and EIGRP 90, the router will use the EIGRP route, since this protocol has a better (*lower*) administrative distance value.

exam
ⓦatch

Here are some important protocols to know and their administrative distances: connected (0), static (0 or 1), EIGRP (90), OSPF (110), and RIP (120).

The protocol with a lower distance is preferred over a higher one, where the most believable route is a directly connected one.

CERTIFICATION OBJECTIVE 15.02

Dynamic Routing Protocols

Unlike static routes that require manual configuration to tell the router where destination networks are, *dynamic routing protocols* learn about destination networks from neighboring routers through a sharing process. Dynamic routing protocols fall under one of three categories: distance vector, link state, and hybrid. Each of these routing protocol types takes a different approach in sharing routing information with neighboring routers and choosing the best path to a destination.

Because of the differences between the various routing protocol types, each has advantages and disadvantages. One choice you'll have to make will be which routing protocol you'll run on the routers in your network. You'll have to examine the following factors when choosing a routing protocol:

- Routing metrics used to choose paths
- How routing information is shared
- Convergence speed of the routing protocol
- How routers process routing information
- Overhead of the routing protocol

The following sections discuss these topics.

Routing Metrics

As mentioned in the "Administrative Distance" section, if your router has two types of routes, such as RIP and EIGRP, for the same network number, the router uses the administrative distance to choose the best one. However, a situation might arise where two paths to the destination network exist, and the *same* routing protocol, RIP, for instance, discovers these multiple paths to the destination network. If this is the case, a routing protocol will use a measurement called a *metric* to determine which path is the best path to place in the routing table.

Table 15-3 lists some common metrics, the IP routing protocols that use them, and brief descriptions of the metrics. As you can see from this table, some routing

TABLE 15-3   Routing Protocol Metrics

Metric	Routing Protocols	Description
Bandwidth	EIGRP	The capacity of the links in Kbps (T1 = 1554)
Cost	OSPF	Measurement in the inverse of the bandwidth of the links
Delay	EIGRP	Time it takes to reach the destination
Hop count	RIP	How many layer 3 hops away from the destination
Load	EIGRP	The path with the least utilization
MTU	EIGRP	The path that supports the largest frame sizes
Reliability	EIGRP	The path with the least amount of errors or down time

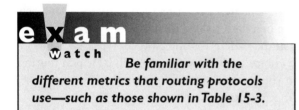

protocols use only a single metric. For instance, RIP uses hop count as a metric, and OSPF uses cost. Other routing protocols use multiple metric values to choose a best path to a destination. For instance, EIGRP can use bandwidth, delay, reliability, load, and maximum transmission unit (MTU) when choosing a best path to a destination.

Distance Vector Protocols

Of the three types of routing protocols—distance vector, link state, and hybrid—distance vector protocols are the simplest in their implementation. Distance vector routing protocols use distance (accumulated metric value) and direction (vector) to find paths to destinations. Most distance vector protocols use the Bellman-Ford algorithm (discussed shortly) for finding paths to destination networks. Sometimes these protocols are referred to as *routing by rumor*, since the routers learn routing information from directly connected neighbors, and these neighbors might have learned these networks from other neighboring routers. RIP is an example of a routing protocol that is a distance vector, and it is discussed in more depth in Chapter 19.

Advertising Updates

One of the mechanisms of a routing protocol is to share routing and reachability information with neighboring routers. Some protocols use local broadcasts to disseminate information, some use multicasts, and some use unicasts. Distance vector protocols typically use periodic local broadcasts with a destination IP address of 255.255.255.255 to share routing information. These protocols do this religiously, whether or not something has changed: Once their periodic timer expires, they broadcast their routing information to any devices connected to their interfaces. Note that distance vector protocols really don't care who listens to these updates, nor do they verify whether neighboring routers received the broadcast update.

Routers running distance vector protocols learn who their neighbors are by listening for routing broadcasts on their interfaces. No formal handshaking process or hello process occurs to discover who are the neighboring routers. Distance vector protocols assume that through the broadcast process, neighbors will be learned, and if a neighbor fails, the missed broadcasts from these neighbors will eventually be detected. And even if changes occur and your router misses an update from a neighbor, it is assumed that your router will learn about the change in the next broadcast update.

Processing Updates

When a distance vector protocol receives a routing update from a neighboring router, it performs these steps:

1. Increments the metrics of the incoming routes in the advertisement (for RIP, add 1 to the advertised hop count of the route).

2. Compares the network numbers in the routing update from the neighbor to what the router has in its routing table.

3. If the neighbor's information is better, places it in the routing table and remove the old entry.

4. If the neighbor's information is worse, ignores it.

5. If the neighbor's information is exactly the same as the entry already in the table, resets the timer for the entry in the routing table (in other words, the router already learned about this route from the same neighbor).

6. If the neighbor's information is a different path to a known destination network, but with the same metric as the existing network in the routing table, the router will add it to the routing table along with the old one. This assumes you have not exceeded the maximum number of equal-cost paths for this destination network number. In this situation, your router is learning about the same network number from two *different* neighbors, and both neighbors are advertising the network number with the same metric.

These six steps are generally referred to as the *Bellman-Ford algorithm*. As you can see from step 6, Cisco supports load balancing for equal-cost paths to a destination within a particular route type, such as RIP routes.

Since distance vector protocols are the simplest of the three protocol types, they are easy to set up and troubleshoot. They have very low overhead on the router, requiring few CPU cycles and memory to process updates: they receive an incoming update, increment the metrics, compare the results to the existing routes in the routing table, and update the routing table if necessary.

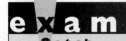

Link State Protocols

Link state protocols use an algorithm called the *Shortest Path First (SPF)* algorithm, invented by Edsger W. Dijkstra, to find the best path to a destination. Whereas distance vector protocols rely on *rumors* from other neighbors about remote routes, link state protocols will learn the complete topology of the network: which routers are connected to which networks. Because of the size of a network, this can create scalability problems. Therefore, link state protocols typically contain capabilities to limit the scope of their learning process, limiting a router's knowledge of the network topology to a smaller number of routers and routes.

Examples of link state protocols include OSPF and IS-IS. OSPF is covered in more depth in Chapter 20. IS-IS is an ISO link state protocol. It was originally developed by DEC as the DECnet Phase V routing protocol. It can route for both TCP/IP traffic and Connectionless Network Protocol (CLNP) and Connectionless Network Service (CLNS) traffic. IS-IS provides for more scalability than OSPF but is more complex to configure. Some ISPs use IS-IS as the routing protocol for their own networks. IS-IS is covered in Cisco's CCNP exams.

Advertising Updates

Whereas distance vector protocols use local broadcasts to disseminate routing information, link state protocols use multicasts. A distance protocol will send out its routing table religiously on its periodic interval whether there are changes or not. Link state protocols are smarter. They multicast what is called a *link state advertisement (LSA)*, which is a piece of routing information that contains who originated the advertisement and what the network number is.

LSAs are typically generated only when changes are made in the network, which is more resource-friendly to your network devices. In other words, periodic updates are rare occurrences. Whereas distance vector protocols use local broadcasts, which are processed by every machine on the segment, link state protocols use multicasts, which are processed only by other devices running the link state protocol. Plus, link state protocols send their updates reliably. A destination router, when receiving an LSA update, will respond to the source router with an acknowledgment. This process is different from distance vector protocols, which don't verify that a routing update was received from neighboring routers.

As a router learns routes from the LSAs of routers in the network, it builds a complete topology of the network—what routers are connected to other routers and what the network numbers are. This is stored in a local topological database. Whereas distance vector protocols are referred to as *routing by rumor*, link state protocols are referred to as *routing by propaganda,* since link state routers are learning which routers are sourcing (connected to) a network number. The LSAs gathered by a link state router are then stored in a local database, sometimes referred to as a *topology table.* Any time there is a change in the database, the router runs the SPF algorithm. The SPF algorithm builds an inverted tree, with the router itself at the top, and other routers and their connected network segments beneath it. This algorithm is somewhat similar to the STP algorithm that layer 2 devices use to remove loops. Depending on the tree structure and the metrics used, the link state router then populates the routing table with the best (shortest) paths to the networks in the SPF tree.

Advantages of Link State Protocols

One of the advantages of link state protocols is that they use a hierarchical structure that helps limit the distance that an LSA travels. This reduces the likelihood that a change in the network will impact every router. This process is different from that of distance vector protocols, which use a flat topology. With distance vector protocols, a change in one part of the network will eventually impact every router in the network. Depending on the configuration of routers in a link state protocol, this is not necessarily true. For instance, OSPF uses areas to help contain changes; therefore, a change in one area won't necessarily impact other areas.

A second advantage of link state protocols is that they use multicasts to share routing information. Multicasts are sent to a group of devices, whereas broadcasts are sent to everyone. Only other routers running the link state protocol will process these LSA packets. Plus, link state routers send out only *incremental* updates. Incremental updates are updates sent out when a change occurs in the state of the network. This is much more advantageous than what distance vector protocols do: broadcast updates based on a periodic timer, which is typically either 30 or 60 seconds. Once all the link state routers are booted up and they learn the topology of the network, updates are typically sent out only when changes take place, which shouldn't be that often. The advantage of this process is that you are using your network's bandwidth and resources more efficiently than with distance vector protocols.

A third advantage that link state protocols have over distance vector protocols is that they support classless routing. Classless routing allows you to summarize a large group of contiguous routes into a smaller number of routes. This process is called *Variable-Length Subnet Masking (VLSM)* and *Classless Interdomain Routing (CIDR)*. These concepts were discussed in depth in Chapter 8.

By summarizing routes, you are making the routing process more efficient. First, you are advertising a smaller number of routes. And second, in order for the summarized route to fail, all of the subnets or networks in the summarization must fail. As an example, you might have a WAN link that is *flapping*. A flapping route is going up and down, up and down, over and over again. This can create serious performance problems for link state protocols. When you perform summarization, if the specific route within a summarized route is flapping, this will not affect the status of the summarized route and thus won't impact many of the routers in your network. Third, by summarizing routes, you reduce the size of your router's routing link state database, which will reduce the number of CPU cycles required to run the SPF algorithm and update the routing table, as well as reduce your router's memory requirements for the routing protocol.

A fourth advantage is that with the use of the SPF algorithm, routing loops will not be included in the population of the routing table: by examining the inverted tree, loops can be easily detected and not included in a routing table. Routing loops can create problems with distance vector protocols, however—this problem is discussed in the section "Distance Vector Protocol Problems and Solutions" section later in this chapter.

Disadvantages of Link State Protocols

Given the advantages of link state protocols, they do have disadvantages. For instance, even though link state protocols can scale a network to a much larger size than distance vector protocols, link state protocols are more CPU- and memory-intensive. Link state protocols have to maintain more tables in memory: a neighbor table, a link state database, and a routing table. When changes take place in the network, the routers must update the link state database, run the SPF algorithm, build the SPF tree, and then rebuild the routing table, which requires a lot more CPU cycles than a distance vector protocol's approach: increment the metrics of incoming routes and compare this to the current routes in the routing table.

As an example, a flapping route in a link state network can affect the processing on many routers, especially if the change is occurring every 10 to 15 seconds. The advantage that distance vector protocols have is that the only time the routers have to perform a function is when they receive the periodic updates, and then processing these updates is router-friendly.

exam

watch *Link state protocols use the SPF algorithm to choose the best path. They are more CPU- and memory-intensive than distance vector protocols. However, they are more network-friendly in that*

they use multicasts to disseminate routing information and only advertise changes. Plus, with route summarization and hierarchical routing, link state protocols can scale to very large network sizes.

Hybrid Protocols

A *hybrid* protocol takes the advantages of both distance vector and link state protocols and merges them into a new protocol. Typically, hybrid protocols are based on a distance vector protocol but contain many of the features and advantages of link state protocols. Examples of hybrid protocols include RIPv2, EIGRP, and BGP. RIPv2 is covered in more depth in Chapter 19, and EIGRP is covered in Chapter 21. BGP is beyond the scope of this book but is heavily emphasized in the CCNP certification.

As an example of a hybrid protocol's approach, Cisco's EIGRP reduces the CPU and memory overhead by acting like a distance vector protocol when it comes to processing routing updates; but instead of sending out periodic updates like a distance vector protocol, EIGRP sends out incremental, reliable updates via multicast messages, providing a more network- and router-friendly environment. EIGRP supports many other features of link state protocols, such as VLSM and route summarization.

BGP is also a hybrid protocol, drawing a lot of its functionality from distance vector protocols. It is based on a standard (RFC 1772) and is used as the de facto routing protocol to interconnect ISPs, and sometimes companies, on the Internet. Unlike most of the other protocols that use multicasts or broadcasts for dissemination, BGP sets up a TCP connection (port 179) to a neighboring peer and uses TCP to share connection information. Like EIGRP and OSPF, BGP supports route summarization. Unlike these protocols, BGP was meant to route between autonomous systems.

on the job

It used to be that running a distance vector protocol such as RIP was sufficient for small to medium networks, given the overhead involved with link state protocols. With the advancement of hardware, distance vector protocols are not commonly used today, even in smaller networks; the most common dynamic IGP protocol is OSPF, with EIGRP a distant second. In SOHO networks, static routes are the most common routing mechanism used.

CERTIFICATION OBJECTIVE 15.03

Distance Vector Protocol Problems and Solutions

The remainder of this chapter focuses on the problems that pertain to distance vector routing protocols: they converge slowly and they are prone to routing (layer 3) loops. The next few sections cover these problems, as well as present solutions implemented by distance vector protocols to solve these problems.

Problem: Convergence

The term *convergence*, in routing parlance, refers to the time it takes for all of the routers to understand the current topology of the network. Link state protocols tend to converge very quickly, while distance vector protocols tend to converge slowly.

Convergence Example

To understand the issue that distance vector protocols have with convergence, let's look at an example. The network is shown in Figure 15-1. In this example, assume that the periodic timer for the distance vector protocol is set to 60 seconds. Also assume that the distance vector protocol is using hop count as a metric and no special features are implemented in this example to solve convergence or routing loop problems.

FIGURE 15-1   Convergence example after routers are turned on

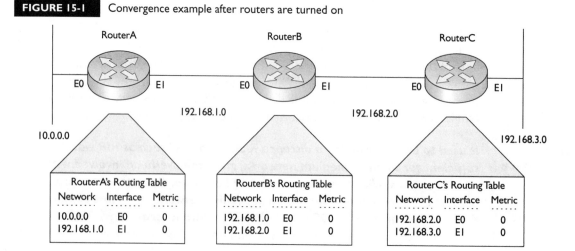

RouterA's Routing Table		
Network	Interface	Metric
10.0.0.0	E0	0
192.168.1.0	E1	0

RouterB's Routing Table		
Network	Interface	Metric
192.168.1.0	E0	0
192.168.2.0	E1	0

RouterC's Routing Table		
Network	Interface	Metric
192.168.2.0	E0	0
192.168.3.0	E1	0

This example has three routers, RouterA, RouterB, and RouterC, where these routers were just turned on. As you can see from the routers' routing tables, the only routes these routers initially know about are their directly connected routes, which they learn by examining the status of their interfaces, making sure that they are *up* and *up*; they then take the network numbers of these interfaces (learned from the configured IP address and subnet mask) and put this information in their routing tables. Currently, each router contains two routes in its routing table. Also notice the metric: these routes have a hop count of 0, since they are directly connected.

Now that their interfaces are active and the routers have an initial routing table, they'll send out their first routing broadcast on these interfaces (they don't wait for their periodic timer in this instance, since the interfaces just went active). This broadcast contains the entries that they have in their routing tables. Assume that all routers are synchronized when they advertise their routing broadcasts, even though this would be highly unlikely in a production environment. This list shows which routers are advertising which routes on their active interfaces:

- **RouterA** Networks 10.0.0.0 and 192.168.1.0
- **RouterB** Networks 192.168.1.0 and 192.168.2.0
- **RouterC** Networks 192.168.2.0 and 192.168.3.0

After this first exchange of routing tables, each router will process its neighbor's received update and incorporate these changes, if necessary. Figure 15-2 displays the contents of the routing tables on the routers after this first exchange.

FIGURE 15-2   Convergence example after first routing update

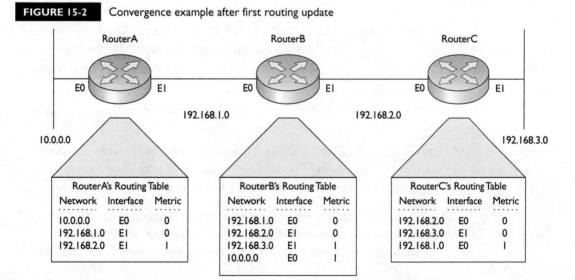

RouterA's Routing Table

Network	Interface	Metric
10.0.0.0	E0	0
192.168.1.0	E1	0
192.168.2.0	E1	1

RouterB's Routing Table

Network	Interface	Metric
192.168.1.0	E0	0
192.168.2.0	E1	0
192.168.3.0	E1	1
10.0.0.0	E0	1

RouterC's Routing Table

Network	Interface	Metric
192.168.2.0	E0	0
192.168.3.0	E1	0
192.168.1.0	E0	1

Let's break this process down one router at a time, starting with RouterA:

1. Receives networks 192.168.1.0 and 192.168.2.0 from RouterB and increments the metric by one hop for each route.

2. Compares the advertised routes from RouterB to what it has in its routing table.

3. Adds 192.168.2.0 because it is not in the routing table.

4. Ignores 192.168.1.0 from RouterB because RouterB has a hop count of 1, while the current routing table entry in the routing table has a hop count of 0.

Let's look at RouterC next:

1. Receives networks 192.168.1.0 and 192.168.2.0 from RouterB and increments the metric by one hop.

2. Compares the advertised routes from RouterB to what it has in its routing table.

3. Adds 192.168.1.0 because it is not in the routing table.

4. Ignores 192.168.2.0 from RouterB because RouterB has a hop count of 1 while the current routing table entry has a metric of 0.

RouterB is saved for last, since it presents a more complicated situation: it is receiving routes from both RouterA and RouterB. Here are the steps RouterB goes through:

1. Receives networks 10.0.0.0 and 192.168.1.0 from RouterA and 192.168.2.0 and 192.168.3.0 from RouterC and increments the metric by one hop.

2. Compares the advertised routes from RouterA and RouterC to what it has in its routing table.

3. Adds 10.0.0.0 and 192.168.3.0 because they are not currently in the routing table.

4. Ignores 192.168.1.0 and 192.168.2.0 from RouterA and RouterC, respectively, because RouterA and RouterC have a metric of 1 for these routes, while the current routing table entries have a metric of 0.

Looking at Figure 15-2, have the routers converged? Remember the definition of convergence: the routers understand the complete topology of the network. Given this definition, the routers have not yet converged. RouterA's routing table doesn't contain 192.168.3.0 and RouterC's routing table doesn't contain 10.0.0.0. Note, however, that RouterB has converged, but RouterA and RouterC still need additional routes.

After their periodic timers expire, the routers again generate local routing broadcast updates on each of their interfaces. Again, they broadcast their entire routing tables on these interfaces. Figure 15-3 shows the network after these routers process these new updates. The routers in this network go through the same process again when receiving the updates. Notice that RouterA's routing table now contains 192.168.3.0, with a hop count of 2, while RouterC's routing table contains 10.0.0.0, with a hop count of 2. Both of these routers learned these networks via RouterB. And since these networks have a hop count of 1 on RouterB, when the edge routers receive the routing table from RouterB, they increment the hop count to 2 for these network numbers.

Given the routing tables shown in Figure 15-3, the routers have fully converged. The problem is, however, that convergence took place only after two updates. The first update took place as soon as the interface was active, and the second update took place 60 seconds later. So in this example, it took more than 60 seconds for convergence to occur. You can imagine that if you have a few hundred routers in your network, it might take many minutes before your network converges and each router knows about all of the destinations that are reachable.

FIGURE 15-3   Convergence example after second routing update

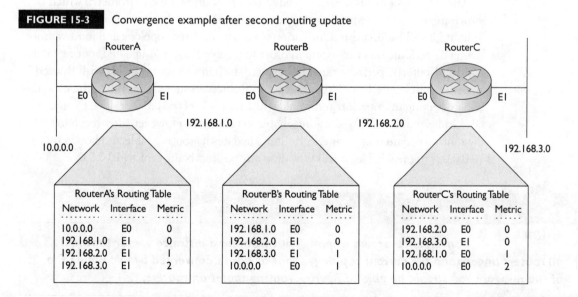

FIGURE 15-4   RouterA's E0 interface has failed.

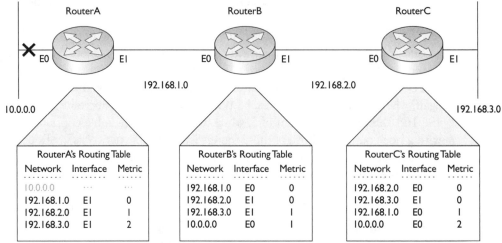

RouterA's Routing Table		
Network	Interface	Metric
10.0.0.0	···	···
192.168.1.0	E1	0
192.168.2.0	E1	1
192.168.3.0	E1	2

RouterB's Routing Table		
Network	Interface	Metric
192.168.1.0	E0	0
192.168.2.0	E1	0
192.168.3.0	E1	1
10.0.0.0	E0	1

RouterC's Routing Table		
Network	Interface	Metric
192.168.2.0	E0	0
192.168.3.0	E1	0
192.168.1.0	E0	1
10.0.0.0	E0	2

Let's use the same network, but assume that RouterA's E0 interface has failed and that RouterA has lost its connection to network 10.0.0.0, as shown in Figure 15-4. As you can see in this example, RouterA's routing table lists the network as unreachable. Unfortunately, RouterA cannot tell the rest of the network concerning the downed route until its periodic timer expires.

After the timer expires, RouterA advertises its routing table to RouterB, which is shown in Figure 15-5. After RouterB receives its update, it has converged. However, RouterC is still lacking this information about the updated topology and must wait for RouterB's periodic timer to expire in order to receive RouterB's updated routing table.

After RouterB's periodic timer has expired, it shares its routing table with RouterC, as is shown in Figure 15-6. Up to this point, RouterC assumed that it had the most up-to-date routing information and would still send packets to 10.0.0.0, since the routing table indicated that 10.0.0.0 was reachable via RouterB. However, after receiving the routing update from RouterB, RouterC updates its routing table and knows that 10.0.0.0 is not reachable; it will now drop any packets being sent to 10.0.0.0.

FIGURE 15-5 RouterB receives the updated information.

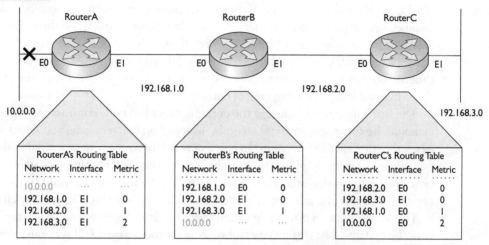

Now all three routers have converged. Here are the three things that affected convergence in this example: the time it took for RouterA to discover that E0 failed (a few seconds); the periodic timer on RouterA to advertise this to RouterB (up to 60 seconds); and the periodic timer on RouterB to advertise this to RouterC (up to 60 seconds). Given these three items, it could take more than 2 minutes to converge. As you can see from the past two examples, convergence with distance vector protocols is a slow process.

FIGURE 15-6 RouterC receives the updated information.

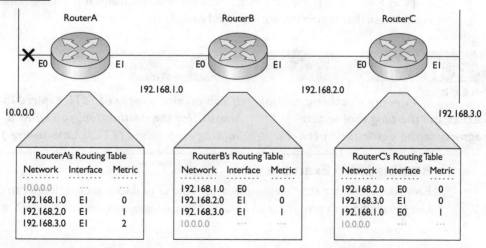

Solution: Triggered Updates

Now that you understand some of the problems associated with convergence in distance vector protocols, consider one possible solution. Given the three things listed in the preceding paragraph that affected convergence with the unreachable network (10.0.0.0), the two things that slowed down convergence were periodic timers. You can actually use two solutions to speed convergence: change the periodic timer interval and/or use triggered updates.

The first solution is to change the periodic timer interval. For instance, in our example the timer was set to 60 seconds. To speed up convergence, you might want to set the interval to 10 seconds. In this example, then, convergence would take only about 20 seconds. However, in today's networks, even waiting this amount of time creates network disruptions. Also, by setting the timer to 10 seconds, you are creating six times the amount of routing broadcast traffic, which is not very efficient.

The second solution is to implement triggered updates. Triggered updates complement periodic updates. The distance vector routing protocol would still generate periodic updates; however, whenever a change took place, the router would immediately generate an update without waiting for the periodic timer to expire. This can decrease convergence times, but it also creates a problem. If you had a flapping route, an update would be triggered each time the route changed state, which would create a lot of unnecessary broadcast traffic in your network and could cause a broadcast storm.

Problem: Routing Loops

The other main problem of distance vector protocols is that they are prone to routing loops. A *routing loop* is a layer 3 loop in the network. Basically, it is a disagreement about how a destination network should be reached.

watch
To verify whether a routing loop exists, use the ping tool to test connectivity to the destination network: if you receive a reply of "TTL expired in transit" for the destination, you know a routing loop exists. (TTL is time-to-live.)

Routing Loop Example

Let's take a look at a simple example of the kind of problems routing loops can create. Use the network shown in Figure 15-7. In this example, assume that RouterX was originally advertising 192.168.4.0 to RouterA, which passed this on to RouterB. RouterX, though, has failed and is no longer advertising 192.168.4.0. RouterA will eventually learn this by missing routing updates from RouterX. RouterA then incorporates the change into its routing table. RouterA must then wait for its periodic timer to expire before forwarding this update to RouterB. Before this happens, however, RouterB advertises its routing table to RouterA, which includes the 192.168.4.0 route, making it appear to RouterA that this network is reachable via RouterB. Since both RouterA and RouterB advertise 192.168.4.0 to each other, this creates confusion about how to reach 192.168.4.0, if it can even be reached (and in this case, it can't). In this example, RouterA thinks that to reach 192.168.4.0, it should send these packets to RouterB. RouterB, on the other hand, thinks that to reach 192.168.4.0, it should use RouterA. This is a very simple example of a routing loop. Typically, routing loops are created because of confusion in the network related to the deficiencies of using periodic timers.

Distance vector protocols use several mechanisms to deal with routing loop problems. However, these solutions slow down convergence. Link state and some hybrid protocols deal with routing loops better by using more intelligent methods that don't slow down convergence. The following sections cover the methods that a distance vector protocol might implement to solve routing loop problems.

FIGURE 15-7   Simple routing loop example

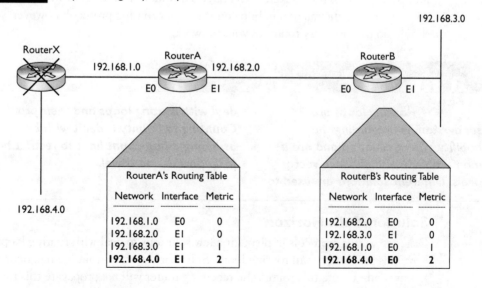

Counting to Infinity Solution: Maximum Hop Count

One problem with a routing loop is called the *counting to infinity* symptom. When a routing loop occurs and a packet or packets are caught in the loop, they continuously circle around the loop, wasting bandwidth on the segments and CPU cycles on the routers that are processing these packets.

To prevent packets from circling around the loop forever, distance vector protocols typically place a hop count limit as to how far a packet is legally allowed to travel. As a packet travels from router to router, a router keeps track of the hops in the TTL field in the IP datagram header: for each hop a packet goes through, the packet's TTL field is decremented by 1. If this value reaches 0, the packet is dropped by the router that decremented the value from 1 to 0. (The function of the TTL field was covered in Chapter 6.)

Placing a maximum hop count limitation on packets, however, doesn't solve routing loop problems—the loop still exists. This solution only prevents packets from getting stuck in the loop. Another issue with placing a hop count limit on packets is that, in some instances, the destination that the packet is trying to reach exceeds the maximum hop count allowed. A router doesn't distinguish between valid destinations and routing loop destinations when examining the TTL field; if the maximum is reached, then the packet is dropped.

RIP sets a hop count limit of 15. When a packet comes into an interface of a router, it decrements the TTL field, and if the hop count falls to 0, the router immediately drops the packet. If you have a destination that is beyond these limits, you can change the maximum hop count for your routing protocol; however, you should do this on every router in your network.

Solution: Split Horizon

Distance vector protocols implement a few solutions to deal with routing loops. *Split horizon* is used with small routing loops. Split horizon states that if a neighboring router sends a route to a router, the receiving router will *not* propagate this route back to the advertising router on the same interface.

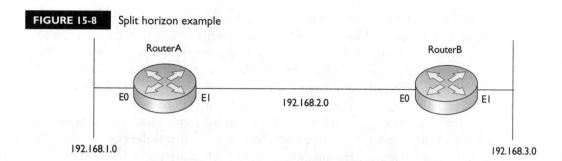

FIGURE 15-8   Split horizon example

RouterA

RouterB

E0   E1   192.168.2.0   E0   E1

192.168.1.0   192.168.3.0

Consider Figure 15-8 to see how split horizon functions. RouterA advertises 192.168.1.0 to RouterB out its E1 interface. Without split horizon in effect, RouterB could advertise this network right back to RouterA. Obviously, RouterA would ignore this, since the directly connected path is better than RouterB's advertised path. However, what would happen if RouterA's E0 interface failed and it received an update from RouterB stating that it had an *alternative* path to 192.168.1.0? In this situation, the network obviously has connectivity problems. With split horizon, though, RouterB would never advertise 192.168.1.0 back to RouterA. Therefore, if RouterA's E0 interface would fail, both RouterA and RouterB would realize that there is no alternative path to reach this network until RouterA's E0 connection is fixed.

Split horizon prevents a router from advertising a route back out the same interface where the router originally learned the route.

Solution: Route Poisoning and Hold-Down Timers

While split horizon is used to solve small routing loop problems, distance vector protocols use two mechanisms to deal with large routing loop problems: *route poisoning* and *hold-down timers*. Route poisoning is a derivative of split horizon. When a router detects that one of its connected routes has failed, the router will *poison* the route by assigning an infinite metric to it. In RIP, the route is assigned a hop count of 16 (15, by default, is the maximum), thus making it an *unreachable* network. When a router advertises a poisoned route to its neighbors, its neighbors break the rule of split horizon and send back to the originator the same poisoned route, called a *poison reverse*. This ensures that everyone received the original poisoned route update.

A poisoned route has an infinite metric assigned to it. A poison reverse causes the router to break the split horizon rule and advertise the poisoned route out all interfaces.

In order to give the routers enough time to propagate the poisoned route and to ensure that no routing loops occur while propagation of the poisoned route occurs, the routers implement a *hold-down* mechanism. During this period, the routers will freeze the poisoned route in their routing tables for the period of the hold-down timer, which is typically three times the interval of the routing broadcast update.

When hold-down timers are used, a poisoned route will remain in the routing table until the timer expires. However, if a router with a poisoned route receives a routing update from a neighboring router with a metric that is the same or better than the original route, the router will abort the hold-down period, remove the poisoned route, and put the new route in its table. Also, if a router receives a worse route from a neighboring router, the router treats this as a suspect route and assumes that this route is probably part of a routing loop, ignoring the update. Of course, the worse metric route really might be a valid alternative path to the network; however, the function of hold-down timers and poisoning routes prohibits the use of this route until the hold period expires. While in a hold-down state, a poisoned route in the routing table will appear as *possibly down*.

One of the problems of using hold-down timers is that they cause the distance vector routing protocol to converge very slowly—if the hold-down period is 180 seconds, you can't use a valid alternative path with a worse metric until the hold-down period expires. Therefore, your users will lose their connections to this network for at least 3 minutes.

e x a m

ⓦ a t c h   *Hold-down timers are used to keep the poisoned route in the routing table long enough so that the poisoned route has a chance to be propagated to all other routers in the network. One downside to hold-down timers is that they slow down convergence.*

Example of Route Poisoning and Hold-Down Timers

Understanding how poisoned routes and hold-down timers work can become complex. Let's take a look at an example to see how these two mechanisms work hand-in-hand to solve large routing loop problems. Use the network shown in Figure 15-9. In this example, assume the routers are running RIPv1.

In this example, RouterA's E0 interface fails, causing it to lose its connection to 192.168.1.0. Since RIPv1 doesn't use triggered updates, the routing protocol must wait for its periodic timer to expire before broadcasting its routing information to

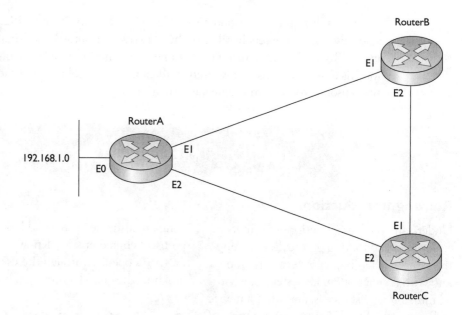

FIGURE 15-9

Route poisoning
and hold-down
timer example

RouterB and RouterC. In RIPv1, the periodic update timer is set to 30 seconds.
RouterA will poison the route (assign an infinite metric of 16 to 192.168.1.0) and
send this to the other two routers when the periodic update timer expires.

When RouterB and RouterC receive the routing update with the poisoned
route from RouterA, they will send back a poison reverse to RouterA. All
routers will freeze the poisoned route in their routing tables for the period of the
hold-down timer. In RIPv1, this defaults to 180 seconds. RouterB and RouterC
also advertise the poisoned route in their routing updates out any other active
interfaces (once their periodic timers expire). As the propagation of the poisoned
route is occurring, the routers that have already received it are counting down
from their hold-down timer value.

If another router in the network advertises a worse path to 192.168.1.0 (this has
to be a worse hop count than the route originally advertised from RouterA), the
three routers shown in the network diagram won't use it, since they have frozen the
poisoned route in their routing tables. The reason for this hold-down period is that
someone else might be advertising 192.168.1.0, but it might not be a valid path.
In other words, another router might be advertising reachability to 192.168.1.0,
but it is assuming that this network is reachable via RouterA. In this situation, this
rogue router hasn't received the poisoned route—the hold-down timer for the other
routers, however, ensures that these rogue routers don't corrupt the routing tables by
introducing incorrect or bad routing information, causing a routing loop.

During this process, if RouterA is able to fix its connection to 192.168.1.0, it will start advertising the reachability of the network to RouterB and RouterC. Since the metric RouterA is advertising is the same as the metric it had previously announced for this route, RouterB and RouterC will cancel their hold-down times and replace the poisoned route with the new information.

INSIDE THE EXAM

Routing Introduction

Understand the basic functions of routers and routed and routing protocols. Knowing the terms in this chapter is very important: know what an autonomous system is, what administrative distance is, and what a metric is. Remember the administrative distances of the different IP routing protocols—be able to pick out what route will show up in the routing protocol based on multiple routing protocols learning the same route.

Dynamic Routing Protocols

Remember the metric components that routing protocols use. Be familiar with how distance vector protocols operate using the Bellman-Ford algorithm, and be able to

compare distance vector and link state protocol characteristics. Know how link state protocols operate through the use of LSAs and how they build a routing table.

Distance Vector Protocol Problems

Understand the problems with distance vector protocols and the solutions employed to solve them. Understand how to find a routing loop by examining a routing table and the solutions used to solve routing loop problems: counting to infinity, split horizon, hold-down timers, poisoned routes, and poisoned reverse. Be familiar with these terms and know what they mean.

CERTIFICATION SUMMARY

Routers find layer 3 paths to destination networks and switch packets from one interface to another to get the packets to their respective destinations. Routers learn about neighboring routers, find locations to destination locations, choose the best paths, and maintain up-to-date routing information. A routed protocol is a layer 3 protocol, such as IP or IPX. A routing protocol defines how to find destinations for a routed protocol, such as RIP or OSPF. Some routing protocols, such as EIGRP, use autonomous systems, which group networks under a single administrative control. Administrative distance is used by a Cisco router to choose among multiple routing protocols to put a destination in the routing table. The routing protocol with the lowest administrative distance with a path to the destination is placed in the routing table.

There are two types of routing protocols: static and dynamic. When choosing a dynamic routing protocol, you should consider routing metrics, how routing information is shared, convergence time, how routing information is processed, and routing overhead. Routing metrics define the method used to calculate a cost to a destination. For instance, RIP uses hop count.

Distance vector protocols use broadcasts to share routing information and don't verify whether neighbors receive routing updates. They use the Bellman-Ford algorithm to process updates, which requires very little CPU processing and memory: They receive an update, increment the metrics, compare the results to the routing table, and update the routing table if necessary.

Link state protocols use the SPF algorithm to build the routing table, providing a loop-free topology. They use multicasts to share routing information incrementally and verify that neighbors received this information. Link state protocols support classless routing and allow you to summarize networking information in your routing table. The main downside of these protocols is that they require more CPU cycles and memory to process and store routing information. They are also prone to flapping route problems.

Hybrid protocols are based on the simplicity of a distance vector protocol but borrow from many features of link state protocols to make them more efficient and scalable. RIPv2, EIGRP, and BGP are examples of hybrid protocols.

Distance vector protocols have problems with convergence and routing loops. Convergence is the amount of time it takes for all of the routers in the network to understand the current topology. Triggered updates can be used to speed up convergence. A routing loop is basically a disagreement about how to reach a particular network. Counting to infinity is resolved by placing a hop count limit to prevent packets from circling around the loop forever. Split horizon is used to prevent the creation of small routing loops: It prevents a router from advertising a route out the same interface from which the route was learned.

Route poisoning, poison reverse, and hold-down timers are used to prevent large routing loops. A route is poisoned if a network connected to a router goes down. Poison reverse has a router advertise a poisoned route out all interfaces, including the interface from which it was learned. Hold-down timers keep the poisoned route in the routing table to ensure the poisoned route is propagated to all routers before any (worse) alternative paths are chosen.

TWO-MINUTE DRILL

Routing Introduction

❑ Routers learn about neighboring routers, find locations of destination networks, choose the best paths to each destination, and maintain routing tables.

❑ A static route is a manually configured route. A connected route is a network to which the router is directly connected on an interface.

❑ An autonomous system (AS) is a group of networks under a single administrative control, which could be your company, a division within your company, or a group of companies.

❑ Administrative distance is a Cisco-proprietary mechanism used to rank IP routing protocols, and it helps the router populate the routing table with best paths to destinations. If you are running more than one routing protocol, administrative distance can determine which routing protocol to use when populating the routing table. The lower the administrative distance number, the more preferred the protocol.

Dynamic Routing Protocols

❑ Internally, a routing protocol will use a metric to choose a best path to reach a destination when more than one path exists to a destination within the same routing protocol.

❑ Distance vector protocols, such as RIPv1, use distance and direction to find paths to a destination and are referred to as routing by rumor. They generate periodic updates as broadcasts and build no formal relationships with other routers. They require little processing and memory, since they simply need to increment metrics and compare these to current networks in the routing table.

❑ Link state protocols, such as OSPF, use the SPF algorithm and understand the complete topology of the network (routing by propaganda). They multicast LSAs, which are specific routes, when changes occur in the network. The LSAs are stored in a link state database. These protocols converge fast, since they use incremental updates, but they require more memory and processing power. They also support a hierarchical structure and route summarization.

❏ Hybrid protocols, such as RIPv2 and EIGRP, take the advantages of both distance vector and link state protocols and merge them together.

Distance Vector Protocol Problems and Solutions

❏ Distance vector protocols converge slowly because of periodic updates. Some protocols overcome this by using triggered updates.

❏ Distance vector protocols are prone to routing loops. To solve this, they use these mechanisms: hop count limits, split horizon, poisoned routes, and hold-down timers.

❏ To prevent packets from circling around the loop forever, distance vector protocols typically place a hop count limit as to how far a packet is legally allowed to travel, referred to as maximum hop count or TTL.

❏ Split horizon states that if a neighboring router sends a route to a router, the receiving router will not propagate this route back to the advertising router on the same interface.

❏ With route poisoning, when a router detects that one of its connected routes has failed, the router will *poison* the route by assigning an infinite metric to it and advertising it to neighbors. When a router advertises a poisoned route to its neighbors, its neighbors break the rule of split horizon and send back to the originator the same poisoned route, called a *poison reverse*. In order to give the routers enough time to propagate the poisoned route and to ensure that no routing loops occur while propagation occurs, the routers implement a hold-down mechanism.

SELF TEST

The following Self Test questions will help you measure your understanding of the material presented in this chapter. Read all the choices carefully, as there may be more than one correct answer. Choose all correct answers for each question.

Routing Introduction

1. _____ is/are a routed protocol.
   A. RIP
   B. OSPF
   C. Both RIP and OSPF
   D. Neither RIP nor OSPF

2. A(n) _____ routes between different autonomous systems.
   A. BPG
   B. EGP
   C. IPP
   D. IGP

3. Your router is running RIP and OSPF and both routing protocols are learning 192.168.1.0/24. Which routing protocol will your router use for this route?
   A. RIP
   B. OSPF

Dynamic Routing Protocols

4. A routing protocol will use a(n) _____ to determine which path is the best path.
   A. Administrative distance
   B. Metric
   C. Hop count
   D. Cost

5. Which type of routing protocol uses the Shortest Path First algorithm?
   A. Distance vector
   B. Link state
   C. Hybrid

6. Which is an example of a hybrid protocol?
   A. IS-IS
   B. EIGRP
   C. RIPv1
   D. OSPF

Distance Vector Protocol Problems and Solutions

7. What would you use to prevent a packet from traveling around a routing loop forever?
   A. Split horizon
   B. Poison reverse
   C. Hold-down timer
   D. TTL

8. _____ states that if a neighboring router sends a route to a router, the receiving router will not propagate this route back to the advertising router on the same interface.
   A. Split horizon
   B. Poison reverse
   C. Hold-down timer
   D. Hop count limit

9. How would you know that a route has been poisoned in the routing table?
   A. It has a metric of 0 assigned to it.
   B. It has an infinite metric assigned to it
   C. It has an administrative distance of 0 assigned to it.
   D. It has an infinite administrative distance assigned to it.

10. You are 10 hops away from a destination network and intermediate routers are running RIP as a routing protocol. You ping a host in the destination network, but the ICMP message you receive back is "TTL expired in transit." What could cause this problem?
    A. A link is down between an intermediate router and the destination network.
    B. There is a mismatch in the administrative distances of RIP.
    C. A routing loop exists.
    D. The destination host has a physical layer problem.

SELF TEST ANSWERS

Routing Introduction

1. ☑ **D.** RIP and OSPF are *routing* protocols, not *routed* protocols. Routed protocols are TCP/IP, IPX, AppleTalk, and so on.
   ☒ Answers **A**, **B**, and **C** are routing protocols, not routed protocols.

2. ☑ **B.** An Exterior Gateway Protocol (EGP) routes between autonomous systems.
   ☒ D routes within an AS. **A** and **C** are nonexistent routing protocols.

3. ☑ **B.** OSPF has a lower administrative distance of 110. The lower one is given preference.
   ☒ A is incorrect because it has a higher administrative distance of 120.

Dynamic Routing Protocols

4. ☑ **B.** A routing protocol will use a metric to determine which path is the best path.
   ☒ A is incorrect because administrative distance is used to choose between different routing protocols, not within a routing protocol. Answers **C** and **D** are types of metrics.

5. ☑ **B.** Link state protocols use the SPF algorithm, developed by Dijkstra, to choose the best path to a destination.
   ☒ A is incorrect because a distance vector uses distance and direction when choosing best paths. C is incorrect because hybrid protocols typically use methods based on distance vector protocols.

6. ☑ **B.** EIGRP is a hybrid protocol, along with RIPv2.
   ☒ A and D are incorrect because IS-IS and OSPF are link state protocols. C is incorrect because RIPv1 is a distance vector protocol.

Distance Vector Protocol Problems and Solutions

7. ☑ **D.** TTL, which implements a hop count limit, prevents an IP packet from traveling around a routing loop forever.
   ☒ A is incorrect because a split horizon is used to prevent small routing loops, preventing the advertisement of a route out the same interface it was learned on. **B** and **C** are used to prevent large routing loops: they allow network stabilization by waiting until every router learns about the downed route before accepting an alternative path.

8. ☑ **A.** Split horizon is used to prevent small routing loops, preventing the advertisement of a route out the same interface on which it was learned.

☒ **B** is incorrect because poison reverse assigns an infinite metric to the route, sends it to a neighboring router, and has the neighbor advertise this back to you. **C** is incorrect because a hold-down timer sets a timer that a poisoned route is held in the routing table. **D** is incorrect because a hop count limit is used to prevent a packet from traveling around a routing loop forever.

9. ☑ **B.** A poisoned route has an infinite metric assigned to it.
   ☒ **A** is incorrect because this would be a directly connected route. Administrative distance ranks different routing protocols, making **C** and **D** incorrect as well.

10. ☑ **C.** If you see a "TTL expired in transit" ICMP message, either the destination is more hops away than the routing protocols supports or a routing loop exists (RIP supports up to 15 hops).
   ☒ **A** and **D** are incorrect because you would receive a network or destination unreachable message from an intermediate router if these were true. **B** is incorrect because administrative distance is used to rank local routing protocols to choose which network is placed in a routing table when two routing protocols tell you about the same network.

16

Initial Router Configuration

his chapter builds upon the configuration concepts discussed in Chapter 11, covering some of the basic commands that you can use to access and configure a Cisco IOS router, which are, as you will see, much like those on the Catalyst IOS switches. The advantage this provides is that you don't have to learn a complete new command-line interface (CLI). The first thing covered is the components of the router and its bootup process, including the use of the *System Configuration Dialog* script: this prompts you for information about how you want to configure your router. You'll also learn about a new feature introduced in version 12.3T code, called *AutoSecure*. Finally, the chapter covers the commands used to create a very basic configuration on your IOS router, including setting up an interface for trunking.

Router Hardware Components

Each IOS device has two main components: hardware and software. Almost every IOS-based router uses the same hardware and firmware components to assist during the bootup process, including the following: ROM (read-only memory), RAM (random access memory), flash, NVRAM (nonvolatile RAM), a configuration register, and physical lines and interfaces. All of these components can affect how the router boots up and finds and loads the operating system and its configuration file. The following sections cover these components in more depth.

Read-Only Memory (ROM)

The software in ROM cannot be changed unless you actually swap out the ROM chip on your router. ROM is nonvolatile—when you turn off your device, the contents of ROM are not erased. ROM contains the firmware necessary to boot up your router and typically has the following four components:

- **POST (power-on self-test)**   Performs tests on the router's hardware components.
- **Bootstrap program**   Brings the router up and determines how the IOS image and configuration files will be found and loaded.

- **ROM Monitor (ROMMON mode)** A mini–operating system that allows you to perform low-level testing and troubleshooting; for instance, ROMMON is used during the password recovery procedure. To abort the router's normal bootup procedure of loading the IOS, use the CTRL-BREAK control sequence to enter ROMMON mode. The prompt in ROMMON mode is either > or rommon>, depending on the router model.

- **Mini-IOS** A stripped-down version of the IOS that contains only IP code. This should be used in emergency situations where the IOS image in flash can't be found and you want to boot up your router and load in another IOS image. This stripped-down IOS is referred to as *RXBOOT* mode. If you see Router(rxboot)# in your prompt, then your router has booted up with the ROM IOS image. Not every router has a Mini-IOS image; on the other hand, some routers, such as the 7200, can store a full-blown IOS image here.

on the
ⓙob

RXBOOT mode, also known as Boot ROM mode, isn't part of newer routers and switches, such as the 1800 and 2600-1 series routers. It does appear on older router models, such as the 2500 series.

eⓍam
ⓦatch

POST performs self-tests on the hardware. The bootstrap program brings the router up and finds the IOS image. ROMMON contains a mini–operating system used for low-level testing and debugging. The Mini-IOS is a stripped-down version of the IOS used for emergency booting of a router and is referred to as RXBOOT mode. All of these components are stored in ROM.

Other Components

Your router contains other components that are used during the bootup process, including RAM, flash, NVRAM, the configuration register, and the physical lines and interfaces. The following paragraphs explain these components.

RAM is like the memory in your PC. On a router, RAM (in most cases) contains the running IOS image, the active configuration file, any tables (including routing, ARP, and other tables), and internal buffers for temporarily storing information such as interface input and output buffers and logging messages. The IOS is responsible for managing memory. When you turn off your router, everything in RAM is erased.

Flash is a form of nonvolatile memory in that when you turn the router off, the information stored in flash is not lost. Routers store their IOS image in flash, but other information can also be stored here, such as a secondary configuration file. Note that some lower end Cisco routers actually run the IOS directly from flash (not RAM). Flash is slower than RAM, a fact that can create performance issues.

NVRAM is like flash in that its contents are not erased when you turn off your router. It is slightly different, though, in that it uses a battery to maintain the information when the Cisco device is turned off. Routers (and switches) use NVRAM to store their configuration files.

The *configuration register* is a special register in the router that determines many of its bootup and running options, including how the router finds the IOS image and its configuration file. The configuration uses a part of memory space in NVRAM. As you will see later in this chapter, you can manipulate this register to affect how your router boots up. You can also use the **boot** command to influence the location from which the IOS and configuration file are loaded (discussed in the "Bootstrap Program" section later).

Every router has at least one line and one physical interface. *Lines* or ports are typically used for management access; the console and auxiliary lines are examples. *Interfaces* are used to move traffic through the router; they can include media types such as Ethernet, Fast Ethernet, serial, and others. These interfaces can be used during the bootup process—you can have the bootstrap program load the IOS from a remote Trivial File Transfer Protocol (TFTP) server (instead of flash), assuming that you have a sufficient IP configuration on your router.

<table>
<tr><td>

e x a m

ⓦatch   *Flash is used to store the operating system and NVRAM is used to store the configuration file. The configuration register is used to determine how the router will boot up.*
</td></tr>
</table>

CERTIFICATION OBJECTIVE 16.02

Router Bootup Process

A router typically goes through five steps when booting up:

1. The router loads and runs POST (located in ROM), testing its hardware components, including memory and interfaces.

2. The bootstrap program is loaded and executed.

3. The bootstrap program finds and loads an IOS image: Possible locations of the IOS image include flash, a TFTP server, or the Mini-IOS in ROM.

4. Once the IOS is loaded, the IOS attempts to find and load a configuration file, which is normally stored in NVRAM—if the IOS cannot find a configuration file, it starts up the System Configuration Dialog.

5. After the configuration is loaded, you are presented with the CLI interface (remember that the first mode you are placed into is User EXEC mode).

16.01. The CD contains a multimedia demonstration of booting up a Cisco router.

If you are connected to the console line, you'll see the following output as your router boots up:

```
System Bootstrap, Version 11.0(10c), SOFTWARE
Copyright (c) 1986-1996 by cisco Systems
2500 processor with 6144 Kbytes of main memory

F3: 5593060+79544+421160 at 0x3000060

Cisco Internetwork Operating System Software
IOS (tm) 2500 Software (C2500-I-L), Version 12.0(5)
Copyright (c) 1986-1999 by cisco Systems, Inc.
Compiled Tue 15-Jun-99 19:49 by phanguye
Image text-base: 0x0302EC70, data-base: 0x00001000
.
.
.

cisco 2504 (68030) processor (revision N) with
    6144K/2048K bytes of memory.
Processor board ID 18086269, with hardware revision
    00000003
Bridging software.
X.25 software, Version 3.0.0.
Basic Rate ISDN software, Version 1.1.
2 Ethernet/IEEE 802.3 interface(s)
2 Serial network interface(s)
32K bytes of non-volatile configuration memory.
16384K bytes of processor board System flash (Read ONLY)

00:00:22: %LINK-3-UPDOWN: Interface Ethernet0, changed
    state to up
```

```
00:00:22: %LINK-3-UPDOWN: Interface Ethernet1, changed
     state to up
  .
  .
  .
Cisco Internetwork Operating System Software
IOS (tm) 2500 Software (C2500-I-L), Version 12.0(5)
Copyright (c) 1986-1999 by cisco Systems, Inc.
Compiled Tue 15-Jun-99 19:49 by phanguye

Press RETURN to get started!
```

You should notice a few things about this output. First, notice that the router is loading the bootstrap program—System Bootstrap, Version 11.0(10c)— and then the IOS image —IOS (tm) 2500 Software (C2500-I-L), Version 12.0(5). During the bootup process, you cannot see the actual POST process (unlike Catalyst switches). However, you will see information about the interfaces going up and/or down—this is where the IOS is loading the configuration and bringing up those interfaces that you previously activated. Sometimes, if the router has a lot of interfaces, the Press RETURN to get started! message is mixed in with the interface messages. Once the display stops, just press ENTER to access User EXEC mode. This completes the bootup process of the router.

When a router boots up, it runs POST, loads the bootstrap program, *finds and loads the IOS, and loads its configuration file—in that order.*

Bootstrap Program

As you saw in the bootup code example, the bootstrap program went out and found the IOS and loaded it. The bootstrap program goes through the following steps when trying to locate and load the IOS image:

1. Examine the configuration register value. This value is a set of four hexadecimal digits. The last digit affects the bootup process. If the last digit is between 0x2 and 0xF, then the router proceeds to the next step. Otherwise, the router uses the values shown in Table 16-1 to determine how it should proceed next.

2. Examine the configuration file in NVRAM for **boot system** commands, which tell the bootstrap program where to find the IOS. These commands are shown in the following paragraph.

3. If no **boot system** commands are found in the configuration file in NVRAM, use the first valid IOS image found in flash.

4. If there are no valid IOS images in flash, generate a TFTP local broadcast to locate a TFTP server (this is called a *netboot* and is not recommended because it is very slow and not very reliable for large IOS images).

5. If no TFTP server is found, load the Mini-IOS in ROM (RXBOOT mode).

6. If there is a Mini-IOS in ROM, then the Mini-IOS is loaded and you are taken into RXBOOT mode; otherwise, the router either retries finding the IOS image or loads ROMMON and goes into ROM Monitor mode.

exam
ⓦatch   *The configuration register is used to influence how the IOS boots up. Remember the values in Table 16-1.*

Table 16-1 contains the three common configuration register values in the fourth hex character of the configuration register that are used to influence the bootup process. The values in the configuration register are represented in *hexadecimal*, the register being 16 bits long.

For step 2 of the bootup process, here are the **boot system** commands that you can use to influence the order that the bootstrap program should use when trying to locate the IOS image:

```
Router(config)# boot system flash name_of_IOS_file_in_flash
Router(config)# boot system tftp IOS_image_name
                            IP_address_of_server
Router(config)# boot system rom
```

TABLE 16-1	Value in *Last* Digit	Bootup Process
Fourth Hex Character Configuration Register Values	0x0	Boot the router into ROMMON mode.
	0x1	Boot the router using the first IOS image in flash or the Mini-IOS in ROM (RXBOOT mode), if the latter exists.
	0x2–0xF	Boot the router using the default boot sequence.

CertCam

16.02. The CD contains a multimedia demonstration of using boot system *commands on a router.*

The **boot system flash** command tells the bootstrap program to load the specified IOS file name in flash when booting up. Note that, by default, the bootstrap program loads the *first* valid IOS image in flash. This command tells the bootstrap program to load an image that's different from the first one. This might be necessary if you perform an upgrade and you have two IOS images in flash—the old one and new one. By default, the old one still loads first (because it appears first in flash) unless you override this behavior with the **boot system flash** command or delete the old IOS flash image. You can also have the bootstrap program load the IOS from a TFTP server—this is not recommended for large images, since the image is downloaded via the User Datagram Protocol (UDP), which is slow. And last, you can tell the bootstrap program to load the Mini-IOS in ROM with the **boot system rom** command. To remove any of these commands, just preface them with the **no** parameter.

on the

job

The order that you enter the boot system *commands is important, since the bootstrap program processes them in the order that you configure them— once the program finds an IOS, it does not process any more* boot system *commands in the configuration file. These commands are also supported on Catalyst IOS switches.*

exam

watch

The boot system *commands can be used to modify the default behavior of where the bootstrap program should load the IOS. When the bootstrap program loads, it examines the configuration file stored in NVRAM for* boot system *commands. If they are found, the IOS uses these commands to find the IOS. If no* boot system *commands are found, the router uses the default behavior in finding and loading the IOS image (first image in flash, a broadcast to a TFTP server, and then the IOS in ROM, if it exists). When the router is booting and you see the message* boot: cannot open "flash:"; *this indicates you misconfigured a* boot system *command and the corresponding IOS image filename in flash doesn't exist.*

System Configuration Dialog

When a router boots up, runs its hardware diagnostics, and loads the IOS software, the IOS then attempts to find a configuration file in NVRAM. If it can't find a configuration file to load, the IOS then runs the System Configuration Dialog, commonly referred to as *Setup* mode, which is a script that prompts you for configuration information. The purpose of this script is to ask you questions that will allow you to set up a basic configuration on your router: It is not intended as a full-functioning configuration tool. In other words, the script doesn't have the ability to perform all the router's configuration tasks. Instead, it is used by novices who are not that comfortable with the IOS CLI. Once you become familiar with the CLI and many of the commands on the router, you'll probably never use this script again.

Running the System Configuration Dialog

As mentioned in the last paragraph, one way to access the System Configuration Dialog is to boot up a router without a configuration in NVRAM. The second way is to use the **setup** Privilege EXEC mode command, shown here:

```
Router# setup
        --- System Configuration Dialog ---
Continue with configuration dialog? [yes/no]: yes
At any point you may enter a question mark '?' for help.
Use ctrl-c to abort configuration dialog at any prompt.
Default settings are in square brackets '[]'.

Basic management setup configures only enough connectivity
for management of the system, extended setup will ask you
to configure each interface on the system

First, would you like to see the current interface summary? [yes]:
Interface IP-Address  OK? Method Status                Protocol
Ethernet0 unassigned  YES unset  administratively down down
Ethernet1 unassigned  YES unset  administratively down down
Serial0   unassigned  YES unset  administratively down down

Would you like to enter basic management setup? [yes/no]: no
Configuring global parameters:
  Enter hostname [Router]:
  The enable secret is a password used to protect access to
  privileged EXEC and configuration modes. This password, after
  entered, becomes encrypted in the configuration.
```

```
Enter enable secret: dealgroup1
The enable password is used when you do not specify an
enable secret password, with some older software versions,
and some boot images.
Enter enable password: dealgroup2
The virtual terminal password is used to protect
access to the router over a network interface.
Enter virtual terminal password: cisco
Configure SNMP Network Management? [no]:
Configure LAT? [yes]: no
Configure AppleTalk? [no]:
Configure DECnet? [no]:
Configure IP? [yes]:
  Configure IGRP routing? [yes]: no
  Configure RIP routing? [no]:
.
.
.
Configuring interface parameters:
Do you want to configure Ethernet0  interface? [no]: yes
  Configure IP on this interface? [no]: yes
    IP address for this interface: 172.16.1.1
    Subnet mask for this interface [255.255.0.0] : 255.255.255.0
    Class B network is 172.16.0.0, 24 subnet bits; mask is /24
Do you want to configure Serial0  interface? [no]:
.
.
.
The following configuration command script was created:
hostname Router
enable secret 5 $1$/CCk$4r7zDwDNeqkxFO.kJxC3G0
enable password dealgroup2
line vty 0 4
 password cisco
.
.
.
end

[0] Go to the IOS command prompt without saving this config.
[1] Return back to the setup without saving this config.
[2] Save this configuration to nvram and exit.
Enter your selection [2]: 2
```

Information included in brackets ([ ]) are default values—if you press ENTER, the value in the brackets is used. One problem with the script is that if you make a mistake, you can't go back to the preceding question. Instead, you must use the CTRL-C break sequence to abort the script and start over. The following sections break down the different components of the script.

The questions that the script asks you might differ from router to router, depending on the hardware model, the interfaces installed in it, and the software running on it.

Status and Global Configuration Information

At the beginning of the script, you are asked whether or not you want to continue. If you answer **yes** or **y**, the script will continue; otherwise, if you answer **no** or **n**, the script is aborted and you are returned to Privilege EXEC mode. The second thing that you are asked is if you want to see the status of the router's interfaces. If you answer **yes**, you'll see all of the interfaces on the router, the interfaces' IP addresses, and the status of the interfaces.

After the status information, you are taken into the actual configuration. The first part of the configuration deals with all configuration information for the router except for the interfaces, which is the second part. In this part of the configuration, you are asked for things like the Privilege EXEC password, VTY password (telnet and SSH), which network protocols you want to activate globally, and other global configuration information.

Note that you are prompted for two Privilege EXEC passwords in the script: `enable secret` *and* `enable password`. *Even though you would normally configure only one, the script requires you to enter both and also requires that both passwords be different.*

Protocol and Interface Configuration Information

After configuring the global information for the router, you are then led through questions about which interfaces you want to use and how they should be configured. The script is smart enough to ask only configuration questions based on how you answered the global questions. As an example, if you activate IP, the script asks you for each activated interface, if you want the interface to process IP, and, if yes, the IP addressing information for the interface.

Exiting Setup Mode

After you answer all of the script's configuration questions, you are shown the router configuration the script created using your answers to the script's questions. Note that the IOS hasn't yet activated the configuration file. Examine the configuration closely and then make one of the three choices shown in Table 16-2. Also, if you enter **1** as your option, when the script starts over again, the information that you previously entered appears in brackets and will be the default values when you press the ENTER key on an empty line.

CertCam

16.03. The CD includes a multimedia demonstration of using the System Configuration Dialog on a Cisco router.

ⓦatch *Remember that the System Configuration Dialog script is started when the router boots up and there is no configuration in NVRAM, or you use the* `setup` *command from Privilege EXEC mode. Also, know the three options at the end of the Setup dialog script. You can press* CTRL-C *to abort the script.*

Configuration Register

As mentioned in the preceding section, the configuration register is used by the bootstrap program to determine the location from which the IOS image and configuration file should be loaded. Once the router is booted up, you can view the configuration register value with the **show version** command:

```
Router> show version
Cisco IOS Software, 1841 Software (C1841-ADVIPSERVICESK9-M),
    Version 12.4(6)T7, RELEASE SOFTWARE (fc5)
Technical Support: http://www.cisco.com/techsupport
```

TABLE 16-2	Option	Description
Options at the End of the System Configuration Dialog	0	Discard the script's configuration and return to Privilege EXEC mode.
	1	Return to the beginning of the script.
	2	Activate the script's configuration, save the configuration to NVRAM, and return to Privilege EXEC mode.

```
Copyright (c) 1986-2007 by Cisco Systems, Inc.
Compiled Thu 29-Mar-07 03:28 by khuie

ROM: System Bootstrap, Version 12.4(13r)T, RELEASE SOFTWARE (fc1)

Router1 uptime is 3 days, 22 hours, 5 minutes
System returned to ROM by reload at 19:06:33 UTC Fri Dec 7 2007
System image file is "flash:c1841-advipservicesk9-mz.124-6.T7.bin"
.
.
.
125K bytes of non-volatile configuration memory.
32768K bytes of processor board System flash (Read/Write)
Configuration register is 0x2102
```

You need to go to the very bottom of the display in order to view the register value.

You can see the system image the router used upon bootup in the `show version` command (`system image file is`). If you misconfigured **the `boot system` commands or are using TFTP for the download, the router might not be able to find and load an IOS.**

Changing the Configuration Register from Configuration Mode

You can change the configuration register value from Configuration mode or from ROMMON mode. If you already have Privilege EXEC access to the router and want to change the register value, use this command:

```
Router(config)# config-register 0xhexadecimal_value
```

The register value is four hexadecimal digits, or 16 bits, in length. Each bit position in the register, though, indicates a function that the bootstrap program should take. Therefore, you should be very careful when configuring this value on your router.

Many sites on the Internet have downloadable configuration register utility programs for Cisco routers. Boson has a free one at this location: http://www .boson.com/FreeUtilities.html. With Boson's utility, you can select or deselect specific boot options, which will automatically generate the correct register value for you.

When entering the register value, you must always precede it with *0x*, indicating that this is a hexadecimal value. If you don't do so, the router assumes the value is decimal and *converts* it to hexadecimal. On Cisco routers, the default configuration register value is *0x2102*, which causes the router to use the default bootup process in finding and locating IOS images and configuration files. If you change this to *0x2142*, this tells the bootstrap program that, upon the next reboot, it should locate the IOS using the default behavior, but *not* to load the configuration file in NVRAM; instead, you are taken directly into the System Configuration Dialog. This is the value that you will use to perform the password recovery procedure.

Changing the Configuration Register from ROM Monitor

Of course, one problem with the Configuration mode method of changing the register value is that you must gain access to Privilege EXEC mode first. This can be a problem if you don't know the passwords on the router. A second method, though, allows you to change the register value without having to log into the router. To use this method, you'll need console access to the router—you can't do this from the auxiliary line or from a VTY session. Next, you'll turn off the router and then turn it back on. As the router starts booting, you'll break into ROMMON mode with the router's break sequence. To break into the router, once you see the bootstrap program has loaded, you can, in most cases, use the CTRL-BREAK control sequence to break into ROMMON mode. Note that this control sequence may differ, depending on the terminal emulation program you are using on your PC.

Once in ROMMON mode, you can begin the process of changing the register value using one of two methods, depending on the router model that you have. Some of Cisco's routers, such as the 1800 and 2600-1, use the **confreg** command. This script asks you basic questions about the function and bootup process of the router. What's nice about the script is that you don't need to know the hexadecimal values for the configuration register, since the router will create them for you as you answer these questions. Here is an example of using this script:

```
rommon 5 > confreg
    Configuration Summary
enabled are:
load rom after netboot fails
console baud: 9600
boot: image specified by the boot system commands
    or default to: cisco2-C3600

do you wish to change the configuration? y/n   [n]:  y
enable  "diagnostic mode"? y/n   [n]:
enable  "use net in IP bcast address"? y/n   [n]:
disable "load rom after netboot fails"? y/n   [n]:
enable  "use all zero broadcast"? y/n   [n]:
enable  "break/abort has effect"? y/n   [n]:
enable  "ignore system config info"? y/n   [n]:
change console baud rate? y/n   [n]:
change the boot characteristics? y/n   [n]:

    Configuration Summary
enabled are:
load rom after netboot fails
console baud: 9600
boot: image specified by the boot system commands
    or default to: cisco2-C3600
do you wish to change the configuration? y/n   [n]:  n
rommon 6 >
```

16.04. The CD contains a multimedia demonstration of changing the configuration register in ROMMON mode (`confreg`) and using the IOS CLI `config-register` command on a router.

Just as in the System Configuration Dialog, any information in brackets ([ ]) represents default values. The first question that it asks is if you want to "change the configuration," which means change the register: answer y to continue. If you answer **y** to ignore system config info, the third hexadecimal digit becomes 4, making a router's register value appear as *0x2142*. This option is used when you want to perform the password recovery procedure. The next-to-last question is change the boot characteristics—this question, if you answer y, will repeat the questions again. Answer **n** to exit the script. If you make any changes, you are asked to save them (do you wish to change the configuration?)—answer y to save your new register value. Once you are done changing the register, reboot the router. On many routers, just type in the letter **i** or **b** in ROMMON mode to boot it up.

As a shortcut, you could also execute the following command from ROMMON mode: `confreg 0x2142`.

exam watch

When performing the password recovery procedure, break into ROMMON mode and change the configuration register value to 0x2142 and boot up the router. Once booted up, the router will ignore the configuration in NVRAM and take you into the System Configuration Dialog. Using CTRL-C will break you out of this utility and take you to User EXEC mode. Enter Privilege EXEC mode and restore your configuration with the `copy startup-config running-config` command. The `no shutdown` command is not listed in the router's NVRAM configuration, so you will have to enable the interfaces manually. This is also true if you copy and paste a configuration into a router with its interfaces disabled, such as a newly booted router.

CERTIFICATION OBJECTIVE 16.03

AutoSecure

AutoSecure is a new IOS feature on newer model routers, such as the 870s and 1800s, that allows you to put a basic security configuration on your router. It was introduced in IOS 12.3 and 12.3T. It is a Privilege EXEC script similar to the System Configuration Dialog: where the latter creates a basic configuration for a router, AutoSecure focuses only on security functions for securing a router. Like the setup script, AutoSecure asks you basic questions about securing your router. It will automatically enable or disable specific services running on your router; set up a stateful firewall by configuring Context-Based Access Control (CBAC), which requires a security IOS image; configure access control lists (ACLs are discussed in Chapter 22); and perform other tasks.

To run the AutoSecure script, from Privilege EXEC mode execute the **auto secure** command:

```
Router#  auto secure [management | forwarding] [no-interact]
```

You can run AutoSecure in two modes:

- **Interactive**   You are prompted for security information during the scripting process.
- **Non-interactive**   The IOS performs all security functions based on a set of defaults from Cisco.

AutoSecure basically secures the router at two levels:

- Management plane (traffic destined to the router)
- Forwarding plane (traffic going through the router)

With no extra parameters with the **auto secure** command, the router will secure both the management and forwarding planes while asking you questions about the security process.

Here is an example of running the AutoSecure script:

```
Router# auto secure
               --- AutoSecure Configuration ---

*** AutoSecure configuration enhances the security of
the router, but it will not make it absolutely resistant
to all security attacks ***

AutoSecure will modify the configuration of your device.
All configuration changes will be shown. For a detailed
explanation of how the configuration changes enhance security
and any possible side effects, please refer to Cisco.com for
Autosecure documentation.
At any prompt you may enter '?' for help.
Use ctrl-c to abort this session at any prompt.

Gathering information about the router for AutoSecure

Is this router connected to internet? [no]: yes
Enter the number of interfaces facing the internet [1]: 1

Interface        IP-Address   OK? Method Status   Protocol
FastEthernet0/0  10.0.6.2     YES NVRAM  up       up
```

```
FastEthernet0/1   172.30.6.2  YES NVRAM  up          up
Enter the interface name that is facing the internet:
  FastEthernet0/1

Securing Management plane services...
Disabling service finger
Disabling service pad
Disabling udp & tcp small servers
Enabling service password encryption
Enabling service tcp-keepalives-in
Enabling service tcp-keepalives-out
Disabling the cdp protocol
  .
  .
  .
Here is a sample Security Banner to be shown
at every access to device. Modify it to suit your
enterprise requirements.

Authorized Access only
   This system is the property of So-&-So-Enterprise.
   UNAUTHORIZED ACCESS TO THIS DEVICE IS PROHIBITED.
  .
  .
  .
Enter the security banner {Put the banner between
k and k, where k is any character}:
$
Keep Out...This means you!
$
Enable secret is either not configured or
 is the same as enable password
Enter the new enable secret: cisco1234
Confirm the enable secret : cisco1234
Enter the new enable password: cisco5678
Confirm the enable password: cisco5678

Configuration of local user database
Enter the username: richard
Enter the password: mypassword123
Confirm the password: mypassword123
Configuring AAA local authentication
Configuring Console, Aux and VTY lines for
 local authentication, exec-timeout, and transport
Securing device against Login Attacks
```

```
Configure the following parameters
Blocking Period when Login Attack detected: 3
Maximum Login failures with the device: 3
Maximum time period for crossing the failed login attempts: 30
Configure SSH server? [yes]: yes
Enter the domain-name: richarddeal.com

Configuring interface specific AutoSecure services
Disabling the following ip services on all interfaces:
 no ip redirects
 no ip proxy-arp
 no ip unreachables
 no ip directed-broadcast
 no ip mask-reply
Disabling mop on Ethernet interfaces

Securing Forwarding plane services...
Enabling CEF (This might impact the memory requirements for
 your platform)
Enabling unicast rpf on all interfaces connected to internet

Configure CBAC Firewall feature? [yes/no]: yes

This is the configuration generated:
no service finger
no service pad
no service udp-small-servers
no service tcp-small-servers
service password-encryption
service tcp-keepalives-in
service tcp-keepalives-out
no cdp run
.
.
.
banner motd ^C
Keep Out...This means you!
^C
.
.
.
enable secret 5 $1$yc/V$99CEHvCR7KoZ/ZznqByyx0
enable password 7 045802150C2E1D1C5A
username richard password 7 083145560E0C1702
.
.
.
```

```
ip domain-name cisco.com
crypto key generate rsa general-keys modulus 1024
ip ssh time-out 60
ip ssh authentication-retries 2
line vty 0 15
 transport input ssh telnet
 .
 .
 .
interface FastEthernet0/0
 no ip redirects
 no ip proxy-arp
 no ip unreachables
 no ip directed-broadcast
 no ip mask-reply
 no mop enabled
interface FastEthernet0/1
 .
 .
 .
ip cef
interface FastEthernet0/1
 ip verify unicast source reachable-via rx allow-default 100
 .
 .
 .
ip inspect name autosec_inspect ftp timeout 3600
ip inspect name autosec_inspect http timeout 3600
 .
 .
 .
ip inspect name autosec_inspect udp timeout 15
ip inspect name autosec_inspect tcp timeout 3600
ip access-list extended autosec_firewall_acl
 permit udp any any eq bootpc
 deny ip any any
interface FastEthernet0/1
 ip inspect autosec_inspect out
 ip access-group autosec_firewall_acl in
end
Apply this configuration to running-config? [yes]: yes
Applying the config generated to running-config
The name for the keys will be: Router6.richarddeal.com
% The key modulus size is 1024 bits
% Generating 1024 bit RSA keys, keys will be non-
    exportable...[OK]
000018: *Oct  5 16:09:57.467 UTC: %AUTOSEC-1-MODIFIED:
    AutoSecure configuration has been Modified on this device
```

During any of the prompts, you can type in the *?* to bring up help, or press CTRL-C to abort the script. At the beginning of the script, you are asked if the router is connected to the Internet. If so, tell AutoSecure which interface (or interfaces) is connected to the Internet so that it can set up its security policies correctly. In the preceding example, Fast Ethernet0/1 is connected to the Internet.

16.05. The CD contains a multimedia demonstration of running AutoSecure.

At this point, global services for the Management plane are enabled or disabled. In this section you are asked to create a login banner, where an example is provided. To start the banner, enter a delimiting character that won't show up in the text, such as ^ or #. When you type in this character the second time, this will end the banner (just as with the **banner** command discussed in Chapter 11). Authentication, authorization, and accounting (AAA) and SSH are then configured. Following this, AutoSecure disables certain services under all of the router's interfaces.

At this point, AutoSecure will enable Cisco Express Forwarding (CEF), enable Context-Based Access Control (CBAC), and create an ACL to block unwanted IP traffic. This finishes the script and AutoSecure displays the configuration it will activate on the router. Press the ENTER key or enter *yes* to accept and activate the configuration.

Cisco recommends running the AutoSecure script after you run the System Configuration Dialog, but before you begin any other advanced configuration tasks from the CLI. If you don't run the System Configuration Dialog, put a basic configuration on your router, such as configuring and enabling the interfaces and configuring a routing protocol, and then run AutoSecure.

CERTIFICATION OBJECTIVE 16.04

Router Configuration

This chapter builds upon the basic IOS configuration commands discussed in Chapter 11, where you were shown how to move around the CLI, change the name of the device, configure passwords, configure hardware characteristics for an interface, and enable an interface. This section discusses these fundamentals in addition to router-specific commands to use for a basic configuration.

Interface Configuration

This section on router configuration covers additional interface configurations, such as configuring assigning an IP address to an interface and changing the bandwidth metric. Following sections will discuss some **show** commands to verify your interface's configuration.

IP Addressing Information

You can use many commands on the router to set up your IP addressing information. One of the most common is to assign an IP address to an interface; however, many more commands, including the setup of DNS, restricting directed broadcasts, and others, can be used. The following sections cover some of these configurations.

Unlike layer 2 switches (such as the 2960), which need only a single IP address for remote management, routers need a unique IP address on each interface that will route IP traffic. Actually, each interface on a router is a separate network or subnet, and therefore you need to plan your IP addressing appropriately and assign a network number to each router segment and then take an unused host address from the segment and configure it on the interface of the router. This address then becomes the default gateway for devices connected to that interface. IP addressing and its components are discussed in Chapter 7.

Let's look at a couple of examples of incorrectly and correctly assigning IP addresses to a router's interfaces. Figure 16-1 shows an invalid configuration example. In this example, only one network number is used: 192.168.1.0/24. Notice that *each* interface on the router has an address from this same network number. Actually, if you would try to configure this addressing scheme on a router, you would get an overlapping address error and be prevented from completing the addressing configuration.

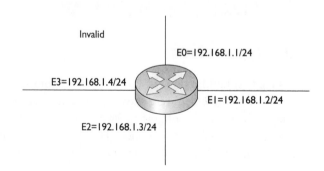

FIGURE 16-1

Invalid addressing
configuration for
a router

Invalid

E0=192.168.1.1/24

E3=192.168.1.4/24

E1=192.168.1.2/24

E2=192.168.1.3/24

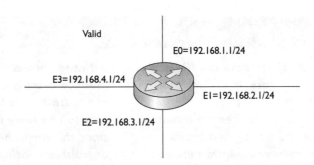

FIGURE 16-2

Correct
addressing
configuration for
a router

Each interface needs a unique host address, as is shown in Figure 16-2. Notice
that in this example, each interface has an address from a *different* network number
when compared to the other interfaces on the router. Which host address you
choose for the router interface is up to personal preference. Many administrators use
either the first or last host address in the network number for the router's interface,
but any valid, unused host address from that network number can be used.

As you have probably already guessed, configuring an IP address on a router requires
that you be in Interface Subconfiguration mode. Here is the syntax of this command:

```
Router(config)# interface type [slot_#/]port_#
Router(config-if)# ip address IP_address subnet_mask
```

This syntax, as you can see, is the same as that used for configuring an IP address on
the 2960 switch (but under the VLAN interface). You can verify your IP addressing
configuration with the **show interfaces** or **show ip interfaces** command,
discussed later in this section.

*16.06. The CD includes a multimedia demonstration of configuring an IP
address on an interface of a Cisco router.*

Using the example in Figure 16-2, the following would be the router's IP
addressing configuration:

```
Router(config)# interface ethernet 0
Router(config-if)# ip address 192.168.1.1 255.255.255.0
Router(config-if)# no shutdown
Router(config-if)# exit
Router(config)# interface ethernet 1
Router(config-if)# ip address 192.168.2.1 255.255.255.0
Router(config-if)# no shutdown
```

If you omit the IP address on a router's interface, it will not process any IP traffic on that interface. If you misconfigured an IP address on a router's interface, use the `no ip address` command to remove it. Optionally, you can use the `ip address` command

with the correct IP address and subnet mask to overwrite the existing IP address configuration on the interface. Remember how to configure IP addressing on a router, since this might be part of a configuration or troubleshooting simulation question.

Bandwidth Parameter

All interfaces have a bandwidth value assigned to them. This is used by certain routing protocols, such as Open Shortest Path First (OSPF) and Enhanced Interior Gateway Routing Protocol (EIGRP), when making routing decisions. (Routing protocols are covered in Chapters 15, 19, 20, and 21.) For LAN-based interfaces, the speed of the interface becomes the bandwidth value, where the bandwidth is measured in kilobits per second (Kbps). However, on synchronous serial interfaces, the bandwidth defaults to 1554 Kbps, or the speed of a T1 link. This is true no matter what the physical clock rate is on the interface (discussed in Chapter 11 with the **clock rate** command). To change the bandwidth value for an interface, use the **bandwidth** Interface Subconfiguration mode command:

```
Router(config)# interface serial [slot_#/]port_#
Router(config-if)# bandwidth rate_in_Kbps
```

As an example, a serial interface clocked at 56,000 bps should have its bandwidth value changed to 56 Kbps, like this:

```
Router(config)# interface serial 0
Router(config-if)# bandwidth 56
```

Note that the `bandwidth` command does not change the clock rate on an interface: the `clock rate`

command does this. The `bandwidth` command affects only routing protocols that use bandwidth as a metric.

The show ip interface Command

Common verification commands that you will use on a router are the **show interfaces** (discussed in Chapter 11) and **show ip interface** commands. The latter command displays the IP configuration of your router's interfaces, including its IP address and subnet mask:

```
Router> show ip interface [type [slot_#/]port_#]
```

Here is an abbreviated output of the **show ip interface** command:

```
Router# show ip interface
Ethernet1 is up, line protocol is up
  Internet address is 192.168.1.1/24
  Broadcast address is 255.255.255.255
  Address determined by setup command
  MTU is 1500 bytes
  Helper address is not set
  Directed broadcast forwarding is disabled
  Outgoing access list is not set
  Inbound  access list is 100
  .
  .
  .
```

Use the show ip interface command to determine whether an ACL is applied to an interface.

As you can see from this command, the status of the interface is shown, the IP address and mask are displayed, and direct broadcasts will be dropped if received on the interface. Any access list applied to the interface is also displayed. Access lists are explained in Chapter 22.

An additional parameter to the preceding command, **brief**, will display a single-line description for each interface, as shown here:

```
Router# show ip interface brief
Interface   IP-Address  OK? Method Status                Protocol
Ethernet0   192.168.1.1 YES NVRAM  up                    up
Ethernet1   192.168.2.1 YES NVRAM  administratively down down
```

16.07. The CD includes a multimedia demonstration of using the show ip interface command.

This is an extremely useful command when you want to see a quick overview of all of the interfaces on the router, their IP addresses, and their statuses. This command also works on switches.

Use the `show ip` `interface brief` command to see	a quick overview of the IP addresses on interfaces and their operational state.

Subnet Zero Configuration

Starting with IOS 12.0, Cisco automatically allows you to use IP subnet zero networks—the first network number in a subnetted network (subnet zero is discussed in Chapter 7). Prior to IOS 12.0, you were not, by default, allowed to use these subnets. However, you could enable their use if you needed extra networks by configuring the **ip subnet-zero** command:

```
Router(config)# ip subnet-zero
```

In IOS 12.0 and later, this command will already be in the router's configuration.

Understand the use of the `ip subnet-zero` command and be able	to pick out subnet zero subnets.

Static Host Configuration

As you are well aware, in the IP world, we typically don't type in an IP address to reach a destination. For example, if you want to reach Cisco's site, in your web browser address bar, you type *www.cisco.com* or *http://www.cisco.com*. Your web browser then resolves the host and domain names to an IP address. The router also supports hostnames for certain operations, such as ping and telnet (discussed in Chapter 17).

You can have your router resolve hostnames to IP addresses in two ways: static and dynamic (using DNS). You can create a static resolution table using this command:

```
Router(config)# ip host name_of_host [TCP_port_#]
                    IP_address_of_host [2nd_IP_address...]
```

You must first specify the name of the remote host. Optionally, you can specify a port number for the host—this defaults to 23 for telnet if you omit it. After this, you can list up to eight IP addresses for this host. The router will try to reach the host with the first address, and if that fails, it will try the second address, and so on and so forth. Use the **show hosts** command to examine your static entries, which are discussed following the next section.

DNS Resolution Configuration

If you have access to a DNS server or servers, you can have your router use these to resolve names to IP addresses. This is configured with the **ip name-server** command:

```
Router(config)# ip name-server IP_address_of_DNS_server
                    [2nd_server's_IP address ...]
```

You can list up to six DNS servers for the router to use with this command. Use the **show hosts** command to examine your static and dynamic entries. This command is discussed in the next section.

Many administrators don't like using DNS to resolve names to addresses on routers, because of one nuisance feature on the router: Whenever you type a nonexistent command on the router, the router assumes you are trying to telnet to a device by that *name* and tries to resolve it to an IP address. This is annoying because either you have to wait for the DNS query to time out or you must execute the break sequence (CTRL-SHIFT-6).

o n   t h e
job

One of the first things I typically configure on a router is the no ip domain-lookup *command so that when I mistype commands, I don't have to wait for the router to attempt to resolve the mistyped command to an IP address.*

You have another option, though, and that is to disable DNS lookups on the router with the following command:

```
Router(config)# no ip domain-lookup
```

16.08. The CD includes a multimedia demonstration of using and disabling name resolution on a Cisco router.

The show hosts Command

To view the static and dynamic DNS entries in your router's resolution table, use this command:

```
Router# show hosts
Default domain is CHECK.COM
Name/address lookup uses domain service
Name servers are 255.255.255.255
Host            Flag       Age   Type   Address(es)
a.check.com     (temp, OK) 1     IP     172.16.9.9
b.check.com     (temp, OK) 8     IP     172.16.1.1
f.check.com     (perm, OK) 0     IP     172.16.1.2
```

The first two entries in the table were learned via a DNS server (temp flag), whereas the last entry was configured statically on the router with the **ip host** command (perm flag).

EXERCISE 16-1

Using IOS Features

The last few sections have covered how you configure basic IP addressing features on your Cisco router. You can perform the following exercises on a Cisco router to enforce these skills. Use the router simulator included on the CD-ROM, or you can use a real Cisco router. You can find a picture of the network diagram for the simulator in the Introduction to this book.

Access the simulator and click the Lab Navigator button. Double-click Exercise 16-1, click the Load Lab button, and then click the OK button. This will load a basic configuration on devices in the network topology, including IP addresses on the Host PCs, based on exercises in Chapters 11 and 12.

1. Access the 2600-1 router. Click the eRouters button and choose 2600-1.
2. Configure an IP address of 192.168.1.1/24 on fastethernet0/0 of the 2600-1 router and bring the interface up.
   Go to Privilege EXEC mode and type this: **configure terminal**, **interface fastethernet0/0**, **ip address 192.168.1.1 255.255.255.0**, **no shutdown**, and **exit**.

3. Configure an IP address of 192.168.2.1/24 on the serial0 interface, set the clock rate to 64,000 bps, and enable the interface.

   Configure serial0: **interface serial0**, **ip address 192.168.2.1 255.255.255.0**, **clock rate 64000**, **no shutdown**, and **exit**. Return to Privilege EXEC mode by typing **end**.

4. Save the configuration file on the router: **copy running-config startup-config**.

5. Test connectivity between the Host-1 PC and the 2600-1.
   Click the eStations icon within the simulator and select Host-1. Test the connection from Host-1 by pinging the 2600-1: **ping 192.168.1.1**. The ping should be successful.

6. Access the 2600-2 router: Click the eRouters button and choose 2600-2.

7. Configure an IP address of 192.168.3.1/24 on fastethernet0/0 of the 2600-2 router and bring up the interface.
   Go to Privilege EXEC mode and type this: **configure terminal**, **interface fastethernet0/0**, **ip address 192.168.3.1 255.255.255.0**, **no shutdown**, and **exit**.

8. Configure an IP address of 192.168.2.2/24 on the serial0 interface and enable the interface.
   Configure serial0: **interface serial0**, **ip address 192.168.2.2 255.255.255.0**, **no shutdown**, and **exit**. Return to Privilege EXEC mode by typing **end**.

9. Save the configuration file on the router: **copy running-config startup-config**.

10. Test connectivity between the 2600-2 and 2600-1 router: **ping 192.168.2.1**. The ping should be successful.

11. Test connectivity between the Host-3 PC and the 2600-2.
    Click the eStations icon within the simulator and select Host-3. Test the connection from Host-3 by pinging the 2600-2: **ping 192.168.3.1**. The ping should be successful.

You should now be more familiar with configuring IP addressing information on a router.

CERTIFICATION OBJECTIVE 16.05

Router-on-a-Stick

Typically, we think of routing as traffic coming in one physical interface and leaving another physical interface. As you learned in Chapter 13, however, trunks can be used to support multiple VLANs, where each VLAN has a unique layer 3 network or subnet number. Certain router models and interface combinations, such as the 1800 series, support trunk connections. A *router-on-a-stick* is a router that has a single trunk connection to a switch and routes between the VLANs on this trunk connection. You could easily do this without a trunk (access-link connections), but each VLAN would require a separate access-link (physical) interface on the router, and this would increase the price of the router solution.

For instance, if you had five VLANs, and your router didn't support trunking, you would need five physical LAN interfaces on your router in order to route between the five VLANs. However, with a trunk connection, you can route between all five VLANs on a *single* interface. Because of cost and scalability, most administrators prefer using a router-on-a-stick approach to solve their routing problems in switched networks.

watch   *A router-on-a-stick is a router that has a single trunk connection to a switch and routes between different VLANs on this trunk. Subinterfaces are used on the router to designate the VLAN with which they are associated.*

Subinterface Configuration

To set up a router-on-a-stick, you need to break up your router's physical interface into multiple logical interfaces, called *subinterfaces*. Cisco supports up to 1000 interfaces on a router, which includes both physical and logical interfaces. Once you create a subinterface, a router will treat this logical interface just like a physical interface: you can assign layer 3 addressing to it, enable, it, disable it, and do many other things.

To create a subinterface, use the following command:

```
Router(config)# interface type port_#.subinterface_#
                        [point|multipoint]
Router(config-subif)#
```

After entering the physical interface type and port identifier, follow this with a dot (.) and a subinterface number. The subinterface number can range from 0 to 4,294,967,295. The number that you use for the subinterface number is only for reference purposes within the IOS, and the only requirement is that when creating a subinterface, you use a unique subinterface number. Many administrators prefer to use the VLAN number that the subinterface will handle for the subinterface number; however, this is not a requirement and the two numbers are not related in any way.

At the end of the statement, you must specify the type of connection *if* the interface is of type serial; otherwise, you can omit it. The **point** parameter is used for point-to-point serial connections, and **multipoint** is used for multipoint connections (many devices connected to the interface). The **multipoint** parameter is used for connections that have more than one device connected to them (physically or logically). For a router-on-a-stick configuration, you can omit the connection type, since the default is **multipoint** for LAN interfaces.

Interface Encapsulation

Once you create a subinterface, you'll notice that your CLI prompt has changed and that you are now in Subinterface Configuration mode. If you are routing between VLANs, you'll need an interface that supports trunking. Some things are configured on the major interface and some things are configured on the subinterface. Configurations such as duplexing and speed are done on the major (or physical) interface. Most other tasks are done on the subinterface (the logical interface), including to which VLAN the subinterface belongs and its IP addressing information.

CertCam

16.09. The CD contains a multimedia demonstration of setting up a router-on-a-stick.

When setting up your subinterface for a router-on-a-stick, one thing that you must configure is the type of trunking—ISL or 802.1Q—and the VLAN with which the subinterface is associated, like this:

```
Router(config)# interface type port_#.subinterface_#
Router(config-subif)# encapsulation isl|dot1q VLAN_#
```

Use the **encapsulation** command to specify the trunk type and the VLAN associated with the subinterface. The VLAN number you specify here *must* correspond to the correct VLAN number in your switched network. You must also set up a trunk connection on the switch for the port to which the router is connected. Once you do this, the switch will send tagged frames to the router, and the router, using your encapsulation, will understand how to read the tags. The router will be able to see from which VLAN the frame came and match it up with the appropriate subinterface that will process it. Remember that only a few of Cisco's switches today support ISL: all of them support 802.1Q, which is denoted with the **dot1q** parameter.

Be familiar with how to create a subinterface with the `interface` **command. The router and switch must be** **using the same VLAN encapsulation type: 802.1Q or ISL.**

Router-on-a-Stick Example Configuration

Let's look at an example to see how a router-on-a-stick is configured. Figure 16-3 shows this configuration. Assume that this is a 3800 router, that the Fast Ethernet interface is the first interface in the first slot, and that the switch is using 802.1Q trunking on the connected interface.

Here's the code example for this router:

```
Router(config)# interface fastethernet0/0
Router(config-if)# duplex full
Router(config-if)# no shutdown
```

FIGURE 16-3

Router-on-a-stick example

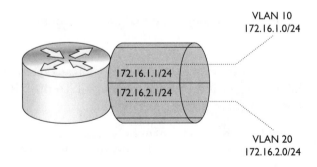

VLAN 10
172.16.1.0/24

172.16.1.1/24

172.16.2.1/24

VLAN 20
172.16.2.0/24

```
Router(config-if)# exit
Router(config)# interface fastethernet0/0.1
Router(config-subif)# encapsulation dot1q 10
Router(config-subif)# ip address 172.16.1.1 255.255.255.0
Router(config-subif)# exit
Router(config)# interface fastethernet0/0.2
Router(config-subif)# encapsulation dot1q 20
Router(config-subif)# ip address 172.16.2.1 255.255.255.0
Router(config-subif)# exit
```

Notice in this example that the subinterface numbers in the **interface** command (1 and 2) do not match the VLAN numbers in the **encapsulation** command (10 and 20); remember that the subinterface numbers are used by the IOS only to reference the particular subinterface and do not have to match any configuration on the subinterface.

on the Job *If you are configuring static routes and want to route traffic out of a particular subinterface, specify the major interface along with the subinterface number, such as `fastethernet0/0.2`. Static routes are discussed in Chapter 19.*

INSIDE THE EXAM

Router Hardware Components

You should be familiar with the different hardware components, what they are used for, and how they affect the bootup process.

Router Bootup Process

You should be familiar with how the router boots up and finds its IOS and configuration file. Understand the use of the configuration register, especially the difference between 0x2102 and 0x2142. Be able to interpret the configuration register value based on the last hexadecimal digit in the configuration

register and how this affects the router's bootup process. Understand the use of the **boot system** commands and issues if you misconfigured these commands. Use the **show version** command to verify these settings. Remember that the System Configuration Dialog will start automatically if the router boots up and can't find its configuration file in NVRAM. Be familiar with how the password recovery process is performed from ROMMON mode.

(Continued)

AutoSecure

Understand what the AutoSecure feature does in the IOS.

Router Configuration

A router must have an IP address on its interface or it will not process any IP packets on the interface. You should be able to put a basic configuration on a router in a short time period. This includes assigning a hostname, configuring the Privilege EXEC and line passwords, creating a login banner, enabling interfaces, assigning a clock rate to a serial DCE interface, and assigning IP addresses to interfaces. You might see a simulation question that has you do this on three to five routers, including turning on a routing protocol. You should be able to perform these basic tasks in less than three minutes on each router. Remember to test connectivity

from a host in a subnet to the router's IP address connected to the subnet (the default gateway). Be able to interpret the output of the `show ip interface brief` command. Understand the use of the `ip subnet-zero` command.

Router-on-a-Stick

Understand how to configure a router-on-a-stick, especially how subinterfaces are created and how the `encapsulation` command associates a VLAN to the subinterface. Remember that the trunking protocol must match between the switch and the router: either 802.1Q or ISL. The IP address on the subinterface is the default gateway address for devices associated with that VLAN.

CERTIFICATION SUMMARY

The router contains the following components in ROM: POST, bootstrap program, ROM Monitor (ROMMON), and Mini-IOS. POST performs hardware tests. The bootstrap program finds and loads the IOS. ROMMON provides basic access to the router to perform testing and troubleshooting.

The configuration register affects how the router boots up. By default, POST is run, the bootstrap program is loaded, the IOS image is located, and the configuration file is executed. You can change this by using `boot system` commands or by changing the configuration register value. The `show version` command displays the current register value and what it will be upon a reload. The default register value is typically 0x2102. For the password recovery, use 0x2142.

The router needs an IP address on each interface where it will be processing IP traffic. This is configured on an interface with the **ip address** command. Use the **show ip interface brief** command to view the status and configuration of your interfaces.

A router-on-a-stick uses a single trunk connection from a router to a switch to route among multiple VLANs. You must create a subinterface on your router for each VLAN. Each subinterface requires the **encapsulation isl|dot1q** command and a layer 3 address or addresses.

✓ # TWO-MINUTE DRILL

Router Hardware Components

❑ ROM stores the Mini-IOS, the bootstrap program, ROMMON, and POST.

❑ Flash stores the IOS images.

❑ NVRAM stores the configuration files.

❑ RAM stores the active configuration, including tables and buffers.

Router Bootup Process

❑ The configuration register and **boot system** commands can be used to override the default router bootup behavior.

❑ Use the **show version** command to see the IOS version being used by the router as well as the register value.

❑ If the fourth hexadecimal character of the configuration register is 0x0, the router boots into ROMMON mode; if 0x1, the router boots the Mini-IOS or the first file in flash if a Mini-IOS doesn't exist; if 0x2–0xF, the router uses the default boot sequence. The default configuration register value is 0x2102. For the password recovery, it's 0x2142. Use the **config-register** IOS command to change this value.

❑ Here is the default bootup process: The bootstrap program examines the configuration register to determine how to boot up. If it is the default, the bootstrap program looks for **boot system** commands in the configuration file in NVRAM. If none are found, it looks for the IOS in flash. If no files are found in flash, the bootstrap program generates a TFTP local broadcast to locate the IOS. If no TFTP server is found, the bootstrap program loads the Mini-IOS in ROM. If there is no Mini-IOS in ROM, the bootstrap program loads ROMMON.

❑ The System Configuration Dialog (setup script) will run when the router boots up and there is no configuration file in NVRAM.

❑ Use the **confreg** command from ROMMON mode to change the configuration register to 0x2142 to perform the password recovery process.

AutoSecure

❑ AutoSecure puts a basic security configuration on a router, such as passwords, CBAC, ACLs, SSH, and other information. It is run from Privilege EXEC mode using the **auto secure** command.

Router Configuration

❑ IP addresses are configured on each interface of the router that will process IP packets with the **ip address** Interface Subconfiguration mode command. The **bandwidth** command changes the metric of the interface, which is used by some routing protocols.

❑ The **show ip interface brief** command displays a brief configuration and status of each interface on the router.

Router-on-a-Stick

❑ A router-on-a-stick is a router with a single trunk connection to a switch; a router routes between the VLANs on this trunk connection.

❑ To route between VLANs with a router-on-a-stick, use subinterfaces and specify the VLAN with the **encapsulation isl|dot1q** command on the subinterface.

SELF TEST

The following Self Test questions will help you measure your understanding of the material presented in this chapter. Read all the choices carefully, as there may be more than one correct answer. Choose all correct answers for each question.

Router Hardware Components

1. Which of the following are stored in ROM? (choose two)
    A. POST
    B. ROMMON
    C. Configuration file
    D. System recovery file

2. Which type of memory does not maintain its contents during a power-off state?
    A. NVRAM
    B. ROM
    C. RAM
    D. Flash

Router Bootup Process

3. Which router command would you use to view the configuration register value?
    A. `show register`
    B. `show interfaces`
    C. `show configuration`
    D. `show version`

4. Enter the router IOS Configuration mode command to change the configuration register to 0x2142: _____.

AutoSecure

5. When is AutoSecure run on a router?
    A. Manually from Privilege EXEC mode
    B. Manually from Configuration mode
    C. Automatically when the router boots up without a configuration
    D. Automatically when the router boots up without a configuration or manually from Privilege EXEC mode

Router Configuration

6. You need to configure an IP address on a router's serial interface (s0/0). Use the last host address in 192.168.1.128/30. The interface is a DCE and you need to enable the interface. The speed of the connection is 64 Kbps. Set the bandwidth metric to match the speed of the interface. Enter the commands to accomplish this.

7. Enter the router Global Configuration mode command that will allow you to use the first address in the first subnet of a subnetted C class network: _____.

8. Examine this output:

```
Interface  IP-Address   OK? Method Status                Protocol
Ethernet0  192.168.1.1  YES NVRAM  up                    up
Ethernet1  192.168.2.1  YES NVRAM  administratively down down
```

Enter the router command that created this output: _____.

Router-on-a-Stick

9. When configuring a router-on-a-stick, the configuration is done on _____.

A. Physical interfaces

B. Major interfaces

C. Subinterfaces

10. Which router-on-a-stick command defines the VLAN for the interface?

A. `vlan`

B. `encapsulation`

C. `trunk`

D. `frame-type`

SELF TEST ANSWERS

Router Hardware Components

1. ☑ **A** and **B.** POST, ROMMON, the Mini-IOS, and the bootstrap program are in ROM.
   ☒ **C** is incorrect because the configuration file is stored in NVRAM, and **D** is a nonexistent file.

2. ☑ **C.** RAM contents are erased when you turn off the device.
   ☒ **A, B,** and **D** are incorrect; NVRAM, ROM, and flash maintain their contents when the device is turned off.

Router Bootup Process

3. ☑ **D.** Use the **show version** command to view the configuration register value.
   ☒ **A** is a nonexistent command. **B** is incorrect because **show interfaces** shows only interface statistics. **C** is the old command version for **show startup-config**.

4. ☑ Enter the **config-register 0x2142** command in Configuration mode to cause the router to boot up and not load the configuration file in NVRAM.

AutoSecure

5. ☑ **A.** AutoSecure can be run manually only from Privilege EXEC mode with the **auto secure** command.
   ☒ **B, C,** and **D** are incorrect.

Router Configuration

6. ☑ The router's configuration will look like this:
   ```
   interface serial0/0
     ip address 192.168.1.130 255.255.255.252
     clock rate 64000
     bandwidth 64
     no shutdown
   ```

7. ☑ The **ip subnet-zero** command allows you to use the first and last subnet when configuring IP addresses on interfaces of your router.

8. ☑ **show ip interface brief**

Router-on-a-Stick

9. ☑ C. Trunking with a router-on-a-stick is done on subinterfaces.
   ☒ Hardware characteristics are configured on **A** (physical interfaces) when trunking, not VLANs. Sometimes the term in **B** (major interfaces) is used to refer to a physical interface.

10. ☑ B. Use the `encapsulation` command to specify the trunking encapsulation and the VLAN number for the subinterface.
    ☒ **A**, **C**, and **D** are nonexistent router commands.

17
IOS Device Management

T his chapter covers important IOS features that you can use to manage your IOS device. Many of these features are supported across all IOS devices, but some of them are supported on only certain devices. This chapter offers an in-depth discussion of configuration files. It also discusses how to upgrade your IOS device and remotely access it via the Secure Shell (SSH). You can use many tools on your IOS device for troubleshooting connection problems, including the Cisco Discovery Protocol (CDP), ping, traceroute, telnet, and debug. These tools are discussed at the end of the chapter.

CERTIFICATION OBJECTIVE 17.01

Router Configuration Files

You had a basic introduction to configuration files in Chapter 11. Remember that a configuration file contains the commands used to configure an IOS device. Configuration files are typically located in one of three places: RAM, NVRAM, and/or an external server, such as a TFTP, FTP, HTTP, or secure copy (SCP) server. The configuration that the router is currently using is in RAM. You can back up, or save, this configuration either to NVRAM or an external server.

As you may recall from Chapter 11, the commands *related* to configuration files, even **show** commands, require you to be at Privilege EXEC mode. Also, the running configuration of an IOS device is not automatically saved to NVRAM—you must manually do this with the **copy running-config startup-config** command. The following sections show you how to manipulate your configuration files.

Saving Configuration Files

Chapter 11 explained how to save your configuration from RAM to NVRAM with the **copy running-config startup-config** command. When you execute this command, whatever filename (the default is *startup-config*) you are copying to in NVRAM is completely overwritten. If you want to keep an old copy and a newer one in NVRAM, you'll need to specify a name other than *startup-config*. Note that the **copy** command has two parameters: The first parameter refers to where the source information is (what you want to copy it from), and the second parameter refers to where the destination is (where you want to copy it to).

You can copy your running-config or startup-config configuration file to flash, like this:

```
IOS# copy running-config|startup-config flash:file_name
```

This allows you to have multiple configuration files stored locally on your IOS device; however, when booting up, your IOS device, by default, will use the startup-config file in NVRAM to load its configuration.

on the
Ö o b

It is not common practice to copy configuration files to flash; for exam purposes, however, this is not where you back them up. However, I commonly do this when an FTP or TFTP server currently isn't reachable and I am too lazy to copy the configuration to the Windows Notepad application.

You can also back up your configuration to an external server. This requires you to have the server software on a server or PC and IP configured correctly on your IOS device in order to access the server. The syntax looks like this on your IOS device:

```
IOS# copy running-config URL_location
```

For example, to back up your configuration file to a TFTP server, the configuration would look like this:

```
IOS# copy running-config tftp://192.168.1.10/mybackupfile.txt
```

The configuration is backed up to an ASCII text file. If you don't supply the full URL, just the protocol information, you'll be prompted for the additional information, like this:

```
IOS# copy running-config tftp
Address or name of remote host []? 192.168.1.10
Destination filename [router-confg]? mybackupfile.cfg
!!
781 bytes copied in 5.8 secs (156 bytes/sec)
IOS#
```

If the filename already exists on the server, the server *overwrites* the old file. After entering this information, you should see bang symbols (!) indicating the successful transfer of UDP segments to the TFTP server. If you see periods (.), this indicates an unsuccessful transfer. Plus, upon a successful transfer, you should also see how many bytes were copied to the server.

17.01. The CD contains a multimedia demonstration of backing up the configuration file of a router.

Restoring Configuration Files

There may be situations when you have misconfigured your router or switch and want to take a saved configuration file and load it back into your Cisco device. You can do this by reversing the source and destination information in the **copy** command:

```
IOS# copy URL_location running-config|startup-config
```

Three variations of the **copy** command can restore your configuration. A TFTP server is used in this example for the first two options. Here is the first one:

```
IOS# copy tftp startup-config
Address or name of remote host []? 192.168.1.10
Source filename []? mybackupfile.cfg
Destination filename [startup-config]?
Accessing tftp://192.168.1.10/mybackupfile.cfg...
Loading mybackupfile.cfg from 192.168.1.10 (via Ethernet0): !
[OK - 781/1024 bytes]
[OK]
781 bytes copied in 11.216 secs (71 bytes/sec)
```

In this example, the configuration file is copied from a TFTP server to NVRAM (the startup-config file); if the file already exists in NVRAM, it will be overwritten.

You can also restore your configuration from a TFTP server to active memory:

```
IOS# copy tftp running-config
```

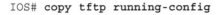
17.02. The CD contains a multimedia demonstration of restoring the configuration file on a router.

There is one main difference between moving the configuration from TFTP to NVRAM and moving it from TFTP to RAM. With the former method, the file in NVRAM is replaced with the one being copied; with the latter method, a *merge* process is used. During a merge process, the IOS updates commands that are common to both places—the new file and in RAM. The IOS also executes any new commands it finds in the uploaded configuration file and adds them to the running-config. However, the IOS does not delete any commands in RAM that it does not find in the uploaded configuration file. In other words, this is *not* a replacement process. As an example, assume that you have a configuration file on a TFTP server that has IPX and IP information in it, but your RAM configuration has IP and AppleTalk. In this example, the router updates the IP configuration, adds the IPX commands, but leaves the AppleTalk commands as they are.

This process is also true if you want to restore your configuration from NVRAM to RAM with this command (the third restore option):

```
IOS# copy startup-config running-config
```

If your backed-up configuration is in flash, use this syntax to restore it:

```
IOS# copy flash:file_name running-config|startup-config
```

exam
watch

The copy *command backs up and restores configuration files:* copy running-config startup-config *and* copy running-config tftp *back up the configuration file. The* copy startup-config running-config *and* copy tftp running-config *or* copy tftp startup-config *commands restore the configuration file. The* erase startup-config *command deletes the configuration file.*

Creating and Deleting Configuration Files

Along with knowing how to back up and restore configuration files, you also need to know how to create and delete them. Actually, you already know how to create a basic configuration file by going into Configuration mode with the Privilege EXEC **configure terminal** command. When you are executing commands within this mode (whether by typing them or pasting them in), the IOS is using a merge process (unless you use the **no** parameter for a command to delete or negate it).

CertCam

17.03. The CD contains a multimedia demonstration of deleting the NVRAM configuration file of a router.

You can also delete your configuration file in the startup-config file in NVRAM by using the following command:

```
IOS# erase startup-config|nvram
```

The 11.1 and earlier versions of this process, which are still supported, use the **write erase** command.

To verify the erasure, use the **show startup-config** command:

```
IOS# show startup-config
%% Non-volatile configuration memory is not present
```

Configuration File Nomenclature

Starting with IOS 12.0 and later, Cisco introduced command and naming nomenclatures that follow IOS File System (IFS) guidelines (what you are used to when you are entering a URL in a web browser address text box). Therefore, instead of entering a command and having a router prompt you for additional information, such as the IP address of a TFTP server as well as the filename, you can now put all of this information on a single command line. Commands that reference configuration files and IOS images contain prefixes in front of the file type, as shown in Table 17-1.

Let's take a look at an example. For instance, say that you want to back up your router's configuration from RAM to NVRAM. With the new syntax, you could type in the following:

```
IOS# copy system:running-config nvram:startup-config
```

You don't always have to put in the type; for instance, in this example, you could easily have entered this:

```
IOS# copy running-config startup-config
```

In many cases, the IOS knows, based on the name of the file, which location you're referring to. For example, when you use *running-config*, the IOS assumes you're referring to RAM, or "system:" as the location.

TABLE 17-1	Location	Description
File Locations	bootflash	Bootflash memory
	flash	Flash memory on the motherboard
	flh	Flash load helper log files
	ftp	FTP server
	nvram	Nonvolatile RAM (NVRAM)
	rcp	Remote Copy Protocol (RCP) server
	scp	Secure Copy (SCP)—uses RCP through an SSH tunnel
	slot0	PCMCIA slot 0
	slot1	PCMCIA slot 1
	system	RAM
	tftp	TFTP server

To view the active configuration, you can use this command:

```
IOS# more system:running-config
```

If you want to delete a file in flash, such as a backed-up configuration file, use the following command:

```
IOS# delete flash:file_name
```

You'll be asked to verify whether you want to delete the file. You can also use this command to delete any file in flash.

on the
!
Ø o b   *The older style of entering configuration and IOS commands is still supported along with the new one. One command that I constantly use in production environments is the* write memory *command, which can be abbreviated as* wr. *This performs the equivalent of the* copy running-config startup-config *command, but it requires only two keystrokes to perform! Please note, however, that the older command syntax is not supported on Cisco exams!*

Review of Configuration Files

It is important that you understand what action the IOS will take when it is either backing up or restoring a configuration file to a particular location. Table 17-2 summarizes this information for the routers.

TABLE 17-2   Overview of IOS Process When Dealing with Configuration Files

Location (From)	Location (To)	Command	IOS Process
RAM	NVRAM	copy running-config startup-config	Overwrite
RAM	TFTP	copy running-config tftp	Overwrite
NVRAM	RAM	copy startup-config running-config	Merge
NVRAM	TFTP	copy startup-config tftp	Overwrite
TFTP	RAM	copy tftp running-config	Merge
TFTP	NVRAM	copy tftp startup-config	Overwrite
CLI	RAM	configure terminal	Merge

exam
ⓦatch

Here is a quick way of remembering whether the IOS is using a merge or overwrite process. Anything copied into RAM uses a merge *process,* *whereas any other copy operation uses an* overwrite *process. Be familiar with the commands listed in Table 17-2 and what they do.*

EXERCISE 17-1

ON THE CD

Manipulating Your Router's Configuration Files

The last few sections dealt with the router's configuration files and how you manipulate them. This exercise will help you reinforce this material. You'll perform these steps on a 2600 router using Boson's NetSim simulator. You can find a picture of the network diagram for the simulator in the Introduction of this book. After starting up the simulator, click the Lab Navigator button. Next, double-click Exercise 17-1 and click the Load Lab button. This will load the lab configuration based on the exercises in Chapters 11 and 16.

1. Access the 2600-1 router.
   At the top of the simulator in the menu bar, click the eRouters icon and choose 2600-1.

2. Access the 2600-1 router's Privilege EXEC mode and view the running configuration.
   Access Privilege EXEC mode: **enable**. Use the **show running-config** command.

3. Save your router's active configuration to NVRAM. Verify the copy.
   Use the **copy running-config startup-config** command. Verify the copy: **show startup-config**.

4. Change the hostname on the router to *different* and then reload the saved configuration from the NVRAM into RAM. What is the hostname?

Access Configuration mode (**configure terminal**) and use the **hostname different** command to change the router's name to *different*. Exit Configuration mode: **end**. Restore your configuration with **copy startup-config running-config**. Your prompt should change back to the previous name of the router (2600-1). (You might have to wait a few seconds for this to complete.)

5. Erase your router's saved configuration in NVRAM. Examine the configuration file in NVRAM. Save the active configuration file to NVRAM. Examine the configuration file in NVRAM.
Use the **erase startup-config** command to erase your configuration in NVRAM. Press ENTER to confirm the erase. Use the **show startup-config** command to verify the configuration file was deleted.

6. Save your configuration file in RAM to NVRAM. View the newly saved configuration file in NVRAM.
Use the **copy running-config startup-config** command to save your configuration to NVRAM. Use the **show startup-config** command to verify that your router's configuration was backed up from RAM to NVRAM.

Now you should be more comfortable with manipulating a router's configuration files. In the next section, you will learn how you should deal with changes in your network.

CERTIFICATION OBJECTIVE 17.02

Changes in Your Network

When you decide to make changes to your network, including the addition or deletion of devices, you should always do some preparation work *before* you make the changes. Making changes can cause things to not function correctly, or not function at all, so you should always prepare beforehand. The following two sections cover the basics of handling changes.

Adding Devices

Before you add an IOS device to your network, you should gather the following information and perform the following tasks:

1. Decide which IP address you'll assign to the device for management purposes.
2. Configure the ports of the device, including the console and VTY ports.
3. Set up your passwords for User and Privilege EXEC access.
4. Assign the appropriate IP addresses to the device's interface(s).
5. Create a basic configuration on the device so that it can perform its job.

Changing Devices

You will constantly be making configuration changes to your network to enhance performance and security. *Before* you make any changes to your network, you should *always* back up your configuration files. Likewise, before you perform a software upgrade on your Cisco device, you should always back up the old IOS image.

You should check a few things before loading the new image on your IOS device. First, does the new image contain all of the features that your previous image had? Or at least the features that you need? Also, does your IOS device have enough flash *and* RAM to store and load the IOS image? You need to check these items before proceeding to load the new image.

At times, you may need to upgrade the hardware or add a new module to your Cisco device. Some devices require that you turn them off before doing the upgrade, while other devices can be left powered on. It is extremely important that you read the installation manual that comes with the hardware before performing the installation. If you install a hardware component into a device that requires that the device be turned off, and the device is running, you could damage your new component or, worse, electrocute yourself.

on the
job

Remember that it is much easier to restore a backup copy than it is to re-create something from scratch. Also, whenever you make changes, always test the change to ensure that your Cisco device is performing as expected.

CERTIFICATION OBJECTIVE 17.03

IOS Image Files

The default location of IOS images is in flash. Some IOS devices have flash built into the motherboard, some use PCMCIA cards for storage, and some use a combination of both. At times, you will have to deal with the device's flash when you want to perform an upgrade, for instance. To view your files in flash, use the **show flash** command:

```
IOS# show flash
-#- --length-- -----date/time------ path
1             0 Sep 18 2007 15:42:20 +00:00 .Trashes
2          4096 Sep 18 2007 15:42:20 +00:00 ._.Trashes
3         12292 Sep 18 2007 15:55:12 +00:00 .DS_Store
4          1159 Sep 9 2007 18:01:42 +00:00 udp.phdf
5       4787200 Oct 3 2007 14:33:50 +00:00 sdm.tar
6          2679 Sep 9 2007 18:01:28 +00:00 ip.phdf
7        113152 Oct 3 2007 14:34:02 +00:00 home.tar
8          2227 Dec 4 2007 16:02:28 +00:00 pre_autosec.cfg
.
.
.
16     23787192 Sep 9 2007 17:45:30 +00:00
                        c1841-advipservicesk9-mz.124-6.T7.bin
.
.
.
31946752 bytes available (31922176 bytes used)
```

In this example, you can see that a router's flash holds many files. Below the list of files, you can see how much flash is used (about 32MB), how much is available (about 32MB), and the total amount of flash on the router (64MB). You can also see how much flash you have installed on your IOS device with the **show version** command.

Use the show flash, show version, *or* dir *command to see how much flash memory is installed on your IOS device.*

In addition to using the **show flash** command, you can also use the **dir** command:

```
IOS# dir
Directory of flash:/
    1  drw-           0  Sep 18 2007 15:42:20 +00:00   .Trashes
    2  -rw-        4096  Sep 18 2007 15:42:20 +00:00   ._.Trashes
    .
    .
    .
   16  -rw-    23787192  Sep 9 2007 17:45:30 +00:00
                                c1841-advipservicesk9-mz.124-6.T7.bin
63868928 bytes total (31946752 bytes free)
```

17.04. The CD contains a multimedia demonstration of viewing the contents of flash on a router.

Naming Conventions for IOS Images

■ Cisco has implemented a naming convention for its IOS images, allowing you to see the platform, software version, and features included in the image just by looking at the name of the image file. As an example, consider the image name from the preceding **show flash** command: *c1841-advipservicesk9-mz.124-6.T7.bin*, which is from a router. Here's an explanation of the nomenclature that Cisco uses for their IOS image names: The *c1841* refers to the name of the platform on which the image will run. This is important because different router models have different processors, and an image compiled for one processor or router model will typically *not* run on a different model. Therefore, it is very important that you load the appropriate image on your device.

■ The *advipservicesk9* refers to the features included in this IOS version, commonly referred to as the *feature set*. In this example, the IOS is the advanced IP services and the *k9* refers to the inclusion of encryption support.

■ The *mz* or *z* means that the image is compressed and must be uncompressed before loading/running. If you see *l* (the letter *l*, not the number *1*) here, this indicates where the IOS image is run from. The *l* indicates a relocatable image and that the image can be run from RAM. Remember that some images can run directly from flash, depending on the router model.

- The *124-6.T7* indicates the software version number of the IOS. In this instance, the version is 12.4(6)T7. Images names with *T* indicate new features, and without the *T* the mainline (only bug fixes are made to it).
- Finally, the *.bin* at the end indicates that this is a binary image.

on the
job

The naming nomenclature discussed here applies to IOS images that are either included on your IOS device when you buy it from Cisco or applied when you download them from Cisco's web site. However, the name, in and of itself, has no bearing on the actual operation of the IOS when it is loaded on your IOS device. For instance, you can download an image from Cisco and rename it poorperformance.bin, and this will have no impact on the IOS device's performance.

Before Upgrading the IOS Image

This and the next section discuss how to upgrade and back up the IOS software on your router. Before you upgrade the IOS on your device, you should first back up the existing image to an external server, for two reasons. First, your flash might not be large enough to support two images—the old one and the new. If you load the new one and you experience problems with it, you'll probably want to load the old image back onto your device. Second, Cisco doesn't keep every software version available on its web site. Older versions of the IOS are hard to locate, so if you are upgrading from an old version of the IOS, I would highly recommend backing it up first.

Before you back up your IOS image to an external server, you should perform the following checks:

- Is the server reachable (test with the **ping** command)?
- Is there enough disk space on the server to hold the IOS image?
- Does the server support the file nomenclature that you want to use?
- Does the file have to exist on the server before you can perform the copy? (This is true with certain TFTP Unix servers.)

Once you have performed these checks, you are ready to continue with the backup process.

Backing Up an IOS Image

To back up your IOS image, you'll use the **copy flash** *URL* command. Optionally, you can specify the name of the IOS in flash in the command line. The URL specifies a URL-style syntax and includes the protocol, such as TFTP, the IP address of the server, possibly the directory to put it in, and the name the image will be called on the server. Optionally, you can just specify the protocol in the URL, and you'll be prompted for the rest of the information, like this:

```
Router# copy flash tftp
Source filename []? c3640-js-mz.120-11
Address or name of remote host []? 192.168.1.10
Destination filename [c3640-js-mz.120-11]?
!!!!!!!!!!!!!!!!!!!!!!!!!!!!!!!!!!!!!!!!!!!!!!!!!!!!!!!!!!!!!!
.
.
.
6754416 bytes copied in 64.452 secs (105537 bytes/sec)
```

As the image is backed up, you should see a bunch of exclamation points filling up your screen (as shown here)—this indicates the successful copy of a packet. If you see a sequence of periods (.) instead, this indicates a failure. After a successful copy operation, you should see the number of bytes copied as well as how long it took. Compare the number of bytes copied to the file length in flash to verify that the copy was actually successful.

CertCam

17.05. The CD contains a multimedia demonstration of backing up the IOS flash image on a router.

Loading an IOS Image

If you want to upgrade your IOS or load a previously saved IOS image, you'll need to place the IOS image on an external server and use the **copy** *URL* **flash** command. You'll be prompted for the same information you needed when you used the **copy flash tftp** command; however, the process that takes place after you enter your information is different. After you enter your information, the IOS first verifies that the image exists on the TFTP server. If the file exists on the server, the IOS then asks you if you want to erase flash. Answer **y** if you don't have enough space in flash for the older image(s) as well as the new one. If you answer **y**, flash is erased and reprogrammed; as this step proceeds, you will see a list of "e"s appear on the screen.

After flash is initialized, your router pulls the IOS image from the TFTP server. Just as in the copy operations with configuration files, a bunch of exclamation marks indicate successful copies, while periods indicate unsuccessful copies.

Here is example of loading an IOS image into your router:

```
Router# copy tftp flash
Address or name of remote host []? 192.168.1.10
Source filename []? c3640-js-mz.120-7
Destination filename [c3640-js-mz.120-7]?
%Warning:There is a file already existing with this name
Do you want to over write? [confirm] y
Accessing tftp://192.168.1.1/c3640-js-mz.120-7...
Erase flash: before copying? [confirm] y
Erasing the flash filesystem will remove all files! Continue?
[confirm] y
Erasing device... eeeeeeeeeeeeeeeeeeeeeeeeeeeeeee ...erased
Erase of flash: complete
Loading c3640-js-mz.120-7 from 192.168.1.1 (via FastEthernet0/0):
!!!!!!!!!!!!!!!!!!!!!!!!!!!!!!!!!!!!!!!!!!!!!!!!!!!!!!!!!!!!!
.

.

.
[OK - 6754416/13508608 bytes]

Verifying checksum...  OK (0xCAF2)
6754416 bytes copied in 66.968 secs (102339 bytes/sec)
Router#
```

In this example, the router noticed that the name of the image that exists on the TFTP server is the same name that is in flash and verifies that you want to overwrite it. After the router copies the IOS image to flash, you must reboot your router in order for it to use the new image. You can reboot your router in two ways: turn it off and back on, or use the Privilege EXEC `reload` command. The first method is a hard reboot, and the second one is a soft reboot.

17.06. The CD contains a multimedia demonstration of loading an IOS flash image on a router.

If you place an incorrect image on your router—for instance, a 3600 series image on a 2800 series router—the router will not boot up. You'll need to break into ROMMON mode and either do a TFTP boot or boot from the Mini-IOS in ROM (if this exists).

Use the `copy flash URL` command to back up the IOS image and the `copy URL flash` command to restore or upgrade the IOS. The `reload` command reboots the router. When doing an upgrade and either the server is not reachable or you have misconfigured the IP address or filename, you'll get an error message on your CLI.

If you encounter a problem with accessing a remote server when performing the upgrade, you'll receive an error message. This could be because you configured the wrong IP address of the server in the **copy** command, or you entered a nonexistent IOS image name. Here's an example illustrating this problem:

```
Router# copy tftp://192.168.101.66/iosimage.bin flash
Destination filename [iosimage.bin]?
Accessing tftp://192.168.101.66/iosimage.bin...
%Error opening tftp://192.168.101.66/iosimage.bin (Timed out)
```

on the job
Not every IOS version has the same upgrade process, so what you see on your router may be different from what appears in this book, especially if you are running IOS version 11.x or earlier.

CERTIFICATION OBJECTIVE 17.04

Remote Access to Your IOS Device

In many instances, it might not be possible to be physically in front of your IOS device to manage it. You can optionally manage it remotely by accessing its CLI via telnet or SSH, or you can manage it with a GUI interface with a web browser. To access your IOS device's CLI remotely, you must first set up its virtual type terminals (VTYs), as discussed in Chapter 11. If you're accessing a layer 2 IOS switch, you'll need to assign an IP address to a VLAN interface (discussed in Chapter 12); if you're accessing a router, you'll need to assign an IP address to one of its interfaces and enable it (discussed in Chapter 16). By default, only telnet is enabled on the router; this section will discuss how you enable SSH.

One common solution for accessing a console remotely is to connect the console ports of your IOS devices to a terminal server and access them via the terminal server. You'll need to log into the terminal server first, either via its console line or remotely via SSH or telnet. From there, you can jump directly into an IOS device's console port to manage it. Many IOS routers support multiport async cards that can be used as this function: I commonly use Cisco routers for terminal servers.

SSH vs. Telnet Access

One of the most common tools used by network administrators to manage their devices remotely is the telnet application. Telnet allows you access to the CLI of a device. However, the problem with telnet is that all information sent between you and the IOS device is sent in clear text, including your username and/or password. Since you don't want someone eavesdropping on your connection and seeing everything you do—logging in, viewing the operation of the device, and configuring the device—you want to protect yourself by encrypting the traffic.

The easiest way to accomplish this is to replace the use of telnet with SSH (secure shell). SSH uses RSA as an encryption algorithm to encrypt any data sent between you and your networking device. SSH is actually disabled, by default, on your IOS device.

exam
watch

Telnet sends traffic in clear text, making it susceptible to an eavesdropping attack. To secure remote access to your IOS device and prevent eavesdropping on the commands you're entering and the configurations you're viewing, use SSH as your remote access

terminal connection: SSH encrypts traffic. To prevent an access attack against your IOS device, you should combine SSH with filtering of management access to your device by using access control lists (which indicate what IP addresses can manage it).

SSH Configuration

To set up SSH on your IOS device so you can use an SSH client to access it, you'll need to configure the following:

- **A local username and password**   SSH requires both (**username** command)
- **A hostname and a domain name**   This is required to label the RSA key pair on the IOS device (**hostname** and **ip domain-name** commands)
- **The SSH version to use**   The default is version 1, but the recommended version to use is 2 (**ip ssh version** command)
- **RSA public and private keys**   These are used to encrypt and decrypt the remote access connection (**crypto key generate rsa** command)
- **Restricting VTY access**   By default, telnet is allowed on the VTYs—you should ensure that only SSH access is allowed (**login local** and **transport input** Line Subconfiguration commands)

17.07. The CD includes a multimedia demonstration of configuring SSH on an IOS device.

Here is an example configuration setting up SSH:

```
IOS(config)# username richard secret mypassword
IOS(config)# hostname alina
alina(config)# ip domain-name deal.com
alina(config)# ip ssh version 2
Please create RSA keys to enable SSH.
alina(config)# crypto key generate rsa
The name for the keys will be: alina.deal.com
Choose the size of the key modulus in the range of 360 to 2048 for
    your General Purpose Keys. Choosing a key modulus greater than 512
    may take a few minutes.
How many bits in the modulus [512]: 1024
% Generating 1024 bit RSA keys, keys will be non-exportable...[OK]
*Oct  5 16:48:23.455: %SSH-5-ENABLED: SSH 2.0 has been enabled
alina(config)# line vty 0 15
alina(config-line)# login local
alina(config-line)# transport input ssh
alina(config-line)# exit
```

Notice in this example that when you execute the `crypto key generate rsa` command, you are prompted for the length of the RSA keys. The longer the keys, the more secure your connection will be, with 2048-bit keys being the strongest. Choosing a higher value, however, will take longer for the IOS device to generate. On IOS devices shipped today, this shouldn't take that long: it took me about 30 seconds to generate 2048-bit keys on an 1841 router.

Another item to point out about this configuration is the two commands on the VTYs. The `login local` command specifies the use of the local database (`username` command) for authentication: this causes the IOS device to prompt for both a username *and* password for authentication. Without the `local` parameter, the IOS prompts only for a password, using the `password` command on the line to do the authentication (this process was discussed in Chapter 11). SSH requires the use of both usernames and passwords. The `transport input ssh` command restricts access to the VTYs to SSH use only; by default, all forms of remote access, including telnet, are allowed.

on the
job   *If you will be using SSH to access your IOS device, you must use either a local username database, as described here, for your VTYs, or an authentication server (AAA). Also, I commonly use PuTTY as a console access program (instead of HyperTerminal), telnet client, and SSH client. It's a great little program that does all these things, and it's free!*

CERTIFICATION OBJECTIVE 17.05

Basic Troubleshooting

The remainder of this chapter focuses on troubleshooting tools that you can use on your routers and switches. One of your first troubleshooting tasks is to figure out in which layer of the OSI Reference Model things are not working. By narrowing down the problem to a specific layer, you've greatly reduced the amount of time that you'll need in order to fix the problem or problems.

TABLE 17-3	OSI Reference Model Layer	Command
	Layer 2	`show ip arp`
IOS Troubleshooting Commands	Layer 2	`show interfaces` (covered in Chapter 11)
	Layer 2	`show cdp neighbors`
	Layer 3	`ping`
	Layer 3	`traceroute`
	Layer 7	`telnet`
	Layers 2–7	`debug`

ⓦ**a t c h**   *Remember at which layer of the OSI Reference Model the commands shown in Table 17-3 operate.*

Cisco offers a wide variety of tools that you can use. Table 17-3 has a list of the more common IOS commands and what layer of the OSI Reference Model that they can be used for in troubleshooting. The following sections cover most of these commands in more depth.

Local ARP Table

Recall from Chapters 6 and 10 that ARP is used to resolve layer 3 IP addresses to layer 2 MAC addresses. When a LAN device in a subnet needs to access resources beyond the subnet, it must forward its frames to the MAC address of the default gateway (router) and uses ARP for the resolution. The router builds a local ARP table when it receives traffic on an interface, keeping track of the IP-to-MAC address mappings. This can be viewed with the **show arp** or **show ip arp** command:

```
IOS# show ip arp
Protocol  Address     Age (min) Hardware Addr   Type  Interface
Internet  10.0.6.2        -      0007.0e46.4070  ARPA  FastEthernet0/0
Internet  172.30.6.2      -      0007.0e46.4071  ARPA  FastEthernet0/1
Internet  172.30.6.7      0      0050.5480.7e01  ARPA  FastEthernet0/1
```

A dash ("-") in the (min) column means the address is local to the router; a time value indicates that the router learned the IP/MAC addressing mapping dynamically. The last entry in this example was dynamically learned within the last minute. If a particular MAC address isn't seen for a period of time, it is aged out of the ARP table. Likewise, when a frame matches an existing entry in the table, its aging time is reset to zero in the table. The Type column denotes the Ethernet encapsulation type (ARPA, SNAP, or SAP) used in the frame: TCP/IP uses ARPA for Ethernet.

The `show ip arp` command is important because if you see at least the router's own mappings in the table for its interfaces and entries are being learned and updated in the table, then you have layer 2 connectivity on those interfaces.

17.08. The CD includes a multimedia demonstration of examining an ARP table on a router.

Cisco Discovery Protocol (CDP)

CDP is a Cisco proprietary data link layer protocol that was made available in version 10.3 of the router IOS. Many, but not all, Cisco devices support CDP, including Cisco routers and Catalyst switches. For those devices that support CDP, CDP is *enabled* by default. CDP messages received from one Cisco device, by default, are not forwarded to any other devices behind it. In other words, you can see CDP information about only other Cisco devices *directly* connected to your device. Most people misunderstand this, since CDP uses multicasts to disseminate its information. You would think that a Cisco switch would flood this kind of traffic; however, CDP is an exception to the rule in a network of Cisco devices.

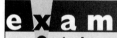

About CDP, you should know that if you are receiving CDP frames from a directly connected Cisco neighbor, then at least the data link layer is functioning correctly. CDP information is not propagated to other Cisco devices behind your directly connected neighboring Cisco devices.

CDP Information

CDP, as mentioned, works at the data link layer. However, since CDP uses a Subnetwork Access Protocol (SNAP) frame type, not every data link layer media type is supported. The media types that are supported are Ethernet, Token Ring, fiber distributed data interface (FDDI), Point-to-Point Protocol (PPP), High-Level Data Link Control (HDLC), Asynchronous Transfer Mode (ATM), and Frame Relay.

The information shared in a CDP packet about a Cisco device includes the following:

- Name of the device configured with the **hostname** command
- IOS software version
- Hardware capabilities, such as routing, switching, and/or bridging
- Hardware platform, such as 2800 or 2960
- The layer 3 address(es) of the device
- The interface on which the CDP update was generated

CDP Configuration

As mentioned in the last section, CDP is enabled on all Cisco CDP–capable devices when you receive your product from Cisco. On Cisco routers and switches, you can globally disable or enable it with this command:

```
IOS(config)# [no] cdp run
```

You can also enable or disable CDP on an interface-by-interface basis:

```
IOS(config)# interface type [slot_#/]port_#
IOS(config-if)# [no] cdp enable
```

Since CDP doesn't use many resources by the IOS (a small frame is generated once a minute), it is recommended that you keep it enabled unless your router is connected to the Internet or untrusted devices; then you should at least disable CDP on these interfaces. At a minimum, the information is only 80 bytes in length. Other, optional commands are related to CDP, such as changing the update and hold-down timers, but these commands are beyond the scope of this book.

CDP Status

To see the status of CDP on your Cisco device, use this command:

```
IOS# show cdp
Global CDP information:
Sending CDP packets every 60 seconds
Sending a holdtime value of 180 seconds
Sending CDPv2 advertisements is  enabled
```

As you can see from this output, CDP is enabled and generating updates every 60 seconds. The hold-down timer is 180 seconds. This timer determines how long a

CDP neighbor's information is kept in the local CDP table without seeing a CDP update from that neighbor. These are the default timers for CDP.

You can also see the CDP configuration on an interface-by-interface basis by adding the **interface** parameter to the **show cdp** command:

```
Router# show cdp interface
Serial0 is up, line protocol is up, encapsulation is HDLC
   Sending CDP packets every 60 seconds
   Holdtime is 180 seconds
Ethernet0 is up, line protocol is up, encapsulation is ARPA
   Sending CDP packets every 60 seconds
   Holdtime is 180 seconds
```

CDP Neighbors

To see a summarized list of the CDP neighbors to which your Cisco device is connected, use the **show cdp neighbors** command:

```
IOS# show cdp neighbors
Capability Codes: R - Router, T - Trans Bridge, B - Source Route
                  Bridge S - Switch, H - Host, I - IGMP,
                  r - Repeater

Device ID   Local Intrfce  Holdtme  Capability  Platform  Port ID
Router-A    Eth 0/0          176        R          2621    Fas 0/1
```

In this example, one device is connected with a device ID of *Router-A*, which is a 2621 router. If you see a MAC address for the device ID, this indicates that the connected Cisco device wasn't assigned a name with the **hostname** command. This update was received on ethernet0/0 on this device 4 seconds ago (hold-down timer of 176 seconds subtracted from the hold-down time of 180 seconds). The Port ID refers to the port at the remote side from which the device advertised the CDP message.

You can add the optional **detail** parameter to the preceding command to see the details concerning the connected Cisco device. You can also use the **show cdp entry *** command. Here is an example of a CDP detailed listing:

```
Router# show cdp neighbor detail
-------------------------
Device ID: Router-A
Entry address(es):
  IP address: 192.168.1.1
```

```
Platform: cisco 2621,  Capabilities: Router
Interface: Ethernet0/0,  Port ID (outgoing port): FastEthernet0/1
Holdtime : 127 sec

Version :
Cisco Internetwork Operating System Software
IOS (tm) C2600 Software (C2600-IK9O3S3-M), Version 12.2(15)T9,
      RELEASE SOFTWARE (fc2)
TAC Support: http://www.cisco.com/tac
Copyright (c) 1986-2003 by cisco Systems, Inc.
Compiled Sat 01-Nov-03 04:43 by ccai

advertisement version: 2
Duplex: half
    .
    .
    .
```

In this example, you can see that the connected device is a 2621 series router running IOS 12.2(15)T9 and has an IP address of 192.168.1.1 configured on the connected interface.

To list the details of a specific neighbor, use this command:

```
Router# show cdp entry neighbor's_name
```

The advantage of this approach over that in the preceding example is this command lists only the specified neighbor's information.

17.09. The CD contains a multimedia demonstration of using CDP on a router.

IOS devices support one additional CDP command, which allows you to view CDP traffic statistics:

```
IOS# show cdp traffic
Total packets output: 350, Input: 223
Hdr syntax: 0, Chksum error: 0, Encaps failed: 0
No memory: 0, Invalid: 0, Fragmented: 0
```

If you are receiving CDP traffic (Input parameter is incrementing with each execution of the command every minute), then the data link layer is functioning correctly.

Layer 3 Connectivity Testing

As you saw in the preceding section, CDP can be very useful in determining whether the data link layer is working correctly with another directly-connected Cisco device. You can even see the layer 3 address(es) configured on your neighboring device and use this for testing layer 3 connectivity. In addition to using CDP, you could also use the **show interfaces** command for data link layer testing (Chapter 11).

However, the main limitation of these two tools is that they don't test layer 3 problems. Cisco does offer tools for testing layer 3 connectivity, however. This section focuses on two of these commands: **ping** and **traceroute**. Both of these commands come in two versions: one for User EXEC mode and one for Privilege EXEC mode. The Privilege EXEC version provides additional options and parameters that can assist you in your troubleshooting process. The following sections cover these tools in more depth.

Using Ping

Ping (Packet Internet Groper) was originally developed for the IP protocol stack to test layer 3 connectivity. The Internet Control Message Protocol (ICMP) is used to implement ping. However, Cisco's IOS has expanded the **ping** command to support other protocols, including Apollo, AppleTalk, CLNS, DECnet, IP, IPX, Vines, and XNS. Cisco uses ping to test layer 3 connectivity with other, non-IP protocols in a (typically) proprietary fashion. However, Cisco follows the standard when using **ping** to test IP connectivity.

on the
job

Ping was originally never intended to be an acronym. It was developed by Mike Muuss, who named it ping simply because it worked like sonar. Later on, David Mils created an acronym for it: Packet Internet Groper. Muuss was, apparently, not amused by the acronym.

exam
ⓦatch

Ping uses ICMP echo messages to initiate the test. If the destination is reachable, the destination responds with an echo reply message for each echo sent by the source. If the destination is not reachable, an intermediate router, if it exists, will respond with a destination unreachable message, indicating where the problem begins. Both the ping and traceroute commands test layer 3 connectivity.

Simple ping Command   To execute a simple ping from either User mode or Privilege EXEC mode, enter the **ping** command on the CLI and follow it with the IP address or hostname of the destination:

```
IOS> ping destination_IP_address_or_host_name
```

Here is a simple example of using this command:

```
IOS> ping 192.168.1.10
Type escape sequence to abort.
Sending 5, 100-byte ICMP Echos to 192.168.1.10,
    timeout is 2 seconds:
!!!!!
Success rate is 100 percent (5/5),
    round-trip min/avg/max = 2/4/6 ms.
```

In this example, five test packets were sent to the destination and the destination responded to all five, as is shown by the exclamation marks (!). The default timeout to receive a response from the destination is 2 seconds—if a response is not received from the destination for a packet within this time period, a period (.) is displayed.

Table 17-4 shows examples of ping messages that you might see in displayed output. The bottom of the output shows the success rate—how many replies were received and the minimum, average, and maximum round-trip times for the ping packets sent (in milliseconds). This information can be used to detect whether a delay exists between you and the destination.

TABLE 17-4	Ping Output	Explanation
Output Codes for the `ping` Commands	.	A response was not received before the timeout period expired.
	!	A response was received within the timeout period.
	U	A remote router responded that the destination is unreachable—the network segment is reachable, but not the host.
	N	A remote router responded that the network is unreachable—the network cannot be found in the routing table.
	P	A remote device responded that the protocol is not supported.
	Q	Source quench, telling the source to slow its output.
	M	The ping packet needed to be fragmented, but a remote router couldn't perform fragmentation.
	A	The ping packet was filtered by a device with an access control list (administratively prohibited).
	?	The ping packet type is not understood by a remote device.
	&	The ping exceeded the maximum number of hops supported by the routing protocol (see Chapter 19).

on the **Job**

You might see a period (.) in the output for a couple of reasons: a response was received, but after the timeout period; or no response was seen at all. If a response was received, but after the timeout period, this might be because an ARP had to take place to learn the MAC address of a connected device or because of congestion—and this process could have occurred on multiple segments. Consider two examples: . ! ! ! ! and ! ! . . !. If devices have to perform ARPs to get the MAC address of the next-hop device, you'll typically see the first example in your output. However, if your output looks like the second example, you're probably experiencing congestion or performance problems.

exam

Watch   *Be familiar with the output descriptors used by the `ping` command in Table 17-4.*

Extended ping Command   IOS devices support an extended **ping** command, which can be executed only at Privilege EXEC mode.

17.10. The CD contains a multimedia demonstration of using the simple and extended `ping` ***commands on a router.***

To execute this command, just type **ping** by itself on the command line:

```
Router# ping
 Protocol [ip]:
 Target IP address: 192.168.1.10
 Repeat count [5]:
 Datagram size [100]:
 Timeout in seconds [2]:
 Extended commands [n]: y
 Source address:
 Type of service [0]:
 Set DF bit in IP header? [no]:
 Data pattern [0xABCD]:
 Loose, Strict, Record, Timestamp, Verbose[none]:
 Number of hops [9]:
 Loose, Strict, Record, Timestamp, Verbose[RV]:
 Sweep range of sizes [n]:
Type escape sequence to abort.
Sending 5, 100-byte ICMP Echos to 192.168.1.10,
     timeout is 2 seconds:
 .
 .
 .
```

Following is an explanation of the parameters that might be required when you execute this command:

- `Protocol`   The protocol to use for the ping (defaults to IP).
- `Target IP address`   The IP address or hostname of the destination to test.
- `Repeat count`   How many echo requests should be generated for the test (defaults to 5).
- `Datagram size`   The size, in bytes, of the ping packet (defaults to 100).
- `Timeout in seconds`   The amount of time to wait before indicating a timeout for the echo (defaults to 2 seconds). When seeing a mix of periods and bangs in the displayed output, increasing this value can help determine if you are experiencing congestion problems with a slow response time between your IOS device and the destination.

- **Extended commands** Whether or not the remaining questions should also be asked (defaults to no).
- **Source address** The IP address that should appear as the source address in the IP header (defaults to the IP address of the interface the ping will use to exit the IOS device).
- **Type of service** The IP level for QoS (defaults to 0).
- **Set DF bit in IP header?** Whether or not the ping can be fragmented when it reaches a segment that supports a smaller MTU size (the default is no—don't set this bit). Sometimes a misconfigured MTU can cause performance problems. You can use this parameter to pinpoint the problem, since a device with a smaller MTU size will not be able to handle the larger packet.
- **Data pattern** The data pattern that is placed in the ping. It is a hexadecimal four-digit (16-bit) number (defaults to 0xABCD) and is used to solve cable problems and crosstalk on cables.
- **Loose, Strict, Record, Timestamp, Verbose** IP header options (defaults to none of these). The record parameter records the route that the ping took—this is somewhat similar to traceroute. If you choose record, you will be asked for the maximum number of hops that are allowed to be recorded by the ping (defaults to 9, and can range from 1 to 9).
- **Sweep range of sizes** Send pings that vary in size. This is helpful when trying to troubleshoot a problem related to a segment that has a small MTU size (and you don't know what that number is). This defaults to n for no.

---

exam

ωatch

When troubleshooting PC problems, first determine whether the user can ping the loopback address of their PC: ping 127.0.0.1. If this fails, you know something is wrong with the TCP/IP protocol stack installation on the PC. Next, have the user try to ping the configured IP address. If this fails, you know that something is wrong with their IP address configuration. Next, have the user ping the default gateway. If this fails, either something is wrong with the configured default gateway address, the default gateway itself, the subnet mask value configured on the user's PC, or the layer 2 switch connecting them together (perhaps a mismatch in the VLAN on the router and PC interfaces of the switch).

Using Traceroute

One limitation of ping is that it will not tell you where, between you and the destination, layer 3 connectivity is broken. Traceroute, on the other hand, will list each router along the way, including the final destination. Therefore, if a layer 3 connection problem exists, traceroute will tell you at least where the problem begins. Like the **ping** command, **traceroute** has two versions: one for User EXEC mode and one for Privilege EXEC mode. The following two sections cover the two different versions.

Simple traceroute Command   The simple **traceroute** command, which works at both User and Privilege EXEC modes, has the following syntax:

```
Router> traceroute destination_IP_address_or_host_name
```

Here is an example of this command:

```
Router> traceroute 65.32.13.33
Type escape sequence to abort.
Tracing the route to 65.32.13.33
  1 10.98.240.1 20 msec 24 msec 16 msec
  2 65.32.15.254 16 msec 16 msec 12 msec
  3 65.32.13.33 12 msec 12 msec 12 msec
```

In this example, the destination was three hops away—each hop is listed on a separate line. For each destination, three tests are performed, where the round-trip time is displayed for each test. If you don't see a round-trip time, typically indicated by an asterisk ("*"), this indicates a possible problem or timeout in the response.

on the
Job

To break out of a ping or traceroute command, use the CTRL-SHIFT-6 break sequence. Also, instead of using the script to perform an extended ping or traceroute, you can execute by specifying all of the parameters on a single command line.

Table 17-5 shows other values that you might see instead of the round-trip time.

In certain cases, for a specific destination, you might see three asterisks (***) in the output; don't be alarmed if you see this, since it can occur for a variety of reasons: for instance, there may be an inconsistency in how the source and destination devices have implemented traceroute, or the destination may be configured not to reply to these messages. However, if you continually find the same destination repeated in the output with these reply messages, this indicates a layer 3 problem starting with either this device or the device preceding it.

TABLE 17-5	Traceroute Messages	

Traceroute Output	Explanation
*	Either the wait timer expired while waiting for a response or the device did not respond at all.
A	The trace packet was filtered by a remote device (administratively prohibited).
U	The port of the device is unreachable (the destination received the trace packet but discarded it).
H	The destination is unreachable (the destination segment was reachable, but not the host).
I	The user interrupted the traceroute process.
N	The network is unreachable (the destination segment was not reachable).
P	The protocol is unreachable (the device doesn't support traceroute).
Q	Source quench.
T	The trace packet exceeded the configured timeout value.
?	The device couldn't identify the specific trace type in the trace packet.

on the ❗ job

If you have DNS lookups enabled on your IOS device (this is the `ip domain-lookup` command), the IOS will attempt to resolve the IP address to a domain name before printing the output line for that device. If your traces seem to take a long time, this is usually the culprit. You can disable DNS lookups on your router with the `no ip domain-lookup` command.

Extended traceroute Command   The extended `traceroute` command is similar to the extended `ping` command and requires Privilege EXEC mode access to execute it:

```
Router# traceroute
Protocol [ip]:
Target IP address: IP_address_of_the_destination
Source address:
Numeric display [n]:
Timeout in seconds [3]:
Probe count [3]:
Minimum Time to Live [1]:
Maximum Time to Live [30]:
Port number [33434]:
Loose, Strict, Record, Timestamp, Verbose [none]:
  .
  .
  .
```

CertCam

Some of these options are the same ones used by ping.

17.11.The CD contains a multimedia demonstration of using the simple and extended `traceroute` *commands on a router.*

Here is an explanation of the other options:

- `Numeric Display`   Turns off a DNS lookup for the names of the routers and the destination.
- `Time to Live`   Specifies how many hops the trace is allowed to take.
- `Loose`   Tells the router that the hops you specify must appear in the trace path, but other routers can appear as well.
- `Strict`   Restricts the trace path only to those routers that you specify.
- `Record`   Specifies the number of hops to leave room for in the trace packet.
- `Timestamp`   Allows you to specify the amount of space to leave room for in the trace packet for timing information.
- `Verbose`   Automatically selected whenever you choose any of the options from this question; it prints the entire contents of the trace packet.

One important item to point out about the **traceroute** command is that if more than one path exists to reach the destination, this command will test *each* path, which can take the trace process longer. And like the extended **ping** command, instead of using the script to perform the test, you can enter the command and all of its parameters on a single command line.

e x a m

watch   *The* ping *command uses ICMP to test layer 3 connectivity to a device. The* traceroute *command*   *lists each router along the way to the destination and is typically used to troubleshoot routing problems.*

Layer 7 Connectivity Testing

The **ping** and **traceroute** commands can test only layer 3 connectivity. If you can reach a destination with either of these two commands, this indicates that layer 3 and below are functioning correctly. You can use other tools, such as telnet, to test the application layer. If you can telnet to a destination, then all seven layers of the

OSI Reference model are functioning correctly. As an example, if you can telnet to a machine but can't send an e-mail to it, then the problem is *not* a networking problem, but an application problem (with the e-mail program). Of course, if you are filtering traffic with an access control list (Chapter 22), this could also be the culprit.

e x a m

ⓦ a t c h
The telnet application is used to test layer 7 (application layer) connectivity. To test telnet, the remote destination must have telnet configured and enabled. If the remote device is an IOS device, you must minimally configure the `login` and `password` commands on the VTYs (Chapter 11).

Using Telnet

If you've configured your Cisco devices correctly (with IP addressing and routing information and the appropriate commands on the VTYs), you should be able to telnet to them successfully. However, if you have followed the advice mentioned earlier in the "Remote Access to Your IOS Device" section, you might have to test connectivity with SSH instead. Cisco routers and switches support both incoming and outgoing telnet and SSH. This assumes you have set up the VTYs and configured your IP addressing correctly.

To open up a telnet session from your IOS device, you can use any of the following three methods:

```
IOS# name_of_the_destination | destination_IP_address
```

or

```
IOS# telnet name_of_the_destination | destination_IP_address
```

or

```
IOS# connect name_of_the_destination | destination_IP_address
```

All three of these methods work in the same manner: they all have the IOS attempt to telnet the specified destination.

on the

ⓙ o b

As I mentioned in Chapter 11, if you mistype a command name from the CLI, the IOS assumes you're trying to use the first telnet method listed above and attempts to resolve the name to an IP address using the local host table, a DNS server, or a DNS broadcast. To stop this behavior, configure the `no ip domain-lookup` *command.*

Suspending Telnet Sessions

If you are on an IOS device and telnet to a remote destination, you might want to go back to your IOS device. One way of doing this is to exit the remote device; however, you might just want to go back to your source Cisco device, make a quick adjustment, and then return to the remote device. Logging off and back onto the remote device is a hassle, in this instance.

Cisco, however, has solved this problem by allowing you to *suspend* a telnet session, return to your original router or switch, do what you need to do, and then jump right back into your remote device—all without your having to log off and back onto the remote device. To suspend a telnet session, use the CTRL-SHIFT-6, X (hold down the CTRL, SHIFT, and 6 keys simultaneously, let go, and then press the X key) or CTRL-^ control sequence, depending on your keyboard.

On your source IOS, if you want to see the open telnet sessions that are currently suspended, use the **show sessions** command:

```
IOS# show sessions
Conn Host        Address      Byte    Idle    Conn Name
   1 10.1.1.1    10.1.1.1       0       1      10.1.1.1
*  2 10.1.1.2    10.1.1.2       0       2      10.1.1.2
```

This example shows two open telnet sessions. The one with the * preceding it is the default (last accessed) session. To resume the last session, all you have to do is press ENTER on an empty command line.

To resume a specific session, use this command:

```
Router# resume connection_#
```

The connection number to enter is the number in the Conn column of the **show sessions** command. As a shortcut, you can just list the number of the connection without typing **resume**, and this will accomplish the same thing. If you are on the source router or switch and want to terminate a suspended telnet session without having to resume the telnet session and then log out it, you can use this command:

```
Router# disconnect connection_#
```

17.12. The CD contains a multimedia demonstration of using telnet on a router.

Verifying and Clearing Connections

If you are logged into an IOS device, you can view the other users that are also logged in with this command:

```
Router# show users
    Line          User      Host(s)   Idle     Location
    0   con 0                         idle
    2   vty 0               idle         0     10.1.1.1
*   3   vty 1               idle         0     10.1.1.2
```

If you see a * in the first column, this indicates your current session. If you want to terminate someone's session, use the Privilege EXEC **clear line** command:

```
Router# clear line line_#
```

The line number that you enter can be found in the Line column of the output of the **show users** command.

Use the CTRL-SHIFT-6, X **control sequence to suspend a telnet session. Pressing** ENTER **on a blank command line resumes the last suspended telnet session. Use the** resume **command to**	**resume a suspended telnet connection. Use the** show sessions **command to see your suspended telnet sessions. Use the** disconnect **command to disconnect a suspended telnet session.**

Debug Overview

One problem with using **show** commands is that they display only what is currently stored somewhere in the router's RAM, and this display is *static*. You have to re-execute the command to get a refreshed update. And **show** commands, unfortunately, do not always display detailed troubleshooting information. For instance, perhaps you want the router to tell you when a particular event occurs and display some of the packet contents of that event. The **show** commands cannot do this; however, **debug** commands can. One of the most powerful troubleshooting tools of the IOS is the **debug** command, which enables you to view events and problems, in real time, on your Cisco device.

The **debug** commands, however, do have a drawback: Since the router has to examine and display many different things when this feature is enabled, the performance of the IOS will suffer. As an example, if you want to see every IP packet that travels through a router, the router has to examine each packet, determine whether it is an IP packet, and then display the packet or partial packet contents on the screen. On a very busy router, this debug process can cause serious performance degradation. Therefore, you should be very careful about enabling a debug process on your router; you might want to wait till after hours or periods of lesser inactivity before using this tool.

on the **You should never use the** `debug all` **command—this enables debugging for every process related to IOS features enabled on your router. In this situation, you'll see pages and pages of output messages on all kinds of things and, on a busy router, probably crash it.**

Typically, you will use **debug** commands for detailed troubleshooting. For instance, you may have tried using **show** commands to discover the cause of a particular problem, but without any success. You should then turn to using a particular **debug** command to uncover the source of the problem. This command has many, many options and parameters—use context-sensitive help to view them. Many of the remaining chapters in this book will cover specific **debug** commands and their uses. To enable debug, you must be at Privilege EXEC mode.

17.13. The CD contains a multimedia demonstration of using debug on a router.

Once you've fixed your problem or no longer need to see the debug output, you should always disable the debug process. You can disable it either by prefacing the **debug** command with the **no** parameter or executing one of the following two commands:

```
IOS# no debug all
```

or

```
IOS# undebug all
```

These two commands disable all running **debug** commands on your router. You can first use the **show debug** command to see which events or processes you have enabled.

If you want to see timestamps displayed in your debug output, enter the following command:

```
Router(config)# service timestamps debug datetime msec
```

The **datetime** parameter displays the current date and time, while the **msec** parameter displays an additional timing parameter: milliseconds.

on the **If you think your** `debug` **commands are causing performance problems, use the** `show processes cpu` **command to check your CPU utilization for the device's various processes, including debug.**

EXERCISE 17-2

ON THE CD

Using the Router's Troubleshooting Tools

The last few sections dealt with the router's troubleshooting tools. This exercise will
help you reinforce this material. You'll perform these steps using Boson's NetSim
simulator. You can find a picture of the network diagram for the simulator in the
Introduction of this book. After starting up the simulator, click the LabNavigator
button. Next, double-click Exercise 17-2 and click the Load Lab button. This will
load the lab configuration based on the exercises in Chapters 11 and 16.

1. Access the 2600-1 router in the simulator on the CD. See what neighbors are
   directly connected to the router. What is the IP address of the 2600-2 router?

   At the top of the simulator in the menu bar, click the eRouters icon and
   choose 2600-1. Use the **show cdp neighbors** command to view
   the 2600-1's neighbors—you may have to wait 60 seconds to see all the
   neighbors connected to this device (repeat the command as necessary). You
   should see one of the 2950 switches and the 2600-2 router. Use the **show
   cdp neighbors detail** command to view the 2600-2's address: it is
   192.168.2.2.

2. Access the 2950-2 switch in the simulator on the CD. See what neighbors are
   directly connected to the router. Which neighbors do you see? What are their
   IP addresses?

   At the top of the simulator in the menu bar, click the eSwitches icon and
   choose 2950-2. Use the **show cdp neighbors** command to view your
   neighbors. You should see the 2950-1 switch and 2600-1 router. You'll see the
   2950-1 twice since there are two connections between these two switches.
   Add the **detail** parameter to the preceding command to see the neighbors'
   IP addresses.

You should be more comfortable with the some of the router's troubleshooting tools.

INSIDE THE EXAM

Router Configuration Files

You should be intimately familiar with configuration files and when they are overwritten versus merged when using the `copy` command: re-examine Table 17-2 for an overview of this process.

Changes in Your Network

No Exam Watches are in this section: only practical knowledge you should always apply before making any changes on your IOS devices.

IOS Image Files

You should be familiar with the commands to verify the files located in flash as well as what IOS image your device loaded from flash. You need to understand how to upgrade your IOS with the `copy` command and know what happens during the upgrade, as well as how to determine whether the upgrade failed.

Remote Access to Your IOS Device

You need to be able to compare telnet and SSH, and you should know how both are set up: review Chapter 11 for setting up your VTYs for telnet access. Understand the basic

configuration to allow SSH access into your IOS device, as well as how to disable the use of telnet on the VTYs.

Basic Troubleshooting

You should be able to determine what router commands you can use to troubleshoot problems at the various OSI Reference Model layers. Know how CDP, including its timers, works and the kinds of information shared between directly connected Cisco devices. Be able to display the CDP tables on an IOS device and understand their output.

Know how to troubleshoot layer 3 problems with `ping` and `traceroute`, starting with testing of the TCP/IP protocol stack on a user's computer. Understand the different message responses you can see when using the `ping` command and what they mean from a troubleshooting perspective.

You should know how to configure your VTYs to allow telnet access, and be able to determine whether this is not set up correctly. Remember how to suspend a telnet from an IOS device, resume it, and display your open sessions. Know how to disable `debug` commands on your IOS device.

CERTIFICATION SUMMARY

Use the **copy** commands to manipulate files, including configuration files and IOS images. Any time you copy something into RAM, the IOS uses a merge process. For any other location, the IOS uses an overwrite process. On IOS devices, use the **erase startup-config** command to delete the startup-config file in NVRAM. SSH should be used instead of telnet for remote terminal (CLI) access to the router since it encrypts traffic between your desktop and an IOS device.

CDP is a Cisco-proprietary protocol that functions at the data link layer. Every 60 seconds, Cisco devices generate a multicast on each of their interfaces containing basic information about themselves, including the device type, the version of software they're running, and their IP address(es). To disable CDP globally, use the **no cdp run** command. To see a list of your neighbors, use the **show cdp neighbors** command.

The **ping** and **traceroute** commands support an extended version at Privilege EXEC mode. If you want to suspend an active telnet session, use the CTRL-SHIFT-6, X control sequence. Pressing ENTER on a blank command line resumes the last suspended telnet session. Use the **resume** command to resume a telnet connection. Use the **show sessions** command to see your open telnet session. Use the **disconnect** command to disconnect a suspended telnet session. To disable debug on your IOS device, use **undebug all** or **no debug all**. Debug functions only at Privilege EXEC mode.

TWO-MINUTE DRILL

Router Configuration Files

❑ These commands perform a merge process: `copy startup-config running-config`, `copy tftp running-config`, and `configure terminal`. These commands perform an overwrite process: `copy running-config startup-config` and `copy running-config tftp`.

❑ IOS devices do not automatically save their configuration in RAM: you must execute the `copy running-config startup-config` command to save the active configuration file to NVRAM.

Changes in Your Network

❑ Always back up your configuration before making any changes to it—preferably to a remote server using SCP, which encrypts it.

IOS Image Files

❑ When upgrading your IOS, make sure you download the version of IOS from Cisco that contains the features that you purchased and verify that your router has enough flash and RAM for the new image. Use the `copy` *URL* `flash` command to perform an IOS upgrade.

❑ Use the `reload` command to reboot your router.

Remote Access to Your IOS Device

❑ Use SSH for an encrypted remote access terminal session to your router. The `transport input` command can be used to limit what management protocols are allowed on the VTYs.

Basic Troubleshooting

❑ For layer 2 troubleshooting, use the `show interfaces` command and CDP. For layer 3 troubleshooting, use `ping` and `traceroute`. For layer 7 troubleshooting, use telnet. For detailed troubleshooting, use `debug`.

❑ CDP is used to learn basic information about directly connected Cisco devices. It uses a SNAP frame format and generates a multicast every 60 seconds. It is enabled, by default, on a Cisco device.

❏ To execute an extended **ping** or **traceroute**, you must be at Privilege EXEC mode. Ping tests only if the destination is reachable, while **traceroute** lists each layer 3 device along the way to the destination.

❏ To suspend a telnet session, use the CTRL-SHIFT-6, X, or CTRL-^ control sequence.

❏ The **debug** commands require Privilege EXEC access. To disable all **debug** commands, use **no debug all** or **undebug all**.

SELF TEST

The following Self Test questions will help you measure your understanding of the material presented in this chapter. Read all the choices carefully, as there may be more than one correct answer. Choose all correct answers for each question.

Router Configuration Files

1. Which router commands perform an overwrite process? (choose two)

    A. `copy running-config startup-config`

    B. `copy startup-config running-config`

    C. `copy tftp running-config`

    D. `copy running-config tftp`

2. Enter the router command to delete your configuration file in NVRAM: _____.

3. You have executed the `show startup-config` command and see the following message: "%%Non-volatile configuration memory is not present". Which of the following answers are correct about these two things? (choose two)

    A. This command displays the running configuration in NVRAM.

    B. This command displays the saved configuration in NVRAM.

    C. This command displays the saved configuration in flash.

    D. The message indicates that flash needs to be reformatted.

    E. This message indicates that NVRAM needs to be reformatted.

    F. This message indicates that there is nothing stored in this memory location.

IOS Image Files

4. When backing up your IOS image from flash, which of the following will the `copy flash tftp` command prompt you for? (choose three)

    A. TFTP server IP address

    B. Verification to copy

    C. Source filename

    D. Destination filename

5. What IOS command will display the version of software your device is running?

    A. `show startup-config`

    B. `show flash`

C. `show version`

D. `dir` and `show version`

Remote Access to Your IOS Device

6. Enter the IOS configuration on the first five VTYs to allow only SSH access and to prompt for both a username and password for line authentication: _____.

7. Enter the IOS command that will create RSA public and private keys to encrypt and decrypt traffic for an SSH session: _____.

Basic Troubleshooting

8. Which of the following is true of CDP?

A. The `show cdp neighbor` command displays what version of software the neighbor is running.

B. The `no cdp run` command disables CDP on an interface.

C. CDP sends out broadcasts every 60 seconds.

D. CDP can be used to validate layer 2 connectivity.

9. Which router command would you use to test only layer 3 connectivity?

A. `telnet`

B. `show cdp traffic`

C. `show interfaces`

D. `traceroute`

10. How would you suspend a telnet session?

A. CTRL-SHIFT-X, 6

B. CTRL-SHIFT-6, X

C. CTRL-6, X

D. CTRL-C

SELF TEST ANSWERS

Router Configuration Files

1. ☑ **A** and **D**. Copying to any other place besides RAM (*running-config*) causes an overwrite.
   ☒ **B** and **C** are wrong because copying to RAM is a merge process, not an overwrite process.

2. ☑ Use the **erase startup-config** command to delete your configuration file in NVRAM.

3. ☑ **B** and **F**. The **show startup-config** command displays a backed-up configuration in NVRAM. If no configuration is stored there, you see the "%%Non-volatile configuration memory is not present" message.
   ☒ **A** is incorrect because a saved configuration, not the running configuration, is found in NVRAM. **C** and **D** are incorrect because these commands save the configuration to flash, not NVRAM. You cannot reformat NVRAM; you can only copy over it or erase it, making **E** incorrect.

IOS Image Files

4. ☑ **A, C,** and **D**. When you use the **copy flash tftp** command, you are prompted for the TFTP server's IP address, the source filename of the IOS in flash, and the name you want to call the IOS image on the TFTP server.
   ☒ **B** is incorrect because you are not prompted for a verification before the command is executed; however, you are prompted for this information if you are doing the reverse: upgrading the IOS device.

5. ☑ **C**. The **show version** command will display the current software version your IOS device is running.
   ☒ **B** is incorrect because **show flash** displays the saved configuration file in NVRAM. **B** and **D** (**dir** command) are incorrect because these commands display the files in flash, but not necessarily the IOS version currently running on the router.

Remote Access to Your IOS Device

6. ☑ `line vty 0 4`
       `transport input ssh`
       `login local`

7. ☑ `crypto key generate rsa`

Basic Troubleshooting

8. ☑ **D.** CDP can be used to validate that you have layer 2 connectivity with a connected device.

☒ **A** is incorrect because **show cdp neighbor** displays neighbors, but not their configuration, software version, or model number; you need the **detail** parameter for this information. **B** is incorrect because **no cdp run** disables CDP globally. **C** is incorrect because CDP uses multicasts, not broadcasts.

9. ☑ **D.** The **traceroute** command tests layer 3.

☒ **A** is incorrect because **telnet** tests layer 7. **B** and **C** are incorrect because **show cdp traffic** and **show interfaces** test layer 2.

10. ☑ **B.** Use CTRL-SHIFT-6, x to suspend a telnet session.

☒ **D** is incorrect because this break sequence is used to break out of the System Configuration Dialog. **A** and **C** are incorrect because these are nonexistent break sequences.

18

Security Device Manager

This book has focused on the use of the command-line interface (CLI) to manage IOS devices; however, Cisco also supports graphical user interfaces (GUIs) as an alternative management method. One GUI product Cisco supports for routers is called *Security Device Manager* (SDM). This chapter provides a brief introduction to the product and describes its uses. A more in-depth discussion of SDM is covered in Cisco's Securing Cisco Network Devices (SND) course, which focuses on configuring security features on routers using SDM.

CERTIFICATION OBJECTIVE 18.01

Introduction to SDM

SDM is a web-based application, implemented with Java, that manages the basic administration and security features on a Cisco router. SDM is installed in the router's flash memory and is remotely accessed from an administrator's desktop using a web browser with Java and Secure Sockets Layer (SSL) (HTTPS). Originally, Cisco developed SDM for small office/home office (SOHO) networks, where the administrator performing the configuration is probably not familiar with Cisco's CLI. Actually, using SDM doesn't require knowledge of Cisco's CLI.

e x a m

w a t c h

SDM is a web-based tool, implemented with Java, that lets you manage a single router at a time. SDM uses SSL (configurations) and Secure Shell (SSH) (interactive commands) to protect the interaction between your desktop and the router.

SDM is supported on routers from the 800 through the 7300 series and is automatically included in flash when you buy these routers today from Cisco: beginning in June 2003, all supported routers with supported IOS versions come with SDM. Some enhanced tools it implements include wizards to simplify the setup of basic administration tasks and security features. Wizards allow you to configure a particular feature quickly in a step-by-step fashion, asking you questions to help the router determine how the configuration should be created. Once you have configured a particular feature with a wizard, you can fine-tune your configuration using enhanced editing features, such as inline editing of access control lists (ACLs), inline editing of crypto maps (for virtual private networks, or VPNs), and a preview function to examine IOS commands before a configuration is committed to a router.

SDM was designed by Cisco to allow you to perform basic administration functions and to manage the security features of your router. SDM cannot perform all functions that can be performed from the CLI, such as the configuration of complex QoS policies or the Border Gateway Protocol (BGP) routing protocol, to name a couple. Nor are all interface types supported within SDM, such as ISDN and dialup. However, for the features and interface types not supported, you can still configure these from the CLI of the router. Likewise, most troubleshooting tasks are still done from the CLI with show *and* debug *commands.*

PC Requirements

SDM is supported on Windows-based PCs meeting the following operating system requirements:

- Microsoft Windows Vista (Business Edition)
- Microsoft Windows XP Professional
- Microsoft Windows 2003 Server (Standard Edition)
- Microsoft Windows 2000 Professional or Server (not Advanced Server) with Service Pack 4

SDM is browser-based and requires the use of a web browser to access it on the router and download it. Supported web browsers include the following:

- Firefox 1.0.6 and later
- Internet Explorer 5.5 and later
- Netscape Navigator 7.1, 7.2, and 9.0

Your PC will also need Java installed. Minimally you'll need version 1.4.2(08) of Sun's Java Runtime Environment (JRE).

SDM requires a minimum screen resolution of 1024x768; a resolution lower than this will not allow you to view the entire Java-based screen. Java has a big problem resizing applications to fit a screen, so if your settings don't meet the above resolution criteria, you won't be able to see all the components on SDM's screens.

Router Requirements and SDM Files

As mentioned in the last section, SDM is not supported on all IOS routers. For a list of router models and IOS images on which SDM is supported, visit Cisco's web site at www.cisco.com/go/sdm. If your router currently doesn't have SDM installed, you can easily add SDM by downloading it from Cisco's web site. Your router will need to be under a maintenance contract and you'll need a Cisco Connection Online (CCO) account to download the SDM software; however, Cisco does not charge you to use the software. On your router, you'll minimally need IOS version 12.2 for SDM to function; and depending on the version of SDM, you will need between 5MB and 8MB of available flash on your router.

If SDM has already been installed on your router, you'll see various files in flash. Depending on the version of SDM, the names and numbers of the files will differ. With version 2.3 and later, you'll see the files listed in Table 18-1.

on the **Job** *Before adding SDM to flash on your router, use the* `dir` *or* `show flash` *command to make sure you have enough flash to fit all the SDM files.*

TABLE 18-1 SDM Files

Filename	Description
common.tar	Support file for SDM
es.tar	Application file for SDM
home.shtml	Support HTML file for SDM
home.tar	Support file for SDM
sdmconfig-xxxx.cfg	Default router configuration with commands necessary to access SDM, where xxxx represents the model number of the router
sdm.tar	SDM application file
xxxx.sdf	IPS signature files (some common names are attack-drop.sdf, 128MB.sdf, 256MB.sdf, and sdmips.sdf)
securedesktop-ios-xxxx-k9.pkg	Cisco Secure Desktop (CSD) client software for the SSL VPN client, where xxxx represents the version number of CSD
sslclient-win-xxxx.pkg	SSL VPN Client (SVC) tunneling software, where xxxx represents the version of SVC
wlanui.tar	Wireless application setup program for a radio module installed in the router

If you don't have SDM installed on your router, you can download the SDM package from Cisco and install it via the router's CLI using the **copy** *URL* **flash** command (discussed in Chapter 17). Optionally, you can order the SDM CD from Cisco and perform the install from the CD. If SDM is already installed on your router, you can upgrade SDM directly through the SDM interface.

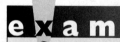

ᗯatch

Use the *show flash* or *dir* command to determine whether you have SDM installed on your router before trying to copy SDM to your router. The files you need in flash in order to run SDM include common.tar, es.tar, home.shtml, home.tar, and sdm.tar.

Necessary Router Configuration

Before you can begin using SDM, the router needs a basic configuration installed. Some of these basic commands were discussed in Chapters 11 and 16, such as assigning IP addresses to your interfaces and enabling them. Beyond this, your router will need additional commands. One of the files included in the SDM package on Cisco's site is named sdmconfig-*xxxx*.cfg. This file contains the necessary commands to configure the router; if you have purchased an 800 series router from Cisco, this is the default configuration on the router. Otherwise, you'll either need to copy and paste the commands from the configuration file into your router or manually type them in:

```
Router(config)# hostname router_name
Router(config)# ip domain-name domain_name
Router(config)# ip http server
Router(config)# ip http secure-server
Router(config)# ip http authentication local
Router(config)# username username privilege 15 secret 0 password
Router(config)# ip http timeout-policy idle seconds
                        life seconds requests number
Router(config)# line vty 0 15
Router(config-line)# privilege level 15
Router(config-line)# login local
Router(config-line)# transport input ssh
```

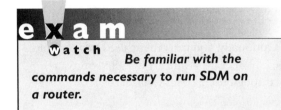

SDM uses SSL to send configurations to the router and SSH to deliver actual interactive commands and the resulting output of those commands, such as **show** commands, back to the SDM's GUI. Both SSL and SSH require an RSA key pair. The generation of RSA keys for SSH was discussed in Chapter 17. To generate these keys, the router needs a host and domain name (the first two commands listed in the preceding code). However, unlike the configuration in Chapter 17, you do not need to create the RSA key pair manually; instead, the first time you access the router using SDM, the router will generate the key pair, which it will use for SSH as well as using these keys to create a self-signed SSL certificate.

Since SDM is web-based and uses SSL, the **ip http server** and **ip http secure-server** commands are used to enable the web server and SSL features of the router. The **ip http authentication** command specifies the use of the local user database (**username** commands) to authenticate SDM access to the router. The user account on the router must have a privilege level of 15 if it is to be able to configure the router using SDM.

o n t h e
ⓙ o b   *The default user account and passwords in the sdmconfig-xxxx.cfg file*
included with SDM are sdm and sdm—don't use these! Change them before
copying and pasting the configuration from the sdmconfig file into the router.
Everyone knows these passwords, and these are the first passwords an
attacker will guess to break into the router.

The **ip http timeout-policy** command is optional, but it is recommended: this command determines how long an SDM connection to the HTTP server on the router should remain open. The **idle** parameter specifies the number of seconds a web connection should remain open if no data is sent or received on the connection: the default is 180 seconds. The **life** parameter specifies the number of seconds a web connection will be kept open to the server from when the time the connection is established to the web server. The default is 180 seconds but can be increased up to 86,400 seconds (1 day). The **requests** parameter limits the number of concurrent requests processed on an existing connection before it is closed: the default is 1.

The last part of the configuration requires you to configure the VTYs on the router: this is necessary for any type of SSH access SDM might need for accessing the router to perform interactive commands. Since SDM requires the highest privilege level when implementing changes on the router (level 15), the VTYs must be assigned this level of access (`privilege level 15`). Second, the router will need to authenticate access using a local user database (`login local`). And last, you should restrict access to the VTYs to just SSH access (`transport input ssh`).

Accessing SDM

Assuming you have placed the necessary configuration on your router to access SDM, you can now open a web browser on your desktop and access it. You'll need to know the IP address of the router's interface. On an 800 series router that shipped from Cisco, the default IP address of the inside interface is 10.10.10.1; just connect your PC to the inside interface with the correct cable type (straight if connecting to a switch port on the router or a crossover cable if connecting to a stand-alone Ethernet port).

To access SDM, enter the following syntax in your web browser's address bar:

`https://router's_IP_address`

Your web browser will attempt to do a DNS lookup of the fully-qualified domain name on the router's self-signed certificate (the router created it when you attempted to access it the first time). If your router's IP address is not listed in a DNS server, you'll see a pop-up window with this error message: "Security Error: Domain Mismatch." Click OK to close this window. You'll be prompted for a username and password: use one of the names listed on your router with the `username` commands. Remember that the account must have a privilege level of 15. Enter a correct username and password and click the OK button.

A new window will pop up, as shown in Figure 18-1. If this window does not open, it is probably because you have pop-up blocking enabled. In your web browser, you'll need to make an exception to pop-up blocking for the IP address of the router you're trying to access. You might be prompted to accept the Java script code and to log in again, via Java, to SDM (this depends on the version of SDM being used).

on the
job

The original web browser window, where you typed in the URL to access the router, can be closed; however, the pop-up window needs to remain open. SDM, via Java, uses this window to communicate to the router using SSL.

Startup Wizard

Certain router models and SDM versions support a *Startup* wizard. The Startup wizard, if supported, will appear the first time you access SDM on a router where a default configuration is detected. The function of the Startup wizard is to put a basic

FIGURE 18-1

SSL interface to
your router

configuration on the router. The wizard will lead you through a handful of screens
where you can configure the following information:

- The LAN interface's configuration, such as its IP addressing information (this
  is the inside interface)
- A DHCP server's configuration for devices connected to the LAN interface,
  including an IP address pool, a default gateway address (this should be the
  router itself), DNS and WINS server addresses, and other information
- The router's hostname and domain name
- The enable secret password
- A level 15 user account and password

Part of the function of the wizard is to enable certain services to enhance the
router's security and disable services that might create a security risk to the router.
At the end of the wizard, SDM will display a brief summary of the configuration it
will push down to the router once you complete the wizard. The Startup wizard is

only run once unless you reset the router back to its factory defaults and configure a basic default configuration on it.

on the
Job

If you change the LAN interface's IP addressing information, at the end of the Startup wizard, you'll lose your connection to SDM: you'll need to re-access SDM using the new IP address on the LAN interface and log back into SDM.

Home Page

After running the Startup wizard and every subsequent time you access SDM, a new window will open, shown in Figure 18-2: this is SDM's home page. At this point you're dealing with Java. At the very top is a menu bar where you can access the File, Edit, View, Tools, and Help menus. Below the menu bar are buttons, explained here:

- **Home**   Clicking this takes you to the screen shown in Figure 18-2.
- **Configure**   Clicking this takes you to the configuration screen, where you can change the configuration of the router.
- **Monitor**   Clicking this takes you to the monitoring screen, where you can view different information on the router, such as logging and interface statistics.
- **Refresh**   Clicking this button will pull in the running configuration of the router into SDM, replacing any configuration SDM might currently have.
- **Save**   Clicking this button sends the `copy running-config startup-config` command down to the router, causing the router to save its active configuration to NVRAM.
- **Search**   Clicking this button displays a screen where you can type in a key word or words to find different screens within SDM. Hyperlinks will appear next to the displayed results that you can click and be taken directly to the selected Configure or Monitor screen.
- **Help**   Clicking this button pulls up help on how to use SDM to configure your router.

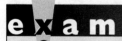

On the Home screen shown in Figure 18-2, you can view information about the router. In the About Your Router section, you can view the model number of the router, the amount of RAM and flash installed in the router, the versions of the IOS and SDM, and the available security features based on the IOS installed on the router.

Under the About Your Router section is the Configuration Overview section, where you can view the following:

- The hardware interfaces installed and their statuses
- A summary of the status of the firewall configuration on the router
- A summary of the status of the VPN connections on the router
- A summary of the routing configuration on the router
- A summary of the IPS (Intrusion Prevention System) configuration on the router

on the
job

Between the About Your Router and Configuration Overview sections on the Home screen is a View Running Config button. Clicking this button will pop up a window and display the current configuration running in RAM on the router.

FIGURE 18-2

SDM Home
screen

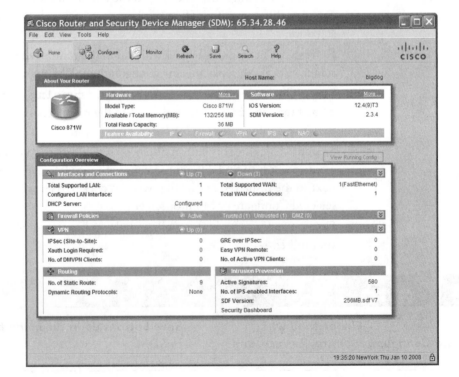

CERTIFICATION OBJECTIVE 18.02

Basic Router Configuration Using SDM

As mentioned in the introduction to this chapter, all the configuration and management aspects of SDM are not covered here: this is a course in-and-of itself called SND, which discusses the use of the product over a four-day period. Instead, this chapter briefly introduces some of the basic configuration tasks you'll perform in SDM and then discusses some of the wizards SDM offers.

Configure Screens

To access the configuration screens, click the Configure button at the top of the SDM window. This will take you to the screen in Figure 18-3. On the left side of the screen are buttons you can click to navigate to the different configuration sections:

- **Interfaces and Connections** You can set up interface trunking, configure properties for an interface, and display the status and configuration of the interfaces.

- **Firewall and ACL** You can create your firewall policies for two or more interface routers, edit access control lists (ACLs are discussed in Chapter 22), change your firewall policies, and view the ACL and firewall policies.

- **VPN** You can create, edit, and view IPSec site-to-site, IPSec remote access, and SSL VPNs, which Cisco refers to as WebVPN (VPNs are discussed in Chapter 25).

- **Security Audit** You can perform a security audit of the router, which has the IOS make recommendations of security features that should be enabled or IOS features that should be disabled.

- **Routing** You can configure your static and dynamic routing protocols (routing configuration is discussed in Chapters 19, 20, and 21).

- **NAT** You can configure static and dynamic address translation policies (address translation is discussed in Chapter 23).

- **Intrusion Prevention** You can configure your intrusion prevention system (IPS) policies to look for network and host attacks.

■ **Quality of Service**   You can define a quality of service (QoS) policy to prioritize your traffic as it goes through the router.

■ **NAC**   You can define a network access control (NAC) server to perform posture validation before allowing a user access through the router.

■ **Additional Tasks**   You can perform all other management tasks by clicking this button, such as setting up a DHCP server, defining local user accounts, restricting access to the VTYs, setting up SSH, and many other management functions.

on the
job   *One handy feature of SDM is that once you have completed a configuration task within the GUI and before you deploy it down to the router, you can see the actual commands SDM will configure on the router. By default, this feature is turned off. To turn it on, choose Edit > Preferences and select the checkbox labeled Preview Commands Before Delivering To Router. Then, when you apply changes to the router, a window will pop up with the actual IOS commands that will be executed on the router. Click the Deliver button to complete the delivery process of the commands to the router.*

FIGURE 18-3

Configure screen

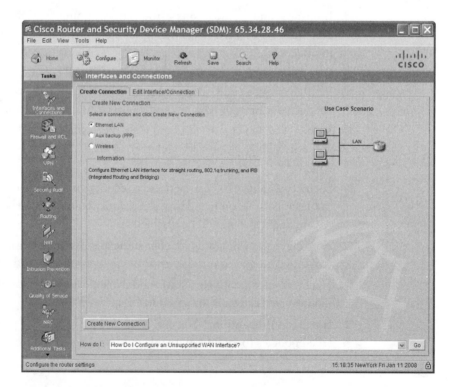

SDM Wizards

At the top of most configuration screens you'll typically find two tabs: Create and Edit. The Create tab allows you to use a wizard to configure the specified feature. Cisco uses wizards to minimize misconfigurations when you are initially setting up the router and certain features on it. Wizards are basically used once, when setting up a particular feature. Once you have completed the configuration task with a wizard, any changes you need to make, as well as viewing the current configuration of the feature, are done from the Edit tab.

e x a m
w a t c h

SDM uses wizards to minimize any misconfiguration of common administrative and security configurations, *including firewall, VPN, address translation, and IPS functions.*

When using a wizard, SDM will lead you through a series of screens that will ask you questions about how you want to configure a particular feature. Based on your answers, SDM will create the necessary commands to implement the feature. At the end of the wizard, the commands are delivered directly to the router and activated in the router's running-config.

Cisco recommends you run the wizards in this order initially:

1. Interfaces and Connections (previously these were two separate buttons, called LAN and WAN, in older SDM versions)
2. Firewall and ACL
3. VPN
4. NAT
5. IPS
6. Security Audit

The Security Audit wizard actually doesn't perform any configurations; instead, it examines the current configuration on your router and compares it to best configuration practices by Cisco's Technical Assistance Center (TAC) and the International Computer Security Association (ICSA). If the wizard sees that you are not following these recommended practices, it can fix these issues for you. In certain cases, you'll have to provide the Security Audit wizard with additional information to complete its tasks. For example, you must define what interfaces are considered trusted and untrusted; and if the wizard needs to fix something, such as create a login banner, you'll need to provide the information to do this.

The Security Audit wizard can be run in two modes: *Perform security audit* and *One-step lockdown*. With the former approach, the wizard will display any issues it discovers and gives you the option of which ones you want the wizard to fix; with the latter approach, the wizard just fixes any issues that it sees.

on the
ⓙⓞⓑ

Cisco recommends that you periodically run the Security Audit wizard to uncover any security issues that may have cropped up based on daily configurations you've performed on your router.

Configuration Changes

One limitation of using a wizard is that the wizard process will not necessarily offer you every configuration option for an IOS feature. To configure these components or to make any changes to components you've configured using a wizard, click the Edit tab for a particular Configure button.

exam
ⓦatch

The Apply Changes, Deliver, and OK buttons are used to send commands SDM creates down to the router, which are then applied.

When you are making changes, in a few instances when you are in a particular configuration screen, they are directly applied to the router. However, in most cases, you make all your changes once on a configuration screen, such as adding and editing ACLs from the Firewall and ACL button's Edit Firewall/ACL Policy tab and then at the bottom of the screen clicking the Apply Changes button. If you don't like your changes and want to abandon them (assuming you haven't already pushed them down to the router), you can click the Discard Changes button (to the right of the Apply Changes button).

on the
ⓙⓞⓑ

When either using a wizard from the Create tab or making configuration changes from the Edit tab, you can take advantage of the built-in help on the router. Clicking the Help button at the top of the window will open a new web browser window that displays the configuration options of the screen in which you are currently working.

Interfaces

Chapters 11 and 16 discussed how you set up your router's interfaces, such as enabling and assigning an IP address and subnet mask to them. You can perform the same tasks via SDM by clicking the Configure button, clicking the Interfaces and Connections button, and then clicking the Edit Interface/Connection tab (displayed in Figure 18-4).

Interface Information

In Figure 18-4, the Details button is selected, which splits the screen into two areas: Interface List and Details About Interface. In the Interface List portion of the screen, you can see the list of interfaces, the IP addresses, the operational statuses of the interfaces, and a description of the interfaces. If you see (DHCP Client) appear next to an IP address, the router acquired the address via DHCP (acting as a DHCP client) on the respective interface.

FIGURE 18-4

Edit Interface/
Connection tab

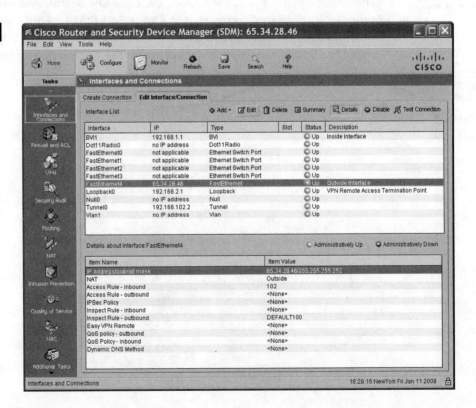

When you click the row for an interface in this section, you'll see some of the policies configured on the selected interface in the Details About Interface section. In Figure 18-4, FastEthernet4 is selected in the top section, and in the bottom section you can see the IP address and subnet mask on the interface as well as any ACL applied to the interface (in this example, ACL 102 is applied in the inbound direction).

Interface Changes

To make changes to an interface, from the Edit Interface/Connection tab, click the interface first. To enable or disable it, click the Enable or Disable button in the top-right corner. To change the properties of an interface, click the Edit button. A new window will pop up, as shown in Figure 18-5.Tabs at the top allow you to change the various properties of the interface. The Connection tab is in the foreground, where you can change the IP address and subnet mask of the interface. Once you make your changes, click the OK button to apply them directly to the router.

on the job

When making changes to Interfaces, click the OK button and they are immediately delivered to the router. Other Edit tabs typically allow you to make multiple changes within SDM, where you then deliver them to the router by clicking the Apply Now button at the completion of your changes.

FIGURE 18-5

Interface Feature
Edit Dialog

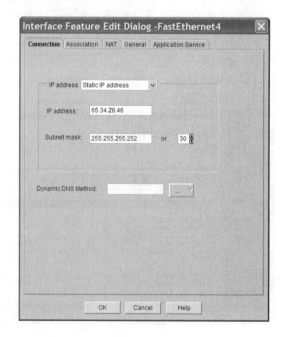

DHCP Setup

The operation of DHCP was discussed in Chapter 6. Using SDM, you can set up your router as a DHCP server, which is common in SOHO settings. Cisco supports a full DHCP server implementation, which allows the router to assign the following addressing information to a client: an IP address, a subnet mask, a default gateway address, a DNS domain name, up to two DNS server addresses, up to two WINS server addresses, and the length of the lease on the IP address.

DHCP Server Configuration

The configuration of a DHCP server is initially done when running the Startup wizard. If you didn't configure the DHCP server then, or you need to make changes afterward, click the Configure button, click the Additional Tasks button, expand the DHCP option, and then click the DHCP Pool option, where you'll seen the screen shown in Figure 18-6.

FIGURE 18-6

DHCP Pools
screen

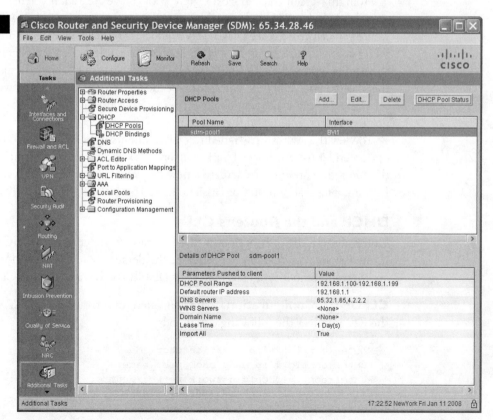

FIGURE 18-7

Edit DHCP Pool
window

From this screen you can see a DHCP pool you've created. If you're starting from scratch, click the Add button at the top of the screen: a new window will pop up, where you can create your DHCP server policies. To make changes to a current DHCP server configuration, from the DHCP Pools screen, select the Pool Name. You can see the configuration of the DHCP server at the bottom of the screen. To make changes to the selected pool, click the Edit button at the top of the screen: a new window will pop up where you can make your changes (shown in Figure 18-7). Table 18-2 explains the fields you can configure on this screen.

To view the addresses assigned to DHCP clients in SDM, from the DHCP Pools option under the Additional Tasks button, click the DHCP Pool Status button at the top-right corner of the screen: a new window will pop up, shown in Figure 18-8. In this example, the router has assigned 192.168.1.103 to a DHCP client.

DHCP and the Router's CLI

Unfortunately, the only option in SDM to view the operation of DHCP was shown in the last section in Figure 18-8. To see the details about the operation of DHCP and to troubleshoot problems related to DHCP, you have to use the CLI.

CLI DHCP Configuration   The equivalent of setting up a DHCP server from the CLI involves the following commands:

```
Router(config)# [no] service dhcp
Router(config)# ip dhcp pool pool_name
Router(config-dhcp)# network network_number
                    [subnet_mask | /prefix_length]
Router(config-dhcp)# domain-name domain_name
```

TABLE 18-2	DHCP Server Configuration Parameters

Parameter	Description
DHCP Pool Name	The unique name of the DHCP configuration
DHCP Pool Network and Subnet Mask	The network number and subnet mask for the range of addresses to be assigned to DHCP clients
Starting IP and Ending IP	The lowest and highest IP addresses in the DHCP Pool Network that can be assigned to DHCP clients
Lease Length	The amount of time the DHCP is allowed to keep the assigned IP address before it must be renewed
DNS Server1 and Server2	Up to two DNS server addresses assigned to the DHCP clients
Domain Name	The domain name assigned to the DHCP clients
WINS Server1 and Server2	Up to two WINS server addresses assigned to the DHCP clients
Default Router	The router's own IP address on the interface connected to the DHCP clients (the clients will use this address to reach other subnets)
Import All DHCP Options Into The DHCP Server Database	The DHCP options will be imported for a higher-level server (if the router is a DHCP client when connected to the ISP and is learning some of the DHCP parameters from the ISP DHCP server, these are passed into and used by the DHCP pool)

```
Router(config-dhcp)# dns-server IP_address [IP_address_2]
Router(config-dhcp)# netbios-name-server IP_address [IP_address_2]
Router(config-dhcp)# netbios-node-type node_type
Router(config-dhcp)# default-router IP_address
Router(config-dhcp)# lease days [hours][minutes] | infinite
Router(config-dhcp)# import all
Router(config-dhcp)# exit
Router(config)# ip dhcp ping timeout milliseconds
Router(config)# ip dhcp excluded-address beginning_IP_address
                      [ending_IP_address]
```

FIGURE 18-8

DHCP Pool
Status window

DHCP Pool Status

DHCP Pool Name: sdm-pool1

IP addresses leased

192.168.1.103

OK

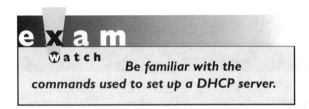

e x a m

ⓦ a t c h

Be familiar with the commands used to set up a DHCP server.

The **service dhcp** command enables and disables the DHCP server feature on your router. By default, this is enabled on your router. Precede the command with the **no** parameter to disable it. The **ip dhcp pool** command creates an addressing pool. The name you give this pool must be unique. Notice that when you execute this command, you are placed in DHCP Subconfiguration mode.

The **network** command specifies the range of IP addresses to be assigned to clients. You specify a network number followed by either a subnet mask or a slash and the number of networking bits in the network. If you omit the subnet mask value, it defaults to the subnet mask of the Class A, B, or C network.

The **domain-name** command assigns the domain name to the client. The **dns-server** command allows you to assign DNS server addresses to the client. Separate each address from the next with a space. The **netbios-name-server** command allows you to assign WINS server addresses to the client. The **netbios-node-type** command assigns the node type to a Microsoft client. This identifies how Microsoft clients perform resolution. These types can be **b** (broadcast only), **p** (WINS only), **m** (broadcast, then WINS), or **h** (WINS, then broadcast). The **default-router** command allows you to assign a gateway address (this should be the router's interface address). The **lease** command specifies the duration of the lease. If you omit this, it defaults to one day. If you specify the **infinite** parameter, the IP address assigned to the client is assigned permanently. The **import all** command performs the equivalent of selecting the Import All DHCP Options Into The DHCP Server Database parameter in SDM (see Table 18-2).

The second to the last command in the preceding code listing is not done within DHCP Subconfiguration mode. The **ip dhcp ping timeout** command is used by the DHCP server to test whether an available address the server has in its pool is or is not being used. Before a server will send an address in a DHCPOFFER message, it pings the address. This command is used to define how long the server should wait for a reply. By default, this is 500 milliseconds. If the server doesn't receive a reply in this time period, the server will assume the address is not being used and offer this to the client. The **ip dhcp excluded-address** command excludes addresses from your network pool—these addresses are already statically assigned to devices, perhaps servers, on the same segment as the client.

If you refer back to Figure 18-7, the configuration pushed down to the CLI is as follows:

```
Router(config)# service dhcp
Router(config)# ip dhcp excluded-address 192.168.1.1 192.168.1.99
Router(config)# ip dhcp excluded-address 192.168.1.200 192.168.1.254
Router(config)# ip dhcp pool sdm-pool1
Router(dhcp-config)# import all
Router(dhcp-config)# network 192.168.1.0 255.255.255.0
Router(dhcp-config)# dns-server 65.32.1.65 4.2.2.2
Router(dhcp-config)# default-router 192.168.1.1
```

CLI DHCP Verification   Once you have your DHCP server up and running, you can view the addresses assigned to clients with the following command:

```
Router# show ip dhcp binding [client_address]
```

Here's an example of the use of this command:

```
Router# show ip dhcp binding
Bindings from all pools not associated with VRF:
IP address      Client-ID/           Lease expiration       Type
                Hardware address/
                User name
192.168.1.103   0100.18f8.29a3.a6  Jan 11 2008 10:12 PM  Automatic
```

On a DHCP server, you can clear an assigned client address with the following command:

```
Router# clear ip dhcp binding client_address | *
```

Entering an asterisk at the end of the command line will clear all of the bounded addresses for clients.

To display any address conflicts discovered by the DHCP server on your router, use the **show ip dhcp conflict** command; here's an example:

```
Router# show ip dhcp conflict
IP address      Detection method   Detection time
192.168.1.107  Ping               Jan 10 2008 11:37 AM
192.168.1.109  Gratuitous ARP     Jan 10 2008 15:22 PM
```

The Detection Method column describes how the router detected an address conflict. The first entry here was discovered by the router through the router itself using ping. The second entry was discovered when the client advertised a gratuitous ARP (discussed in Chapter 6). When the router discovers a conflicting address, it removes the address from the pool and won't assign it to any requesting DHCP requests until the address conflict is resolved by an administrator.

For more detailed troubleshooting, you can use the following **debug** command:

```
Router# debug ip dhcp server events|packet|linkage
```

CERTIFICATION OBJECTIVE 18.03

Basic Router Monitoring Using SDM

You can view basic information about the operation of your router in SDM, including some statistics of the behavior of the router; however, most information can be viewed only by using the **show** or **debug** command from the router's CLI. The following sections briefly cover some of the statistics you can view in SDM.

To view the statistics in SDM, click the Monitor button, where you'll see the screen in Figure 18-9. The statistics you can view from the Monitor section include the following:

- **Overview**   Displays an overview of the operation of the router
- **Interface Status**   Displays the statuses of the interfaces on the router, where you can create near real-time graphs of various interface statistics, such as the bandwidth being utilized on an interface
- **Firewall Status**   Displays the log messages of matches on ACL statements
- **VPN Status**   Displays the statuses of VPN tunnels terminated on the router
- **Traffic Status**   Displays traffic statistics if you have the network-based application recognition (NBAR) feature enabled
- **NAC Status**   Displays information about the interaction with the NAC policy server
- **Logging**   Displays logging messages stored in the router's RAM
- **IPS Status**   Displays the IPS alerts from attacks

FIGURE 18-9

Monitor screen

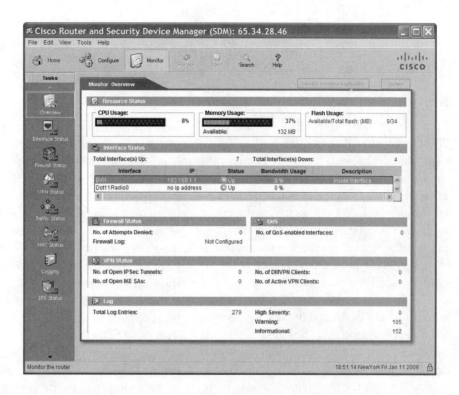

To access any of these statistics, click the appropriate button from the Tasks list on the left side of the screen.

When entering the SDM Monitor section, the statistics are pulled from the router but are not automatically updated unless you click the Update button. The exception to this is the Interface Status screen, which automatically updates the interface statistics every 10 seconds.

When you click the Monitor button, you are automatically taken to the Overview statistics that provide an overview of the statistics found on other screens in SDM, including the CPU, memory (RAM), and flash usage on the router; the status of the router's interfaces; the number of denied packets by ACLs; the number of interfaces that have QoS enabled; the number of VPN tunnels on the router; and a breakdown of the log messages in the router's RAM.

18.01. The CD contains a multimedia demonstration of accessing and using SDM.

INSIDE THE EXAM

Introduction to SDM

Even though SDM has been around since 2003, Cisco recently added it to its CCNA curriculum. However, Cisco only lightly covers the topic in its CCNA courses, so don't expect many questions from this chapter to show up on the exam (at least not yet). This doesn't mean that the material in this chapter isn't important, since even a single question about the material might be the difference between passing and failing the exam.

You should remember that SDM is a web-based GUI tool developed in Java. It provides a secure connection using SSL (HTTPS) and SSH to a Cisco router. Only a single router can be managed at a time using SDM. You should be familiar with the files that are used in flash in SDM. You should also be able to examine a router's configuration to determine what command is missing that is causing SDM not to start up. The Startup wizard runs only once unless you reset the router back to its factor default configuration. Be familiar with the various buttons in the toolbar of SDM and how to move around the various screens within SDM.

Basic Router Configuration Using SDM

You shouldn't be expected to configure anything within SDM; however, you should be familiar with the configuration sections available: *Interfaces and Connections*, *Firewall and ACL*, *VPN*, *Security Audit*, *Routing*, *NAT*,

Intrusion Prevention, *Quality of Service*, *NAC*, and *Additional Tasks*. Remember that most configuration sections support a wizard to configure a component of a router, minimizing any type of misconfiguration on your part. Click the Create tab within the appropriate section to access a wizard. To send changes to the router, you typically click either the Apply Changes, Deliver, or OK button, depending on the screen or window.

As to setting up DHCP, you should actually be more familiar with the IOS commands than using SDM. Be able to examine a DHCP configuration and spot any missing or incorrectly configured commands. Understand some of the things a router will use in order to determine whether an address conflict exists with DHCP.

Currently, no simulation questions are included on Cisco's CCNA exams pertaining to SDM; however, Cisco's professional certification exams, such as the CCSP, do have testlets and simulations covering the Device Manager products Cisco has for its hardware platforms. So don't be surprised to see changes on the CCNA exam in this regard with the addition of a testlet or simulation question on SDM at some future date.

Basic Router Monitoring Using SDM

Understand how to access the Monitor section of SDM by clicking the Monitor button.

CERTIFICATION SUMMARY

This chapter introduced you to Cisco's SDM GUI tool to manage a router. SDM is a web-based tool implemented in Java that allows you to manage a single router at a time. SDM currently ships in flash on all routers up to the 7300 series. SDM uses SSL and SSH to protect communications between your desktop and the router. For features not supported by SDM, as well as detailed troubleshooting, the CLI is still the main tool of choice.

SDM is not contained in a single file but requires many files to be copied to flash before it can be used. On top of this, your router needs a basic configuration on it in order to access SDM. This includes a name and domain name, a web server, a privilege level 15 account, and the correct setup on your VTYs. In the SDM packaged zip file, a configuration file is included with the necessary commands that can be used to configure your router initially.

To access SDM, enter **https://** *router's_IP_address* in a supported web browser's address bar. Depending on the router model and SDM version, the Start up wizard will begin the very first time you use SDM. The Startup wizard leads you through the steps of putting a basic configuration on your router. Every time you start up SDM after this, you are presented with the Home screen. The Configure button takes you to a screen where you can configure components on your router; the Monitor button takes you to a screen where you can view various status and statistical information on the router; the Refresh button replaces the configuration SDM has for the router with the router's current running configuration; and the Save button executes the **copy running-config startup-config** command on the router.

✓ TWO-MINUTE DRILL

Introduction to SDM

❑ SDM is a web-based Java tool that allows you to access a single router securely via SSL and SSH.

❑ SDM is supported on Windows operating systems and supports the Firefox, Internet Explorer, and Netscape Navigator web browsers.

❑ Use the **show flash** or **dir** command to determine whether SDM is installed on your router. Minimally, you need these SDM files in flash: common.tar, es.tar, home.shtml, home.tar, and sdm.tar.

❑ The sdmconfig-*xxxx*.cfg file in the SDM package has the necessary commands to configure a router so that you can access SDM using a web browser.

❑ Enter **https://*router's_IP_address*** in your web browser address bar to access SDM on your router.

❑ The Startup wizard runs only the first time you access SDM unless you reset the router back to its factory defaults.

❑ The Refresh button pulls in the current configuration of the router into SDM, and the Save button saves the router's running configuration to NVRAM.

Basic Router Configuration Using SDM

❑ SDM supports wizards to simplify the setting up of common features, as well as to minimize the misconfiguration of them.

❑ Not all IOS features can be configured with SDM.

❑ Click the Apply Changes, Deliver, or OK button to send an SDM configuration down to the router.

❑ A DHCP server will not function on a router unless it has an IP address configuration on the interface where the DHCP clients are located and the interface has been activated.

❑ The router should advertise itself as the default gateway in its DHCP OFFER message to a requesting client.

Basic Router Monitoring Using SDM

❑ Click the Monitor button to view information about the overview and operation of the router.

SELF TEST

The following Self Test questions will help you measure your understanding of the material presented in this chapter. Read all the choices carefully, as there may be more than one correct answer. Choose all correct answers for each question.

Introduction to SDM

1. What communication protocols are used between a user's desktop running SDM and a router? (choose two)
   A. HTTP
   B. SSL
   C. SSH
   D. FTP

2. Which of the following SDM files does not have to be in flash in order to access SDM from your desktop?
   A. common.tar
   B. home.shtml
   C. home.tar
   D. sdmconfig-*xxxx*.cfg
   E. None of the above

3. Enter the router command to enable a web server on it: _____.

4. What button do you click to pull in the router's current running configuration into SDM?
   A. Deliver
   B. Apply Changes
   C. Refresh
   D. Save
   E. Update

5. A router has an IP address of 10.10.10.1. Enter the URL to access SDM on it: _____.

Basic Router Configuration Using SDM

6. What SDM wizard would you run to find any security misconfiguration issues on your router?
   A. Security Alert
   B. Firewall and ACL
   C. Security Audit
   D. IPS

7. What button would you click on from a Configuration screen to send changes you've made in SDM to your router?

   A. Download

   B. Deliver

   C. Execute

   D. Activate Changes

8. Examine the following configuration. Why can't a user connected to fastethernet0/1 acquire DHCP addressing information from the router?

```
Router(config)# service dhcp
Router(config)# ip dhcp excluded-address 192.168.1.1 192.168.1.99
Router(config)# ip dhcp excluded-address 192.168.1.200 192.168.1.254
Router(config)# ip dhcp pool sdm-pool1
Router(dhcp-config)# import all
Router(dhcp-config)# network 192.168.1.0 255.255.255.0
Router(dhcp-config)# dns-server 65.32.1.65 4.2.2.2
Router(dhcp-config)# default-router 192.168.1.1
Router(dhcp-config)# exit
Router(config)# interface fastethernet0/0
Router(config-if)# ip address 192.168.2.1 255.255.255.0
Router(config-if)# shutdown
Router(config-if)# exit
Router(config)# interface fastethernet0/1
Router(config-if)# speed 100
Router(config-if)# duplex full
Router(config-if)# no shutdown
```

   A. The interface is not enabled.

   B. The DHCP server has not been enabled.

   C. The interface needs an IP address and subnet mask.

   D. The DHCP server does not have a WINS server configured.

9. What methods or tools can a router use to detect address conflicts for DHCP? (choose two)

   A. Ping

   B. Traceroute

   C. Gratuitous ARP

   D. RARP

Basic Router Monitoring Using SDM

10. What SDM button would you click to view the interface statistics and the firewall logs?

   A. View

   C. Status

   B. Configure

   D. Monitor

SELF TEST ANSWERS

Introduction to SDM

1. ☑ **B and C.** SSL (HTTPS) and SSH are used to communicate between a user's desktop running SDM and a Cisco router. SSL is used to communicate configuration commands and updates to the router while SSH is used to deliver **show** commands and the resulting output back to the desktop.

   ☒ **A and D**, HTTP and FTP, are not used and therefore are incorrect.

2. ☑ **D.** The sdmconfig-*xxxx*.cfg provides the necessary router configuration commands in order to access SDM from your desktop. It is provided as a quick start to get SDM up and running on the router; however, the file is not necessary to run SDM itself.

   ☒ **A, B,** and **C** are required files and therefore are incorrect answers. Since there is a correct answer, **E** is incorrect.

3. ☑ The **ip http server** command enables a web server on the router.

4. ☑ **C.** Click the Refresh button to replace SDM's configuration for the router with the current running configuration on the router.

   ☒ **A and B**, the Deliver and Apply Changes buttons, deliver SDM configuration changes to the router. **D**, the Save button, causes SDM to execute the **copy running-config startup-config** command on the router. **E** is incorrect because Update is a nonexistent button.

5. ☑ Enter **https://10.10.10.1** to access SDM on this router.

Basic Router Configuration Using SDM

6. ☑ **C.** The Security Audit wizard compares your router's configuration with the security practices recommended by Cisco's TAC and ICSA and looks for differences and allows you to fix the differences.

   ☒ **A**, Security Alert, is a nonexistent wizard. **B** is incorrect because the Firewall and ACL wizard allows you to set up the initial firewall and ACL features on the router. **D** is incorrect because the IPS wizard allows you to set up the initial IPS features to look for attacks directed at your router or going through your router.

7. ☑ **B.** The Deliver, Apply Changes, and OK buttons are used to deliver configurations from SDM to the router; as to which one is used, it depends on the screen and if you have the command-preview feature enabled.

   ☒ **A and C** are nonexistent buttons. **D** should be Apply Changes, not Activate Changes.

8. ☑ **C.** To perform DHCP server functions on an interface, the router must have an IP address and subnet mask assigned to it and the interface must be enabled—the IP address and subnet mask are missing from this configuration.

☒ **A** is incorrect since the `no shutdown` command was executed on the interface. **B** is incorrect since the `service dhcp` command was executed. **D** is incorrect since WINS is necessary only to resolve names to addresses in a Windows domain infrastructure and is an optional command.

9. ☑ **A** and **C.** The router can use ping to determine whether an address is already in use by someone else. The router will also listen to ARP replies (gratuitous ARPs) to see if someone is attempting to use an address already assigned by the router to someone else.

☒ **B** is incorrect because traceroute is used to troubleshoot layer 3 connectivity problems. **D** is incorrect because RARP is used by BOOTP to acquire addressing information on a device.

Basic Router Monitoring Using SDM

10. ☑ **D.** Clicking the Monitor button allows you to see status and statistics information on the router.

☒ **A** and **C** are nonexistent buttons. **B** is incorrect because the Configure button takes you to the configuration screens.

Part V

Routing

19

Basic Routing

In Chapter 15, you read about routing protocols, including the different types and their advantages and disadvantages. You performed a basic configuration of a router from the command-line interface (CLI) in Chapter 16 and Security Device Manager (SDM) in Chapter 18. This chapter covers the basic configuration of static routes and distance vector protocols, specifically the IP Routing Information Protocol (RIP). The section on RIP focuses on the basics of this protocol; advanced configuration of RIP is beyond the scope of this book. However, by the end of the chapter, you'll be able to configure routers using static routes or a running RIP that will route traffic in a network between the router's interfaces.

CERTIFICATION OBJECTIVE 19.01

Static Routes

A *static route* is a manually configured route on your router. Static routes are typically used in smaller networks and when few networks or subnets exist, or with WAN links that have little available bandwidth. With a network that has hundreds of routes, static routes are not scalable, since you would have to configure each route and any redundant paths for that route on each router. This section covers the configuration of static routes and some of the issues associated with them.

---

exam ⓦatch

Dynamic routing protocols are preferred over static routes when many networks or subnets exist in a network, since the configuration of static routes would be prone to misconfiguration given *the number of destinations. Static routes are typically used in small networks with few segments and little bandwidth, such as WAN links.*

Static Route Configuration

To configure a static route for IP, use one of these two commands:

```
Router(config)# ip route destination_network_# [subnet_mask]
                IP_address_of_next_hop_neighbor
                [administrative_distance] [permanent]
```

or

```
Router(config)# ip route destination_network_# [subnet_mask]
                interface_to_exit
                [administrative_distance] [permanent]
```

The first parameter that you must specify is the destination network number. If you omit the subnet mask for the network number, it defaults to the Class A (255.0.0.0), B (255.255.0.0), or C (255.255.255.0) default subnet mask, depending on the network number of the destination.

After the subnet mask parameter, you can specify how to reach the destination network in one of two ways: you can tell the router the next hop neighbor's IP address or the interface the router should exit to reach the destination network. You should use the former method if the link is a multi-access link (the link has more than two devices on it—three routers, for instance). You can use the latter method if it is a point-to-point link. In this instance, you must specify the *name* of the interface on the router, like so: **serial0**.

Optionally, you can change the administrative distance of a static route. If you omit this value, it will have one of two defaults, depending on the configuration of the previous parameter. If you specified the next hop neighbor's IP address, then the administrative distance defaults to 1. If you specified the interface on the router it should use to reach the destination, the router treats the route as a connected route and assigns an administrative distance of 0 to it.

Note that you can create multiple static routes to the *same* destination. For instance, you might have primary and backup paths to the destination. For the primary path, use the default administrative distance value. For the backup path, use a number higher than this, such as 2. Once you have configured a backup path, the router will use the primary path, and if the interface on the router fails for the primary path, the router will use the backup route.

The **permanent** parameter will keep the static route in the routing table even when the interface the router uses for the static route fails. If you omit this parameter, and the interface used by the static route fails, the router will remove this route from its routing table and attempt to find an alternative path to place in the routing table.

You might want to use the **permanent** parameter if you never want packets to use another path to a destination, perhaps because of security reasons.

Default Route Configuration

A *default route* is a special type of static route. Where a static route specifies a path a router should use to reach a specific destination, a default route specifies a path the router should use if it *doesn't know how to reach the destination*. Note that if a router does not have any path in its routing table telling it how to reach a destination, and the router receives a packet destined for this network, the router will *drop* the packet. This is different from a switch, which will flood unknown destinations. Therefore, a default route can serve as a *catch-all*: if no path to the destination is specified, the router will use the default route to reach it.

To set up a default route, use the following syntax for a static route:

```
Router(config)# ip route 0.0.0.0 0.0.0.0
                IP_address_of_next_hop_neighbor
                [administrative_distance] [permanent]
```

or

```
Router(config)# ip route 0.0.0.0 0.0.0.0
                interface_to_exit
                [administrative_distance] [permanent]
```

The network number of 0.0.0.0/0 at first appears a bit strange. Recall from Chapter 7, however, that network 0.0.0.0 represents all networks, and a mask of all 0s in the bit position represents all hosts in the specified network.

Default Routes and Distance Vector Protocols

A default route sometimes causes problems for certain routing protocols. A routing protocol can fall under two additional categories: *classful* and *classless*. Examples of classful protocols include RIPv1 and IGRP (no longer supported by Cisco). Examples of classless protocols include RIPv2, Open Shortest Path First (OSPF), Enhanced Interior Gateway Routing Protocol (EIGRP), Intermediate System-Intermediate System (IS-IS), and Border Gateway Protocol (BGP).

A classful routing protocol understands only class subnets. For instance, if you have 192.168.1.0/23 in a routing update, a classful routing protocol wouldn't understand it, since a Class C network requires 24 bits of network numbers. This can create problems with a default route, which has a /0 mask.

Also, when a classful router advertises a route out its interface, it does not include the subnet mask. For example, you might have 192.168.1.1/26 configured on your router's interface, and the router receives a routing updated with 192.168.1.0. With a classful routing protocol, the router will comprehend subnet masks only for network numbers configured on its interfaces. In this example, the router assumes that for 192.168.1.0, the only valid mask is /26. Therefore, if the routers sees the 192.168.1.0/26 as the network number, but the network is really 192.168.1.0/27, a lot of routing confusion results.

Classless protocols, on the other hand, do not have any issues accepting routing updates with any bit value for a subnet mask. However, for classful protocols, you must configure the following command to accept nonconforming subnet masks, such as a default route:

```
Router(config)# ip classless
```

This command is also used to deal with *discontiguous* subnets in a network that is using a classful protocol: subnets separated by a different class network. For example, assume that you have networks 172.16.1.0/24, 172.16.2.0/24, and 172.16.3.0/24. However, a different class network, 192.168.1.0/24, sits between the first two Class B subnets and 172.16.3.0/24. In this situation, the router connected to 172.16.1.0/24 and 172.16.2.0/24, when it receives 172.16.0.0 from the side of the network connected to the discontiguous subnet, will *ignore* this routing entry.

Remember that when routes cross a class boundary in a classful protocol, the network number is sent as its classful number. Therefore, the router connected to 192.168.1.0/24 and 172.16.3.0/24, when it advertises updates across the 192.168.1.0/24 subnet, will advertise 172.16.0.0—not the actual subnet number.

Since the router connected to 172.16.1.0/24 and 172.16.2.0/24 ignores the 172.16.0.0 routing information, it will not be able to reach 172.16.3.0. On top of this problem, even if you have a default route configured, since the router is connected to the 172.16.0.0 subnets, it assumes that 172.16.3.0 must also be connected; and if it isn't in the routing table, then the route cannot be reached. This topic was discussed in Chapter 8.

By using the **ip classless** command, you are overriding this behavior; you're allowing your classful router to use a default route to reach discontiguous subnets. Not that this is a recommended design practice, but it does allow you to solve reachability problems for discontiguous subnets.

Classful protocols, such as IP RIPv1, understand only classful subnets—you can apply only one subnet mask to a class address. Classless protocols, such as RIPv2, EIGRP, OSPF, and IS-IS, do not have this restriction.

The ip classless command allows a classful protocol to use a default route; omitting this command will cause the router to drop packets that don't match a specific destination network entry in the routing table.

Static Route Verification and Troubleshooting

To verify the configuration of static and default routes on your router, use the **show ip route** command:

```
Router# show ip route
Codes: C - connected, S - static, I - IGRP, R - RIP,
       M - mobile, B - BGP, D - EIGRP, EX - EIGRP external,
       O - OSPF, IA - OSPF inter area, N1 - OSPF NSSA
       external type 1, N2 - OSPF NSSA external type 2,
       E1 - OSPF external type 1, E2 - OSPF external type 2,
       E - EGP, i - IS-IS, L1 - IS-IS level-1, L2 - IS-IS level-2,
       * - candidate default, U - per-user static route, o - ODR,
       T - traffic engineered route
Gateway of last resort is 0.0.0.0 to network 0.0.0.0

     172.16.0.0/24 is subnetted, 3 subnets
C       172.16.1.0 is directly connected, Ethernet0
C       172.16.2.0 is directly connected, Serial0
S       172.16.3.0 is directly connected, Serial0
*S       0.0.0.0/0 is directly connected, Serial1
```

This command displays the IP routing table on your router and can contain directly connected subnets, static and default routes, and dynamically learned routes from a routing protocol. The top portion of the display for this command has a table of codes. These codes, which describe a type of route that may appear in the routing table, are shown in the first column at the bottom part of the display. In this example, there are two connected routes (C) and two static routes (S). The first static route is treated as a directly connected route, since it was created by specifying the interface to exit the router. The second static route is a default route—the asterisk (*) indicates the gateway of last resort: the path the router should use if no other specific path is available.

19.01. The CD contains a multimedia demonstration of setting up static routes on a router.

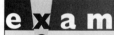

Be familiar with the output of the show ip route *command and be able to determine, based on a router's* *configuration, what routes should appear in a router's routing table.*

EXERCISE 19-1

Static Route Configuration

These last few sections have dealt with static routes and their configuration. This exercise will help you reinforce this material for the configuration of static routes. You'll perform this lab using Boson's NetSim simulator. In this exercise, you'll set static routes on the two routers (2600-1 and 2600-2). You can find a picture of the network diagram for Boson's NetSim simulator in the Introduction of this book. After starting up the simulator, click the LabNavigator button. Next, double-click Exercise 19-1 and then click the Load Lab button. This will load the lab configuration based on the exercises in Chapters 11 and 16.

1. Access the 2600-1 router. At the top of the simulator in the menu bar, click the eRouters icon and choose 2600-1.

2. On the 2600-1, verify that the fa0/0 and s0 interfaces are up. If not, bring them up. Examine the IP addresses configured on the 2600-1.

Use the **show interfaces** command to verify your configuration. If fa0/0 and s0 are not up, go into the interfaces (fa0/0 and s0) and enable them using the **no shutdown** command. Use the **show interfaces** command to verify that the IP addresses you configured in Chapter 16 are still there.

3. Examine the routing table on the 2600-1.

   Use the **show ip route** command. You should have two connected networks: 192.168.1.0 connected to fa0/0 and 192.168.2.0 connected to s0.

4. Access the 2600-2 router. At the top of the simulator in the menu bar, click the eRouters icon and choose 2600-2.

5. On the 2600-2, verify that the fa0/0 and s0 interfaces are up. If not, bring them up. Examine the IP addresses configured on the 2600-2 and look at its routing table.

   On the 2600-2, use the **show interfaces** command to verify your configuration. If fa0/0 and s0 are not up, go into the interfaces (fa0/0 and s0) and enable them using the **no shutdown** command. Use the **show interfaces** command to verify that the IP addresses you configured in Chapter 16 are still there.

6. Examine the routing table on the 2600-2 router.

   Use the **show ip route** command. You should have two connected networks: 192.168.3.0 connected to fa0/0 and 192.168.2.0 connected to s0.

7. Test connectivity between Host-1 and the 2600-1.

   At the top of the simulator in the menu bar, click the eStations icon and choose Host-1. From Host-1, ping the 2600-1: **ping 192.168.1.1**. The ping should be successful. If it is not, you may have used the configuration from the VLAN lab in Chapter 13 and may have a VLAN configuration problem.

8. Test connectivity between Host-3 and the 2600-2.

   At the top of the simulator in the menu bar, click the eStations icon and choose Host-3. From Host-3, ping the 2600-2 router: **ping 192.168.3.1**. The ping should be successful.

9. Test connectivity between Host-3 and Host-1.

   From Host-3, ping Host-1: **ping 192.168.1.10**. The ping should fail: there is no route from the 2600-2 to this destination.

10. Look at the 2600-2's routing table: **show ip route**. It doesn't list 192.168.1.0/24.

11. On the 2600-2, configure a static route to 192.168.1.0/24, which is connected to the 2600-1.

    At the top of the simulator in the menu bar, click the eRouters icon and choose 2600-2. Configure a static route to reach 192.168.1.0/24 via the 2600-1 router.
    Configure the static route: **configure terminal, ip route 192.168.1.0 255.255.255.0 192.168.2.1**, and **end**.

12. View the routing table on the 2600-2 router.

    View the connected and static routes: **show ip route**. Make sure that 192.168.1.0/24 shows up in the routing table as a static route (S).

13. On the 2600-1, configure a static route to 192.168.3.0/24, which is connected to the 2600-2.

    At the top of the simulator in the menu bar, click the eRouters icon and choose 2600-1. Configure the static route: **configure terminal, ip route 192.168.3.0 255.255.255.0 192.168.2.2**, and **end**.

14. View the routing table on the 2600-1.

    View the connected and static routes: **show ip route**. Make sure that 192.168.3.0/24 shows up in the routing table as a static route (S).

15. From Host-3, ping the **fa0/0** interface of the 2600-1.

    At the top of the simulator in the menu bar, click the eStations icon and choose Host-3. Access Host-3 and ping the **fa0/0** interface of the 2600-1 router: **ping 192.168.1.1**. The ping should be successful.

16. From Host-3, ping Host-1.

    Ping Host-1: **ping 192.168.1.10**. The ping should be successful.

Now you should be more comfortable with configuring static routes.

EXERCISE 19-2

Basic IP and Routing Troubleshooting

This chapter has covered the basics of routers and routing. This exercise is a troubleshooting exercise and is different from the other exercises you have performed so far. In previous exercises, you were given a configuration task.

In this exercise, the network is already configured; however, three problems exist in this network and you'll need to find and fix them to make it operate correctly. All of these problems deal with IP (layer 3) connectivity.

You'll perform this exercise using Boson's NetSim simulator. You can find a picture of the network diagram for Boson's NetSim simulator in the Introduction of this book. The addressing scheme is the same. After starting up the simulator, click the LabNavigator button. Next, double-click Exercise 19-2 and click the Load Lab button. This will load the lab configuration based on the exercises in Chapters 11 and 16 and static routing, with problems, of course.

Let's start with your problem: Host-1 cannot ping Host-3. Your task is to find the three problems causing this problem and fix them. You should try this troubleshooting process on your own first; if you have problems, come back to the steps and solutions provided here.

1. Use ping to test connectivity from Host-1 to Host-3.

   At the top of the simulator in the menu bar, click the eStations icon and choose Host-1. On Host-1, ping Host-3: `ping 192.168.3.10`. Note that the ping fails.

2. Examine the IP configuration on Host-1.

   Execute `ipconfig /all`. Make sure the IP addressing information is correct: IP address of 192.168.1.10, subnet mask of 255.255.255.0, and default gateway address of 192.168.1.1.

3. Test connectivity from Host-1 to its default gateway by using ping.

   Ping the default gateway address: `ping 192.168.1.1`. The ping should be successful, indicating that at least layer 3 is functioning between Host-1 and the 2600-1.

4. Verify Host-3's IP configuration.

   At the top of the simulator in the menu bar, click the eStations icon and choose Host-3. Examine the IP configuration on Host-3 by executing `ipconfig /all`. Make sure the IP addressing information is correct: IP address of 192.168.3.10, subnet mask of 255.255.255.0, and default gateway address of 192.168.3.1.

5. Test connectivity from Host-3 to its default gateway by using ping.

   Ping the default gateway address: `ping 192.168.3.1`. The ping should fail, indicating that there is a problem between Host-3 and the 2600-2. In this example, assume layer 2 is functioning correctly; therefore, it must be a problem with the 2600-2.

6. Check the 2600-2's IP configuration.

   At the top of the simulator in the menu bar, click the eRouters icon and choose 2600-2. From the 2600-2, ping Host-3: **ping 192.168.3.10**. The ping should fail. Examine the interface on the 2600-2: **show interface fa0/0**. The interface is disabled, but it has the correct IP address: 192.168.3.1. Enable the interface: **configure terminal, interface fa0/0, no shutdown,** and **end**. The interface should come up. Retry the ping test: **ping 192.168.3.10**. The ping should be successful.

7. Access Host-1 and retry pinging Host-3.

   At the top of the simulator in the menu bar, click the eStations icon and choose Host-1. Test connectivity to Host-3: **ping 192.168.3.10**. The ping should still fail. So far, there is connectivity within 192.168.1.0 and 192.168.3.0, but there is still a problem between these two networks.

8. Check the interface statuses on the 2600-1 and verify connectivity to the 2600-2.

   At the top of the simulator in the menu bar, click the eRouters icon and choose 2600-1. Check the status of the interfaces: **show ip interface brief**. Notice that the fa0/0 and s0 are both up. Try pinging the 2600-2's s0 interface: **ping 192.168.2.2**. The ping fails. Examine CDP information that the 2600-1 has learned about the 2600-2: **show cdp entry 2600-2**. Notice that the 2600-2 has no IP address.

9. Fix the IP addressing problem on the 2600-2 and retest connectivity across the serial connection.

   At the top of the simulator in the menu bar, click the eRouters icon and choose 2600-2. Fix the IP address: **configure terminal, interface s0, ip address 192.168.2.2 255.255.255.0,** and **end**. Retest the connection to the 2600-1: **ping 192.168.2.1**. The ping should be successful.

10. Examine the routing table on the 2600-2 and verify that 192.168.1.0/24 shows up as a static route.

    Examine the routing table: **show ip route**. As you can see, 192.168.1.0 shows up as a static route and points to 192.168.2.1.

11. Access Host-3 and try connectivity between its default gateway and the 2600-1 router.

    At the top of the simulator in the menu bar, click the eStations icon and choose Host-3. Test the connection to the 2600-2: **ping 192.168.3.1**. The ping should be successful, considering you already tested it. Test connectivity to the 2600-1: **ping 192.168.2.1**. The ping should fail.

This presents an interesting problem. Host-1 can ping the 2600-1. The 2600-1 can ping the 2600-2. Host-3 can ping the 2600-2. Therefore, on a hop-by-hop basis, you have IP connectivity. And the 2600-2 can even ping Host-1, indicating that some routing functioning is working.

12. Access the 2600-1 router and examine its routing table. Fix the problem.

At the top of the simulator in the menu bar, click the eRouters icon and choose 2600-1. Examine the routing table: **show ip route**. Does the 2600-1 know how to reach 192.168.3.0/24? It does not. The 2600-2 router could ping Host-1 since the 2600-1 router is directly connected to these segments, but any traffic from the 2600-1 to 192.168.3.0/24 will fail since the router doesn't have a path. Add a static route to 192.168.3.0/24: **configure terminal, ip route 192.168.3.0 255.255.255.0 192.168.2.2**, and **end**. Test connectivity to Host-3: **ping 192.168.3.10**. The ping should be successful.

13. Now test connectivity between Host-1 and Host-3.

At the top of the simulator in the menu bar, click the eStations icon and choose Host-1. Test connectivity to Host-3: **ping 192.168.3.10**. The ping should be successful.

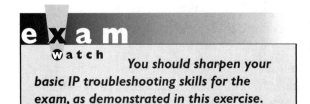

e x a m

ⓦ a t c h *You should sharpen your basic IP troubleshooting skills for the exam, as demonstrated in this exercise.*

You should now feel comfortable troubleshooting routers that are using static routes for routing.

CERTIFICATION OBJECTIVE 19.02

Dynamic Routing Protocol Basics

Before learning about how to configure a dynamic routing protocol such as RIP, consider some basic configuration tasks that are required no matter what dynamic routing protocol you are running. You need to perform two basic steps when setting up IP routing on your router:

- Enable the routing protocol.
- Assign IP addresses to your router's interfaces.

Remember the two steps required to set up IP routing on a router.

Note that the order of these tasks is not important. You already know how to configure an IP address on the router's interface: this was discussed in Chapter 16. The following sections cover the first bullet point in more depth.

The router Command

Enabling an IP routing protocol is a two-step process. First, you must go into Router Subconfiguration mode. This mode determines the routing protocol that you'll be running. Within this mode, you'll configure the characteristics of the routing protocol. To enter the routing protocol's configuration mode, use the following command:

```
Router(config)# router name_of_the_IP_routing_protocol
Router(config-router)#
```

The **router** command is used to access the routing protocol that you want to configure; it doesn't enable it. If you are not sure of the name of the routing protocol that you want to enable, use the context-sensitive help feature:

```
Router(config)# router ?
  bgp                 Border Gateway Protocol (BGP)
  eigrp               Enhanced Interior Gateway Routing
                        Protocol (EIGRP)
  isis                ISO IS-IS
  iso-igrp            IGRP for OSI networks
  mobile              Mobile routes
  odr                 On Demand stub Routes
  ospf                Open Shortest Path First (OSPF)
  rip                 Routing Information Protocol (RIP)
Router(config)#
```

As you can see from the context-sensitive help output, you have a lot of IP routing protocols at your disposal.

on the **Job**
One important item to point out is that the router *command doesn't turn on the routing protocol. This process is done in the protocol's Router Subconfiguration mode, indicated by the* (config-router) *prompt.*

The network Command

Once in the routing protocol, you need to specify what interfaces are to participate in the routing process. By default, no interfaces participate in the routing process. To specify which interfaces will participate, use the **network** Router Subconfiguration mode command:

```
Router(config-router)# network IP_network_#
```

As soon as you enter a network number, the routing process becomes *active*. For distance vector protocols such as RIP, you need to enter only the Class A, B, or C network number or numbers that are associated with your interface or interfaces. In other words, if you have subnetted 192.168.1.0 with a subnet mask of 255.255.255.192 (/26), and you have subnets 192.168.1.0/26, 192.168.1.64/26, 192.168.1.128/26, and 192.168.1.192/26, you don't need to enter each specific subnet. Instead, just enter **192.168.1.0**, and this will accommodate all interfaces that are associated with this Class C network. If you specify a subnet, the router will *convert* it to the class address, because RIP is a classful protocol.

Let's take a look at a simple example of the configuration, shown in Figure 19-1. This example focuses on the configuration of the **network** commands, assuming

FIGURE 19-1

Simple network example

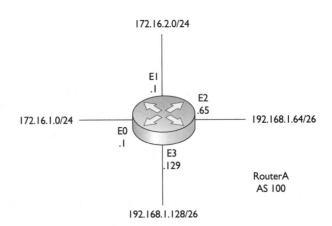

that the routing protocol is a classful protocol, such as RIP. In this example, the router is connected to a Class B network (172.16.0.0) and a Class C network (192.168.1.0), both of which are subnetted.

Assume that you forgot that you need to enter only the classful network numbers, and you entered the subnetted values instead, like this:

```
Router(config-router)# network 172.16.1.0
Router(config-router)# network 172.16.2.0
Router(config-router)# network 192.168.1.64
Router(config-router)# network 192.168.1.128
```

When entering your **network** statements, you need to include any network that is associated with your router's interfaces; if you omit a network, your router will not include the omitted interface in the routing process. As you can see from the preceding example, all the subnets were included. Remember, however, that the router requires only that you enter the class addresses. If you were to execute a **show running-config** command, you would not see the four networks just listed, but only the Class B and C network numbers. You shouldn't worry about this; it's just that you entered more commands than were necessary. In reality, you needed to enter only these two **network** commands:

```
Router(config-router)# network 172.16.0.0
Router(config-router)# network 192.168.1.0
```

Both ways of entering your statements are correct, but the latter is what the router will use if you type in all of the specific subnets.

CertCam

19.02. The CD contains a multimedia demonstration of an introduction to basic IP routing protocol configuration.

CERTIFICATION OBJECTIVE 19.03

RIP

IP RIP comes in two different versions: 1 and 2. Version 1 is a distance vector protocol and is defined in RFC 1058. Version 2 is a hybrid protocol and is defined in RFCs 1721 and 1722. The CCNA exam now primarily focuses on version 2. However, you still need to know a few things about RIPv1, specifically its characteristics. This section covers the basics of configuring and troubleshooting your network using IP RIP.

RIP Operation

As you'll recall from Chapter 15, RIP is a distance vector protocol. RIP is an old protocol and therefore is very stable—in other words, Cisco doesn't do that much development on the protocol, unlike other, more advanced protocols. Therefore, you can feel safe that when you upgrade your IOS to a newer version, RIP will function the same way it did in the previous release. This section includes brief overviews of both versions of RIP.

RIPv1

RIPv1 uses local broadcasts to share routing information. These updates are periodic in nature, occurring, by default, every 30 seconds, with a hold-down period of 180 seconds. Both versions of RIP use *hop count* as a metric, which is not always the best metric to use. For instance, if you had two paths to reach a network, where one was a two-hop Ethernet connection and the other was a one-hop 64 Kbps WAN connection, RIP would use the slower 64 Kbps connection because it has a lesser accumulated hop-count metric. You have to remember this little tidbit when looking at how RIP will populate your router's routing table. To prevent packets from circling around a loop forever, both versions of RIP solve counting to infinity by placing a hop-count limit of 15 hops on packets. Any packet that reaches the sixteenth hop will be dropped.

And as mentioned in the last section, RIPv1 is a *classful* protocol. This is important for configuring RIP and subnetting your IP addressing scheme: you can use only one subnet mask value for a given Class A, B, or C network. For instance, if you have a Class B network such as 172.16.0.0, you can subnet it with only one mask. As an example, you couldn't use 255.255.255.0 and 255.255.255.128 on 172.16.0.0—you can choose only one.

Another interesting feature is that RIP supports up to six equal-cost paths to a single destination, where all six paths can be placed in the routing table and the router can load-balance across them. The default is actually four paths, but this can be increased up to a maximum of six. Remember that an equal-cost path is where the metric for the multiple paths to a destination is the same. RIP will not load-balance across *unequal*-cost paths.

Figure 19-2 illustrates equal-cost-path load balancing. In this example, RouterA has two equal-cost paths to 10.0.0.0 (with a hop count of 1) via RouterB and RouterC. Putting both of these paths in RouterA's routing table offers two advantages:

- The router can perform load balancing to 10.0.0.0, taking advantage of the bandwidth on both of these links.

- Convergence is sped up if one of the paths fails. For example, if the connection between RouterA and RouterB fails, RouterA can still access network 10.0.0.0 via RouterC and has this information in its routing table; therefore, convergence is instantaneous.

For these two reasons, many routing protocols support parallel paths to a single destination. Some protocols, such as EIGRP, even support unequal-cost load balancing, which is discussed in Chapter 21.

FIGURE 19-2

Equal-cost-path
load balancing

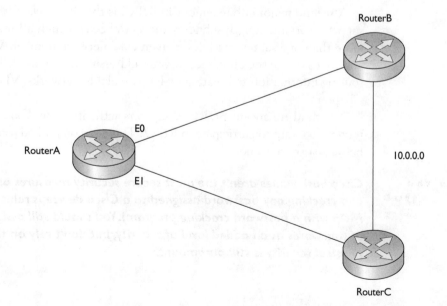

exam

IP RIPv1, a classful protocol, broadcasts updates every 30 seconds and has a hold-down period of 180 seconds. Hop count is used as a **metric: the path or paths with the least accumulated hop count are used and placed in the routing table.**

RIPv2

One thing you should keep in the back of your mind when dealing with RIPv2 is that it is based on RIPv1 and is, at heart, a distance vector protocol with routing enhancements built into it. Therefore, it is commonly called a *hybrid protocol*. You read about some of the characteristics that both versions of RIP have in common in the preceding section. This section focuses on the characteristics unique to RIPv2.

One major enhancement to RIPv2 pertains to how it deals with routing updates. Instead of using broadcasts, RIPv2 uses *multicasts*: updates are advertised to 224.0.0.9, which all RIPv2 routers will process. And to speed up convergence, RIPv2 supports *triggered* updates—when a change occurs, a RIPv2 router will immediately propagate its routing information to its connected neighbors.

A second major enhancement in RIPv2 is that it is a *classless* protocol. RIPv2 supports variable-length subnet masking (VLSM), which allows you to use more than one subnet mask for a given class network number. VLSM allows you to maximize the efficiency of your addressing design as well as summarize routing information to create very large, scalable networks. VLSM is discussed in Chapter 8.

As a third enhancement, RIPv2 supports authentication. You can restrict what routers you want to participate in RIPv2. This is accomplished using a clear-text or hashed password value.

on the
Üob

Cisco hash values aren't the most secure security measures on the planet, and cracking any password assigned to a Cisco device is relatively easy (even MD5 with a password cracking program). You should still assign these kinds of passwords as an added level of security, but don't rely on them totally: physical security is still paramount.

e**x**a**m**

ⓦatch *Even with all of its advanced characteristics, RIPv2 is still, at heart, a distance vector protocol. It uses hop count as a metric, supports the same solutions to solve routing loop problems, has a 15-hop count limit, and shares other characteristics of RIPv1. RIPv2 is a hybrid protocol, based on RIPv1. It uses multicasts to disseminate routing information and* *supports triggered updates. Unlike RIPv1, RIPv2 supports VLSM (advertises subnet masks with associated network numbers), which allows you to summarize routing information, and authentication of routing updates. Otherwise, its characteristics are like those of RIPv1.*

RIP Configuration

As you will see in this section, configuring RIP is an easy and straightforward process. The basic configuration of RIP involves the following two commands:

```
Router(config)# router rip
Router(config-router)# network IP_network_#
```

As explained in the preceding section, RIPv1 is classful and RIPv2 is classless. However, whenever you configure *either* version of RIP, the **network** command assumes *classful*: You need to enter only the Class A, B, or C network number, not the subnets, as was discussed earlier in this chapter. If you refer back to Figure 19-1, the router's RIPv1 configuration would look like this:

```
Router(config)# router rip
Router(config-router)# network 172.16.0.0
Router(config-router)# network 192.168.1.0
```

CertCam

19.03. The CD contains a multimedia demonstration of a basic RIP configuration on a router.

e**x**a**m**

ⓦatch *Use the* `router rip` *and* `network` *commands to configure RIP routing. Remember to put the class address* *(not the subnetted network number) in the* `network` *statement.*

Specifying RIP Version 1 and 2

By default, the IOS *accepts* both RIPv1 and RIPv2 routing updates; however, it *generates* only RIPv1 updates. You can configure your router to

- accept and send RIPv1 only
- accept and send RIPv2 only
- use a combination of the two, depending on your interface configuration

To accomplish either of the first two items in the list, you need to set the version in your RIP configuration:

```
Router(config)# router rip
Router(config-router)# version 1|2
```

When you specify the appropriate version number, your RIP routing process will send and receive only the version packet type that you configured.

You can also control which version of RIP is running on an interface-by-interface basis. For instance, suppose a bunch of new routers at your site support both versions and a remote office understands only RIPv1. In this situation, you can configure your routers to generate RIPv2 updates on all their LAN interfaces, but for the remote access connection at the corporate site, you could set the interface to run only RIPv1.

To control which version of RIP should handle generating updates on an interface, use the following configuration:

```
Router(config)# interface type [slot_#/]port_#
Router(config-router)# ip rip send version 1 | version 2 |
                                     version 1 2
```

With the **ip rip send** command, you can control which version of RIP the router should use on the specified interface when *generating* RIP updates. You can be specific by specifying version 1 or 2, or you can specify both.

To control what version of RIP should be used when receiving RIP updates on a particular interface, use the following configuration:

```
Router(config)# interface type [slot_#/]port_#
Router(config-router)# ip rip receive version 1 | version 2 |
                                     version 1 2
```

on the
job

Unless you need to run RIPv1 because of backward compatibility with an older router or host running RIP, you should use version 2 because of some of its enhancements over version 1, such as classless routing, multicasts, and triggered updates.

19.04. The CD contains a multimedia demonstration of RIPv2 configuration on a router.

A Cisco router running RIP, by default, generates only RIPv1 updates but processes received version 1 and 2 updates. *Use the* `version` *command to change the RIP version.*

Configuration Example

Let's use a simple network example, shown in Figure 19-3, to illustrate configuring RIPv2. Here's RouterA's configuration:

```
RouterA(config)# router rip
RouterA(config-router)# network 192.168.1.0
RouterA(config-router)# network 192.168.2.0
RouterA(config-router)# version 2
```

Here's RouterB's configuration:

```
RouterB(config)# router rip
RouterB(config-router)# network 192.168.2.0
RouterB(config-router)# network 192.168.3.0
RouterB(config-router)# version 2
```

As you can see, configuring RIPv2 is very easy.

FIGURE 19-3

RIPv2 configuration example

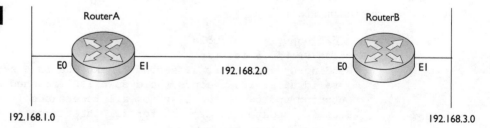

RouterA   RouterB

E0   E1   192.168.2.0   E0   E1

192.168.1.0   192.168.3.0

RIP Verification and Troubleshooting

Once you have configured IP RIP, a variety of commands are available to view and troubleshoot your RIP configuration and operation:

- `clear ip route`
- `show ip protocols`
- `show ip route`
- `debug ip rip`

The following sections cover these commands in more depth.

The clear ip route Command

The `clear ip route *` is a Privilege EXEC mode command. This command clears and rebuilds the IP routing table. Any time you make a change to a routing protocol, you should clear and rebuild the routing table with this command. You can replace the asterisk (`*`) with a specific network number; if you choose to do so, this will only clear the specified route from the routing table. Note that the `clear` command clears only routes learned from a routing protocol (dynamic routes); static and directly connected routes cannot be cleared from the routing table using the `clear` command. Static routes must be cleared manually using the `no ip route` command, and directly connected routes are persistent and cannot be removed from the routing table unless the interface they are associated with is not operational.

The show ip protocols Command

The `show ip protocols` command displays all the IP routing protocols, including RIP, which you have configured and are running on your router. Here's an example of this command:

```
Router# show ip protocols
Routing Protocol is "rip"
  Sending updates every 30 seconds, next due in 5 seconds
  Invalid after 180 seconds, hold down 180, flushed after 240
  Outgoing update filter list for all interfaces is not set
  Incoming update filter list for all interfaces is not set
  Redistributing: rip
  Default version control: send version 2, receive version 2
    Interface        Send  Recv  Triggered RIP Key-chain
    Ethernet0        2     2
    Ethernet1        2     2
```

```
Automatic network summarization is in effect
Maximum path: 4
Routing for Networks:
   192.168.1.0
   192.168.2.0
Routing Information Sources:
   Gateway          Distance         Last Update
   192.168.2.2           120         00:00:22
   192.168.3.2           120         00:03:30
Distance: (default is 120)
```

In this example, RIPv2 is running on the router. The routing update interval is 30 seconds, with the next update being sent in 5 seconds. You can see that two interfaces are participating: `Ethernet0` and `Ethernet1`. On these interfaces, RIPv2 is being used to generate and receive updates on these two interfaces. You can see the two networks specified with the **network** commands: 192.168.1.0 and 192.168.2.0. In this example, this router received an update 22 seconds ago from a neighboring router: 192.168.2.2. For the second gateway, 192.168.3.2, the router hasn't seen an update from it in 210 seconds. Given that the flush timer is 240 seconds, if the local router doesn't receive an update from 192.168.3.2 within 30 seconds, 192.168.3.2 and its associated routes are removed from the local router (flushed). And last, the default administrative distance of RIP is 120.

CertCam

19.05. The CD contains a multimedia demonstration of the `show ip protocols` command for RIP on a router.

e x a m

ⓦ a t c h

RIP advertises routes every 30 seconds. Its hold-down period is 180 seconds, and its flush period is *240 seconds. Be familiar with the output of the `show ip protocols` command: the version of RIP and when routes are flushed.*

The show ip route Command

Your router keeps a list of the best paths to destinations in a routing table. A separate routing table is kept for each *routed* protocol. For instance, if you are running IP and IPX, your router will have two routing tables: one for each. However, if you are running two *routing* protocols for a single routed protocol, such as IP RIP and EIGRP, your router will have only one routing table for IP, with both sets of routes, possibly, in the same table.

e x a m

ⓦatch

Remember the output of the show ip route command for the RIP routing protocol, including being able *to identify the administrative distance and metric values.*

To view the routing table, use the **show ip route** command. Here's an example of a RIPv2 router's table:

```
Router# show ip route
Codes: C - connected, S - static, I - IGRP, R - RIP,
       M - mobile, B - BGP, D - EIGRP, EX - EIGRP external,
       O - OSPF, IA - OSPF inter area, N1 - OSPF NSSA
       external type 1, N2 - OSPF NSSA external type 2,
       E1 - OSPF external type 1, E2 - OSPF external type 2,
       E - EGP, i - IS-IS, L1 - IS-IS level-1,
       L2 - IS-IS level-2, * - candidate default,
       U - per-user static route, o - ODR,
       T - traffic engineered route

Gateway of last resort is not set
     172.16.0.0/24 is subnetted, 2 subnets
C       172.16.1.0 is directly connected, Ethernet0
R       172.16.2.0 [120/1] via 172.16.1.2, 00:00:21, Ethernet0
     192.168.1.0/24 is subnetted, 2 subnets
C       192.168.1.0 is directly connected, Serial0
R    192.168.2.0/24 [120/2] via 192.168.1.2, 00:00:02, Serial2
```

In this example, you can see that two types of routes are in the routing table: R is for RIP and C is for a directly connected route. For the RIP entries, you can see two numbers in brackets: the administrative distance of the route and the metric. For instance, 172.16.2.0 has an administrative distance of 120 and a hop count of 1. Following this information is the neighboring RIP router that advertised the route (172.16.1.2), how long ago an update for this route was received from the neighbor (21 seconds), and on which interface this update was learned (Ethernet0).

19.06. The CD contains a multimedia demonstration of the show ip route command for RIP on a router.

The debug ip rip Command

Remember that the **show** commands show a static display of what the router knows, and they sometimes don't display enough information concerning a specific issue or problem. For instance, you might be looking at your routing table with the **show ip route** command and expect a certain RIP route to appear from a connected neighbor, but this network is not shown. Unfortunately, the **show ip route** command won't tell you why a route is or isn't in the routing table. However, you can resort to **debug** commands to assist you in your troubleshooting.

For more detailed troubleshooting of IP RIP problems, you can use the **debug ip rip** command, shown here:

```
Router# debug ip rip
RIP protocol debugging is on
Router#
00:12:16: RIP: received v1 update from 192.168.1.2 on Serial0
00:12:16:       192.168.2.0 in 1 hops
00:12:25: RIP: sending v1 update to 255.255.255.255 via Ethernet0
172.16.1.1)
00:12:26:       network 192.168.1.0, metric 0
00:12:26:       network 192.168.2.0, metric 1
```

This command displays the routing updates sent and received on the router's interfaces. In this code example, the router received a V1 update from 192.168.1.2 on Serial0. This update contained one network, 192.168.2.0, indicating that this network is reachable from this and the advertising routers. After this update, you can see that your router generated a RIP update (local broadcast—255.255.255.255) on its Ethernet0 interface. This update contains two networks: 192.168.1.0 and 192.168.2.0. Also notice the metrics associated with these routes: 192.168.1.0 is connected to this router, while 192.168.2.0 is one hop away. When the neighboring router connected to Ethernet0 receives this update, it will increment the hop count by 1 for each route in the update.

If the two routers are running different RIP versions—v1 and v2—you'll see output like the following on your router when running the preceding **debug** command:

```
00:12:25: RIP: sending v1 update to 255.255.255.255
                      via Ethernet0 172.16.1.1)
00:12:26:        network 192.168.1.0, metric 0
00:12:26:        network 192.168.2.0, metric 1
00:12:32: RIP: ignored v2 packet from 192.168.2.1
                      (illegal version)
```

on the **Job** *When using debug commands, you must be at Privilege EXEC mode. To disable a specific debug command, negate it with the no parameter. To turn off debugging for all debug commands, use either the undebug all or no debug all command.*

19.07. The CD contains a multimedia demonstration of the debug ip rip command for RIP on a router.

EXERCISE 19-3

Configuring RIP

These last few sections dealt with configuring RIP on a router. This exercise will help you reinforce the material for setting up and troubleshooting RIP. You'll perform this lab using Boson's NetSim simulator. You can find a picture of the network diagram for Boson's NetSim simulator in the Introduction of this book. In this exercise, you set IP RIPv1 on the two routers (2600-1 and 2600-2). After starting up the simulator, click the LabNavigator button. Next, double-click Exercise 19-3 and click the Load Lab button. This will load the lab configuration based on the exercises in Chapters 11 and 16.

   1. On the 2600-1, verify that the fa0/0 and s0 interfaces are up. If not, bring them up. At the top of the simulator in the menu bar, click the eRouters icon and choose 2600-1. On the 2600-1, use the **show interfaces** command to verify your configuration. If fa0/0 and s0 are not up, go into the interfaces (fa0/0 and s0) and enable them: **configure terminal, interface type** [*slot_#/*] *port_#*, **no shutdown**, and **end**.

2. Examine the IP addresses configured on the 2600-1.

   Use the **show ip interface brief** command to verify that the IP addresses you configured in Chapter 16 are still there.

3. Examine the routing table on the 2600-1.

   Use the **show ip route** command. You should have two connected networks: 192.168.1.0 connected to fa0/0 and 192.168.2.0 connected to s0.

4. On the 2600-2, verify that the fa0/0 and s0 interfaces are up. If not, bring them up.

   At the top of the simulator in the menu bar, click the eRouters icon and choose 2600-2. On the 2600-2, use the **show interfaces** command to verify your configuration. If fa0/0 and s0 are not up, go into the interfaces (fa0/0 and s0) and enable them: **configure terminal, interface type port_#, no shutdown**, and **end**. Use the **show interfaces** command to verify your interface configuration.

5. Examine the IP addresses configured on the 2600-2.

   Use the **show ip interface brief** command to verify that the IP addresses you configured in Chapter 16 are still there.

6. Examine the routing table on the 2600-2.

   Use the **show ip route** command. You should have two connected networks: 192.168.3.0 connected to fa0/0 and 192.168.2.0 connected to s0.

7. Test connectivity between Host-1 and the 2600-1.

   At the top of the simulator in the menu bar, click the eStations icon and choose Host-1. From Host-1, ping the 2600-1 router (the default gateway): **ping 192.168.1.1**. The ping should be successful.

8. Test connectivity between Host-3 and the 2600-2.

   At the top of the simulator in the menu bar, click the eStations icon and choose Host-3. From the Host-3, ping the 2600-2 router (the default gateway): **ping 192.168.3.1**. The ping should be successful.

9. Test connectivity between Host-3 and Host-1.

   From the Host-3, ping Host-1: **ping 192.168.1.10**. The ping should fail. Why? There is no route from the 2600-2 to this destination. (Look at the 2600-2's routing table: it doesn't list 192.168.1.0/24.)

10. Access the 2600-2 and examine the routing table to see why the ping failed.

    At the top of the simulator in the menu bar, click the eRouters icon and choose 2600-2. Examine the routing table: **show ip route**. Notice that it doesn't list 192.168.1.0/24, which explains why Host-3 can't reach Host-1.

11. Enable RIPv1 on the 2600-1 router.

    At the top of the simulator in the menu bar, click the eRouters icon and choose 2600-1. On the 2600-1, execute the following: **configure terminal, router rip, network 192.168.1.0, network 192.168.2.0**, and **end**.

12. Enable RIPv1 on the 2600-2 router.

    At the top of the simulator in the menu bar, click the eRouters icon and choose 2600-2. On the 2600-2, execute the following: **configure terminal, router rip, network 192.168.2.0, network 192.168.3.0**, and **end**.

13. On the 2600-1, verify the operation of RIP.

    At the top of the simulator in the menu bar, click the eRouters icon and choose 2600-1. Use the **show ip protocols** command to make sure that RIP is configured—check for the neighboring router's IP address. Use the **show ip route** command and look for the remote LAN network number as a RIP (R) entry in the routing table. On the 2600-1, you should see 192.168.3.0, which was learned from the 2600-2.

14. On the 2600-2, verify the operation of RIP.

    At the top of the simulator in the menu bar, click the eRouters icon and choose 2600-2. Use the **show ip protocols** command to make sure that RIP is configured—check for the neighboring router's IP address. Use the **show ip route** command and look for the remote LAN network number as a RIP (R) entry in the routing table. On the 2600-2, you should see 192.168.1.0, which was learned from the 2600-1.

15. On Host-1, test connectivity to Host-3.

    At the top of the simulator in the menu bar, click the eStations icon and choose Host-1. On Host-1, test connectivity: **ping 192.168.3.10**. The ping should be successful.

EXERCISE 19-4

Basic RIP Troubleshooting

This exercise is a troubleshooting exercise and is similar to Exercise 19-3, in which you were given a configuration task to set up RIP. In this exercise, the network is already configured; however, three problems exist in this network and you'll need to find and fix them in order for the network to operate correctly. All of these problems deal with IP (layer 3) connectivity. You'll perform this exercise using Boson's NetSim simulator. You can find a picture of the network diagram for Boson's NetSim simulator in the Introduction of this book. The addressing scheme is the same as that configured in Chapter 16. After starting up the simulator, click the LabNavigator button. Next, double-click Exercise 19-4 and click the Load Lab button. This will load the lab configuration based on Chapter 16's exercises (with problems, of course).

Let's start with your problem: Host-1 cannot ping Host-3. Your task is to identify and fix the three problems. In this example, RIPv2 has been preconfigured on the routers. Try this troubleshooting process on your own first; if you have problems, come back to the steps and solutions provided here.

1. Use the ping tool to test connectivity from Host-1 to Host-3.

   At the top of the simulator in the menu bar, click the eStations icon and choose Host-1. On Host-1, ping Host-3: **ping 192.168.3.10**. Note that the ping fails.

2. Examine the IP configuration on Host-1.

   Execute **ipconfig /all**. Make sure the IP addressing information is correct: IP address of 192.168.1.10, subnet mask of 255.255.255.0, and default gateway address of 192.168.1.1.

3. Use the ping tool to test connectivity from Host-1 to its default gateway.

   Ping the default gateway address: **ping 192.168.1.1**. The ping should fail, indicating that at least layer 3 is not functioning between Host-1 and the 2600-1.

4. Check the 2600-1's IP configuration.

   At the top of the simulator in the menu bar, click the eRouters icon and choose 2600-1. From the 2600-1, ping Host-1: **ping 192.168.1.10**.

The ping should fail. Examine the interface on the 2600-1: **show interface fa0/0**. The interface is enabled, but it has an incorrect IP address: 192.168.11.1. Fix the IP address: **configure terminal, interface fa0/0, ip address 192.168.1.1 255.255.255.0,** and **end**. Verify the IP address: **show interface fa0/0**.

5. Retest connectivity with ping.

   Retry the ping test: **ping 192.168.1.10**. The ping should be successful. Save the configuration on the router: **copy running-config startup-config**.

6. Test connectivity from Host-1 to Host-3 with ping, as well as to the default gateway.

   At the top of the simulator in the menu bar, click the eStations icon and choose Host-1. On Host-1, ping Host-3: **ping 192.168.3.10**. Note that the ping still fails.

7. Examine Host-3's IP configuration.

   At the top of the simulator in the menu bar, click the eStations icon and choose Host-3. Examine the IP configuration on Host-3 by executing **ipconfig /all**. Make sure the IP addressing information is correct: IP address of 192.168.3.10, subnet mask of 255.255.255.0, and default gateway address of 192.168.3.1.

8. Test connectivity from Host-3 to its default gateway.

   Ping the default gateway address: **ping 192.168.3.1**. The ping should fail, indicating that there is a problem between Host-3 and the 2600-2. In this example, assume layer 2 is functioning correctly; therefore, it must be a problem with the 2600-2.

9. Check the interface statuses and IP configuration on the 2600-2.

   At the top of the simulator in the menu bar, click the eRouters icon and choose 2600-2. Check the status of the interfaces: **show interfaces**. Notice that the fa0/0 is disabled, but s0 is enabled (*up* and *up*). Go into fa0/0 and enable it: **configure terminal, interface fa0/0, no shutdown**, and **end**. Verify the status of the fa0/0 interface: **show interface fa0/0**.

10. Verify connectivity from the 2600-2 to the 2600-1.

    Try pinging Host-3: **ping 192.168.3.10**. The ping should succeed. Try pinging the 2600-1's s0 interface: **ping 192.168.2.1**. The ping succeeds.

11. Verify RIP's configuration on the 2600-2.

    Examine the RIP configuration: **show ip protocol**. You should see RIP as the routing protocol and networks 192.168.2.0 and 192.168.3.0 included. From the output, it looks like RIP is configured correctly on the 2600-2. Save the configuration on the router: **copy running-config startup-config**.

12. Test connectivity from the 2600-2 to Host-1. Examine the routing table.

    Test the connection to Host-1: **ping 192.168.1.10**. The ping should fail. This indicates a layer 3 problem between the 2600-2 and Host-1.

13. View the routes in the 2600-2's routing table.

    Examine the routing table: **show ip route**. Notice that there are only two connected routes (192.168.2.0/24 and 192.168.1.0/24), but no RIP routes.

14. Access the 2600-1 router and examine RIP's configuration.

    At the top of the simulator in the menu bar, click the eRouters icon and choose 2600-1. Examine the routing table: **show ip protocol**. What networks are advertised by the 2600-1? You should see 192.168.1.0 and 192.168.11.0. Obviously, serial0's interface isn't included since 192.168.2.0 is not configured.

15. Fix the problem with the 2600-1's RIP configuration.

    Fix this configuration problem: **configure terminal**, **router rip**, **no network 192.168.11.0**, **network 192.168.1.0**, and **end**. Examine the routing protocol configuration: **show ip protocol**.

16. Test connectivity to Host-3 using ping.

    Test connectivity to Host-3: **ping 192.168.3.10**. The ping should be successful. Save the configuration on the router: **copy running-config startup-config**.

17. Now test connectivity between Host-1 and Host-3.

    At the top of the simulator in the menu bar, click the eStations icon and choose Host-1. Test connectivity to Host-3: **ping 192.168.3.10**. The ping should be successful.

Now you should be more comfortable with configuring IP RIP on your IOS router.

INSIDE THE EXAM

Static Routes

Be familiar with when static routes are used versus a dynamic routing protocol. Understand the syntax of the `ip route` command and the default values, if omitted. Know how to configure a default route. Be able to find misconfigured static routes in a router's configuration. Know how to read the output of the `show ip route` command and to find the administrative distance and metric values of dynamic routing protocols in this output.

Dynamic Routing Protocol Basics

Remember the two things that need to happen to enable routing on a router: enabling the routing protocol by assigning networks to it and activating interfaces by enabling and assigning addresses to them.

Don't be surprised if you see a simulation question on the exam for which you have to configure or troubleshoot a dynamic routing protocol—RIPv2, OSPF, or EIGRP—on multiple routers.

RIP

Understand the differences between RIPv1 and RIPv2 and be able to compare and contrast these protocols. Be able to configure RIPv2 successfully on a router. Understand the output of the `show ip protocols` and `debug ip rip` commands to troubleshoot routing and connectivity problems. Understand the problems `debug` commands can create on a router and how to disable `debug`.

CERTIFICATION SUMMARY

Two types of routing protocols can be used to define or learn destination networks: static and dynamic. To create a static route, use the **ip route** command. For a default route, use 0.0.0.0/0 as the network number and subnet mask. To view your router's routing table, use the **show ip route** command.

When setting up IP routing, you must enable the routing protocol and configure IP routing on your router's interfaces. The **router** command takes you into the routing process, while the **network** command specifies what interfaces will participate in the routing process. Use the **ip address** command to assign IP addresses to your router's interfaces.

RIPv1 generates local broadcasts every 30 seconds to share routing information, with a hold-down period of 180 seconds. Hop count is used as the metric for choosing paths. RIP can load-balance across six equal-cost paths to a single destination. RIPv2 uses multicasts instead of broadcasts and also supports VLSM for hierarchical routing and route summarization. RIPv2, to speed up convergence, uses triggered updates. Use the **router rip** command to go into the routing process and the **network** command to specify your connected networks. When specifying your connected networks, specify only the Class A, B, or C network number (not subnet numbers), since RIPv1 is classful: even though RIPv2 is classless, configure it as a classful protocol. Use the **version** command to enable RIPv2. The **debug ip rip** command will display the actual routing contents that your router advertises in its updates or receives in neighbors' updates.

The **show ip protocols** command displays information about the IP routing protocols currently configured and running on your router. It shows metric information, administrative distances, neighboring routers, and routes that are being advertised. The **show ip route** command displays the IP routing information currently being used by your router. An R in the left-hand column indicates a RIP route.

✓ # TWO-MINUTE DRILL

Static Routes

- ❑ Use the `ip route` command to configure a static route.
- ❑ After the subnet mask parameter, you have two ways of specifying how to reach the destination network: you can tell the router either the next hop neighbor's IP address or the interface the router should exit to reach the destination network. The former has an administrative distance of 1 and the latter, 0 (a directly connected route).

Dynamic Routing Protocol Basics

- ❑ To set up IP on your router, you need to enable the routing protocol and assign IP addresses to your router's interfaces.
- ❑ Use the `router` and `network` commands to enable routing. With classful protocols, use the class address in the `network` command.

RIP

- ❑ RIP uses hop count as a metric and has a hop-count limit of 15. IP RIP supports up to six equal-cost paths to a single destination.
- ❑ RIPv1 sends out periodic routing updates as broadcasts every 30 seconds. The hold-down timer is 180 seconds. It is a classful protocol.
- ❑ RIPv2 uses triggered updates and sends its updates out as multicasts. It is a classless protocol and supports VLSM and route summarization. Optionally, RIPv2 updates can be authenticated.
- ❑ Use the `router rip` and `network` commands to set up RIP. Use the `version` command to hard code the version. Use the following commands for troubleshooting: `show ip protocols`, `show ip route`, and `debug ip rip`.
- ❑ After making a change to an IP routing protocol, use the `clear ip route *` command to clear the IP routing table and rebuild it.

SELF TEST

The following Self Test questions will help you measure your understanding of the material presented in this chapter. Read all the choices carefully, as there may be more than one correct answer. Choose all correct answers for each question.

Static Routes

1. Enter the command to set up a static route to 192.168.1.0/24, where the next hop address is 192.168.2.2: _____.

2. What subnet mask would you use to set up a default route?
   A. 0.0.0.0
   B. 255.255.255.255
   C. Depends on the type of network number
   D. None of these answers

3. What is the default administrative distance of a static route where the next hop specified is the IP address of a neighboring router?
   A. 0
   B. 1
   C. 90
   D. 120

Dynamic Routing Protocol Basics

4. You have a distance vector protocol such as RIP. You've entered the RIP process by executing: **router rip**. On one of your router's interfaces, you have the following IP address: 192.168.1.65 255.255.255.192. Enter the command to include this interface in the RIP routing process: _____.

RIP

5. RIP generates routing updates every _____ seconds.
   A. 15
   B. 30
   C. 60
   D. 90

6. RIP has a hold-down period of _____ seconds.

    A. 60

    B. 120

    C. 180

    D. 280

7. RIP has a maximum hop count of _____ hops.

    A. 10

    B. 15

    C. 16

    D. 100

8. RIP supports load balancing for up to _____ _____ paths.

    A. Six, unequal-cost

    B. Four, unequal-cost

    C. Four, equal-cost

    D. Six, equal-cost

9. Which of the following is true concerning RIPv2?

    A. It uses triggered updates.

    B. It uses broadcasts.

    C. It is classful.

    D. It doesn't support route summarization.

10. Enter the router command used to view which routing protocols are active on your router, as well as their characteristics and configuration: _____.

SELF TEST ANSWERS

Static Routes

1. ☑ `ip route 192.168.1.0 255.255.255.0 192.168.2.2`

2. ☑ **A.** A default route is set up with an IP address and mask of 0.0.0.0 0.0.0.0.
    ☒ **B** is incorrect because this number indicates that the complete IP address is a network number, commonly called a host route. **C** is incorrect because the network number would use a standard subnet mask based on the network you're trying to reach: 0.0.0.0 as a subnet mask indicates all hosts. And since there is a correct answer, **D** is incorrect.

3. ☑ **B.** The default administrative distance of a static route pointing to a neighbor's IP address is 1.
    ☒ **A** is incorrect because 0 is the value of a static route with an interface or a connected route. **C** is incorrect because 90 is EIGRP's administrative distance and **D**, 120, is RIP's administrative distance.

Dynamic Routing Protocol Basics

4. ☑ `network 192.168.1.0`. Remember that RIPv1 is classful.

RIP

5. ☑ **B.** RIP generates routing updates every 30 seconds.
    ☒ **A, C,** and **D** are invalid update intervals.

6. ☑ **C.** RIP has a hold-down period of 180 seconds.
    ☒ **A, B,** and **D** are invalid hold-down periods.

7. ☑ **B.** RIP has a maximum hop count of 15 hops.
    ☒ **A, C,** and **D** are invalid maximum hop-count values.

8. ☑ **D.** RIP supports load-balancing for up to six equal-cost paths.
    ☒ **A** and **B** are invalid because RIP doesn't support unequal-cost paths. **C** is incorrect because four is the default, but six is the maximum.

9. ☑ **A.** RIPv2 supports triggered updates.
    ☒ **B** is incorrect because RIPv2 uses multicasts. **C** is incorrect because RIPv2 is classless. **D** is incorrect because RIPv2 supports VLSM and route summarization.

10. ☑ To view the IP routing protocols running on your router, use **show ip protocols**.

20

OSPF Routing

The Open Shortest Path First (OSPF) protocol is a link state protocol that handles routing for IP traffic. Version 2 of OSPF, which is explained in RFC 2328, is an open standard, such as Routing Information Protocol (RIP) v1 and RIPv2. Chapter 15 offered a brief introduction to link state protocols. As you will see in this chapter, OSPF draws heavily on the concepts described in Chapter 15, but it also has some unique features of its own. Besides covering the characteristics of OSPF, you'll be presented with enough information to undertake a basic routing configuration using OSPF. A more thorough discussion is covered in Cisco's CCNP certification.

CERTIFICATION OBJECTIVE 20.01

OSPF Overview

OSPF was created in the mid-1980s to overcome many of the deficiencies and scalability problems that RIP had in large enterprise networks. Because it is based on an open standard, OSPF is very popular in many corporate networks today and has many advantages, including these:

- It will run on most routers, since it is based on an open standard.
- It uses the SPF algorithm, developed by Edsger Dijkstra, to provide a loop-free topology.
- It provides fast convergence with triggered, incremental updates via link state advertisements (LSAs).
- It is a classless protocol and allows for a hierarchical design with VLSM and route summarization.
- It has an intelligent metric (cost), which is the inverse of the bandwidth of an interface.

Given its advantages, OSPF does have its share of disadvantages:

- It requires more memory to hold the adjacency (list of OSPF neighbors), topology (a link state database containing all of the routers and their routes/links), and routing tables.
- It requires extra CPU processing to run the SPF algorithm, which is especially true when you first turn on your routers and they are initially building the adjacency and topology tables.

- For large networks, it requires careful design to break up the network into an appropriate hierarchical design by separating routers into different *areas*.
- It is more complex to configure and more difficult to troubleshoot than distance vector protocols.

Knowing the advantages and disadvantages of any routing protocol is useful when it comes to picking a protocol. Typically, OSPF is used in large enterprise networks that have either a mixed routing vendor environment or a policy that requires an open standard for a routing protocol, which gives a company flexibility when it needs to replace any of its existing routers.

Remember the advantages and disadvantages of OSPF: it's an open standard, it supports a hierarchical design using areas, and it uses cost as a metric.*

on the job *Typically, when you start having more than 50 routers, Cisco recommends you use a more advanced routing protocol such as OSPF or EIGRP. In a mixed-vendor environment there is basically one choice between these two: OSPF.*

Hierarchical Design: Areas

To provide scalability for very large networks, OSPF supports two important concepts: autonomous systems and areas. Autonomous systems (ASs) were discussed in Chapter 15. Within an AS, *areas* are used to provide hierarchical routing. An area is a group of contiguous networks. Basically, areas are used to control when and how much routing information is shared across your network. In flat network designs, such as those that use IP RIP, if a change occurs on one router (perhaps a flapping route problem), it affects *every* router in the entire network. With a correctly designed hierarchical network, these changes can be contained within a single area.

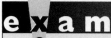

Remember that OSPF supports a two-layer hierarchy: the backbone (area 0 or 0.0.0.0) and areas connected to the backbone.*

OSPF implements a two-layer hierarchy: the backbone and areas off the backbone, as shown in Figure 20-1. This network includes a backbone and three areas connected to the backbone. Each area is given a unique number that is 32 bits in length. The area number can be represented by a single decimal number, such as 1, or in a dotted decimal format, such as 0.0.0.1. Area 0 is a special area and represents the top-level hierarchy of the OSPF network, commonly called the *backbone*. Through a correct IP addressing design, you should be able to summarize routing information between areas. By summarizing your routing information, perhaps one summarized route for each area, you are reducing the amount of information that routers need to know about. For instance, each area in Figure 20-1 is assigned a separate Class B network number. Through summarization on the border routers between areas, other areas would not need to see all the Class B subnets—only the summarized network numbers for each respective area (the Class B network numbers themselves).

FIGURE 20-1 OSPF hierarchical design

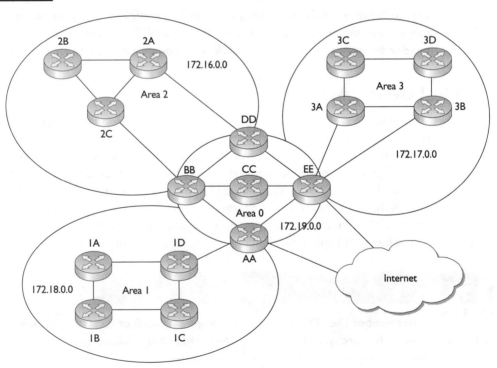

Area 2, for instance, doesn't need to see all of the subnets of Area 1's 172.18.0.0 network number, since only two paths exist out of Area 2 to the backbone. Area 2, however, needs to see all of its internal subnets to create optimized routing tables to reach its own internal networks within Area 2. Therefore, in a correctly designed OSPF network, each area should contain specific routes only for its own areas and summarized routes to reach other areas. By performing this summarization, the routers have a smaller topology database (they know only about links in their own area and the summarized routes) and their routing tables are smaller (they know only about their own area's routes and the summarized routes). Through a correct hierarchical design, you can scale OSPF to very large sizes. Chapter 8 discussed route summarization.

Note that the CCNA exam focuses on only single-area designs, and the material throughout the rest of the sections of this chapter covers only single-area concepts. The CCNP-level material, however, spends a lot of time on both single- *and* multi-area designs. Designing a multi-area OSPF network can become very complicated and requires a lot of networking knowledge and skill.

on the
(J) o b

An excellent resource for OSPF, called the "OSPF Design Guide," can be found free on Cisco's web site: http://www.cisco.com/warp/public/104/1.html. It covers both single- and multi-area designs in much depth.

Metric Structure

Unlike RIP, which uses hop count as a metric, OSPF uses cost. Cost is actually the inverse of the bandwidth of a link: the faster the speed of the connection, the lower the cost. The most preferred path is the one with the lowest accumulated cost value. By using cost as a metric, OSPF will choose more intelligent paths than RIP (metrics are discussed in more depth in the "OSPF Metric Values" section later in the chapter).

Remember that on synchronous serial links, no matter what the clock rate of the physical link is, the bandwidth always defaults to 1544 Kbps. You'll want to code this correctly with the `bandwidth` Interface Subconfiguration mode command (discussed in Chapter 16). This is important if you have multiple synchronous serial paths to a destination, especially if they have different clock rates. OSPF supports load balancing of up to 16 equal-cost paths to a single destination; however, only four equal-cost paths are used by default. Remember that if you don't configure the bandwidth metric correctly on your serial interfaces, your router might accidentally include paths with different clock rates, which can cause load-balancing issues.

watch

OSPF uses cost as a metric, which is the inverse of the bandwidth of a link.

For example, if you have one serial connection clocked at 1544 Kbps and another clocked at 256 Kbps and you don't change the bandwidth values, OSPF will see *both* connections as 1544 Kbps and attempt to use both when reaching a single destination across these links. This can create throughput problems when the router is performing load balancing—half of the connections will go down one link and half down the other, creating congestion problems for the 256 Kbps connection.

CERTIFICATION OBJECTIVE 20.02

OSPF Operation

As mentioned, OSPF is a link state protocol like that generically described in Chapter 15. However, each link state protocol, such as OSPF and IS-IS, has its own unique features and characteristics. This section introduces you to how OSPF operates in a single-area design.

Router Identities

Each router in an OSPF network needs a unique ID—this must be unique not just within an area, but within the entire OSPF network. The ID is used to provide a unique identity to the OSPF router. The ID is included in any OSPF messages the router generates that other OSPF routers will process. The router ID is chosen according to one of the following criteria:

- The highest IP address on the router's active loopback interfaces is used (this is a logical interface on a router).
- If no loopback interface exists with an IP address, the highest IP address on its active interfaces is used when the router boots up.

The router ID is used by the router to announce itself to the other OSPF routers in the network. This ID must be unique. If no loopback interfaces are configured, the router will use the highest IP address from one of its active physical interfaces.

If no active interface exists, the OSPF process will not start and therefore you will not have any OSPF routes in your routing table. It is highly recommended, therefore, that you use a loopback interface because it is always up and thus the router can obtain a router ID and start OSPF.

Finding Neighbors

An OSPF router learns about its OSPF neighbors and builds its adjacency and topology tables by sharing link state advertisements (LSAs), which exist in different types. When learning about the neighbors to which a router is connected, as well as keeping tabs on known neighbors, OSPF routers will generate LSA hello messages every 10 seconds. When a neighbor is discovered and an adjacency is formed with the neighbor, a router expects to see hello messages from the neighbor. If a neighbor's hello is not seen within the dead interval time, which defaults to 40 seconds, the neighbor is declared dead. When this occurs, the router will advertise this information, via an LSA message, to other neighboring OSPF routers.

Whereas RIP accepts routing updates from just about any other RIP router (unless RIPv2 with authentication is configured), OSPF has some rules concerning if and how routing information should be shared. First, before a router will accept any routing information from another OSPF router, the routers must build an *adjacency* between them, on their connected interfaces. When this adjacency is built, the two routers (on the connected interfaces) are called *neighbors*, indicating a special relationship between the two. In order for two routers to become neighbors, the following must match on each router:

- The area number
- The hello and dead interval timers on their connected interfaces
- The OSPF password (optional), if it is configured
- The area stub flag, indicating the type of area; a stub is used to contain OSPF messages and routing information, which is beyond the scope of this book
- MTU sizes on the connected interfaces

If these items do not match, the routers will not form an adjacency and will ignore each other's routing information.

Let's assume that you turned on all your routers simultaneously on a segment. In this case, the OSPF routers will go through three states, called the *exchange process*, in determining whether they will become neighbors:

1. **Down state**   The routers have not exchanged any OSPF information with any other router.

2. **Init state**   A destination router has received a new router's hello and adds it to its neighbor list (assuming that values in the preceding bullet points match). Note that communication is only unidirectional at this point.

3. **Two-way state**   The new router receives a unidirectional reply (from the destination router) to its initial hello packet and adds the destination router to its neighbor database.

Once the routers have entered a *two-way* state, they are considered neighbors. At this point, an election process takes place to elect the designated router (DR) and the backup designated router (BDR) on the segment.

Designated and Backup Designated Routers

An OSPF router will not form adjacencies to just any router. Instead, a client/server design is implemented in OSPF on *each* broadcast segment. For each multi-access broadcast segment, such as Ethernet, there is a DR and a BDR as well as other OSPF routers, called *DROTHERs*. As an example, if you have 10 VLANs in your switched area, you'll have 10 DRs and 10 BDRs. The one exception of a segment not having these two routers is on a WAN point-to-point link.

When an OSPF router comes up, it forms adjacencies with the DR and the BDR on each multi-access segment to which it is connected; if it is connected to three segments, it will form three sets of adjacencies. Any exchange of routing information is between these DR/BDR routers and the other OSPF neighbors on a segment (and vice versa). An OSPF router talks to a DR using the IP multicast address of 224.0.0.6. The DR and the BDR talk to all OSPF routers using the 224.0.0.5 multicast IP address.

The OSPF router with the highest priority becomes the DR for the segment. If there is a tie, the router with the highest *router ID* (not IP address on the segment) will become the DR. By default, all routers have a priority of 1 (priorities can range from 0 to 255—it's an 8-bit value). If the DR fails, the BDR is promoted to DR and another router is elected as the BDR. Figure 20-2 shows an example of the election process, where router E is elected as the DR and router B, the BDR. Note that in this example, each router has the default priority, 1; therefore, router E is chosen as the DR since it has the highest router ID and router B as the BDR because it has the second highest router ID. If a router has a priority of 0, it will never become the DR or BDR.

FIGURE 20-2

DR and BDR election process

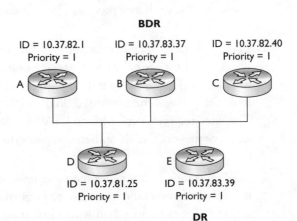

on the
job

The DR and BDR priority is changed on an interface-by-interface basis and is configured with the `ip ospf priority` *command within the Interface Subconfiguration mode. Once the DR/BDR are elected, they maintain these roles even if other routers form adjacencies with them that have higher priorities: an election or re-election will occur only if no DR or BDR exists.*

e x a m

ⓦatch
The router with the highest priority (or highest router ID) becomes the DR—note that it is not the highest IP address on the link. This process is true for multi-access segments, but not point-to-point links, where DRs/BDRs are not used. Setting the priority to 0 will mean the router will never become the DR or BDR.

Sharing Routing Information

After electing the DR/BDR pair, the routers continue to generate hellos to maintain communication. This is considered an *exstart* state, in which the OSPF routers are ready to share link state information. The process the routers go through is called an *exchange protocol*, and is outlined here:

1. **Exstart state** The DR and BDR form adjacencies with the other OSPF routers on the segment. Then, within each adjacency, the router with the highest router ID becomes the master and starts the exchange process first (shares its link state information). Note that the DR is not necessarily the master for the exchange process. The remaining router in the adjacency will be the slave.

2. **Exchange state** The master starts sharing link state information first with the slave. These are called *database description packets (DBDs)*, also referred to as DDPs. The DBDs contain the link state type, the ID of the advertising router, the cost of the advertised link, and the sequence number of the link. The slave responds back with an LSACK—an acknowledgment to the DBD from the master. The slave then compares the DBD's information with its own.

3. **Loading state** If the master has more up-to-date information than the slave, the slave will respond to the master's original DBD with a link state request (LSR). The master will then send a link state update (LSU) with the detailed

information of the links to the slave. The slave will then incorporate this into its local link state database. Again, the slave will generate an LSACK to the master to acknowledge the fact that it received the LSU. If a slave has more up-to-date information, it will repeat the exchange and loading states.

4. **Full state**   Once the master and the slave are synchronized, they are considered to be in a full state.

To summarize these four steps, OSPF routers share a type of LSA message in order to disclose information about available routes; basically, an LSA update message contains a link and a state, as well as other information. A *link* is the router interface on which the update was generated (a connected route). The *state* is a description of this interface, including the IP address configured on it as well as the relationship this router has with its neighboring router. However, OSPF routers will not share this information with just any OSPF router: just between themselves and the DR/BDR on a segment.

OSPF routers share information about their connected routes with the DR/BDR, which includes the link state type, the ID of the advertising router, the cost of the advertised link, and the sequence number of the link. This is different from distance vector protocols.

Distance vector protocols share their entire routing table with their neighbors with the exception of routes learned from the same interface of the neighbor (split horizon) and the connected route of the interface where the neighbor resides.

OSPF uses incremental updates after entering a full state. This means that whenever changes take place, only the change is shared with the DR, which will then share this information with other routers on the segment. Figure 20-3 shows an example of this. In this example, Network Z, connected to router C, goes down. Router C sends a multicast to the DR and the BDR (with a destination multicast address of 224.0.0.6), telling them about this change. Once the DR and the BDR incorporate the change internally, the DR then tells the other routes on the segment (via a multicast message sent to 224.0.0.5, which is all OSPF routers) about the change concerning Network Z. Any router receiving the update will then share this update to the DRs of other segments to which they are connected.

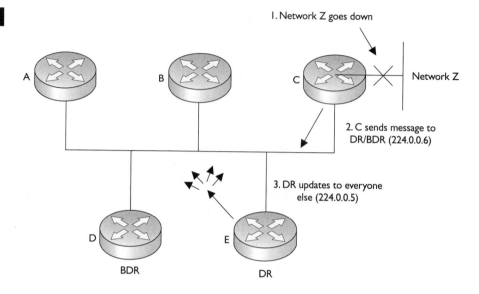

FIGURE 20-3

LSA update process

1. Network Z goes down

Network Z

2. C sends message to DR/BDR (224.0.0.6)

3. DR updates to everyone else (224.0.0.5)

A   B   C

D   E

BDR   DR

Note that the communications between OSPF routers is connection-oriented, even though multicasts are used. For example, if a router tells a DR about a change, the DR acknowledges this new piece of information with the source of the communication. Likewise, when the DR shares this information with the other routers on the segment, the DR expects acknowledgments from each of these neighbors. Remember that when an OSPF router exchanges updates with another, the process requires an acknowledgment: this ensures that a router or routers have received the update.

The exception to the incremental update process is that the DR floods its database every 30 minutes to ensure that all of the routers on the segment have the most up-to-date link state information. It does this with a destination address of 224.0.0.5 (all OSPF routers on the segment).

When building the routing table using link state information, an OSPF router can keep up to 16 paths to a destination in its routing table. The only restriction is that the paths must have the same accumulated cost metric.

e x a m

w a t c h

A two-way state indicates that two OSPF routers are neighbors. A full state indicates the completion of sharing of links between routers.

OSPF Configuration

Configuring OSPF is slightly *different* from configuring RIP. When configuring OSPF, use the following syntax:

```
Router(config)# router ospf process_ID
Router(config-router)# network IP_address wildcard_mask
                        area area_#
```

The *process_ID* is locally significant and is used to differentiate between OSPF processes running on the same router. Your router might be a boundary router between two OSPF autonomous systems, and to differentiate them on your router, you'll give them unique process IDs. Note that these numbers do *not* need to match between different routers and that they have nothing to do with autonomous system numbers. (The process of configuring two OSPF processes on the same router is beyond the scope of this book.)

e x a m

ᴡ a t c h
When configuring the OSPF routing process, you must specify a process ID (identifier). This uniquely identifies an instance of the OSPF database on *the router and is only* locally *significant: it doesn't have to match on each router in the AS.*

When specifying what interfaces go into an OSPF area, use the **network** command. As you can see in the preceding code listing, the syntax of this command is different from that of RIP's configuration, where you specify only a class address. OSPF is classless. With this command, you can be very specific about what interface belongs to a particular area. The syntax of this command lists an IP address or network number, followed by a *wildcard mask*, which is different from a subnet mask. A wildcard mask tells the router the interesting component of the address—in other words, what part of the address it should match on. This mask is also used with access lists, which are discussed thoroughly in Chapter 22.

A wildcard mask is 32 bits in length. A 0 in a bit position means there must be a match, and a 1 in a bit position means the router doesn't care. Actually, a wildcard mask is an *inverted* subnet mask, with the 1s and 0s switched. Using a wildcard mask, you can be very specific about which interfaces belong to which areas. The last part of the command tells the router to which area these addresses on the router belong.

Let's look at some code examples to see how the wildcard mask works. Use the router shown in Figure 20-4 as an illustration.

```
Router(config)# router ospf 1
Router(config-router)# network 10.1.1.1 0.0.0.0 area 0
Router(config-router)# network 10.1.2.1 0.0.0.0 area 0
Router(config-router)# network 172.16.1.1 0.0.0.0 area 0
Router(config-router)# network 172.16.2.1 0.0.0.0 area 0
```

In this example, the interfaces with addresses of 10.1.1.1, 10.1.2.1, 172.16.1.1, and 172.16.1.1 all are associated with area 0. A wildcard mask of 0.0.0.0 says that there

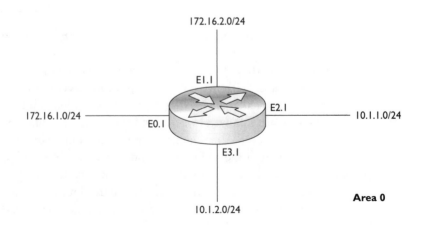

FIGURE 20-4

OSPF network configuration example

must be an exact match against the address on the router's interface in order to place it in area 0.

Here's another example that accomplishes the same thing:

```
Router(config)# router ospf 1
Router(config-router)# network 10.0.0.0 0.255.255.255 area 0
Router(config-router)# network 172.16.0.0 0.0.255.255 area 0
```

In this example, interfaces beginning with an address of 10 or 172.16 are to be included in area 0. Or, if all the interfaces on your router belonged to the same area, you could use this configuration:

```
Router(config)# router ospf 1
Router(config-router)# network 0.0.0.0 255.255.255.255 area 0
```

In this example, all interfaces are placed in area 0. As you can see, OSPF is very flexible in allowing you to specify which interface or interfaces will participate in OSPF and to which area they will belong.

20.01. The CD contains a multimedia demonstration of configuring OSPF on a router.

Loopback Interfaces

A *loopback interface* is a logical, virtual interface on a router. By default, the router doesn't have any loopback interfaces, but they can be easily created. All IOS platforms support loopback interfaces, and you can create as many of these interfaces as you need. These interfaces are treated as physical interfaces on a router: you can assign addressing information to them, include their network numbers in routing updates, and even terminate IP connections on them, such as telnet and SSH.

A loopback interface is a logical interface that always remains up. Use the `interface loopback` command to create it.

Here are some reasons you might want to create a loopback interface:

- To assign a router ID to an OSPF router
- To use for testing purposes, since this interface is always up
- To terminate special connections, such as GRE tunnels or IPSec connections, since this interface is always up

on the job

The router ID for OSPF is chosen when the OSPF routing process is started. This occurs when you execute the `router ospf` *command manually or when the router's configuration is loaded when booting up. Therefore, if you create a loopback interface after enabling OSPF, the loopback won't be used as the router ID; however, if you reboot the router, the loopback interface will be used, by default. Therefore, I recommend that you create your loopback interface and assign an IP address to it first and then enable OSPF to eliminate any confusion about what your router's router ID is.*

To create a loopback interface, use the following command:

```
Router(config)# interface loopback port_#
Router(config-if)# ip address IP_address subnet_mask
```

As you can see, creating a loopback interface is easy. You can specify port numbers from 0 to 2147483647. The number you use is only locally significant. Once you enter the loopback interface, you can execute almost any interface command on it; for instance, you can assign it an IP address with the `ip address` command.

CertCam

20.02. The CD contains a multimedia demonstration of creating a loopback interface on a router.

Default Route Propagation

On your perimeter OSPF router connected to the ISP, you typically have a default route pointing to the ISP. To take this route and redistribute it into your OSPF process, basically making your perimeter router an autonomous system boundary router (ASBR), use the following configuration:

```
Router(config)# ip route 0.0.0.0 0.0.0.0
                         ISP_interface_or_IP_address
Router(config)# router ospf process_ID
Router(config-router)# default-information originate
```

exam
watch

Make sure your default route doesn't point to your internal network, but your ISP's network; otherwise you'll be creating a routing loop.

OSPF Metric Values

You can affect the cost metric that OSPF uses in picking the best-cost routes for the routing table in two ways. First, remember that the cost metric is the inverse of the accumulated bandwidth values of routers' interfaces. The default measurement that Cisco uses in calculating the cost metric is: $cost = 10^8/(interface\ bandwidth)$. You can also affect the value of the cost by changing the 10^8 value with the **auto-cost reference-bandwidth** command.

Table 20-1 contains some default costs for different interface types.

To change the cost of an interface manually, use the following configuration:

```
Router(config)# interface type [slot_#/]port_#
Router(config-if)# ip ospf cost cost_value
```

Notice that the cost is assigned within an interface. This value can range from 1 to 65,535. Note that each vendor might use a different calculation to come up with a cost value.

on the
ⓙob

It is very important that the costs for a link match for every router on a given segment. Mismatched cost values on a segment can cause routers to run the SPF algorithm continually, greatly affecting the routers' performance.

Normally, you won't be changing the default cost values on an interface. However, since OSPF uses the inverse of bandwidth as a metric, and serial interfaces default to a bandwidth of 1544 Kbps, you will definitely want to match the bandwidth metric on the serial interface to its real clock rate. To configure the bandwidth on your router's interfaces, use the following command:

```
Router(config) interface type [slot_#/]port_#
Router(config-if)# bandwidth speed_in_Kbps
```

TABLE 20-1	Cost Value	Interface Type
OSPF Costs for Different Interfaces	1785	56 Kbps serial line
	1652	64 Kbps serial line
	64	T1
	10	Ethernet
	1	Fast Ethernet and FDDI

As an example, if the clock rate were 64,000, you would use the following command to configure the bandwidth correctly: **bandwidth 64**. Note that the speed is in *Kbps* for the **bandwidth** command. For example, assume you configured the bandwidth with this: **bandwidth 64000**. By doing this, the router would assume the bandwidth metric of the interface is 64 Mbps, not Kbps.

By default, the router will place up to four equal-cost OSPF paths to a destination in the router's routing table. This can be increased up to 16 equal-cost paths with the following configuration:

```
Router(config)# router ospf process_ID
Router(config-router)# maximum-paths #_of_max_paths
```

20.03. The CD contains a multimedia demonstration of changing OSPF metrics on a router.

@atch

The bandwidth command should be used on synchronous serial interfaces to match the bandwidth metric to the clocked rate of the interface.

Synchronous serial interfaces, no matter what they are clocked at, default to a bandwidth metric of 1544 Kbps.

OSPF Authentication

OSPF supports authentication of neighbors and routing updates. This is used to prevent rogue OSPF routers from injecting bad or misleading routing information into your topological databases. Authentication can be done with a clear-text password or a digital signature created with the MD5 algorithm. Of the two, the latter is the more secure: clear-text passwords can be seen by an eavesdropper between two OSPF neighbors. When using MD5, to prevent against a replay attack where the same information is always sent to a neighbor, such as a hello message, a nondecreasing sequence number is included in the message to ensure that the message and the signature are unique. The authentication information is placed in every LSA and validated before being accepted by an OSPF router. To become neighbors, the keying information—clear-text password or key for the MD5 algorithm—must match on the two peers.

Remember that if the password/key values on two OSPF neighbors don't match, an adjacency will not occur. Of the two methods, using MD5 is definitely much more secure than a clear-text password.

Configuring authentication is a two-step process: specifying the password/key to use and enabling authentication. The configuration of the key is done on an interface-by-interface basis, which means that every neighboring OSPF router off of the same interface must use the password/key. Here's the command to configure the password/key value:

```
Router(config)# interface type [slot_#/]port_#
Router(config-if)# ip ospf authentication-key password
```

Starting in IOS 12.4, any password greater than eight characters is truncated to eight characters by the router. The password is stored in clear text in the router's configuration. To encrypt it, use the **service password-encryption** command, discussed in Chapter 11.

Next, you must specify whether the password is sent in clear text or used by MD5 to create a digital signature. This can be done on the interface or on an area-by-area basis. To specify the interface method, use this configuration:

```
Router(config)# interface type [slot_#/]port_#
Router(config-if)# ip ospf authentication [message-digest]
```

If you omit the **message-digest** parameter, the key is sent as a clear-text password. Your other option is to configure the use of the password/key for an area with which the router is associated:

```
Router(config)# router ospf process_ID
Router(config-router)# area area_# authentication
                        [message-digest]
```

If you omit the **message-digest** parameter, the key is sent as a clear-text password.

Of the two approaches, the latter is the older method: the interface method (former method) was added in IOS 12.0 and is the preferred approach.

20.04. The CD contains a multimedia demonstration of setting up MD5 authentication on a router.

CERTIFICATION OBJECTIVE 20.04

OSPF Troubleshooting

Once you have configured OSPF, a variety of commands are available to view and troubleshoot your OSPF configuration and operation:

- `show ip protocols`
- `show ip route`
- `show ip ospf`
- `show ip ospf interface`
- `show ip ospf neighbor`
- `debug ip ospf adj`
- `debug ip ospf events`
- `debug ip ospf packet`

The following sections cover these commands.

The show ip protocols Command

The `show ip protocols` command displays all of the IP routing protocols that you have configured and that are running on your router. Here's an example of this command with OSPF:

```
Router# show ip protocols
Routing Protocol is "ospf 1"
  Outgoing update filter list for all interfaces is not set
 Incoming update filter list for all interfaces is not set
  Router ID 192.168.100.1
  Number of areas in this router is 1. 1 normal 0 stub 0 nssa
  Maximum path: 4
  Routing for Networks:
    0.0.0.0 255.255.255.255 area 0
  Routing Information Sources:
    Gateway          Distance      Last Update
    192.168.1.100         110      00:00:24
    192.168.100.1         110      00:00:24
  Distance: (default is 110)
```

In this example, the router's ID is 192.168.100.1. All interfaces are participating in OSPF (0.0.0.0 255.255.255.255) and are in area 0. There are two OSPF routers in this network: 192.168.1.100 (another router) and 192.168.100.1 (this router). Notice that the default administrative distance is 110.

20.05. The CD contains a multimedia demonstration of using the `show ip protocols` command on an OSPF router.

The show ip route Command

Your router keeps a list of the best IP paths to destinations in a routing table. To view the routing table, use the **show ip route** command:

```
Router# show ip route
Codes: C - connected, S - static, I - IGRP, R - RIP,
       M - mobile, B - BGP, D - EIGRP, EX - EIGRP external,
       O - OSPF, IA - OSPF inter area, N1 - OSPF NSSA
       external type 1, N2 - OSPF NSSA external type 2,
       E1 - OSPF external type 1, E2 - OSPF external type 2,
       E - EGP, i - IS-IS, L1 - IS-IS level-1,
       L2 - IS-IS level-2, * - candidate default,
       U - per-user static route, o - ODR,
       T - traffic engineered route
Gateway of last resort is not set
       10.0.0.0/24 is subnetted, 1 subnets
O       10.0.1.0 [110/65] via 192.168.1.100, 00:04:18, Serial0
C       192.168.1.0/24 is directly connected, Serial0
C       192.168.100.0/24 is directly connected, Ethernet0
```

In this example, there is one OSPF route (O): 10.0.1.0. This route has an administrative distance of 110, a metric cost of 65, and can be reached via neighbor 192.168.1.100.

20.06. The CD contains a multimedia demonstration of using the `show` ***`ip route` command on an OSPF router.***

The show ip ospf Command

To view an overview of your router's OSPF configuration, use the **show ip ospf** command:

```
Router# show ip ospf
  Routing Process "ospf 1" with ID 10.1.1.1 and Domain ID
10.1.1.1
  Supports only single TOS(TOS0) routes
  Supports opaque LSA
  SPF schedule delay 5 secs, Hold time between two SPFs 10 secs
  Minimum LSA interval 5 secs. Minimum LSA arrival 1 secs
  LSA group pacing timer 100 secs
  Interface flood pacing timer 55 msecs
  Retransmission pacing timer 100 msecs
  Number of external LSA 0. Checksum Sum 0x0
  Number of opaque AS LSA 0. Checksum Sum 0x0
  Number of DCbitless external and opaque AS LSA 0
  Number of DoNotAge external and opaque AS LSA 0
  Number of areas in this router is 1. 1 normal 0 stub 0 nssa
  External flood list length 0
    Area BACKBONE(0)
        Number of interfaces in this area is 2
        Area has message digest authentication
        SPF algorithm executed 4 times
        Area ranges are
        Number of LSA 4. Checksum Sum 0x29BEB
        Number of opaque link LSA 0. Checksum Sum 0x0
        Number of DCbitless LSA 3
        Number of indication LSA 0
        Number of DoNotAge LSA 0
        Flood list length 0
```

This command shows the OSPF timer configurations and other statistics, including the number of times the SPF algorithm is run in an area.

20.07. The CD contains a multimedia demonstration of using the show *ip* ospf *command on an OSPF router.*

The show ip ospf interface Command

On an interface-by-interface basis, your OSPF router keeps track of what area an interface belongs to and what neighbors, if any, are connected to the interface. To view this information, use the **show ip ospf interface** command:

```
Router# show ip ospf interface
Ethernet 1 is up, line protocol is up
Internet Address 172.16.255.1/24, Area 0
Process ID 100, Router ID 172.16.255.1, Network Type BROADCAST, Cost: 10
Transmit Delay is 1 sec, State DROTHER, Priority 1
Designated Router id 172.16.255.11, Interface address 172.16.255.11
Backup Designated router id 172.16.255.10, Interface addr 172.16.255.10
Timer intervals configured, Hello 10, Dead 40, Wait 40, Retransmit 5
Hello due in 0:00:03
Neighbor Count is 3, Adjacent neighbor count is 2
  Adjacent with neighbor 172.16.255.10  (Backup Designated Router)
  Adjacent with neighbor 172.16.255.11  (Designated Router)
```

exam
ⓦatch

The show ip ospf interface *command displays your router's ID, the ID of the DR and BDR, the hello timer (10 seconds), the dead interval (40 seconds), the number of neighbors, and* *the number of adjacencies. Remember that the hello and deal interval time values must match to become a neighbor with another OSPF router.*

In this example, the router ID is 172.16.255.1. Its state is DROTHER, which means that it is *not* the DR or BDR. Actually, the DR is 172.16.255.11 and the BDR is 172.16.255.10 (these are their router IDs). A total of three neighbors have two adjacencies—remember that adjacencies are built only between routers and the DR and BDR, not all routers on the segment.

20.08. The CD contains a multimedia demonstration of using the `show ip ospf interface` *command on an OSPF router.*

The show ip ospf neighbor Command

To see all of your router's OSPF neighbors, use the **show ip ospf neighbor** command:

```
Router# show ip ospf neighbor
   ID        Pri   State          Dead Time   Address          Interface
172.16.255.11  1    FULL/DR        0:00:31     172.16.255.11    Ethernet0
172.16.255.10  1    FULL/BDR       0:00:33     172.16.255.10    Ethernet0
172.16.255.9   1    2WAY/DROTHER   0:00:35     172.16.255.9     Ethernet0
172.16.254.2   1    FULL/DR        0:00:39     172.16.254.2     Serial0.1
```

e x a m

ⓦatch
Remember that the `show ip ospf neighbor` *command lists all of the router's OSPF neighbors, their OSPF states, their router IDs, and which interface the neighbors are connected to.*

In this example, three routers are connected to `Ethernet0`: 172.16.255.11 is a DR, 172.16.255.10 is a BDR, and 172.16.255.9 is another OSPF router (DROTHER). Notice that for the DR and the BDR, the state is *full*, which is to be expected, since this router and the DR/BDR share routing information with each other. The DROTHER router is in a *two-way* state, which indicates that the router is a neighbor, but this router and the DROTHER router will not share routing information directly with each other since the other router is *not* a DR or BDR. Optionally, you can add the ID of the neighbor to the **show ip ospf neighbor** command to get more information about a particular neighbor.

on the ⓙob
If the MTU sizes are different on the OSPF routers' interfaces, they will not become neighbors; verify the MTU size on each neighbor with the `show interfaces` *or* `show ip interfaces` *command.*

20.09. The CD contains a multimedia demonstration of using the `show ip ospf neighbor` *command on an OSPF router.*

The debug ip ospf adj Command

For more detailed troubleshooting, you can use **debug** commands. If you want to view the adjacency process that a router builds to other routers, use the **debug ip ospf adj** command:

```
Router# debug ip ospf adj
172.16.255.11 on Ethernet0, state 2WAY
OSPF: end of Wait on interface Ethernet0
OSPF: DR/BDR election on Ethernet0
OSPF: Elect BDR 172.16.255.10
OSPF: Elect DR 172.16.255.11
      DR: 172.16.255.11 (Id) BDR: 172.16.255.10 (Id)
OSPF: Send DBD to 172.16.255.11 on Ethernet0
      seq 0x10DB opt 0x2 flag 0x7 len 32
OSPF: Build router LSA for area 0, router ID 172.16.255.11
```

In this example, you can see the election process for the DR and BDR and the sharing of links (DBDs) with the DR.

If two routers have misconfigured the authentication type for OSPF, such as clear-text passwords on one and MD5 on the other, you'll see the following with the above **debug** command:

```
OSPF: Rcv pkt from 192.168.1.1, Serial1/0:
Mismatch Authentication type. Input packet specified
                        type 0, we use type 1
```

However, if you have mismatched the passwords (keys) on the two OSPF routers, you'll see something like this:

```
OSPF: Rcv pkt from 192.168.1.1, Serial1/0 :
Mismatch Authentication Key - Clear Text
```

20.10. *The CD contains a multimedia demonstration of using the* debug ip ospf adj *command on an OSPF router.*

The debug ip ospf events Command

If you want to view OSPF events on your router, use the **debug ip ospf events** command:

```
Router# debug ip ospf events
4d02h: OSPF: Rcv hello from 192.168.1.100 area 0 from Serial0 192.168.1.100
4d02h: OSPF: End of hello processing
```

In this example, the router received a hello packet from 192.168.1.00, which is connected to `Serial0`. You might see the following kinds of information as well:

- Hello intervals that do not match for routers on a segment
- Dead intervals that do not match for routers on a segment
- Mismatched subnet masks for OSPF routers on a segment

20.11. The CD contains a multimedia demonstration of using the debug ip ospf events *command on an OSPF router.*

The debug ip ospf packet Command

If you want to view OSPF packet contents of LSAs, use the **debug ip ospf packet** command:

```
Router# debug ip ospf packet
4d02h: OSPF: rcv. v:2 t:1 l:48 rid:192.168.1.100
        aid:0.0.0.0 chk:15E4 aut:0 auk: from Serial0
```

Table 20-2 explains the values shown in this command.

Field Value	Explanation
Aid:	OSPF Area ID number
Auk:	OSPF authentication key used for neighbor authentication
Aut:	Type of OSPF authentication (0–none, 1–simple password, 2–MD5 hashing)
Keyid:	MD5 key value if this authentication mechanism is enabled
L:	Length of the packet
Rid:	OSPF router ID
Seq:	Sequence number
T:	OSPF packet type (1–hello, 2–data description, 3–link state request, 4–link state update, 5–link state acknowledgment
V:	OSPF version number

20.12. The CD contains a multimedia demonstration of using the debug
ip ospf packet *command on an OSPF router.*

EXERCISE 20-I

Configuring OSPF

The last few sections dealt with configuring OSPF on a router. This exercise will
help you reinforce this material for setting up and troubleshooting OSPF. You'll
perform this lab using Boson's NetSim simulator. You can find a picture of the
network diagram for Boson's NetSim simulator in the Introduction of this book. In
this exercise, you'll set OSPF on the two routers (2600-1 and 2600-2). After starting
up the simulator, click the LabNavigator button. Next, double-click Exercise 20-1
and then click the Load Lab button. This will load the lab configuration based on
the exercises in Chapters 11 and 16.

1. On the 2600-1, verify that the fa0/0 and s0 interfaces are up. If not, bring
   them up. Examine the IP addresses configured on the 2600-1 and look at its
   routing table.

   At the top of the simulator in the menu bar, click the eRouters icon and
   choose 2600-1. On the 2600-1, use the **show interfaces** command to
   verify your configuration. If fa0/0 and s0 are not up, go into the interfaces
   (fa0/0 and s0) and enable them: **configure terminal, interface**
   type port, **no shutdown**, **end**, and **show interfaces**. Use the
   show ip route command. You should have two connected networks:
   192.168.1.0 connected to fa0/0 and 192.168.2.0 connected to s0.

2. On the 2600-2, verify that the fa0/0 and s0 interfaces are up. If not, bring
   them up. Examine the IP addresses configured on the 2600-2 and look at its
   routing table.

   At the top of the simulator in the menu bar, click the eRouters icon and
   choose 2600-2. On the 2600-2, verify that the fa0/0 and s0 interfaces are
   up. If not, bring them up: **configure terminal**, **interface** *type*
   port, **no shutdown**, **end**, and **show interfaces**. Use the **show
   interfaces** command to verify that the IP addresses you configured
   on Chapter 16 are still there. Use the **show ip route** command. You
   should have two connected networks: 192.168.3.0 connected to fa0/0 and
   192.168.2.0 connected to s0.

3. Test connectivity between Host-1 and the 2600-1.

   At the top of the simulator in the menu bar, click the eStations icon and choose Host1. From Host1, ping the 2600-1: **ping 192.168.1.1**. The ping should be successful.

4. Test connectivity between Host-3 and the 2600-2.

   At the top of the simulator in the menu bar, click the eStations icon and choose Host3. From Host3, ping the 2600-2 router: **ping 192.168.3.1**. The ping should be successful.

5. Test connectivity between Host3 and Host1.

   From Host3, ping Host 1: **ping 192.168.1.10**. The ping should fail: there is no route from the 2600-2 to this destination (look at the 2600-2's routing table; it doesn't list 192.168.1.0/24).

6. Enable OSPF on the 2600-1 router, using a process ID of 1, and put all interfaces in area 0.

   At the top of the simulator in the menu bar, click the eRouters icon and choose 2600-1. On the 2600-1 router, configure the following: **configure terminal**, **router ospf 1**, **network 0.0.0.0 255.255.255.255 area 0**, and **end**.

7. Enable OSPF on the 2600-2 router, using a process ID of 1, and put all interfaces in area 0.

   At the top of the simulator in the menu bar, click the eRouters icon and choose 2600-2. On the 2600-2 router, configure the following: **configure terminal**, **router ospf 1**, **network 0.0.0.0 255.255.255.255 area 0**, and **end**.

8. On the 2600-2, verify the operation of OSPF. Is either router a DR or BDR on the WAN link?

   At the top of the simulator in the menu bar, click the eRouters icon and choose 2600-2. Use the **show ip protocols** command to make sure that OSPF is configured—check for the neighboring router's update. Use the **show ip route** command and look for the remote LAN network number as a OSPF (O) entry in the routing table. Use the **show ip ospf neighbor** command to view your neighboring router. Neither should be a DR or BDR on the serial link, since point-to-point connections don't use DRs and BDRs.

9. On the 2600-1, verify the operation of OSPF.

At the top of the simulator in the menu bar, click the eRouters icon and choose 2600-1. Use the **show ip protocols** command to make sure that OSPF is configured—check for the neighboring router's update. Use the **show ip route** command and look for the remote LAN network number as an OSPF *(O)* entry in the routing table. Use the **show ip ospf neighbor** command to view your neighboring router.

10. On Host1, test connectivity to Host3.

At the top of the simulator in the menu bar, click the eStations icon and choose Host1. On Host1, execute this: **ping 192.168.3.10**. The ping should be successful.

EXERCISE 20-2

ON THE CD

Troubleshooting OSPF

This exercise will help introduce you to an already configured network, but with some configuration issues that are preventing OSPF connectivity. You'll perform this lab using Boson's NetSim simulator. You can find a picture of the network diagram for Boson's NetSim simulator in the Introduction of this book. After starting up the simulator, click the LabNavigator button. Next, double-click Exercise 20-2 and click the Load Lab button. This will load the lab configuration based on the exercises in Chapters 11 and 16 (with problems in the configurations, of course).

Let's start with the problem: Host1 cannot ping Host3. Your task is to figure out the multiple problems and fix them. In this example, OSPF has been preconfigured on the routers. Try this troubleshooting process on your own first; if you have problems, come back to the following steps and solutions provided here.

1. Test connectivity from Host1 to Host3 with ping as well as from Host1 to its default gateway.

At the top of the simulator in the menu bar, click the eStations icon and choose Host1. On Host1, ping Host3: **ping 192.168.3.10**. Note that the ping fails. Ping the default gateway address: **ping 192.168.1.1**. The ping should fail, indicating that at least layer 3 is not functioning between

Host1 and the 2600-1. Examine the IP configuration on Host1 by executing **winipcfg**. Make sure the IP addressing information is correct: IP address of 192.168.1.10, subnet mask of 255.255.255.0, and default gateway address of 192.168.1.1. Notice that the IP address is 192.168.100.10. Change this address to 192.168.1.10. Click the OK button to save your changes and close **winipcfg**. Try pinging the 2600-1 again: **ping 192.168.1.1**. The ping should succeed. On Host1, ping Host3: **ping 192.168.3.10**. Note that the ping still fails.

2. Test connectivity from Host3 to its default gateway.

   At the top of the simulator in the menu bar, click the eStations icon and choose Host3. Examine the IP configuration on Host3 by executing **ipconfig /all**. Make sure the IP addressing information is correct: IP address of 192.168.3.10, subnet mask of 255.255.255.0, and default gateway address of 192.168.3.1. Ping the default gateway address: **ping 192.168.3.1**. The ping should fail, indicating that there is a problem between Host3 and the 2600-2. In this example, assume layer 2 is functioning correctly; therefore, it must be a problem with the 2600-2.

3. Check the interface statuses and IP configuration on the 2600-2.

   At the top of the simulator in the menu bar, click the eRouters icon and choose 2600-2. Check the status of the interfaces: **show interfaces**. Notice that the fa0/0 has the wrong IP address (192.168.30.1) and is disabled. Go into fa0/0, fix the IP address, and enable it: **configure terminal**, **interface fa0/0**, **ip address 192.168.3.1**, **no shutdown**, and **end**. Verify the status of the fa0/0 interface: **show interface fa0/0**. Try pinging Host3: **ping 192.168.3.10**. The ping should succeed.

4. Verify connectivity from the 2600-2 to the 2600-1.

   Try pinging the 2600-1's serial1/0 interface: **ping 192.168.2.1**. The ping succeeds.

5. Verify OSPF's configuration on the 2600-2.

   Examine the 2600-2's OSPF configuration: **show ip protocol**. You should see OSPF as the routing protocol and networks 192.168.2.0 and 192.168.3.0 included (0.0.0.0 255.255.255.255). From this output, it looks like OSPF is configured correctly on the 2600-2.

6. Save the configuration on the 2600-2: `copy running-config startup-config`.

7. Test connectivity from the 2600-2 to Host1. Examine the routing table.

   From the 2600-2 router, test the connection to Host1: `ping 192.168.1.10`. The ping should fail. This indicates a layer 3 problem between the 2600-2 and Host1. Examine the routing table: `show ip route`. Notice that there are only two connected routes (192.168.2.0/24 and 192.168.1.0/24), but no OSPF routes.

8. Access the 2600-1 router and examine OSPF's configuration. Fix the problem.

   At the top of the simulator in the menu bar, click the eRouters icon and choose 2600-1. Examine the routing table: `show ip protocol`. What networks are advertised by the 2600-1? You should see 192.168.100.0 and 192.168.2.0. Obviously, `fa0/0`'s interface isn't included since 192.168.1.0 is not configured. Fix this configuration problem: `configure terminal`, `router ospf 1`, `no network 192.168.100.0 0.0.0.255 area 0`, `network 192.168.1.0 0.0.0.255 area 0`, and `end`. Test connectivity to Host3: `ping 192.168.3.10`. The ping should be successful. Save the configuration on the router: `copy running-config startup-config`.

9. Examine the routing table on the 2600-2. Test connectivity from the 2600-2 to Host1.

   At the top of the simulator in the menu bar, click the eRouters icon and choose 2600-2. Examine the routing table: `show ip route`. Notice that there are only two connected routes (192.168.2.0/24 and 192.168.1.0/24) and one OSPF route (192.168.1.0/24). From the 2600-2 router, test the connection to Host1: `ping 192.168.1.10`. The ping should succeed.

10. Now test connectivity between Host1 and Host3.

    At the top of the simulator in the menu bar, click the eStations icon and choose Host1. Test connectivity to Host3: `ping 192.168.3.10`. The ping should be successful.

Now you should be more comfortable with configuring and troubleshooting OSPF.

INSIDE THE EXAM

OSPF Overview

Remember that OSPF is an open-standard protocol and it, or EIGRP, should be used when dealing with large layer 3 networks: it supports hierarchical routing (two layers—backbone and others) and uses cost as an intelligent metric.

OSPF Operation

Be able to determine an OSPF router's ID based on the interfaces that are active and the loopbacks, if any, which are configured. Understand how OSPF routers form a neighbor relationship and the components that must match between them. Remember the differences between a two-way and full state. Know how LSAs are disseminated and the multicast addresses used for transmitting LSAs. Know the differences between DRs, BDRs, and DROTHERs and when DRs and BDRs are used: broadcast and multi-access segments. Be familiar with how DRs and BDRs are elected and be able to choose which routers will perform which role based on output of router **show** commands and example network illustrations.

OSPF Configuration

Be familiar with the basic configuration of OSPF on Cisco routers: you might have to set up and/or troubleshoot a basic configuration of OSPF on *multiple* routers (perhaps three to five routers) in a simulation question. Be able to define a process ID. Remember that a wildcard mask is used to associate an interface or interfaces with an area in the **network** command. Understand why loopback interfaces are typically configured for OSPF. Be familiar with metrics of OSPF routes and the load balancing process the routing protocol uses.

OSPF Troubleshooting

Expect questions on OSPF configurations that have problems and be able to pinpoint the problem or problems. Be very familiar with the various **show** and **debug** commands for OSPF. Know how to read the routing table and pick out OSPF routes and their associated costs. Understand the output of the **show** and **debug** commands and be able to pinpoint problems related to failed neighbor relationships: mismatched timers, incorrect authentication, and mismatched subnets.

CERTIFICATION SUMMARY

OSPF is an open-standard routing protocol for IP, which uses cost as a metric. It uses the Dijkstra algorithm (SPF) to provide a loop-free routing topology and uses incremental updates with route summarization support. OSPF is hierarchical, supporting two layers: backbone (area 0) and areas connected to the backbone. Its downside is that OSPF requires more memory and CPU processes than distance vector protocols, and it is more difficult to configure and troubleshoot.

Each OSPF router has a router ID, which is either the highest IP address on a loopback interface or the highest IP address on an active interface. LSAs are used to develop neighbor relationships and are sent as multicasts every 10 seconds. For LAN segments, a DR and a BDR are elected (highest router ID) to disseminate routing information. Routers use 224.0.0.6 to send information to the DR/BDR. OSPF is connection-oriented in that any routing information sent to another router requires a responding ACK. When DRs share routing information to their neighbors, the multicast address used is 224.0.0.5.

Configuring OSPF requires you to specify a process ID, which is locally significant to the router. When configuring the **network** command, you specify an IP address or network number, a wildcard mask (inverted subnet mask), and a number for the area to which the address or network belongs. The **show ip ospf interface** command displays OSPF information about the router's ID, the DR and BDR, and timer information. The **show ip ospf neighbor** command displays your router's neighbors as well as their OSPF states.

✓ TWO-MINUTE DRILL

OSPF Overview

❑ OSPF is an open-standard, link state protocol. It's classless and supports hierarchical routing and route summarization. It uses cost as a metric, which is the inverse of the bandwidth of a link.

❑ OSPF requires more memory and faster processors to handle its additional information.

OSPF Operation

❑ Each OSPF router has an ID, which is either the highest IP address on a loopback interface, if one exists, or the highest IP address on an active interface.

❑ Routers use LSAs to learn the topology of the network. To share information with another router, the routers must be neighbors: their area numbers and types, timers, and passwords must match.

❑ DRs and BDRs assist in sharing topology information. Traffic sent to a DR/BDR pair is multicast to 224.0.0.6. Traffic sent to all routers on a segment has a destination address of 224.0.0.5. Hello messages are sent out every 10 seconds, with a dead interval timer of 40 seconds. The DR sends a periodic update every 30 minutes.

OSPF Configuration

❑ You must give the OSPF routing process a process ID, which is locally significant to the router. You use a wildcard mask when specifying which interfaces are in which areas and are participating in OSPF: **network** *IP_address wildcard_mask* **area** *area_#.*

❑ Loopback interfaces are always active unless manually disabled and are used to give an OSPF router an ID.

❑ The **bandwidth** command is used to derive a cost value for an interface metric; it should be configured on serial interfaces since the bandwidth defaults to 1544 Kbps on these.

❑ By default, OSPF load balances across four equal-cost paths to a destination.

OSPF Troubleshooting

❑ The administrative distance for OSPF is 110.

❑ The `show ip ospf interface`, `show ip ospf neighbor`, `debug ip ospf adj`, and `debug ip ospf events` commands can be used to troubleshoot neighbor relationship problems.

SELF TEST

The following Self Test questions will help you measure your understanding of the material presented in this chapter. Read all the choices carefully, as there may be more than one correct answer. Choose all correct answers for each question.

OSPF Overview

1. Which of the following is false concerning OSPF?
    A. It provides a loop-free topology.
    B. It is a classful protocol and allows for a hierarchical design.
    C. It requires more memory and processing cycles than distance vector protocols.
    D. It is complex to configure and difficult to troubleshoot.

2. OSPF uses _____ as a metric.
    A. bandwidth
    B. delay
    C. cost
    D. hop count

OSPF Operation

3. An OSPF's router ID is based on _____.
    A. the lowest IP address on its loopback interface, if configured, or the lowest IP address on its active interfaces
    B. the highest IP address on its loopback interface, if configured, or the highest IP address on its active interfaces
    C. the highest IP address on its active interfaces, if configured, or the highest IP address on its loopback interfaces
    D. the lowest IP address on its active interfaces, if configured, or the lowest IP address on its loopback interfaces

4. OSPF hellos are sent every _____ seconds on a multi-access medium.
    A. 5
    B. 10
    C. 15
    D. 40

5. Which of the following is true concerning OSPF?

    A. Setting an interface priority to 0 causes a router to become a DR on that interface.

    B. If the dead interval timer doesn't match between two OSPF routers, they will not become neighbors.

    C. DRs are elected on broadcast, multi-access, and point-to-point segments.

    D. Routers use a multicast address of 224.0.0.5 to send LSAs to the DR/BDR.

OSPF Configuration

6. The OSPF process ID is _____.

    A. locally significant and is the router ID

    B. globally significant and must match on every router

    C. locally significant

    D. OSPF doesn't use a process ID, but an AS number.

7. Enter the OSPF command to include all of its interfaces in area 0: _____.

OSPF Troubleshooting

8. When examining routes in the routing table, enter the code used to represent OSPF routes: _____.

9. Which of the following can you not see from the `show ip ospf interface` command?

    A. Process and router ID of you and the neighboring OSPF routers

    B. Hello and dead interval timers

    C. Priority of your router

    D. Cost of the interface

10. Two OSPF routers cannot form a neighbor relationship. Which of the following would not cause this problem?

    A. Hello and dead intervals don't match.

    B. MTU sizes don't match.

    C. Subnet masks don't match.

    D. Router IDs don't match.

SELF TEST ANSWERS

OSPF Overview

1. ☑ **B.** OSPF is a classless, not a classful, protocol.
   ☒ **A**, **C**, and **D** are true concerning OSPF.

2. ☑ **C.** OSPF uses cost as a metric.
   ☒ **A**, bandwidth, is used to compute the cost, where cost is the inverse of the bandwidth. **B** is incorrect because delay is used by EIGRP. **D** is incorrect because hop count is used by RIP.

OSPF Operation

3. ☑ **B.** An OSPF's router ID is based on the highest IP address on its loopback interface, if configured, or the highest IP address on its active interfaces.
   ☒ **A** is incorrect because it specifies the lowest IP address. **C** is incorrect because the loopback is used first, if configured. **D** is incorrect because the loopback is checked first.

4. ☑ **B.** OSPF hellos are sent every 10 seconds.
   ☒ **A** and **C** are incorrect timers. **D** is incorrect because 40 is the dead interval timer.

5. ☑ **B.** The hello and dead interval timers, the area number, the OSPF router, the area type, and the MTU sizes must match on a segment for routers to form a neighbor relationship.
   ☒ **A** is incorrect because an interface priority of 0 will cause a router never to become a DR/BDR. **C** is incorrect because point-to-point segments don't use DRs/BDRs. **D** is incorrect because 224.0.0.6 is used when sending LSAs to the DR/BDR.

OSPF Configuration

6. ☑ **C.** The OSPF process ID is locally significant.
   ☒ **A** is not true, because the router ID is based on the highest IP address of a loopback or active interface. **B** is not true, because it is locally significant. **D** is not true, because OSPF requires a process ID to be configured.

7. ☑ `network 0.0.0.0 255.255.255.255 area 0`.

OSPF Troubleshooting

8. ☑ The code used to represent OSPF routes is O. The letter O is used to represent OSPF routes in an IP routing table.

9. ☑ **A.** You can see the router IDs of the other routers off an interface, but not their process IDs, which are locally significant.

☒ **B, C,** and **D** can be viewed and are therefore incorrect answers.

10. ☑ **D.** Router IDs in an AS must be unique and cannot match.

☒ **A, B,** and **C** must match, as well as the area type, to form a neighbor relationship.

21
EIGRP Routing

In Chapter 19, you were introduced to the configuration of Routing Information Protocol (RIPv1 and v2), a distance vector routing protocol, and in Chapter 20, you learned about the configuration of Open Shortest Path First (OSPF), a link state protocol. This chapter focuses on Cisco's proprietary routing protocol for TCP/IP: the Enhanced Interior Gateway Routing Protocol (EIGRP). EIGRP is a hybrid protocol; fundamentally, it is a distance vector protocol with many link state protocol advantages built into it. This chapter covers only the basic operation and configuration of EIGRP. A more thorough discussion is covered in Cisco's CCNP-level courses and exams.

CERTIFICATION OBJECTIVE 21.01

EIGRP Overview

EIGRP is a Cisco-proprietary routing protocol for TCP/IP. It's actually based on Cisco's proprietary IGRP routing protocol, with many enhancements built into it. Because it has its roots in IGRP, the configuration is similar to IGRP; however, it has many link state characteristics that were added to it to allow EIGRP to scale to enterprise network sizes. These characteristics include the following:

- Fast convergence
- Loop-free topology
- Variable Length Subnet Masking (VLSM) and route summarization
- Multicast and incremental updates
- Multiple *routed* protocols

The following sections cover some of the characteristics of EIGRP, its operation, and its configuration.

As of IOS release 12.3, Cisco no longer supports its older sibling, IGRP; EIGRP is still supported and widely deployed, however.

EIGRP has the following characteristics:

- Uses multicast addresses to disseminate routing information
- Offers load balancing across six paths to a destination (equal or unequal metrics)
- Supports an intelligent and complex metric structure

- Has fast convergence (triggered updates when changes occur and saves neighbors' routing tables locally)
- Has little network overhead, since it uses incremental updates

Metrics and Interoperability

Like its older cousin IGRP, EIGRP uses the same metric structure, based on these components: bandwidth, delay, reliability, load, and maximum transmission unit (MTU). By default, only *bandwidth* and *delay* are used in the metric computation and the other values are turned off; however, you can manually enable these values in the metric algorithm.

One interesting point about the IGRP and EIGRP routing protocols is that if you have some routers in your network running IGRP and others running EIGRP, and both sets have the same autonomous system number configured, routing information will *automatically* be shared between the two. This makes it easy to migrate from IGRP to EIGRP. When sharing routes between the two routing protocols, the routers have to perform a conversion concerning the metrics. Even though both protocols use the same metric components, they store them in different size values: EIGRP uses a 32-bit metric, while IGRP uses a 24-bit metric. When integrating the two protocols together, EIGRP routes are divided by 256 to fit a 24-bit metric structure when passed to IGRP and IGRP routes are multiplied by 256 to fit a 32-bit metric structure when passed to EIGRP.

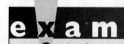

Routing Tables and Updates

EIGRP uses the Diffusing Update Algorithm (DUAL) to update the local routing table. This algorithm enables very fast convergence by storing a neighbor's routing information in a local topology table. If a primary route in the routing table fails, DUAL can take a backup route from the topology table (a neighbor's routing table) and place this into the routing table without necessarily having to talk to other EIGRP neighboring routers to find an alternative path to the destination.

EIGRP supports both automatic and manual summarization. Remember that EIGRP is, at heart, a distance vector protocol, and therefore it will automatically summarize routes across Class A, B, and C network boundaries, as was discussed in Chapter 8. You can also manually summarize within a class network, at your discretion. Configuration of summarization is beyond the scope of this book, but it is covered in depth at Cisco's CCNP-level material.

One really unique feature of EIGRP is that it supports three routed protocols: IP (IPv4 and IPv6), Internetwork Packet Exchange (IPX), and AppleTalk. In other words, EIGRP can route for all three of these protocols simultaneously. If you are running these routed protocols in your environment, EIGRP is a perfect fit. You need to run only one routing protocol for all three instead of a separate routing protocol for each, definitely reducing your routing overhead.

EIGRP supports route summarization and routing for IPv4, IPv6, IPX, and AppleTalk. The DUAL algorithm is used to build a loop-free routing topology.

CERTIFICATION OBJECTIVE 21.02

EIGRP Operation

Unlike most distance vector routing protocols, EIGRP learns a partial topology of the network beyond its directly connected neighbor. Like OSPF, EIGRP uses hello packets to discover and maintain neighbor relationships (stored in a neighbor table) and to share routing information (stored in the topology and routing tables). EIGRP uses the multicast address of 224.0.0.10 for the destination in its hello packets. EIGRP generates hello packets every 5 seconds on LAN, point-to-point, and multipoint connections of at least T1/E1 speeds. Otherwise, hellos are generated every 60 seconds. The dead interval period is three times the hello interval.

EIGRP supports multicast and incremental updates. Hello packets are generated every 5 seconds on LAN interfaces as multicasts (224.0.0.10). Hellos are used to maintain the EIGRP neighbor and the EIGRP topology tables in RAM.

Building Neighbor Relationships

For EIGRP routers to become neighbors, the following information must match in their hello packets:

- The autonomous system (AS) number
- The K-values (these enable/disable the different metric components used in the DUAL algorithm)

Unlike OSPF, the hello and hold-down timers on the two routers do *not* need to match in order for the routers to become neighbors.

When two routers determine whether they will become neighbors, they go through the following process:

1. The first router generates a hello with its configuration information.
2. If the configuration information matches (AS number and K-values), the second router responds with an Update message with its local topology information.
3. The first router responds with an ACK message, acknowledging the receipt of the second's Update.
4. The first router then sends its topology to the second router via an Update message.
5. The second router responds with an ACK.

At this point, the two routers have converged. This process differs from that of OSPF, where routing information is disseminated via a designated router. With EIGRP, any router can share routing information with any other router. As you can see from the preceding steps, EIGRP, like OSPF, is connection-oriented: certain EIGRP messages sent by a router will cause it to expect an acknowledgment (ACK) from the destination(s). Here are the message types for which an EIGRP router expects an ACK back:

- **Update**   Contains a routing update
- **Query**   Asks a neighboring router to validate routing information
- **Reply**   Responds to a query message

If an EIGRP router doesn't receive an ACK from these three packet types, the router will try a total of 16 times to resend the information. After this, the

router declares the neighbor dead. When a router sends a hello packet, however, no corresponding ACK is expected in return.

Choosing Routes

EIGRP can use the following metric components when choosing a route: bandwidth, delay, reliability, load, and MTU. By default, however, only bandwidth and delay are activated (the MTU size, however, is exchanged between the peers, even though it's not used, by default). Bandwidth and delay are the K1 and K3 values.

o n t h e
ⓘo b   *Because bandwidth is used in EIGRP's metric computation, it is important that you match up this value correctly with the correct speed of your serial interfaces. Cisco assumes that a serial interface is connected to a T1 connection, so if this is incorrect, use the* `bandwidth` *command to correct it (discussed in Chapter 16). Remember to put the bandwidth value in Kbps.*

Table 21-1 explains important terms used by EIGRP.

TABLE 21-1	Important EIGRP Terms

Term	Definition
Neighbor table	Contains a list of the EIGRP neighbors and is similar to the adjacencies that are built in OSPF between the designated router/backup DR and the other routers on a segment. Each routed protocol (IP, IPX, and AppleTalk) for EIGRP has its own neighbor table.
Topology table	Similar to OSPF's database, contains a list of all destinations and paths the EIGRP router learned—it is basically a compilation of the neighboring routers' routing tables. A separate topology table exists for each routed protocol.
Successor	The best path to reach a destination within the topology table.
Feasible successor	The best backup path to reach a destination within the topology table—multiple successors can be feasible for a particular destination.
Routing table	This is all of the *successor* routes from the topology table. There is a separate routing table for each routed protocol.
Advertised distance	The distance (metric) that a neighboring router is advertising for a specific route.
Feasible distance	The distance (metric) that your router has computed to reach a specific route: the advertised distance from the neighboring router plus the local router's interface metric.

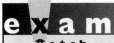

EIGRP uses a less complicated approach than OSPF when choosing best-path routes to a destination and is thus less CPU-intensive; however, it does have more overhead than a distance vector protocol, such as RIPv2. EIGRP routers keep topology information in a *topology table*. The topology table contains the routes that neighbors are advertising, the advertised distances (metrics) of the neighbor for these routers, and the feasible distances of this router to reach these network destinations. A *successor route* is a path in the topology table that has the best metric (feasible distance) compared to all the other alternative paths to the same network destination. A *feasible successor* is a valid backup route to the successor route.

Not just any route can be chosen as a feasible successor. For a route to be considered a feasible successor in the topology table, the neighbor router's advertised distance must be *less than* that of the original route's feasible distance. If a successor route in the routing table fails and a feasible successor exists in the topology table, the EIGRP router goes into a *passive* state—it immediately takes the feasible successor route from the topology table and puts it in the routing table, converging almost instantaneously. If the EIGRP router does not have a feasible successor in the topology table, it will go into an *active* state and generate a query packet for the route in question. This query is sent to the neighbor or neighbors that originally advertised this route.

The concern that EIGRP has with nonfeasible successor routes is that the path these routers are advertising might be part of a routing loop. EIGRP goes into an active state for these paths to verify this by double-checking with these neighbors. The neighbors will verify the information that they have in their topology table and reply to the requester with the appropriate information concerning these alternative paths. The terms *passive* and *active* can be misleading—passive means that a valid alternative route exists and can be immediately used in the routing table without contacting any of the advertising neighbors, while active indicates that an alternative path exists but might or might not be valid.

When a successor route is no longer available and no feasible successor route exists in the topology table, a multicast EIGRP query is sent to all other neighbors advertising the same route to determine whether they have a valid path (successor route) to the destination network.

CERTIFICATION OBJECTIVE 21.03

EIGRP Configuration

Setting up EIGRP is almost as simple as configuring RIPv2:

```
Router(config)# router eigrp autonomous_system_#
Router(config-router)# network IP_network_# [subnet_mask]
```

As you can see from these commands, enabling EIGRP is straightforward: you need to enter an autonomous system (AS) number and **network** statements for interfaces that will participate in EIGRP. Note that the network numbers you specify are *classful* network numbers, even though EIGRP is *classless*. Optionally, you can qualify the network number with a subnet mask value, including only certain subnets of a class address in the EIGRP AS.

You must specify the AS number when configuring EIGRP. Even though EIGRP is classless, by default you configure it as a classful protocol when specifying your network numbers with the `network` command. For example, `network 172.16.0.0` would include the interfaces associated with subnets 172.16.1.0/24 and 172.16.100.0/24.

EIGRP Configuration Example

Let's look at a simple example, shown in Figure 21-1, to help illustrate how to configure EIGRP on a router.

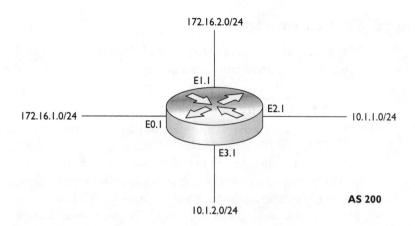

FIGURE 21-1

EIGRP network
example

21.01. The CD contains a multimedia demonstration of configuring EIGRP on a router.

Here's the routing configuration of the router for Figure 21-1:

```
Router(config)# router eigrp 200
Router(config-router)# network 172.16.0.0
Router(config-router)# network 10.0.0.0
```

This router has four interfaces: 172.16.1.1/24, 172.16.2.1/24, 10.1.1.1/24, and
10.1.2.1/24. Remember that when configuring your **network** commands, put in
only the Class A, B, or C network numbers, or qualify them with a subnet mask. In
the preceding example, the Class B and A network numbers were entered, activating
EIGRP routing on all four interfaces.

You could also have been more specific with your **network** statements, by including
the subnet mask value to include specific interfaces in the EIGRP AS, like this:

```
Router(config)# router eigrp 200
Router(config-router)# network 172.16.1.0 255.255.255.0
Router(config-router)# network 172.16.2.0 255.255.255.0
Router(config-router)# network 10.1.1.0 255.255.255.0
Router(config-router)# network 10.1.2.0 255.255.255.0
```

on the
job

*Either of these two approaches will work in the example in Figure 21-1;
however, in practice, I recommend using the latter; especially in situations
where your router might be running more than one routing protocol, such
as EIGRP and OSPF, and you want only certain subnets of a class address
included in each routing protocol.*

Other EIGRP Commands

You should be aware of three other configurations when enabling EIGRP: load balancing, summarization, and authentication of routing updates.

Load Balancing

EIGRP supports load balancing across six paths to the same destination. By default, EIGRP will do only equal-cost load balancing. With equal-cost load balancing, EIGRP will only use successor routers that have the same metric value. However, you can enable *unequal*-cost load balancing of EIGRP routes by using the **variance** and **traffic-share** Router Subconfiguration mode commands.

To enable unequal-cost paths for EIGRP, use the **variance** Router Subconfiguration mode command:

```
Router(config)# router eigrp autonomous_system_#
Router(config-router)# variance multiplier
```

The *multiplier* value is a positive integer. By default, the variance is equal to one. To use an unequal-cost path (less preferred), the router multiplies the best metric path (feasible distance) by the multiplier value; if the less preferred path's metric (advertised distance) is less than this value, the router will include it in the routing table along with the best metric path.

The multiplier can range from 1 to 128. The default is 1, which means the EIGRP router will use only the best metric path(s). If you increase the multiplier, the router will use any route that has a metric less than the best metric route multiplied by the variance value. Care must be taken, however, to ensure that you do not set a variance value too high; otherwise routing loops may accidentally be created.

To illustrate how this is used, examine Table 21-2. In this example, three neighbors are advertising the same route, 192.168.1.0/24, to your router. By default, RouterB has the best feasible distance and is thus used in your router's routing table as a successor route. If you set the variance to 2, then RouterC's alternative path could also be included in the routing table along with RouterB's successor route:

TABLE 21-2	Network Number	Neighboring Router	Feasible Distance (FD)	Advertised Distance (AD)
Example EIGRP Topology Table for Variance Computation	192.168.1.0/24	RouterB	40	20
		RouterC	60	20
		RouterD	85	35

RouterC's FD (60) is less than 2 times RouterB's FD (40). In other words 60 < 2 × 40 (or 80). RouterD's path is not used since its FD is greater than 2 times RouterB's FD.

Be able to correctly	**added to the routing table by using a**
compute additional successor routes	**variance multiplier.**

When load balancing, the router will do the process intelligently. In other words, if you have two WAN links (64 Kbps and 128 Kbps) included in the routing table to reach a single destination, it makes no sense to send half of the traffic down the 64 Kbps link and the other half down the 128 Kbps link. In this situation, you would probably saturate your slower-speed 64 Kbps link. EIGRP, instead, will load-balance traffic in proportion to the inverse of the metric for the path. So, given this example, about one-third of the traffic would be sent down the 64 Kbps link and two-thirds down the 128 Kbps link.

You can override this behavior with the **traffic-share** Router Subconfiguration mode command:

```
Router(config)# router eigrp autonomous_system_#
Router(config-router)# traffic-share balanced
```

or

```
Router(config-router)# traffic-share min across-interfaces
```

The first command provides the default behavior for load balancing, as was explained in the preceding paragraph. The **min** parameter has the router put the unequal-cost paths in the router's routing table; however, the router won't use these routes unless the best metric route fails. This is used when you don't want to use the worse connections, which perhaps are slower connections such as dial-up, but you still want to take advantage of fast convergence: when the primary path fails, the secondary path is already in the routing table.

Note that by using the variance feature, you can introduce additional paths to a destination in your IP routing table. By doing this, when one path fails, you already have a backup path in the routing table, so convergence is instantaneous. If you want your router to use only the best path, but you want to put the alternative paths in the routing table, use the **traffic-share min across-interfaces** command.

on the ● job

When testing load balancing from a router, be careful to not use ping *or* traceroute *since these packets are process-switched instead of fast-switched, which can produce confusing results in the load balancing tests: each possible path is tested. Instead, preferably perform the test from any other device* behind *the load balancing router.*

ⓦatch

Use the variance command to load-balance across unequal-   *cost paths. The default is to place only equal-cost paths in the routing table.*

Summarization

EIGRP automatically summarizes routes on a class boundary (shown in the top part of Figure 21-2). For example, if a router is connected to subnets in 172.16.0.0/16 and a separate network, such as 192.168.1.0/24, then EIGRP will send the 172.16.0.0/16 route out the 192.168.1.0/24 interface (instead of the specific subnets of 172.16.0.0/16). If your network is split into two parts, 172.16.1.0/24 and 172.16.2.0/24, but is connected by 192.168.1.0/24, this would cause reachability problems, since the two sides would advertise 172.16.0.0/16 at the network boundary. This problem was discussed in Chapter 8.

FIGURE 21-2

Discontiguous subnets

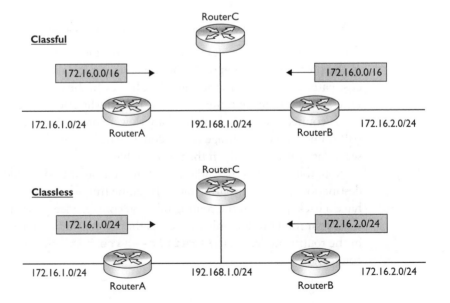

To turn off automatic summarization for an AS, use the following configuration:

```
Router(config)# router eigrp autonomous_system_#
Router(config-router)# no auto-summary
```

By turning off automatic summarization, you are turning the EIGRP process into a classless protocol, like that shown in the bottom of Figure 21-2. Manual summarization of routes using EIGRP is beyond the scope of this book.

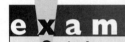

Neighbor Authentication

EIGRP supports authentication of routing updates from neighboring peers using the Message Digest 5 (MD5) algorithm. Using MD5 to authenticate routing updates ensures that your routers accept updates only from authorized routers and prevents unsupported routers from injecting bad routing updates into your routing process.

Setting up EIGRP authentication is a three-step process: enabling EIGRP, defining a key to use for MD5 authentication, and enabling authentication. Enabling EIGRP was discussed earlier. This section will focus on the latter two steps.

To define the keys used for MD5 authentication, use the following configuration:

```
Router(config)# key chain name_of_key_chain
Router(config-keychain)# key key_number
Router(config-keychain-key)# key-string key_value
Router(config-keychain-key)# accept-lifetime start_time
               {infinite | end_time | duration seconds}
Router(config-keychain-key)# send-lifetime start_time
               {infinite | end_time | duration seconds}
```

The **key chain** command specifies the name of the keying information to use; the name is locally significant and takes you into a subcommand mode. The **key** subcommand mode command specifies the number of the key, which must match on all routers on the segment using the authentication key; this command takes you into a second subcommand mode. The **key-string** command specifies the actual authentication key, which can be up to 16 characters in length. Each key can have a separate lifetime value, allowing different keys to be used at different times; however, if you use this approach, it's recommended that you use the Network Time Protocol (NTP) to synchronize the date and time on your routers. The **accept-lifetime** command specifies when you'll accept the key value, and the **send-lifetime** command specifies when you'll use this key to create authenticated EIGRP routing updates. If you don't specify either set of time values, the default to the current time are valid indefinitely.

To enable authentication, you set up your EIGRP configuration on an interface:

```
Router(config)# interface type number
Router(config-if)# ip authentication mode eigrp AS_# md5
Router(config-if)# ip authentication key-chain
            eigrp AS_# key_chain_name
```

As you can see from this configuration, you must enable authentication for the EIGRP AS number and then specify the name of the key chain you'll use. Note that since you are referencing a key chain, you can have different keys being used for different interfaces; however, all routers in the same subnet need to use the same keying information.

Let's look at a simple example of two routers' configurations using authentication. Both routers are connected to the same Ethernet segment and/or VLAN. Here's RouterA's configuration:

```
RouterA(config)# key chain RouterAchain
RouterA(config-keychain)# key 1
RouterA(config-keychain-key)# key-string 0123456789
Router(config)# interface fastethernet 0/0
Router(config-if)# ip authentication mode eigrp 100 md5
Router(config-if)# ip authentication key-chain eigrp 100
            RouterAchain
```

Here's RouterB's configuration:

```
RouterB(config)# key chain RouterBchain
RouterB(config-keychain)# key 1
RouterB(config-keychain-key)# key-string 0123456789
RouterB(config)# interface fastethernet 1/0
Router(config-if)# ip authentication mode eigrp 100 md5
Router(config-if)# ip authentication key-chain eigrp 100
            RouterBchain
```

CERTIFICATION OBJECTIVE 21.04

EIGRP Troubleshooting

Following are some of the common commands you'll use when viewing and troubleshooting EIGRP on your router:

- `show ip protocols`
- `show ip route`
- `show ip eigrp neighbors`
- `show ip eigrp topology`
- `show ip eigrp interfaces`
- `show ip eigrp traffic`
- `debug ip eigrp`
- `debug eigrp packets`

The following sections cover these commands.

The show ip protocols Command

You can use the **show ip protocols** command to display the IP routing protocols that have been configured and are running on your router. Here is an example of this command for EIGRP:

```
Router# show ip protocols
Routing Protocol is "eigrp 200"
  Outgoing update filter list for all interfaces is not set
  Incoming update filter list for all interfaces is not set
  Default networks flagged in outgoing updates
  Default networks accepted from incoming updates
  EIGRP metric weight K1=1, K2=0, K3=1, K4=0, K5=0
  EIGRP maximum hopcount 100
  EIGRP maximum metric variance 1
  Redistributing: eigrp 200
  Automatic network summarization is in effect
  Automatic address summarization:
    10.0.0.0/8 for Serial0
  Maximum path: 4
  Routing for Networks:
```

```
     10.0.0.0
     192.168.4.0
   Routing Information Sources:
     Gateway          Distance       Last Update
     (this router)          90       00:00:08
     192.168.4.101          90       00:00:06
   Distance: internal 90 external 170
```

In this command, you can see that the AS is 200 and the variance is 1 (only equal-cost load balancing). The K1 and K3 metrics are enabled, which means that only bandwidth and delay are used by the DUAL algorithm when computing a metric. Two **network** statements are configured: 10.0.0.0 and 192.168.4.0. There is one neighboring router, 192.168.4.101. The administrative distance of internal EIGRP (routers in the same AS number) is 90.

21.02. The CD contains a multimedia demonstration of the show
ip protocols *command for EIGRP on a router.*

The show ip route Command

21.03. The CD contains a multimedia demonstration of the show ip route
command for EIGRP on a router.

To view the EIGRP routes in your router's routing table, use the **show ip route** command:

```
Router# show ip route
Codes: C - connected, S - static, I - IGRP, R - RIP,
       M - mobile, B - BGP, D - EIGRP, EX - EIGRP external,
       O - OSPF, IA - OSPF inter area, N1 - OSPF NSSA
       external type 1, N2 - OSPF NSSA external type 2,
       E1 - OSPF external type 1, E2 - OSPF external type 2,
       E - EGP, i - IS-IS, L1 - IS-IS level-1,
       L2 - IS-IS level-2, * - candidate default,
       U - per-user static route, o - ODR,
       T - traffic engineered route
Gateway of last resort is not set
     10.0.0.0/8 is variably subnetted, 2 subnets, 2 masks
C       10.0.4.0/24 is directly connected, FastEthernet0
D    192.168.100.0/24 [90/2195456] via 192.168.4.101, 00:00:08, Serial0
D    192.168.101.0/24 [90/2195837] via 192.168.3.1, 00:00:05, Ethernet0
                      [90/2195837] via 192.168.3.2, 00:00:03, Ethernet0
C    192.168.4.0/24 is directly connected, Serial0
```

At the bottom of the display, a D in the first column refers to an EIGRP route. In this example, there is one EIGRP route that was learned from 192.168.4.101. For an EIGRP route, you'll see two sets of values in brackets ([ ]). The first value indicates the administrative distance of the route (90) and the second the feasible distance of the router (the metric). Following this you can see the peer with which the route is associated, how long ago an update was received concerning this route or neighbor, and which local interface on the router to use to reach the neighbor. Notice that for network 192.168.101.0/24 there are two successor routers with the same metric, which means the router will load-balance traffic across these two paths to this destination.

A D in the routing table indicates an EIGRP route. EIGRP has an administrative distance of 90.

If you are not seeing EIGRP routes in the routing table for a peer, check the following on your router:

- Make sure the interface is operational and that you don't have a layer 2 or layer 3 problem: **show interfaces**.
- Make sure you have EIGRP neighbors with the **show ip eigrp neighbors** command.
- Make sure the correct K-values are enabled on both EIGRP routers, the **network** commands are configured correctly, and that both routers are in the same EIGRP AS: use the **show ip protocols** command to verify this.

To view only the EIGRP routes in the routing table, use the `show ip route eigrp` command. The `show ip route` command displays routes for all routing protocols: connected, static, and dynamic protocols.

The show ip eigrp neighbors Command

21.04. The CD contains a multimedia demonstration of the `show ip eigrp neighbors` command for EIGRP on a router.

To view the list of EIGRP neighbors that your router has learned, use the **show ip eigrp neighbors** command:

```
Router# show ip eigrp neighbors
IP-EIGRP neighbors for process 200
Address         Interface  Hold  Uptime    SRTT  RTO   Q    Seq
                           (sec)           (ms)        Cnt  Num
192.168.4.101 Se0          13    00:02:10  610   3660  0    4
```

This example has one neighbor (192.168.4.101). Table 21-3 explains the output of this command.

on the Job *If you see a log message on your router about your router and a neighboring EIGRP router "not on a common subnet," then you have misconfigured the IP addressing on either your router or the peer router (they're in different subnets).*

TABLE 21-3   Fields from the **show ip eigrp neighbors** Command

Field	Description
Process	AS number of the EIGRP routing process for the neighbor; if your router is running more than one AS, you'll see different sections of neighbors, each listed under a different AS number
Address	IP address of the EIGRP neighbor
Interface	Your router's interface on which you are receiving the neighbor's hellos
Hold	The remaining time left before you declare your neighbor dead when you are not seeing hello messages from the neighbor
Uptime	Length of time that you have known your neighbor
SRTT (smooth round-trip time)	The measured amount of time, in milliseconds, that it takes for your router to send EIGRP information to a neighbor and to get an ACK back
RTO	The amount of time, in milliseconds, that your router will wait before resending an EIGRP packet from the transmission queue to a neighbor
Q Cnt	The number of update/query/reply packets that you have queued up, ready to be sent to the neighbor
Seq Num	The sequence number of the update/query/reply packet that your neighbor last sent

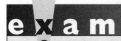

The show ip eigrp topology Command

To see the list of successor and feasible successors, as well as other types of EIGRP routes learned from EIGRP neighbors, use the **show ip eigrp topology** command:

```
Router# show ip eigrp topology
IP-EIGRP Topology Table for AS(200)/ID(192.168.4.100)

Codes: P - Passive, A - Active, U - Update, Q - Query,
       R - Reply,r - Reply status
P 10.10.10.0 255.255.255.0, 2 successors, FD is 0
          via 10.10.1.1    (46251776/46226176), Ethernet0
          via 10.10.2.1    (46251776/46226176), Ethernet1
          via 10.10.1.3    (46277376/46251776), Ethernet0
```

21.05. The CD contains a multimedia demonstration of the `show ip eigrp topology` command for EIGRP on a router.

When a route is listed for a neighbor, you'll see two values in parentheses. The first value is the feasible distance (the metric value for your router to reach the destination), while the second value is the advertised distance (the metric value the neighbor is advertising). In this example, you can see two successor routes (the first two), but no feasible successor routes (FD is 0). Also notice that 10.10.10.0 is in a passive state (P), since it has two successor routes. Remember that for there to be a feasible successor, the advertised distance of the route has to be less than (not less than or equal to) the current successor route. In this case, the third route's advertised distance is the same as the two successor routes, so it's not a feasible successor. In addition to seeing a passive code (P), other codes you can see are active (A—where EIGRP is computing possible paths to a destination), update (U—where an update was sent to the destination), query (Q—where a query was sent to the destination), reply (R—where a reply packet was sent to a destination), and reply status (r—where the router sent a query and is waiting for a reply).

The show ip eigrp interfaces Command

To see information about the interfaces on which EIGRP is enabled, use the following command:

```
Router# show ip eigrp interfaces
IP EIGRP interfaces for process 100
              Xmit Queue  Mean  Pacing Time  Multicast  Pending
Int    Peers  Un/Reliable SRTT  Un/Reliable  Flow Timer Routes
Et0/0  1        0/0        337    0/10          0         0
Se1/0  1        0/0        10     1/63          103       0
```

Optionally, you can qualify the output by specifying an interface after the **interfaces** parameter. Table 21-4 explains the information found in the

| | TABLE 21-4 | Fields from the show ip eigrp interfaces Command |

Field	Description
Int	Interface on which the EIGRP process is enabled
Peers	Number of EIGRP peers in the AS seen off of the associated interface
Xmit Queue Un/Reliable	Number of EIGRP packets remaining queued up in the Unreliable and Reliable queues
Mean SRTT	Average smooth round-trip time (SRTT) time in milliseconds between all neighbors off of the interface
Pacing Time Un/Reliable	Number of milliseconds the router waits after transmitting Unreliable and Reliable EIGRP packets
Multicast Flow Timer	Number of milliseconds to wait for an acknowledgment of a sent EIGRP multicast packet before transmitting another multicast packet
Pending Routes	Number of EIGRP routes in packets waiting to be sent from the transmit queue on the specified interface

preceding output. In this example, EIGRP is enabled for Ethernet0/0 and Serial1/0 in AS 100 and one EIGRP peer is off of each interface.

The show ip eigrp traffic Command

To see information about traffic statistics for EIGRP, use the following command:

```
Router# show ip eigrp traffic
IP-EIGRP Traffic Statistics for process 200
 Hellos sent/received: 274/139
 Updates sent/received: 3/4
 Queries sent/received: 1/0
 Replies sent/received: 0/1
 Acks sent/received: 4/3
 Input queue high water mark 1, 0 drops
 SIA-Queries sent/received: 0/0
 SIA-Replies sent/received: 0/0
```

As you can see from this output, the router is sending and receiving hellos and updates and is sharing information with neighboring EIGRP routers.

21.06. The CD contains a multimedia demonstration of the `show ip eigrp traffic` *command for EIGRP on a router.*

The debug ip eigrp Command

To troubleshoot EIGRP routing problems, you can use **debug** commands. The following command displays EIGRP events (other parameters are available for this command):

```
Router# debug ip eigrp
IP-EIGRP: 10.0.4.0/24 - don't advertise out Serial0
IP-EIGRP: 192.168.4.0/24 - do advertise out Serial0
IP-EIGRP: 10.0.0.0/8 - do advertise out Serial0
IP-EIGRP: Int 10.0.0.0/8 metric 28160 - 25600 2560
IP-EIGRP: Processing incoming UPDATE packet
IP-EIGRP: Int 192.168.100.0/24 M 2195456 - 1657856
          537600 SM 281600 - 56000 25600
IP-EIGRP: 192.168.100.0/24 routing table not updated
IP-EIGRP: 10.0.4.0/24 - don't advertise out Serial0
IP-EIGRP: 192.168.4.0/24 - do advertise out Serial0
IP-EIGRP: 10.0.0.0/8 - do advertise out Serial0
IP-EIGRP: Int 10.0.0.0/8 metric 28160 - 25600 2560
IP-EIGRP: Processing incoming UPDATE packet
IP-EIGRP: Int 10.0.0.0/8 M 4294967295 - 1657856
          4294967295 SM 4294967295 - 1657856 4294967295
```

In this example, I disabled and re-enabled Serial0. As you can see, it is advertising 192.168.4.0 to its neighbor connected to this interface.

21.07. The CD contains a multimedia demonstration of the debug ip eigrp *command for EIGRP on a router.*

The debug eigrp packets Command

If you see an EIGRP neighbor as a peer and/or see EIGRP routing updates from the peer in the routing table, the two peers are using matching keys for authentication. If you don't see a router as a neighbor (**show ip eigrp neighbors**) when you expect to see a peer as a neighbor, this could indicate an authentication problem. When using the **debug eigrp packets** command and you see "authentication mismatch" and "dropping peer, invalid authentication" messages, then the two peers have an authentication configuration problem:

```
Router# debug eigrp packets
EIGRP Packets debugging is on
    (UPDATE, REQUEST, QUERY, REPLY, HELLO, IPXSAP, PROBE,
      ACK, STUB, SIAQUERY, SIAREPLY)
EIGRP: pkt key id = 2, authentication mismatch
EIGRP: Serial0/1: ignored packet from 192.168.1.2,
    opcode = 5 (invalid authentication)
EIGRP: Dropping peer, invalid authentication
EIGRP: Sending HELLO on Serial0/1
AS 100, Flags 0x0, Seq 0/0 idbQ 0/0 iidbQ un/rely 0/0
%DUAL-5-NBRCHANGE: IP-EIGRP(0) 100: Neighbor 192.168.1.2
  (Serial0/1) is down: Auth failure
```

Make sure the lifetime values match between peer routers so that when changing from one key to another, the right key value is used to authenticate the routing updates successfully—this is a common misconfiguration that causes authentication to fail.

If you see a "Mismatched adjacency values" or "K-Value mismatch" message in the preceding **debug** command output, it could be caused by a mismatch in the AS number or a mismatch in the K-values enabled on the two EIGRP routers.

21.08. The CD contains a multimedia demonstration of the debug eigrp packets *command for EIGRP on a router.*

INSIDE THE EXAM

EIGRP Overview

Remember that EIGRP is proprietary to Cisco, and remember the components it uses in its metric structure and the routing protocols it supports.

EIGRP Operation

Be familiar with the operation of EIGRP, including how neighbor adjacencies are built using multicast hello messages and how this information is maintained in local neighbor and topology tables. Be familiar with the EIGRP message types and how they are used. Memorize and understand the terms used in Table 21-1.

EIGRP Configuration

Know the basic commands in enabling EIGRP: `router eigrp` and `network`. Be able to detect misconfigured EIGRP routing processes on routers by looking for misconfigured `network` commands. Be able to pick out successor routes, feasible successor routes, and successor routers created by using the `variance` command from the topology table. Remember when the `no auto-summary` command is used for EIGRP.

EIGRP Troubleshooting

Expect a few questions on troubleshooting EIGRP problems. You should be able to understand and interpret the output of the various `show` commands for EIGRP to find problems with an EIGRP configuration.

CERTIFICATION SUMMARY

Cisco's proprietary EIGRP routing protocol is based on IGRP. Enhancements of EIGRP include fast convergence, a loop-free topology, route summarization, multicast and incremental updates, and routing for IP, IPX, and AppleTalk. Hellos are sent every 5 seconds as multicasts to develop and maintain a neighbor relationship. EIGRP's metrics are bandwidth, delay, reliability, load, and MTU.

The DUAL algorithm is used to provide a loop-free topology. This algorithm provides fast convergence by storing a neighbor's routing information locally in a topology table. The best path is called a successor route, and any valid alternative paths are called feasible successors. The advertised distance is a neighbor's metric to reach a destination, while the feasible distance is your router's metric to reach the same destination. There are five EIGRP messages: hello, update, query, reply, and acknowledgment.

Enabling EIGRP is simple: you must specify an AS number with the **router** command and you enter connected network numbers with the **network** command. The **show ip eigrp neighbors** command displays adjacent neighbors and issues with building an adjacency with other EIGRP routers. The **show ip eigrp topology** command shows the topology table the DUAL algorithm uses to build the routing table. EIGRP routes show up as *D* in the IP routing table.

✓ TWO-MINUTE DRILL

EIGRP Overview

❑ EIGRP, which is based on IGRP, is a hybrid protocol with many link state protocol characteristics: it supports fast convergence, provides a loop-free topology, supports route summarization and VLSM, and uses multicasts and incremental updates.

❑ EIGRP uses bandwidth and delay, by default, in its metric computation, but it can also use reliability, load, and MTU.

EIGRP Operation

❑ EIGRP sends hello multicasts (224.0.0.10) out every 5 seconds on its interfaces. To form a neighbor relationship, EIGRP routers must have matching AS numbers and K-values.

❑ EIGRP uses the DUAL algorithm to maintain the topology table and update the routing table. A successor route is the route with the best path to the destination. A feasible successor route is a valid backup route (not part of a routing loop). The advertised distance is the distance for a neighbor to reach a destination network, and the feasible distance is the distance for this router to reach the same network.

❑ EIGRP maintains separate neighbor, topology, and routing tables for each routed protocol.

EIGRP Configuration

❑ Configuring EIGRP requires an AS number. Remember to use classful network numbers in your **network** statements or include a subnet mask value to qualify the network number.

❑ Use the **variance** command to include other nonsuccessor EIGRP routes in your routing table.

❑ Use the **no auto-summary** command when you have discontiguous subnets for a classful address in your EIGRP network.

EIGRP Troubleshooting

❑ To verify your EIGRP configuration, use the following commands: **show ip protocols**, **show ip eigrp neighbors**, **show ip eigrp topology**, and **show ip eigrp traffic**.

SELF TEST

The following Self Test questions will help you measure your understanding of the material presented in this chapter. Read all the choices carefully, as there may be more than one correct answer. Choose all correct answers for each question.

EIGRP Overview

1. EIGRP will route for _____.
   A. IP
   B. IP and IPX
   C. IP and AppleTalk
   D. IP, IPX, and AppleTalk

2. EIGRP uses the _____ algorithm to update its routing table.
   A. Bellman-Ford
   B. Dijkstra
   C. DUAL
   D. Integrated

EIGRP Operation

3. EIGRP generates hellos every _____ seconds on LAN segments.
   A. 5
   B. 10
   C. 15
   D. 30

4. A _____ route is the best path to reach a destination within the EIGRP topology and routing tables.
   A. Successor
   B. Feasible successor
   C. Advertised distance
   D. Feasible distance

5. When a successor route is no longer available and no feasible successor route exists in the topology table, a _____ is sent to all other neighbors advertising the same route to determine whether they have a valid path to the destination network.
   A. Multicast active message
   B. Broadcast query message
   C. Multicast reply message
   D. Multicast query message

EIGRP Configuration

6. Enter the EIGRP command or commands to include the interfaces with 192.168.1.1/26, 192.168.1.65/26, and 192.168.1.129/26 in the routing process: _____.

7. Enter the EIGRP command to advertise specific subnets, instead of advertising summarized classful routes, across a class boundary: _____.

EIGRP Troubleshooting

8. When examining the IP routing table, an EIGRP route will be shown as what letter?
   A. I
   B. R
   C. O
   D. D

9. Enter the EIGRP command to view only the successor routes: _____.

10. Enter the EIGRP command to view both the successor and feasible successor routes: _____.

SELF TEST ANSWERS

EIGRP Overview

1. ☑ **D.** EIGRP supports three routed protocols: IP, IPX, and AppleTalk.
☒ **A** is incorrect because it omits IPX and AppleTalk. **B** is incorrect because it omits AppleTalk. **C** is incorrect because it omits IPX.

2. ☑ **C.** EIGRP uses the DUAL algorithm to update its routing table.
☒ **A** is incorrect because Bellman-Ford is used by the distance vector protocols. **B** is incorrect because Dijkstra is used by link state protocols. **D** is a nonexistent routing algorithm.

EIGRP Operation

3. ☑ **A.** EIGRP generates hellos every 5 seconds.
☒ **B, C,** and **D** are incorrect hello periods.

4. ☑ **A.** A successor route is the best path to reach a destination within the topology table.
☒ **B** is incorrect because a feasible successor is a valid backup route. **C,** advertised distance, refers to a neighbor's distance to a route. **D,** feasible distance, refers to a router's distance to a route.

5. ☑ **D.** A multicast query message is sent to neighbors to determine whether a nonfeasible successor route to a destination is valid.
☒ **A** is incorrect because this is the state the route is in, not the message sent. **B** is incorrect because EIGRP uses multicasts, not broadcasts. **C** is incorrect because a reply message is in response to a query.

EIGRP Configuration

6. ☑ `network 192.168.1.0`

7. ☑ `no auto-summary`

EIGRP Troubleshooting

8. ☑ **D.** A D in the routing table indicates an EIGRP route.
☒ **A** is incorrect because an *I* indicates an IGRP route. **B** is incorrect because an *R* indicates a RIP route. **C** is incorrect because an *O* is an OSPF route.

9. ☑ `show ip route`. Successor routes are populated in the router's IP routing table.

10. ☑ `show ip eigrp topology`.

Part VI

Advanced Cisco Router Features

22
Access Control Lists

T he last few chapters introduced you to routing protocols and their basic configuration. By default, once you set up routing, your router will allow any packet to flow from one interface to another. You may want to implement policies to restrict the flow of traffic, for security or traffic policy reasons. Cisco allows you to control the flow of traffic from one interface to another by using access control lists (ACLs). ACLs, pronounced *ackles,* are a powerful feature of the Internetwork Operating System (IOS). Cisco actually supports ACLs for protocols other than IP, including Internetwork Packet Exchange (IPX), AppleTalk, layer 2 traffic, and others. This chapter focuses only on IP ACLs.

CERTIFICATION OBJECTIVE 22.01

ACL Overview

ACLs, known for their ability to filter traffic as it either comes into or leaves an interface, can also be used for other purposes, including restricting remote access (virtual type terminal, or VTY) to an IOS device, filtering routing information, prioritizing traffic with queuing, triggering phone calls with dial-on-demand routing (DDR), changing the administrative distance of routes, and specifying traffic to be protected by an IPSec VPN, among many others. This chapter focuses on restricting the flow of traffic to or through a router.

ACLs can be used for filtering of traffic through the IOS device *as well as remote access traffic to the IOS's VTY lines.*

Definition

ACLs are basically a set of commands, grouped together by a number or name, that are used to filter traffic entering or leaving an interface. ACL commands define specifically which traffic is permitted and denied. ACLs are created in Global Configuration mode.

Once you create your group of ACL statements, you must activate them. For filtering traffic between interfaces, the ACL is activated in Interface Subconfiguration mode. This can be a physical interface, such as `ethernet0` or `serial0`, or a logical interface, such as `ethernet0.1` or `serial0.1`. When activating an ACL on an interface, you must specify in which direction the traffic should be filtered:

■ Inbound (as the traffic comes into an interface from an external source)

■ Outbound (before the traffic exits an interface to the network)

With inbound ACLs, the IOS compares the packet to the interface ACL before the IOS forwards it to another interface. With outbound ACLs, the packet is received on an interface and forwarded to the exit interface; the IOS then compares the packet to the ACL.

One restriction that ACLs have is that they cannot filter traffic that the router itself originates. For example, if you execute a ping or traceroute from the router, or if you telnet from the router to another device, ACLs applied to the router's interfaces cannot filter these connections outbound. However, if an external device tries to ping, traceroute, or telnet *to* the router or *through* the router to a remote destination, the router can filter these packets.

Types

ACLs come in two varieties: *numbered and named* and *standard and extended.* Numbered and named ACLs define how the router will reference the ACL. You can think of this as something similar to an index value. A numbered ACL is assigned a unique number among all ACLs, whereas a named ACL is assigned a unique name among all named ACLs. These are then used by the router to filter traffic.

Each of these references to ACLs supports two types of filtering: *standard* and *extended.* Standard IP ACLs can filter only on the source IP address inside a packet, whereas an extended IP ACLs can filter on the source and destination IP addresses in the packet, the IP protocol (TCP, UDP, ICMP, and so on), and protocol information (such as the TCP or UDP source and destination port numbers or ICMP message types).

Filtered Information	Standard IP ACL	Extended IP ACL
Source address	Yes	Yes
Destination address	No	Yes
IP protocol (i.e., TCP or UDP)	No	Yes
Protocol information (i.e., port number)	No	Yes

TABLE 22-1

Standard and Extended ACL Comparison

ⓦatch *Remember the filtering abilities of standard versus extended ACLs in Table 22-1.*

With an extended ACL, you can be very precise in your filtering. For example, you can filter a specific telnet session from one of your user's PCs to a remote telnet server. Standard ACLs do not support this form of granularity. With a standard ACL, you can either permit or deny all traffic from a specific source device. Table 22-1 compares the two types of filtering for IP traffic.

Processing

ACLs are basically statements that are grouped together by either a name or number. Within this group of statements, when a packet is processed by an ACL, the IOS will go through certain steps in finding a match against the ACL statements. ACLs are processed *top-down* by the IOS. Using a top-down approach, a packet is compared to the first statement in the ACL, and if the IOS finds a match between the packet and the statement, the IOS will execute one of two actions included with the statement: *permit* or *deny*.

If the IOS doesn't find a match of packet contents to the first ACL statement, the IOS will proceed to the next statement in the list, again going through the same matching process. If the second statement matches the packet contents, the IOS executes one of the two actions. If there is no match on this statement, the IOS will keep on going through the list until it finds a match. If the IOS goes through the entire list and doesn't find a match in the ACL statements to the ACL contents, the router will *drop* the packet. The top-down processing of ACLs brings out the following very important points:

- Once a match is found, no further statements are processed in the list.
- The order of statements is important, since after the first match, the rest of the statements are not processed.
- If no match is found in the list, the packet is dropped.

Statement Ordering

If a match is found on a statement, no further statements are processed. Therefore, the order of the statements is *very* important in an ACL. If you have two statements, one denying a host and one permitting the same host, whichever one appears *first* in the list will be executed and the second one will be ignored. Because order of statements is important, you should always place the most specific ACL statements at the top of the list and the least specific at the bottom of the list.

Let's take a look at an example to illustrate this process. In this example, you have an ACL on your router with two statements in this order:

1. Permit traffic from subnet 172.16.0.0/16.

2. Deny traffic from host 172.16.1.1/32.

Remember that the router processes these statements *top-down*. Let's assume that a packet is received on the router with a source IP address of 172.16.1.1. Given the preceding ACL, the router compares the packet contents with the first statement. Does the packet have a source address from network 172.16.0.0/16? Yes. Therefore, the result indicates that the router should permit the packet. Notice that the second statement is never processed once the router finds a match on a statement. In this example, any traffic from the 172.16.0.0/16 subnet is permitted, even traffic from 172.16.1.1.

Let's reverse the order of the two statements in the ACL and see how this reordered ACL will affect traffic flow:

1. Deny traffic from host 172.16.1.1.

2. Permit traffic from subnet 172.16.0.0/16.

If 172.16.1.1 sends traffic through the router, the IOS first compares these packets with the first ACL statement. Since the source address matches 172.16.1.1, the router drops the packet and stops processing statements in the ACL. In this example, it doesn't matter what traffic 172.16.1.1 is sending, because it's dropped. If another device, say 172.16.1.2, sends traffic through the router, the router compares the packet contents to the first ACL statement. Since the source address in the packet doesn't match the source address in the ACL statement, the router proceeds to the next statement in the list. Comparing the packet contents to the statement, there is a match. Therefore, the router will execute the results, permitting the traffic from 172.16.1.2. As you can see from both of these ACL examples, the order of statements in the ACL is very important and *definitely* impacts what traffic is permitted or denied.

Implicit Deny

Another important aspect of the top-down process is that if the router compares a packet to every statement in the list and does not find a match against the packet contents, the router will *drop* the packet. This process is referred to as *implicit deny*. At the end of every ACL is an invisible statement that drops all traffic that doesn't match any of the preceding statements in the ACL. Given this process, it makes no sense to have a list of only deny statements, since the implicit deny drops all traffic anyway. Therefore, every ACL should have at least *one permit* statement; otherwise, an ACL with only deny statements will drop all traffic, given the deny statements and the hidden implicit deny statement.

Important Configuration Guidelines

Configuring an ACL is not a simple process. To get the configuration process right, you should be guided by the following list:

- Order of statements is important: Put the most restrictive statements at the top of the list and the least restrictive at the bottom.

- ACL statements are processed top-down until a match is found, and then no more statements in the list are processed.

- If no match is found in the ACL, the packet is dropped (implicit deny).

- Each grouping of ACL statements needs either a unique number or a unique name.

- The router cannot filter traffic that it, itself, originates.

- Only one IP ACL can be applied to an interface in each direction (inbound and outbound)—two or more ACLs cannot be applied inbound or outbound to the same interface. (Actually, one ACL for each protocol, such as IP and IPX, can be applied to an interface in each direction.)

■ Applying an empty ACL to an interface permits all traffic by default: in order for an ACL to have an implicit deny statement, you need at least one actual permit or deny statement in the ACL.

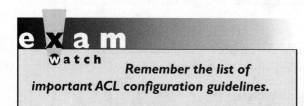

e x a m

⍵ a t c h *Remember the list of important ACL configuration guidelines.*

As you can see from this list of guidelines, ACLs are not a simple matter. ACLs are one of the IOS's more complex, yet powerful, features. The configuration, management, and troubleshooting of ACLs can become very complex and create many headaches for you. Therefore, it is important for you to understand the process the router uses when it compares packets to ACLs and how to create and maintain them. The following sections cover the basic configuration of ACLs on your router.

CERTIFICATION OBJECTIVE 22.02

Basic ACL Configuration

This section provides a brief introduction to the two basic commands you'll use to configure IP ACLs. The sections following this cover the actual details of configuring numbered versus named and standard versus extended ACLs.

Creating an ACL

To create a numbered ACL, use the following general syntax:

```
Router(config)# access-list ACL_# permit|deny conditions
```

Prior to IOS 11.2, you could give an ACL only a number as an identifier. Starting with IOS 11.2, an ACL can be referenced by a number or name. The purpose of the ACL_# is to group your statements together into a single list or policy. You cannot choose just any number for an ACL. Each layer 3 protocol is assigned its own range or ranges of numbers.

Table 22-2 shows the valid ACL numbers for IP ACLs. As you can see from this table, numbered ACLs give you a limited number of lists that you can create, which is based on the range of numbers assigned to a protocol type. However, named ACLs

TABLE 22-2	ACL Type	ACL Numbers
ACL Types and Numbers	IP Standard	1–99, 1300–1999
	IP Extended	100–199, 2000–2699

do not have this restriction. Basically, the number of named ACLs on a router is restricted only by the amount of RAM and NVRAM your router has.

Remember the numbers you can use for IP ACLs. Standard ACLs can use numbers ranging from 1–99 and *1300–1999, and extended ACLs can use 100–199 and 2000–2699.*

The *condition* in an ACL statement tells the router what contents in the packet need to match in order for the router to execute the action (**permit** or **deny**). The condition can include matching of IP addresses and protocol information. When the IOS compares a packet to the condition, if it finds a match, no more ACL statements are processed; if it doesn't find a match, the IOS proceeds to compare the packet to the next ACL statement in the list.

Matching on Addresses: Wildcard Masks

When dealing with IP addresses in ACL statements, you can use *wildcard masks* to match on a range of addresses instead of manually entering every IP address that you want to match on. Wildcard masks were briefly discussed in Chapter 20. This section goes into more depth about wildcard masks and how they are used in ACLs.

First, a wildcard mask is *not* a subnet mask. Like an IP address or a subnet mask, a wildcard mask is composed of 32 bits. Table 22-3 compares the bit values in a subnet mask and a wildcard mask. With a wildcard mask, a 0 in a bit position means that the corresponding bit position in the address of the ACL statement *must* match the same bit position in the IP address in the examined packet. A 1 in a bit position means that the corresponding bit position in the address of the ACL statement does *not* have to match the bit position in the IP address in the examined packet. In other words, the wildcard mask and the address in the ACL statement work in tandem. The wildcard mask tells the router which addressing bits in the address of the ACL statement must match the bits in the packet to which it is being compared.

TABLE 22-3	Bit Value	Subnet Mask	Wildcard Mask
	0	Host component	Must match
Subnet Mask Versus Wildcard Mask	1	Network component	Ignore

In reality, a wildcard mask is more like an *inverted* subnet mask. For instance, if you want to match on any address in a subnet or network, you can simply take the subnet mask, invert its bit values (change the 1s to 0s and the 0s to 1s), and you have a corresponding wildcard mask.

Let's look at a simple example of performing a binary conversion of a subnet mask to a wildcard mask. Assume that you have subnet mask of 255.255.0.0. Its binary representation is 11111111.11111111.00000000.00000000. When you convert this to a wildcard mask, invert the bits, like this: 00000000.00000000.11111111.11111111. Then convert this to decimal: 0.0.255.255. This is the corresponding wildcard mask for the subnet mask of 255.255.0.0. In this example, the wildcard mask tells the router that the first 16 bits of the corresponding IP address in the ACL statement must match the first 16 bits in the IP address of the examined packet for the router to continue processing the statement; otherwise, the router will proceed to the next ACL statement. As you can see, this example was easy to convert.

Let's look at a more difficult example. Assume that you want to match on a subnet that has a subnet mask of 255.255.240.0. Here's the entire subnet mask in binary: 11111111.11111111.11110000.00000000. In this example, the first, second, and fourth octets are easy to convert: the difficult conversion is in the third octet. To convert the subnet mask to a wildcard mask, invert all the bits, as shown here: 00000000.00000000.00001111.11111111. Next convert this back to decimal. This results in a wildcard mask of 0.0.15.255.

As you can see from the last two examples in the previous paragraph, if a subnet mask has 0 in an octet, the wildcard mask has a value of 255; if the subnet mask has 255 in an octet, the wildcard mask has a value of 0. However, the third octet in the second example makes this process more difficult.

Here's a shortcut to alleviate the conversion of a subnet mask to a wildcard mask. When doing the conversion, subtract each byte in the subnet mask *from* 255. The result will be the corresponding byte value for the wildcard mask. Going back to the 255.255.240 example, here is the shortcut:

- First byte: 255 – 255 (first subnet byte value) = 0 (wildcard mask value)
- Second byte: 255 – 255 (second subnet byte value) = 0 (wildcard mask value)

■ Third byte: 255 – 240 (third subnet byte value) = 15 (wildcard mask value)

■ Fourth byte: 255 – 0 (fourth subnet byte value) = 255 (wildcard mask value)

As you can see, this results in a wildcard mask of 0.0.15.240. This simple trick makes converting subnet masks to wildcard masks (and vice versa) very easy.

Special Wildcard Masks

Two special types of wildcard masks exist: 0.0.0.0 and 255.255.255.255. A wildcard mask of 0.0.0.0 tells the IOS that all 32 bits of the address in the ACL statement must match those found in the IP packet in order for the IOS to execute the action for the statement. A 0.0.0.0 wildcard mask is called a *host mask*. Here's a simple example of this information in an ACL statement: 192.168.1.1 0.0.0.0. This statement tells the IOS to look for the exact same IP address (192.168.1.1) in the IP packet. If the IOS doesn't find a match, the IOS will go to the next ACL statement. If you configure 192.168.1.1 0.0.0.0, the IOS will covert this to the following syntax: **host 172.16.1.1** (note the keyword *host* that precedes the IP address).

A wildcard mask of 255.255.255.255 tells the router the exact opposite of a 0.0.0.0 mask. In this mask, all of the bit values are 1s, which tells the IOS that it doesn't matter what is in the packet that it is comparing to the ACL statement—*any* address will match. Typically, you would record this as an IP address of 0.0.0.0 and a wildcard mask of 255.255.255.255, like this: 0.0.0.0 255.255.255.255. If you enter this, the IOS will convert the address and mask to the keyword **any**. Actually, the IP address that you enter with this mask doesn't matter. For instance, if you enter 192.168.1.1 255.255.255.255, this still matches any IP address. Remember that it's the wildcard mask that determines what bits in the IP address are *interesting* and should match.

Wildcard Mask Examples

Since the concept of a wildcard mask can be confusing, let's look at some examples. Table 22-4 shows some examples of addresses and wildcard masks.

TABLE 22-4	IP Address	Wildcard Mask	Matches
Wildcard Mask Examples	0.0.0.0	255.255.255.255	Match on any address (keyword `any` in an ACL statement).
	172.16.1.1	0.0.0.0	Match only if the address is 172.16.1.1 (preceded by the keyword `host`).
	172.16.1.0	0.0.0.255	Match only on packets that are in 172.16.1.0/24 (172.16.1.0–172.16.1.255).
	172.16.2.0	0.0.1.255	Match only on packets that are in 172.16.2.0/23 (172.16.2.0–172.16.3.255).
	172.16.0.0	0.0.255.255	Match only on packets that are in 172.16.0.0/16 (172.16.0.0–172.16.255.255).

Some wildcard masks can be confusing, such as 0.0.1.255. For masks like these, it's sometimes easier to look at them from a subnet mask perspective. In this example, the corresponding subnet mask would be 255.255.254.0. You can use a simple trick here by subtracting the wildcard mask from a local broadcast address (255.255.255.255) to come up with the correct wildcard mask. Based on this little trick, it's easier to see why row 4 of Table 22-4 matches on a range of addresses from 172.16.2.0 to 172.16.3.255.

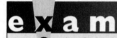

Be familiar with how wildcard masks work, as well as the special *notation Cisco uses for a match on all devices or a specific host, as shown in Table 22-4.*

Activating an ACL

Once you have built your IP ACL, it will do nothing until you apply it to a process in the IOS. This chapter focuses primarily on filtering traffic through interfaces. Therefore, to have the IOS filter traffic between interfaces, you must enter the appropriate interface or interfaces and activate your ACL. Here's the command to activate an ACL on an interface:

```
Router(config)# interface type [slot_#]port_#
Router(config-if)# ip access-group ACL_# in|out
```

At the end of the **ip access-group** command, you must specify which ACL you are activating and in which direction:

- **in**   As traffic comes into the interface
- **out**   As traffic leaves the interface

Note that you can apply the same ACL to multiple interfaces on a router, or you can activate the same ACL twice on the same interface: inbound and outbound. You can also apply a nonexistent ACL to an interface. A nonexistent ACL is an ACL that has no statements in it—an empty ACL will permit *all* traffic. For an ACL to have an implicit deny, it needs at least one **permit** or **deny** statement. It is highly recommended that you do *not* apply nonexistent ACLs to a router's interface. In this situation, when you create the very first statement in the list, the implicit deny is automatically placed at the bottom, which might create reachability issues for your router.

Let's take a look at an example that has a nonexistent ACL and examine the kinds of problems that you might experience. Assume that you have applied an ACL (#10) to a router's ethernet0 interface and this ACL currently doesn't have any **permit** or **deny** statements (it's empty). You are connected to the router via telnet on this interface, and your PC has an IP address of 192.168.1.1. You create an entry in ACL #10 that permits traffic from 172.16.0.0/16. As soon as you do this, you lose your telnet connection. If you guessed that the implicit deny caused the router to drop your connection, you guessed correctly. As soon as the router has one statement in it, the implicit deny is added at the bottom. In this example, since your PC had a source address of 192.168.1.1, and this wasn't included in the first statement, the router dropped your connection because it couldn't find any matching statements in ACL #10.

on the
job

A lot of confusion exists among published authors about an empty ACL: *some say an empty ACL drops all traffic, some say it permits all traffic, and some say that it depends on the IOS version. I've worked with ACLs since they first came out in version 7 of the IOS, and from that version all the way up to 12.4T code (the latest), an empty ACL has always allowed traffic to and through the interface. I encourage you to test this by applying an inbound ACL to the router's interface that has no statements and then ping that interface: the ping will work.*

CERTIFICATION OBJECTIVE 22.03

ACL Types

The following sections cover the configuration of both numbered and named ACLs. The first two sections deal with configuring numbered standard and extended ACLs; they are followed by a section on configuring named ACLs and then a section on how to verify your ACL configuration. Last, you'll be introduced to a feature called *sequenced* ACLs, which allows you to edit ACLs easily from the CLI of your IOS device.

Standard Numbered ACLs

Standard IP ACLs are simple and easy to configure. First, standard IP ACLs filter on only the *source IP address* in an IP packet. Use the following command to create an entry in a standard numbered IP ACL:

```
Router(config)# access-list 1-99|1300-1999 permit|deny
                    source_IP_address
                    [wildcard_mask] [log]
```

With a standard numbered IP ACL, you can use list numbers of 1–99 and 1300–1999. Following this is the action the router should take if there is a match on the condition. The condition is based solely on the source IP address. You enter this followed by an optional wildcard mask. If you omit the mask, it defaults to 0.0.0.0—an exact match is required in order to execute the action.

Be very familiar with the syntax of a standard ACL, as well as the fact that it can filter only on source addresses in a packet. If you omit the wildcard mask in a standard ACL, it defaults to 0.0.0.0 (an exact match is required).

Following this is the optional **log** parameter, which is new to standard ACLs in IOS 12.0. This parameter will cause any match of this statement to be printed to the console port of the router. These messages, by default, will not appear on a non-console connection to the IOS device unless you execute the following:

```
Router# terminal monitor
```

The terminal monitor command is good only for your current session: when you log out and then log back into the IOS device, you'll need to re-execute it to see logging output on your VTY or TTY session.

You can also forward these ACL logging messages to a syslog server. This setup is useful for debugging and security purposes. Once you have created your ACL, you can proceed to activate it on an interface with the **ip access-group** *ACL_#* **in | out** command.

Standard IP ACL Examples

Now that you have been introduced to the two basic commands to create and activate a standard numbered IP ACL, let's look at some examples to help you further your understanding. Here's the first example:

```
Router(config)# access-list 1 permit 192.168.1.1
Router(config)# access-list 1 deny 192.168.1.2
Router(config)# access-list 1 permit 192.168.1.0 0.0.0.255
Router(config)# access-list 1 deny any
Router(config)# interface serial 0
Router(config-if)# ip access-group 1 in
```

In this example, the first ACL statement in ACL #1 says that in order to execute the **permit** action, the IP packet must have a source address of 192.168.1.1—if it doesn't, the IOS proceeds to the second statement. Remember that if you omit the wildcard mask on a standard ACL, it defaults to 0.0.0.0—an exact match of the corresponding address in the ACL statement. The second ACL statement says that in order to execute the **deny** action, the IP packet must have a source address of 192.168.1.2; if it doesn't, the IOS proceeds to the third statement. The third ACL statement says that in order to execute the **permit** action, the IP packet must have a source address between 192.168.1.0 and 192.168.1.255—if it doesn't, the IOS proceeds to the fourth statement. The fourth statement is actually not necessary: it drops any packet. You don't need this statement since an invisible implicit deny any statement occurs at the end of every ACL. The last two commands in the ACL example activate ACL #1 on serial0 as traffic comes into the interface.

Actually, you could have written the preceding ACL like this:

```
Router(config)# access-list 1 deny 192.168.1.2
Router(config)# access-list 1 permit 192.168.1.0 0.0.0.255
Router(config)# interface serial 0
Router(config-if)# ip access-group 1 in
```

This example reduces your configuration from four ACL statements in the list down to two.

22.01. The CD contains a multimedia demonstration of configuring a standard numbered ACL on a router.

Here's another example of a standard ACL:

```
Router(config)# access-list 2 deny 192.168.1.0
Router(config)# access-list 2 deny 172.16.0.0
Router(config)# access-list 2 permit 192.168.1.1
Router(config)# access-list 2 permit 0.0.0.0 255.255.255.255
Router(config)# interface ethernet 0
Router(config-if)# ip access-group 1 out
```

This ACL example has a few problems. Examine it and see if you can spot them.

The first ACL statement appears to deny all traffic from 192.168.1.0/24. In reality, it will accomplish nothing. Remember that if you omit the wildcard mask for the address, it defaults to 0.0.0.0—an exact match. The problem is that you'll never have a packet with a source address of 192.168.1.0, since this is a network number, and not a host address. The second statement has the same problem. The third and fourth statements are okay.

As you can see, configuring ACLs can be tricky. For the preceding example, here's the updated configuration:

```
Router(config)# access-list 2 deny 192.168.1.0 0.0.0.255
Router(config)# access-list 2 deny 172.16.0.0 0.0.255.255
Router(config)# access-list 2 permit 192.168.1.1
Router(config)# access-list 2 permit 0.0.0.0 255.255.255.255
Router(config)# interface ethernet 0
Router(config-if)# ip access-group 1 out
```

In this example, the first statement now says that any packet with a source address from network 192.168.1.0/24 should be dropped. The second statement will drop any traffic from the Class B network 172.16.0.0/16. The third statement will permit traffic from 192.168.1.1. The fourth statement will permit traffic from anywhere. Actually, there is *still* a problem with this configuration—look at the first and third statements. Will the third statement ever be executed? If you answered *no*, you are correct. In this situation, you need to put the more specific entry before the less specific one. Another minor point to make is that the fourth statement in the list could represent the address as the keyword **any**. Here's the updated configuration:

```
Router(config)# access-list 2 permit 192.168.1.1
Router(config)# access-list 2 deny 192.168.1.0 0.0.0.255
Router(config)# access-list 2 deny 172.16.0.0 0.0.255.255
Router(config)# access-list 2 permit any
Router(config)# interface ethernet 0
Router(config-if)# ip access-group 1 out
```

There's actually one more problem with this ACL. If you guessed the ACL number used on the interface is not correct, then you guessed correctly. Notice that the ACL created has a number of 2, while the application of the ACL on the interface uses 1. To fix this, use the following configuration:

```
Router(config)# interface ethernet 0
Router(config-if)# no ip access-group 1 out
Router(config-if)# ip access-group 2 out
```

Note that you must first remove the old ACL from the interface before applying the new ACL.

exam

⚙ a t c h *Be able to troubleshoot ACL configurations by examining the order of statements in the list. The preceding example with misconfigured ACL statements is an excellent example of issues to look for in configuring ACLs.*

Restricting VTY Access to the Router

In addition to using standard IP ACLs to filter traffic as it enters and/or leaves an interface, you can also use them to restrict VTY access (telnet and SSH) to your router. You might want to do this to allow only network administrators to access the CLI of your IOS device remotely. Setting this up is almost the same as setting up restricted access on an interface.

First, you need to create a standard ACL that has a list of **permit** statements that allow your corresponding network administrators remote access; include the IP addresses of their PCs in this list. Next, you need to activate your ACL. However, you will not do this on any of the router's interfaces. If you were to activate this ACL on an interface, it would allow any type of traffic from your administrators but drop *all* other traffic. As you may recall from Chapter 17, when someone telnets or SSH's into your router, the router associates this connection with a virtual type terminal (VTY) line. Therefore, you'll apply your standard ACL to the VTYs, like this:

```
Router(config)# line vty 0 4
Router(config-line)# access-class standard_ACL_# in|out
```

Remember that your router supports five telnets by default (0–4), and more on certain IOS devices. You can configure all VTYs simultaneously by specifying the beginning and ending line numbers after the **vty** parameter. If you don't apply the restriction to all of your VTYs, you are leaving a backdoor into your router, which might cause a security problem.

Also, notice the command used to apply the ACL to the line: **access-class**. This is different from activating an ACL on a router's interface. If you use the **in** parameter, you are restricting telnet and SSH access to the router itself. The **out** parameter is kind of unique. By using this parameter, you are restricting what destinations this router can telnet or SSH to when someone uses the **telnet**, **connect**, or **ssh** commands. This creates an exception to a standard ACL and has the router treat the address in the ACL statements as a destination address; it causes the router to compare this address to the address in the **telnet** command before allowing the user on the router to telnet to the specified destination.

Here's a simple example of using a standard ACL to filter telnet traffic to a router:

```
Router(config)# access-list 99 permit 192.168.1.0 0.0.0.255
Router(config)# line vty 0 4
Router(config-line)# access-class 99 in
```

In this example, only traffic from 192.168.1.0/24 is allowed to telnet or SSH into this router. Because of the implicit deny at the end of **access-list 99**, all other connections to this router (via the VTYs) will be dropped.

22.02. The CD contains a multimedia demonstration of configuring a standard numbered ACL to restrict telnet access on a router.

As you will see in the next section, you can also use extended ACLs to restrict access to the IOS device, but this configuration is much more complex. Second, extended ACLs are applied to interfaces and thus won't be able to restrict telnet access *from* the router to a remote destination. And third, whenever you apply an ACL to an interface on the router, you'll affect the performance of the router on that interface. Depending on the router model, the IOS version, and the features you have enabled, the degradation in performance will vary (today's most current IOS versions take very little of a performance hit when using ACLs on interfaces). Therefore, if you only want to restrict telnet or SSH access to or from the router, using a standard ACL and the **access-class** statement on your VTYs is the best approach.

EXERCISE 22-1

Configuring Standard Numbered ACLs

The last few sections dealt with the configuration of standard numbered ACLs. This exercise will help you reinforce this material by letting you configure a standard numbered ACL on a router to restrict access through it. You'll perform this lab using Boson's NetSim simulator. You can find a picture of the network diagram for Boson's NetSim simulator in the Introduction of this book. In this exercise, you'll first set up static routes on the two routers (2600-1 and 2600-2) and verify network connectivity. Next, you'll configure your ACL. After starting up the simulator, click the LabNavigator button. Next, double-click Exercise 22-1 and click the

Load Lab button. This will load the lab configuration based on the exercises in Chapters 11 and 16.

1. On the 2600-2, configure a static route to 192.168.1.0/24, which is off of the 2600-1. View the routing table.

   At the top of the simulator in the menu bar, click the eRouters icon and choose 2600-2. Configure the static route: **configure terminal, ip route 192.168.1.0 255.255.255.0 192.168.2.1**, and **end**. View the static route: **show ip route**. Make sure that 192.168.1.0/24 shows up in the routing table as a static route (**S**).

2. On the 2600-1, configure a static route to 192.168.3.0/24, which is off of the 2600-2. View the routing table.

   At the top of the simulator in the menu bar, click the eRouters icon and choose 2600-1. Configure the static route: **configure terminal, ip route 192.168.3.0 255.255.255.0 192.168.2.2**, and **end**. View the static route: **show ip route**. Make sure that 192.168.3.0/24 shows up in the routing table as a static route (**S**).

3. From Host-3, test connectivity to the 2600-1.

   At the top of the simulator in the menu bar, click the eStations icon and choose Host3. Ping the **serial0** and **fa0/0** interface of the 2600-1 router: **ping 192.168.2.1** and **ping 192.168.1.1**. The pings should be successful.

4. From Host-3, test connectivity to Host-1.

   Ping Host-1: **ping 192.168.1.10**. The ping should be successful.

5. Check network connectivity between the 2950-1 switch, the 2600-2 router, and the 2600-1 router.

   At the top of the simulator in the menu bar, click the eSwitches icon and choose 2950-1. From the 2950-1 switch, ping the 2600-1 router: **ping 192.168.1.1**. At the top of the simulator in the menu bar, click the eRouters icon and choose 2600-2. From the 2600-2 router, ping the 2600-1 router: **ping 192.168.1.1**. At the top of the simulator in the menu bar, click the eRouters icon and choose 2600-1. From the 2600-1 router, ping the 2950-1 switch: **ping 192.168.1.2**. From the 2600-1 router, ping the 2600-2 router: **ping 192.168.2.2**.

6. Configure a standard numbered ACL on the 2600-1 to allow traffic from the 2950-1 switch, but to deny all other traffic.

   At the top of the simulator in the menu bar, click the eRouters icon and choose 2600-1. On the 2600-1, create a standard ACL statement to permit access from the 2950-1 switch, logging matches: **configure terminal** and **access-list 1 permit host 192.168.1.2**. Create a second ACL statement to deny all traffic, logging matches: **access-list 1 deny any**. Exit configuration mode: **end**. Examine the ACL configuration: **show access-lists**.

7. Activate the ACL on the 2600-1 router on fa0/0 in the inbound direction. Access the interface: **interface fa0/0**. Apply the ACL: **ip access-group 1 in**. Exit configuration mode: **end**.

8. Access the 2950-1 and verify its IP address configuration.

   At the top of the simulator in the menu bar, click the eSwitches icon and choose 2950-1. View the IP address for VLAN 1: **show ip interface brief**.

9. Test the ACL from the 2950-1 by pinging 192.168.1.1.

   From the 2950-1 switch, ping the 2600-1: **ping 192.168.1.1**. The ping should be successful.

10. Examine the ACL statement matches on the 2600-1.

    At the top of the simulator in the menu bar, click the eRouters icon and choose 2600-1, and then use the **show access-lists** command to examine the ACL configuration. There should be five matches on the **permit** statement.

11. Test the ACL from the 2950-2 by pinging 192.168.1.1.

    At the top of the simulator in the menu bar, click the eSwitches icon and choose 2950-2. From the 2950-2 switch, ping the 2600-1: **ping 192.168.1.1**. The ping should fail.

12. Examine the ACL statement matches on the 2600-1.

    At the top of the simulator in the menu bar, click the eRouters icon and choose 2600-1 and then use **show access-lists** to examine the ACL configuration. There should be five matches on the **deny** statement.

13. Remove the ACL configuration from the interface.

At the top of the simulator in the menu bar, click the eRouters icon and choose 2600-1. On the 2600-1 router, remove the application of the ACL. Go into the interface: **configure terminal** and **interface fa0/0**. Deactivate the ACL: **no ip access-group 1 in**. Go back to Global Configuration mode: **exit**.

14. Remove ACL 1 from the configuration.

   Delete the ACL statements: **no access-list 1**. Exit configuration mode: **end**. Use the **show access-list** command to verify the ACL no longer exists.

15. Test connectivity from both switches.

   At the top of the simulator in the menu bar, click the eSwitches icon and choose 2950-1. From the 2950-1 switch, ping the 2600-1: **ping 192.168.1.1**. At the top of the simulator in the menu bar, click the eSwitches icon and choose 2950-2. The ping should be successful. From the 2950-2 switch, ping the 2600-1: **ping 192.168.1.1**. Both pings should also be successful.

Now you should be more comfortable with configuring standard numbered ACLs on a router.

Extended Numbered ACLs

Extended IP ACLs are much more flexible in what you can match on than standard ACLs. Extended ACLs can match on all of the following information:

- Source *and* destination IP addresses
- TCP/IP protocol (IP, TCP, UDP, ICMP, and so on)
- Protocol information, such as port numbers for TCP and UDP, or message types for ICMP

The following sections cover the configuration and use of extended numbered IP ACLs.

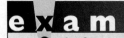

Command Syntax

Here is the generic command to configure an extended numbered IP ACL:

```
Router(config)# access-list 100-199|2000-2699 permit|deny
                    IP_protocol
                    source_address source_wildcard_mask
                        [protocol_information]
                    destination_address destination_wildcard_mask
                        [protocol_information] [log]
```

As you can see from this command, the configuration of an extended ACL is more complicated than that of a standard one. Extended IP numbered ACLs can use list numbers in the ranges 100–199 and 2000–2699. After the action (**permit** or **deny**) comes the IP protocol that you want to match on. This is the first major difference between an extended ACL and a standard one. These IP protocols include the following: **ip**, **icmp**, **tcp**, **gre**, **udp**, **igrp**, **eigrp**, **igmp**, **ipinip**, **nos**, and **ospf**. If you want to match on any IP protocol—TCP, UDP, ICMP, and so on—use the **ip** keyword for the protocol. If Cisco doesn't have a name for the IP protocol you want to specify, use the number of the protocol instead, such as **6** for TCP.

The second major difference is that you must specify both the source and destination addresses and their respective wildcard masks. With a standard ACL, you can specify only the source address, and the wildcard mask is optional. Depending on the IP protocol, you might be able to add protocol information for the source and/or destination. For example, TCP and UDP allow you to specify both source and destination port numbers, and ICMP allows you to specify ICMP message types. As with standard ACLs, you can log messages to the console or a syslog server with the **log** parameter.

Once you have created your extended numbered IP ACL, you must activate it on your router's interface with the **ip access-group** command. Note that this is the same configuration used with a standard ACL. Once you activate the ACL, the router will begin filtering traffic on the interface.

ⓌａｔｃＨ *Be very familiar with the general syntax of an extended ACL* *statement: you might have to configure an extended ACL on the exam.*

TCP and UDP

Use the following syntax to configure an extended ACL for TCP or UDP:

```
Router(config)# access-list 100-199|2000-2699 permit|deny
                tcp|udp
                source_address source_wildcard_mask
                    [operator source_port_#]
                destination_address destination_wildcard_mask
                    [operator destination_port_#]
                [established] [log]
```

After specifying the action (**permit** or **deny**), you configure the IP protocol: **tcp** or **udp**.

Operators With TCP and UDP, you can specify the source, destination, or both source and destination port numbers or names. To specify how to perform the match, you must configure an operator. The operator tells the router how to match on the port number(s) or names. Table 22-5 lists the valid operators for TCP and UDP ACL entries. Note that these operators apply only to TCP and UDP connections. Other IP protocols do not use them. If you omit the port number or name, the ACL looks for a match on all TCP or UDP connections.

Ports Numbers and Names For TCP and UDP connections, you can list either the name or the number of the port. For example, if you wanted to match on telnet traffic, you could use either the keyword **telnet** or the number **23**. Table 22-6 lists some of the most common port names and numbers for TCP connections.

TABLE 22-5	Operator	Explanation
TCP and UDP Operators	lt	Less than
	gt	Greater than
	neq	Not equal to
	eq	Equal to
	range	Range of port numbers

TABLE 22-6	Port Name	Command Parameter	Port Number
Common TCP Port Names and Numbers	FTP Data	`ftp-data`	20
	FTP Control	`ftp`	21
	Telnet	`telnet`	23
	SMTP	`smtp`	25
	WWW	`www`	80
	POP3	`pop3`	110

Table 22-7 shows some of the common UDP port names and numbers.

exam
ⓦatch

One common problem that occurs when setting up an ACL is that the administrator specifies the wrong protocol for the application, such as TCP for TFTP, RIP, or DNS queries, instead of UDP. This is also true of port numbers or names.

You need to be familiar with the TCP/IP protocols and their ports when setting up filtering policies. Remember the TCP and UDP application names and numbers in Tables 22-6 and 22-7.

established Keyword   The `established` keyword is used only for TCP connections. The assumption behind the use of this keyword is that you are originating TCP traffic on the inside of the network and filtering the returning traffic as it comes back into your network. In this situation, this keyword allows (or denies) any TCP traffic that has a certain flag or flag bits set in the TCP segment header, indicating that this is returning traffic back into your network. Refer to Chapter 2 for an explanation of connection-oriented transport protocols

TABLE 22-7	Port Name	Command Parameter	Port Number
Common UDP Port Names and Numbers	DNS Query	`dns`	53
	TFTP	`tftp`	69
	SNMP	`snmp`	161
	IP RIP	`rip`	520

w a t c h *Understand the use of the* **established** *keyword with TCP ACL statements.*

and Chapter 9 for the mechanics of TCP. My book with Cisco Press, *Cisco Router Firewall Security* 2007©, discusses this topic in much more depth, comparing and contrasting the use of the **established** keyword with how stateful firewalls, such as the Cisco ASA, work.

CertCam

22.03. The CD contains a multimedia demonstration of configuring an extended numbered ACL to allow telnet traffic through a router.

ICMP

The following command shows the syntax of filtering ICMP traffic:

```
Router(config)# access-list 100-199|2000-2699 permit|deny icmp
                source_address source_wildcard_mask
                destination_address destination_wildcard_mask
                [icmp_message] [log]
```

Unlike TCP and UDP, ICMP doesn't use ports. Instead, ICMP uses message types. And where TCP and UDP extended ACLs allow you to specify both source and destination ports, ICMP allows you to enter an ICMP message. Table 22-8 shows some of the common ICMP messages and brief descriptions. You can enter the ICMP message by either its name or its number. If you omit the ICMP message type, all message types are included.

TABLE 22-8	Message Type	Message Description
Common ICMP Messages	`administratively-prohibited`	Message that says that someone filtered a packet
	`echo`	Used by ping to check a destination
	`echo-reply`	Is a response to an echo message created by ping
	`host-unreachable`	The subnet is reachable, but the host is not responding
	`net-unreachable`	The network/subnet is not reachable
	`traceroute`	Filters on traceroute information when ICMP is used

on the **job**

If you execute the `no access-list` *command, followed by the ACL number, the entire ACL and its referenced commands are deleted. What most administrators don't realize, or forget, is that if you preface any numbered ACL statement with the* `no` *parameter, it has exactly the same effect: the entire ACL is deleted. For example, executing the* `no access-list 100 permit tcp any any` *command causes the router basically to ignore everything after the* `100` *parameter, causing the router to execute the command as if it were* `no access-list 100`*!*

CertCam

22.04. The CD contains a multimedia demonstration of configuring an extended numbered ACL to permit ICMP traffic through a router.

e x a m

w a t c h   *Use an extended ACL*   *application traffic. Remember the ICMP*
with the ICMP protocol to filter ping   *message types in Table 22-8.*

Extended IP ACL Example

Now that you have seen the syntax for creating extended numbered IP ACLs, take a look at a configuration example:

```
Router(config)# access-list 100 permit tcp
                         any 172.16.0.0 0.0.255.255
                         established log
Router(config)# access-list 100 permit udp
                         any host 172.16.1.1 eq dns log
Router(config)# access-list 100 permit tcp
                         172.17.0.0 0.0.255.255
                         host 172.16.1.2 eq telnet log
Router(config)# access-list 100 permit icmp
                         any 172.16.0.0 0.0.255.255
                         echo-reply log
Router(config)# access-list 100 deny ip any any log
Router(config)# interface ethernet 0
Router(config-if)# ip access-group 100 in
```

The assumption behind this example is that it is restricting what traffic can come into a network. The first statement says that if any TCP session has any source address and is destined to 172.16.0.0/16, it will be permitted if certain TCP flag bits are set (**established**) in the TCP segment header, indicative of returning traffic. Remember that the keyword **any** is the same as 0.0.0.0 255.255.255.255. Also, the **log** keyword will cause a match on this statement to be printed on the console. Since a TCP port isn't specified, all TCP connections will match on this statement.

The second line of this example allows a DNS query from any source device to be sent to an internal DNS server (172.16.1.1). Remember that the 0.0.0.0 wildcard mask is removed and the keyword **host** is inserted in the front of the IP address. A match on this statement is also logged.

The third line allows any telnet connection from devices in the 172.17.0.0/16 network if the destination device is 172.16.1.2. Remember that telnet uses TCP. A match on this statement is also logged.

The fourth line allows any replies to a ping to come back to devices with an address of 172.16.0.0/16. Note that only the echo replies are allowed—echoes are not allowed, preventing someone from this interface from executing pings. A match on this statement is also logged.

The fifth line isn't necessary because all traffic not matching on the previous **permit** statements will be dropped. However, if you want to log what is dropped, you'll need to configure this statement with the **log** parameter, as shown in the example. The last part of the configuration shows the ACL applied inbound on ethernet0.

Go back and look at the extended IP ACL example again and make sure you understand how the ACL functions.

Named ACLs

Starting with IOS 11.2, Cisco routers support both numbered and named ACLs. One of the original limitations of numbered ACLs was that you could create only so many of them. Originally, you could have only 99 standard IP ACLs and 100 extended IP ACLs. The additional numbers weren't added until the last few years. Starting with IOS 11.2, Cisco allowed you to use names to reference your ACLs instead of, or in combination with, numbered ACLs. Unlike in numbered ACLs, in named ACLs you can delete a single entry in the ACL without deleting the entire ACL.

Creating Named ACLs

To create a named IP ACL, use the following command:

```
Router(config)# ip access-list standard|extended ACL_name
```

The first thing you must specify is the type of ACL: standard or extended. Second, you must give the ACL a name that groups the ACL statements together. This name must be unique among all named ACLs. Once you enter this command, you are taken into the appropriate ACL Subconfiguration mode, as is shown here:

```
Router(config-std-acl)#
```

or

```
Router(config-ext-acl)#
```

Once you are in the Subconfiguration mode, you can enter your ACL commands. For a standard named ACL, use the following configuration:

```
Router(config)# ip access-list standard ACL_name
Router(config-std-acl)# permit|deny source_IP_address
                           [wildcard_mask]
```

For an extended named ACL, use the following configuration:

```
Router(config)# ip access-list extended ACL_name
Router(config-ext-acl)# permit|deny IP_protocol
                          source_IP_address wildcard_mask
                             [protocol_information]
                          destination_IP_address wildcard_mask
                             [protocol_information] [log]
```

As you can see, creating a standard or extended named IP ACL is similar to creating a numbered one. Once you have created your extended numbered IP ACL, you must activate it on your IOS device's interface with the **ip access-group** command, referencing a name instead of a number.

Example of a Named Access List

This example converts the extended IP numbered ACL from the "Extended IP ACL Example" section earlier in this chapter to a named ACL:

```
Router(config)# ip access-list extended do_not_enter
Router(config-ext-acl)# permit tcp any 172.16.0.0 0.0.255.255
                          established log
Router(config-ext-acl)# permit udp any
                          host 172.16.1.1 eq dns log
Router(config-ext-acl)# permit tcp 172.17.0.0 0.0.255.255
                          host 176.16.1.2 eq telnet log
Router(config-ext-acl)# permit icmp any 176.16.0.0 0.0.255.255
                          echo-reply log
Router(config-ext-acl)# deny ip any any log
Router(config)# interface ethernet 0
Router(config-if)# ip access-group do_not_enter in
```

Both this example and the numbered example do the *exact same thing*. Therefore, it is a matter of personal preference whether you use a named or numbered ACL. (My preference is to use numbered ACLs, if only because I've been using them since they first came out in IOS version 7.)

CertCam

22.05. The CD contains a multimedia demonstration of configuring a named IP ACL on a router.

ACL Remarks

Starting in IOS 12.0(2)T, you can embed remarks or comments within your ACL statements. Remarks work with named or numbered ACLs. Here's the configuration, based on whether you're using a numbered or named ACL:

```
Router(config)# access-list ACL_# remark remark
```

or

```
Router(config)# ip access-list standard|extended ACL_name
Router(config-{std|ext}-acl)# remark remark
```

The remark can be up to 100 characters in length.

on the **ĵob**

Go ahead and use copious remarks in your ACLs, since some ACLs can have thousands of statements in them! Without the remark feature, you would have an almost impossible task of determining what a statement or group of statements was doing when confronted with so many ACL entries.

Access List Verification

Once you have created and activated your ACLs, you can verify their configuration and operation with various **show** commands. One common command that you can use is the Privilege EXEC **show running-config** command, which will display your ACL and the interface or interfaces on which it is activated. However, you can use many other commands as well.

If you simply want to see which ACLs are activated on your router's interfaces, you can use the **show ip interfaces** command:

```
Router# show ip interfaces
Ethernet0 is up, line protocol is up
   Internet address is 172.16.1.1/24
   Broadcast address is 255.255.255.255
   Address determined by setup command
   MTU is 1500 bytes
   Helper address is not set
   Directed broadcast forwarding is disabled
   Outgoing access list is not set
   Inbound  access list is 100
   Proxy ARP is enabled
   .
   .
   .
```

From the output of this command, you can see that ACL 100, an extended numbered IP ACL, is applied inbound on ethernet0.

22.06. The CD contains a multimedia demonstration of using the show ip interfaces **command on a router to verify the activation of your ACLs.**

To view the statements in your ACLs, use either of the following two commands:

```
Router# show access-lists [ACL_#_or_name]
Router# show ip access-list [ACL_#_or_name]
```

Here is an example of the **show access-lists** command:

```
Router# show access-lists
Extended IP access list 100
    permit tcp 172.16.0.0 0.0.255.255 any established
        (189 matches)
```

```
permit udp host 172.16.1.39 any eq domain
    (32 matches)
permit icmp host 199.199.199.1 any
IPX sap access list 1000
 deny FFFFFFFF 7
 permit FFFFFFFF 0
```

First, notice that the router keeps track of matches on each statement. The first statement in ACL 100 has had 189 matches against it.

It is recommended that you put a `deny ip any any` *command at the end of an extended ACL, even though the implicit deny statement will drop the traffic. By putting this statement at the end of your ACL, you can see the hit counts of all the denied traffic: since the implicit deny command is invisible, you can't see the hit counts for it.*

You can clear these counters with this command:

```
Router# clear access-list counters [ACL_#_or_name]
```

Also notice that using the **show access-lists** command displays all ACLs from all protocols on your router. From the preceding output, two ACLs are shown: an extended numbered IP ACL and an IPX SAP ACL. If you want to view only ACLs for IP, use the following command:

```
Router# show ip access-list
Extended IP access list 100
    permit tcp 172.16.0.0 0.0.255.255 any established
        (189 matches)
    permit udp host 172.16.1.39 any eq domain
        (32 matches)
    permit icmp host 199.199.199.1 any
```

If you want to view only a particular ACL, use either of the following two commands:

```
Router# show access-lists 100
Extended IP access list 100
    permit tcp 172.16.0.0 0.0.255.255 any established
        (189 matches)
    permit udp host 172.16.1.39 any eq domain
        (32 matches)
    permit icmp host 199.199.199.1 any
```

or

```
Router# show ip access-list 100
      .
      .
      .
```

22.07. The CD contains a multimedia demonstration of using the `show [ip]` **`access-list` command on a router to verify the activation of your ACLs.**

Use the `show ip` `interfaces` command to see whether or not an IP ACL is applied to your router's interfaces. Use the `show access-lists` command to view all of the ACLs on your router. The `show ip access-list` lists only the IP ACLs on your router.

ACL Changes

Prior to the addition of the sequenced ACL feature, you basically had to make ACL changes in an external text editor such as Windows Notepad, delete the old ACL on the router, and paste in the new commands. However, starting in IOS 12.3, you can edit ACLs on your IOS device on the fly with the sequenced ACL feature. Sequenced ACLs allow you to insert and delete statements and remarks in an existing ACL.

With sequenced ACLs, each ACL command is given a unique sequence number. By default, the sequence numbers start at 10 and increment by 10. You know that your IOS device supports sequenced ACLs if you display them with the **show access-lists** command and you see sequence numbers in front of the ACL statements:

```
Router# show access-list
Extended IP access list 101
    10 permit ip host 192.168.101.69 any
    20 permit ip host 192.168.101.89 any
```

As you can see from this example, ACL 101 is using sequenced ACLs. The sequence numbers are added when the router boots up and loads the ACL or when you add or change the ACL from the CLI or SDM. Whenever you save the IOS's configuration to NVRAM, the sequence numbers are not stored with the ACL statements: Cisco implemented this feature for backward compatibility with older IOS versions that do not support sequenced ACLs.

Sequenced ACLs work with both named and numbered ACLs; however, to edit a numbered ACL, you must treat it as though it were a named ACL. Once you enter the ACL subcommand mode, you can delete an entry by prefacing the sequence number with the **no** command:

```
Router(config)# ip access-list {standard|extended} ACL_name_or_#
Router(config-{std|ext}-nacl)# no sequence_#
```

To insert a statement in an ACL, enter the ACL subcommand mode and preference the ACL statement with a sequence number that does not currently exist in the list of statements, like this:

```
Router(config)# ip access-list {standard|extended} ACL_name_or_#
Router(config-{std|ext}-nacl)#  sequence_# {permit|deny}
                        ACL_condition
```

Since sequence numbers increment by 10, if you need to insert more than nine statements in the same place in your ACL, you'll first need to resequence the entries in the list:

```
Router(config)# ip access-list resequence ACL_name_or_number
                     starting_seq_#    increment
```

With this command, you need to specify the initial sequence number, and then the increment. In the following example, the initial sequence number is 100 and the increment is 100:

```
Router (config)# ip access-list resequence 101 100 100
Extended IP access list 101
    100 permit ip host 192.168.101.69 any
    200 permit ip host 192.168.101.89 any
```

22.08. The CD contains a multimedia demonstration of the sequenced ACL feature.

CERTIFICATION OBJECTIVE 22.03

ACL Placement

This section covers design issues with ACLs—that is, where you should place ACLs of a given type (standard or extended). In other words, given the source and destination that you are filtering, on what router and what interface on that router should you activate your ACL? This section covers some of the important points you should consider when determining where to put your ACLs.

First, don't go crazy with ACLs and create dozens and dozens of them across all of your routers. This makes testing and troubleshooting your filtering rules almost impossible. In a campus network, for example, ACL configuration and filtering is on the layer 3 switch or router at the distribution layer that connects a building or floor to the campus backbone. This model was discussed in Chapter 14: the core, distribution, and access layers.

The second point is that you will want to limit the number of statements in your ACL. An ACL with hundreds of statements is almost impossible to test and troubleshoot. It's not unusual to see an ACL have a lot of unnecessary and overlapping commands that have been carried over from years past.

As to where you should place your ACLs, the following two rules hold true in most situations:

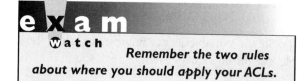

Remember the two rules about where you should apply your ACLs.

- Standard ACLs should be placed as close to the destination devices as possible.
- Extended ACLs should be placed as close to the source devices as possible.

Standard ACLs

You want to place standard ACLs as close to the destination that you want to prevent the source from reaching, since they allow you to filter only on the source IP address in the packet headers. If you put the standard ACL too close to the source, then you could be preventing the source from accessing other valid services in your network. By putting the standard ACL as close to the destination as possible, you are still allowing the source to access other resources, while restricting it from accessing the remote destination device or devices.

Let's take a look at an example to illustrate the placement of standard ACLs. Use the network shown in Figure 22-1. In this example, the user (192.168.5.1) should be prevented from accessing the server (192.168.1.1). Here is the ACL configuration:

```
Router(config)# access-list 1 deny host 192.168.5.1
Router(config)# access-list 1 permit any
```

As you can see from this example, the goal is to prevent 192.168.5.1 from accessing the server at 192.168.1.1, but to allow everyone else to access the server. Let's discuss the options for placing this ACL. Your first choice is to place this ACL on RouterC. If you placed it here, 192.168.5.1 would not be able to reach 192.168.1.1, but the user wouldn't be able to access anything else either. If you placed the ACL on RouterB, the user would be able to access the 192.168.4.0 network, but nothing else. You actually have two choices for placing the ACL on RouterA: interfaces E0 and E1. If you placed it inbound on E1, then the user wouldn't be able to access network 192.168.2.0. Therefore, you would have to place it outbound on E0 of RouterA.

Note that there is still an issue with using standard ACLs—any traffic from 192.168.5.1 is dropped as it attempts to leave this interface. So, the user is prevented from reaching not only the server but anything else on this segment. Another issue with standard ACLs, since you typically place them as close to the destination as possible, is that they are not very network-friendly: packets travel almost all of the way to the destination and *then* they are dropped. This wastes bandwidth in your network, especially if the source is sending a lot of traffic to the destination.

FIGURE 22-1   Placement of ACLs

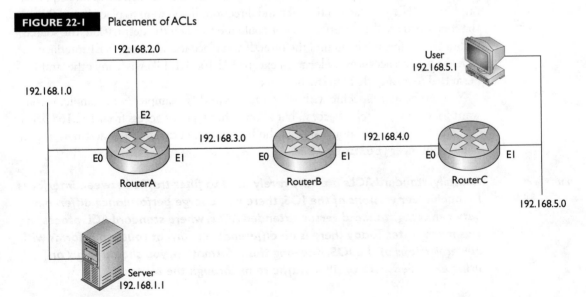

Extended ACLs

Given the preceding example, it would be much better to place the standard ACL as close to the source as possible to prevent unwanted traffic from traversing almost the whole network before being dropped. With a standard ACL, though, you would be preventing the user from accessing most of the resources in the network.

Extended ACLs, however, don't have this limitation, since they can filter on *both* the source and destination addresses in the IP packet headers. Given this ability, it is recommended that you place extended ACLs as *close* to the source as possible, thus preventing unwanted traffic from traversing your network. With an extended ACL, since you can filter on both addresses, you can prevent a source from accessing a particular destination or destinations but still allow it to access others.

With the preceding example, your configuration would look like this when using an extended ACL:

```
Router(config)# access-list 100 deny ip host 192.168.5.1
                                    host 192.168.1.1
Router(config)# access-list 100 permit ip any any
```

This configuration example is preventing only traffic from 192.168.5.1 to 192.168.1.1. Now the question is, where you should place this ACL? Again, you want to put this ACL as close to the source as possible. This means that you should place it on RouterC. RouterC has two interfaces, though. Again, remember that it should be placed as close to the source as possible. This means that the ACL should be placed on RouterC's E1 interface in the inbound direction. If you were to place it on E0, and the router had another interface that it could use to reach the destination, the source still might be able to get around the filter. If you place it on RouterC's E1 interface, 192.168.5.1 can access every location except 192.168.1.1. Likewise, any other traffic is permitted to go anywhere in the network.

You can be more specific with your filtering in this example. For example, if you want to restrict just telnet access, but allow other types of access from 192.168.5.1 to 192.168.1.1, then you should specify the IP protocol (**tcp**) and the destination port name or number (**telnet** or **23**).

on the
job
Actually, standard ACLs are very rarely used to filter traffic between interfaces. In much older versions of the IOS, there was a large performance difference between using standard versus extended ACLs, where standard ACL processing was much faster. Today there is no difference on current router platforms with newer versions of the IOS. Knowing this information, you should focus on using extended ACLs to filter traffic to or through the router.

INSIDE THE EXAM

ACL Overview

Don't be surprised to see a handful of questions on ACLs and ACL troubleshooting on the exam, where you'll see Cisco emphasize this topic more so than others, since ACLs are a commonly used tool on IOS devices. Remember that you can use ACLs for things other than filtering of traffic through the IOS device, such as restricting VTY access to the device. When filtering traffic, the inbound ACL is processed first before traffic is forwarded to a destination interface. Be able to compare and contrast standard and extended IP ACLs and the kinds of information each can filter. Be very familiar with how ACLs are processed and the order that statements occur in an ACL.

Basic ACL Configuration

Be very familiar with the syntax of both IP standard and extended ACLs, including the numbers allowed for both types. You need to be very comfortable with wildcard masks and how they are used to match on a range of addresses. Remember the trick of subtracting a subnet mask from a local broadcast address to get the corresponding wildcard mask. You might see troubleshooting questions in which the wildcard mask is configured incorrectly—be able to identify correct wildcard masks based on the range of addresses that will be matched on. Remember that ACLs are activated on interfaces inbound and/or outbound.

ACL Types

Remember that if you omit the wildcard mask in a standard ACL, it defaults to 0.0.0.0, a particular host—you might see a troubleshooting question related to this type of misconfiguration. Be able to troubleshoot problems based on ACL entries being placed in an incorrect order. Use the **access-class** command to restrict VTY access to an IOS device. Don't be surprised if you have to configure an actual ACL and activate it on a router's interface or VTY lines.

Be comfortable in examining extended ACL examples and determining what the ACL commands are actually filtering. You might also have to configure and activate an extended ACL on a router to filter traffic between locations. You should know how to create an ACL remark and use sequenced ACLs to edit existing ACLs. Be comfortable in using the **show** commands to examine and troubleshoot ACL configurations.

ACL Placement

Remember the two rules for where standard versus extended ACLs are placed:

- Standard ACLs should be placed as close to the *destination* devices as possible.
- Extended ACLs should be placed as close to the *source* devices as possible.

CERTIFICATION SUMMARY

ACLs can be used to filter traffic and routing information, restrict telnet and SSH access to your IOS device, prioritize traffic, trigger dial-on-demand routing (DDR) phone calls, and many other things. ACLs are statements grouped together by a number or name that defines traffic that should be permitted or denied. ACLs can be applied in either the inbound or outbound direction. With an inbound ACL, the ACL is processed first before any other processing is done on the packet. With an outbound ACL, the packet is routed to the outbound interface first and then the ACL is processed.

Standard IP ACLs allow you to filter on the source IP address, while extended IP ACLs allow you to filter on the source and destination IP addresses, the IP protocol, and protocol information (such as port numbers). ACLs are processed top-down until a match is found; at that point, no other statements are processed. Therefore, the order of the statements is important. If no match is found, the implicit deny rule takes place and the packet is dropped. You can have one ACL, per protocol, per interface, per direction on that interface. There are two special filtering rules for ACLs: you cannot filter traffic the router itself originates, and applying an empty ACL to an interface permits all traffic by default.

Standard ACLs can have numbers ranging from 1 to 99 and 1300 to 1999, and extended ACLs can have numbers ranging from 100 to 199 and 2000 to 2699. Standard ACLs should be placed as close to the destination as possible, while extended ACLs should be placed as close to the source as possible.

To create a numbered ACL, use the **access-list** command. Use the **ip access-group** command to activate your ACL on an interface. To filter telnet traffic to and from your router, activate the standard IP ACL on your VTY lines with the **access-class** command. When making changes to ACLs, use the sequenced ACL feature to insert new statements or delete existing ones. To create a named ACL, use the **ip access-list standard|extended** command. This will take you into the appropriate Subconfiguration mode.

Wildcard masks allow you to match a single address, a range of addresses, or all addresses. Basically, a wildcard mask is like an inverted subnet mask. A 0 in a bit position means match, and a 1 means ignore. To convert a subnet mask to a wildcard mask, subtract each octet in the subnet mask from 255, resulting in the corresponding octet value for the wildcard mask. With standard ACLs, if you omit the wildcard mask, it defaults to 0.0.0.0.

The **show ip interfaces** command will display any ACLs that have been activated on your router's interfaces. The **show access-lists** command displays all ACLs configured on your router for all protocols, including hit-count values for each statement in the list. The **show ip access-list** command displays only IP ACLs.

✓ TWO-MINUTE DRILL

ACL Overview

❑ ACLs allow you to filter traffic, restrict telnets to the router, filter routing information, prioritize WAN traffic, trigger dialup connections, change administrative distances of routes, and do many other things.

❑ ACLs can be created using either numbers or names and in two basic types: standard and extended. Standard ACLs allow you to filter only the source IP address, whereas extended IP ACLs allow you to filter on source and destination addresses, TCP/IP protocols, and protocol information.

❑ The router can take one of two actions when a match is found on an ACL: permit or deny. ACLs are processed top-down, where the order of the statements is important. Upon the first match, no other statements are processed.

❑ There is an implicit deny at the end of the list. You cannot filter traffic the router itself originates.

❑ When adding ACL statements, note that they are always added to the bottom. Only named ACLs allow you to delete a specific entry.

Basic ACL Configuration

❑ The **access-list** command creates an ACL and the **ip access-group** command activates the ACL on an interface. You can filter traffic as it enters (**in**) or leaves (**out**) an interface. To delete a complete access control list, use the **no access-list** command, followed by its number.

❑ Standard IP ACLs use numbers in the ranges 1–99 and 1300–1999, and extended IP ACLs use list numbers 100–199 and 2000–2699.

❑ A wildcard mask is like an inverted subnet mask. A 0 in a bit position of the wildcard mask means the corresponding bit position in the condition's address must match that in the IP packet. A 1 in a bit position of the wildcard mask means there doesn't have to be a match.

❑ A wildcard mask of 0.0.0.0 means that the entire address must match. Precede the word **host** before an address accomplishes the same thing. A wildcard mask of 255.255.255.255 indicates that any address matches: you can replace the address and wildcard mask with the keyword **any**.

❏ To invert a subnet mask into a wildcard mask, subtract each octet in the subnet mask from 255, which will result in the corresponding octet value for the wildcard mask.

ACL Types

❏ Standard ACLs can filter only on the source IP address. If you omit the wildcard mask, it defaults to 0.0.0.0. Use the **access-class** command to activate a standard ACL to restrict telnet access to a router.

❏ Use the **terminal monitor** command to view console output on non-console connections, such as VTYs.

❏ Extended IP ACLs allow you to filter on both the source and destination IP addresses (where you must specify the wildcard mask for both), the IP protocol (TCP, UDP, ICMP, and so on), and protocol information (such as ICMP message types or TCP and UDP source and destination port numbers). If you want to match on all IP traffic, use the keyword **ip** for the protocol parameter.

❏ Use the **ip access-list standard|extended** *ACL_name* command to create a named ACL. This takes you into the ACL Subconfiguration mode.

❏ Use the **remark** parameter to add a comment about an ACL statement or statements.

❏ The **show running-config** command will display your configured ACLs and the interfaces on which they are activated. The **show ip interfaces** command shows the ACLs activated on a router's interfaces. The **show [ip] access-lists** command displays the statements in a router's ACLs.

❏ ACLs support sequence numbers that allow you to delete an existing statement in the ACL or insert a statement in your current ACL configuration.

ACL Placement

❏ Standard ACLs should be placed as close to the *destination* devices as possible.

❏ Extended ACLs should be placed as close to the *source* devices as possible.

SELF TEST

The following Self Test questions will help you measure your understanding of the material presented in this chapter. Read all the choices carefully, as there may be more than one correct answer. Choose all correct answers for each question.

ACL Overview

1. Which of the following is not a feature of ACLs?

    A. Restricting telnet access to a router

    B. Prioritizing WAN traffic

    C. Filtering traffic from the router

    D. Triggering dialup phone calls

2. Which of the following is true concerning ACLs?

    A. The order of the statements is automatic.

    B. All statements are processed.

    C. If no match is found, the packet is permitted.

    D. You can delete a specific statement in a named list.

Basic ACL Configuration

3. Which command activates an IP ACL on a router's interface?

    A. `access-list`

    B. `ip access-group`

    C. `access-class`

    D. `access-group`

4. Enter the wildcard mask value to match on every bit position in an address: _____.

5. Enter the wildcard mask value for the subnet mask of 255.255.248.0: _____.

ACL Types

6. Which of the following can a standard IP ACL match on?

    A. Destination address

    B. IP protocol

    C. IP protocol information

    D. None of the above

7. Enter the standard IP ACL command to permit traffic from 192.168.1.0/24, using a list number of 10: _____.

8. Enter the extended IP ACL command to permit all ICMP traffic from 172.16.0.0/16 to 172.17.0.0/17, using a list number of 101: _____.

9. Enter the router command to activate an ACL with a name of test inbound on an interface: _____.

ACL Placement

10. Extended IP ACLs should be placed as close to the _____ device as possible.
   - A. Source
   - B. Destination

SELF TEST ANSWERS

ACL Overview

1. ☑ **C.** ACLs cannot filter outbound traffic the router originates, such as pings or traceroutes.
☒ **A, B,** and **D** are ACL features.

2. ☑ **D.** You can delete a specific ACL statement in a named ACL, but not a numbered ACL (unless using sequenced ACLs).
☒ **A** is not true because all statements are always added at the bottom of the ACL. **B** is not true because as soon as there is a statement match, no more statements are processed. **C** is not true because the implicit deny at the end of every ACL drops a non-matching packet.

Basic ACL Configuration

3. ☑ **B.** The `ip access-group` command activates an ACL on a router's interface.
☒ **A** is incorrect because it creates an ACL statement in a list. **C** is incorrect because it activates a standard ACL on a line, not an interface. **D** is a nonexistent command.

4. ☑ The value 0.0.0.0 is a wildcard mask that says to match on every bit position in an address.

5. ☒ The inverted subnet mask for 255.255.248.0 is 0.0.7.255. The trick is to subtract the subnet mask octets from 255.

ACL Types

6. ☑ **D.** Standard IP ACLs can match only on source IP addresses.
☒ **A, B,** and **C** are things extended IP ACLs can match on, but not standard IP ACLs.

7. ☑ `access-list 10 permit 192.168.1.0 0.0.0.255`.

8. ☒ `access-list 101 permit icmp 172.16.0.0 0.0.255.255 172.17.0.0 0.0.127.255` (notice the subnet mask value for 172.17.0.0, which is 17 bits!)

9. ☑ `ip access-group test in`.

ACL Placement

10. ☑ **A.** Extended IP ACLs should be placed as close to the source device as possible.
☒ **B** is true for standard ACLs.

23

Address Translation

C hapter 22 introduced you to access control lists (ACLs), an advanced feature of the router's Internetwork Operating System (IOS). This chapter covers one more advanced feature: *address translation*. Address translation allows you to change the source or destination address and/or port numbers inside an IP packet. This is typically done if you are using private IP addresses inside your network, or you have overlapping addresses when connecting two companies together. The first half of this chapter provides an overview of address translation, including the terms used and the different types of address translation. The second half of the chapter focuses on the configuration of address translation on an IOS router.

CERTIFICATION OBJECTIVE 23.01

Address Translation Overview

Address translation was originally developed to solve two problems: to handle a shortage of IPv4 addresses and hide network addressing schemes. Most people think that address translation is used primarily to solve the first problem. However, as the first half of this chapter illustrates, address translation provides solutions for many problems and has many advantages.

Running Out of Addresses

Because of the huge Internet explosion during the early and mid 1990s, it was foreseen that the current IP addressing scheme would not accommodate the number of devices that would need public addresses. A long-term solution was conceived to address this; it called for the enhancement of the TCP/IP protocol stack, including the addressing format. This new addressing format was called IPv6. Whereas the current IP addressing scheme (IPv4) used 32 bits to represent addresses, IPv6 uses 128 bits for addressing, creating billions of extra addresses. IPv6 is discussed in Chapter 24.

ⓦatch   *Small companies typically get their public IP addresses directly from their ISPs, which have a limited number. Large companies can sometimes get their public IP addresses from a registration authority, such as the Internet Assigned Numbers Authority (IANA).*

Private Addresses

It took a while for IPv6 to become a standard, and on top of this, its adoption early on was quite slow, even with ISPs on the Internet backbone. The main reason that this standard wasn't embraced for a long time is the success of the two short-term solutions to the address shortage problem: schemes to create additional addresses, called *private addresses*, and translation of these addresses to public addresses using address translation.

RFC 1918, by the Internet Engineering Task Force (IETF), is a document that was created to address the shortage of addresses. When devices want to communicate, each device needs a unique IP address. RFC 1918 created a private address space that any company can use internally. Table 23-1 shows the range of private addresses that RFC 1918 set aside. As you can see from this table, you have 1 Class A, 16 Class B, and 256 Class C addresses at your disposal. Just the single Class A address of 10.0.0.0 has more than 17 million IP addresses, more than enough to accommodate your company's needs.

e x a m
ⓦ a t c h

Remember the private addresses listed in Table 23-1. Private addresses are a scheme developed by IETF to overcome the limited number of available public IP addresses; however, private addresses cannot be placed in packets that will be routed to a public network: they must be translated first. Translation typically takes place on a perimeter device, such as a router or security appliance (such as the ASA or PIX).

One of the main issues of RFC 1918 addresses is that they can be used only internally within a company and cannot be used to communicate to devices in a public network, such as the Internet. For this reason, they are commonly referred to as *private addresses*. If you send packets with RFC 1918 addresses in them to your ISP,

TABLE 23-1	Class	Range of Addresses
RFC 1918 Private Addresses	A	10.0.0.0–10.255.255.255
	B	172.16.0.0–172.31.255.255
	C	192.168.0.0–192.168.255.255

for instance, your ISP will either filter them or not be able to route this traffic back to your devices. Obviously, this creates a connectivity problem, since many of your devices with private addresses need to send and receive traffic from public networks.

Address Translation

A second standard, RFC 1631, was created to solve this problem. It defines a process called *Network Address Translation* (NAT), which allows you to change an IP address in a packet to a different address. When communicating to devices in a public network, your device needs to use a source address that is a public address. Address translation allows you to translate your internal private addresses to public addresses before these packets leave your network.

on the *Job*

Common devices that can perform address translation include firewalls, routers, and servers. Typically address translation is done at the perimeter of the network by either a firewall (more commonly) or a router.

Actually, RFC 1631 doesn't specify that the address you are changing has to be a private address—it can be *any* address. This is useful if you randomly chose someone else's public address space but still want to connect to the Internet. Obviously, you don't own this address space, but address translation allows you to keep your current addressing scheme but translate these source addresses to those your ISP assigned to you before your packets enter the Internet.

Here are some common reasons that you might need to employ address translation:

- You have to use private addressing because your ISP didn't assign you enough public IPv4 addresses.
- You are using public addresses but have changed ISPs, and your new ISP won't support these public addresses.
- You are merging two companies and they are using the same address space—for instance, 10.0.0.0—which creates routing and reachability issues.
- You want to assign the same IP address to multiple machines so that users on the Internet see this offered service as a single logical computer.

CERTIFICATION OBJECTIVE 23.02

Address Translation Types

Address translation comes in a variety of types, such as NAT, Port Address Translation (PAT), dynamic address translation, and static address translation. Because of the many terms used, the concept of address translation can be confusing, especially since many people use the address translation terms incorrectly. The following sections cover the different types of address translation.

Terms and Definitions

Table 23-2 shows some common terms used in address translation, and Table 23-3 shows some terms used for types of address translation.

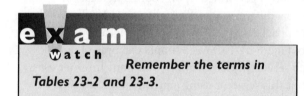

e x a m

ⓦatch   *Remember the terms in Tables 23-2 and 23-3.*

Network Address Translation

NAT translates one IP address to another. This can be a source address or a destination address. Two basic implementations of NAT can be used: *static* and *dynamic*. The following sections cover the mechanics of these implementations.

TABLE 23-2	Term	Definition
Common Address Translation Terms	Inside	Addresses located on the inside of your network
	Outside	Addresses located outside of your network
	Local	The IP address physically assigned to a device
	Global	The public IP address physically or logically assigned to a device
	Inside local IP address	An inside device with an assigned private IP address
	Inside global IP address	An inside device with a registered public IP address
	Outside global IP address	An outside device with a registered public IP address
	Outside local IP address	An outside device with an assigned private IP address

TABLE 23-3	Translation Type	Explanation
Common Address Translation Types	Simple	One IP address is translated to a different IP address.
	Extended	One IP address and one TCP/UDP port number are mapped to a different IP address and, possibly, port number.
	Static	A manual address translation is performed between two addresses and possibly port numbers.
	Dynamic	An address translation device automatically performs address translation between two addresses and possibly port numbers.
	Network Address Translation (NAT)	Only IP addresses are translated (not port numbers).
	Port Address Translation (PAT)	Many inside IP addresses are translated to a single IP address, where each inside address is given a different TCP or UDP port number for uniqueness.

Static NAT

With static NAT, a manual translation is performed by an address translation device, translating one IP address to a different one. Typically, static NAT is used to translate destination IP addresses in packets as they come into your network, but you can translate source addresses also. Figure 23-1 shows a simple example of outside users trying to access an inside web server. In this example, you want Internet users to access an internal web server, but this server is using a private address (10.1.1.1).

FIGURE 23-1

Static NAT example

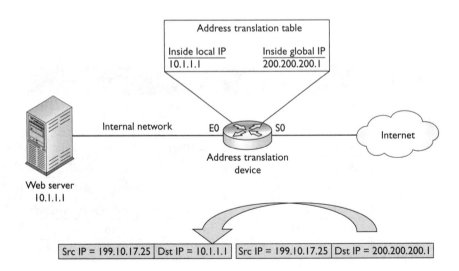

This creates a problem, since if an outside user would put a private address in the destination IP address field, their ISP would drop this. Therefore, the web server needs to be presented as having a public address. This is defined in the address translation device (in this case, it is a Cisco router).

The web server is assigned an inside global IP address of 200.200.200.1 on the router, and your DNS server advertises this address to the outside users. When outside users send packets to the 200.200.200.1 address, the router examines its translation table for a matching entry. In this case, it sees that 200.200.200.1 maps to 10.1.1.1. The router then changes the destination IP address to 10.1.1.1 and forwards it to the inside web server. Note that if the router didn't do the translation to 10.1.1.1, the web server wouldn't know this information was meant for itself, since the outside user sent the traffic originally to 200.200.200.1. Likewise, when the web server sends traffic out to the public network, the router compares the *source* IP address to entries in its translation table, and if it finds a match, it changes the inside local IP address (private source address, 10.1.1.1) to the inside global IP address (public source address, 200.200.200.1).

Dynamic NAT

With static address translation, you need to build the translations manually. If you have 1000 devices, you need to create 1000 static entries in the address translation table, which is a lot of work. Typically, static translation is done for inside resources that outside people want to access. When inside users access outside resources, dynamic translation is typically used. In this situation, the global address assigned to the internal user isn't that important, since outside devices don't directly connect to your internal users—they just return traffic to them that the inside user requested.

With dynamic NAT, you must manually define two sets of addresses on your address translation device. One set defines which inside addresses are allowed to be translated (the local addresses), and the other defines what these addresses are to be translated to (the global addresses). When an inside user sends traffic through the address translation device, say a router, it examines the source IP address and compares it to the internal local address pool. If it finds a match, then it determines which inside global address pool it should use for the translation. It then dynamically picks an address in the global address pool that is not currently assigned to an inside device. The router adds this entry in its address translation table, the packet is translated, and the packet is then sent to the outside world. If no matching entry is found in the local address pool, the address is not translated and is forwarded to the outside world in its original state.

When returning traffic comes back into your network, the address translation device examines the destination IP addresses and checks them against the address translation table. Upon finding a matching entry, it converts the global inside address to the local inside address in the destination IP address field of the packet header and forwards the packet to the inside network.

Port Address Translation

One problem with static or dynamic NAT is that it provides only a one-to-one address translation. Therefore, if you have 5000 internal devices with private addresses, and all 5000 devices try to reach the Internet simultaneously, you need 5000 public addresses in your inside global address pool. If you have only 1000 public addresses, only the first 1000 devices are translated and the remaining 4000 won't be able to reach outside destinations. To overcome this problem, you can use a process called *address overloading*. Many other terms are used to describe this process, including port address translation (PAT) and network address port translation (NAPT).

Same IP Address, Different Port Numbers

With PAT, all devices that go through the address translation device have the same global IP address assigned to them, so the source TCP or UDP port numbers are used to differentiate the different connections. If two devices have the same source port number, the translation device changes one of them to ensure uniqueness. When you look at the translation table in the address translation device, you'll see the following items when PAT is performed on a packet:

- Inside local IP address (original source private IP)
- Inside local port number (original source port number)
- Inside global IP address (translated public source IP)

- Inside global port number (new source port number)
- Outside global IP address (destination public address)
- Outside global port number (destination port number)

One main advantage of NAT over PAT is that NAT will basically work with most types of IP connections. Since PAT relies on port numbers to differentiate connections, PAT works only with TCP and UDP; however, many vendors, including Cisco, also support ICMP with PAT using a proprietary translation method.

on the **Job**

Most vendors use the sequence number in an ICMP echo message, along with the source address, to uniquely identify a translation for ICMP traffic.

Example Using PAT

Let's take a look at an example using PAT, shown in Figure 23-2. In this example, both PCs execute a telnet to 199.199.199.1, and both of these connections use a source port number of 50,000. When these connections reach the address translation device, the translation device performs its PAT translation. For the first connection, say PC-A, the source IP address (inside local) is changed to 200.200.200.7 (inside global). Since this is the first connection and the source port is not found in the

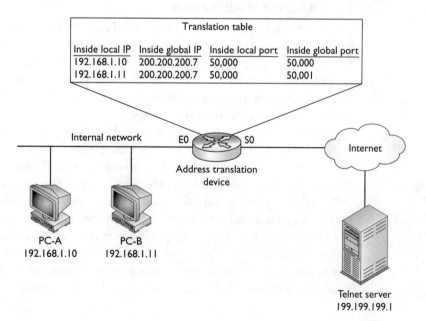

FIGURE 23-2

PAT example

Translation table

Inside local IP	Inside global IP	Inside local port	Inside global port
192.168.1.10	200.200.200.7	50,000	50,000
192.168.1.11	200.200.200.7	50,000	50,001

Internal network   E0   S0   Internet

Address translation
device

PC-A
192.168.1.10

PC-B
192.168.1.11

Telnet server
199.199.199.1

translation table, the source port number is left as is. When PC-B makes a telnet connection to the remote device, since it is using a source port number (50,000) already in the table for a connection to the telnet server, the address translation device changes it from 50,000 to an unused one in the translation table, for example, 50,001. Therefore, when traffic is sent from the telnet server to the inside PCs, the address translation device will be able to differentiate the two connections and undo the translation correctly by examining both the destination IP address *and* port number in the telnet reply packets: the destination port of 50,000 will be redirected to PC-A and the destination port of 50,001 will be changed back to 50,000 and redirected to PC-B. In both cases, the destination IP address is also changed to the inside local address of the device to which the packet will be forwarded.

on the

job

Since the port number in the TCP and UDP header is 16 bits in length, you can theoretically represent 65,536 internal connections with a single public IP address. However, in reality, this number is about 4,000 to 16,000 connections per public address because many port numbers are reserved or private. Note that you don't have to restrict yourself to one type of address translation process. For instance, you can use PAT for inside-to-outside connections and static NAT for outside-to-inside connections.

Port Address Redirection

The last example showed PAT being carried out dynamically by the address translation device. In some situations, however, this will not work. For instance, your ISP might assign you a single public IP address. You need to use this with PAT to allow inside users to access outside resources. However, you have a problem if you want outside users to access an internal service, such as a web server. Dynamic PAT, unfortunately, won't work in this situation.

Another solution to this problem is available: static PAT, often called *port address redirection* (PAR). Let's look at a simple example to illustrate how PAR works. Assume that your ISP has assigned you a single public IP address: 199.199.199.1. You need to use this address for inside users to access the outside world, but you still need the outside world to access an internal web server. With static PAT, you set up your address translation device to look not only at the destination IP address (199.199.199.1), but also the destination port number (80 for a web server). You create a static PAT entry such that when the address translation device sees this combination of address and port numbers, the device translates it to the inside local IP address and, possibly, the port number used for the service on this inside device.

For example, assume you are given the network shown in Figure 23-1. In this example, your ISP has assigned you a single IP address, 200.200.200.1, and this address must be configured on your router's S0 interface. This presents a problem in this example, since you have an internal web server that you want external users to access. Port address redirection can be used to overcome this problem. You would set up a static PAT entry on your router that would take TCP traffic sent to 200.200.200.1 on port 80 and redirect it to 10.1.1.1 on port 80. Without PAR, the router would try to process the web connection itself since this IP address is assigned to its own local interface.

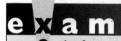

Port address redirection allows you to redirect application traffic directed to one address to a different address.

Advantages of Address Translation

As mentioned at the beginning of this part of the chapter, address translation devices are typically used to give you an almost inexhaustible number of addresses as well as to hide your internal network addressing scheme. Another advantage of address translation is that if you change ISPs or merge with another company, you can keep your current addressing scheme and make any necessary changes on your address translation device or devices, making your address management easier.

Another big advantage that address translation provides is that it gives you tighter control over traffic entering and leaving your network. For example, if you are using private addresses internally, all traffic entering and leaving must pass through an address translation device. Because of this restriction, it is much easier to implement your security and business policies.

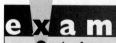

Advantages of address translation include conservation of public addresses, protection of resources with private addresses from external devices, and no need for readdressing of devices when switching from one ISP to another.

Disadvantages of Address Translation

Even though address translation solves many problems and has many advantages, it also has its share of disadvantages. Here are the three main issues with address translation:

- Each connection has an added delay.
- Troubleshooting is more difficult.
- Not all applications work with address translation.

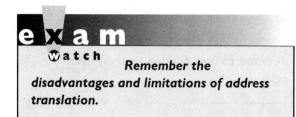

Remember the disadvantages and limitations of address translation.

Since address translation changes the contents of packets and, possibly, segment headers, as well as computing any necessary new checksum values, extra processing is required on each packet. This extra processing, obviously, will affect the throughput and speed of your connections. The more packets that pass through your address translation device needing translation, the more likely your users will notice the delay. Therefore, choosing the appropriate product for address translation becomes very important.

Whenever problems arise with connections involving address translation, it is more difficult to troubleshoot them. When troubleshooting, it becomes more difficult to track down the real source and destination of a connection—you have to log into your address translation device and look at your translation tables. And if the packet is going through multiple layers of translation, possibly at both the source and destination sites, this can be a hair-pulling experience. Also, even though one of the advantages of address translation is that it hides your internal addressing scheme, it also creates security issues—an external hacker can more easily hide his identity by sending his packets through a translation device or multiple translation devices, trying to hide his true IP address.

Probably the most difficult issue with address translation is that not all applications will work with it. For instance, some applications embed IP addressing or port information in the actual data payload (such as FTP, for example), expecting the destination device to use this addressing information in the payload instead of what is in the packet and segment headers. This can pose a problem with address translation, since address translation, by default, doesn't translate data payload information, only header information. Multimedia and NetBIOS applications are notorious for embedding addressing information in data payloads. In some instances, some vendors' address translation devices can detect this process for certain applications and fix it when building the appropriate translation in the translation table. For instance, Cisco routers with the IOS firewall feature set and PIX and ASA security appliances support a fix-up process that covers many of these application issues, including embedded addressing information. However, if your product doesn't support this feature, you'll need to disable address translation for the affected devices.

CERTIFICATION OBJECTIVE 23.03

Address Translation Configuration

The configuration of the different types of address translation, such as NAT and PAT, is very similar. The following sections cover the configuration and verification of some of the types of address translation discussed so far.

on the job

Even though Cisco routers support address translation capabilities, by far the address translation features of the ASA and PIX security appliances provide more granularity and flexibility in implementing your address translation policies than do Cisco routers. For more complex address translation policy configurations on Cisco routers, read my book with Cisco Press, Cisco Router Firewall Security *(ISBN: 1587051753). For information on configuring address translation on PIXs and ASAs, read my book with McGraw-Hill,* Cisco PIX Firewalls *(ISBN: 0072225238).*

NAT Configuration

As mentioned, the two types of NAT are static and dynamic. The configuration process is similar for both types. Probably the most difficult process of configuring address translation is understanding the difference between the terms *inside* and *outside*. These terms refer to where your devices are located (inside) and where the external network (the Internet, for instance) is (outside). This is important when it comes to the configuration of address translation. In the IOS, you must perform two basic configuration steps:

- Define the address translation type (Global Configuration mode commands).
- Define the location of devices (Interface Subconfiguration mode commands).

The following sections cover the configuration of both static and dynamic NAT.

Configuring Static NAT

As mentioned earlier, static NAT is typically used when devices on the outside of your network want to access resources, such as web, DNS, and e-mail servers, on the inside. Here are the two commands used to define the static translations for NAT:

```
Router(config)# ip nat inside source static
                    inside_local_source_IP_address
                    inside_global_source_IP_address
Router(config)# ip nat outside source static
                    outside_global_destination_IP_address
                    outside_local_destination_IP_address
```

The **inside** and **outside** parameters specify the direction in which translation will occur. For instance, the **inside** keyword specifies that the inside source local IP addresses are translated to an inside global IP address when *leaving* the network; and the destination global IP addresses are translated to inside local IP addresses when *entering* your network. The **outside** keyword changes the outside *destination* global IP address to an outside local address (the latter command is used when you are connecting two company networks together and their addresses overlap).

After you configure your translations, you must specify which interfaces on your router are considered to be on the inside and which are on the outside. This is done with the following configuration:

```
Router(config)# interface type [slot_#/]port_#
Router(config-if)# ip nat inside|outside
```

Specify **inside** for interfaces connected to the inside of your network and **outside** for interfaces connected to external networks, such as your ISP.

Let's take a look a simple static NAT example. I'll use the network shown in Figure 23-3 for this example. In this example, an internal web server (192.168.1.1) will

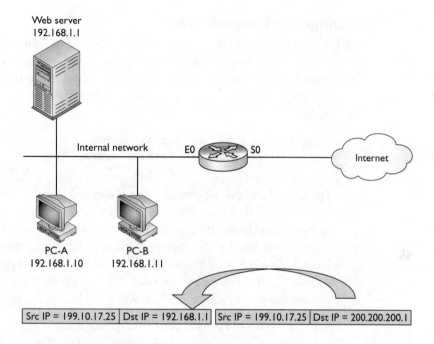

FIGURE 23-3

Network
translation
example

be assigned a global IP address of 200.200.200.1. Here's the router's configuration to
accomplish this static translation:

```
Router(config)# ip nat inside source static
                    192.168.1.1 200.200.200.1
Router(config)# interface ethernet 0
Router(config-if)# ip nat inside
Router(config-if)# exit
Router(config)# interface serial 0
Router(config-if)# ip nat outside
```

The **ip nat inside source static** command defines the translation.
The **ip nat inside** and **outside** commands specify what interfaces are on
the inside (E0) and what interfaces are on the outside (S0). Note that any packets
that don't match the address translation rule will pass between these two interfaces
untranslated. If you want only translated packets to pass between these interfaces,
you'll need to configure an appropriate ACL or ACLs.

**23.01. The CD contains a multimedia demonstration of configuring static NAT
on a router.**

Configuring Dynamic NAT

When you are configuring dynamic NAT, you'll need to configure three things: what inside addresses are to be translated, what global addresses will be used for the dynamic translation, and what interfaces are involved in the translation. To specify what internal devices will have their source address translated, use the following command:

```
Router(config)# ip nat inside source
                  list standard_IP_ACL_name_or_#
                  pool NAT_pool_name
```

The **ip nat inside source list** command requires you to configure a standard IP ACL that has a list of the inside source addresses that will be translated—any addresses listed with a **permit** statement will be translated, and any addresses listed with a **deny**, or the implicit deny, statement will not be translated. Following this is the name of the address pool: this ties together the address pool you'll use that contains your global source IP addresses.

To create the pool of source inside global IP addresses, use this command:

```
Router(config)# ip nat pool NAT_pool_name
                  beginning_inside_global_IP_address
                  ending_inside_global_IP_address
                  netmask subnet_mask_of_addresses
```

The pool name that you specify references the inside addresses that will be translated from the **ip nat inside source list** command. Next, list the beginning and ending IP addresses in the pool, followed by the subnet mask for the addresses. Once you have done this, the last thing you need to configure is which interfaces are considered to be on the inside and outside of your network. Use the **ip nat inside** and **ip nat outside** Interface Subconfiguration mode commands discussed earlier.

---

exam

🅦 **a t c h**   *The ip nat inside source list command specifies which internal addresses will be dynamically translated. Remember that translation takes place only when a packet matches a permit statement in the ACL: matching a deny statement or the implicit deny exempts the packet from translation. The ip nat pool command specifies the global addresses to use when performing dynamic translation of local addresses.*

The network shown in Figure 23-3 is used to illustrate how dynamic NAT is configured. In this example, the two PCs will have dynamic NAT performed on them.

```
Router(config)# ip nat inside source list 1 pool nat-pool
Router(config)# access-list 1 permit host 192.168.1.10
Router(config)# access-list 1 permit host 192.168.1.11
Router(config)# ip nat pool nat-pool 200.200.200.2
                        200.200.200.3 netmask 255.255.255.0
Router(config)# interface ethernet 0
Router(config-if)# ip nat inside
Router(config-if)# exit
Router(config)# interface serial 0
Router(config-if)# ip nat outside
```

The **ip nat inside source list** command specifies the inside source IP addresses that will be translated. Notice that these are addresses in ACL 1— 192.168.1.10 and 192.168.1.11. They are associated with the global address pool called *nat-pool*. The **ip nat pool** command specifies the global addresses that the inside source addresses will be translated to. And finally, ethernet0 is specified as being on the inside and serial0 is on the outside.

23.02. The CD contains a multimedia demonstration of configuring dynamic NAT on a router.

PAT Configuration

The last example showed an example of dynamic NAT. This section covers how to configure PAT on your router. This configuration, which is very similar to configuring dynamic NAT, requires three basic translation commands. The first thing you specify is which inside devices will have their source addresses translated. You'll use the same command as you used in dynamic NAT, but you'll add the **overload** parameter to specify that PAT is to be performed:

```
Router(config)# ip nat inside source
                    list standard_IP_ACL_#
                    pool NAT_pool_name overload
```

Next, you specify the global pool to use. Again, you'll use the same command you used in dynamic NAT:

```
Router(config)# ip nat pool NAT_pool_name
                    beginning_inside_global_IP_address
                    ending_inside_global_IP_address
                    netmask subnet_mask_of_addresses
```

You can specify more than one address to use in PAT, or you can specify a single IP address (use the same address for the beginning and ending addresses). And last, you have to tell the IOS which interfaces are inside and outside, respectively, in terms of the **ip nat inside** and **ip nat outside** commands.

Now we'll use Figure 23-3 to see how PAT is configured. In this example, 200.200.200.1 is being used in the static translation for the internal server. Only a single, additional, IP address is placed in the address pool (200.200.200.2) and the address translation is restricted to performing PAT for only two devices: 192.168.1.10 and 192.168.1.11. Here's the configuration:

```
Router(config)# ip nat inside source list 1 pool
                       nat-pool overload
Router(config)# access-list 1 permit host 192.168.1.10
Router(config)# access-list 1 permit host 192.168.1.11
Router(config)# ip nat pool nat-pool 200.200.200.2
                       200.200.200.2
                       netmask 255.255.255.0
Router(config)# interface ethernet 0
Router(config-if)# ip nat inside
Router(config-if)# exit
Router(config)# interface serial 0
Router(config-if)# ip nat outside
```

23.03. The CD contains a multimedia demonstration of configuring PAT on a router.

Address Translation Verification

Once you have configured address translation, you can use many different commands to verify and troubleshoot the operation of address translation on your router. For instance, if you want to see the address translation table on your router, use the **show ip nat translations** command:

```
Router# show ip nat translations
Pro  Inside global  Inside local  Outside local  Outside global
---  200.200.200.1  192.168.1.1   ---            ---
---  200.200.200.2  192.168.1.2   ---            ---
```

In this example, two addresses are being translated: 192.168.1.1 (inside local) to 200.200.200.1 (inside global) and 192.168.1.2 (inside local) to 200.200.200.2

(inside global). Notice that no protocol is listed (`Pro`) or port numbers, indicating that these are NAT translations, not PAT.

Here's an example of the **show** command with PAT translations in the translation table:

```
Router# show ip nat translations
Pro Inside global     Inside local    Outside local Outside global
tcp 200.200.200.1:1080 192.168.1.1:1080 201.1.1.1:23   201.1.1.1:23
tcp 200.200.200.1:1081 192.168.1.2:1080 201.1.1.1:23   201.1.1.1:23
```

In this example, both 192.168.1.1 and 192.168.1.2 are accessing the same outside device (201.1.1.1) using telnet. Notice that both also use the same source port number (1080 under the `Inside local` column). The IOS has noticed this and changed the second connection's source port number from 1080 to 1081 in order to differentiate the two connections.

CertCam

23.04. The CD contains a multimedia demonstration of the `show ip nat translations` command on a router.

You can even see address translations statistics on your router with this command:

```
Router# show ip nat statistics
Total translations: 2 (0 static, 2 dynamic; 0 extended)
Outside interfaces: Serial0
Inside interfaces: Ethernet0
Hits: 98 Misses: 4
Expired translations: 1
Dynamic mappings:
-- Inside Source
access-list 1 pool nat-pool refcount 2
pool nat-pool: netmask 255.255.255.255
start 200.200.200.10 end 200.200.200.254
type generic, total addresses 12, allocated 1 (9%), misses 0
```

In this example, there are currently two dynamic translations in the translation table. `Hits` refers to the number of times the IOS looked into the translation table and found a match (an existing translation that can be used for the packet), while `Misses` indicates the number of times the IOS looked in the table for a translation, didn't find one, and had to create an entry in the translation table for the packet.

CertCam

23.05. The CD contains a multimedia demonstration of the `show ip nat statistics` command on a router.

For dynamic entries in the translation table, you can clear all of the entries, or specific entries, using the following commands:

```
Router# clear ip nat translation *
Router# clear ip nat translation inside
                    global_IP_address local_IP_address
Router# clear ip nat translation outside
                    global_IP_address local_IP_address
Router# clear ip nat translation protocol inside
                    global_IP_address global_port
                    local_IP_address local_port
```

The first command clears all dynamic entries in the table. Note that to clear static entries, you need to delete your static NAT configuration commands from within Configuration mode.

CertCam

23.06. The CD contains a multimedia demonstration of the `clear ip nat translation` *command on a router.*

In addition to **show** commands, you can also use **debug** commands for troubleshooting. The **debug ip nat** command, for instance, will show the translations the IOS is doing on every translated packet. This is useful in determining whether the IOS is translating your packet and segment header addressing information correctly. Please note that on a busy network, this command will require a lot of CPU cycles on your router.

e x a m
ⓦatch

Use the `show ip nat translations` command to display the router's translations. Use the `clear ip nat translations` command to clear dynamic translations from the translation table. The `debug ip nat` command shows the router performing address translation in a real-time fashion.

Here's an example of the **debug ip nat** command:

```
Router# debug ip nat
05:32:23: NAT: s=192.168.1.10->200.200.200.2, d=201.1.1.1 [70]
05:32:23: NAT*: s=201.1.1.1, d=200.200.200.2->192.168.1.10 [70]
```

In the first line of this example, an internal machine (192.168.1.10), which is the source address in the packet (s=), is having its address translated to 200.200.200.2 where the packet is being sent to the destination of 201.1.1.1 (d=). The second line shows the returning traffic from 201.1.1.1 and the translation from the global to the local inside address. An asterisk (*) indicates that the packet was fast-switched. The number in the brackets ([]) is an identification number of the packet and can be used to correlate this information to packet traces done with an external protocol analyzer or sniffer product.

You can add the `detailed` *parameter to the* `debug ip nat` *command that displays a description of each packet that is a candidate for translation, as well as any errors, such as no more addresses in the global pool to assign to an outbound user.*

23.07. The CD contains a multimedia demonstration of the `debug ip nat` *command on a router.*

CERTIFICATION OBJECTIVE 23.04

Translation Process and Troubleshooting

When troubleshooting problems, it is important that you understand the order of features the router goes through when processing a packet. The following sections discuss the steps the routers take before address translation actually takes place.

Local-to-Global Translation

In *local-to-global translation*, the packets are being translated from the inside to the outside. Here are the steps the IOS takes in processing a packet from an inside interface to an outside interface, including any necessary address translation:

1. If an inbound ACL is applied to the inbound interface, the ACL is processed.
2. If you've configured IPSec (discussed in Chapter 25), crypto ACLs are checked to see whether the encrypted traffic terminates on the router; if so, the router decrypts the packets.
3. If any inbound rate limit policies are configured, these are then processed and enforced.
4. If input accounting is enabled, it is performed.
5. If policy routing is configured, this is performed.

6. The packet is routed to the correct interface.

7. The packet is compared to the inside-to-outside NAT rules to see whether address translation is necessary; if so, translation takes place.

8. If you've configured IPSec, crypto ACLs are checked to see whether the packet needs to traverse a tunnel to a remote destination; if so, the packet is encrypted.

9. If an outbound ACL on the outside interface is configured, the packet is checked to make sure it is allowed to leave the router.

Global-to-Local Translation

In *global-to-local translation*, the packets are being translated from the outside to the inside. Here are the steps the IOS takes in processing a packet from an outside interface to an inside interface, including any necessary address translation:

1. If an inbound ACL is applied to the inbound interface, the ACL is processed.

2. If you have IPSec configured on the router, the packet is compared to the crypto ACLs and any necessary de-encryption is performed on protected packets.

3. If any inbound rate limit policies are configured, these are processed and enforced.

4. If input accounting is enabled, it is performed.

5. If the traffic matches an address translation policy, the global-to-local translation takes place.

6. If policy routing is configured, this is performed.

7. The packet is routed to the correct interface.

8. If you've configured IPSec, crypto ACLs are checked to see whether the packet needs to traverse a tunnel to a remote destination; if so, the packet is marked for encryption.

9. If an outbound ACL on the outside interface is configured, the packet is checked to make sure it is allowed to leave the router.

10. If context-based access control (CBAC) is configured, the inspection process on the packet takes place.

11. If TCP intercept is configured, the packet is compared to the thresholds to deal with TCP SYN flood attacks.

12. If encryption is necessary, it is performed.

13. The packet is queued up on the inside interface and then processed.

Address Translation Troubleshooting

Troubleshooting problems of traffic flowing through a router is not necessarily an easy task. It can become complicated depending on what features you have enabled, as you can see from the preceding two sections. Follow these steps when troubleshooting problems you think are related to address translation:

1. Verify your NAT commands to ensure that your configuration is correct, including the ACL with the **permit** statements that specify traffic that should be dynamically translated.

2. Check to see whether the router is actually translating the packets for the user with the **show ip nat translations** command.

3. Use the **show ip nat statistics** command to see whether translations are actually occurring—remember that the output is static and you'll need to re-execute it multiple times to update the statistics. For example, by sending 5 ICMP echoes through the router that match a NAT translation rule, you should see the hit-count increment by 5.

4. Use the **debug ip nat [detailed]** command to see if translation is occurring or not; make sure enough addresses are available in a corresponding global NAT pool when performing dynamic NAT.

5. Verify that you have correctly configured the router's interfaces for NAT as inside or outside with the **ip nat inside** and **ip nat outside** Interface Subconfiguration mode command.

6. Use the **show access-lists** command to see if hit counts appear on the permit statements for packets that should be translated.

7. Make sure the router can route the packet to the destination by looking at the routing table: **show ip route**.

8. If the packet is being translated, but you are not getting any replies for the user traffic, such as echo replies when using ping, examine any ACLs on the router to make sure that the traffic can get back through the router with the **show access-lists** command: look for incrementing hit counts on **deny** statements.

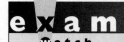

Be comfortable with the troubleshooting steps listed here *in troubleshooting address translation problems.*

EXERCISE 23-1

Configuring Static Address Translation

The last few sections dealt with the configuration of address translation on IOS routers. This exercise will help you reinforce this material by configuring a simple static NAT translation. You'll perform this lab using Boson's NetSim simulator. You can find a picture of the network diagram for Boson's NetSim simulator in the Introduction of this book. This exercise has you first set static routes on the two routers (2600-1 and 2600-2) and verify network connectivity. Following this, you'll configure your translation policy. After starting up the simulator, click the Lab Navigator button. Next, double-click Exercise 23-1 and click the Load Lab button. This will load the lab configuration based on the exercises in Chapters 11 and 16.

1. On the 2600-2, configure a static route to 192.168.1.0/24, which is off of the 2600-1. View the routing table.

    At the top of the simulator in the menu bar, click the eRouters icon and choose 2600-2. Configure the static route: `configure terminal`, `ip route 192.168.1.0 255.255.255.0 192.168.2.1`, and `end`. View the static route: `show ip route`. Make sure that 192.168.1.0/24 shows up in the routing table as a static route (`S`).

2. On the 2600-1, configure a static route to 192.168.3.0/24, which is off of the 2600-2. View the routing table.

    At the top of the simulator in the menu bar, click the eRouters icon and choose 2600-1. Configure the static route: `configure terminal`, `ip route 192.168.3.0 255.255.255.0 192.168.2.2`, and `end`. View the static route: `show ip route`. Make sure that 192.168.3.0/24 shows up in the routing table as a static route (`S`).

3. From Host3, ping the `fa0/0` interface of the 2600-1.

    At the top of the simulator in the menu bar, click the eStations icon and choose Host3. Ping the `serial0` and `fa0/0` interface of the 2600-1 router: `ping 192.168.2.1` and `ping 192.168.1.1`. The pings should be successful.

4. From Host-3, ping Host-1.

    Ping Host1: `ping 192.168.1.10`. The ping should be successful.

5. Check network connectivity between the two 2950 switches and the Host3.

    At the top of the simulator in the menu bar, click the eSwitches icon and choose 2950-1. From the 2950-1 switch, ping Host3: `ping 192.168.3.10`. At the top of the simulator in the menu bar, click the eSwitches icon and choose 2950-2. From the 2950-2 switch, ping Host3: **ping 192.168.3.10**. At the top of the simulator in the menu bar, click the eStations icon and choose Host3. From Host3, ping the 2950-1 switch: **ping 192.168.1.2**. From Host3, ping the 2950-2 switch: **ping 192.168.1.3**.

6. Set up a static route on the 2600-2 to reach 10.0.0.0/8, which are the global addresses behind the 2600-1. Remove the 192.168.1.0/24 static route.

   At the top of the simulator in the menu bar, click the eRouters icon and choose 2600-2. On the 2600-2, set up a static route: **configure terminal** and **ip route 10.0.0.0 255.0.0.0 192.168.2.1**. Remove the old static route: **no ip route 192.168.1.0 255.255.255.0 192.168.2.1**. Exit Configuration mode: **end**.

7. Verify the 2600-2's routing table.

   View the routing table: **show ip route**. Verify that 10.0.0.0/8 is configured correctly.

8. On the 2600-1 router, set up a static NAT translation for 2950-1 (10.0.0.2).

   At the top of the simulator in the menu bar, click the eRouters icon and choose 2600-1. Access Configuration mode: **configure terminal**. Set up static NAT statement on the 2600-1 router for 2950-1: **ip nat inside source static 192.168.1.2 10.0.0.2**.

9. Configure **fa0/0** as the inside and **s0** as the outside for NAT.

   Specify **fa0/0** as the inside: **interface fa0/0**, **ip nat inside**, and **exit**. Specify **s0** as the outside: **interface s0**, **ip nat outside**, and **end**.

10. View your static translation: **show ip nat translations**.

11. Test the translation from Host3 by pinging the 2950-1 with its global and local addresses.

    At the top of the simulator in the menu bar, click the eStations icon and choose Host3. From Host3, ping 2950-1's global address: **ping 10.0.0.2**. The ping should be successful. From Host3, ping 2950-1's local address: **ping 192.168.1.2**. The ping should fail (no route).

12. Test connectivity by pinging the 2950-2 local addresses.

    From Host3, ping 2950-2's local address: **ping 192.168.1.3**. The ping should fail (no route).

Now you should be more comfortable with configuring static address translation on a router.

EXERCISE 23-2

ON THE CD

Configuring Dynamic Address Translation

In Exercise 23-1, you configured static translation. In this exercise, you'll configure dynamic address translation. You'll perform this lab using Boson's NetSim simulator. You can find a picture of the network diagram for Boson's NetSim simulator in the Introduction of this book. This exercise has you first set static routes on the two routers (2600-1 and 2600-2) and verify network connectivity. Following this, you'll configure your translation policy. After starting up the simulator, click the Lab Navigator button. Next, double-click Exercise 23-2 and click the Load Lab button. This will load the lab configuration based on the exercised in Chapters 11 and 16.

1. On the 2600-2, configure a static route to 192.168.1.0/24, which is off of the 2600-1. View the routing table.

   At the top of the simulator in the menu bar, click the eRouters icon and choose 2600-2. Configure the static route: **configure terminal**, **ip route 192.168.1.0 255.255.255.0 192.168.2.1**, and **end**. View the static route: **show ip route**. Make sure that 192.168.1.0/24 shows up in the routing table as a static route (S).

2. On the 2600-1, configure a static route to 192.168.3.0/24, which is off of the 2600-2. View the routing table.

   At the top of the simulator in the menu bar, click the eRouters icon and choose 2600-1. Configure the static route: **configure terminal**, **ip route 192.168.3.0 255.255.255.0 192.168.2.2**, and **end**. View the static route: **show ip route**. Make sure that 192.168.3.0/24 shows up in the routing table as a static route (S).

3. From Host3, ping the fa0/0 interface of the 2600-1. From Host3, ping Host1.

   At the top of the simulator in the menu bar, click the eStations icon and choose Host3. Ping the serial0 and fa0/0 interface of the 2600-1 router: **ping 192.168.2.1** and **ping 192.168.1.1**. The pings should be successful. Ping Host1: **ping 192.168.1.10**. The ping should be successful.

4. Set up a static route on the 2600-2 to reach 10.0.0.0/8, which are the global addresses behind the 2600-1. Remove the 192.168.1.0/24 static route.

At the top of the simulator in the menu bar, click the eRouters icon and choose 2600-2. On the 2600-2, set up a static route: **configure terminal** and **ip route 10.0.0.0 255.0.0.0 192.168.2.1**. Remove the old static route: **no ip route 192.168.1.0 255.255.255.0 192.168.2.1**. Exit Configuration mode: **end**.

5. Verify the routing table on the 2600-2.

   View the routing table: **show ip route**.

6. On the 2600-1 router, set up address overloading for all devices in network 192.168.1.0/24, translating them to 10.0.0.1 through 10.0.0.100. The ACL number should be 1 and the pool name with the global addresses should be called nat-pool.

   At the top of the simulator in the menu bar, click the eRouters icon and choose 2600-1. Access Configuration mode: **configure terminal**. Set up the standard ACL for the local inside addresses to be translated: **access-list 1 permit 192.168.1.0 0.0.0.255**. Configure the global address pool with a single address in it: **ip nat pool nat-pool 10.0.0.1 10.0.0.100 netmask 255.255.255.0**. Set up the address overload statement on the 2600-1 router for inside network: **ip nat inside source list 1 pool nat-pool overload**.

7. Configure **fa0/0** as the inside and **s0** as the outside for NAT. View your static translations.

   Specify **fa0/0** as the inside: **interface fa0/0**, **ip nat inside**, and **exit**. Specify **s0** as the outside: **interface s0**, **ip nat outside**, and **end**.

8. Clear the translation table: **clear ip nat translations ***.

9. View the static translations: **show ip nat translations**.

10. Test the translation from Host1 by pinging Host3.

    At the top of the simulator in the menu bar, click the eStations icon and choose Host1. From Host1, ping Host3: **ping 192.168.3.10**. The ping should be successful.

11. Test the translation from Host2 by pinging Host3.

    At the top of the simulator in the menu bar, click the eStations icon and choose Host2. From Host2, ping Host3: **ping 192.168.3.10**. The ping should be successful.

12. View the translation table on the 2600-1 router.

At the top of the simulator in the menu bar, click the eRouters icon and choose 2600-1. Examine the translation table: **show ip nat translation**. You should have two sets of translations for ICMP—for ICMP, each echo is treated as a separate connection since the IOS is using the sequence numbers in the ICMP payload to differentiate the connections.

Now you should be more comfortable with configuring dynamic address translation on a router.

INSIDE THE EXAM

Address Translation Overview

Understand from where companies commonly get their public IP addresses: ISPs and registration authorities (IANA, for example). Remember the ranges of addresses specified in RFC 1918, why private addresses are used, and their shortcomings. Be familiar with the reasons address translation is necessary.

Address Translation Types

Be able to compare and contrast the definitions in Tables 23-2 and 23-3: for example, the difference between an inside and outside global address. Understand how dynamic NAT and overloading (use of source TCP/UDP port numbers) works for inside translations and why overloading is necessary in certain situations. Know when PAR is necessary: when you have a single IP address from the ISP, but need Internet users to access internal resources. Be familiar with the advantages and disadvantages of address translation.

Address Translation Configuration

I cannot begin to stress how important it is to know the commands for configuring address translation: static, dynamic NAT, and overloading. Don't be surprised if you are asked to configure address translation in a simulation question on the exam.

Translation Process and Troubleshooting

Again, be very comfortable with the syntax of the address translation commands. You might be given configuration scenarios and asked questions about them: for example, given a certain group of users, what will happen to their traffic when it is sent to the Internet? Or why isn't address translation occurring given a particular configuration? Be familiar with the troubleshooting commands, including the use of the **show** and **debug** commands.

CERTIFICATION SUMMARY

Private addresses are defined in RFC 1918: 10.0.0.0/8, 172.16.0.0/16–172.31.0.0/16, and 192.168.0.0/24–192.168.255.0/24. If you use private addresses, you must have these translated to a public address before these packets reach a public network. Address translation is used when you don't have enough public addresses, you change ISPs but keep your existing addresses, you are merging companies with overlapping address spaces, or you want to assign the same IP address to multiple machines.

The term *inside local IP address* refers to packets with a private or original IP address. The term *inside global IP address* refers to packets with a public, or translated, address. NAT translates one IP address to another, while PAT (address overloading) translates many IP addresses to the same global address, where the source port numbers are changed to ensure the translation device can differentiate the connections. PAR redirects traffic destined to a port on one device to a different device.

Address translation allows access to an almost inexhaustible group of addresses and enables you to hide your internal network design from outsiders. It also gives you tighter control over traffic entering and leaving your network. However, address translation adds delay to your traffic, makes troubleshooting more difficult, and won't work with all applications, especially multimedia applications.

The **ip nat inside source static** command sets up static NAT. The **ip nat inside source list** and **ip nat pool** (add **overload** to do PAT) commands set up dynamic translations. The **ip nat inside|outside** Interface Subconfiguration mode command defines which interfaces are considered internal and external for address translation.

Use the **show ip nat translations** command to view the router's address translation table. The **clear ip nat translation *** command clears all dynamic address translation entries in the router's translation table. The **debug ip nat** command will show the translations the IOS is doing on every translated packet.

✓ TWO-MINUTE DRILL

Address Translation Overview

❑ RFC 1918 private addresses include 10.0.0.0/8, 172.16.0.0/16–172.31.0.0/16, and 192.168.0.0/24–192.168.255.0/24.

❑ Reasons to use address translation include not having enough public addresses, changing ISPs, merging networks with overlapping addresses, and representing multiple devices as a single logical device.

❑ Disadvantages of address translation include connection delays, difficult troubleshooting, and that it doesn't work with all applications.

Address Translation Types

❑ An inside local IP address is a private address assigned to an inside device. An inside global IP address is a public address associated with an inside device.

❑ NAT does a one-to-one address translation. PAT translates multiple IP addresses to a single address, using the source TCP/UDP port number to differentiate connections.

❑ Port address redirection is a form of static PAT, where traffic sent to a specific address and port is redirected to another machine (and possibly a different port).

Address Translation Configuration

❑ To define inside and outside, use the `ip nat inside|outside` Interface Subconfiguration mode command.

❑ To configure static NAT, use the `ip nat inside|outside source static` command.

❑ To set up dynamic NAT, use the `ip nat inside source list` command, with a standard ACL specifying the inside local addresses. Add `overload` to this command to do PAT. Use the `ip nat pool` command to specify the global addresses.

❑ Use the `show ip nat translations` command to view the static and dynamic address translations. Use the `clear ip nat translation *` command to clear the dynamic translations from the address translation table. Use `debug ip nat` to see the actual translation process.

Translation Process and Troubleshooting

❑ When troubleshooting address translation problems, first verify your address translation configuration. Examine the translation table with the **show ip nat translations** command. Use the **show ip nat statistics** command to see whether translations are actually occurring.

❑ Use the **debug ip nat [detailed]** command to see whether translation is occurring or not. Verify that you have correctly configured the router's interfaces for NAT as inside or outside. Use the **show access-lists** command to see whether hit counts appear on the permit statements for packets that should be translated.

❑ Make sure the router can route the packet to the destination by looking at the routing table: **show ip route**.

SELF TEST

The following Self Test questions will help you measure your understanding of the material presented in this chapter. Read all the choices carefully, as there may be more than one correct answer. Choose all correct answers for each question.

Address Translation Overview

1. Which of the following is a private address?
   A. 192.169.7.17
   B. 172.32.28.39
   C. 10.1.256.8
   D. 172.16.255.89

2. For which of the following reasons might you need to use address translation?
   A. You have to use public addressing because your ISP didn't assign you enough private addresses.
   B. You are using private addresses but have changed ISPs, and your new ISP won't support these private addresses.
   C. You want to assign public addresses to devices and need to access the Internet.
   D. You are merging two companies that use the same address space.

Address Translation Types

3. _____ translates one (and only one) IP address to another.
   A. NAT
   B. PAT
   C. PAR
   D. NAT and PAT

4. An _____ is a public IP address associated with an inside device.
   A. inside global IP address
   B. inside local IP address
   C. outside global IP address
   D. outside local IP address

Address Translation Configuration

5. Which command is used to define the local addresses that are statically translated to global addresses?

   A. `ip nat inside source static`

   B. `ip nat inside`

   C. `ip nat inside source list`

   D. `ip nat pool`

6. You have 30 internal machines that need to access the Internet: 192.168.1.32/27. You've been given six public IP addresses for this access: 199.1.1.41–199.1.1.46. Interface fastethernet0/0 is connected to the inside and serial1/0 to the ISP on your router. Enter the commands to perform PAT with this information.

7. When configuring the `ip nat inside source` command, which parameter must you specify to perform PAT?

   A. `pat`

   B. `overload`

   C. `load`

   D. `port`

Translation Process and Troubleshooting

8. Examine the following configuration. There are more than 100 internal devices. Some devices can access the Internet, but some can't. What is the possible problem with this situation?

   ```
   ip nat pool mypool 199.1.1.2 199.1.1.62
           netmask 255.255.255.192
   access-list 1 permit 192.168.1.0 0.0.0.255
   ip nat inside source list 1 pool mypool overload
   interface fastethernet0/0
      ip address 192.168.1.1 255.255.255.0
      ip nat inside
   interface serial1/0
      ip address 199.1.1.1 255.255.255.192
      ip nat outside
   ```

   A. The ACL is misconfigured.

   B. The `ip nat inside` command should be configured on serial1/0.

   C. There are not enough public IP address in the mypool address pool.

   D. The serial1/0 IP address is not configured in the correct subnet.

9. Examine the following configuration. Which of the following is true concerning the source address the Internet will see if a device with an IP address of 192.168.1.5 sends a packet through the router?

```
ip nat pool mypool 199.1.1.2 199.1.1.3
        netmask 255.255.255.252
access-list 1 permit 192.168.1.0 0.0.0.255
ip nat inside source list 1 pool mypool overload
interface fastethernet0/0
   ip address 192.168.1.1 255.255.255.0
   ip nat inside
interface serial1/0
   ip address 199.1.1.1 255.255.255.252
```

   A. It will be seen as 192.168.1.5.
   B. It will be seen as 199.1.1.2.
   C. It will be seen as 192.1.1.3.
   D. It will be seen as either 192.1.1.2 or 192.1.1.3.

10. When doing a local-to-global translation, which of the following occurs first?
   A. Policy routing
   B. Inside-to-outside NAT rules
   C. Inbound ACL
   D. Inbound rate limiting policies

SELF TEST ANSWERS

Address Translation Overview

1. ☑ **D.** The address 172.16.255.89 is a private address.

   ☒ **A** and **B** are public addresses. **C** is an invalid address (256 is an invalid value).

2. ☑ **D.** Overlapping addresses between networks requires address translation to make them look unique to each other so that they can successfully communicate with each other.

   ☒ **A** is not true, because the words *public* and *private* should be reversed. **B** is not true, because it refers to private, not public addresses. Address translation is not necessary if you already have public addresses, making **C** false.

Address Translation Types

3. ☑ **A.** NAT translates only one IP address to another.

   ☒ **B** and **D** are incorrect because PAT translates many addresses to one address. **C** is incorrect because PAR can translate a port number to another port number.

4. ☑ **A.** An inside global IP address is a public IP address assigned to an inside device.

   ☒ **B** is incorrect because it refers to an inside private address. **C** is incorrect because it refers to an outside public address. **D** is incorrect because it refers to an outside private address.

Address Translation Configuration

5. ☑ **A.** The `ip nat inside source static` command configures static NAT translations.

   ☒ **B** specifies an interface as being inside. **C** and **D** are used to configure dynamic NAT.

6. ☑
   ```
   ip nat pool mypool 199.1.1.41 199.1.1.46
        netmask 255.255.255.248
     access-list 1 permit 192.168.1.32 0.0.0.31
     ip nat inside source list 1 pool mypool overload
     interface fastethernet0/0
        ip nat inside
     interface serial1/0
        ip nat outside
   ```

7. ☑ **B.** Use the `overload` parameter with the `ip nat inside source` command to set up PAT.

   ☒ **A**, **C**, and **D** are invalid parameters.

Translation Process and Troubleshooting

8. ☑ **C.** The address pool has 61 addresses, but more than 100 are needed and address overloading is not configured.

   ☒ **A** is not correct since the ACL includes addresses off of the fa0/0 interface. **B** is incorrect because the fa0/0 interface is the inside interface. **D** is incorrect because the IP address and mask is configured correctly.

9. ☑ **A.** The `ip nat outside` command is missing on serial1/0, so no translation will take place.

   ☒ Since translation is misconfigured, **B**, **C**, and **D** are incorrect answers.

10. ☑ **C.** ACLs are processed before the other three.

    ☒ **A** is incorrect because policy routing is done after inbound rate limiting policies. **B** is incorrect because inside-to-outside NAT rules occur after policy routing. **D** is incorrect because inbound rate limiting policies are done after the inbound ACLs.

24

IPv6

T his chapter introduces you to the next generation of TCP/IP: IP version 6 (IPv6). Because of the many deficiencies found in IPv4, as well as the poor scalability for hierarchical addressing in IPv4, IPv6 was developed to meet the rapidly growing needs of small companies, corporations, and the explosive growth of the Internet, especially in emerging markets such as China and India. In this chapter you'll discover why IPv6 is necessary, the different kinds of IPv6 addresses, routing with IPv6, and how to configure a basic IPv6 setup. The CCNP certification goes into much more depth than what you'll find in this chapter.

CERTIFICATION OBJECTIVE 24.01

Necessity of IPv6

Given that an IP address is 32 bits in length, there are 2^{32} actual IP addresses, which is 4.3 billion addresses. Not all of these are usable, however: only 3.7 billion of these are actually usable. Many addresses are reserved, such as the research (239–254), broadcast (255), multicast (224–239), private (10, 172.16, and 192.168), and loopback addresses (127). And, of course, many of the usable addresses are already assigned, leaving about 1.3 billion addresses for new growth.

Unlike 32-bit IPv4 addresses, IPv6 uses a 128-bit address. This allows for 3.4×10^{38} addresses, which is enough for many IP addresses for each person on Earth, and probably multiple planets.

Growth Issues

During the early-to-mid-1990s, concern began to grow about the diminishing number of IPv4 addresses. The temporary solution to solve this problem was to set aside an address space, called *private addresses*, which anyone could use in a public network. Recall from Chapters 7 and 23 that these addresses are defined in RFC 1918: 10.0.0.0/8, 172.16.0.0–172.31.255.255, and 192.168.0.0–192.168.255.255. And to access a public network, address translation was used to translate the private addressing information to a public address, commonly with static Network Address Translation (NAT) translations for internal services and dynamic overloading (Port Address Translation, or PAT) for user connection.

However, many changes in the marketplace are quickly reaching the point where address translation won't be enough: there won't be any public addresses left to translate to. Here are some valid reasons why companies are beginning to migrate to an IPv6 environment:

- Currently more than 1 billion people are connected to the Internet, and this is exponentially increasing based on fast-emerging technical markets such as China and India.
- More than 1 billion mobile phones are currently on the market, most of which support limited data services, and this is expected to grow not only in numbers, but also with the enhanced offerings of data services these phone and providers are capable of delivering.
- More than 30 million PDAs and similar devices offer common data services such as e-mail and web browsing, and this number is expected to grow as more and more businesses implement mobile applications.
- More data services are being offered on consumer products, such as automobiles, household appliances, and industrial devices, and this number is expected to grow into the billions.

As you can see, it's not a matter of *if* this is going to happen, and not even *when* it's going to happen, but *how soon* in the near future this is going to happen. Some people have predicted that IPv4 addresses will run out in 2008 or 2009, and some as late as 2013. Some countries have already begun the conversion process. For example, as of 2003, the US Department of Defense has mandated that all new network equipment support IPv6. Likewise, beginning in 2008, the US government has mandated that all government agencies' core networks run IPv6. Other countries such as Japan and China are quickly adopting the new standard.

Imagine a future in the next decade where from your cell phone you can change the channels on your TV, call home and program the microwave to turn on, or stream content from your TV provider to your PC and then to a network storage device that your TV can quickly access. As you can see, for communication to take place between all these devices, they'll need an addressing structure, and most companies are basically relying on TCP/IP to provide this. For example, Sony has already mandated that, as of 2005, all of its products support IPv6.

IPv6 Features

Obviously, the replacement for IPv4 needs to support enough addresses for this growing demand, but it also needs to provide ease of use and configuration, enhanced security, and the ability to interoperate with IPv4 as the transition takes place. Here are some features built into IPv6:

- **Very large address space**   IPv6's large address space deals with global growth, where route prefixes can be easily aggregated in routing updates. Support for multihoming to ISPs with a single address space is easily accomplished. Autoconfiguration of addressing information, including the capability of including MAC addresses in the IP address, as well as plug-and-play options, simplifies address management. Renumbering and modification of addresses is easily accommodated, as well as public-to-private readdressing without involving address translation.

- **Security**   IP security (IPSec) is built into IPv6, whereas it is an awkward add-on in IPv4. With IPv6, two devices can dynamically negotiate security parameters and build a secure tunnel between them with no user intervention.

- **Mobility**   With the growth of mobile devices, such as PDAs and smart phones, devices can roam between wireless networks without breaking their connections.

- **Streamlined encapsulation**   The IPv6 encapsulation is simpler than IPv4, providing faster forwarding rates by routers and better routing efficiency. No checksums are included, reducing processing on endpoints. No broadcasts are used, reducing utilization of devices within the same subnet. QoS information is built into the IPv6 header, where a flow label identifies the traffic; this alleviates intermediate network devices from having to examine contents inside the packet, the TCP/UDP headers, and payload information to classify the traffic for QoS correctly.

- **Transition capabilities**   Various solutions exist to allow IPv4 and IPv6 to successfully coexist when migrating between the two. One method, dual stack, allows you to run both protocols simultaneously on an interface of a device. A second method, tunneling, allows you to tunnel IPv6 over IPv4 and vice versa to transmit an IP version of one type across a network using another type. Cisco supports a third method, referred to as Network Address Translation-Protocol Translation (NAT-PT), to translate between IPv4 and IPv6 (sometimes the term *Proxy* is used instead of Protocol).

CERTIFICATION OBJECTIVE 24.02

IPv6 Addressing

What scares most administrators about IPv6 addresses is how different they appear when compared to IPv4 addresses. Learning to deal with an address four times longer seems impossible; however, as you will see in this chapter, the standards body for TCP/IP has simplified it as much as possible.

IPv6 Address Format

Whereas IPv4 addresses use a dotted-decimal format, where each byte ranges from 0 to 255, IPv6 addresses use eight sets of four hexadecimal addresses (16 bits in each set), separated by a colon (:), like this: *xxxx:xxxx:xxxx:xxxx:xxxx:xxxx:xxxx:xxxx* (*x* would be a hexadecimal value). This notation is commonly called *string* notation. Recall from Chapter 3 that hexadecimal numbers range from 0 to F.

Here are some important items concerning IPv6 addresses:

- Hexadecimal values can be displayed in either lower- or upper-case for the numbers A–F.
- A leading zero in a set of numbers can be omitted; for example, you could either enter *0012* or *12* in one of the eight fields—both are correct.
- If you have successive fields of zeroes in an IPv6 address, you can represent them as two colons (::). For example, *0:0:0:0:0:0:0:5* could be represented as *::5*; and *ABC:567:0:0:8888:9999:1111:0* could be represented as *ABC:567::8888:9999:1111:0*. However, you can only do this *once* in the address: *ABC::567::891::00* would be invalid since :: appears more than once in the address. The reason for this limitation is that if you had two or more repetitions, you wouldn't know how many sets of zeroes were being omitted from each part.
- An unspecified address is represented as ::, since it contains all zeroes.

Types of IPv6 Addresses

Recall from Chapter 7 that many types of IPv4 addresses exist: unicast, broadcast, multicast, research, private, and so on. IPv6 also has different types of addresses. Following are the three main types:

- **Anycast**   Very different from an IPv4 broadcast—one-to-the-nearest interface, where many interfaces can share the same address
- **Multicast**   Similar to a multicast in IPv4—one to a group of devices
- **Unicast**   Represents a single interface

IETF defines support for many data link layer types; however, Cisco supports only Ethernet, Point-to-Point Protocol (PPP), High-Level Data Link Control (HDLC), Asynchronous Transfer Mode (ATM) (using PVCs only), and Frame Relay (using PVCs only). The following sections discuss these in more depth.

Anycast

One of the problems with addressing in IPv4 was the use of broadcasts, which every device had to process on a segment (even when the broadcast wasn't ultimately destined to a device). IPv4 relied heavily on broadcasts to discover devices on a segment, such as ARP, and to acquire addressing, such as Dynamic Host Control Protocol (DHCP). In IPv6, broadcasts no longer exist: they've been replaced with anycast and multicast addresses.

An anycast address identifies one or more _interfaces_. Notice that I don't use the term _device_, since a device can have more than one interface. Sometimes people use the term _node_ to designate an interface on a device. Basically, an anycast is a hybrid of a unicast and multicast address. With a unicast, one packet is sent to one destination; with a multicast, one packet is sent to all members of the multicast group; and with an anycast, a packet is sent to any one member of a group of devices that are configured with the anycast address. By default, packets sent to an anycast address are forwarded to the closet interface (node), which is based on the routing process employed to get the packet to the destination. Given this process, anycast addresses are commonly referred to as *one-to-the-nearest* address. And, interestingly enough, anycast addresses are allocated from the global pool of unicast addresses in IPv6, making a unicast and anycast address indistinguishable from each other when you look at them in a packet. And since multiple devices can be configured with the same anycast address, they are commonly used in situations where load balancing traffic, such as web content, to two different destinations is needed.

on the **job** *Anycast addresses and their uses are still in their infancy and some known problems can occur when using them. Until administrators gain more experience in how anycast addresses work and people in the industry agree upon how to solve these problems, you should follow these guidelines: Don't assign these addresses to hosts—only routers. Don't put an anycast address in the source of a packet—only the destination.*

Multicast

Multicasts in IPv6 serve a function similar to their counterpart in IPv4: they represent a group of interfaces interested in seeing the same traffic. A multicast packet example for IPv6 is shown in Figure 24-1. The first 8 bits are set to FF. The next 4 bits are the lifetime of the address: 0 is permanent and 1 is temporary. The next 4 bits indicate the scope of the multicast address (how far the packet can travel): 1 is for a node, 2 is for a link, 5 is for the site, 8 is for the organization, and E is global (the Internet). For example, a multicast address that begins with FF02::/16 is a permanent link address, whereas an address of FF15::/16 is a temporary address for a site.

FIGURE 24-I	
IPv6 multicast packet	

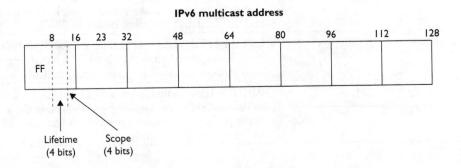

IPv6 multicast address

Unicast

IPv6 unicast addresses are assigned to each node (interface), and their uses are
discussed in RFC 4291. The five types of unicast addresses are listed in Table 24-1.
Interestingly enough, multiple addresses of any type can be assigned to a device's
interface: unicast, multicast, and anycast.

Private Addresses   As mentioned in Table 24-1, private addresses are used for
devices that don't need to access a public network. There are two kinds of private
addresses:

- **Site-local**   FEC:: through FFF::
- **Link-local**   FE8:: through FEB::

Site-local addresses are similar to the RFC 1918 addresses and represent a
particular site or company. These addresses can be used within a company without
having to waste any public IP addresses—not that this is a concern, given the large
number of addresses available in IPv6. However, by using private addresses, you can
easily control who is allowed to leave your network and get returning traffic back by
setting up address translation policies for IPv6.

TABLE 24-1   IEEE Ethernet Components

Address	Value	Description
Global	2000::/3	These are assigned by the IANA and used on public networks. They are equivalent to IPv4 global (sometimes called public) addresses. ISPs summarize these to provide scalability in the Internet.
Reserved	(range)	Reserved addresses are used for specific types of anycast as well as for future use. Currently about 1/256th of the IPv6 address space is reserved.
Private	FE80::/10	Like IPv4, IPv6 supports private addressing, which is used by devices that don't need to access a public network. The first two digits are FE, and the third digit can range from 8 to F.
Loopback	::1	Like the 127.0.0.1 address in IPv4, 0:0:0:0:0:0:0:1, or ::1, is used for local testing functions; unlike IPv4, which dedicates a complete A class block of addresses for local testing, only one is used in IPv6.
Unspecified	::	0.0.0.0 in IPv4 means "unknown" address. In IPv6, this is represented by 0:0:0:0:0:0:0:0, or ::, and is typically used in the source address field of the packet when an interface doesn't have an address and is trying to acquire one dynamically.

Link-local addresses are a new concept in IPv6. These kinds of addresses have a smaller scope as to how far they can travel: just the local link (the data link layer link). Routers will process packets destined to a link-local address, but they will not forward them to other links. Their most common use is for a device to acquire unicast site-local or global unicast addressing information, discovering the default gateway, and discovering other layer 2 neighbors on the segment. When a device is using link-local addresses, it must specify an outbound interface, since every interface is connected to a "link."

Global Addresses   With the exception of the multicast address space of FF00::/8, unicast and anycast addresses make up the rest. However, IANA has currently assigned only 2000::/3 addresses to the global pool, which is about 1/6th of the available IPv6 addresses. Of these addresses, only 2001::/16 are assigned to various Internet address registries. Global unicast addresses are made up of two components, shown in Figure 24-2: subnet ID (64 bits) and an interface ID (64 bits). The subnet ID contains the registry of the address (which is responsible for assigning it, such as IANA), the ISP prefix (which ISP is associated with the address), the site prefix (which company is assigned the address space), and a subnet prefix (subnets within the site). ISPs are assigned an ISP prefix range that allows them easily to aggregate their prefixes, advertising just a single route to the Internet backbone; this alleviates one main problem today with how the Internet grew and how ISPs, initially, were assigned IPv4 address spaces that could not easily be summarized. Another advantage of this address allocation is that the subnet prefix is 16 bits in length. Therefore, with a single global site address, a company can address up to 65,536 subnets.

FIGURE 24-2

IPv6 unicast packet

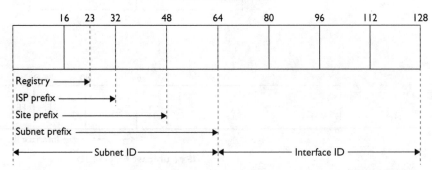

IPv6 unicast address

The last half of the IPv6 address, the interface ID, represents a particular interface within the site. One requirement with addresses from 2000::/3 through E000::/3 is that the interface ID must have a 64-bit value in it to be considered valid. Therefore, addresses that have 0s for the last 64 bits are considered invalid IPv6 unicast addresses. For example, 2004:1234:5678:90AB:: is invalid, since the interface ID (the last 64 bits—that is, the last four sets of numbers) are binary zeroes.

The interface ID is typically composed of a part of the MAC address of the interface. When this is done, the interface ID is commonly called an *extended unique identifier 64* (EUI-64). Figure 24-3 shows an example of the frame with a EUI-64 format. The OUI part of the LAN NIC's MAC address is mapped into the first 24 bits of the interface ID. The seventh bit in the highest order byte is set to 1, indicating that the interface ID is unique across the site, or 0, indicating that it is unique within the local scope only. The OUI mapping is followed by the 16-bit value of FFFE. The last 24 bits of the MAC address are then mapped into the last part of the interface ID.

Addresses that have 0s for the interface ID part of a unicast IPv6 address are invalid. For example, this *would be an invalid IPv6 unicast address: 2001:5005::.*

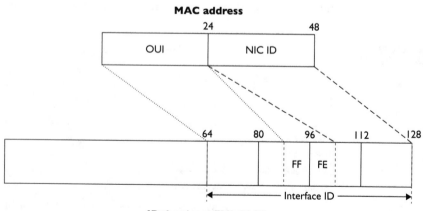

FIGURE 24-3

EUI-64 interface ID

IPv6 unicast EUI-64 ID

CERTIFICATION OBJECTIVE 24.03

Address Assignment

You can use four methods to assign an interface an IPv6 address: two are done statically and two dynamically. The following three sections discuss these four options.

Static Address Assignment

One option you have is to statically assign a unicast address to a device's interface using either of these two approaches:

- Specify all 128-bits manually
- Use EUI-64

You can manually specify the entire 128-bit address, or you can specify the subnet ID and have the device use the EUI-64 method to create the interface ID part of the address. If you're manually entering the entire address, remember that sets of fields that have 0s in them can be abbreviated with ::. The EUI-64 method is the more common approach by most network administrators.

DHCPv6

DHCPv6 is an update of the DHCP protocol in IPv4 and works similarly to the previous version with a few differences. Before the client can begin, it must first detect a router on the link via a neighbor discovery process. If the client detects a router, the client examines the router advertisement messages to determine whether DHCPv6 has been set up. If the router specifies that DHCPv6 is supported, or no router advertisement messages are seen, the client will begin to find a DHCPv6 server by generating a DHCP solicit message. This message is sent to the ALL-DHCP-Agents multicast address, using the link-local scope to ensure the message isn't forwarded, by default, beyond the local link. An agent is either a DHCPv6 server or a relay, such as a router.

In DHCPv4 (IPv4 addressing), you had to configure the IP Helper feature on Cisco routers when the DHCP server was not on the same segment as the requesting clients. IP Helper had the router redirect a DHCP request either to a particular server or a directed broadcast address of the segment that had one or more DHCP servers. This is no longer necessary in DHCPv6: if no server is on the link, a relay can forward the request to the ALL-DHCP-Agents multicast address with the site-local scope. You still have the option of doing this statically: this is necessary if you want to control which DHCPv6 server or servers should process the request.

Stateless Autoconfiguration

Stateless autoconfiguration is an extension of DHCPv6. Like DHCPv6, clients can still acquire their addressing dynamically; however, with stateless autoconfiguration, no server is necessary to assign IPv6 addressing information to the clients. Instead, the client uses information in router advertisement messages to configure an IPv6 address for the interface. This is accomplished by taking the first 64 bits in the router advertisement source address (the prefix of the router's address) and using the EUI-64 process to create the 64-bit interface ID. Stateless autoconfiguration was designed primarily for cell phones, PDAs, and home network and appliance equipment to assign addresses automatically without having to manage a DHCP server infrastructure.

W a t c h   *Stateless autoconfiguration assigns addresses dynamically without needing a DHCP server. The device learns the IPv6 prefix from a router advertisement and uses EUI-64 to create the interface ID part of the address dynamically.*

Normally, routers generate periodic router advertisement (RA) messages the client can listen to and then use to generate its link address automatically; however, when the client is booting up, waiting for the RA might take awhile. In this situation, the client will generate a router solicitation message, asking the router to reply with an RA so the client can generate its interface address.

CERTIFICATION OBJECTIVE 24.04

Routing and IPv6

As in IPv4, routers in IPv6 find best paths to destinations based on metrics and administrative distances; and like IPv4, IPv6 routers look for the longest matching prefix in the IPv6 routing table to forward a packet to its destination. The main difference is that the IPv6 router is looking at 128 bits when making a routing decision instead of 32 bits.

RFC 2461 requires that a router must be able to identify the link-local address of each neighboring router, which is used in the routing process. Because of this, the use of global unicast addresses as a next-hop address is not recommended by the RFC.

Supported Routing Protocols

IPv6 supports both static and dynamic routing protocols. IPv6 supports these routing protocols: static, RIPng, OPSFv3, IS-IS for IPv6, MP-BGP4, and EIGRP for IPv6. This book covers only RIPng; the other dynamic routing protocols are covered in Cisco's CCNP certification.

RIPng

Routing Information Protocol next generation (RIPng) is defined in RFC 2080. It is actually similar to RIP for IPv4, with these characteristics:

- It's a distance vector protocol.
- The hop-count limit is 15.
- Split horizon and poison reverse are used to prevent routing loops.
- It is based on RIPv2.

Cisco routers running 12.2(2)T and later support RIPng.

These are the enhancements in RIPng:

- An IPv6 packet is used to transport the routing update.
- The ALL-RIP routers multicast address (FF02::9) is used as the destination address in routing advertisements and is delivered to UDP port 521.
- Routing updates contain the IPv6 prefix of the router and the next-hop IPv6 address.

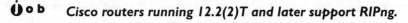

RIPng uses UDP port 521 for its connections. Its destination multicast address is FF02::9.

Implementation Strategies

One nice feature of moving your network to IPv6 is that you don't have to do it all in one step. Various migration strategies support both IPv4 and IPv6 as you migrate from

TABLE 24-2	IPv4-to-IPv6 Transition Options

Transition Method	Description
Dual stacking	Devices such as PCs and routers run both IPv4 and IPv6, and thus have two sets of addresses.
Manual IPv6-over-IPv4 (6to4) tunneling	IPv6 packets are tunneled across an IPv4 network by encapsulating them in IPv4 packets. This requires routers configured with dual stacks.
Dynamic 6to4 tunneling	Allows IPv6 localities to connect to other IPv6 localities across an IPv4 backbone, such as the Internet, automatically. This method applies a unique IPv6 prefix to each locality without having to retrieve IPv6 addressing information from address registries or ISPs.
Intra-Site Automatic Tunnel Addressing Protocol (ISATAP) tunneling	Uses virtual links to connect IPv6 localities together within a site that is primarily using IPv4. Boundary routers between the two addressing types must be configured with dual stacks.
Teredo tunneling	Instead of using routers to tunnel packets, Teredo tunneling has the hosts perform the tunneling. This requires the hosts to be configured with dual stacks. It is commonly used to move packets through an IPv4 address translation device.
NAT Proxying and Translation (NAT-PT)	Has an address translation device translate addresses between an IPv6 and IPv4 network and vice versa.

the former to the latter. Table 24-2 briefly lists these. Of these, the next two sections discuss dual stacking and manual tunneling, the two most common methods.

e x a m

ⓦ a t c h   *Routers running both IPv6 and IPv4 are referred to as being dual stacked. Connecting IPv6 networks by* *tunneling it in IPv4 packets is referred to as 6to4 tunneling.*

Dual Stacking   In dual stacking, a device runs both protocol stacks: IPv4 and IPv6. Of all the transition methods, this is the most common one. Dual stacking can be accomplished on the same interface or different interfaces of the device. The top part of Figure 24-4 shows an example of dual stacking on a router, where NetworkA has a mixture of devices configured for the two different protocols, and the router configured in a dual stack mode. Older IPv4-only applications can still work while

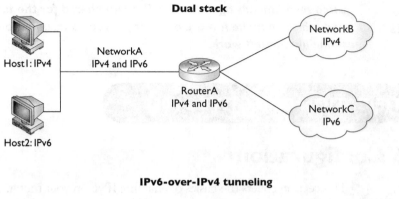

Dual stack and
IPv6 tunneling

they are migrated to IPv6 by supporting newer APIs to handle IPv6 addresses and
DNS lookups with IPv6 addresses.

on the
job

> ***The main disadvantage of dual stacking on a segment is that devices configured***
> ***using only one stack must forward their traffic to a dual-stacked device, such as***
> ***a router, which must then forward the traffic back to the same segment using***
> ***the other stack. This is an inefficient use of bandwidth, but it does allow devices***
> ***using both protocol stacks to coexist on the same network segment.***

IPv6 Tunneling   IPv6 tunneling allows you to tunnel IPv6 packets by carrying
them as payloads in an IPv4 packet, as shown at the bottom of Figure 24-4.
Tunneling allows you to connect IPv6 networks together across an intermediate
IPv4 network. When tunneling IPv6 packets in an IPv4 payload, the IPv4 protocol
field contains a value of *41*, indicating that IPv6 tunneling is occurring. The two
routers performing the tunneling must be configured using dual stacking, since they
need to communicate with both IPv6 and IPv4 devices on different segments.

  If you are configuring the tunnel manually, you'll need to configure both the IPv4
and IPv6 addresses statically. You'll also need to ensure that routing is performing
normally to tunnel the IPv6 packets across the IPv4 network, as well as allowing the
two IPv6 networks, as shown in Figure 24-4, to see each other's routes.

on the **Ôob** *Cisco recommends against using IP unnumbered for the tunnel endpoints, since this can make it more difficult for you to troubleshoot problems when tunneling doesn't work.*

CERTIFICATION OBJECTIVE 24.05

IPv6 Configuration

This section covers the basics of enabling IPv6 on your router, assigning IPv6 addresses to your interfaces, and enabling RIPng.

Enabling IPv6 and Assigning Addresses

To use IPv6 on your router, you must, at a minimum, enable the protocol and assign IPv6 addresses to your interfaces, like this:

```
Router(config)# ipv6 unicast-routing
Router(config)# interface type [slot_#/]port_#
Router(config-if)# ipv6 address ipv6_address_prefix/prefix_length
                       [eui-64]
```

The **ipv6 unicast-routing** command globally enables IPv6 and must be the first IPv6 command executed on the router. The **ipv6 address** command assigns the prefix, the length, and the use of EUI-64 to assign the interface ID. Optionally, you can omit the **eui-64** parameter and configure the entire IPv6 address. You can use the **show ipv6 interface** command to verify an interface's configuration. Here's an example configuration, with its verification:

```
Router(config)# ipv6 unicast-routing
Router(config)# interface fastethernet0/0
Router(config-if)# ipv6 address 2001:1cc1:dddd:2::/64 eui-64
Router(config-if)# end
Router# show ipv6 interface fastethernet0/0
FastEthernet0/0 is administratively down, line protocol is down
   IPv6 is enabled, link-local address is FE80::207:EFF:FE46:4070
      [TEN]
```

```
No Virtual link-local address(es):
Global unicast address(es):
  2001:1CC1:DDDD:2:207:EFF:FE46:4070, subnet is
    2001:1CC1:DDDD:2::/64 [EUI/TEN]
Joined group address(es):
  FF02::1
  FF02::2
  .
  .
  .
```

CertCam

24.01. The CD contains a multimedia demonstration of enabling IPv6 and configuring IPv6 on a router's interfaces.

To set up a static DNS resolution table on the router, use the **ipv6 host** command; you can also specify a DNS server with the **ip name-server** command:

```
Router(config)# ipv6 host hostname [port_#] ipv6_address1
                                 [ipv6_address2...]
Router(config)# ip name-server DNS_server_IPv6_address
```

The **ip name-server** command can be used to assign both IPv4 and IPv6 DNS servers.

---

exam

⚥atch *First, enable IPv6 with the* ***ipv6 unicast-routing command.*** *Then create IPv6 addresses on the* *interfaces with the* ***ipv6 address*** *ipv6_address_prefix/prefix_length* ***eui-64 command.***

RIPng

Enabling RIPng is a little bit different than enabling RIP for IPv4. First, you use the **ipv6 router rip** *tag* command to enable RIPng globally:

```
Router(config)# ipv6 router rip tag
```

This takes you into a subcommand mode, where you can change some of the global values for RIPng, such as disabling split horizon, the administrative distance, and timers. The tag is a locally significant identifier used to differentiate between multiple RIP processes running on the router.

Unlike RIP for IPv6, there is no **network** command to include interfaces in RIPng. Instead, you must enable RIPng on a per-interface basis with the **ipv6 rip** *tag* **enable** command:

```
Router(config)# interface type [slot_#/]port_#
Router(config-if)# ipv6 rip tag enable
```

The *tag* parameter associates the interface with the correct RIPng routing process.

w a t c h   ***Use the*** `ipv6 router`   ***globally and the*** `ipv6 rip tag enable`
`rip` `tag` ***command to enable RIPng***   ***command to enable it on an interface.***

To view the routing protocol configuration, use the **show ipv6 rip** command:

```
Router# show ipv6 rip
RIP process "RIPPROC1", port 521, multicast-group FF02::9,
     pid 187
     Administrative distance is 120. Maximum paths is 16
     Updates every 30 seconds, expire after 180
     Holddown lasts 0 seconds, garbage collect after 120
     Split horizon is on; poison reverse is off
     Default routes are not generated
     Periodic updates 2, trigger updates 0
  Interfaces:
    FastEthernet0/0
  Redistribution:
    None
```

In this example, the tag is RIPPROC1 for the name of the RIPng routing process and RIPng is enabled on FastEthernet0/0. To view the IPv6 routing table for RIPng, use the **show ipv6 route rip** command.

24.02. The CD contains a multimedia demonstration of enabling and verifying RIPng on a router.

INSIDE THE EXAM

Necessity of IPv6

IPv6 is a new addition to the CCNA exam; at this point, expect only basic questions on addressing and types of routing, but in future updates of the exam, expect to see questions related to configuration of IPv6 on routers. Remember that IPv6 addresses are 128 bits in length.

IPv6 Addressing

Be familiar with the format of an IPv6 address, including how sets of 0s can be summarized using double colons (::) one time in an IPv6 address. Be able to compare and contrast the three kinds of addresses: anycast, multicast, and unicast. Multicast addresses begin with FF. Be able to pick out invalid, global, and private (FE80::/10) addresses. The loopback address is ::1. Remember that IPv6 addresses have two components: subnet ID and interface ID. The interface ID is commonly made up from part of the MAC address (EUI-64).

Address Assignment

Be able to compare and contrast DHCPv6 and stateless autoconfiguration.

Routing and IPv6

You should be able to compare and contrast RIP with IPv4 and IPv6. Be familiar with the transition options available when moving from IPv4 to IPv6, including dual stack and 6to4 tunneling.

IPv6 Configuration

Remember that you must first execute the `ipv6 unicast-routing` command to enable IPv6. Know the command to create an EUI-64 address for a router's interface: `ipv6 address`. Remember how to enable RIP: `ipv6 router rip` *tag* (global) and `ipv6 rip` *tag* `enable` (interface).

CERTIFICATION SUMMARY

This chapter focused on an introduction to IPv6. Because of the limited number of addresses left in IPv4, IPv6 was designed to bring the Internet into its next generation. IPv6 addresses use eight sets of 4 hexadecimal addresses (16 bits in each set), separated by a colon (:), like this: *xxxx:xxxx:xxxx:xxxx:xxxx:xxxx:xxxx:xxxx*. If you have successive fields of zeroes in an IPv6 address, you can represent them as ::. However, you can only use this *once* in the address.

IPv6 addresses have three basic types: anycast, multicast and unicast. An anycast address is very different from an IPv4 broadcast: it represents one-to-the-nearest interface, where many interfaces can share the same address. A multicast address is similar to a multicast in IPv4: one-to-many. A unicast address represents a single interface. Global unicast addresses are 2000::/3. A loopback is ::1. Site-local private addresses range from FEC:: through FFF:: and link-local addresses range from FE8:: through FEB::.

The most common way of assigning static addresses to an interface is to use the EUI-64 method. DHCPv6 and stateless autoconfiguration allow a device to acquire an address dynamically. Stateless autoconfiguration accomplishes this by requesting a router to give the subnet ID and the device using EUI-64 to acquire an interface ID dynamically.

Routing protocols supported in IPv6 include static, RIPng, OSPFv3, IS-IS for IPv6, MP-BGP4, and EIGRP for IPv6. RIPng uses UDP port 521 for its connections. Its destination multicast address is FF02::9. The most common transition methods to move from IPv4 to IPv6 include dual stacking and 6to4 tunneling. In dual stacking, a device runs both protocol stacks. In 6to4 tunneling, IP6 packets are encapsulated in an IPv4 packet to move across an IPv4 backbone to another IPv6 network.

You must first execute the **ipv6 unicast-routing** command to enable IPv6. An address must be assigned to each interface, typically using the EUI-64 method, for it to process IPv6 packets. RIPng must be configured globally and then enabled on a per-interface basis. A tag is used to specify the RIPng routing process to which an interface belongs.

✓ TWO-MINUTE DRILL

Necessity of IPv6

❑ IPv6 addresses are 128 bits in length.

❑ IPSec is built into the IPv6 protocol and allows for device roaming without losing connectivity.

IPv6 Addressing

❑ IPv6 addresses use eight sets of four hexadecimal addresses (16 bits in each set), separated by a colon (:), like this: *xxxx:xxxx:xxxx:xxxx:xxxx:xxxx:xxxx:xxxx*.

❑ If you have successive fields of zeroes in an IPv6 address, you can represent them using two colons (::), but this can be used only once in an address.

❑ An anycast address represents the nearest interface to a device, where many devices can share an anycast address. Multicast addresses begin with *FF*.

❑ Global unicast addresses begin with *2000::/3*. Private addresses range from FE8 through FFF. A loopback address is ::1.

❑ The subnet ID is the first 64 bits and the interface ID is the last 64 bits. EUI-64 allows dynamic creation of the interface ID portion by using the MAC address on the interface.

Address Assignment

❑ DHCPv6 and stateless autoconfiguration allow interfaces to acquire their addressing dynamically.

❑ Stateless autoconfiguration allows an interface to learn the subnet ID from a router and dynamically create the interface ID using the EUI-64 method.

Routing and IPv6

❑ Supported routing protocols for IPv6 include static, RIPng, OPSFv3, IS-IS for IPv6, MP-BGP4, and EIGRP for IPv6.

❑ RIPng is based on RIPv2. The ALL-RIP router multicast address is FF02::9 and is sent via UDP to port 521.

❑ Dual stack is where a device runs both the IPv4 and IPv6 protocol stacks. 6to4 tunneling tunnels IPv6 packets in an IPv4 payload to connect two IPv6 networks via an intermediate IPv4 network.

IPv6 Configuration

❑ The **ipv6 unicast-routing** command globally enables IPv6 and must be the first IPv6 command executed on the router. The **ipv6 address** command assigns the prefix, the length, and the use of EUI-64 to assign the interface ID.

❑ The **ipv6 router rip** *tag* command enables an RIPng routing process on the router. The **ipv6 rip** *tag* **enable** command associates an interface to a particular RIPng routing process. The **show ipv6 rip** command displays the configuration of the RIPng routing process. The **show ipv6 route rip** command displays the RIPng routes in the IPv6 routing table.

SELF TEST

The following Self Test questions will help you measure your understanding of the material presented in this chapter. Read all the choices carefully, as there may be more than one correct answer. Choose all correct answers for each question.

Necessity of IPv6

1. IPv6 addresses are _____ bits in length.

IPv6 Addressing

2. Which of the following are valid IPv6 unicast addresses? (choose two)
   A. 2001::567::891::
   B. 2000::57
   C. 2000:FFEE:7878:1111:1:2:7:E
   D. 2001::

3. Which of the following best describes an anycast address?
   A. one-to-all
   B. one-to-many
   C. single interface
   D. one-to-nearest

4. Which of the following is a global address?
   A. 2001:FFEE:7880::
   B. FF80::9868:1122:ABCD:1234
   C. ::1
   D. None of the above

Address Assignment

5. Which of the following allows a router to forward a DHCP request to a remote DHCP server?
   A. DHCP solicit
   B. stateless autoconfiguration
   C. stateful autoconfiguration
   D. IP Helper

Routing and IPv6

6. Which of the following is true concerning RIPng?

   A. Uses 6to4 to share routing information with neighboring routers

   B. Uses a multicast address of FF02::9

   C. Uses TCP as a transport

   D. Uses port 520

7. Match the transition method with its description.
   Transition method: dual stack, 6to4 tunneling, ISATAP, and Teredo tunneling.
   Description: host-to-host tunneling, virtual links connect IPv6 localities, IPv6 packets are encapsulated in IPv4 payloads, both protocol stacks are operational on a device.

IPv6 Configuration

8. Which IPv6 command must first be entered on a Cisco router?

   A. `router ipv6-unicast`

   B. `ipv6 address`

   C. `ipv6 unicast-routing`

   D. `ipv6 support enable`

9. Enter the router command that globally enables RIPng, where the RIPng process is called *RP1*: _____.

10. Which router command enables RIPng on an interface?

    A. `ipv6 rip` *tag* `enable`

    B. `network`

    C. `ipv6 router rip` *tag*

    D. `ripng enable` *tag*

SELF TEST ANSWERS

Necessity of IPv6

1. ☑ IPv6 addresses are 128 bits in length.

IPv6 Addressing

2. ☑ **B** and **C.** 2000::57 and 2000:FFEE:7878:1111:1:2:7:E are valid IPv6 unicast addresses.
☒ **A** has multiple :: representations, making it invalid. **D** has the interface ID value of 0s, which is also invalid.

3. ☑ **D.** An anycast is one-to-nearest.
☒ **A** is incorrect because one-to-all represents a broadcast, which IPv6 doesn't support. **B**, one-to-many, represents a multicast address and **C**, single interface, represents a unicast address.

4. ☑ **D.** None of these is a global address.
☒ **A** is incorrect because 2001:FFEE:7880:: has an interface ID of 0s. **B** is incorrect because FF80::9868:1122:ABCD:1234 is a private address. **C** is incorrect because ::1 is a loopback address.

Address Assignment

5. ☑ **D.** IP Helper is the feature that allows the router to forward a DHCP solicit message to a remote DHCP server.
☒ **A**, DHCP solicit, is what a DHCP client generates to acquire its addressing information. **B**, stateless autoconfiguration, is what a client performs when DHCP is not configured but the client still wants to acquire its addressing dynamically. **C**, stateful autoconfiguration, is a nonexistent term.

Routing and IPv6

6. ☑ **B.** RIPng uses a multicast address of FF02::9.
☒ **A** is incorrect because 6to4 is not used to share routing information with neighbors, but instead to move IPv6 packets across an IPv4 backbone. **C** and **D** are incorrect because RIPng uses UDP on port 521.

7. ☑ Dual stack: both protocol stacks are operational on a device. 6to4 tunneling: IPv6 packets are encapsulated in IPv4 payloads. ISATAP: virtual links connect IPv6 localities. Teredo tunneling: host-to-host tunneling.

IPv6 Configuration

8. ☑ C. The `ipv6 unicast-routing` command globally enables IPv6 and must be the first IPv6 command executed on the router.

   ☒ A and D are invalid commands. B assigns an IPv6 address to an interface.

9. ☑ `ipv6 router rip RP1`.

10. ☑ A. The `ipv6 rip` *tag* `enable` command enables RIPng on an interface.

    ☒ B is incorrect because **network** is used in IPv4 to associate an interface with the RIP routing process. C and D are invalid commands.

Part VII

Cisco Routers and WANs

25

WAN Introduction

T he preceding few chapters introduced you to configuring advanced IP features on your Cisco router. This chapter introduces you to wide area networking (WAN) concepts and some basic point-to-point configurations, including High-Level Data Link Control (HDLC) and Point-to-Point Protocol (PPP). This chapter also introduces the use of virtual private networks (VPNs) in a WAN, briefly covering the most popular VPN implementation, IPSec.

CERTIFICATION OBJECTIVE 25.01

Wide Area Networking Overview

Typically, LAN connections are used within a company and WAN connections allow you to connect to remote locations or sites. With a WAN, you don't own the infrastructure for WAN connections—another company, such as a telephone company or cable provider, provides the infrastructure. WAN connections are usually slower than LAN connections. A derivative of WAN solutions is the metropolitan area network (MAN). MANs sometimes use high-speed LAN connections in a small geographic area between different companies or divisions within a company. MANs are becoming more and more popular in large cities and even provide connections over a LAN medium, such as Ethernet.

Equipment and Components

WAN connections are made up of many types of equipment and components. Figure 25-1 shows some of the WAN terms used for these, and Table 25-1 shows the terms and definitions. As you may recall from Chapters 2 and 11, data communications equipment (DCE) terminates a connection between two sites and provides clocking and synchronization for that connection; it connects to data termination equipment (DTE). The DCE category includes equipment such as channel service units/data service units (CSU/DSUs), Network Terminator Type 1 (NT1), and cable and analog modems. A DTE is an end-user device, such as a router or PC, which connects to the WAN via the DCE. In some circumstances, the function of the DCE might be built into the DTE's physical interface. For instance, certain Cisco routers can be purchased with built-in NT1s or CSU/DSUs in their WAN interfaces. Or you might have a laptop with a built-in analog modem.

FIGURE 25-1

WAN terms

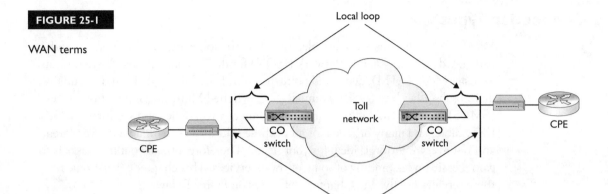

TABLE 25-1   WAN Terms and Definitions

Term	Definition
Customer premises equipment (CPE)	Your network's equipment, which includes the DCE (modem, NT1, CSU/DSU) and your DTE (router, access server)
Demarcation point	Where the responsibility of the carrier is passed on to you; this could be inside or outside your local facility; note that this is a *logical* boundary, not necessarily a physical boundary
Local loop	The connection from the carrier's switching equipment to the demarcation point
Central office (CO) switch	The carrier's switch within the toll network
Toll network	The carrier's internal infrastructure for transporting your data

Connection Types

Many WAN solutions are available, including the following: analog modems and Integrated Services Digital Network (ISDN) for dialup connections, Asynchronous Transfer Mode (ATM), dedicated point-to-point leased lines (dedicated circuits), digital subscriber line (DSL), Frame Relay, Switched Multi-megabit Data Services (SMDS), wireless (including cellular, laser microwave, radio, and satellite), X.25, DSL, cable, and many others. Not all of these solutions are available in every area, and not every solution is ideal for your needs. Therefore, one of your first tasks is to gain a basic understanding of some of these services. This chapter covers some of these services briefly, and Chapter 26 focuses on Frame Relay.

Typically, WAN connections fall under one of four categories:

- Leased lines, such as dedicated circuits or connections
- Circuit-switched connections, such as analog modem and digital ISDN dialup connections
- Packet-switched connections, such as Frame Relay and X.25
- Cell-switched connections, such as ATM and SMDS

The following sections introduce you to these four connection types.

WANs primarily operate at the physical and data link layers.

Leased-Line Connections

A leased-line connection is basically a dedicated circuit connection between two sites. It simulates a single cable connection between the local and remote sites. Leased lines are best suited when both of these conditions hold:

- The distance between the two sites is small, making the least-line connection cost-effective.
- A constant amount of traffic occurs between two sites and you need to guarantee bandwidth for certain applications.

Even though leased lines can provide guaranteed bandwidth and minimal delay for connections, other available solutions, such as ATM, can provide the same features. The main disadvantage of leased lines is their cost—they are typically the most expensive WAN solution. Another disadvantage is that each connection to a site requires a separate interface on your router. For example, if you had a central office router that needed access to four remote sites, the central office router would need four WAN interfaces for terminating the four leased lines. With Frame Relay and ATM, you could use one WAN interface to provide the same connectivity.

Leased lines use synchronous serial connections, with their data rates ranging from 2400 bps all the way up to 45 Mbps, in what is referred to as a *DS3* connection. A synchronous serial connection allows you to send and receive information simultaneously without having to wait for any signal from the remote side. Nor does a synchronous connection need to indicate when it is beginning to send something or the end of a transmission. These two things, plus how clocking is done, are the three major differences between synchronous and asynchronous connections—asynchronous connections are typically used for dialup connections, such as modems.

If you purchase a leased line, you will need the following equipment:

■ **DTE** A router with a synchronous serial interface: this provides the data link framing and terminates the WAN connection.

■ **DCE** A CSU/DSU to terminate the carrier's leased-line connection: this provides the clocking and synchronization for the connection.

Serial interfaces are used for WAN services like dedicated circuits (leased lines) and Frame Relay.

Figure 25-2 shows an example of the equipment required for a leased-line connection. The CSU/DSU is responsible for handling the

FIGURE 25-2

Leased line example

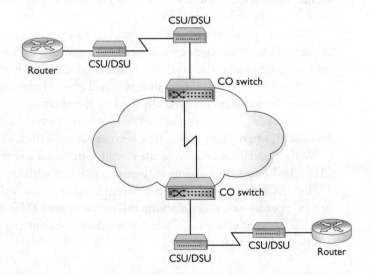

physical layer framing, clocking, and synchronization of the connection. Common data link layer protocols you can use for dedicated connections include PPP and HDLC.

Circuit-Switched Connections

Circuit-switched connections are dialup connections, like those that are used by a PC with a modem when dialing up an ISP. Circuit-switched connections include the following types:

- **Asynchronous serial connections** These include analog modem dialup connections and the standard telephone system, which is commonly referred to as Plain Old Telephone Service (POTS) by the telephone carriers.
- **Synchronous serial connections** These include digital ISDN Basic Rate Interface (BRI) and Primary Rate Interface (PRI) dialup connections; they provide guaranteed bandwidth.

Asynchronous serial connections are the cheapest form of WAN services but are also the slowest and most unreliable of the services. For instance, every time you make a connection using an analog modem, there is no guarantee of the connection rate you'll get. With these connections, the top connection rate in the United States is 53 Kbps, but depending on the quality of the connection, you might get something as low as 300 bps. In the United States, the Federal Communications Commission (FCC) restricts analog data rates to 53 Kbps or less. Other countries might support higher data rates.

The main problem with circuit-switched connections is that they are expensive if you need to make connections over long distances, with a per-minute charge that varies, depending on the destination: the more data you have to send, the more time it will take, and the more money it will cost. Therefore, asynchronous circuit-switched connections are typically used for home office and low-speed backup connections, as well as temporary low-speed connections for additional boosts in bandwidth when your primary link becomes congested or when it fails.

With leased lines, as soon as the circuit is installed and you have configured your DTE, the line remains up unless there is a problem with the carrier's network or the DTE or DCE equipment. This is different from circuit-switched connections, which are temporary—you make a phone call to the remote DTE and when the line comes up, you transmit your data. Once you are done transmitting your data, the phone connection is terminated.

If you will be using a circuit-switched analog connection, you'll need this equipment:

- **DTE**   A router with an asynchronous serial interface
- **DCE**   A modem

If you will be using a circuit-switched digital connection, you'll need this equipment:

- **DTE**   A router with an ISDN interface
- **DCE**   An NT1 for a BRI or a CSU/DSU for a PRI

Figure 25-3 shows an example of an analog circuit-switched connection. With this connection, you'll typically use PPP or HDLC for the encapsulation: SLIP is rarely used since it lacks authentication and supports only IP as a transported protocol.

Packet-Switched Connections

With leased lines and circuit-switched connections, a physical circuit is used to make the connection between the two sites. With a leased line, the same circuit path is always used. With circuit-switched connections, the circuit path is built every time a phone call is made, making it highly probable that the same circuit path will not be used for every phone call.

Packet-switched connections use logical circuits to make connections between two sites. These logical circuits are referred to as *virtual circuits* (VCs). One advantage that a logical circuit has over a physical one is that a logical circuit is not tied to any particular physical circuit. Instead, a logical circuit is built across any available physical connection. Another advantage of logical circuits is that you can build multiple logical circuits over the same physical circuit. Therefore, with a

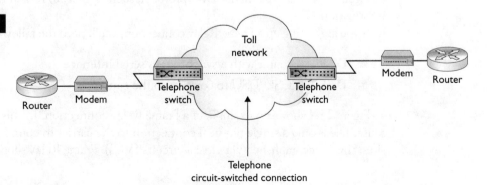

FIGURE 25-3

Analog circuit-switched connection

single physical connection to a carrier, you can connect to multiple sites. This is not possible with leased lines: for each location to which you want to connect, you need a *separate* physical circuit, making the cost of the solution much higher than one that uses logical circuits. Technologies that use packet switching and logical circuits include ATM, Frame Relay, SMDS, and X.25. From a cost perspective, packet-switched solutions fall somewhere between circuit-switched solutions and leased lines.

on the
O o b
Both Frame Relay and ATM are in regression in their usage in the marketplace. The advent of cable modems, DSL, fiber to the home, and other technologies have drastically cut into the deployment of Frame Relay and ATM. X.25 usage is very uncommon today because of the proliferation of reliable digital circuits.

X.25 The oldest of these four technologies is X.25, which is an ITU-T standard. X.25 is a network layer protocol that runs across both synchronous and asynchronous physical circuits, providing a lot of flexibility for your connection options. X.25 was actually developed to run across unreliable medium. It provides error detection *and* correction, as well as flow control, at both the data link layer (by LAPB) and the network layer (by X.25). In this sense, it performs a function similar to what TCP, at the transport layer, provides for IP. Because of its overhead, X.25 is best delegated to asynchronous, unreliable connections. If you have a synchronous digital connection, another protocol, such as Frame Relay or ATM, is much more efficient.

Frame Relay Frame Relay is a digital packet-switched service that can run only across synchronous digital connections at the data link layer. Because it uses digital connections (which have very few errors), it does not perform any error correction or flow control as X.25 does. Frame Relay will, however, detect errors and drops bad frames. It is up to a higher layer protocol, such as TCP, to resend the dropped information.

If you are setting up a Frame Relay connection, you'll need the following equipment:

- **DTE** A router with a synchronous serial interface
- **DCE** A CSU/DSU to connect to the carrier

Figure 25-4 shows an example of a Frame Relay connection. In this example, the router needs only a single physical connection to the carrier to connect to multiple sites: this is accomplished via virtual circuits (VCs). Frame Relay supports speeds

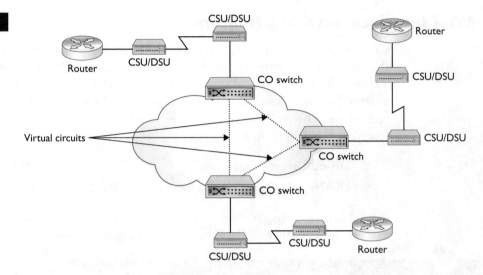

FIGURE 25-4

Frame Relay
packet-switched
connection

from fractional T1 or E1 connections (56–64 Kbps) up to a DS3 (45 Mbps). Frame Relay is discussed in Chapter 26.

ATM ATM is also a packet-switched technology that uses digital circuits. Unlike Frame Relay and X.25, however, this service uses fixed-length (53 byte) packets, called *cells*, to transmit information. Therefore, this service is commonly called a cell-switched service. It has an advantage over Frame Relay in that it can provide guaranteed throughput and minimal delay for a multitude of services, including voice, video, and data. However, it does cost more than Frame Relay services. ATM (sort of an enhanced Frame Relay) can offer a connection guaranteed bandwidth, limited delay, limited number of errors, Quality of Service (QoS), and more. Frame Relay can provide some minimal guarantees to connections, but not to the degree of precision that ATM can. Whereas Frame Relay is limited to 45 Mbps connections, ATM can scale to very high speeds: OC-192 (SONET), for instance, affords about 10 Gbps of bandwidth.

exam
watch

Remember that packet-switched and cell-switched services are typically used when a router has only a *single WAN interface but needs to connect to multiple remote sites.*

WAN Interfaces on Cisco Routers

Cisco supports a wide variety of serial cables for its serial router interfaces. Some of the cable types supported for synchronous serial interfaces are EIA/TIA-232, EIA/TIA-449, EIA/TIA-530, V.35, and X.21. The end that connects to the DCE device is defined by these standards. However, the end that connects to the Cisco router is proprietary in nature. Cisco's cables have two different end connectors that connect to a router's serial interfaces:

- **DB-60** Has 60 pins
- **DB-26** Has 26 pins and is flat, like a USB cable

Note that these connectors are for synchronous serial connections. Cisco has other cable types, typically with RJ-45 connectors, for asynchronous connections.

WAN Cabling

In WAN connections, your router is the DTE and the equipment to which it attaches, such as a modem, CSU/DSU, or an NT1, is a DCE. The DCE is responsible for providing the clocking and synchronization of the physical layer connection. The cabling discussed in this section applies only to DTE-to-DCE connections. The cabling used for the WAN connection is dependent on the technology and speed of access that you are using.

Table 25-2 lists the connectors/cables and when they are used. Each cable has two ends: one connects to the DCE and the other to the DTE. The DCE endpoint is defined in the Cable Standards column in Table 25-2. However, the DTE end is proprietary to Cisco.

Encapsulation Methods

Many different methods are available for encapsulating data for serial connections. Table 25-3 shows the most common ones. The following sections cover HDLC and PPP in more depth.

TABLE 25-2	Cable Standards	HDLC	PPP	Frame Relay	HSSI
WAN Cable Types	EIA/TIA-232	Yes	Yes	Yes	No
	EIA/TIA-449	Yes	Yes	Yes	No
	EIA/TIA-612/613	No	No	No	Yes
	X.21	Yes	Yes	Yes	No
	V.24	Yes	Yes	Yes	No
	V.35	Yes	Yes	Yes	No

e x a m

w a t c h   *Be familiar with the* *data link encapsulation types listed in*   *Table 25-2, such as HDLC, PPP, and LAPB (Frame Relay).*

TABLE 25-3	Protocol	Explanation
Common Encapsulation Methods	High-Level Data Link Control (HDLC)	Based on ISO standards, it is used with synchronous and asynchronous connections.
	Synchronous Data Link Control Protocol (SDLC)	Used in IBM SNA environments, it has been replaced by HDLC.
	Link Access Procedure Balanced (LAPB)	Used in X.25, it has extensive error detection and correction.
	Link Access Procedure D Channel (LAPD)	It is used by ISDN to signal call setup and teardown of phone connections.
	Link Access Procedure Frame mode bearer services (LAPF)	It is used in Frame Relay between a DTE and a DCE and is similar to LAPD.
	Point-to-Point Protocol (PPP)	Based on RFC standards, PPP is the most common encapsulation used for dialup and dedicated circuits. It provides for authentication, handling multiple protocols, compression, multilink, and error detection.

HDLC

Based on ISO standards, the HDLC protocol can be used with synchronous and asynchronous connections and defines the frame type and interaction between two devices at the data link layer. The following sections cover how Cisco implements HDLC and how it is configured on a router's serial interface.

Frame Type

Cisco's implementation of HDLC is based on ISO's standards, but Cisco has made a change in the frame format, making it proprietary. In other words, Cisco's HDLC will work only if the remote end also supports Cisco's HDLC. Figure 25-5 shows examples of some WAN frame formats, including ISO's HDLC, Cisco's HDLC, and PPP. Notice that the main difference between ISO's HDLC and Cisco's frame format is that Cisco has a proprietary field: *Type*. One of the problems with ISO's HDLC is that it does not define how to carry multiple protocols across a single link, as does Cisco's HDLC with the Type field. Therefore, ISO's HDLC is typically used on serial links where there is only a single protocol to transport. The *default* encapsulation on Cisco's synchronous serial interfaces is HDLC. Actually, Cisco supports only its own implementation of HDLC, not ISO's implementation.

Cisco's HDLC has a proprietary Type field in the frame header.

FIGURE 25-5

WAN frame types

ISO's HDLC

Flag	Address	Control	Data	FCS	Flag

Cisco's HDLC

Flag	Address	Control	Type	Data	FCS	Flag

PPP

Flag	Address	Control	Protocol	Data	FCS	Flag

Configuring HDLC

As mentioned in the preceding section, the default encapsulation on Cisco's synchronous serial interfaces is HDLC. You need to use the following configuration only if you changed the data link layer protocol to something else and then need to set it back to HDLC:

```
Router(config)# interface serial [slot_#/]port_#
Router(config-if)# encapsulation hdlc
```

Notice that you must be in the serial interface (Interface Subconfiguration mode) to change its data link layer encapsulation. If you had a different encapsulation configured on the serial interface, executing this command would set the frame format to Cisco's HDLC. Note that the other side must be set to Cisco's HDLC or the data link layer will fail on the interface (the interface will be "up, line protocol is down").

HDLC is the default encapsulation on synchronous serial interfaces of Cisco routers. Use the show interfaces *command to see the encapsulation type. Use the* encapsulation hdlc *command to change the serial interface's encapsulation to Cisco's HDLC. Note that if one router is a Cisco router and the other a non-Cisco router when using HDLC, the interface will show as "up, line protocol is down". This would also be true if one side was using PPP and the other HDLC or if a DCE was not providing any clocking to the router (DTE).*

After you have configured HDLC, use the **show interfaces** command to view the data link layer encapsulation:

```
Router# show interfaces serial 1
Serial1 is up, line protocol is up
  Hardware is MCI Serial
  Internet address is 192.168.2.2 255.255.255.0
  MTU 1500 bytes, BW 1544 Kbit, DLY 20000 usec, rely 255/255, load 1/255
  Encapsulation HDLC, loopback not set, keepalive set (10 sec)
  Last input 0:00:02, output 0:00:00, output hang never
  .
  .
  .
```

Notice in this example that the physical and data link layers are up and that the encapsulation is set to Cisco's HDLC (`Encapsulation HDLC`).

on the
ⓙob

Remember that the `encapsulation hdlc` command is the default on a serial interface and is thus not displayed with the `show running-config` command. Use the `show interfaces` command to view the encapsulation type on a serial interface. Notice (from the `show interfaces` output) that HDLC sends keepalives and expects responses back (the default keepalive timer is 10 seconds). If no responses to the keepalives are seen, the interface will show as "up, line protocol is down".

CertCam

25.01. The CD contains a multimedia demonstration of configuring HDLC on a router.

CERTIFICATION OBJECTIVE 25.03

PPP

Whereas Cisco's HDLC is a proprietary protocol, PPP is based on an open standard defined in RFCs 1332, 1661, and 2153. PPP works with asynchronous and synchronous serial connections as well as High-Speed Serial Interfaces (HSSI) and ISDN interfaces (BRI and PRI). The following sections offer an overview of PPP and how to configure it, including authentication.

exam
ⓦatch

HDLC on Cisco routers is proprietary and can be used only on a point-to-point connection between two Cisco routers. When connecting Cisco and non-Cisco routers on point-to-point connections, PPP should be used since it is an open standard.

PPP Components

PPP has many more features than HDLC. Like HDLC, PPP defines a frame type and how two PPP devices communicate with each other, including the multiplexing of network and data link layer protocols across the same link. However, PPP also does the following:

- Performs dynamic configuration of links
- Allows for authentication
- Compresses packet headers
- Tests the quality of links
- Performs error detection and correction
- Allows multiple PPP physical connections to be bound together as a single logical connection (referred to as *multilink*)

PPP supports handling multiple encapsulated protocols, authentication, compression, multilink, *error detection/correction, and can be used over synchronous and asynchronous circuits.*

PPP has three main components:

- Frame format (encapsulation)
- Link Control Protocol (LCP)
- Network Control Protocol (NCP)

Each of these three components plays an important role in the setup, configuration, and transfer of information across a PPP connection. The following sections cover these components.

Frame Format

The first component of PPP is the frame format, or encapsulation method, it uses. The frame format defines how network layer packets are encapsulated in a PPP frame, as well as the format of the PPP frame. PPP is typically used for serial WAN connections because of its open-standard character. It works on asynchronous (modem) and synchronous (ISDN, point-to-point, and HSSI) connections. If you are dialing up to your ISP, you'll be using PPP. PPP's frame format is based on ISO's HDLC, as you can see in Figure 25-5. The main difference is that the PPP frame has a Protocol field, which defines the protocol of the network layer data that is encapsulated.

LCP and NCP

The second and third components of PPP are LCP and NCP. LCP is responsible for establishing, configuring, authenticating, and testing a PPP connection. It handles all of the up-front work in setting up a connection. Here are some of the things that LCP will negotiate when setting up a PPP connection:

- Authentication method used (PPP Authentication Procedure [PAP] or Challenge-Handshake Authentication Protocol [CHAP]), if any
- Compression algorithm used (Stacker or Predictor), if any
- Callback phone number to use, if defined
- Multilink: other physical connections to use, if configured

LCP and NCP go through three steps to establish a PPP connection:

1. Link establishment (LCP)
2. Authentication (LCP)
3. Protocol negotiation (NCP)

The first step is the link establishment phase. In this step, LCP negotiates the PPP parameters that are to be used for the connection, which may include the authentication method and compression algorithms. If authentication has been configured, the authentication type is negotiated. This can either be PAP or CHAP. These are discussed later in the "PPP Authentication" section. If authentication is configured and there is a match on the authentication type on both sides, authentication is performed in the second step. If this is successful, NCP, in the third step, will negotiate the upper layer protocols, which can include protocols such as IP and IPX as well as data link layer protocols (bridged traffic, such as Ethernet, and Cisco's CDP) that will be transmitted across the PPP link. Once LCP and NCP perform their negotiation and the connection has been authenticated (if this has been defined), the data link layer will come up (the status of a router's interface will be "up, line protocol is up").

Once a connection is enabled, LCP uses error detection to monitor dropped data on the connection as well as loops at the data link layer. The Quality and Magic Numbers protocol is used by LCP to ensure that the connection remains reliable.

Configuring PPP

The configuration of PPP is almost as simple as that of HDLC. To specify that PPP is to be used on a WAN interface, use the following configuration:

```
Router(config)# interface type [slot_#]port_#
Router(config-if)# encapsulation ppp
```

As you can see, you need to specify the **ppp** parameter in the **encapsulation** Interface Subconfiguration mode command. With the exception of authentication, other PPP options are not discussed in this book.

25.02. The CD contains a multimedia demonstration of configuring PPP on a router.

Troubleshooting PPP

Once you have configured PPP on your router's interface, you can verify the status of the interface with the **show interfaces** command:

```
Router# show interfaces serial 0
Serial0 is up, line protocol is up
  Hardware is MCI Serial
  Internet address is 192.168.1.2 255.255.255.0
  MTU 1500 bytes, BW 1544 Kbit, DLY 20000 usec, rely 255/255, load 1/255
  Encapsulation PPP, loopback not set, keepalive set (10 sec)
  lcp state = OPEN
  ncp ccp state = NOT NEGOTIATED   ncp ipcp state = OPEN
  ncp osicp state = NOT NEGOTIATED   ncp ipxcp state = NOT NEGOTIATED
  ncp xnscp state = NOT NEGOTIATED   ncp vinescp state = NOT NEGOTIATED
  ncp deccp state = NOT NEGOTIATED   ncp bridgecp state = NOT NEGOTIATED
  ncp atalkcp state = NOT NEGOTIATED   ncp lex state = NOT NEGOTIATED
  ncp cdp state = OPEN
  .
  .
  .
```

In the fifth line of output, you can see that the encapsulation is set to PPP. Below this is the status of LCP (`lcp state = OPEN`). An OPEN state indicates that LCP has successfully negotiated its parameters and brought up the data link layer. The statuses of the protocols by NCP follow. In this example, only two protocols are running across this PPP connection: IP (`ncp ipcp state = OPEN`) and CDP (`ncp cdp state = OPEN`).

e x a m

ⓦatch   *If one side is configured for PPP and the other side is configured with a different encapsulation type (such as HDLC), the interface status will be "up, line protocol is down". If the physical and data link layers are "up, line protocol is up" and you don't have layer 3 connectivity, there is probably a problem with the IP addressing on the two peers: you're using the wrong address when doing a ping or the addresses on the two peers are in the wrong subnets.*

If you are having problems with the data link layer coming up when you've configured PPP, you can use the following **debug** command to troubleshoot the connection:

```
Router# debug ppp negotiation
PPP protocol negotiation debugging is on
Router# configure terminal
Enter configuration commands, one per line.  End with CNTL/Z.
Router(config)# interface serial 0
Router(config-if)# no shutdown
%LINK-3-UPDOWN: Interface Serial0, changed state to up
ppp: sending CONFREQ, type = 5 (CI_MAGICNUMBER), value = 4FEFE5
PPP Serial0: received config for type = 0x5 (MAGICNUMBER) value = 0x561036 acked
PPP Serial0: state = ACKSENT fsm_rconfack(0xC021): rcvd id 0x2
ppp: config ACK received, type = 5 (CI_MAGICNUMBER), value = 4FEFE5
ipcp: sending CONFREQ, type = 3 (CI_ADDRESS), Address = 192.168.2.1
ppp Serial0: Negotiate IP address: her address 192.168.2.2 (ACK)
ppp: ipcp_reqci: returning CONFACK.
ppp: cdp_reqci: returning CONFACK
PPP Serial0: state = ACKSENT fsm_rconfack(0x8021): rcvd id 0x2
ipcp: config ACK received, type = 3 (CI_ADDRESS), Address = 192.168.2.1
PPP Serial0: state = ACKSENT fsm_rconfack(0x8207): rcvd id 0x2
ppp: cdp_reqci: received CONFACK
%LINEPROTO-5-UPDOWN: Line protocol on Interface Serial0, changed state to up
```

In this example, **debug** was first enabled and then the serial interface was enabled. Notice that the two connected routers go through a negotiation process. They first verify their IP addresses, 192.168.2.1 and 192.168.2.2, to make sure they are not the same address, and then they negotiate the protocols (`ipcp_reqci` and `cdp_reqci`). In this example, IP and CDP are negotiated and the data link layer comes up after the successful negotiation.

25.03. The CD contains a multimedia demonstration of troubleshooting PPP on a router.

ex**a m**
w a t c h

Use the encapsulation ppp *command to change a serial interface's encapsulation to PPP. When you look at the output of the* show interfaces *command, any protocol* *listed as* OPEN *has been negotiated correctly. If you are having problems with the LCP negotiation, use the* debug ppp negotiation *command.*

PPP Authentication

PPP, unlike HDLC, supports device authentication. Two methods can be used to implement authentication: PAP and CHAP. Both of these authentication methods are defined in RFC 1334; RFC 1994 replaces the CHAP component of RFC 1334. The authentication process is performed (by LCP) before the network and data link layer protocols are negotiated for the PPP connection by NCP. If the authentication fails, the data link layer will not come up. Authentication is optional and adds very little overhead to the connection. As you will see in the following sections, the setup and troubleshooting of PAP and CHAP are easy.

PAP

Of the two PPP authentication protocols, PAP is the simplest but the least secure. During the authentication phase, PAP goes through a two-way handshake process. In this process, the source sends its username (or hostname) and password, in clear text, to the destination. The destination compares this information to a list of locally stored usernames and passwords. If it finds a match, the destination sends back an *accept* message. If it doesn't find a match, it sends back a *reject* message. The top part of Figure 25-6 shows an example of PAP authentication.

FIGURE 25-6

PAP and CHAP authentication

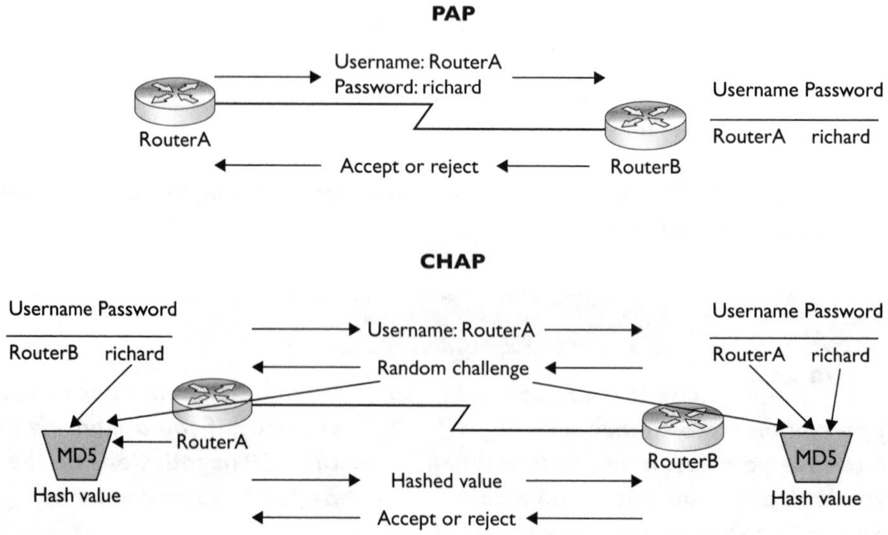

The configuration of PAP is straightforward. First, you need to determine which side will be the client side (sends the username and password) and which will be the server side (validates the username and password). To configure PAP for a PPP client, use this configuration:

```
Router(config)# interface type [slot_#]port_#
Router(config-if)# encapsulation ppp
Router(config-if)# ppp pap sent-username your_hostname
                       password password
```

The first thing you must do on the router's interface is to define the encapsulation type as PPP. Second, you must specify that PAP will be used for authentication and provide the username and password that will be used to perform the authentication on the server side. This is accomplished with the **ppp pap sent-username** command.

To configure the server side of a PPP PAP connection, use the following configuration:

```
Router(config)# hostname your_router's_hostname
Router(config)# username remote_hostname
                       password matching_password
Router(config)# interface type [slot_#/]port_#
Router(config-if)# encapsulation ppp
Router(config-if)# ppp authentication pap
```

The first thing you must do is to give your router a unique hostname. Second, you must list the remote hostnames and passwords these remote hosts will use when authenticating to your router. This is accomplished with the **username** command. Please note that the password you configure on this side must match the password on the remote side (it's case-sensitive). On your router's WAN interface, you need to enable PPP with the **encapsulation ppp** command. Then you can specify PAP authentication with the **ppp authentication pap** command.

The preceding client and server code listings perform a one-way authentication— the client authenticates to the server and not vice versa. If you want to perform two-way authentication, where each side must authenticate to the other side, configure both devices as PAP servers and clients.

25.04. The CD contains a multimedia demonstration of configuring PPP authentication using PAP on a router.

CHAP

One main problem with PAP is that it sends the username and password across the connection in clear text. If someone is tapping into the connection and eavesdropping on the PPP communication, she will see the actual password that is being used, making it an insecure authentication method. CHAP, on the other hand, uses a one-way hash function based on the Message Digest 5 (MD5) hashing algorithm to hash the password. This hashed value is then sent across the wire. In this situation, the actual password is never sent. Anyone tapping the wire will not be able to reverse the hash to come up with the original password. This is why MD5 is referred to as a one-way function—it cannot be reverse-engineered.

CHAP uses a three-way handshake process to perform authentication. The bottom part of Figure 25-6 shows the CHAP authentication process. First, the source sends its username (not its password) to the destination. The destination sends back a challenge, which is a random value generated by the destination. The challenge contains the following information:

- **Packet identifier**   Set to 01 for a challenge, 02 for the reply to a challenge, 03 for allowing the PPP connection, and 04 for denying the connection
- **ID**   A local sequence number assigned by the challenger to distinguish among multiple authentication processes
- **Random number**   The random value used in the MD5 hash function
- **Router name**   The name of the challenging router (the server), which is used by the source to find the appropriate password to use for authentication

Both sides then take the source's username, the matching password, and the challenge and run them through the MD5 hashing function. The source then takes the result of this function and sends it to the destination. The destination compares this value to the hashed output that it generated—if the two values match, the password used by the source must have been the same as that which was used by the destination, and thus the destination will permit the connection.

The following configuration shows how to set up two-way CHAP authentication:

```
Router(config)# hostname your_router's_hostname
Router(config)# username remote_hostname
                          password matching_password
Router(config)# interface type [slot_#/]port_#
Router(config-if)# encapsulation ppp
Router(config-if)# ppp authentication chap
```

Notice that this is the same configuration used with server-side PAP, with the exception of the omission of the sent username. The only difference is that the **chap** parameter is specified in the **ppp authentication** command.

25.05. The CD contains a multimedia demonstration of configuring PPP authentication using CHAP on a router.

Actually, here is the full syntax of the PPP authentication command:

```
Router(config-if)# ppp authentication chap|pap|ms-chap
                          [chap|pap|ms-chap]
```

If you specify **pap chap** or **chap pap**, the router will negotiate both authentication parameters in the order that you specified them. For example, if you configure **chap pap**, your router will first try to negotiate CHAP; if this fails, then it will negotiate PAP.

on the **job**

Microsoft has its own implementation of CHAP, which is not compatible with the RFC version of CHAP. Therefore, if you are connecting to a Microsoft device, choose ms-chap for your authentication parameter.

Troubleshooting Authentication

To determine whether authentication was successful, use the **show interfaces** command:

```
Router# show interfaces serial 0
Serial0 is up, line protocol is down
  Hardware is MCI Serial
  Internet address is 192.168.1.2 255.255.255.0
  MTU 1500 bytes, BW 1544 Kbit, DLY 20000 usec, rely 254/255, load 1/255
```

```
Encapsulation PPP, loopback not set, keepalive set (10 sec)
lcp state = ACKRCVD
ncp ccp state = NOT NEGOTIATED    ncp ipcp state = CLOSED
ncp osicp state = NOT NEGOTIATED    ncp ipxcp state = NOT NEGOTIATED
ncp xnscp state = NOT NEGOTIATED    ncp vinescp state = NOT NEGOTIATED
ncp deccp state = NOT NEGOTIATED    ncp bridgecp state = NOT NEGOTIATED
ncp atalkcp state = NOT NEGOTIATED    ncp lex state = NOT NEGOTIATED
ncp cdp state = CLOSED
        .
        .
        .
```

Notice the lcp state in this example: it's not OPEN. Also, notice the states for IP and CDP: CLOSED. These things indicate that something is wrong with the LCP setup process, causing the data link layer to fail ("up, line protocol is down"). In this example, the CHAP passwords on the two routers didn't match.

25.06. The CD contains a multimedia demonstration of troubleshooting PPP authentication on a router.

Of course, looking at the preceding output, you don't really know that this was an authentication problem. To determine this, use the **debug ppp authentication** command. Here's an example of the use of this command with two-way CHAP authentication:

```
RouterA# debug ppp authentication
%LINK-3-UPDOWN: Interface Serial0, changed state to up
Se0 PPP: Treating connection as a dedicated line
Se0 PPP: Phase is AUTHENTICATING, by both
Se0 CHAP: O CHALLENGE id 2 len 28 from "RouterA"
Se0 CHAP: I CHALLENGE id 3 len 28 from "RouterB"
Se0 CHAP: O RESPONSE id 3 len 28 from "RouterA"
Se0 CHAP: I RESPONSE id 2 len 28 from "RouterB"
Se0 CHAP: O SUCCESS id 2 len 4
Se0 CHAP: I SUCCESS id 3 len 4
%LINEPROTO-5-UPDOWN: Line protocol on Interface Serial0, changed
state to up
```

In this example, notice that both routers—RouterA and RouterB—are using CHAP for authentication. Both routers send a CHALLENGE, and both receive a corresponding RESPONSE. Notice the I and O following Se0 CHAP:, which indicates the direction of the CHAP message: I is for inbound and O is for outbound. Following this is the status of the hashed passwords: SUCCESS. And, last, you can see the data link layer coming up for the serial interface.

Here's an example of a router using PAP with two-way authentication:

```
RouterA# debug ppp authentication
%LINK-3-UPDOWN: Interface Serial0, changed state to up
Se0 PPP: Treating connection as a dedicated line
Se0 PPP: Phase is AUTHENTICATING, by both
Se0 PAP: O AUTH-REQ id 2 len 18 from "RouterA"
Se0 PAP: I AUTH-REQ id 3 len 18 from "RouterB"
Se0 PAP: Authenticating peer RouterB
Se0 PAP: O AUTH-ACK id 2 len 5
Se0 PAP: I AUTH-ACK id 3 len 5
%LINEPROTO-5-UPDOWN: Line protocol on Interface Serial0, changed
state to up
```

In this example, notice that the authentication messages are different. The AUTH-REQ shows the server requesting the authentication from a router, and the AUTH-ACK acknowledges the successful password matching by a router. Notice that since both routers are requesting authentication, both routers are set up in server mode for PAP.

exam
ⓦatch
PAP authentication sends the username and password across the wire in clear text. CHAP doesn't send the password in clear text—instead, a hashed value from the MD5 algorithm is sent. Use the ppp authentication *command to specify which PPP authentication method to use. The* username *command allows you to build a local authentication table, which lists the remote names and passwords to use for authentication. The* debug ppp authentication *command can help you troubleshoot PPP problems—be familiar with the output of this command.*

EXERCISE 25-1

Configuring PPP

The last few sections dealt with the configuration of PPP on IOS routers. This exercise will help you reinforce this material by configuring PPP and authentication. You'll perform this lab using Boson's NetSim simulator. You can find a picture of the network diagram for Boson's NetSim simulator in the Introduction of this book. After starting the simulator, click the LabNavigator button. Next, double-click Exercise 25-1 and click the Load Lab button. This will load the lab configuration based on the exercises in Chapters 11 and 16.

1. Check network connectivity between the two routers.

   At the top of the simulator in the menu bar, click the eRouters icon and choose 2600-1. From the 2600-1 router, verify the status of the serial interface: **show interface s0**. Make sure the encapsulation is HDLC. From the 2600-1 router, ping the 2600-2: **ping 192.168.2.2**. The ping should be successful.

2. On the 2600-1 router, set up PPP as the encapsulation on the serial0 interface.

   At the top of the simulator in the menu bar, click the eRouters icon and choose 2600-1. On the 2600-1, enter the serial interface: **configure terminal** and **interface serial0**. Set up PPP as the data link frame type: **encapsulation ppp** and **end**.

3. Verify the status of the serial0 interface.

   View the status of the interface: **show interface serial0**. The physical layer should be *up* and the data link layer should be *down*—the 2600-2 still has HDLC configured. Also, examine the output of the **show** command to verify that the encapsulation is PPP.

4. On the 2600-2 router, set up PPP as the encapsulation on the serial0 interface.

   At the top of the simulator in the menu bar, click the eRouters icon and choose 2600-2. On the 2600-2, enter the serial interface: **configure terminal** and **interface serial0**. Set up PPP as the data link frame type: **encapsulation ppp** and **end**.

5. Verify the status of the serial0 interface.

View the status of the interface: **show interface serial0**. The physical and data link layers should be *up* (this should also be true on the 2600-1 router). Also check to make sure the encapsulation is PPP.

6. Test connectivity by pinging the 2600-1's **serial0** interface.

   Test connectivity: **ping 192.168.2.1**. The ping should be successful.

7. Set up PPP CHAP authentication on the 2600-1. Use a password of *richard*. Test the authentication.

   At the top of the simulator in the menu bar, click the eRouters icon and choose 2600-1. Access Configuration mode: **configure terminal**. On the 2600-1, set up your username and password: **username 2600-2 password richard**. Enter the serial interface: **interface serial0**. Set the authentication to CHAP: **ppp authentication chap**. Shut down the interface: **shutdown**. Bring the interface back up: **no shutdown**. Exit Configuration mode: **end**.

8. Examine the status of the **serial0** interface.

   Examine the status of the interface: **show interface serial0**. The data link layer should be down, and the LCP should be ACKRCVD. Please note that you don't really need to bring the interface down and back up, because after a period of time, LCP will notice that authentication configuration and will perform it.

9. Set up PPP CHAP authentication on the 2600-2. Use a password of *richard*. Test the authentication. Test the connection.

   At the top of the simulator in the menu bar, click the eRouters icon and choose 2600-2. Access Configuration mode: **configure terminal**. On the 2600-2, set up your username and password: **username 2600-1 password richard**. Enter the serial interface: **interface serial0**. Set the authentication to CHAP: **ppp authentication chap**. Shut down the interface: **shutdown**. Bring the interface back up: **no shutdown**. Exit Configuration mode: **end**.

10. Examine the status of the **serial0** interface.

    Examine the status of the interface: **show interface serial0**. The data link layer should come up and the LCP should be OPEN. IP and CDP should be the two protocols in an OPEN state.

11. Test connectivity to the 2600-1.

    Ping the 2600-1: **ping 192.168.2.1**. The ping should be successful.

EXERCISE 25-2

Basic PPP Troubleshooting

This exercise is a troubleshooting exercise and is different from Exercise 25-1. In that exercise, you set up a PPP CHAP connection between the 2600-2 and 2600-1 routers. In this exercise, the network is already configured; however, there are three problems in this network you'll need to find and fix in order for it to operate correctly. All of these problems deal with connectivity between the 2600-2 and 2600-1 routers. You'll perform this exercise using Boson's NetSim simulator. You can find a picture of the network diagram for Boson's NetSim simulator in the Introduction of this book. The addressing scheme is the same. After starting up the simulator, click the LabNavigator button. Next, double-click Exercise 25-2 and click the Load Lab button. This will load the lab with a PPP configuration on your routers.

Let's start with your problem: The PPP data link layer between the 2600-2 and 2600-1 won't come up. Your task is to figure out and fix three problems. Try this troubleshooting process on your own first; if you have problems, come back to the steps and solutions provided here.

1. Examine the status of the serial interface on the 2600-1.

   At the top of the simulator in the menu bar, click the eRouters icon and choose 2600-1. Examine serial0: **show interfaces serial0**. Note that the interface is up and line protocol is down. This indicates a physical or data link layer problem.

2. Check the status of serial0 on the 2600-2.

   At the top of the simulator in the menu bar, click the eRouters icon and choose 2600-2. Examine the status of the interface: **show interfaces serial0**. Notice that the interface is administratively down. Activate the interface: **configure terminal**, **interface serial0**, **no shutdown**, and **end**. Wait a few seconds and examine the status of the interface: **show interfaces serial0**. Notice that the status of the interface is up and down, indicating that there is a problem with the data link layer. Notice that the encapsulation, though, is set to PPP.

3. Check the 2600-1's serial encapsulation and the rest of its configuration.

Examine the status of the interface: **show interfaces serial0**. Notice that the status of the interface is up and down, indicating that there is a problem with the data link layer. Notice that the encapsulation, though, is set to PPP. Since both sides are set to PPP, there must be an authentication problem. Examine the 2600-1's active configuration: **show running-config**. CHAP is configured for authentication on serial0. Notice, though, that the **username** has the 2600-1's, and not the 2600-2's. Fix this by doing the following: **configure terminal**, **no username 2600-1 password cisco**, **username 2600-2 password cisco**, and **end**. Re-examine the router's configuration: **show running-config**. Examine the status of the interface: **show interfaces serial0**. The data link layer is still down, so there must be a problem on the 2600-2 router.

4. Access the 2600-2 router and determine the PPP problem.

   At the top of the simulator in the menu bar, click the eRouters icon and choose 2600-2. Examine the active configuration: **show running-config**. The **username** command is correct, with the 2600-1's hostname and a password of *cisco*. However, there is a problem with the PPP authentication method on the serial interface: CHAP is missing. Fix this problem: **configure terminal**, **interface serial0**, and **ppp authentication chap**. Bounce the interface: **shutdown**, **no shutdown**, and **end**. Re-examine the router's configuration: **show running-config**. Wait a few seconds and examine the status of the interface: **show interfaces serial0**. The data link layer should now be up and line protocol is up.

5. Now test connectivity between the 2600-2 and 2600-1.

   Test connectivity to the 2600-1: **ping 192.168.2.1**. The ping should be successful. If you want to allow connectivity for all devices, you'll need to add a static route on both the 2600-2 (to reach 192.168.1.0/24) and the 2600-1 (to reach 192.168.3.0/24).

Now you should be more comfortable with configuring PPP on a router.

Virtual Private Networks

One WAN solution becoming more common today is virtual private networks, commonly called VPNs. The *network* part of the term refers to the use of a public network, such as the Internet, to implement the WAN solution. The *virtual* part of the term hides the public network from the internal network components, such as users and services. This is similar to using virtual circuits (VCs) to connect remote locations, such as a corporate office, remote access users and SOHOs, branch and regional offices, and business partners, as shown in Figure 25-7. Actually, a VPN is similar to a Frame Relay network; however, a VPN uses a public network for its connectivity and Frame Relay uses a private one. The *private* part of the term specifies that the traffic should remain private—not viewable by eavesdroppers in the network. This is accomplished using encryption to keep the data confidential.

Many VPN technologies exist, such as IPSec, Point-to-Point Tunneling Protocol (PPTP), Layer 2 Transport Protocol (L2TP), SSL, and others; however, this chapter

FIGURE 25-7

Network using a VPN

Intranet: same company sites
Extranet: third-party and business partners
Remote access: users and SOHOs

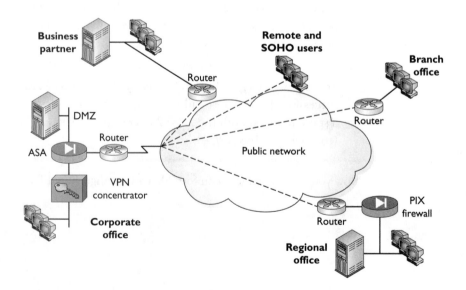

serves as a quick introduction to VPNs. A detailed introduction to VPNs—the different types and the technologies they use, how they work, how to configure them on Cisco devices, and how to troubleshoot them—is covered extensively in my book *The Complete Cisco VPN Configuration Guide* with Cisco Press (ISBN: 978-1587052040).

Benefits

VPNs provide four main benefits over setting up a private WAN network, such as those used by Frame Relay, point-to-point circuits, and ATM:

- **Security** Security is provided through data encryption to protect confidentiality, data integrity checking to validate packets, and authentication to prevent unauthorized access.
- **Cost** Public networks, such as the Internet, can be used instead of building a private WAN infrastructure, greatly reducing a company's WAN infrastructure cost.
- **Bandwidth** Inexpensive high-bandwidth connections, such as DSL and cable, can be used to interconnect offices to allow for fast and secure access to corporate resources.
- **Scalability** Companies can easily add large numbers of users and offices without building a significant WAN infrastructure.

VPN Types

VPNs fall under two implementation types:

- Site-to-Site
- Remote Access

The following sections will expand on these types.

Site-to-Site

Site-to-Site VPNs, sometimes called *LAN-to-LAN* or *L2L* VPNs, connect two locations or sites together, basically extending a classical WAN design. Two intermediate devices, commonly called *VPN gateways*, protect the traffic between the two LANs. This type of VPN tunnels packets between the locations: the original IP packet from one LAN is encrypted by one gateway, forwarded to the destination gateway, and then decrypted and forwarded to the local LAN at its end to the destination. From the real source and destination's perspective, the VPN is *virtual*—they don't even know their traffic is being protected between the two VPN gateways. The most common site-to-site protocol used to protect traffic is IPSec. Routers are commonly used as the VPN gateway product, though other products can be used, such as firewalls. Cisco products that support IPSec L2L VPNs include routers, ASA and PIX security appliances, and the VPN 3000 concentrators. Because of scalability features such as dynamic multipoint VPNs (DMVPNs), Cisco routers are the preferred choice for IPSec L2L gateways.

L2Ls come in two flavors: *intranet* and *extranet*. An intranet L2L basically connects two offices of the same company together, such as a corporate office and a regional or branch office. An extranet is an L2L VPN that connects two different companies together, such as a corporate office and another company that is a business partner. Address translation is commonly required here because the two companies might be using the same private address space.

Remote Access

Remote access VPNs are an extension of the classic circuit-switching networks, such as POTS and ISDN. They securely connect remote users or SOHOs to a corporate or branch office. With a remote access VPN, the VPN provides a virtualization process, making it appear that the remote access user or office is physically connected to the corporate office network. Common protocols used for remote access VPNs include IPSec, SSL, PPTP, and L2TP. Cisco supports all four of these protocols; however, most of the Cisco's development effort is based on IPSec and SSL. These are discussed in the next two sections.

Easy VPN   Cisco's IPSec remote access solution is called *Easy VPN*. Easy VPN is a design approach Cisco took to make it easy to deploy, scale to a large number of users, and centralize policy configurations. Easy VPN involves two components:

- Easy VPN Server
- Easy VPN Remote or Client

The Easy VPN Server centralizes the policy configurations for the Easy VPN Remotes and provides access to corporate resources. All of your IPSec remote access policies are configured on the Servers and pushed down to the Remotes, which implement the policies. This makes it easy to change policies, since they need to be changed only on a small number of Servers, not on any of the Remotes. Easy VPN Server products that Cisco supports include the ASA and PIX security appliances, routers, and the VPN 3000 concentrators. Since the concentrators are end-of-sale, the recommended platform for Easy VPN Servers is the ASA security appliances.

The Easy VPN Remote allows the user or users to access corporate resources securely via the Easy VPN Server. Very little configuration is required on the Remote to bring up a tunnel—another reason the term *easy* is used to describe this solution. Easy VPN Remotes include the following products from Cisco: the Cisco VPN Client (runs on Windows, Macintosh, Solaris, and Linux); the Certicom and Movian clients (runs on PDAs and smart phones), and hardware clients such as the 3002, the PIX 501 and 506E; the ASA 5505; and small-end routers such as the 800s through the 3800s. Easy VPN allows users to use their applications as they would without having a VPN in place; the downside of Easy VPN is that special software must be installed on user desktops, laptops, PDAs, or smart phones, or a hardware client must be deployed.

e x a m
w a t c h

Cisco's main remote access VPN solutions are IPSec using Easy VPN and SSL using WebVPN. Easy VPN has two components: Server and Remote.

WebVPN   Unlike IPSec, which is an open standard, SSL VPNs, even though they use SSL as their protection protocol, are implemented differently by each vendor, making them proprietary. SSL VPNs are one of the newest VPNs in the marketplace today. Cisco's SSL VPN solution is called WebVPN and provides three secure connection methods: clientless, thin client, and the SSL VPN Client. The clientless and thin client implementations use a normal web browser, with JavaScript installed, to provide the VPN solution. The main advantage of this is that no special software has to be installed on a user's desktop—they use the web browser that is already there! The downside of this is that the applications must be either web-based or a supported handful of non–web-based applications, such as telnet. The SSL VPN Client provides network-layer protection and allows users to use their day-to-day applications without any modifications. And on the VPN gateway side, they are easy to set up, change policies, and add new users. However, they are not as scalable or as secure as using IPSec.

It is not uncommon to see a company use both Easy VPN and WebVPN: Easy VPN is used for situations in which hardware clients are used at SOHOs or when users are using company computers, such as laptops, where it is acceptable to install the Cisco VPN Client. WebVPN is commonly used when it is not possible to install Easy VPN client software, such as for business partners accessing your network or employees using airport Internet kiosks when they are traveling.

IPSec

IPSec, short for IP Security, is an open standard defined across quite a few different RFCs. IPSec functions at the network layer and protects IP packets. IPSec can be used for L2L VPNs as well as remote access. Compared to all other VPNs, it is the most secure commercial solution today, the most widely used, but the most difficult to set up and troubleshoot. The next two sections will briefly cover the services IPSec offers, as well as the protocols it uses to provide for protection.

IPSec Services

IPSec provides four main services:

- **Authentication** Verifying the identity of remote peers; digital signatures are used to provide identity verification via pre-shared keys or digital certificates
- **Confidentiality** Guaranteeing that no intermediate device can decipher the contents of the payload in a packet; encryption is used to "hide" the real data
- **Integrity** Guaranteeing that the contents of a packet have not been tampered with (changed) by an intermediate device; a derivative of hashing functions, called HMAC functions, is used to verify the source of every packet as well as checking if it was tampered or not
- **Anti-replay protection** Verifying that each packet is unique and not duplicated; ensuring that copies of a valid packet are not used to create a denial of service attack; protected sequence numbers are used to detect duplicate packets and drop them

IPSec provides the following services: peer authentication via pre-shared keys or certificates (RSA signatures), confidentiality via encryption, packet integrity via HMAC functions, and anti-replay protection via unique sequence numbers in packets.

IPSec Components

The following sections discuss the components of IPSec, including keys, encryption algorithms, HMAC functions, and protocols. The following information provides only a brief introduction to these components.

Confidentiality: Keys and Encryption   A *key* is a term used in security to protect information. Just as you would use a password to protect a user account, or a PIN to protect your ATM card, a key in the data world is used to protect your information. Keys can be used in two ways: to perform encryption and decryption and to provide authentication and integrity of your transmission. Typically, the longer the key, the more difficult it is for a man-in-the-middle (MTM) attack to break the encryption process by doing some reverse-engineering to discover the key.

Two methods are used for implementing keying solutions: symmetric and asymmetric keys. With symmetric keys, the same key is used to protect your information. Because it uses the same key for both encryption and de-encryption, the algorithm used is much simpler and thus the protection process is very fast; therefore, symmetric keys are commonly used for encrypting large amounts of data. However, the problem with symmetric keys is that somehow the keys need to be shared between the two peers. Two methods of accomplishing this securely:

- *Pre-share the keys out-of-band*. This is not very scalable if you need to manage hundreds of keys.
- *Share the keys across a secure connection*. The Diffie-Hellman (DH) protocol accomplishes this for IPSec.

Examples of symmetric encryption algorithms supported by IPSec include Data Encryption Standard (DES), Triple DES (3DES), and Advanced Encryption Standard (AES) (128-bit, 192-bit, and 256-bit, respectively). Of the three, AES is the most secure. Cisco's routers, concentrators, PIXs, and ASAs support modular cards to perform these types of encryption in hardware at very high speeds.

When using asymmetric keys, two keys are generated for a unidirectional communication: one is kept by the source (private key), and the other is given to the destination (public key). When the destination wants to send something to the source, it uses the source's public key to encrypt the information and then, when the source receives the data, the source uses its corresponding private key to decrypt it. Since only the corresponding private key can decrypt the information, the private key is never shared. And because communication is a two-way process, the destination will also have to generate two keys and share its public key with the original source. Asymmetric keys are much more secure than symmetric keys; however, the former is much, much slower when protecting information—about 1500 times slower than symmetric key algorithms. Therefore, asymmetric keys are usually used either to share symmetric keys or perform authentication of a peer.

DH and RSA are two examples of asymmetric keying algorithms. IPSec uses DH to share keys (a key exchange protocol) and RSA to authenticate VPN peers. Within IPSec, DH supports 368-, 768-, 1024-, and 1536-bit keys. RSA supports key sizes from 512 bits to 2048 bits (up to eight times longer than AES-256).

Integrity: HMAC Functions   Hashing functions are used to verify whether information was changed. Hashed message authentication code (HMAC) functions are a derivative of hashing functions and are used specifically for security functions: they take a variable length input and a symmetric key and run these through the HMAC function, resulting in a fixed-length output. The fixed-length output is commonly called a *digital signature*. IPSec supports two HMAC functions:

- Message Digest 5 (MD5)
- Secure Hashing Algorithm version 1 (SHA-1)

MD5 is defined in RFC 1321 and creates a 128-bit digital signature. MD5 is used in many other protocols, including PPP's CHAP and authentication of routing updates in RIPv2, EIGRP, OSPF, BGP, and others. SHA-1 is defined in RFC 2404 and creates a longer signature of 160 bits in length. Of the two, SHA-1 is more secure, but slower.

In IPSec, HMAC functions are used to validate that a packet is coming from a trusted source (packet authentication) and that the packet hasn't been tampered with (packet integrity). The source takes information from the packet being sent, along with the symmetric key, and runs it through the HMAC function, creating a digital signature. The signature is then added to the original packet and sent to the destination. The destination repeats the process: it takes the original packet input along with the same symmetric key, and should be able to generate the same signature that was sent in the packet. If the signature generated is the same, then the packet must come from someone who knows the symmetric key and knows that the packet hasn't been tampered with; if the computed signature is not the same, then the packet is dropped since the signature in it is either a fake or the packet was tampered with between the source and destination.

Authentication: Peer Validation   Another important component of any VPN solution, including IPSec, is validating the peer's identity through some form of authentication. IPSec supports two forms of authentication: device and user (commonly called extended authentication or XAUTH for short). L2L sessions support only device authentication while remote access supports both. Device authentication supports two methods of validating a peer:

- **Pre-shared keys (PSKs)**   PSKs require that a pre-shared symmetric key be configured on each VPN peer. This key is then used, along with identity information from the peer, to generate a signature. The remote end can then validate the signature using the same PSK.

- **RSA signatures**   RSA signatures use asymmetric keys for authentication. Hashes of signatures (created with a private key) are placed on digital certificates generated by a central certificate authority (CA). The signatures can then be validated with the associated public key.

Of the two, PSK is the easier to implement; however, certificates using RSA signatures are a much more scalable solution.

IPSec Protocols

IPSec is actually a group of standards, protocols, and technologies that work together to build a secure session, commonly called a *tunnel*, to a remote peer. An IPSec tunnel comprises three connections: one management connection and two unidirectional data connections. The tunnel is built across two phases. The management connection is built during Phase 1 and is used to share IPSec-related information between the two peers. The two data connections are built during Phase 2 and are used to transmit user traffic. All three connections are protected. Here is a brief description of these protocols used to build a tunnel:

- **ISAKMP**   The *Internet Security Association and Key Management Protocol* is used to build and maintain the tunnel; it defines the format of the management payload, the mechanics of a key exchange protocol for the encryption algorithms and HMAC functions, negotiates how the tunnel will be built between the two devices, and authenticates the remote device.

- **IKE** The *Internet Key Exchange Protocol* is responsible for generating and managing keys used for encryption algorithms and HMAC functions. Actually, it is a combination of ISAKMP and IKE working together that secures the tunnel between two devices: they use UDP as a transport and connect on port 500.

- **DH** The *Diffie-Hellman* process is used to securely exchange the encryption and HMAC keys that will be used to secure the management and data connections.

- **AH** The *Authentication Header* protocol is used only to validate the origination and validity of data packets (on the data connections) received from a peer; it accomplishes this by using HMAC functions, where the signature created is based on almost the entire IP packet. Its two main disadvantages are that it breaks if it goes through any type of address translation device and it does not support encryption.

- **ESP** The *Encapsulation Security Payload* protocol is used to provide packet confidentiality and authentication. It provides confidentiality through encryption and packet authentication through an HMAC function. Because it supports encryption, it is the protocol companies use to protect the data connections; however, its downside is that its signature process does not protect the outer IP header and thus cannot detect packet tampering in the header, whereas AH can. ESP's other main advantage is that it can work through address translation devices doing NAT without any changes, but it requires an encapsulation in a UDP packet to work through a PAT or firewall device. This part of the IPSec standard is called NAT Transparency or Traversal, or NAT-T for short.

w a t c h

Remember the IPSec protocols (ISAKMP, IKE, DH, AH, and ESP) and their descriptions in the above bullets.

INSIDE THE EXAM

Wide Area Networking Overview

Remember that WANs operate at the physical and data link layers. You should be familiar with what a DCE and DTE are, what their main functions are, and examples of these kinds of devices. WAN services that use VCs, such as Frame Relay and ATM, are used to connect multiple locations together using a single WAN interface. Be able to compare and contrast different data link layer encapsulation types, such as HDLC and PPP, as shown in Table 25-2. Serial interfaces are used for synchronous connections.

HDLC

Remember that Cisco's implementation of HDLC is proprietary: the frame header has a proprietary Type field. Know how to troubleshoot problems with HDLC interfaces: mismatch in encapsulation types, Cisco and non-Cisco devices, misconfigured IP addressing, and missed keepalive responses—this statement also applies to the section on configuring PPP. Remember that when you execute the **show running-config** command, if no **encapsulation** command is displayed in the configuration for a synchronous serial interface, the default encapsulation is HDLC.

PPP

PPP should be used in a mixed-vendor environment. Know the services PPP provides: authentication via CHAP and PAP, support for multiple encapsulated protocols, compression, multilink, error detection/correction, and support for synchronous and asynchronous circuits. Be able to explain what LCP and NCP do within PPP and the differences between PAP and CHAP authentication. As with HDLC, know how to troubleshoot PPP connections by examining the status of the LCP state with the **show interfaces** command, and be able to identify problems with misconfigured PAP or CHAP authentication by examining a router's configuration with the **show running-config** command.

Virtual Private Networks

VPNs are not currently emphasized on the exam; however, you might be asked a general question about when VPNs are most recommended, the different kinds of VPNs Cisco offers, and some of the basic terms used by a VPN, such as IPSec.

CERTIFICATION SUMMARY

The CPE is your WAN equipment. The demarcation point is the point where the carrier's responsibility for the circuit ends. The local loop is the connection from the demarcation point to the carrier's WAN switching equipment. There are four main WAN connection categories. Leased lines include dedicated circuits, which are useful for short connections where you have constant traffic and need guaranteed bandwidth. Circuit-switched connections provide dialup capabilities, as are needed for analog modems and ISDN. These connections are mostly used for backup of primary connections and for an additional bandwidth boost. Packet-switched connections include Frame Relay and X.25. They are used to connect multiple sites together at a reasonable cost. If you need guaranteed bandwidth or need to carry multiple services, cell-switched services, such as ATM, provide a better solution.

Cisco synchronous serial interfaces support DB-60 and DB-26 connectors. The default encapsulation on these interfaces is Cisco's HDLC. Cisco's HDLC and ISO's HDLC are not compatible with each other. Use the **encapsulation hdlc** command to change an interface's encapsulation to Cisco's HDLC. The **show interfaces** command displays the data link layer encapsulation for a serial interface.

PPP is one of the most commonly used data link encapsulations for serial interfaces. It is an open standard. It defines three things: frame type, LCP, and NCP. When building a PPP connection, LCP takes place first, then authentication, and last NCP. LCP is responsible for negotiating parameters, and setting up and maintaining connections, which include authentication, compression, link quality, error detection, multiplexing network layer protocols, and multilink. NCP handles the negotiation of the upper layer protocols that the PPP connection will transport. To set up PPP as an encapsulation type on your serial interface, use the **encapsulation ppp** command. Use the **debug ppp negotiation** command to troubleshoot LCP and NCP problems.

There are two forms of PPP authentication: PAP and CHAP. PAP sends the password across the wire in clear text, while CHAP sends a hashed output value from the MD5 hash algorithm—the password is not sent across the connection. PAP goes through a two-way handshake, while CHAP goes through a three-way handshake. Authentication is optional but can be configured with the **ppp authentication pap|chap** Interface Subconfiguration mode command. To build a local authentication table with usernames and passwords, use the **username** command. If you have authentication problems, troubleshoot them with the **debug ppp authentication** command.

VPNs are becoming a common and inexpensive solution for providing protected connectivity across a public network. VPN implementation types include site-to-site and remote access. The most common VPN implementations are IPSec and SSL. Cisco's remote access VPNs include Easy VPN for IPSec and WebVPN for SSL. Easy VPN has two components: Server and Remote. The Server centralizes policy configurations. Cisco supports both hardware and software Remote devices. IPSec is an open standard for implementing site-to-site and remote access VPNs. It provides authentication, confidentiality, integrity, and anti-replay protection. Protocols used to implement IPSec include ISAKMP, IKE, DH, AH, and ESP.

✓ TWO-MINUTE DRILL

Wide Area Networking Overview

❏ DCEs provide synchronization and clocking on a serial connection. Examples of DCEs include modems, NT1s, and CSU/DSUs (T1 lines).

❏ Leased lines are dedicated circuits. Circuit-switched connections use analog modems or ISDN for dialup connections. Packet-switched services, such as ATM, Frame Relay, and X.25, use VCs for transmitting data. Of these, leased lines are the most costly. Packet-switched services are used when you need to connect a router to multiple destinations, but the router has only a single serial interface.

HDLC

❏ ISO's HDLC and Cisco's HDLC are not compatible. Cisco's frame format has a proprietary Type field that allows for the transport of multiple protocols. Cisco's HDLC is the default encapsulation on synchronous serial interfaces and is not displayed with the **show running-config** command.

❏ To configure this frame format on an interface, use this command: **encapsulation hdlc**. Use the **show interfaces** command to verify your encapsulation and to troubleshoot problems when the data link layer is down.

PPP

❏ PPP is an open standard that provides dynamic configuration of links, authentication, error detection, compression, and multiple links.

❏ LCP sets up, configures, and transfers information across a PPP connection. NCP negotiates the data link and network protocols that will be transported across this link. The PPP frame format is based on ISO's HDLC.

❏ Use this interface command to specify PPP: **encapsulation ppp**. Use the **show interfaces** command to view the PPP status. OPEN indicates successful negotiation, and CLOSED indicates a problem. Use the **debug ppp negotiation** command for detailed troubleshooting of LCP and NCP.

❑ PAP uses a two-way handshake and sends the password across in clear text. CHAP uses a three-way handshake and sends a hashed value, which is created by MD5 by inputting a challenge, the hostname, and the password.

❑ To set up authentication, use the `ppp authentication chap|pap` command. Use the `debug ppp authentication` command to troubleshoot. CHALLENGE, RESPONSE, and SUCCESS messages are from CHAP, and AUTH-REQ and AUTH-ACK are from PAP.

Virtual Private Networks

❑ VPNs provide protection connections between different networks (L2L) and networks and users (remote access).

❑ Cisco's two main remote access technologies are IPSec with Easy VPN and SSL with WebVPN.

❑ IPSec provides peer authentication via pre-shared keys or certificates (RSA signatures), confidentiality via encryption, packet integrity via HMAC functions, and anti-replay protection via unique sequence numbers in packets.

SELF TEST

The following Self Test questions will help you measure your understanding of the material presented in this chapter. Read all the choices carefully, as there may be more than one correct answer. Choose all correct answers for each question.

Wide Area Networking Overview

1. Which device provides clocking and synchronization on a synchronous serial interface on a router connected to a DTE cable?

   A. The router itself

   B. Modem

   C. CSU/DSU

   D. Carrier switch

2. At what layer or layers does a WAN typically operate at within the OSI Reference Model?

   A. Physical only

   B. Data link only

   C. Physical and data link

   D. Physical, data link, and network

HDLC

3. Which frame field is different between ISO HDLC and Cisco's HDLC?

   A. Address

   B. Control

   C. Flag

   D. Type

4. The default encapsulation on a synchronous serial interface is _____.

   A. HDLC

   B. PPP

   C. neither HDLC nor PPP

   D. auto-sensed on synchronous serial interfaces

PPP

5. PPP can do all of the following except _____.

   A. authentication

   B. compression

C. quality of service

D. All answers are correct.

6. _____ negotiates the data link and network layer protocols that will traverse a PPP connection.

A. LCP

B. NCP

C. CDP

D. PAP

7. When you have configured PPP on an interface and use the **show interfaces** command, what state indicates the successful negotiation of a network layer protocol?

A. ACK

B. CHALLENGE

C. CLOSED

D. OPEN

8. Which of the following is false concerning CHAP?

A. It sends an encrypted password.

B. It sends a challenge.

C. It is more secure than PAP.

D. It uses a three-way handshake.

Virtual Private Networks

9. Which VPN technology implements confidentiality?

A. MD5

B. AES

C. DH

D. IKE

10. What are the two components of Easy VPN?

A. Server

B. Gateway

C. Host

D. Remote

SELF TEST ANSWERS

Wide Area Networking Overview

1. ☑ **C.** CSU/CSUs are used to terminate synchronous digital circuits and provide DCE services such as clocking and synchronization.
   ☒ **A** is incorrect because a router can provide clocking only when connected to the DCE end of the cable. **B** is incorrect because a modem is used for asynchronous services, and **D** is incorrect because it is a DTE and doesn't provide clocking/synchronization.

2. ☑ **C.** WANs primarily operate at the physical and data link layers.
   ☒ Therefore **A**, **B**, and **D** are incorrect.

HDLC

3. ☑ **D.** The Type field is unique between the Cisco HDLC frame format and ISO's HDLC.
   ☒ **A**, **B**, and **C** are incorrect because they are in both frame formats.

4. ☑ **A.** HDLC is the default encapsulation on synchronous serial interfaces.
   ☒ **B** is incorrect because PPP is not the default on any type of a serial interface. **C** is incorrect because HDLC is the default. **D** is incorrect because no auto-sensing feature is supported on serial interfaces for the encapsulation method to use.

PPP

5. ☑ **C.** PPP does error detection and correction, but not quality of service.
   ☒ **A** and **B** are supported by PPP, and since answer C is correct, **D** is incorrect.

6. ☑ **B.** NCP negotiates the data link and network layer protocols that will traverse a PPP connection.
   ☒ **A** is incorrect because LCP sets up and monitors the PPP connection. **C** is incorrect because CDP is a proprietary Cisco protocol that allows Cisco devices to share some basic information. **D** is incorrect because PAP performs authentication for PPP.

7. ☑ **D.** OPEN indicates a successful negotiation of a network layer protocol in the **show interfaces** output.
   ☒ **A** is a nonexistent state. **B** shows up as a message type in the output of the **debug ppp authentication** command. **C** indicates an unsuccessful negotiation.

8. ☑ **A.** CHAP doesn't send the encrypted password—it sends a hashed value created from the MD5 algorithm.
   ☒ **B**, **C**, and **D** are true concerning CHAP.

Virtual Private Networks

9. ☑ **B.** Confidentiality is provided by encryption algorithms such as DES, 3DES, and AES.

    ☒ **A** is incorrect because MD5 is an HMAC function, which provides for packet integrity;
    C is incorrect because DH is used to exchange keys for encryption and HMAC functions; **D** is
    incorrect because IKE is used to manage create and manage keys on a VPN device.

10. ☑ **A** and **D.** The two components of Easy VPN are Server and Remote (sometimes called
    Client).

    ☒ **B** and **C,** Gateway and Host, are nonexistent terms in Easy VPN.

26

Frame Relay

C hapter 25 introduced you to wide area networking and point-to-point connections using High-Level Data Link Control (HDLC) and Point-to-Point Protocol (PPP) for a data link layer encapsulation. These protocols are common with leased lines and circuit-switched connections. This chapter introduces you to the second WAN topic: Frame Relay. Frame Relay is a data link layer packet-switching protocol that uses digital circuits to transmit data and thus is virtually error-free. Therefore, it performs only error detection—it leaves error correction to an upper layer protocol, such as TCP or the application itself.

Frame Relay is actually a group of separate standards, including those from ITU-T and ANSI. Interestingly enough, Frame Relay defines only the interaction between the Frame Relay customer premises equipment (CPE) and the Frame Relay carrier switch. The connection across the carrier's network is *not* defined by the Frame Relay standards. Most carriers, however, use Asynchronous Transfer Mode (ATM) as a transport to move Frame Relay frames between different sites.

CERTIFICATION OBJECTIVE 26.01

Virtual Circuits

Frame Relay is connection-oriented: a layer 2 connection must be established before information can be sent to a remote device. The connections used by Frame Relay are provided by virtual circuits (VCs). A VC is a logical connection between two devices; therefore, many VCs can exist on the same physical interface. The advantage that VCs have over leased lines is that they can provide full connectivity (fully meshed) at a much lower price. VCs are also full-duplex: you can simultaneously send and receive on the same VC. Other packet- and cell-switching technologies, such as ATM and X.25, also use VCs. Most of the information covered in this section concerning VCs is true of Frame Relay as well as these other technologies.

Fully Meshed Design

As mentioned, VCs are more cost-effective than leased lines because they reduce the number of physical connections required to fully mesh your network, but still allowing a fully meshed topology. Let's assume you have two choices for connecting four WAN devices together: leased lines and VCs. The top part of Figure 26-1 shows

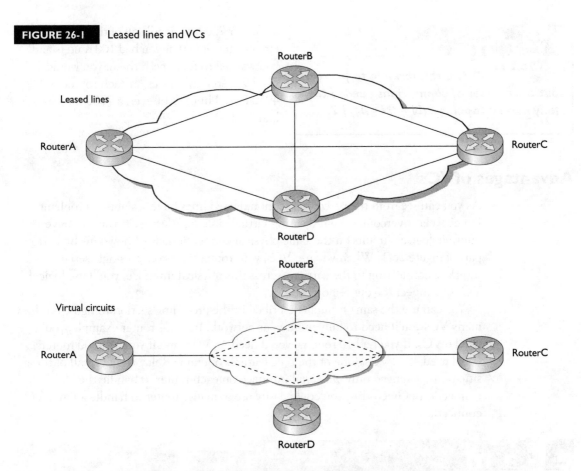

FIGURE 26-1 Leased lines and VCs

an example of connecting these devices using leased lines. Notice that to fully mesh this network (every device is connected to every other device), a total of six leased lines is required, including three serial interfaces on each router.

To figure out the number of connections required, you can use the following formula: $(N \times (N - 1)) / 2$. In this formula, N is the number of devices you are connecting together. In our example, this was four devices, resulting in $(4 \times (4 - 1)) / 2 = 6$ leased lines. The more devices that you have, the more leased lines you need, as well as additional serial interfaces on each router. For instance, if you have 10 routers you want to fully mesh, you would need a total of 9 serial interfaces on each router and a total of 45 leased lines! If you were thinking of using a smaller end router, such as a 2600, this would be unrealistic. Therefore, you would need a larger router, such as

> *Use this formula to figure out the number of connections needed to fully mesh a topology: (N × (N – 1)) / 2.*

a 3800 or 7200, to handle all of these dedicated circuits. Imagine that you had 100 routers and you wanted to fully mesh them: you would need 99 serial interfaces on each router and 4950 leased lines! Not even a 7700 router can handle this!

Advantages of VCs

As you can see from the preceding section, leased lines have scalability problems. Frame Relay overcomes them by using virtual circuits. With VCs, you can have multiple logical circuits on the same physical connection, as is shown in the bottom part of Figure 26-1. When you use VCs, your router needs only a single serial interface connecting to the carrier. Across this physical interface, you'll use logical VCs to connect to your remote sites.

You can use the same formula described in the preceding section to figure out how many VCs you'll need to fully mesh your network. In our 4-router example, you'd need 6 VCs. If you had 10 routers, you'd need 45 VCs; and if you had 100 routers, you'd need 4950 VCs. One of the nice features of Frame Relay is that in all of these situations, you need only *one* serial interface on each router to handle the VC connections. Given this, you could easily use a smaller router to handle a lot of VC connections.

e x a m

W a t c h

> *Frame Relay with VCs is a good solution if your router has a single serial interface, but needs to connect to multiple WAN destinations.*

Actually, VCs use a process similar to what T1 and E1 leased lines use in sending information. With a T1, for instance, the physical layer T1 frame is broken up into 24 logical time slots, or channels, with 64 Kbps of bandwidth each. Each of these time slots is referred to as a DS0, the smallest fixed amount of bandwidth in a channelized connection.

For example, you can have a carrier configure your T1 so that if you have six sites you want to connect to, the carrier can separate these time slots so that a certain number of time slots are redirected to each remote site, as is shown in Figure 26-2.

FIGURE 26-2 Leased lines and time slots

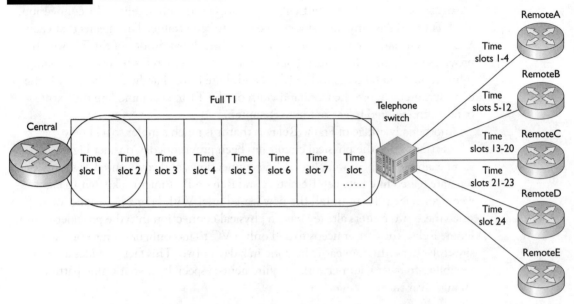

In this example, the T1 has been split into five connections: Time slots 1–4 go to RemoteA, time slots 5–12 go to RemoteB, time slots 13–20 go to RemoteC, time slots 21–23 go to RemoteD, and time slot 24 goes to Remote E.

As you can see from the figure, this is somewhat similar to the use of VCs. However, breaking up a T1's or E1's time slots does have disadvantages. For instance, assume that the connection from the central site needs to send a constant rate of 128 Kbps of data to RemoteE. You'll notice that the T1 was broken up and only one DS0, time slot 24, was assigned to this connection. Each DS0 has only 64 Kbps' worth of bandwidth. Therefore, unfortunately, this connection will become congested until traffic slows down to a data rate below 64 Kbps. With this type of configuration, it is difficult to reconfigure the time slots of the T1, because you must also have the carrier involved. If your data rates change to remote sites, you'll need to reconfigure the time slots on your side to reflect the change as well as have the carrier reconfigure its side. With this process, adapting to data rate changes is a very slow and inflexible process. Even for slight data rate changes to remote sites—say, for example, a spike of 128 Kbps to RemoteE—there will be a brief period of congestion. This is true *even if* the other time slots are empty—remember that these time slots are configured to have their traffic sent to a specific destination and only that destination.

Frame Relay, using VCs, has an advantage over leased lines in this regard. VCs are *not* associated with any particular time slots on the channelized T1 connection. With Frame Relay, any time slot can be used to send traffic. This means that each VC to a destination has the potential to use the full bandwidth of the T1, which provides much more flexibility. For example, if the RemoteE site has a brief bump in its traffic from 64 Kbps to 128 Kbps, and there is free bandwidth on the T1, the central router can use the free bandwidth on the T1 to accommodate the extra bandwidth required to get traffic to RemoteE.

Another advantage of Frame Relay is that it is much simpler to add new connections once the physical circuit has been provisioned. Consider Figure 26-2 as an example. If these were leased-line connections, and you wanted to set up a separate leased line between RemoteA and RemoteB, it might take four to eight weeks for the carrier to install the new leased line! With Frame Relay and VCs, since these two routers already have a physical connection into the provider running Frame Relay, the carrier needs to add only a VC to its configuration to tie the two sites together—this can easily be done in a day or two. This fact provides a lot of flexibility to meet your network's requirements, especially if your traffic patterns change over time.

Types of VCs

There are two types of VCs: *permanent VCs (PVCs)* and *switched* or *semi-permanent VCs (SVCs)*. A PVC is similar to a leased line: it is configured up front by the carrier and remains up as long as a physical circuit path exists from the source to the destination. SVCs are similar to telephone circuit-switched connections: whenever you need to send data to a connection, an SVC is dynamically built and then torn down once your data has been sent. PVCs are typically used when you have data that is constantly being sent to a particular site, while SVCs are used when data is sent periodically. Cisco routers support both types of VCs; however, this book focuses on the configuration of PVCs for Frame Relay.

PVCs

A PVC is similar to a leased line, which is why it is referred to as a *permanent*
VC. PVCs must be configured or dynamically learned on each router and built
on the carrier's switches before you can send any data. One disadvantage of PVCs
is that they require a lot of manual configuration up front to establish the VC.
Another disadvantage is that they aren't very flexible: if the PVC fails, there is no
dynamic rebuilding of the PVC around the failure. However, once you have a PVC
configured, it will always be available, barring any failures between the source and
destination. One advantage that PVCs have over SVCs is that SVCs must be set up
when you have data to send, a fact that introduces a small amount of delay before
traffic can be sent to the destination.

SVCs

SVCs are similar to making a telephone call. For example, when you make a
telephone call in the United States, you need to dial a 7-, 10-, or 11-digit telephone
number. This number is processed by the carrier's telephone switch, which uses
its telephone routing table to bring up a circuit to the destination phone number.
Once the circuit is built, the phone rings at the remote site, the destination person
answers the phone, and *then* you can begin talking. Once you are done talking, you
hang up the phone. This causes the carrier switch to tear down the circuit-switched
connection.

SVCs use a similar process. Each SVC device is assigned a unique address, similar
to a telephone number. To reach a destination device using an SVC, you'll need
to know the destination device's address. In WAN environments, this is typically
configured manually on your SVC device. Once your device knows the destination's
address, it can forward the address to the carrier's SVC switch. The SVC switch
then finds a path to the destination and builds a VC to it. Once the VC is built, the
source and destination are notified about this, and both can start sending data across
it. Once the source and destination are done sending data, they can signal their
connected carrier switch to tear the connection down.

One advantage of SVCs is that they are temporary. Therefore, since you are using
the SVC only part of the time, the cost of the SVC is less than that of a PVC, since
a PVC, even if you are not sending data across it, has to be sustained in the carrier's
network.

The problem with SVCs, however, is that the more you use them, the more
they cost. Compare this to making a long-distance telephone call where you are
being billed for each minute—the more minutes you talk, the more expensive the
connection becomes. At some point in time, it will be actually cheaper to use a fixed

PVC instead of a dynamic SVC. SVCs are actually good for backup purposes—you might have a primary PVC to a site that costs X dollars a month and a backup SVC that costs you money only if you use it, and then that cost is based on how much you use it—perhaps based on the number of minutes used or the amount of traffic sent. If your primary PVC fails, the SVC is used only until the primary PVC is restored.

To determine whether you should be using an SVC or PVC, you'll need to weigh in factors such as the amount of use and the cost of a PVC versus that of an SVC given this level of use. Another advantage of SVCs is that they are adaptable to changes in the network—if there is a failure of a physical link in the carrier's network, the SVC can be rebuilt across a redundant physical link inside the carrier's network.

The main disadvantages of SVCs are the initial setup and troubleshooting efforts associated with them as well as the time they take to establish. For example, to establish an SVC, you'll need to build a manual resolution table for each network layer protocol that is used between your router and the remote router. If you are running IP, IPX, and AppleTalk, you'll need to configure all three of these entries in your resolution table. Basically, your resolution table maps the remote's network layer address to its SVC address. Depending on the number of protocols that you are running and the number of sites to which you are connecting, this process can take a lot of time. And when you experience problems with SVCs, they become more difficult to troubleshoot because of the extra configuration involved on your side as well as the layer 2 routing table used on the carrier's side. Setting up PVCs is actually much easier. Plus, each time an SVC doesn't exist to a remote site, your router has to establish one, and it has to wait for the carrier switch to complete this process before your router can start sending its information to the destination.

on the *Even though Frame Relay is a much more cost-effective solution than a*
job *dedicated circuit, it is slowly being replaced by other options, such as VPNs using the Internet via DSL and cable modem connections. However, for delay-sensitive traffic such as voice and video, a private network such as Frame Relay or ATM is used; even so, these two private network technologies are being supplanted by multiprotocol label switching (MPLS) across Ethernet or ATM in carrier networks.*

Supported Serial Connections

A typical Frame Relay connection looks similar to Figure 26-3. As you can see in this example, serial cables connect from the router to the CSU/DSU and from the carrier switch to the CSU/DSU. The serial cables that you can use include

FIGURE 26-3   Typical Frame Relay connection

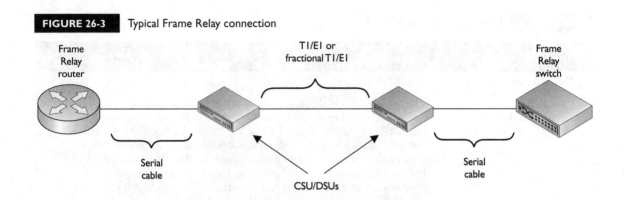

the following: EIA/TIA-232, EIA/TIA-449, EIA/TIA-530, V.35, and X.25. The connection between the two CSU/DSUs is a channelized connection; it can be a fractional T1/E1 that has a single or multiple time slots, a full T1/E1 (a T1 has 24 time slots and an E1 has 30 usable time slots), or a DS3 (a T3 is clocked at 45 Mbps and an E3 is clocked at 34 Mbps).

CERTIFICATION OBJECTIVE 26.02

Frame Relay Terms

When compared to HDLC and PPP, Frame Relay is much more complex in operation, and many more terms are used to describe its components and operation. Table 26-1 contains an overview of these terms. Only the configuration of LMI is discussed in this book—the configuration of other parameters, such as B_C and B_E, is beyond the scope of this book. The proceeding sections describe the operation of Frame Relay and cover these terms in more depth.

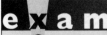
ⓦatch

Remember the terms in Table 26-1. LMI is a keepalive mechanism used between the DTE and DCE to ensure *that both are operational and VCs are not inadvertently deleted or disabled by either side.*

| TABLE 26-1 | Common Frame Relay Terms |

Term	Definition
LMI (local management interface)	This defines how the DTE (the router or other Frame Relay device) interacts with the DCE (the Frame Relay switch).
DLCI (data link connection identifier)	This value is used to uniquely identify each VC on a physical interface: it's the address of the VC. Using DLCIs, you can multiplex traffic for multiple destinations on a single physical interface. DLCIs are locally significant and can change on a segment-by-segment basis. In other words, the DLCI that your router uses to get to a remote destination might be 45, but the destination might be using 54 to return the traffic—and yet it's the *same* VC. The Frame Relay switch will do a translation between the DLCIs when it is switching frames between segments. This is similar to the use of MAC addresses in layer 3 networks.
Access rate	This is the speed of the physical connection (such as a T1) between your router and the Frame Relay switch.
CIR (committed information rate)	This is the average data rate, measured over a fixed period of time, that the carrier guarantees for a VC.
B_C (committed burst rate)	This is the average data rate (over a period of a smaller fixed time than CIR) that a provider guarantees for a VC; in other words, it implies a smaller time period but a higher average than the CIR to allow for small bursts in traffic.
B_E (excessive burst rate)	This is the fastest data rate at which the provider will ever service the VC. Some carriers allow you to set this value to match the access rate.
DE (discard eligibility)	This is used to mark a frame as low priority. You can do this manually, or the carrier will do this for a frame that is nonconforming to your traffic contract (exceeding CIR/B_C values).
Oversubscription	When you add up all of the CIRs of your VCs on an interface, they exceed the access rate of the interface: you are betting that all of your VCs will not run, simultaneously, at their traffic-contracted rates.
FECN (forward explicit congestion notification)	This value in the Frame Relay frame header is set by the carrier switch (typically) to indicate congestion inside the carrier network to the destination device at the end of the VC; the carrier may be doing this to your traffic as it is on its way to its destination.
BECN (backward explicit congestion notification)	This value is set by the destination DTE (Frame Relay device) in the header of the Frame Relay frame to indicate congestion (from the source to the destination) to the source of the Frame Relay frames (the source DTE, the router). Sometimes the carrier switches can generate BECN frames in the backward direction to the source to speed up the congestion notification process. The source can then adapt its rate on the VC appropriately.

LMI

LMI is used only locally, between the Frame Relay DTE (a router) and the Frame Relay DCE (a carrier switch), as is shown in Figure 26-4. In other words, LMI information originating on one Frame Relay DTE will *not* be propagated across the carrier network to a remote Frame Relay DTE: it is processed only between the Frame Relay DTEs and DCEs, which is why the term *local* is used in LMI. LMI is used for management purposes and allows two directly connected devices to share information about the status of VCs, as well as their configuration.

Three different standards are defined for LMI and its interaction with a Frame Relay DTE and DCE:

- ANSI's Annex D standard, T1.617
- ITU-T's Q.933 Annex A standard
- The *Gang of Four*, for the four companies that developed it: Cisco, DEC, StrataCom, and NorTel (Northern Telecom). This standard is commonly referred to as Cisco's LMI.

FIGURE 26-4  LMI example

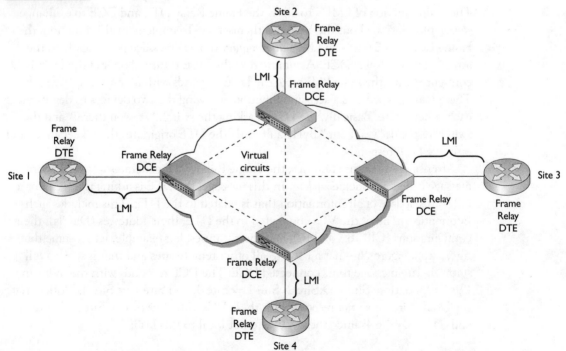

Because LMI is locally significant, each Frame Relay DTE in your network does not have to use the same LMI type. For example, Site 1 and Site 2, shown in Figure 26-4, might have a PVC connecting them together. The Site 1 router might be using ANSI for an LMI type, and the Site 2 router might be using the Q.933 LMI type. Even though they have a PVC connecting them, the LMI process is local and can therefore be different. Actually, the LMI type is typically dependent on the carrier and the switch that it is using. Most carrier switches support all three types, but some carrier switches don't. Likewise, those that do support all three might have standardized on a particular type. Cisco routers support all three LMI standards.

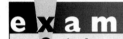

LMI's Functions

The main function of LMI is to allow the Frame Relay DTE and DCE to exchange status information about the VCs and themselves. To implement this function, the Frame Relay DTE sends an LMI *status enquiry* (query) message periodically to the attached Frame Relay DCE. Assuming that the DCE is turned on and the DCE is configured with the same LMI type, the DCE responds with a *status reply* message. These messages serve as a *keepalive* function, allowing the two devices to determine each other's state. Basically, the DTE is asking the switch "are you there?" and the switch responds "yes, I am." By default, only the DTE originates these keepalives and only the DCE responds.

After so many status enquiries, the Frame Relay DTE generates a special query message called a *full status update*. In this message, the DTE is asking the DCE for a full status update of all information that is related to the DTE. This includes such information as all of the VCs connected to the DTE, their addresses (DLCIs), their configurations (CIR, B_C, and B_E), and their statuses. For example, let's assume that Site 1 from Figure 26-4 has a PVC to all other remote sites and that it sends a full status update message to its connected DCE. The DCE responds with the following PVC information: Site 1 → Site 2, Site 1 → Site 3, and Site 1 → Site 4. Notice that the DCE switch does *not* respond with these VCs: Site 2 → Site 3, Site 3 → Site 4, and Site 2 → Site 4, since these VCs are not local to this DTE.

LMI Standards

For the LMI communication to occur between the DTE and the DCE, the LMI information must use a VC. In order for the DTE and DCE to know that the Frame Relay frame contains LMI information, a reserved VC is used to share LMI

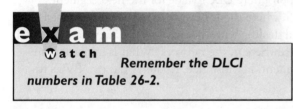

information. The LMI type that you are using will determine the DLCI address that is used in the communication. Table 26-2 shows the DLCI addresses assigned to the three LMI types. DLCIs are discussed in more depth in the following section.

DLCIs

Each VC has a unique *local* address, called a DLCI. This means that as a VC traverses various segments in a WAN, the DLCI numbers can be *different* for each segment. The carrier switches take care of converting a DLCI number from one segment to the corresponding DLCI number used on the next segment.

DLCI Example

Figure 26-5 shows an example of how DLCIs are used. This example shows three routers and three carrier switches. RouterA has a PVC to RouterB, and RouterA has

TABLE 26-2	LMI Type	DLCI #
LMI Addresses	ANSI Annex D	0
	ITU-T Annex A	0
	Gang of Four (Cisco)	1023

another PVC to RouterC. Let's take a closer look at the PVC between RouterA and RouterB. Starting from RouterA, the PVC traverses three physical links:

- RouterA → Switch 1 (DLCI 200)
- Switch 1 → Switch 2 (DLCI 200)
- Switch 2 → RouterB (DLCI 201)

Note that DLCIs are locally significant: they need to be unique only on a segment-by-segment basis and do *not* need to be unique across the entire Frame Relay network. This is similar to the use of MAC addresses in Ethernet (refer to Chapter 10 for an example of this). Given this statement, the DLCI number can change from segment to segment, and it is up to the carrier switch to change the DLCI in the frame header to the appropriate DLCI value for the next segment. This fact can be seen in Figure 26-5, where the DTE segments have different DLCI values (200 and 201), but we're still dealing with the same PVC. Likewise, the DLCI numbers of 200 and 201 are used elsewhere in the network. What is important are the DLCI numbers on the *same* segment. For instance, RouterA has two PVCs to

FIGURE 26-5 DLCI addressing example

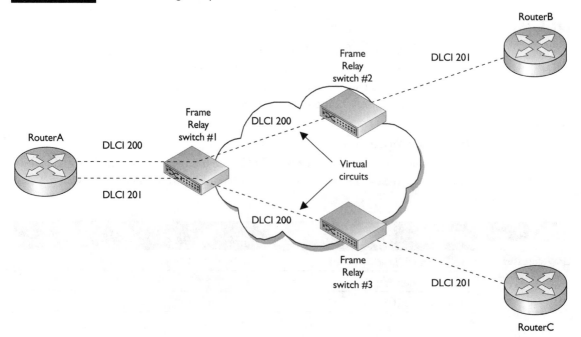

two different destinations. On the RouterA → Switch 1 connection, each of these PVCs needs a unique address value (200 and 201); however, these values do not have to be the same for each segment to the destination.

This can become confusing unless you look at the DLCI addressing from a device's and segment's perspective. As an example, if RouterA wants to send data to RouterB, it encapsulates it in a Frame Relay frame and puts a DLCI address of 200 in the header. When Switch 1 receives the frame, it looks at the DLCI address *and* the interface on which it was received and compares these to its DLCI switching table. When it finds a match, the switch takes the DLCI number for the next segment (found in the same table entry), substitutes it into the frame header, and forwards the frame to the next device. In this case, the DLCI number remains the same (200). When Switch 2 receives the frame from Switch 1, it performs the same process and realizes it needs to forward the frame to RouterB, but that before doing this, it must change the DLCI number to 201 in the frame header. When RouterB receives the frame, it also examines the DLCI address in the frame header. When it sees 201 as the address, RouterB knows that the frame originated from RouterA.

This process, at first, seems confusing. However, to make it easier, look at it from the router's perspective:

- When RouterA wants to reach RouterB, RouterA uses DLCI 200.
- When RouterB wants to reach RouterA, RouterB uses DLCI 201.
- When RouterC wants to reach RouterA, RouterC uses DLCI 201.

When the carrier creates a PVC for you between two sites, it assigns the DLCI number that you should use at each site to reach the other site. Certain DLCI numbers are reserved for management and control purposes, such as LMI's 0 and 1023 values. Reserved DLCIs are 0–15 and 1008–1023. DLCI numbers from 16–1007 are used for data connections.

---

exam

watch

DLCIs are locally significant: Your router uses a local DLCI number in the frame relay frame header to indicate the destination peer to which the frame is to be forwarded. The carrier's switches take care of mapping DLCI numbers for a VC between DTEs and DCEs.

Network and Service Interworking

As mentioned earlier in this chapter, Frame Relay is implemented between the Frame Relay DTE and the Frame Relay DCE. How the frame is carried across the Frame Relay carrier's network is not specified. In almost all situations, ATM is used as the layer 2 transport. ATM, like Frame Relay, uses VCs. ATM, however, uses a different nomenclature in assigning an address to a VC. In ATM, two identifiers are assigned to a VC: a virtual path identifier (VPI) and a virtual channel identifier (VCI). These two numbers serve the same purpose that a DLCI serves in Frame Relay. Like DLCIs, the VPI/VCI value is locally significant.

Two standards, FRF.5 and FRF.8, define how the frame and address conversion takes place between Frame Relay and ATM:

- **FRF.5 (Networking Interworking)** The two DTEs are Frame Relay and the carrier uses ATM as a transport.
- **FRF.8 (Service Interworking)** One DTE is a Frame Relay device and the other is an ATM device, and the carrier uses ATM as a transport.

Figure 26-6 shows an example of these two standards. FRF.5 defines how two Frame Relay devices can send frames back and forth across an ATM backbone, as is shown between RouterA and RouterB. With FRF.5, the Frame Relay frame

| FIGURE 26-6 | Network and service interworking example |

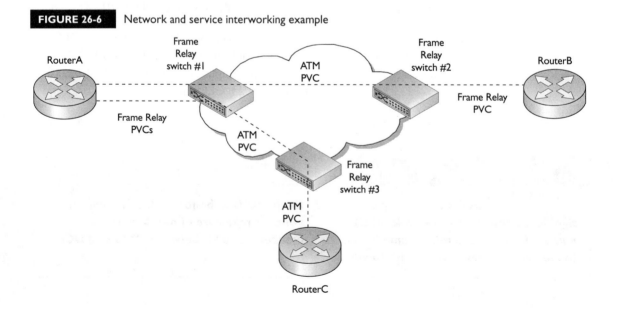

is received by the connected switch. The switch figures out which ATM VC is to be used to get the information to the destination and *encapsulates* the Frame Relay frame into an ATM frame, which is then chunked up into ATM cells. When the ATM cells are received by the destination carrier switch, the switch reassembles the ATM cells back into an ATM frame, extracts the Frame Relay frame that was encapsulated, and then looks up the DLCI in its switching table. When switching the frame to the next segment, if the local DLCI number is different, the switch changes the DLCI in the header and recomputes the CRC.

The connection between RouterA and RouterC is an example of an FRF.8 connection. With FRF.8, one DTE is using Frame Relay and the other DTE is using ATM. The carrier uses ATM to transport the information between the two DTEs. For example, in Figure 26-6, RouterA sends a Frame Relay frame to RouterC. The carrier's switch *converts* the Frame Relay frame into an ATM frame, which is different from what FRF.5 does. The switch then segments the ATM frame into cells and assigns the correct VPI/VCI address to the cells to get to the remote ATM switch. In this example, RouterA thinks it's talking to another Frame Relay device (RouterC). RouterC, on the other hand, thinks it's talking to an ATM device (RouterA).

VC Data Rates

Each data VC has a few parameters associated with it that affect its data rate and throughput. These values include the following: CIR (committed information rate), B_C (committed burst rate), B_E (excessive burst rate), and access rate. This section covers these four values and how the Frame Relay switch uses them to enforce the traffic contract for the VC.

CIR is the average contracted rate of a VC measured over a period of time. This is the guaranteed rate that the carrier is giving to you, barring any major outages the carrier might experience in its network.

Two burst rates allow you to go above the CIR limit temporarily, assuming the provider has enough bandwidth in its network to support this temporary burst. B_C allows you to burst up to a higher average than CIR for a VC, but the time period of the burst is smaller than the time period over which CIR is measured. If you send information above the CIR, but below the B_C value, the carrier will permit the frame into its network.

The B_E value indicates the maximum rate you are allowed to send into the carrier on a VC. Any frames that exceed this value are dropped. If you send traffic at a rate between B_C and B_E, the carrier switch marks the frames as discard eligible, using the 1-bit Discard Eligible (DE) field in the Frame Relay frame header. By marking this bit, the carrier is saying that the frame is allowed in the network; however, as soon as the carrier experiences congestion, these are the first frames that are dropped. From the carrier's perspective, frames sent at a rate between B_C and B_E are bending the rules but will be allowed if enough bandwidth is available for them.

It is important to point out that *each* VC has its own CIR, B_C, and B_E values. However, depending on the carrier's implementation of Frame Relay, or how you purchase the VCs, the B_C and B_E values might not be used. In some instances, the B_E value defaults to the access rate—the speed of the physical connection from the Frame Relay DTE to the Frame Relay DCE. This could be a fractional T1 running at, say, 256 Kbps, or a full T1 (1.544 Mbps).

No matter how many VCs you have, or what their combined CIR values are, you are always limited to the access rate—you can't exceed the speed of the physical connection. It is a common practice to oversubscribe the speed of the physical connection: this occurs when the total CIR of all VCs exceeds the access rate. Basically, you're betting that all VCs will not simultaneously run at their CIRs, but that most will run below their CIR values at any given time, requiring a smaller speed connection to the carrier. A Frame Relay setup incurs two basic costs: the cost of each physical connection to the Frame Relay switch and the cost of each VC, which is usually dependent on its rate parameters.

Figure 26-7 shows an example of how these Frame Relay traffic parameters affect the data rate of a VC. The graph shows a linear progression of frames leaving a router's interface on a VC. As you can see from this figure, as long as the data rate of the VC is below the CIR/B_C values, the Frame Relay switch allows the frames into the Frame Relay network. However, those frames (4 and 5) that exceed the B_C value will have their DE bits set, which allows the carrier to drop these frames in times of internal congestion. Also, any frames that exceed B_E are dropped: in this example, Frames 6 and 7 are dropped.

ⓦatch   *Typically, frames that exceed the B_C value have their DE bits set by the carrier.*

Some carriers don't support B_C and B_E. Instead, they mark all frames that exceed the CIR as discard eligible. This means that you can send all your frames into the carrier network at the access rate speed and the carrier will permit them in (after marking the DE bit). All of these options and implementations can make it confusing when you're trying to find the right Frame Relay solution for your network. For example, one carrier might sell you a CIR of 0 Kbps, which causes the carrier to permit all your traffic into the network but marks all of the frames

| **FIGURE 26-7** | VC traffic parameters |

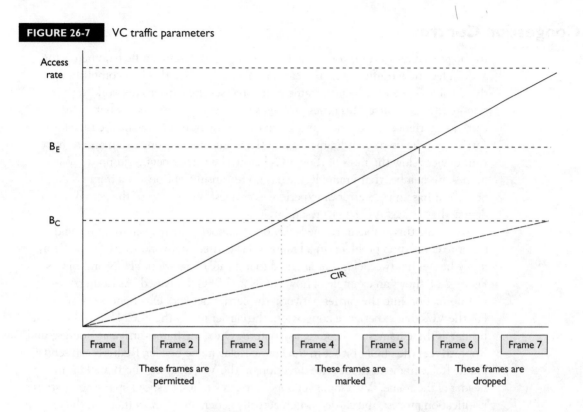

as discard eligible. Assuming the carrier experiences no congestion problems, you're getting a great service. Of course, if the carrier is constantly experiencing congestion, you are getting very poor service, since some or most of your frames are dropped.

If you need a guaranteed rate for a VC or VCs, you can obtain this from most carriers, but this costs more money than a CIR of 0 Kbps VC. The more bandwidth you require, the more expensive the circuit, since the carrier must reserve this bandwidth inside its network to accommodate your traffic rate needs. And what makes this whole process complex is looking at the traffic rates for all your connections and trying to get the best value for your money. Some network administrators oversubscribe their access rates, expecting that not all VCs will simultaneously send traffic at their CIR traffic rates. How Frame Relay operates and how your traffic behaves can make it difficult to pick the right Frame Relay service for your network.

Congestion Control

In the preceding section, you were shown how the different traffic parameters for a VC affect how traffic enters the carrier's network. Once this is accomplished, these values have no effect on traffic as it traverses the carrier's network to your remote site. Of course, this poses problems in a carrier's network—what if the carrier experiences congestion and begins dropping frames? It would be nice for the carrier to indicate to your Frame Relay DTEs that there is congestion and to have your devices slow the rates of their VCs before the carrier begins dropping your frames. Remember that Frame Relay has no retransmit option—if a frame is dropped because it has an FCS error or experiences congestion, it is up to the actual source device that *created* the data to resend it.

To handle this problem, Frame Relay has a standard mechanism to signify and adapt to congestion problems in a Frame Relay carrier's network. Every Frame Relay frame header has two fields that are used to indicate congestion: FECN and BECN. Figure 26-8 shows an example of how FECN and BECN are used. As RouterA sends its information into the carrier network, the carrier network experiences congestion. For the VCs that experience congestion, the carrier marks the FECN bit in the frame header as these frames are heading *to* RouterB. Once the frames arrive at RouterB and RouterB sees the FECN bit set in the Frame Relay frame header, RouterB can send a Frame Relay frame in the reverse direction on the VC, marking the BECN bit in the header of the frame. With some vendors' carrier switches, to speed up the congestion notification process, the carrier switch actually generates a BECN frame in the reverse direction of the VC, back to the source, to indicate congestion issues. Once RouterA receives the BECN frames, it can then begin to slow down the data rate on the VC.

FIGURE 26-8 FECN and BECN illustration

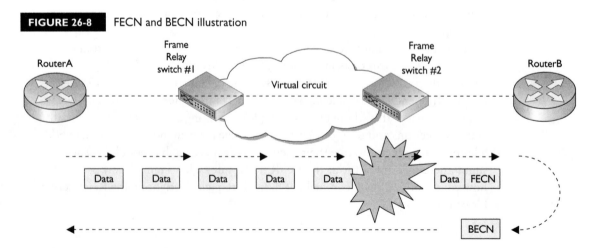

One of the main drawbacks of using the FECN/BECN method of congestion notification is that it is not a very efficient form of flow control. For example, the carrier might begin to mark the FECN bit in frames as they are headed to the destination to indicate a congestion problem. As the destination is responding to the source with BECN frames, the congestion disappears. When the source receives the BECN frames, it begins to slow down even though the congestion problem no longer exists. On top of this, there is no way of notifying the source or destination how much congestion exists—the source might begin slowing down the VC too slowly or too quickly without any decent feedback about how much to slow down. Because of these issues, many companies have opted to use ATM. ATM also supports flow control, but its implementation is more sophisticated than Frame Relay and allows VCs to adapt to congestion in a real-time fashion.

FECN is used to indicate congestion as frames go from the source to the destination. BECN is used by the *destination (and sent to the source) to indicate that there is congestion from the source to the destination.*

CERTIFICATION OBJECTIVE 26.03

Frame Relay Configuration

The remainder of this chapter focuses on the different ways of configuring Frame Relay on your router. Like the other WAN encapsulations, PPP and HDLC, Frame Relay's configuration is done on your router's serial interface.

Encapsulation Configuration

To set the data link layer encapsulation type to Frame Relay, use this configuration:

```
Router(config)# interface serial [slot_#/]port_#
Router(config-if)# encapsulation frame-relay [cisco|ietf]
```

Notice that the **encapsulation** command has options for two different frame types. The frame type you configure on your router must match the frame type configured on the Frame Relay DTEs at the remote side of your VCs. The default is **cisco** if you don't specify the encapsulation type. This frame type is proprietary to Cisco equipment. In most instances, you'll use the standardized frame type (**ietf**). IETF has defined a standardized Frame Relay frame type in RFC 1490, which is interoperable with all vendors' Frame Relay equipment.

on the

ⓘo b *Most Frame Relay providers use IETF as the data link layer frame type.*

Once you have configured your frame type, use the **show interfaces** command to verify your frame type configuration:

```
Router# show interfaces serial 1/0
Serial 1/0 is up, line protocol is up
    Hardware is MCI Serial
    Internet address is 172.16.2.1, subnet mask is 255.255.255.0
    MTU 1500 bytes, BW 256 Kbit, DLY 20000 usec, rely 255/255, load 1/255
    Encapsulation FRAME-RELAY, loopback not set, keepalive set
    LMI DLCI    0, LMI sent 1107, LMI stat recvd 1107
    LMI type is ANSI Annex D
    .
    .
    .
```

Notice that the encapsulation type has been changed to FRAME-RELAY in this example.

CertCam

26.01. The CD contains a multimedia demonstration of changing the encapsulation type to Frame Relay on a router.

	Parameter	Standard
TABLE 26-3	`ansi`	ANSI's Annex D standard, T1.617
LMI Parameters	`cisco`	The Gang of Four
	`q933a`	ITU-T's Q.933 Annex A standard

LMI Configuration

Once you have set the encapsulation on your serial interface, you need to define the LMI type that is used to communicate information between your router and the carrier's switch: remember that LMI is a local process. What you configure on your router doesn't have to match what is on the remote routers: What has to match is what your carrier is using on its switch (the DTE to DCE connection).

Use this configuration to configure the LMI type:

```
Router(config)# interface serial [slot_#/]port_#
Router(config-if)# frame-relay lmi-type ansi|cisco|q933a
```

Note that the LMI type is specific to the entire interface, not to a VC. Table 26-3 maps the LMI parameters to the corresponding LMI standard.

Starting with IOS 11.2, Cisco routers can autosense the LMI type that is configured on the carrier's switch. With this feature, the router sends a status enquiry for each of the three LMI types to the carrier's switch, one at a time, and waits to see which one the switch will respond to. The router keeps on doing this until the switch responds to one of them. If you are not getting a response from the carrier, it is most likely that the carrier forgot to turn on and configure LMI on its switch. Remember that a Cisco router generates an LMI status enquiry message every 10 seconds. On the sixth message, the router sends a full status update query. Since Cisco routers can autosense the LMI type used by the carrier, it is not necessary to hard code it.

CertCam

26.02. The CD contains a multimedia demonstration configuring the LMI type on a router.

Troubleshooting LMI

If you are experiencing LMI problems with your connection to the carrier's switch, you can use three commands to assist you in the troubleshooting process:

- `show interfaces`
- `show frame-relay lmi`
- `debug frame-relay lmi`

The following sections cover each of these commands in detail.

The show interfaces Command

Besides showing you the encapsulation type of an interface, the **show interfaces** command also displays the LMI type that is being used as well as some LMI statistics, as is shown here:

```
Router# show interfaces serial 0
Serial 0 is up, line protocol is up
   Hardware is MCI Serial
   Internet address is 172.16.2.1, subnet mask is 255.255.255.0
   MTU 1500 bytes, BW 256 Kbit, DLY 20000 usec, rely 255/255, load 1/255
   Encapsulation FRAME-RELAY, loopback not set, keepalive set
   LMI DLCI    0, LMI sent 1107, LMI stat recvd 1107
   LMI type is ANSI Annex D
   .
   .
   .
```

Notice the two lines below the encapsulation. The first line shows the DLCI number used by LMI (0) as well as the number of status enquiries sent and received. If you re-execute the **show interfaces** command every 10 seconds, both of these values should be incrementing. The second line shows the actual LMI type used (ANSI Annex D).

The show frame-relay lmi Command

If you want to see more detailed statistics regarding LMI than what the **show interfaces** command displays, you can use the **show frame-relay lmi** command, shown here:

```
Router# show frame-relay lmi
LMI Statistics for interface Serial0
                       (Frame Relay DTE) LMI TYPE = ANSI
   Invalid Unnumbered info 0          Invalid Prot Disc 0
   Invalid dummy Call Ref 0           Invalid Msg Type 0
   Invalid Status Message 0           Invalid Lock Shift 0
   Invalid Information ID 0           Invalid Report IE Len 0
   Invalid Report Request 0           Invalid Keep IE Len 0
   Num Status Enq. Sent 12            Num Status msgs Rcvd 12
   Num Update Status Rcvd 2           Num Status Timeouts 2
```

on the job

If you see the Num Status Timeouts *increasing, but the* Num Status msgs Rcvd *is not increasing, this probably indicates that the provider forgot to enable LMI on its switch's interface.*

With this command, you can see both valid and invalid messages. If the Invalid field values are incrementing, this can indicate a mismatch in the LMI configuration: you have one LMI type configured and the switch has another type configured. The last two lines of the output refer to the status enquiries that the router generates. The Num Status Enq Sent field is the number of enquiries your router has sent to the switch. The Num Status msgs Rcvd field is the number of replies that the switch has sent upon receiving your router's enquiries. The Num Update Status Rcvd are the number of full status updates messages the switch has sent. The Num Status Timeouts indicates the number of times your router sent an enquiry and did *not* receive a response.

CertCam

26.03. The CD contains a multimedia demonstration of the show frame-relay lmi *command on a router.*

The debug frame-relay lmi Command

For more detailed troubleshooting of LMI, you can use the **debug frame-relay lmi** command. This command shows the actual LMI messages being sent and received by your router.

Here's an example of the output of this command:

```
Router# debug frame-relay lmi
Serial1/0 (in): Status, myseq 290
RT IE 1, length 1, type 0
RT IE 3, length 2, yourseq 107, my seq 290
PVC IE 0x7, length 0x6, dlci 112, status 0x2 bw 0
```

```
Serial1/0 (out): StEnq, myseq 291, yourseq 107, DTE up
Datagramstart = 0x1959DF4, datagramsize = 13
FR encap = 0xFCF10309
00 75 01 01 01 03 02 D7 D4
```

In this output, the router, on `Serial1/0`, first receives a status reply from the switch to the two hundred ninetieth LMI status enquiry the router sent—this is the very first line of the debug output. Following this on the fifth line is the router's two hundred ninety-first status enquiry (`StEnq`) being sent to the switch.

26.04. The CD contains a multimedia demonstration of the `debug frame-relay lmi` *command on a router.*

PVC Configuration

The preceding two sections showed you how to configure the interaction between your router (DTE) and the carrier's switch (DCE). This section expands upon this and shows you how to send data between two Frame Relay DTEs. As mentioned earlier in the chapter, to send data to another DTE, a VC must first be established. This can be a PVC or an SVC. The CCNA exam focuses on PVCs, so the topic is restricted to the configuration of PVCs in this book.

One of the first issues that you'll have to deal with is the router, which, by default, doesn't know what PVCs to use and which device is off of which PVC. Remember that PVCs are given unique locally significant addresses called DLCIs. Somehow the router has to learn the DLCI numbers and the layer 3 address that is at the remote end of the VC (this is similar to the problem of how devices, with IP addresses, need to talk to each other across Ethernet, which uses MAC addresses). With TCP/IP, the Address Resolution Protocol (ARP) is used to solve this problem. Two methods are available to resolve this issue in Frame Relay: manual and dynamic resolution. These resolutions map the layer 3 address of the remote Frame Relay DTE to the local DLCI number your router uses to reach this DTE. The following sections cover the configuration of both of these resolution types.

Manual Resolution

If you are using manual resolution to resolve layer 3 remote addresses to local DLCI numbers, use the following configuration:

```
Router(config)# interface serial [slot_#/]port_#
Router(config-if)# frame-relay map protocol_name
                        destination_address local_dlci_#
                        [broadcast] [ietf|cisco]
```

The **frame-relay map** command defines the manual resolution process. The *protocol_name* parameter specifies the layer 3 protocol that you are resolving: IP, IPX, or AppleTalk, for instance. If you are running two protocols between yourself and the remote DTE, such as IP and IPX, you will need a separate **frame-relay map** command for each protocol and destination mapping. Following the name of the protocol is the *remote* DTE's layer 3 address (*destination_address*), such as its IP address. Following the layer 3 address is the *local* DLCI number *your* router should use in order to reach the remote DTE. These are the only three required parameters.

The other two parameters, the **broadcast** parameter and the frame type parameter, are optional. By default, local broadcasts and multicasts do not go across a manually resolved PVC. Therefore, if you are running Routing Information Protocol (RIPv2), Open Shortest Path First (OSPF), or Enhanced Interior Gateway Routing Protocol (EIGRP) as a routing protocol, the routing updates these protocols generate will not go across the PVC unless you configure the **broadcast** parameter. If you don't want broadcast traffic going across a VC, then don't configure this parameter. If this is the case, then you'll need to configure static routes on both Frame Relay DTEs.

The beginning of this section described how to change the encapsulation type for Frame Relay frames with the **encapsulation frame-relay** command. This command allows you to specify one of two frame types: **ietf** or **cisco**, with **cisco** being the default. The problem with this command is that it specifies the same encapsulation on every VC for the specified interface. When doing manual resolution, you can specify the encapsulation for *each* VC separately. If you omit this on your manual mapping statement, the encapsulation defaults to that encapsulation type on the serial interface.

Let's look at an example, shown in Figure 26-9, to illustrate how to set up manual resolution for a PVC configuration. Here's the configuration for RouterA:

```
RouterA(config)# interface serial 0
RouterA(config-if)# encapsulation frame-relay ietf
RouterA(config-if)# frame-relay lmi-type q933a
RouterA(config-if)# ip address 192.168.2.1 255.255.255.0
RouterA(config-if)# frame-relay map ip 192.168.2.2 103 broadcast
```

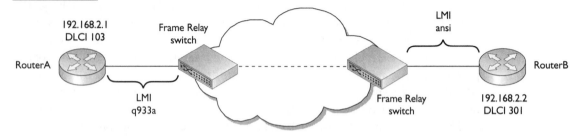

FIGURE 26-9 PVC manual resolution example

Here's the configuration for RouterB:

```
RouterB(config)# interface serial 0
RouterB(config-if)# encapsulation frame-relay ietf
RouterB(config-if)# frame-relay lmi-type ansi
RouterB(config-if)# ip address 192.168.2.2 255.255.255.0
RouterB(config-if)# frame-relay map ip 192.168.2.1 301 broadcast
```

First, notice that the two routers are using *different* LMI types at each end. This is okay, since LMI is used only between the Frame Relay DTE and DCE devices. Second, notice that the DLCI numbers are different at each end. Again, remember that DLCI numbers are locally significant and do not have to be the same on all segments the VC traverses: the carrier will assign these values for you and send you the correct mappings to use for the DLCIs.

26.05. The CD contains a multimedia demonstration of configuring manual resolution for a PVC on a router.

on the
()ob

One common problem of setting up manual resolution is that it is very common for administrators to configure the wrong DLCI for the VC. For example, in the configuration shown for Figure 26-9, some administrators forget that DLCIs are locally significant and configure DLCI 301 on RouterA and DLCI 103 on RouterB. When troubleshooting this problem, examine the status of the VC with the `show frame-relay pvc` *or* `show frame-relay map` *command, looking for a "deleted" status for the VC. These* show *commands are discussed in the next section.*

Dynamic Resolution

Instead of using manual resolution for your PVCs, you can use *dynamic* resolution. Dynamic resolution uses a feature called *Inverse ARP*. This is something like a reverse ARP in TCP/IP. Inverse ARP allows devices to automatically discover the layer 3 protocols and addresses that are used on each VC.

Inverse ARP occurs every 60 seconds on VCs that are not manually configured and it occurs only on VCs that are in an *active* state. Recall from the LMI section that the state of the VCs is learned from the full status update message. For example, once the physical layer for the interface comes up, your router starts sending its LMI enquiries every 10 seconds. On the sixth one, it sends a full status message, which requests the statuses of the VCs that the switch directs to this router's interface. In this example, it will take at least a minute before the router learns of the status of the VC.

Once the router sees an active status for a VC, it *then* does an inverse ARP on the VC if it is not already manually resolved with a **frame-relay map** command. This frame contains the layer 3 protocol and protocol address used by the router. When the frame arrives at the remote DTE, the device takes the protocol, layer 3 address, and *local* DLCI number in the frame header and puts them in its VC resolution table. The remote DTEs do the same thing. Within a short period of time, your router will know the layer 3 addresses at the end of each of its dynamically learned VCs. Once the router knows who is at the other end of the VC, your router can begin transmitting data to the remote DTE.

Inverse ARP allows a router to send a Frame Relay frame across a VC with its layer 3 addressing information. The *destination can then use this, along with the incoming DLCI number, to reach the advertiser.*

Remember the VC statuses in Table 26-4.

VC Status You already know about one of the three states for a VC: active. Table 26-4 shows all three basic statuses for a VC. For Inverse ARP to take place, the VC must have an active status.

TABLE 26-4	Status	Description
VC Statuses	Active	The VC between both Frame Relay DTEs is up and operational.
	Inactive	The VC between your Frame Relay DTE and DCE is up and operational, but something is wrong with the connection between your connected Frame Relay switch and the *destination* DTE.
	Deleted	You are not receiving any LMI messages from the Frame Relay switch for a local VC.

Disadvantages of Dynamic Resolution   Even though dynamic resolution requires no configuration on your router in order to work, it does have some disadvantages. First, one of the main problems of dynamic resolution is that in order for you to send data across the VC, you must wait until you learn the status of the VC and wait for the inverse ARP to occur. This process can sometimes take more than 60 seconds, even if the data link layer is operational and the VC is in place. The advantage of manually resolved PVCs is that as soon as the data link layer is up, your router can immediately begin to send traffic to the destination router. Assuming that the Frame Relay switch replies to your router's first LMI enquiry, this can be less than a second before your router can begin transmitting information to the destination DTE. So even though the manual resolution process requires you to configure all of the manual resolution entries, many network administrators choose to do this so that data can begin to traverse the VCs as soon as the physical and data link layers are "up and line protocol is up".

The second disadvantage of dynamic resolution is that in some instances, with equipment from multiple vendors, you might experience problems with how different vendors implement inverse ARP. In this case, the dynamic resolution fails and you must resort to configuring manual resolution with the **frame-relay map** command. This might even be true between Cisco routers. I have experienced problems with routers running very old and new versions of the IOS trying to perform inverse ARP between them, and it failing. You could either use manual resolution or upgrade the IOS on the older routers.

The third problem with dynamic resolution is that inverse ARP works only with the following protocols: AppleTalk, DECnet, TCP/IP, IPX, Vines, and XNS. If you use another protocol, you will need to configure manual resolution commands to solve your resolution problem.

Configuring Inverse ARP   By default, inverse ARP is already *enabled* on your Cisco router. You can disable it or re-enable it with the following configuration:

```
Router(config)# interface serial [slot_#/]port_#
Router(config-if)# [no] frame-relay inverse-arp
                        [protocol_name] [DLCI_#]
```

Without any options, the **frame-relay inverse-arp** command enables inverse ARP for all VCs on the router's serial interface. You can selectively disable inverse ARP for a particular protocol or VC (DLCI #). Use the **clear frame-relay-inarp** command to clear the Inverse ARP resolution table. To see the Inverse ARP statistics, use this command:

```
Router# show frame-relay traffic
Frame Relay statistics:
ARP requests sent 14, ARP replies sent 0
ARP request recvd 0, ARP replies recvd 10
```

Dynamic Resolution Example   Previously, you saw how to set up manual resolution for the VC connection shown in Figure 26-9. Using the same network, this example implements dynamic resolution to illustrate how this is set up on your router. In this example, assume that your router is autosensing the LMI type. Here's the configuration for RouterA:

```
Router(config)# interface serial 0
Router(config-if)# encapsulation frame-relay ietf
Router(config-if)# ip address 192.168.2.1 255.255.255.0
```

Here's the configuration for RouterB:

```
Router(config)# interface serial 0
Router(config-if)# encapsulation frame-relay ietf
Router(config-if)# ip address 192.168.2.2 255.255.255.0
```

With autosensing of the LMI type, you don't need to configure the LMI type on the interface. And since you are using dynamic resolution with inverse ARP, which is enabled by default, you don't need any additional configuration on your router's serial interface. As you can see from these code examples, the only thing you have to configure is the encapsulation type on the interface, making the setup of Frame Relay a simple and straightforward process.

26.06. The CD contains a multimedia demonstration of configuring dynamic resolution for a PVC on a router.

PVC Status Verification

To see all of the Frame Relay PVCs terminated at your router, as well as their statistics, use the **show frame-relay pvc** command. Optionally, you can look at just one PVC by following this command with the local DLCI number, as shown in this example:

```
Router# show frame-relay pvc 100
PVC Statistics for interface Serial0
                        (Frame Relay DTE) DLCI = 100,
     DLCI USAGE = LOCAL, PVC STATUS = ACTIVE, INTERFACE = Serial0
      input pkts 15        output pkts 26        in bytes 508
```

```
out bytes 638         dropped pkts 1        in FECN pkts 0
in BECN pkts 0        out FECN pkts 0       out BECN pkts 0
in DE pkts 0          out DE pkts 0
out bcast pkts 0      out bcast bytes 0
pvc create time 00:22:01, last time pvc status
            changed 00:05:37
```

In this example, PVC 100's status is ACTIVE, which indicates that the PVC is operational between the two Frame Relay DTEs. You can also see traffic statistics for the PVC. In this example, 15 packets were received and 26 packets were transmitted on this PVC.

exam

watch

Use the `show frame-relay pvc` command to view the statuses of your VCs. If you see an ACTIVE state, this indicates that the VC is operational from this DTE (such as a Cisco router) to the destination DTE. If your router is receiving BECNs, in the output of this command, this indicates congestion in the forward direction from you to your remote Frame Relay peer.

To see the VC resolution table, which maps layer 3 addresses to local DLCI numbers, use the **show frame-relay map** command:

```
Router# show frame-relay map
Serial0 (up): ip 192.168.2.2 dlci 32(0x20, 0x1C80), dynamic,
                      Broadcast, CISCO, status defined, active
```

In this output, one PVC has a local DLCI of 32. At the end of this PVC is a router with an IP address of 192.168.2.2. Notice that this information was learned via Inverse ARP (dynamic), local broadcasts and multicasts are allowed, the default frame type is cisco, and the status of the VC is active. If you had configured manual resolution for this connection, the entry would have listed static instead of dynamic. Also, if the frame type was based on RFC 1490, the frame type would have been listed as IETF.

CertCam

26.07. The CD contains a multimedia demonstration of using the show frame-relay pvc *command.*

If you manually map the layer 3 addresses to DLCIs, and assign a nonexistent DLCI to the resolution, your output will look like this:

```
Router# show frame-relay map
Serial0 (up): ip 192.168.2.2 dlci 32(0x20, 0x1C80), static,
                     Broadcast, CISCO, status defined, deleted
```

Notice that in this example the DLCI has been manually mapped (`static`) and the status is `deleted`.

26.08. The CD contains a multimedia demonstration of using the `show frame-relay map` command on a router.

Use the `show frame-relay map` command to view the manual or Inverse ARP mappings of layer 3 addresses to DLCIs; those learned dynamically via Inverse ARP will have the keyword `dynamic` associated with the VC.

If you statically map the layer 3 address to a DLCI and the status of the DLCI is `deleted`, then you probably misconfigured the DLCI number to one that doesn't exist on the Frame Relay switch.

EXERCISE 26-1

ON THE CD

Configuring Frame Relay

The preceding few sections dealt with the configuration of Frame Relay on a physical serial interface. This exercise will help you reinforce this material by configuring a simple Frame Relay connection. Inverse ARP will be used to resolve the addresses for the VC. The DLCI number on both sides is 100. You'll perform this lab using Boson's NetSim simulator. You can find a picture of the network diagram for Boson's NetSim simulator in the Introduction of this book. After starting up the simulator, click the LabNavigator button. Next, double-click Exercise 26-1 and click the Load Lab button. This will load the lab configuration based on the exercises in Chapters 11 and 16.

 1. On the 2600-1 router, disable `serial0`—this is the dedicated point-to-point connection—and you'll be setting up Frame Relay.

At the top of the simulator in the menu bar, click the eRouters icon and choose 2600-1. Execute the following: **configure terminal**, **interface serial0**, **shutdown**, and **end**. Use the **show interfaces** command to check the status of the interfaces. At this point, only the `fa0/0` interface on the 2600-1 should be enabled.

2. On the 2600-2 router, disable `serial0`—this is the dedicated point-to-point connection—and you'll be setting up Frame Relay.

   At the top of the simulator in the menu bar, click the eRouters icon and choose 2600-2. Execute the following: **configure terminal**, **interface serial0**, **shutdown**, and **end**. Use the **show interfaces** command to check the status of the interfaces. At this point, only the `fa0/0` interface on the 2600-2 should be enabled.

3. Enable Frame Relay on the 2600-1. Enable the `serial1` interface. Use the Cisco frame type for Frame Relay. Set the LMI type to ITU-T. Assign the IP address.

   At the top of the simulator in the menu bar, click the eRouters icon and choose 2600-1. Enable the Frame Relay interface: **configure terminal**, **interface serial1**, and **no shutdown**. Set the encapsulation and frame type: **encapsulation frame-relay**. Set the LMI type: **frame-relay lmi-type q933a**. Assign the IP address on the interface: **ip address 192.168.10.1 255.255.255.0**. Exit Configuration mode: **end**.

4. Verify the operational state of the interface as well as LMI.

   Use the **show interfaces** command to verify that the interface is up and up and that LMI is functioning. Use the **show frame-relay lmi** command to make sure the router is sending and receiving LMI information.

5. Enable Frame Relay on the 2600-2. Enable the `serial1` interface. Use the Cisco frame type for Frame Relay. Set the LMI type to ITU-T. Assign the IP address. Verify the operation of LMI.

   At the top of the simulator in the menu bar, click the eRouters icon and choose 2600-2. From the 2600-2 router, enable the interface: **configure terminal**, **interface serial1**, and **no shutdown**. Set the encapsulation and frame type: **encapsulation frame-relay**. Set the LMI type: **frame-relay lmi-type q933a**. Assign the IP address on the interface: **ip address 192.168.10.2 255.255.255.0**. Exit Configuration mode: **end**.

6. Verify the operational state of the interface as well as LMI.

   Use the **show interfaces** command to verify that the interface is up and up and that LMI is functioning. Use the **show frame-relay lmi** command to make sure the router is sending and receiving LMI information.

7. Verify your PVC configuration and status on the 2600-2.

   View the resolution entry: **show frame-relay map**. View the PVC: **show frame-relay pvc**. The status of the VC should be ACTIVE.

8. Verify your PVC configuration and status on the 2600-1.

   At the top of the simulator in the menu bar, click the eRouters icon and choose 2600-1. View the resolution entry: **show frame-relay map**. View the PVC: **show frame-relay pvc**. The status of the VC should be ACTIVE.

9. Ping the 2600-2's Frame Relay interface address.

   Test connectivity: **ping 192.168.10.2**. The ping should be successful.

10. On the 2600-1 router, set up a static route to the 2600-2's remote network. View the routing table.

    At the top of the simulator in the menu bar, click the eRouters icon and choose 2600-1. On the 2600-1, set up the static route to reach 192.168.3.0/24: **configure terminal** and **ip route 192.168.3.0 255.255.255.0 192.168.10.2**. Exit Configuration mode: **end**. View the routing table and look for the static route: **show ip route**.

11. On the 2600-2 router, set up a static route to the 2600-1's remote network. View the routing table.

    At the top of the simulator in the menu bar, click the eRouters icon and choose 2600-2. On the 2600-2, set up the static route to reach 192.168.3.0/24: **configure terminal** and **ip route 192.168.1.0 255.255.255.0 192.168.10.1**. Exit Configuration mode: **end**. View the routing table and look for the static route: **show ip route**.

12. From Host-1, test the connection to Host-3.

    At the top of the simulator in the menu bar, click the eStations icon and choose Host-1. On Host-1, ping Host-3: **ping 192.168.3.10**. The ping should be successful.

You should now be more familiar with setting up a basic manually resolved Frame Relay connection to a remote site.

CERTIFICATION OBJECTIVE 26.04

Non-Broadcast Multi-Access Environments

Non-broadcast multi-access (NBMA) is a term used to describe WAN networks that use VCs for connectivity. In a broadcast medium in LAN environments such as Ethernet, every device on a segment or VLAN is in the same broadcast domain—when a device generates a broadcast, every other device in the broadcast domain will see the segment, as is shown in the top part of Figure 26-10. As you can see in this example, RouterA generates one broadcast and the other two routers, RouterB and RouterC, receive it. With WAN networks that use VCs, each device is connected to another device via a point-to-point VC—only two devices can be connected to a VC. This poses a problem with NBMA environments.

e x a m

ⓦatch *An NBMA environment is an environment that allows access by multiple devices but doesn't support a traditional broadcast environment such as Ethernet. Frame Relay is an example of an NBMA network.*

FIGURE 26-10 Broadcast versus NBMA environments

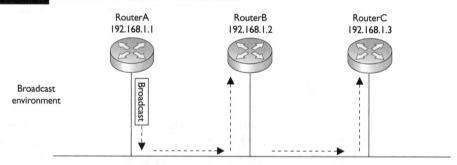

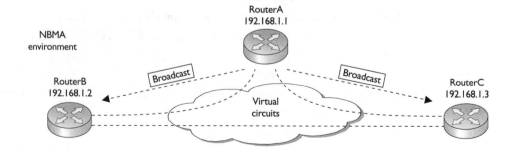

Topology Types

Before reading more about the issues of NBMA environments, consider some of the topologies you can use to connect your devices using VCs. Table 26-5 contains the terms used to describe these various topologies. The bottom part of Figure 26-10 shows an example of a fully meshed network. In such a network, it is easy to emulate a broadcast environment. In this environment, your router *replicates* the local broadcast across every VC in the subnet on that interface. For example, in Figure 26-10, when RouterA wants to send a local broadcast, it sends it across the two VCs to RouterB and RouterC. In a fully meshed environment, every device receives the original broadcast frame. This process is also true if RouterB or RouterC generates a broadcast in this example.

Split Horizon Issues

The main problem of NBMA environments arises when the network is *partially* meshed for a *subnet*. This can create problems with routing protocols that support split horizon. Recall from Chapter 15 that distance vector protocols, such as RIP, use split horizon to prevent routing loops. Split horizon states that if routing information is learned on an interface, this routing information will not be propagated out the same interface.

This is an issue with partially meshed networks that use VCs. For instance, two routers may be in the same subnet but not have a VC between them. With partially meshed networks, this can create routing issues. Look at Figure 26-11 to see the problem. This figure shows a network in which RouterA has a VC to the other three routers, but these three routers must go through RouterA to reach the other routers

TABLE 26-5	Topology	Description
NBMA Topology Types	Fully meshed	Your router has VC connections to every other router.
	Partially meshed	Your router has VC connections to some, but not all, of the other routers.
	Point-to-point	Your router has a VC connection on only one other router (this is used to emulate leased lines/dedicated circuit connections).
	Star	Your router has VC connections to some, but not all, of the other routers. This is sometimes called a *hub-and-spoke* topology, where the routers are partially meshed. Each remote site router has a connection to the central site router.

FIGURE 26-11   NBMA and split horizon issues

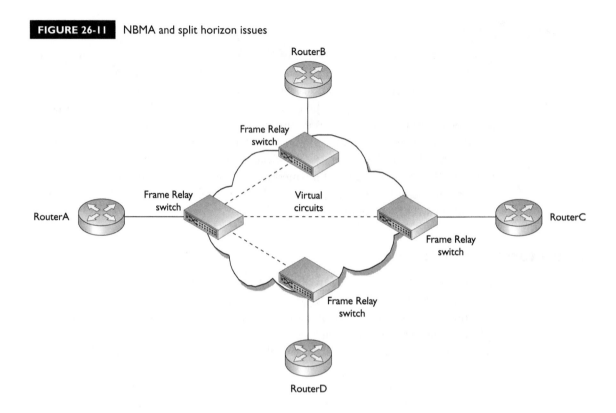

(a hub-and-spoke/star topology). The assumption here is that all of the routers are in the same subnet, and the three VCs terminated at RouterA are going into the same serial interface.

Let's look at this from a routing perspective, assuming that these routers are running RIPv2. RouterB, RouterC, and RouterD have no issues—they have only one VC apiece and can send and receive their routing updates on their VCs. However, RouterA has a problem disseminating routing information from RouterB, RouterC, or RouterD to the other routers in the subnet.

For example, assume that RouterB generates a routing update. Since RouterB doesn't have a VC to RouterC and RouterD, it forwards the update to RouterA, in hopes that RouterA will forward this to the other two routers in the subnet. However, when RouterA receives the routing update from RouterB, RouterA can't forward this to RouterC and RouterD because of split horizon. Even though these two routers are off of different VCs than RouterB, they are off of the *same* physical interface.

Therefore, by default, any routing information from these remote routers will not be propagated by RouterA to the other remote counterparts.

Figure 26-11 shows a prime example of an NBMA environment. Even though it is possible to reach every router in the subnet, even if it takes an extra hop, in the WAN network, broadcasts (and multicasts) don't function correctly.

Solutions to Split Horizon Problems

Given the preceding problem with routing protocols that use split horizon, you can use several solutions to overcome this issue:

- Create a fully meshed network.
- Use static routes.
- Disable split horizon.
- Use subinterfaces on RouterA and associate a single VC and subnet to each subinterface.

These solutions apply to any NBMA environment that uses VCs, including Frame Relay, X.25, and ATM. The following paragraphs deal with each of these solutions individually.

As to the first solution, if you fully mesh your WAN network, you don't have to deal with split horizon problems with distance vector protocols: every router has a VC to every other router in the WAN. Therefore, when any router generates a routing update broadcast, the broadcast is replicated across every VC to all of the destination routers. The main problem with this solution is that to fully mesh your WAN network, you have to purchase a lot of VCs. In many cases, this doesn't make financial sense. For instance, in Figure 26-11, if most of the traffic is from RouterB, RouterC, and RouterD to RouterA, it makes no sense to pay extra money just to replicate the routing updates to the three nonconnected routers.

The second solution has you configure static routes on RouterB, RouterC, and RouterD to solve your routing problems. This works fine if the number of networks and subnets these routers are connected to is small. But if these are major regional sites, with hundreds of networks behind these routers, then setting up static routes becomes a monumental task. Not only does it take a lot of time to configure all of these routes, but you must also test and troubleshoot them, making this solution not scalable.

The third solution has you disable split horizon on RouterA. Some layer 3 protocols allow you to disable split horizon, and some don't. And if the routing protocol allowed you to disable split horizon, it is an all-or-nothing proposition. In other words, Cisco doesn't let you enable or disable split horizon on an interface-by-interface basis. This can create problems if RouterA has multiple LAN connections. By disabling split horizon in this situation, you are allowing RouterB, RouterC, and RouterD to learn each other's routes, but you may be creating routing loops on the LAN side of RouterA.

Subinterfaces

The fourth solution is the *preferred* method for solving split horizon and routing problems in NBMA environments. Recall from Chapter 16 that a subinterface is a logical interface associated with a single physical interface. A physical interface can support many subinterfaces. Cisco routers treat subinterfaces just as they do physical interfaces. You can shut down a physical interface, shutting down all of its associated subinterfaces, or you can shut down a single subinterface while keeping the remaining subinterfaces operational.

When using subinterfaces in a Frame Relay environment, you basically configure two commands on the physical (or major) interface:

- `encapsulation frame-relay`
- `frame-relay lmi-type`

All other configuration commands should be placed under the appropriate *subinterface*.

Overcoming Split Horizon Issues

By using subinterfaces, and placing each subinterface in a *separate* subnet, you make it possible for routing information received on one subinterface to be propagated to other subinterfaces on the same physical interface. Figure 26-12 shows an example of how subinterfaces can be used to overcome split horizon issues in a partially meshed NBMA environment. In this example, you create a separate subinterface on RouterA for each destination. Since RouterA is using a separate *subinterface* for each of these connections, a different subnet is used for each router-to-router VC. With this setup, if RouterB sent a routing update to RouterA, it would be processed on one subinterface and the routing information could be broadcast out the other two subinterfaces. This process allows you to overcome the split horizon problem.

on the **Ø** o b

The main problem with the subinterface solution, however, is that for each subinterface on RouterA, you need a separate network or subnet number. Therefore, it is highly recommended that you use a 255.255.255.252 subnet mask (/30), which allows for two host addresses per subnet, conserving addresses.

FIGURE 26-12   Subinterfaces and split horizon

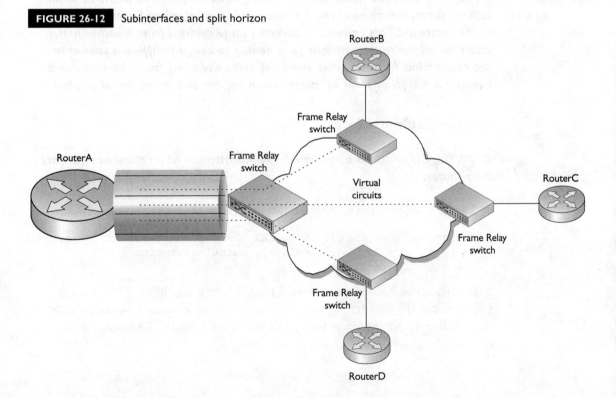

Subinterface Types

As was described in Chapter 16, two types of subinterfaces exist: point-to-point and multipoint. Multipoint subinterfaces (subinterfaces with many VCs terminated on them) are good for fully meshed networks. If the WAN is fully meshed, the devices can be placed in the same subnet and thus require only one network number to address your devices. However, multipoint subinterfaces don't work well in partially meshed network designs. In this situation, they have problems with routing protocols that use split horizon.

Point-to-point subinterfaces work best in partially meshed environments or in environments in which you need to simulate a leased-line connection. Point-to-point subinterfaces are used to overcome routing protocols that use split horizon. But like multipoint subinterfaces, point-to-point subinterfaces have their fair share of problems. In the biggest problem, each point-to-point subinterface requires a separate network or subnet number. If you have 200 subinterfaces on your serial interface, then you need 200 subnets to accommodate your addressing needs.

on the
job

If you are concerned about the addressing needs required of point-to-point subinterfaces, you can use the `ip unnumbered` *Interface Subconfiguration mode command. This command borrows an IP address from another active interface on the router without your having to assign a different subnet to the connection. Most network administrators shy away from this command because it has its own set of issues, which are beyond the scope of this book.*

Creating Subinterfaces

CertCam

26.09. The CD contains a multimedia demonstration of creating subinterfaces on a router.

To create a subinterface, use the following syntax:

```
Router(config)# interface serial [slot_#/]port_#.subinterface_#
                         point-to-point|multipoint
Router(config-subif)#
```

Subinterface numbers can range from 1 to well over 100 million. What number you choose as the subinterface number doesn't matter; it needs to be unique only among all of the subinterfaces for a given physical interface. The router uses this number to differentiate the subinterfaces for each physical interface. Once you create a subinterface, notice that the prompt changed from `Router(config)#` to `Router(config-subif)#`.

Once you create a subinterface, you can delete it by prefacing the `interface` command with the no parameter. However, once you delete the subinterface, the subinterface still exists in the router's memory. To completely remove the subinterface, you need to save your configuration and reboot your router. Also, if you want to change the subinterface type from multipoint to point-to-point or vice versa, you must delete the subinterface, save your configuration, and reboot your router.

Configuring Frame Relay with Subinterfaces

When you are configuring Frame Relay with subinterfaces, you must associate your DLCI or DLCIs with each subinterface by using the **frame-relay interface-dlci** command:

```
Router(config)# interface serial [slot_#/]port_#.subinterface_#
                        point-to-point|multipoint
Router(config-subif)# frame-relay interface-dlci local_DLCI_#
```

If you have a point-to-point subinterface, you can assign only one VC, and thus one DLCI, to it. If it is a multipoint subinterface, you can assign multiple DLCIs to it. When creating your subinterfaces, it is a common practice to match the subinterface number with the DLCI number; however, remember that these two numbers have nothing in common and can be different. Also, make sure that you assign your layer 3 addressing to the subinterface and *not* the physical (main) interface. The frame type and LMI type are, however, configured on the physical interface.

The **frame-relay interface-dlci** command uses dynamic resolution with inverse ARP. If you can't use inverse ARP, or don't want to, then use the **frame-relay map** command on the subinterface to perform manual resolution, like this:

```
Router(config)# interface serial [slot_#/]port_#.subinterface_#
                        point-to-point|multipoint
Router(config-if)# frame-relay map protocol_name
                        destination_address local_dlci_#
                        [broadcast] [ietf|cisco]
```

Example Configuration with Multipoint Subinterfaces

This section offers an example of using multipoint subinterfaces on a router to set up Frame Relay connections. Use the network shown in Figure 26-13. In this example, assume that LMI is being autosensed and a single multipoint subinterface is used on RouterA.

Here's the configuration for RouterA:

```
RouterA(config)# interface serial 0
RouterA(config-if)# encaspulation frame-relay ietf
RouterA(config-if)# no shutdown
RouterA(config-if)# exit
RouterA(config)# interface serial0.1 multipoint
RouterA(config-subif)# ip address 192.168.1.1 255.255.255.0
RouterA(config-subif)# frame-relay interface-dlci 101
RouterA(config-subif)# frame-relay interface-dlci 102
```

Since this is a partially meshed network, and you are terminating two VCs on the same subinterface, you need to do one of the following to solve split horizon issues: disable split horizon on RouterA or configure static routes on RouterB and RouterC.

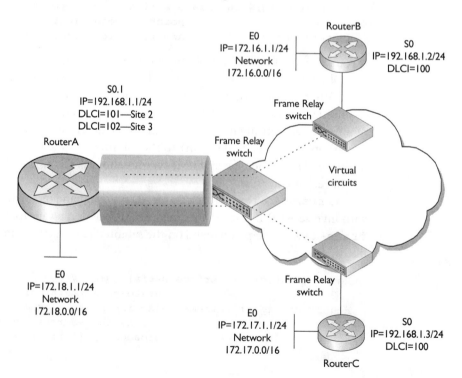

FIGURE 26-13

Multipoint subinterface example

This example configures static routes. Here's the configuration for RouterB:

```
RouterB(config)# interface serial 0
RouterB(config-if)# encaspulation frame-relay ietf
RouterB(config-if)# ip address 192.168.1.2 255.255.255.0
RouterB(config-if)# no shutdown
RouterB(config-if)# exit
RouterB(config)# interface ethernet 0
RouterB(config-if)# ip address 172.16.1.1 255.255.255.0
RouterB(config-if)# no shutdown
RouterB(config-if)# exit
RouterB(config)# ip route 172.17.0.0 255.255.0.0 192.168.1.1
```

Notice in this example that you did not need to configure the DLCI number on the physical interface, since the router will learn this from the full status update via LMI. Also notice the static route on RouterB, which allows it to reach RouterC's network.

Here's the configuration for RouterC:

```
RouterC(config)# interface serial 0
RouterC(config-if)# encaspulation frame-relay ietf
RouterC(config-if)# ip address 192.168.1.3 255.255.255.0
RouterC(config-if)# no shutdown
RouterC(config-if)# exit
RouterC(config)# interface ethernet 0
RouterC(config-if)# ip address 172.17.1.1 255.255.255.0
RouterC(config-if)# no shutdown
RouterC(config-if)# exit
RouterC(config)# ip route 172.16.0.0 255.255.0.0 192.168.1.1
```

26.10. *The CD contains a multimedia demonstration of setting up Frame Relay connections using multipoint subinterfaces on a router.*

Example Configuration with Point-to-Point Subinterfaces

This section offers an example of using point-to-point subinterfaces on a router to set up Frame Relay connections. Use the network shown in Figure 26-14. In this example, assume that LMI is being autosensed and two point-to-point subinterfaces are used on RouterA.

The configurations on RouterB and RouterC are the same as before, with the exception that the static routes are not needed, since point-to-point subinterfaces are being used on RouterA and RouterC will need a different IP address because

FIGURE 26-14

Point-to-point
subinterface
example

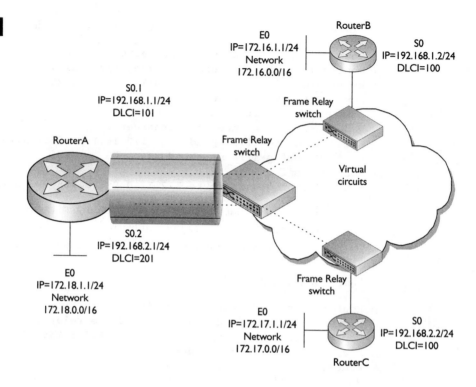

of the two subnets (instead of one). The biggest difference is the configuration on
RouterA, shown here:

```
RouterA(config)# interface serial 0
RouterA(config-if)# encaspulation frame-relay ietf
RouterA(config-if)# no shutdown
RouterA(config-if)# exit
RouterA(config)# interface serial0.1 point-to-point
RouterA(config-subif)# ip address 192.168.1.1 255.255.255.0
RouterA(config-subif)# frame-relay interface-dlci 101
RouterA(config-subif)# exit
RouterA(config)# interface serial0.2 point-to-point
RouterA(config-subif)# frame-relay interface-dlci 201
RouterA(config-subif)# ip address 192.168.2.1 255.255.255.0
```

In this example, subinterface serial0.1 is connected to RouterB and subinterface
serial0.2 is connected to RouterC. Also notice that there is a different subnet
on each subinterface. RouterB's configuration doesn't change, but you'll need
to configure 192.168.2.2 on RouterC's serial interface (RouterB and RouterC are

now in a different subnet). One other item to point out is that if you are running a dynamic routing protocol such as RIPv2 or EIGRP, you could remove the static routes on RouterB and RouterC, since split horizon is solved by RouterA's configuration.

CertCam

26.11.The CD contains a multimedia demonstration of setting up Frame Relay connections using point-to-point subinterfaces on a router.

e x a m

ⓦatch
When configuring Frame Relay with subinterfaces, the Frame Relay encapsulation and LMI type go on the major (physical) interface. The IP address and DLCI number for the VC go on the subinterface. To specify the DLCI number, use the `frame-relay interface-dlci` or `frame-relay map` command.

ON THE CD

EXERCISE 26-2

Configuring Frame Relay with Subinterfaces

The preceding few sections dealt with the configuration of Frame Relay using subinterfaces. This exercise will help you reinforce this material by configuring a simple Frame Relay point-to-point connection. This exercise builds upon Exercise 26-1, moving the configuration from that exercise and placing it on a point-to-point subinterface. Also, inverse ARP is used to perform the resolution. You'll perform this lab using Boson's NetSim simulator. You can find a picture of the network diagram for Boson's NetSim simulator in the Introduction of this book. This exercise has you first set up two routers (2600-1 and 2600-2) and verify network connectivity. Following this, you'll configure your ACL. After starting up the simulator, click the LabNavigator button. Next, double-click Exercise 26-2 and click the Load Lab button. This will load the lab configuration based on Exercise 26-1.

1. Remove the IP address on the physical interface of the 2600-1.

   At the top of the simulator in the menu bar, click the eRouters icon and choose 2600-1. Remove the IP address on the interface: **configure terminal**, **interface serial1**, and **no ip address 192.168.10.1 255.255.255.0**. Exit Configuration mode: **end**.

2. Verify your changes on the 2600-1.

   Use the **show interface serial1** command to verify the removal of the IP address and that the interface is up and up and that LMI is functioning. Use the **show frame-relay lmi** command to make sure the router is still sending and receiving LMI information.

3. Remove the IP address on the physical interface of the 2600-2.

   At the top of the simulator in the menu bar, click the eRouters icon and choose 2600-2. From the 2600-2 router, remove the IP address on the interface: **configure terminal, interface serial1**, and **no ip address 192.168.10.2 255.255.255.0**. Exit Configuration mode: **end**.

4. Verify your changes on the 2600-2.

   Use the **show interface serial1** command to verify the removal of the IP address and that the interface is up and up and that LMI is functioning. Use the **show frame-relay lmi** command to make sure the router is still sending and receiving LMI information.

5. Create a point-to-point subinterface on the 2600-1 router with a subinterface number of 100. Assign the DLCI to the subinterface. The DLCI number used locally is 100. Assign the IP address to the subinterface.

   At the top of the simulator in the menu bar, click the eRouters icon and choose 2600-1. Create the subinterface: **configure terminal** and **interface serial 1.100 point-to-point**. Assign the DLCI: **frame-relay interface-dlci 100**. Assign the IP address: **ip address 192.168.10.1 255.255.255.0**. Exit Configuration mode: **end**.

6. Verify the PVC's configuration on the 2600-1.

   View the PVC: **show frame-relay pvc**.

7. Create a point-to-point subinterface on the 2600-2 router with a subinterface number of 100. Assign the DLCI to the subinterface. The DLCI number used locally is 100. Assign the IP address to the subinterface.

   At the top of the simulator in the menu bar, click the eRouters icon and choose 2600-2. On the 2600-2, create the subinterface: **configure terminal, interface serial 1.100 point-to-point**. Assign the DLCI: **frame-relay interface-dlci 100**. Assign the IP address: **ip address 192.168.10.2 255.255.255.0**. Exit Configuration mode: **end**.

8. Verify the PVC's configuration on the 2600-2.

   View the PVC: **show frame-relay pvc**.

9. On the 2600-1, test the connection to the 2600-2. Verify the router's routing table.

   At the top of the simulator in the menu bar, click the eRouters icon and choose 2600-1. On the 2600-1 router, ping the 2600-2's Frame Relay interface: **ping 192.168.10.2**. The ping should be successful. If it isn't, wait 1 minute and try again—the inverse ARP might be taking place.

10. From Host-1, test the connection to Host-3.

    At the top of the simulator in the menu bar, click the eStations icon and choose Host-1.On Host-1, ping Host-3: **ping 192.168.3.10**. The ping should be successful.

Now you should be more familiar with configuring Frame Relay with subinterfaces.

INSIDE THE EXAM

Virtual Circuits

You should be very familiar with the terms used in Frame Relay, some of the basic configuration commands, and how to interpret the output of the various **show** commands to troubleshoot problems. VCs are a much cheaper solution than using dedicated lines/circuits and are more easily provisioned after the initial line is installed to the carrier's switch.

Frame Relay Terms

You should be very familiar with the terms listed in Table 26-1, including the use of LMI and FECNs and BECNs. Remember that periodically a full status update is received from the carrier switch, containing a list of the VCs, their configurations, and their statuses. You should know how DLCIs are used to reach destinations and that they are locally significant: study Figure 26-5 and the discussion in the "DLCI Example" section.

(continued)

Frame Relay Configuration

Remember the two encapsulation types for a Frame Relay frame: Cisco and IETF. IETF is used in a multi-vendor environment. If you don't configure the LMI type, Cisco routers will autosense it. The `show interfaces` and `show frame-relay lmi` commands will indicate whether you are sending status enquiries and receiving replies from the carrier switch. Know how to resolve layer 3 addresses to local DLCIs with the `frame-relay map` command and how to get routing updates across the VC with the `broadcast` parameter. Know how to troubleshoot misconfigured manually resolved VCs. Be familiar with how inverse ARP works and be able to identify VCs dynamically resolved with the `show frame-relay pvc` command. Know the three states of a VC—inactive, active, and deleted—and how they can be used to troubleshoot problems with a VC.

Non-Broadcast Multi-Access Environments

Be familiar with the problems associated with connectivity and routing across an NBMA network and how to solve split horizon problems. The recommended solution is subinterfaces, where a single VC and subnet is associated with each subinterface. Know how to associate a DLCI to a subinterface with the `frame-relay interface-dlci` command.

CERTIFICATION SUMMARY

Frame Relay uses VCs for connectivity. A VC is a logical connection between devices. There are two types of VCs: PVCs, which are similar to a leased line, and SVCs, which are similar to circuit-switched calls. VCs have advantages over leased lines in that once a physical connection is provisioned, it is easy to add VCs as well as allocate bandwidth for users or applications by using VCs. If you want to fully mesh your Frame Relay routers, use this formula to figure out the number of required connections: $(N \times (N-1)) / 2$.

LMI defines how a Frame Relay DTE (router) interacts with a Frame Relay DCE (carrier switch). There are three types of LMI: Gang of Four, ANSI Annex D, and ITU-T Q.933 Annex A. LMI is local to the two devices (router and Frame Relay switch) and is never forwarded to another device. By default, DTEs originate LMI messages. Cisco routers generate LMI messages every 10 seconds, with a full status update occurring every sixth message. Each VC is given an address, called a DLCI. DLCIs are also locally significant and can change on a segment-by-segment basis. Carrier switches remap DLCI numbers in the Frame Relay header if a DLCI addressing change occurs from one segment to another. Carriers use two methods for transporting Frame Relay frames across their network.

Many parameters can be used to control the rate of traffic and congestion for a VC. CIR is the guaranteed average rate of a VC. B_C is a higher supported average rate, but measured over a shorter period than CIR. If frames exceed this rate, they are marked as discard eligible and are the first frames dropped by the carrier when the carrier experiences congestion problems. B_E is the maximum rate at which the carrier will service the VC; any data sent above this rate is dropped. Oversubscription occurs when the CIRs of all of your VCs exceed your access rate (physical line rate). You are betting that not all VCs will simultaneously run at their CIRs. FECN and BECN are used to indicate congestion from the source to the destination DTE.

There are two Frame Relay encapsulations: Cisco's and IETF's. Use the `encapsulation frame-relay` command to specify the encapsulation type. Cisco routers can autosense the LMI type. To hard-code the LMI type, use the `frame-relay lmi-type` command. The `show interfaces` and `show frame-relay lmi` commands show the number of LMI messages sent and received.

You can perform layer 3 to DLCI resolution in your configuration in two ways: manually and dynamically. To specify a manually resolved VC, use the `frame-relay map` command. Inverse ARP, which occurs every 60 seconds, allows you to dynamically learn the layer 3 addresses from each VC. Inverse ARP requires the VC to be in an active state, which indicates the VC is functioning between the two DTEs. If the VC is in an inactive state, the VC is functioning between the DTE and DCE, but there is a problem between the local DCE and the remote DTE. If the VC is in a deleted state, there is a problem with the VC between the local DTE and the local DCE. Use the `show frame-relay map` command to see your resolutions and the `show frame-relay pvc` command to view your PVCs.

NBMA environments have problems with distance vector routing protocols and split horizon when the network is partially meshed. To overcome split horizon, you can use any of the following solutions: fully mesh the network, use static routes, disable split horizon, or use subinterfaces. The recommended approach is to use subinterfaces. When you are configuring Frame Relay for subinterfaces, the encapsulation type and LMI type go on the main physical interface. All layer 3 addressing and the DLCI number for the VC (`frame-relay interface-dlci`) are configured on the subinterface.

TWO-MINUTE DRILL

Virtual Circuits

- ❑ Use this formula to figure out the number of connections required to fully mesh a network: $(N \times (N-1)) / 2$.
- ❑ VCs are not tied to any particular time slots on a channelized connection and are much easier to add or change than leased lines.
- ❑ A PVC is similar to a leased line and is always up. An SVC is similar to a telephone circuit-switched connection and is brought up when you have data to send and torn down when you are finished transmitting data. PVCs are best used if you have delay-sensitive information or you are constantly sending data. SVCs are used when you occasionally need to send information or for backup purposes.

Frame Relay Terms

- ❑ LMI defines how the Frame Relay DTE and DCE interact and is locally significant. There are three implementations of LMI: ITU-T Annex A, ANSI Annex D, and the Gang of Four. Cisco routers autosense LMI. By default, Cisco routers send out LMI queries every 10 seconds, with a full status update every sixth query.
- ❑ DLCIs are used to locally identity a VC—they are the address of the VC. Since this number has only local significance, it can change on a hop-by-hop basis.
- ❑ Congestion experienced as frames go to a destination will have the FECN bit set. The destination will then send a frame—with the BECN bit set—back to the source, indicating congestion.

Frame Relay Configuration

- ❑ The **encapsulation frame-relay** command specifies the encapsulation type. There are two frame types: **cisco** and **ietf**; **cisco** is the default, but **ietf** is an open standard and used in a multi-vendor environment.
- ❑ Use the **frame-relay lmi-type** command to hard-code the LMI type. Cisco routers can autosense the LMI type. Use these commands to troubleshoot LMI: **show interfaces**, **show frame-relay lmi**, and **debug frame-relay lmi**.

❑ To configure a manually resolved PVC, use the **frame-relay map** command. If you omit the **broadcast** parameter, local broadcasts and multicasts won't traverse the VC. Inverse ARP is used for dynamic resolution. This occurs on a VC after the full status update is received and the VC is not already manually resolved.

❑ There are three statuses of VCs: active (the VC is up and operational between the two DTEs), inactive (the connection is functioning at least between the DTE and DCE), and deleted (the local DTE/DCE connection is not functioning). To view a PVC, use the **show frame-relay pvc** command. To see the resolution entries, use the **show frame-relay map** command.

Non-Broadcast Multi-Access Environments

❑ Partially meshed networks have VC connections to some, but not all, routers. A star (hub-and-spoke) topology is partially meshed. Partially meshed networks with VCs have problems with split horizon, which can be overcome by using one of the following solutions: use a fully meshed network, use static routes, disable split horizon, or use subinterfaces.

❑ When using subinterfaces, the physical interface has the encapsulation and LMI type configured on it. Everything else is configured on the subinterface. When you delete a subinterface, save your configuration and reboot the router to remove it from RAM. Point-to-point subinterfaces should be used to solve split horizon problems.

❑ Use the **frame-relay interface-dlci** command to associate a VC to a particular subinterface.

SELF TEST

The following Self Test questions will help you measure your understanding of the material presented in this chapter. Read all the choices carefully, as there may be more than one correct answer. Choose all correct answers for each question.

Virtual Circuits

1. You have a total of five routers. _____ dedicated circuits are required to fully mesh the network, where every router needs _____ interfaces.
   A. 5, 5
   B. 8, 4
   C. 10, 5
   D. 10, 4

Frame Relay Terms

2. _____ defines how the Frame Relay DTE and DCE interact with each other.
   A. DLCI
   B. CIR
   C. LMI
   D. PMI

3. The address of a Frame Relay VC is called a _____.
   A. data link layer connection identifier
   B. data layer connection index
   C. data link connection index
   D. data link connection identifier

4. When a carrier experiences congestion, it marks the _____ bit in the header of the Frame Relay frame.
   A. CIR
   B. DE
   C. BECN
   D. FECN

Frame Relay Configuration

5. Cisco routers generate LMI enquiries every _____ seconds and a full status update every _____ seconds.

   A. 10, 60

   B. 10, 6

   C. 60, 300

   D. 15, 60

6. Enter the router command to have the serial interface use a frame encapsulation type compatible with a non-Cisco router: _____.

7. When using the `show interfaces` command, which Frame Relay information can you not see?

   A. The DLCI number used for LMI

   B. The number of LMIs sent and received

   C. Statuses of PVCs

   D. The LMI type

8. Which Frame Relay command is used to manually resolve layer 3 addresses to DLCIs?

   A. `frame-relay interface-dlci`

   B. `frame-relay map`

   C. `frame-relay resolve`

   D. `frame-relay lmi-type`

9. If you see a VC with an inactive status, this indicates _____.

   A. The connection between both Frame Relay DTEs is up and operational.

   B. The connection between your Frame Relay DTE and DCE is up and operational, but something is wrong with the connection between your connected Frame Relay switch and the destination DTE.

   C. You are not receiving any LMI messages from the Frame Relay switch.

Non-Broadcast Multi-Access Environments

10. _____ topologies in NBMA environments do not have problems with split horizon.

    A. Partially meshed

    B. Fully meshed

    C. Hub-and-spoke

    D. Star

11. Enter the router command to associate DLCI 500 with a subinterface: _____.

SELF TEST ANSWERS

Virtual Circuits

1. ☑ **D.** Use the (N × (N – 1) / 2) formula for the number of circuits. You need a total of 10 circuits and 4 interfaces on each router.
   ☒ **A** has the wrong number of circuits and interfaces. **B** has the wrong number of circuits. **C** has the wrong number of interfaces.

Frame Relay Terms

2. ☑ **C.** The local management interface (LMI) defines how the Frame Relay DTE and DCE interact with each other.
   ☒ **A** is incorrect because DLCI defines the local address of a VC. **B** is incorrect because CIR defines the average traffic rate for a VC. **D** is incorrect because PMI is a nonexistent acronym in this context.

3. ☑ **D.** The address of a Frame Relay VC is called a data link connection identifier (DLCI).
   ☒ **A** and **B** include the term *layer* and are therefore incorrect. **B** and **C** use the term *index* and are therefore incorrect.

4. ☑ **D.** When a carrier experiences congestion, it marks the FECN bit in the header of the Frame Relay frame.
   ☒ **A** is incorrect because CIR specifies the average rate of a VC. **B** is incorrect because DE is used to mark frames that exceed their allowable rate. **C** is incorrect because BECN is marked by the destination device to indicate congestion and is sent to the source device.

Frame Relay Configuration

5. ☑ **A.** Cisco routers generate LMI enquiries every 10 seconds and a full status update every 60 seconds.
   ☒ **B** specifies the wrong update interval for the full update message. **C** has wrong values for both timers. **D** has a wrong value for the status enquiry timer.

6. ☑ `encapsulation frame-relay ietf`

7. ☑ **C.** When using the `show interfaces` command, you cannot see the statuses of the PVCs—you need to use the `show frame-relay pvc` command.
   ☒ **A**, **B**, and **D** can be seen in the output of this command.

8. ☑ **B.** The `frame-relay map` command is used to manually resolve layer 3 addresses to DLCIs.
   ☒ **A** is incorrect because `frame-relay interface-dlci` associates a DLCI to a subinterface. **C** is a nonexistent command. **D** is incorrect because `frame-relay lmi-type` hard-codes the LMI type for the physical serial interface.

9. ☑ **B.** If you see a VC with an inactive status, this indicates that the connection between your Frame Relay DTE and DCE is up and operational, but something is wrong with the connection between your connected Frame Relay switch and the destination DTE.
   ☒ **A** indicates an active VC. **C** indicates a deleted VC.

Non-Broadcast Multi-Access Environments

10. ☑ **B.** Fully meshed topologies in NBMA environments do not have problems with split horizon.
    ☒ **A, C,** and **D** are incorrect because these topologies have problems with split horizon.

11. ☑ `frame-relay interface-dlci 500`

Part VIII

Appendixes

A

About the CD

T he CD-ROM included with this book comes complete with 100 unique electronic practice exam questions from the author, the Boson NetSim Limited Edition (LE), CertCam video training narrated by the author, an electronic version of the book, Boson Software utilities, and the Boson Exam Environment (BEE). The software is easy to install on any Windows 98/Me/2000 Pro/XP/Vista computer and must be installed to access the Boson NetSim LE and electronic practice exam features. You may, however, browse the electronic book, CertCams, and Boson utilities directly from the CD without installation.

System Requirements

Software requires Windows 98SE or higher and Internet Explorer 5.0 or above and 120MB of hard disk space for full installation. The electronic book requires Adobe Acrobat Reader version 5.0 or higher. To access the CertCams, you must have a Windows-compatible sound card installed and enabled.

Installing and Running the Boson NetSim LE and BEE

If your computer CD-ROM drive is configured to auto run, the CD-ROM should automatically start up upon inserting the disc. If the auto run feature did not launch the CD, browse to the CD and click the Setup icon. From the opening screen, you may install the Boson NetSim LE or the BEE by clicking the Install NetSim LE or the Install BEE link.

For information about technical support related to the content of the practice exam, see "Technical Support" at the end of this appendix. Information about customer support for the Boson Software included on the CD is also shown at the end of the appendix.

Boson NetSim LE

The Boson NetSim LE is a restricted version of the Boson NetSim. Boson NetSim is an interactive network simulator that will allow you to simulate a wide variety of tasks as if you were working on a real network. Once you have installed the NetSim LE, you may access it quickly through Start | Programs | Boson Software.

The first time the simulator runs it requires registration. Enter your Boson account information along with the activation code found inside the CD-ROM sleeve. If you do not have a valid boson.com account, create one by visiting boson.com/account. Once registration is complete, the software will load. To load any of the labs found in this book, select one of them from the Lab Navigator and click the Load Lab button.

BEE and Practice Exams

The BEE is a software-based delivery platform for the electronic practice exams. The electronic practice exams provide you with a simulation of an actual CCNA exam. You have the option to customize your test-taking environment by selecting the number of questions, the type of questions, and the time allowed in order to assist you in your studies. The BEE also allows you to simulate an actual test-taking environment. You also have the option to take exams by chapter or objective and the option to an exam in study mode, including references and answers. This practice exam has been created specifically for McGraw-Hill and is available only by purchasing this McGraw-Hill book.

To access your practice exam, install the BEE and use the Exam Wizard to create a Boson account. Activate the practice exam using the activation code found inside the CD sleeve at the back of the book. An active Internet connection is required for the initial activation and download of the practice exam content.

Follow these steps to access the practice exam on the CD:

1. Install the Exam Engine from the CD menu.
2. The first time you run the software, a wizard will help you create the required Boson account.
3. After creating an account and logging in, the Exam Wizard should start and will guide you through the process of activating and downloading the exam.

If the wizard does not automatically start, choose the Exam Wizard option or use the Unlock An Exam option, available through Exam Tools.

Using the Exam Wizard

1. Select the Activate A Purchased Exam option.
2. Enter your activation key.
3. Select the exam(s) you want to download.

Using the Unlock An Exam tool

1. Select Exam Tools.
2. Select Unlock An Exam.
3. Enter your e-mail address, password, and activation key.
4. Select the My New Exams tab.
5. Select the exam(s) you want to download.
6. Click the Download Exam or Download All button.

Electronic Book

The entire contents of the Study Guide is provided in PDF format. Adobe's Acrobat Reader is used to read PDF files and can be downloaded free of charge from www. adobe.com. Simply select the View Book In Electronic Format link from the main CD launch page.

CertCams

CertCam custom AVI clips demonstrate how to perform complex configurations with IOS commands on Cisco routers and Catalyst switches. These clips walk you step-by-step through various system configurations. You can access the clips directly from the CertCam table of contents by selecting the View CertCam Index link on the main CD launch page. Do not try to play the custom AVI file clips without using the CD-ROM menu program. Each chapter that has CertCams in it references the appropriate link from the screen.

Help

Individual help features are available through Boson's NetSim LE and the BEE. Review the Boson NetSim LE User's Guide for details on registration and how-to directions on completing the practice labs.

Removing Installation(s)

For *best* results for removal of Windows programs, choose Start | Programs | Control Panel | Add/Remove Programs to remove the NetSim or the practice exam software.

Technical Support

For questions regarding the technical content of the book, electronic practice exam, the electronic book, or the CertCams, please visit www.mhprofessional.com (click the Computing tab) or e-mail customer.service@mcgraw-hill.com. For customers outside the 50 United States, e-mail international_cs@mcgraw-hill.com.

For technical problems with the Boson NetSim LE (installation, operation, and removal installations) and the BEE, and for questions regarding the Boson activation, visit www.boson.com, or e-mail supportissues@boson.com, or follow the help instructions in the help features included with the Boson NetSim LE or BEE.

B

Exam Readiness
Checklist

ICNDvI (642–822) Exam

Exam Readiness Checklist

Official Objective	Study Guide Coverage	Ch #	Beginner	Intermediate	Expert
Describe the operation of data networks					
Describe the purpose and functions of various network devices	Networks OSI Reference Model Layer 2 LAN Technologies Bridges and Switches Routers and Routing	1 2 3 4 15			
Select the components required to meet a given network specification	Layer 2 LAN Technologies Bridges and Switches Routers and Routing	3 4 15			
Use the OSI and TCP/IP models and their associated protocols to explain how data flows in a network	OSI Reference Model TCP/IP Internet Layer TCP/IP Transport Layer Sending and Receiving TCP/IP Packets	2 6 7 10			
Describe common networking applications including web applications	OSI Reference Model TCP/IP Transport Layer	2 7			
Describe the purpose and basic operation of the protocols in the OSI and TCP models	OSI Reference Model TCP/IP Internet Layer TCP/IP Transport Layer	2 6 7			
Describe the impact of applications (Voice over IP and Video over IP) on a network	Networks VLANs and Trunks	1 13			
Interpret network diagrams	Layer 2 LAN Technologies Bridges and Switches Sending and Receiving TCP/IP Packets Routers and Routing	3 4 10 15			
Determine the path between two hosts across a network	Bridges and Switches Sending and Receiving TCP/IP Packets Routers and Routing	4 10 15			
Describe the components required for network and Internet communications	Networks Layer 2 LAN Technologies WAN Introduction	1 3 25			

Exam Readiness Checklist

Official Objective	Study Guide Coverage	Ch #	Beginner	Intermediate	Expert
Identify and correct common network problems at layers 1, 2, 3, and 7 using a layered model approach	TCP/IP Internet Layer IOS Device Management	6 17			
Differentiate between LAN/WAN operation and features	WAN Introduction	25			
Implement a small switched network					
Select the appropriate media, cables, ports, and connectors to connect switches to other network devices and hosts	Layer 2 LAN Technologies Bridges and Switches	3 4			
Explain the technology and media access control method for Ethernet technologies	Layer 2 LAN Technologies	3			
Explain network segmentation and basic traffic management concepts	Bridges and Switches VLANs and Trunks Routers and Routing	4 13 15			
Explain the operation of Cisco switches and basic switching concepts	Bridges and Switches	4			
Perform, save, and verify initial switch configuration tasks including remote access management	Cisco IOS Software Initial Switch Configuration IOS Device Management	11 12 17			
Verify network status and switch operation using basic utilities (including ping, traceroute, telnet, SSH, ARP, ipconfig), show and debug commands	Cisco IOS Software IOS Device Management	11 17			
Implement and verify basic security for a switch (port security, deactivate ports)	Initial Switch Configuration	12			
Identify, prescribe, and resolve common switched network media issues, configuration issues, autonegotiation, and switch hardware failures	Cisco IOS Software Initial Switch Configuration	11 12			

Exam Readiness Checklist

Official Objective	Study Guide Coverage	Ch #	Beginner	Intermediate	Expert
Implement an IP addressing scheme and IP services to meet network requirements for a small branch office					
Describe the need and role of addressing in a network	OSI Reference Model TCP/IP Internet Layer	2 6			
Create and apply an addressing scheme to a network	IP Addressing and Subnetting	7			
Assign and verify valid IP addresses to hosts, servers, and networking devices in a LAN environment	TCP/IP Internet Layer IP Addressing and Subnetting	6 7			
Explain the basic uses and operation of NAT in a small network connecting to one ISP	Address Translation	23			
Describe and verify DNS operation	Sending and Receiving TCP/IP Packets	10			
Describe the operation and benefits of using private and public IP addressing	TCP/IP Internet Layer Address Translation	6 23			
Enable NAT for a small network with a single ISP and connection using SDM and verify operation using CLI and ping	Address Translation	23			
Configure, verify, and troubleshoot DHCP and DNS operation on a router (including CLI/SDM)	Security Device Manager	18			
Implement static and dynamic addressing services for hosts in a LAN environment	Security Device Manager	18			
Identify and correct IP addressing issues	IP Addressing and Subnetting Cisco IOS Software IOS Device Management	7 11 17			
Implement a small routed network					
Describe basic routing concepts (including packet forwarding, router lookup process)	VLSM Routers and Routing	8 15			

Exam Readiness Checklist

Official Objective	Study Guide Coverage	Ch #	Beginner	Intermediate	Expert
Describe the operation of Cisco routers (including router bootup process, POST, router components)	Initial Router Configuration	16			
Select the appropriate media, cables, ports, and connectors to connect routers to other network devices and hosts	Layer 2 LAN Technologies Cisco IOS Software WAN Introduction	3 11 25			
Configure, verify, and troubleshoot RIPv2	Basic Routing	19			
Access and utilize the router CLI to set basic parameters	Cisco IOS Software Initial Router Configuration	11 16			
Connect, configure, and verify operation status of a device interface	TCP/IP Internet Layer Cisco IOS Software Initial Switch Configuration Initial Router Configuration IOS Device Management	6 11 12 16 17			
Verify device configuration and network connectivity using ping, traceroute, telnet, SSH, or other utilities	TCP/IP Internet Layer IOS Device Management	6 17			
Perform and verify routing configuration tasks for a static or default route given specific routing requirements	Basic Routing	19			
Manage IOS configuration files (including save, edit, upgrade, restore)	IOS Device Management	17			
Manage Cisco IOS	IOS Device Management	17			
Implement password and physical security	Networks Cisco IOS Software	1 11			
Verify network status and router operation using basic utilities (including ping, traceroute, telnet, SSH, ARP, ipconfig), show and debug commands	TCP/IP Internet Layer IOS Device Management	6 17			

Exam Readiness Checklist

Official Objective	Study Guide Coverage	Ch #	Beginner	Intermediate	Expert
Explain and select the appropriate administrative tasks required for a WLAN					
Describe standards associated with wireless media (including IEEE WI-FI Alliance, ITU/FCC)	Wireless LANs	5			
Identify and describe the purpose of the components in a small wireless network (including SSID, BSS, ESS)	Wireless LANs	5			
Identify the basic parameters to configure on a wireless network to ensure that devices connect to the correct access point	Wireless LANs	5			
Compare and contrast wireless security features and capabilities of WPA security (including open, WEP, WPA-1/2)	Wireless LANs	5			
Identify common issues with implementing wireless networks	Wireless LANs	5			
Identify security threats to a network and describe general methods to mitigate those threats					
Explain today's increasing network security threats and the need to implement a comprehensive security policy to mitigate the threats	Networks	1			
Explain general methods to mitigate common security threats to network devices, hosts, and applications	Networks	1			
Describe the functions of common security appliances and applications	Networks	1			
Describe security recommended practices including initial steps to secure network devices	Networks	1			
Implement and verify WAN links					
Describe different methods for connecting to a WAN	WAN Introduction	26			
Configure and verify a basic WAN serial connection	WAN Introduction	26			

ICNDv2 (642-816) Exam

Exam Readiness Checklist

Official Objective	Study Guide Coverage	Ch #	Beginner	Intermediate	Expert
Configure, verify, and troubleshoot a switch with VLANs and interswitch communications					
Describe enhanced switching technologies (including VTP, RSTP, VLAN, PVSTP, 802.1Q)	VLANs and Trunks Switches and Redundancy	13 14			
Describe how VLANs create logically separate networks and the need for routing between them	VLANs and Trunks	13			
Configure, verify, and troubleshoot VLANs	VLANs and Trunks	13			
Configure, verify, and troubleshoot trunking on Cisco switches	VLANs and Trunks	13			
Configure, verify, and troubleshoot interVLAN routing	VLANs and Trunks Initial Router Configuration	13 16			
Configure, verify, and troubleshoot VTP	VLANs and Trunks	13			
Configure, verify, and troubleshoot RSTP operation	Switches and Redundancy	14			
Interpret the output of various show and debug commands to verify the operational status of a Cisco switched network	Cisco IOS Software Initial Switch Configuration VLANs and Trunks Switches and Redundancy	11 12 13 14			
Implement basic switch security (including port security, unassigned ports, trunk access, etc.)	Cisco IOS Software Initial Switch Configuration VLANs and Trunks	11 12 13			
Implement an IP addressing scheme and IP services to meet network requirements in a medium-size Enterprise branch office network					
Calculate and apply a VLSM IP addressing design to a network	VLSM	8			
Determine the appropriate classless addressing scheme using VLSM and summarization to satisfy addressing requirements in a LAN/WAN environment	VLSM	8			
Describe the technological requirements for running IPv6 (including protocols, dual stack, tunneling, etc.)	IPv6	24			
Describe IPv6 addresses	IPv6	24			
Identify and correct common problems associated with IP addressing and host configurations	TCP/IP Internet Layer IP Addressing and Subnetting	6 7			

Exam Readiness Checklist

Official Objective	Study Guide Coverage	Ch #	Beginner	Intermediate	Expert
Configure and troubleshoot basic operation and routing on Cisco devices					
Compare and contrast methods of routing and routing protocols	Routers and Routing	15			
Configure, verify, and troubleshoot OSPF	OSFP Routing	20			
Configure, verify, and troubleshoot EIGRP	EIGRP Routing	21			
Verify configuration and connectivity using ping, traceroute, and telnet or SSH	IOS Device Management	17			
Troubleshoot routing implementation issues	Basic Routing OSPF Routing EIGRP Routing	19 20 21			
Verify router hardware and software operation using show and debug commands	Cisco IOS Software Initial Router Configuration	11 16			
Implement basic router security	Cisco IOS Software	11			
Implement, verify, and troubleshoot NAT and ACLs in a medium-sized Enterprise branch office network					
Describe the purpose and types of access control lists	Access Control Lists	22			
Configure and apply access control lists based on network filtering requirements	Access Control Lists	22			
Configure and apply an access control list to limit telnet and SSH access to the router	Access Control Lists	22			
Verify and monitor ACLs in a network environment	Access Control Lists	22			
Troubleshoot ACL implementation issues	Access Control Lists	22			
Explain the basic operation of NAT	Address Translation	23			
Configure NAT for given network requirements using CLI	Address Translation	23			
Troubleshoot NAT implementation issues	Address Translation	23			
Implement and verify WAN links					
Configure and verify Frame Relay on Cisco routers	Frame Relay	26			
Troubleshoot WAN implementation issues	WAN Introduction	25			
Describe VPN technology (including importance, benefits, role, impact, components)	WAN Introduction	25			
Configure and verify PPP connection between Cisco routers	WAN Introduction	25			

INDEX